APPLICATIONS IN BEHAVIORAL MEDICINE AND HEALTH PSYCHOLOGY: A CLINICIAN'S SOURCE BOOK

Edited by

James A. Blumenthal, PhD
and
Daphne C. McKee, PhD

Professional Resource Exchange, Inc.

635 South Orange Avenue, Suites 4-6
Sarasota, Florida 33577

Hardbound Edition ISBN: 0-943158-18-4
Library of Congress Catalog Number: 86-062715

The copy editors for this book were Joann M. Bierenbaum
and Janet Nunez, the production supervisor was Debbie
Worthington, the graphics coordinator was Judy Warinner,
the cover designer was Bill Tabler, and the printer was
BookCrafters.

In Memory of Arthur

TABLE OF
CONTENTS

v

Table of Contents

Table of Contents

CONTRIBUTORS

Edward W. Aberger, PhD, Clinical Coordinator, Miriam Hospital Chronic Pain Treatment Program, Providence, RI.

David K. Ahern, PhD, Program Coordinator, Miriam Hospital Chronic Pain Treatment Program, Providence, RI.

Francis Andrasik, PhD, Associate Director, Pain Therapy Centers, Greenville Hospital System, Greenville, SC.

Albert S. Aniskiewicz, PhD, Professor, Counseling Center and Department of Psychology, Michigan State University, East Lansing, MI.

James A. Blumenthal, PhD, Associate Professor of Medical Psychology, Department of Psychiatry, Duke University Medical Center, Durham, NC.

Edmund J. Burke, PhD, Staff Psychologist, Sunnyview Hospital and Rehabilitation Center, Schenectady, NY.

Patricia H. Cotanch, RN, PhD, Associate Professor of Nursing and Assistant Professor of Psychiatry, Duke University Medical Center, Durham, NC.

Linda Wilcoxon Craighead, PhD, Associate Professor, Division of Counseling and Educational Psychology, Pennsylvania State University, University Park, PA.

James E. Crisson, MA, Research Analyst, Pain Management Program, Duke University Medical Center, Durham, NC.

Patricia M. Dubbert, PhD, Acting Chief of Psychology, Jackson VA Medical Center, Jackson, MS.

Randall W. Evans, PhD, Post-Doctoral Research Fellow, Biological Sciences Research Center, University of North Carolina School of Medicine, Chapel Hill, NC.

Jonathan Farber, PhD, Clinical Assistant Professor, Psychology Department, University of North Carolina, Chapel Hill, NC.

Contributors

Michael J. Follick, PhD, Director, Miriam Hospital Chronic Pain Treatment Program, Providence, RI.

Nanette M. Frautschi, PhD, Psychologist, Outpatient Behavioral Medicine Service, Kaiser Permanante Health Care Program, Los Angeles, CA.

Richard Green, LCSW, Licensed Clinical Social Worker, Outpatient Department, Sharp Rehabilitation Center, San Diego, CA.

Robert G. Hall, PhD, Chief, Health Psychology Section and Program Evaluation (Psychiatry), Palo Alto Veterans Administration Hospital, Palo Alto, CA.

Sharon M. Hall, PhD, Associate Professor of Medical Psychology, Langley Porter Psychiatric Institute, University of California, San Francisco, CA.

Priscilla Hastedt, MPH, RD, practicing nutritionist and patient care specialist, Seattle, WA.

Steve Herman, PhD, Assistant Professor of Medical Psychology, Duke University Medical Center, Durham, NC.

Thomas Kamarck, PhD, Post-Doctoral Fellow in Behavioral Medicine, University of Pittsburgh, Pittsburgh, PA.

Francis J. Keefe, PhD, Director, Pain Management Program, Duke University Medical School, Durham, NC.

James D. Lane, PhD, Medical Research Assistant Professor, Division of Medical Psychology, Department of Psychiatry, Duke University Medical Center, Durham, NC.

Rona L. Levy, MSW, MPH, PhD, Professor of Social Work, University of Washington, Seattle, WA.

John E. Martin, PhD, Professor of Clinical Psychology, San Diego State University, San Diego, CA.

Daphne McKee, PhD, Associate Professor, Department of Psychiatry, University of North Carolina School of Medicine, Chapel Hill, NC.

Paul A. Obrist, PhD, Professor, Department of Psychiatry, University of North Carolina, Chapel Hill, NC.

Lynda H. Powell, PhD, Assistant Professor of Epidemiology and Public Health, Yale Medical School, New Haven, CT.

Ronald M. Ruff, PhD, Head, Neuropsychology Unit, University of California Medical Center, San Diego, CA.

Frederick A. Schmitt, PhD, Director, Neuropsychology Service, University of Kentucky Medical Center, Lexington, KY.

Douglas D. Schocken, PhD, Head, Clinical Cardiology, James A. Haley Veterans' Hospital, Tampa, FL.

Contributors

Brian Stabler, PhD, Associate Professor of Psychology and Pediatrics, University of North Carolina School of Medicine, Chapel Hill, NC.

Gary E. Swan, PhD, Senior Health Psychologist, Department of Behavioral Medicine, Stanford Research Institute, Menlo Park, CA.

Carl E. Thoresen, PhD, Professor of Education and Psychology, Stanford University, Stanford, CA.

Mary Trainor, RN, Head Nurse, Clinical Specialty Unit, Inpatient Chronic Pain Unit, Duke University Medical Center, Durham, NC.

Stephen M. Weiss, PhD, Chief, Behavioral Medicine Branch, National Heart, Lung, and Blood Institute, Bethesda, MD.

FOREWORD

Behavioral medicine is a term that was first used by Birk in 1973 to describe the efficacy of biofeedback in treating such medical disorders as asthma, epilepsy, headaches, and Raynaud's disease (Birk, L. 1973. *Biofeedback: Behavioral Medicine.* New York: Grune & Stratton). Birk noted that

> it is perhaps not an exaggeration to point out that a new "behavioral medicine," biofeedback, now still in its infancy may in fact represent a major new developing frontier of clinical medicine and psychiatry. (p. 362)

Over the past 15 years, behavioral medicine has grown to encompass far more than a particular mode of treatment. A philosophy of individual responsibility for disease prevention and health maintenance, known as *behavioral health*, also has emerged, along with the discipline of health psychology, which emphasizes the unique contributions of psychologists to the prevention of disease and promotion of good health through behavior change.

As a result of this rapidly growing interest among health-care professionals, the American Psychological Association established a new division of health psychology (Division 38), and a group of biomedical and behavioral scientists independently established a Society of Behavioral Medicine.

In his Introduction, Dr. Stephen Weiss, Chief of the Behavioral Medicine Branch of the National Heart, Lung, and Blood Institute, reviews the development of this promising new field, and notes the exciting possibilities that behavioral medicine holds for the future.

Much of the appeal of behavioral medicine and behavioral health lies in its efforts to integrate knowledge from the behavioral and biomedical sciences to reach solutions to practical problems of physical health and illness. It is generally conceived as being broad in scope and not restricted to any one discipline or theoretical orientation. Rather, behavioral medicine and behavioral health represent interdisciplinary fields concerned with health promotion and disease prevention, as well as diagnosis, treatment, and rehabilitation. The contributors to this volume reflect this diverse expertise and include contributions from medicine, psychology, nursing, social work, and nutrition.

The book is divided into four sections. In Section I, we focus on issues of assessment. Drs. James Blumenthal and Thomas Kamarck review the various procedures for identifying the Type A behavior pattern and recommend ways to add greater precision to the assessment of the components of Type A, particularly hostility. Drs. Frank Andrasik and Edmund Burke describe procedures for diagnosing different kinds of headaches and provide empirical evidence to support their use. Dr. Francis Keefe, along with his colleagues, James Crisson and Mary Trainor, describe a behavioral strategy for evaluating patients with chronic pain and present new data regarding the reliability and validity of their techniques. Dr. Albert Aniskiewicz presents his approach to the evaluation of cognitive impairment in the elderly, with an emphasis on integrating subjective and objective analysis of test results. In the final chapter, Dr. Steve Herman reviews the sexual dysfunction questionnaire that he developed for evaluating men with impotence.

Section II is devoted to treatment considerations. Dr. Linda Wilcoxon Craighead presents a decision-making approach to weight reduction and includes a step-by-step guide for the practicing clinician. Drs. Lynda Powell and Carl Thoresen describe their innovative program for Type A modification and present data showing that their program is not only effective in modifying Type A behavior, but that it appears to reduce the risk for recurrent myocardial infarction in patients with coronary heart disease. Drs. Frederick Schmitt and Jonathan Farber describe methods for improving memory function in individuals with cognitive deficits. Drs. Michael Follick, David Ahern, and Edward Aberger describe how they are able to tailor their outpatient-based chronic pain treatment program to individual's unique problems. Finally, Drs. Ronald Ruff, Randall Evans, and Richard Green present their observations on the usefulness of group therapy in the rehabilitation of head-injured patients.

Section III deals with issues of health promotion. Drs. Sharon Hall and Robert Hall review treatment strategies for smoking cessation and include a discussion of how to motivate clients to stop smoking and to present relapse. Dr. Brian Stabler reviews efforts directed at health promotion in children and emphasizes the importance of social and parental influences in establishing healthy habits. Drs. John Martin and Patricia Dubbert present a rationale for promoting physical exercise and describe methods for enhancing compliance to exercise programs. Drs. Nanette Frautschi and Gary Swan provide guidelines for establishing and evaluating worksite health promotion programs. The last chapter by Priscilla Hastedt describes the role of diet in health and illness and offers specific suggestions for proper nutrition.

Section IV is comprised of miscellaneous topics of special interest to clinicians. Dr. Patricia Cotanch presents information on the use of relaxation therapies as procedures to reduce some of the unpleasant side-effects of cancer treatment. Dr. Paul Obrist describes the potential uses of ambulatory monitoring of cardiovascular function with a particular emphasis on the value of ambulatory monitoring of blood pressure. Dr. James Lane focuses on the often-neglected problem of excessive caffeine use and suggests specific guidelines for reducing caffeine consumption. Dr. Douglas Schocken offers advice about how to prescribe exercise for different individuals and suggests procedures for implementing and evaluating exercise programs. Finally, Dr. Rona Levy presents 10 basic principles for enhancing compliance in clinical practice.

This volume is intended to be a source book for researchers and clinicians who have an interest in the practical applications of behavioral medicine in their everyday work with students, clients, and patients. The book is not intended to represent a definitive text on the subject. Rather, it attempts to reflect the rich diversity of empirical research on selected problems of health and illness.

We would like to acknowledge many people who made this book possible. First, we would like to extend thanks to our authors for their excellent contributions. We set out to recruit the experts in the field and sought individuals who were not only nationally recognized for their research contributions but who also had practical, "hands-on" clinical experience. Unlike most behavioral medicine texts, we attempted to bring together individuals whose clinical practice reflects the state of the art in their respective fields. We appreciate their taking the time away from their busy practices to communicate what they do and how they do it to those of us less informed. We also are indebted to a number of individuals who directly and indirectly made this book possible. We would like to thank our colleagues at Duke University Medical Center and the University of North Carolina whose support and encouragement were so important during the development of the book. In particular, we would like to thank Drs. Richard Surwit, Redford Williams, Dave Madden, Arthur Prange, and the late David Raft for their enthusiastic support of our work. We would also like to thank Drs. Bernard Carroll, David Janowsky, and members of the Departments of Psychiatry at Duke and UNC for the recognition that they have given us and the behavioral medicine programs at our respective universities. We are indebted to our families and friends for their understanding and encouragement during our work on this book. Most of all, we thank each other and take pride in this book as a product of our mutual respect and love for each other.

J.A.B./D.C.M.

Chapel Hill, North Carolina
September, 1986

INTRODUCTION

Stephen M. Weiss

BEHAVIORAL MEDICINE IN THE "TRENCHES"

Essentially unknown 10 years ago, the term "behavioral medicine" is currently being applied to a growing array of "centers," "institutes," "departments," "laboratories," "units," "sections," and other such entities in academic, clinical, research, and governmental settings. Several national scientific and professional organizations representing this multidisciplinary field have also been established within this time period. This growth has taken place primarily within the United States and Canada, although Great Britain, Eastern and Western Europe, and the Soviet Union have recently developed "biobehavioral" activities in both the clinical and research domains.

In a formal sense, the term "behavioral medicine" can be dated to the Yale Conference on Behavioral Medicine held early in 1977. But the evolution of the basic concept spans thousands of years, beginning with the work of Homer, Plato, and Aristotle who made speculations that are remarkably similar to our current understanding of the relationship between mind and body. Descartes and more recent philosophers added to our understanding of this sometimes elusive relationship (Weiss, 1979). In medicine, concepts of psychosomatic illness did not gain currency until after middle of the 19th century. Sir William Osler observed the association between aggressive behavior and coronary heart disease, and Freud, Mesmer, and others used hypnosis to demonstrate the influence of the mind on the body. By 1930, Franz Alexander had developed the concept that conflict could cause identifiable organ disease through prolonged autonomic arousal (Laman & Evans, 1980). And by 1947 the term "psychosomatic medicine" had gained widespread attention through Flanders Dunbars' publication of *Mind and Body: Psychosomatic Medicine*.

During the 1950s and early 1960s, psychosomatic medicine captured the attention of the biomedical community as both struggled to come to terms with diagnostic, treatment, and rehabilitation problems of the chronic degenerative diseases. By the late 1960s and early 1970s, however, the lack of progress in developing effective treatment strategies, the continuing preoccupation with questions of psychodynamic pathogenesis, and the paucity of experimentally oriented research prompted leaders in psychosomatic medicine to urge a reconceptualization of approach, theory, and method in their efforts to revitalize the relationship between the behavioral and biomedical sciences (Engel, 1977; Lipowski, 1977; Weiner, 1977).

This extensive history notwithstanding, the greatest deterrents to the progression of concept, theory, and ideology in establishing linkages between the behavioral and biomedical sciences have been encountered in the development of research methodology and communication models acceptable to all relevant scientific disciplines. The recent emergence of multifactorial approaches to the pathogenesis of chronic disease has unquestionably facilitated conceptual development in behavioral medicine. Understanding the role of environmental and behavioral factors as synergistic, catalytic, instigative, modulating, and mediating agents in the complex physiologic and biochemical reactions that result over time in organ damage has become a significant challenge to the biomedical and behavioral research communities. Efforts to broaden the attack on chronic disease have identified many nontraditional paths for potentially fruitful exploration. For example, diet, exercise, stress reduction, weight control, smoking behavior, and strategies for compliance and adherence have all recently emerged as legitimate areas of research in the prevention and control of chronic disease.

Most attempts by biomedical and behavioral researchers to *independently* investigate these common problems have not been gratifying. Too often, whether in the behavioral or the biomedical fields, scientists have made serious, disqualifying errors or omissions resulting from an insufficient knowledge of concepts within another discipline's purview. It has become increasingly obvious that successful chronic disease research requires a multifaceted approach through collaborative relationships among scientists who collectively embody the necessary expertise to understand *all* the dimensions of the research problems facing them. Familiarity with one another's terminology, concepts, and perspectives is a prerequisite to model the combination of biobehavioral circumstances responsible for the development of chronic disease.

Although contributions to behavioral medicine come from many disciplines (see Table 1), biomedicine and psychology, particularly *health* psychology, are unquestionably major contributors to the field. To clarify the interrelatedness of the *discipline* of health psychology to the *field* of behavioral medicine, let us define the terms:

Health Psychology: the aggregate of the specific educational, scientific, and professional contributions of the discipline of psychology to the promotion and maintenance of health, the prevention and treatment of illness, and the identification of etiologic and diagnostic correlates of health, illness and related dysfunction, and to the analysis and improvement of the health care system and health policy formation. (Matarazzo, 1982, p. 4)

Behavioral Medicine: the interdisciplinary field concerned with the development and integration of behavioral and biomedical science knowledge and techniques relevant to health and illness and

---

TABLE 1: DISCIPLINES RELATED TO BEHAVIORAL MEDICINE INCLUDE, BUT ARE NOT LIMITED TO:

---

*	Anthropology	*	Nursing
*	Biostatistics	*	Nutrition
*	Dentistry	*	Pharmacology
*	Epidemiology	*	Physiology
*	Health Education	*	Psychiatry
*	Medicine	*	Psychology
	(including relevant specialty areas, e.g., neurology, cardiology, internal medicine, oncology, rehabilitation, etc.)	*	Sociology

---

the application of this knowledge and these techniques to prevention, diagnosis, treatment and
rehabilitation. (Schwartz & Weiss, 1978, p. 250)

As is readily apparent from these definitions (and
reflected in the chapters of this book), behavioral approaches to the assessment, treatment, and prevention of
disease and to health promotion play a major role in the
multifactorial model of health and illness.

Several cautions should be brought to mind as we
endeavor to integrate these approaches into the general
health care system. Above all we should be cautious in
making clinical claims which have not been fully established by clinical trials research. Although in many cases
we may achieve very promising results in clinical experiments, until such findings are replicated in large-scale
clinical trials which are truly representative of the
condition we are studying, we must present such therapies
to patients as being still in the experimental stage and not
completely verified as an accepted standard of treatment.
Thus, it is particularly important for us as clinicians to
remain up to date on the research literature concerning
the various behavioral and biobehavioral treatment techniques so that we may pace our use and modify our
techniques in accordance with new findings as they become available. As a critical mass of clinical research
consistently demonstrates the efficacy of a technique as
well as the specificity or generalizability of such techniques to all individuals with the disease (or at risk), we
can have greater confidence in prescribing this technique
for a given patient.

Parenthetically, it behooves the astute clinician to
follow the basic science as well as clinical research related to specific disease conditions. In certain circumstances, questions pertaining to potential mechanisms of
action can only be addressed in animal research. While
such approaches have recognized limitations, being
familiar with both literatures will provide the clinician a
better understanding of what measures may be useful in
determining treatment effects on the basis of such
mechanism research.

The second issue, as health providers, concerns our
being good health care role models. Particularly for those
clinicians involved in health promotion, we need to assess
our personal suitability as role models with regard to
health-enhancing lifestyles. Having been exposed to

social learning theory and Albert Bandura's concept of social modeling, clinicians must look to their own behavior with regard to known health risk factors. Major changes have taken place among physicians concerning their health behaviors (e.g., smoking). Health psychologists are equally capable of making similar modifications in their own behavior (psychologists, heal thyselves?).

Finally, the biobehavioral approach to chronic illness and health promotion entails bioethical issues which span both biomedical and behavioral domains. Whereas such concerns have been reasonably well debated within the biomedical community, the behavioral sciences have yet to come to terms with many of the more subtle issues relating particularly to our interdisciplinary scientific or clinical activities. In our efforts to focus on measurable endpoints, for example, we might not give sufficient attention to the larger philosophical and moral issues which are related to our actions. As "behavior change experts" we may be increasingly called upon by other health professional colleagues as our skills become more recognized and accepted. However, whenever we are asked to utilize our skills to attain *another's* objectives, we must, as full-fledged health care researchers and professionals, consider how those objectives relate to *our* philosophical and moral "weltanschauung" concerning the proper role of the health care expert in society. To just count pills in compliance studies without first reviewing how such objectives relate to the overall well-being of those on whom we would practice our craft is more in keeping with the *technician* than the *professional*. To participate in behavior change activities which compromise an individual's ability to make informed, personal choices concerning health behavior, or which achieve short-term success at the expense of long-term well-being, raises another set of bioethical concerns. Whether or not to engage in such activities is also a matter of personal and professional choice, but at a minimum, one must *recognize* the implications of one's actions to realize that reflection on many of these issues is warranted. Informed reflection, however, can only occur in the presence of knowledge--having the relevant facts in hand to make rational decisions and recognizing the gray areas which require considered professional judgment as to what action is most appropriate. Thus, it is not a particular path of action which is called for, but rather recognition of the *process* in which one must engage prior to committing oneself to collaborative professional activities where the end objectives and the implications for the patient are equivocal. Inevitably, such consideration and reflection will create some discomfort in our colleagues from other disciplines who may not share our particular concerns. This is insufficient reason, however, not to assure oneself that one's actions are *right* as well as *correct.*

In summary, there is much excitement in the developments which are taking place in behavioral medicine, and health psychologists, physicians, nurses, health educators, epidemiologists, and many others have much to offer each other in developing truly biobehavioral paradigms in seeking solutions to problems of health and illness. Using Neal Miller's classic statement on the subject as our watchword, "we must be bold in what we try, but cautious in what we claim," we can be sure of a long and viable future for our field.

Stephen M. Weiss, PhD, is currently Chief of the Behavioral Medicine Branch of the National Heart, Lung, and Blood Institute in Bethesda, Maryland, and Professor in the Department of Medical Psychology at the Uniformed Services University School of Medicine. He received his PhD in psychology from the University of Arizona in 1965. Dr. Weiss co-edited *Behavioral Health* and six other books. He has written over 60 articles, contributed chapters, and research monographs on behavioral medicine and health psychology. Dr. Weiss may be contacted at the Department of Health and Human Services, National Institutes of Health, National Heart, Lung, and Blood Institute, Bethesda, MD 20892.

RESOURCES

Engel, G. L. (1977). The need for a new medical model: A challenge for biomedicine. *Science, 196,* 129-136.
Laman, C., & Evans, R. I. (1980). Behavioral medicine: The history and the past. *National Forum, LX,* 1.
Lipowski, Z. J. (1977). Psychosomatic medicine in the seventies: An overview. *American Journal of Psychiatry, 134,* 233-244.

Matarazzo, J. D. (1982). Behavioral health's challenge to academic, scientific and professional psychology. *American Psychologist, 37,* 1-14.

Schwartz, G. E., & Weiss, S. M. (1978). Behavioral medicine revisited: An amended definition. *Journal of Behavioral Medicine, 1,* 249-251.

Weiner, H. (1977). *Psychobiology and Human Disease.* New York: Elsevier North-Holland.

Weiss, S. M. (1979). The contribution of psychology to behavioral medicine. In D. G. Oborne, M. M. Gruneberg, & J. R. Eiser, *Research in Psychology and Medicine* (pp. 1-10). London: Academic Press.

SECTION I:

ASSESSMENT

ASSESSMENT OF THE
TYPE A BEHAVIOR PATTERN*

James A. Blumenthal and Thomas Kamarck

The Type A behavior pattern is a particular set of overt behaviors and underlying psychological predispositions displayed by individuals who are at greater risk for the development of coronary heart disease (CHD). The term "Type A behavior pattern" was originally coined by Drs. Meyer Friedman and Ray Rosenman, two practicing cardiologists in the San Francisco Bay area, in the mid-1950s. They noticed that their private patients displayed a particular style of behavior that they believed was responsible for the patients' heart attacks.

In their book, *Type A Behavior and Your Heart*, Friedman and Rosenman (1974) described the Type A behavior pattern as an "action emotion complex that can be observed in any person who is aggressively involved in a chronic incessant struggle to achieve more and more in less and less time, and if required to do so, against the opposing efforts of other things or other persons" (p. 67). The behavioral manifestations of this struggle include explosive, loud, and rapid speech; an accelerated behavioral tempo; impatience; a tendency to simultaneously engage in multiple activities; self-preoccupation; evaluation of self-worth primarily in terms of numbers and accomplishments; an overriding propensity to challenge and compete with others even in noncompetitive situations; and the marked presence of free-floating hostility.

The Western Collaborative Group Study (WCGS) is the landmark study in the Type A literature. In previous retrospective studies, Rosenman and Friedman reported

*Preparation of this chapter was supported by NIH Grants HL30675, AG04238, and by a grant from the John D. and Catherine T. MacArthur Foundation.

3

that in Type A men and women the rate of CHD was 4-7 times that of their Type B counterparts (Friedman & Rosenman, 1959; Rosenman & Friedman, 1961). The WCGS project was initiated in 1960-1961 as a prospective epidemiologic study of the incidence of CHD among more than 3500 middle-aged men employed in 11 participating companies in the San Francisco Bay area. At the beginning of this study, subjects underwent extensive medical testing and were evaluated for the presence of the Type A behavior pattern. Initially, 113 men were found to have clinically manifest CHD, 80 of whom were classified as Type A (Rosenman et al., 1964). The remaining 3154 subjects were diagnosed as being free from CHD and were followed on an annual basis for almost 10 years. The results of the study, shown in Figure 1 (page 5), indicate that of the 257 men who developed CHD during this time interval 178 were classified as Type A while only 79 were considered Type B. Individuals displaying the Type A behavior pattern had 2.37 times the rate of new CHD compared to their Type B counterparts (Rosenman et al., 1975). In addition, Figure 1 shows that the rate of recurring myocardial infarctions (MI) was five times as great for Type As as for Type Bs. In 1978, a conference of experts was assembled by the National Heart, Lung and Blood Institute to review the available evidence. The scientists concluded that Type A behavior was a significant risk factor for coronary disease, over and above the risk imposed by age, blood pressure, elevated cholesterol, and cigarette smoking (Review Panel, 1981).

Over the past two decades, numerous clinical, epidemiological, and laboratory studies have provided evidence that Type A behavior is an independent risk factor for the development of CHD. Interested readers are referred to several excellent reviews of the literature including Dembroski, Weiss, Shields, Haynes, and Feinleib (1978), Price (1982), and Matthews (1982).

In this chapter the most common procedures for assessing Type A behavior will be described along with the strengths and limitations of each.

EARLY EFFORTS TO MEASURE TYPE A BEHAVIOR

Initially Type A classification was performed by lay selectors whose identification of Type A and Type B

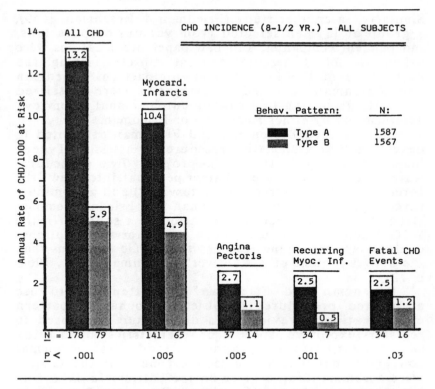

Figure 1. The annual incidence rate of CHD in 3154 subjects studied prospectively in the WCGS project for 8-1/2 years. The higher incidence rates of all forms of CHD is shown.

Note. From Friedman (1971). Copyright © 1971 by Annals of Clinical Research. Reprinted by permission.

individuals was based upon the selectors' knowledge of the core characteristics of the Type A behavior pattern. These characteristics included (a) sustained aggressive drive for achievement, advancement, and recognition; (b) competitiveness and the desire to win; (c) habitual immersion in multiple vocational and avocational involvements subject to the time pressures of deadlines; (d) extraordinary mental and physical alertness; and (e) the habitual propensity to accelerate the pace of execution of most mental and physical functions. In one study (Rosenman & Friedman, 1961), for example, the assessment by Mother Superiors of 19 nuns exhibiting Type A behavior and 20 nuns exhibiting Type B behavior was judged to be accurate in all but one of the cases.

5

Similarly, in another study (Friedman & Rosenman, 1959), a group of laymen selected from various corporations, independent companies, and newspaper organizations were asked to select associates most closely fitting the description of the Type A behavior pattern. Friedman and Rosenman reported the majority were classified correctly according to a subsequent "personal interview" administered by either Rosenman or Friedman.

In 1959-1960, Rosenman and Friedman attempted to develop a more systematic procedure for assessing Type A behavior for use in the WCGS project. Two procedures were used: a 30-minute, 23-item personal interview (the forerunner of the "Structured Interview") and a 16-minute psychophysiological test. Rosenman and Friedman emphasized that "the correct classification of a subject (in the WCGS) depended far more upon the motor and emotional qualities accompanying response to specific questions than the actual content of his answer" (Rosenman et al., 1964, p. 121).

Rosenman and Friedman also attempted to use automated procedures to objectify behavior pattern classification. Previously, a device had been used to register explosive speech characteristics by having subjects read two paragraphs out loud, first in normal conversational tone and a second time as if the subject were a commanding officer on the battlefield exhorting his troops into battle (Friedman, Brown, & Rosenman, 1969). Although the device was found to accurately assess Type A behavior in 84% of the test subjects, this test proved too cumbersome and was abandoned by the time of the WCGS. Instead, WCGS subjects were required to listen to a 16-minute recording of two monologues. One monologue was delivered by a man speaking at his usual conversational rate. However, the monologue was interrupted on 11 occasions by a "challenge" monologue delivered in a deliberately irritating manner by a woman. Behavior pattern classification was based upon qualitative assessments of characteristic motoric behaviors and respiratory abnormalities displayed by Type A subjects (Rosenman et al., 1964). By 1970, however, this test was abandoned, and attention shifted to refining the personal interview. The interview procedure was evolved over the past 20 years to be known variously as a "stress" interview, "semi-structured" interview, and finally the "Structured Interview," as it is presently known.

STRUCTURED INTERVIEW

The Structured Interview (SI) initially consisted of 23 items requiring about 12-15 minutes, in which the respondent was asked a variety of questions about feelings, attitudes, and reactions to various everyday situations. The SI was considered to be a challenge situation to study the response style of the individual, since Rosenman and Friedman were concerned far more with the manner in which the respondent answered questions than with the content of the answers. Thus, the SI assessment was based more upon the stylistics of speech (i.e., the way something is said by the subject) and the overt psychomotor, nonverbal behaviors exhibited during the interview than upon the content of the answers to the questions. For example, subjects were asked about their feelings of ambition and drive (e.g., "Are you satisfied with your present job?" and "Were you on any athletic or other teams or activity in high school or college?"); their competitive and aggressive feelings (e.g., "Do you think of yourself as hard driving and aggressive or as relaxed and easy going?"); and their sense of time urgency (e.g., "Are there many deadlines in your work?" and "Do you like to help your wife with the dishes and housekeeping or do you resent this as a waste of time?"). Since the interview was designed to elicit *behaviors*, several questions were asked solely to observe the presence of speech hurrying (e.g., "Have you ever taken snapshots? Well, uh, when you did take them, uh-the films-uh, the development, uh-did you yourself uh develop uh-uh them?"). A Type A individual would presumably anticipate what was being asked in this deliberately hesitant manner, and answer before the question was completed.

For purposes of classification, Rosenman and Friedman employed five behavioral categories. Subjects were classified as Type A-1 if they exhibited Type A behavior pattern in the most fully developed form and Type A-2 if Type A behavior was exhibited to a lesser degree. Type B subjects (i.e., subjects who exhibited an absence of Type A behaviors) were classified as Type B-4 if they exhibited Type B behavior in its extreme degree and as Type B-3 if Type B behavior was present to lesser degree. Subjects were classified as Type X if they exhibited a pattern with approximately equivalent

7

features of Type A and Type B behaviors. A third type (Type C) was suggested to reflect Type B characteristics with chronically high levels of anxiety and insecurity. However, this latter category is no longer in use. In addition, Types B-3 and B-4 have been merged into a single Type B behavior pattern category, since the subdivisions do not differ in relationship to any meaningful behavioral or clinical outcome measures.

Approximately half of the participants in the WCGS were classified as Type A, although more recent estimates of the prevalence of Type A behavior are 60-70% in the general adult population and more than 80% in coronary samples (e.g., patients undergoing cardiac catheterization or who are on the Coronary Care Unit) (Rosenman et al., 1964). In terms of the reliability of the SI, most studies suggest an interrater agreement between 74% and 84%. Stability of the behavior pattern was studied by reinterviewing the same subjects in the WCGS about 1.5 years after their initial interview. The same behavior pattern classification was made in 80% of the subjects (Jenkins, Rosenman, & Friedman, 1968).

By the late 1970s, a "second generation" of interviewers began to employ a variation of the original SI. The most widely used procedure was proposed by Rosenman (1978) and requires only about 10 minutes to administer. The interview consists of only 22 items and, like the original SI, questions are designed to elicit specific content as well as characteristic Type A behaviors. The revised procedure involves a more challenging and confrontational style of administration than the original SI. The rationale for this approach was that Type A behaviors are most effectively elicited when the respondent is suitably challenged.

A third version of the SI has been developed recently for use in the Recurrent Coronary Prevention Project (Friedman et al., 1982). Four sets of questions are asked of each interviewee. One set is aimed primarily at learning about the habits and beliefs of the interviewee that are suggestive of time-urgency. A second set is asked chiefly to permit the interviewer time to observe the face and body for various psychomotor signs, and to elicit a latent sense of time-urgency. A third set of questions seeks to discover some of the habits and beliefs of the interviewee that may suggest the presence of free-floating hostility, while a fourth set of questions serves to elicit the psychomotor signs of hostility. This interview is videotaped (hence is referred to as the Videotaped Structured Interview or VSI) and takes approximately 15-20 minutes to administer. The manner of administration tends to be more open-ended and less challenging than the Rosenman (1978) version, and it frequently involves follow-up questions to elicit appropriate Type A biographic or behavioral manifestations. The VSI yields a continuous score based upon 38 "behavioral indicators." These indicators are listed in Table 1 (see pages 10-11). Unlike the Rosenman version of the SI, which employs a 4-point discrete categorical system, the VSI uses a continuous score. The cutoff for Type A classification has not been determined, however.

One of the criticisms of the SI is the potential for measurement error due to unstandardized interviewer behavior. Although the evidence is mixed (Scherwitz, Berton, & Leventhal, 1977), some studies have shown that interviewers' behaviors may differ according to the behavior type of the interviewee (Scherwitz, Graham, Grandits, & Billings, 1985). Siegman, Feldstein, Barkley, and Simpson (1985) provided evidence suggesting that interviewer challenge during the SI may be associated with a large number of false positive Type As. They further noted that this emphasis on challenge in the interview may be responsible for the recent failure to replicate findings of a prospective relationship between Type A and CHD in the Multi Risk Factor Intervention Trial (MRFIT) study and for the increasing prevalence of Type A behavior among adult men in the U.S.

The problem of measurement error due to unstandardized interviewer behavior in the SI has not been adequately addressed in the literature. Uncompromising standardization may not be desirable. For example, the use of individualized follow-up questions (as suggested for the VSI) may be necessary in order to obtain necessary information and to keep the interviewee sufficiently engaged. On the other hand, when the interviewer's behavior shows systematic differences as a function of the behavior classification of the respondent, it becomes difficult to know what is really being assessed.

A second criticism of the SI is based upon the subjective scoring system used for Type A classification. Although the reliability of Type A ratings has been found to be adequate when auditors are sufficiently trained,

9

TABLE 1:   DIAGNOSTIC INDICATORS OF TYPE A BEHAVIOR (REVISED)

Score		
	Scale T: Time Urgency	
	A.	Biographic and Self-Appraisal Indicators
0-1-2-3	1.	Self-awareness of presence of Type A.
0-1-2-3	2.	Polyphasic activities (e.g., brushes teeth and showers at same time, thinks of other matters while conversing with others, and so on).
0-1-2-3	3.	Walks fast, eats fast, and quickly leaves table after eating.
0 or 3	4.	Makes fetish of always being on time under all circumstances.
0 or 3	5.	Has been told to slow down in working and living habits by spouse.
0 or 3	6.	Difficulty in sitting and doing nothing.
0 or 3	7.	Subject habitually substitutes numerals for metaphors in speech.
	B.	Psychomotor Manifestations
0-1-2-3	8.	Characteristic facial tautness expressing tension.
0 or 3	9.	Rapid horizontal eyeball movements during ordinary conversation.
0 or 3	10.	Rapid eye blinking (over 40 blinks/minute).
0 or 3	11.	Tic-like retraction of eyelids showing cornea above and below pupil.
0-1-2-3	12.	Knee jiggling or rapid vigorous tapping of fingers.
0 or 3	13.	Rapid, frequently dysrhythmic speech with accelerated expression of the terminal words of sentences.
0-1-2-3	14.	Lip clicking during ordinary speaking.
0-1-2-3	15.	Rapid tic-like eyebrow lifting.
0-1-2-3	16.	Head nodding when **interviewer** speaks.
0 or 3	17.	Sucking in of air during speech.
0 or 3	18.	Humming (tuneless).
0-1-2-3	19.	Hurrying the speech of others.
0 or 3	20.	Tense posture.
0-1-2-3	21.	Motorization accompanying responses.
0-1-2-3	22.	Expiratory sighs.
0-1-2-3	23.	Rapid body movements.
0-1-2-3	24.	Interruption of the speech of others.
	Scale H: Free-Floating Hostility	
0-1-2-3	25.	Irritability if kept waiting for any reason or when encountering the driving errors of other car drivers.
0-1-2-3	26.	General distrust of other people's motives.
0-1-2-3	27.	Necessity to win at games even when playing with children.
0 or 3	28.	Characteristic facial set exhibiting aggression and hostility (eye and jaw muscles).
0-1-2-3	29.	Characteristic tic-like drawing back of corner of lips, almost exposing front teeth.
0 or 3	30.	Hostile, jarring laugh.
0-1-2-3	31.	Use of clenched fist and table pounding or excessively forceful use of hands and fingers.

Score	Scale H (Continued):
0 or 3	32. Explosive, staccato, frequently unpleasant sounding voice.
0 or 3	33. Frequent use of obscenity.
0 or 3	34. Exhibition of psychomotor signs of irritation and rage when asked about past events in which the subject became angered.
0 or 3	35. The interviewer directly challenges the validity of some comment or behavior that the subject has reported. Does the subject react in a hostile or unpleasant manner?
0 or 3	36. The interviewer questions the subject about views on politics, race, women, competitors, and so on. Does the subject respond with absolute, almost angry generalizations?

Scale P: Pathophysiologic Indicators

0 or 3	37. Periorbital pigmentation.
0 or 3	38. Excessive forehead and upper lip perspiration.

Adapted from "The Diagnosis and Quantitative Assessment of Type A Behavior: Introduction and Description of the Videotaped Structured Interview" by M. Friedman and L. H. Powell, 1984, *Integrative Psychiatry*, 2, pp. 123-129.

there is some evidence that the criteria used for Type A ratings may vary across different studies. Scherwitz et al. (1985), for example, found that interviewee speech characteristics were less important in contributing to Type A classification in the MRFIT study than in previous studies that have used the SI. The subjectivity of the global Type A ratings from the SI has led Siegman and Feldstein (1985) to conclude that "from a methodological or measurement point of view, the SI resembles the Rorschach in its early days."

Several investigators have sought to remedy this scoring problem by developing component behavior rating systems for the SI. These coding systems are designed to measure the observable behaviors of the interviewee that are considered to be components of the Type A pattern.

At least six different component scoring systems have been described for use with the SI (see Table 2, pages 12-13). Five of these systems make use of human coders, while the sixth uses a computer for scoring vocal stylistics (Feldstein, Siegman, Simpson, Barkley, & Kobren, 1984; Howland & Siegman, 1982; Siegman & Feldstein, 1985). As previously described, the VSI employs component ratings and includes more extensive use of psychomotor

TABLE 2: SIX COMPONENT SCORING SYSTEMS FOR THE ASSESSMENT OF THE TYPE A BEHAVIOR PATTERN

COMPONENT	DEMBROSKI ET AL. (1978) & MATTHEWS ET AL. (1985)	SCHUCKER & JACOBS (1977)	SCHERWITZ ET AL. (1977)	ANDERSON & WALDRON (1983)	BLUMENTHAL ET AL. (1984)	SIEGMAN & FELDSTEIN (1985)
Verbal Competitiveness:	Combined scoring of 5 characteristics below (1-5)	-----	-----	-----	-----	-----
Interruptions	Frequency count	Frequency count			Frequency count	Frequency**
Affirmations during questions	Frequency count	-----			-----	-----
Expiratory sighs	Frequency count	-----	-----	-----	Frequency count	-----
Tongue clicks	Frequency count	-----	-----	-----	-----	-----
Hissing sounds	Frequency count	-----	-----	-----	-----	-----
Speech Quality:						
Volume	Rated 1-5	Rated 1-3	-----	"strong voice" (Rated 1-3)	Rated 1-5	Subjective ratings***
Overall speed	Rated 1-5	Rated 1-3	Rated 1-7	Rated 1-3	Rated 1-5	Speech rate
Evenness of speech*	-----	Frequency count	-----	-----	Rated 1-5	-----
Repeated words	-----	Frequency count	-----	-----	-----	-----
Clipped words	-----	Frequency count	-----	-----	-----	-----
Explosive voice modulation	Rated 1-5	Number of plosive words	"voice emphasis" Rated 1-7	"Emphasis" Rated 1-3	Number of plosive words minutes 6-9	-----
Latency of response	Rated 1-5	Average latency intervals for 8 questions	Rated 1-7	Average response latency	Average latency intervals for 3 questions	Average response latency

COMPONENT	DEMBROSKI ET AL. (1978) & MATTHEWS ET AL. (1985)	SCHUCKER & JACOBS (1977)	SCHERWITZ ET AL. (1977)	ANDERSON & WALDRON (1983)	BLUMENTHAL ET AL. (1984)	SIEGMAN & FELDSTEIN (1985)
Pause duration	-----	-----	-----	-----	-----	Average pause duration
Responses to Specific Questions:						
Delay questions (latency, interrupt)	-----	Latency interval	-----	-----	Latency interval and interruption (yes/no)	-----
"Anger-in" questions	Rated 1-5	-----	-----	-----	-----	-----
Potential for Hostility (argumentative, condescending, intense, impatient, irritable)	Rated 1-5	-----	-----	Rated 1-3	Rated 1-5	-----
Motoric Activity	-----	-----	-----	"Hurried motor pace" Rated 1-3	Frequency count motoric movements, 3 intervals during interview	-----

*Last words of sentence spoken faster than first.
**Frequency of interruptive and noninterruptive simultaneous speech.
***The authors report that they have since developed the capacity for automated measurement of volume and pitch as well.

characteristics. For example, facial tautness, head nodding, and knee jiggling are scored, along with "pathophysiological" indicators such as periorbital pigmentation and forehead and upper lip perspiration.

Attempts to demonstrate the validity of component interview ratings in the assessment of the Type A behavior pattern have taken two forms. One group of studies has examined associations between component ratings and the global Type A rating of the interviewee. These studies have attempted to objectify the decision rules used by SI raters in assigning the global Type A classification. Scherwitz et al. (1985) reviewed seven recent studies that used interviewee speech characteristics to predict global Type A ratings. In general, more than 50% of the variance in global (4-point) Type A ratings was accounted for by speech characteristics (voice emphasis, speed of speaking, interruptions, and latency for answering) in these studies. It should be noted that speech characteristics accounted for only 15-25% of the variance in behavior judgments in the MRFIT study.

A second group of studies examining component ratings has attempted to determine which elements of Type A are most strongly associated with clinical CHD end points. Anger and hostility have been the most frequently cited Type A components in this group of studies. Jenkins, Rosenman, and Friedman (1966) found that ratings of hostility from the SI distinguished patients with silent myocardial infarctions from age- and employer-matched controls. Matthews, Glass, Rosenman, and Bortner (1977) compared CHD cases and controls in a subsample of the subjects in the WCGS using 44 ratings of interview behavior and content. Seven of these ratings distinguished the group with documented CHD; three of these ratings were directly concerned with self-reports of anger or irritation and one involved potential for hostility. Dembroski, MacDougall, Williams, Haney, and Blumenthal (1985) also found that "potential for hostility" and "anger-in" ratings from the SI were positively related to angiographically documented coronary disease, although explosive speech was negatively correlated with the extent of coronary disease. These studies suggested that aggression, hostility, and anger (AHA!) are the "active ingredients" in contributing to CHD, whereas other Type A characteristics (e.g., speech style, time-urgency, work involvement) may be largely irrelevant for CHD.

14

PSYCHOMETRIC PROCEDURES

JENKINS ACTIVITY SURVEY

In an attempt to design a more objective, convenient, and less expensive procedure for assessment of Type A behavior, the Jenkins Activity Survey (JAS) was developed in 1964 (Jenkins, Rosenman, & Friedman, 1967; Jenkins, Zyzanski, & Rosenman, 1979). Jenkins worked closely with Friedman and Rosenman in devising this self-report, multiple choice questionnaire as an alternative to the SI for the WCGS project. It is recommended for use with adults who can read at least at an eighth grade level, and it requires approximately 15 minutes to complete.

Items are based upon questions from the SI, as well as additional clinical material that appears to distinguish Type A from Type B individuals. The initial 64 items were subjected to a series of empirical tests that identified the items that best discriminated the two groups. The Type A scale for the 1969 edition was derived from discriminant function procedures using as criterion groups those subjects who scored at the extreme ends of the distribution on previous editions of the test, and three subscales were also factor analytically derived: Speed and impatience (S), Hard driving and competitive (H), and Job involvement (J) (Jenkins, Zyzanski, & Rosenman, 1971).

In 1971, Form B of the JAS was developed to allow its use with a broader range of subjects. The present JAS, Form C, consists of 52 of the items in Form B. The Type A scale consists of 21 items, while Speed and impatience includes 21 items, Hard driving 24 items, and Job involvement 20 items. There are a number of items that overlap between scales and are assigned different scale weightings. Correlations between the Type A scale and Factors S (.17), H (.58), and J (.42) are modest, and Jenkins claims that the three factor scores make independent contributions to the assessment of Type A tendencies. The internal consistency for the four JAS scales (overall Type A, S, H, and J) show reliability coefficients ranging from .73 to .85. Test-retest coefficients are generally between .60 and .70 for intervals of 1 to 4 years. Experimental Forms N (for nonworking persons) and Form T (college students) also have been developed but are used only for research purposes.

The normative data published for the JAS manual are based on the 1969 JAS scores of WCGS participants. The sample consisted of 2,588 white, middle-aged, middle-class employed males. The JAS scores were normally distributed in the WCGS validation sample. Scores were transformed to have a mean of 0.0 and a standard deviation of 10.0. Positive scores indicate Type A behavior and negative scores indicate Type B behavior.

The validity of the JAS for assessing the Type A behavior pattern has been established by comparing JAS scores to Type A ratings based upon the SI. Using the 1965 JAS with the WCGS population, the SI ratings and JAS scores corresponded 73% of the time. However, more recent comparisons of the JAS and the SI have reported correlations in the range of .2 to .4. For example, an early study indicated that there is nearly 90% agreement between the JAS and SI for persons scoring more than one standard deviation from the mean (Jenkins, Zyzanski, & Rosenman, 1971). More recently, Blumenthal et al. (1985) found that the JAS misclassified a significant number of subjects even at the extreme ends of the distribution.

A comparison of the JAS and the SI revealed that sources of common variance appeared to be in the measures of self-reported pressured drive, hostility, energy level, and verbal competitiveness. The source of unique variance in the SI is the subjects' speech style, while the source of unique variance in the JAS is self-reported time pressure (Matthews, Krantz, Dembroski, & MacDougall, 1982). The JAS and SI appear to measure different aspects of the Type A behavior pattern, and the JAS should *never* be considered equivalent to the SI.

In addition to its correlation with the SI, the validity of the JAS has been established by demonstrating that it is independently and significantly associated with the prevalence and incidence of CHD. There have been eight case-control/cross-sectional studies showing a positive correlation between JAS scores and CHD. Two prospective studies have also reported associations between the JAS and new and recurrent CHD events. Analyses of JAS scores of 2,750 healthy men in the WCGS showed the Type A scale distinguished the 120 future clinical cases of CHD. Among men scoring in the top third (greater than +5.0) of the Type A distribution the incidence of CHD over a 4-year period was 1.7 times that of those scoring in the lowest third (less than -5.0) (Jenkins, Rosenman, & Zyzanski, 1974). Although statistically significant, this

16

association is weaker than the association of the SI and CHD. Jenkins, Zyzanski, and Rosenman (1976) reported that JAS Type A scores were even more strongly associated with increased risk of reinfarction among persons in the WCGS who had suffered a previous MI.

Negative findings regarding the validity of the JAS include: the failure of any of the three subscales to be associated with any clinical manifestations of CHD, the failure of the JAS to be associated with CHD in numerous angiographic studies (Blumenthal, Williams, Kong, Schanberg, & Thompson, 1978; Dimsdale, Hackett, Hutter, Block, & Catanzano, 1978; Krantz, Sanmarco, Selvester, & Matthews, 1979), and the failure of the JAS to predict recurrent MI in 516 post-MI patients who completed the JAS 2 weeks after their MI (R. B. Case, Heller, N. B. Case, Moss, & Multicenter Post-Infarction Research Group, 1985). Moreover, recent evidence has shown the JAS to have a lower correlation with the SI than previously reported (Byrne, Rosenman, Schiller, & Chesney, 1985).

Thus, the JAS offers little prognostic value on an individual basis, and recent data have failed to find a significant relationship between JAS scores and new cases of CHD. The JAS and SI are only weakly related, and subcomponents of the Type A behavior pattern such as hostility or anger, hastened behavior tempo, and feelings of time pressure may best be evaluated by employing other instruments.

There also are problems inherent in the test itself. Test items are transparent and there are no safeguards for test taking attitudes that may distort responses such as defensiveness, noncompliance, or social desirability. Furthermore, the scoring system is complex and hand scoring is tedious and time-consuming. The JAS may be mailed to Psychological Corporation for scoring, although the cost of $5 may discourage some users.

FRAMINGHAM TYPE A SCALE

The Framingham Type A scale consists of 10 items that appeared relevant to Type A behavior selected from the 300 items of the Extensive Interview Questionnaire administered in the Framingham Heart Study (Haynes, Levine, Scotch, Feinleib, & Kannel, 1978). Each item was unit-weighted and then all items were summed to yield an overall Type A score. Those who score above the sample median are considered Type A, while those who score below the median are considered Type B. Using a 1-7 Likert scale, subjects are asked if they are hard driving and competitive, usually pressed for time, bossy and dominating, eating too quickly, and so on. The Framingham scale has been found to correlate weakly with the SI ($r = .20$) (Chesney, Black, Chadwick, & Rosenman, 1981) but moderately with the JAS ($r = .53$) (Byrne et al., 1985). Unlike the JAS and SI, Type A assessment by the Framingham scale has been related to anxiety, depression, and neuroticism (Chesney et al., 1981). Interestingly, neuroticism appears to be negatively related to coronary disease (Blumenthal, Thompson, Williams, & Kong, 1979), but positively related to complaints of angina pectoris (chest pain) (Costa et al., 1985). The Framingham Type A scale has been found to be predictive of CHD in white collar males and working women, but not blue collar males or housewives (Haynes & Feinleib, 1982; Haynes, Feinleib, & Kannel, 1980).

BORTNER RATING SCALE

The 14-item Bortner Self-Rating Scale was developed from the SI and was intended to serve as a screening measure of Type A behavior (Bortner, 1969). Each of the 14 scales is composed of two adjectives or phrases separated by a horizontal line with 24 gradations. Each pair of items was chosen to represent two contrasting behaviors. Representative items include: never late--casual about appointments; not competitive--very competitive; always rushed--never feels rushed even under pressure. The rating scales were scored by measuring to the nearest 1/16 of an inch from the beginning of the Type B end of the 1.5-inch line to the point marked by the subject. A total score is obtained by adding the scores of each of 14 items. Scores can vary between 1 and 24 for each rating and 14 and 336 for total Type A scores. A 7-item scale subsequently was found to constitute a more efficient combination for assessing Type A behavior. This 7-item scale, known as the Bortner "Short Scale," yields a weighted score that is obtained by multiplying the 7-item raw scale scores by their respective weights and cumulatively adding or subtracting these from a constant in accord with their respective signs. A Belgian study (Belgian-French Pooling Project, 1984) found that the Bortner Scale with weighted scores agreed with the SI

75% of the time. However, this relationship has not been replicated in other populations.

There are data to suggest that Type A assessed by the Bortner Questionnaire is related to CHD end points. In a case-control study of patients with CHD, scores on the 14-item Bortner Scale were found to be significantly greater for patients who had a myocardial infarction than for controls (Heller, 1979). Bortner scores predicted incidence of total CHD events, independent of age, blood pressure, smoking, and cholesterol in the Belgian-French Cooperative Heart Study (Belgian-French Pooling Project, 1984; French-Belgian Collaborative Group, 1982). However, in the Finnish Twin Study, the Bortner Short Scale did not predict CHD mortality in a 6-year follow-up study (Koskenvuo, Kaprio, Langinvainio, & Romo, 1983) and the Bortner Scale was found to be unrelated to coronary artery disease (CAD) in an angiography study (Kornitzer et al., 1982).

TYPE A SELF-REPORT INVENTORY

The Type A Self-Report Inventory (TASRI) was developed by Blumenthal and colleagues (1985) in an effort to provide an easily administered and scored self-report screening device for the assessment of the Type A behavior pattern. Twenty researchers active in Type A research were asked to identify a set of adjectives from among the 300 Gough Adjective Checklist (ACL) items that they considered to be either characteristic or uncharacteristic of the typical Type A individual. These ratings were then pooled, yielding a set of 65 adjectives which were endorsed by at least 50% of the expert raters. An item analysis was undertaken to identify which of the 65 Type A adjectives were endorsed differentially by SI-rated Type A and B subjects. Thirty-eight items met the criteria for statistical significance, and three additional items were added that had been marginally excluded from the original Type A scale but nevertheless discriminated well between Type As and Bs. This pool of items was edited to remove redundancies of content, leaving a 28-item scale, and the response format was changed to a 7-point Likert format.

In a study of 281 cardiac patients, a significant linear relationship was found between SI ratings and scores on the TASRI (Blumenthal et al., 1985). The correlation between the TASRI and JAS was good ($r = .58$), although

19

correlations between the SI and either the JAS or TASRI were relatively low. Moreover, Type A assessed by the TASRI, JAS, and SI all were unrelated to measures of CAD determined by coronary angiography.

Although the TASRI has seen limited application and large scale normative data are not yet available, its simplicity of administration and scoring (5 minutes to complete and 2 minutes to score) may prove to be an advantage over the JAS when large numbers of subjects need to be quickly screened for Type A tendencies. Further work is necessary to evaluate the usefulness of the TASRI as an index of risk for the development of CHD.

OTHER PSYCHOMETRIC INSTRUMENTS

The Milwaukee Questionnaire is a 10-item questionnaire designed to assess global Type A behavior. Representative items include: How do you feel about competition on the job? (A Type A response would be "I enjoy it"); How is your temper? (A Type A response would be "Fiery and hard to control"); and Do you usually wake up well rested? (A Type A response would be "No"). Although the authors claim that this scale is reliably associated with the SI and the JAS, the data are too limited to recommend its use (Young & Barboriak, 1982).

The Rating of Statements List (RSL; Dutch abbreviation BUL) (van Dijl, 1978) is a self-report questionnaire consisting of a number of factors including an 11-item Aggressivity factor (e.g., I am often infuriated, very stubborn, etc.); an 8-item Activity and work factor (e.g., I am immensely active, very precise, etc.); and a 6-item Ambition and dominance factor (e.g., I admire great sporting achievements very much indeed). Although the test has a modest correlation with the SI, it has not been shown to be related to any measure of CHD.

Similarly a 9-item Type A scale developed by Vickers (1973) as part of a University of Michigan study on "Job Demands and Worker Health" has not been shown to be associated with CHD or to correlate significantly with the SI (Caffrey, 1978).

PERFORMANCE TESTS

In 1967, Bortner and Rosenman developed a performance battery to assess Type A behavior. The

Bortner Test Battery consisted of a set of performance measures including time estimation tasks, a rod-and-frame test, an embedded figures test, a flicker fusion test, and an arrow-dot test. Although the authors reported that Type A was correctly assessed in 77% of the cases (Bortner & Rosenman, 1967), the task proved to be far too time-consuming. It is no longer used as a method for assessing Type A behavior.

TYPE A AND PSYCHOPHYSIOLOGIC REACTIVITY

As a result of the epidemiological findings that the Type A behavior pattern was associated with increased risk for the development of CHD, researchers turned their attention to the study of the underlying physiological mechanisms that may be responsible for the association between Type A and CHD. Although the process by which atherosclerosis develops in the coronary arteries is not fully understood, the most popular theory at this time is that exaggerated cardiovascular and neuroendocrine responses promote arterial injury and, ultimately, contribute to the build-up of plaque in the coronary arteries. There have now been numerous studies that have shown that Type As generally exhibit greater reactivity than Type Bs, especially when provoked by challenging, competitive, or hostile situations. However, the reader should also be advised that comparisons of physiological reactivity among Type As and Bs are not always consistent. Krantz and Manuck (1984) present an excellent review of the literature and note that only about 70% of the published studies report greater reactivity among Type As than among Type Bs. Furthermore, it has not been conclusively demonstrated that reactivity is a risk factor for the development of CHD.

There are a number of techniques for assessing cardiovascular and neuroendocrine reactivity in the laboratory. Psychological stressors that have been used in the laboratory include mental challenges such as mental arithmetic, reaction time tasks; vigilance tasks; cognitive problems such as anagrams, Stroop Color Word Test, and Raven's Progressive Matrices; various video games; and simulated public speaking. In addition, tasks that are less structured such as interpersonal games, role playing, and interviews such as the SI have also been used. The degree of reactivity can be manipulated by varying task instructions or demands, such as by providing various incentives, reducing predictability, and increasing frustration or task difficulty.

Evidence suggests that different patterns of physiologic reactivity are produced by different tasks and different task demands. For example, there are tasks that activate the "fight-flight" response. These tasks elicit predominantly beta-adrenergic responses and are associated with increases in cardiac output and skeletal muscle vasodilation. Another pattern is associated with increases in total peripheral resistance. In general, tasks involving active coping, mental effort, conflict, competition, unpredictability, engagement, and frustration elicit beta-adrenergic responses. Tasks that elicit the increases in peripheral resistance appear to be more passive, and involve quiet attentiveness.

A discussion of the instrumentation to measure cardiovascular and neuroendocrine responses in the laboratory is obviously beyond the scope of this chapter. A number of methods are available. Automated units for measuring heart rate and blood pressure are commercially available and are relatively inexpensive. For example, the Dynamap automatic heart rate and blood pressure monitor sells for $2,500 and can be obtained from Critikon, c/o Johnson & Johnson Company, P. O. Box 22800, Tampa, FL 33630-2800. Similarly, an automatic pump for exfusing blood during laboratory tasks to measure catecholamines, cortisol, testosterone, and other hormones can be purchased from Cormed Instruments, 591 Mahar Street, Box 470, Medina, NY 14103, and sells for $1,800.

It is also important to assess physiologic reactivity in the natural environment during normal daily activities. Technological advances in the past 10 years have made it possible to measure physiologic reactivity outside the laboratory. For example, automatic ambulatory determinations of blood pressure and heart rate responses can be obtained at regular intervals for up to 24 hours. A more complete discussion of ambulatory monitoring techniques is presented in Chapter 17.

ASSESSMENT OF TYPE A IN CHILDREN

Since most studies of the Type A behavior pattern have focused on white, middle-aged, employed males or college freshmen, most of the Type A assessment procedures have been designed for use with adults. However, researchers who were interested in the developmental aspects of Type A behavior found that the established instruments (JAS, SI, etc.) were not suitable for children.

Matthews developed the Matthews Youth Test for Health (MYTH) for use with elementary school children (Matthews, 1978, 1979). Many of the items evolved from an earlier test called the Children's Activity Survey (Glass, 1977). The MYTH is a 17-item 5-point rating scale evaluation of the child's behavior in the classroom by the teacher. For example, one representative item is "when this child plays, he or she is competitive." A teacher-rating of 1 is "very uncharacteristic" while a rating of 5 is "very characteristic." Possible MYTH scores range from 17 (extreme Type B) to 85 (extreme Type A).

Each item on the MYTH was designed (a) to measure one of three components of Type A behavior (competitive achievement-striving, aggression-hostility, and time-urgency), and (b) to describe behavior readily observed in the school classroom. Reliability and validity measurements were obtained from a sample of 485 rural, white, middle-class children in grades K, 2, 4, and 6 (Matthews & Angulo, 1980). The MYTH yields an overall Type A score and two subscale scores. One subscale score is the sum of all items describing children's competitive and achievement behaviors. The second is the sum of all items describing hostility, aggression, and time-urgency. The total score and components are internally consistent, and test-retest reliability over 3 months is in the range of .73 to .86.

Although the MYTH has not been related to CHD, children's behavior has been found to be distinguished by their scores on the MYTH. For example, Type A children have been found to be more aggressive with a Bobo doll, impatient on a tracking task, inclined to interrupt the experimenter, squirmy, restless, and able to win a car race by a larger margin (only when the experimenter was female) than Type B children (Matthews & Angulo, 1980).

In contrast to the MYTH, which is scored by an independent observer, that is, teacher, a *self*-administered Type A test has been developed for children by Wolf (Wolf, Hunter, & Webber, 1979). The Hunter-Wolf A-B Rating Scale is patterned after the Bortner Self-Rating Scale. It is composed of 24 scales in the form of a 7-rung ladder. The subject is asked to describe where he/she is on the ladder most of the time. Representative items on the scale include: I am easy going--I am hard driving; It does matter if I'm late--it doesn't matter if I'm late; and I drink fast--I drink slowly. Ratings are scored in the A direction and summed over 24 items to obtain a total Type A score ranging from 24 to 168. Factor analysis has yielded four components: (a) restlessness--aggression, (b) eagerness--energy, (c) leadership, and (d) alienation.

Test-retest reliability data on the A-B Scale over a 6-week period have not been encouraging (correlations under .60). As with the MYTH, however, studies have found that the behaviors of Type A and B children can be distinguished on various tasks. For example, 336 fifth and seventh graders were compared on a battery of performance measures characteristic of Type A. Type A children were found to speak louder, eat faster, walk faster, drop more marbles into a box, and cross out more digits than Type B children did (Wolf, Sklov, Wenzl, Hunter, & Berenson, 1982). These data support the validity of the instrument, although more work is needed.

There are more reliable methods for assessing Type A behavior in older children. For example, the 10-question Butensky-Waldron interview (Butensky, Faralli, Heebner, & Waldron, 1976) is modeled after the SI but relies more on content than on voice stylistics. An adolescent version of the SI (the ASI), developed by Siegel and Leitch (1981), consists of 22 items delivered in a nonchallenging manner. Although the ASI agreed with the Bortner Rating Scale only 54% of the time, certain factors on the ASI (e.g., interview behaviors, impatience, and "hard-drivingness") were related to measures on the Edwards Personality Inventory. The interview behaviors assessed by the ASI such as vigorous and quick responses, interruptions, hostility, and attempts to control the interview are present even in adolescence, and are associated with global Type A behavior classification (Siegel, Matthews, & Leitch, 1981).

MEASURING COMPONENTS OF ANGER

Matthews, Jamison, and Cotlington (1985) listed more than 20 available instruments for anger/hostility assessment in their review of self-report Type A and anger questionnaires. Four instruments appeared to be promising in terms of their psychometric characteristics and their demonstrated relationship with CHD end points. These are the Buss-Durkee Hostility Inventory, the Framingham Anger Scales, the Novaco Anger Scale, and the Cook-Medley Hostility Scale. Each of these instruments is described below, along with the available data on its relationship to cardiovascular disease.

BUSS-DURKEE HOSTILITY INVENTORY

The Buss-Durkee Hostility Inventory is a 75-item true-false scale, designed to measure each of seven subtypes of hostility (physical assault, indirect hostility, irritability, negativism, resentment, suspicion, verbal hostility). A global measure of hostility is also obtained with this scale (Buss & Durkee, 1957). Bendig (1962) derived an overt hostility and a covert hostility subscale from the Buss-Durkee item pool, using factor analysis, and reported internal reliability coefficients for these subscales of .76 and .72, respectively. Two-week test-retest reliability for the global hostility score was .82 (Biaggio, Supplee, & Curtis, 1981) and ranged from .64 to .78 for the seven subscales. Validity data include positive correlations with other self-report anger scales and some inconsistent findings regarding the scale's ability to predict role-playing responses to anger-provoking circumstances, willingness to administer shock to confederates, and aggression ratings by others (Matthews et al., 1985). Hicks and Hodgson (1981) found that JAS-defined Type A college students scored higher than Type Bs on the overt hostility subscale of the Buss-Durkee. In this study, no differences in covert hostility were found.

Although findings regarding the association between Buss-Durkee scores and hypertension are inconsistent (Matthews et al., 1985), Esler et al. (1977) reported that the scale was useful in demonstrating differences between hypertensive subtypes. They found that high renin hypertensives (found to have higher indices of sympathetic activity) scored lower than normal renin hypertensives or normotensives on Buss-Durkee verbal hostility and irritability subscales.

Matthews et al. (1985) described several studies investigating the relationship of Buss-Durkee scores with psychophysiological reactivity. The results in this area appear somewhat complex, and need replication. For example, Diamond et al. (1984) described interactions between the Buss-Durkee and several other personality measures (SI, potential for hostility from SI, Framingham anger-out, Framingham anger-in) and their relationship with systolic blood pressure changes during a challenging

25

laboratory task. In this study, high hostile (Buss-Durkee) subjects showed greater reactivity than low hostile subjects.

FRAMINGHAM ANGER SCALES

Included in the Framingham Heart Study were four short self-report scales designed to measure anger: anger symptoms (five items inquiring about propensity to get tense or worried), anger-in (three items measuring tendency to keep anger to oneself), anger-out (two items measuring tendency to take out anger on others), and anger-discuss (two items, self-explanatory). Items for each of these scales were selected from a 300-item pool by expert judges and were evaluated by factor analysis and item analysis. Internal reliability coefficients for the anger symptoms scale was estimated at .74; no values were reported for the other Framingham anger scales (Haynes et al., 1978).

Although data on the validity of the Framingham scales are relatively limited, their use in the Framingham epidemiological study warranted their inclusion in this chapter. Among women in this study, scores from the anger symptoms, anger-in, and anger-discuss scales were related to diastolic blood pressure, and the anger symptoms scale score was related to CHD prevalence. Low anger-out scores were prospectively related to the development of CHD over an 8-year period for men and women ages 55-64 in this sample. High anger-in and low anger-discuss scores predicted the development of CHD in women as well. Multivariate analyses controlling for other standard risk factors on subsamples of the Framingham study showed significant independent effects of Type A and low anger-out for white collar men, and independent effects of Type A and low anger-discuss scores on CHD among the working women in Framingham (Haynes et al., 1980).

NOVACO ANGER INVENTORY

The Novaco Anger Inventory is an 80-item self-report Likert scale that measures the subject's intensity of reaction to a variety of anger-provoking incidents. Each item represents one incident (e.g., being singled out for correction when the actions of others go unnoticed or someone has chipped paint off your car). Subjects' reactions to each item are rated and summed to provide a total scale score. A principal component analysis suggested that the scale measures a single dimension (Novaco, 1975).

Internal consistency of the Novaco Anger Scale has been shown to be quite high (.90 or above), but test-retest reliability is less consistently high. One study (Biaggio et al., 1981) reported 2-week test-retest correlations of .17. Matthews et al. (1985) reviewed the evidence for the validity of the scale, which consisted mainly of adequate correlations with other self-report anger inventories. No relationships were found between the Novaco and self-reports of actual anger incidents, role-playing response to anger-provoking situations, or physiological reactions to self-reports or role plays. However, the Novaco Scale was used in Friedman's Recurrent Coronary Prevention Project, and preliminary unpublished reports have suggested that it may be a significant predictor of recurrent CHD events.

COOK-MEDLEY HOSTILITY SCALE

The Cook-Medley Hostility (Ho) Scale is one of the more important self-report Type A component measures available. It is a 50-item true-false subscale of the MMPI that was selected from a larger group of items found to discriminate teachers who had the most difficulty getting along with pupils, as measured by the Minnesota Teacher Attitude Inventory (Cook & Medley, 1954).

The Cook-Medley appears to be quite reliable and stable over time. Internal reliability in a group of 200 graduate students was estimated at .86 (Cook & Medley, 1954), and test-retest reliability over a 4-year period has been found to be as high as .89 (Shekelle, Gayle, Ostfeld, & Paul, 1983).

Validity evidence suggests that the Ho scale measures hostility as well as a form of cynicism or distrust. Correlations between Ho and Spielberger's Trait Anger Scale have ranged from .59 to .61 (Smith & Frohm, 1985; Williams et al., 1980) and the scale was also significantly ($r = .37$) associated with potential for hostility ratings from the SI (Dembroski et al., 1985). Smith and Frohm (1985) reported that the Cook-Medley Scale was associated with scores on the Buss-Durkee, especially with the Resentment (.70) and Suspicion (.69) subscales. Evidence for "cynicism" in the Cook-Medley is derived from the fact that this scale shares many items with cynicism factors from the MMPI (Williams, Barefoot, & Shekelle, 1984). Smith and Frohm (1985) reported that Ho scores were negatively associated with scores from the Rotter Trust Scale as well.

In two independent, prospective studies, the Cook-Medley Hostility Scale has been shown to be a significant predictor of CHD morbidity over a 10-25 year time interval, as well as a significant predictor of death from CHD and other causes over a 20-25 year period (Barefoot, Dahlstrom, & Williams, 1983; Shekelle et al., 1983). In one sample (Barefoot et al., 1983), the high Ho group had a four- to five-fold relative risk of developing CHD and a six-fold relative risk of dying over a 25-year period. In addition, the Ho scale has been found to be associated with the extent of coronary atherosclerosis. Whereas 70% of the patients who scored 11 or more on the Ho scale demonstrated significant occlusion in at least one artery, only 48% of the patients scoring 10 or less had a significant occlusion in at least one artery (Williams et al., 1980).

Matthews (1985) noted that one major limitation of the research relating anger/hostility with CHD is its failure to specify the behavioral mechanisms by which this association might occur. She posited four dimensions of anger: environmental elicitors; anger experience (frequency, duration, intensity); mode of expression; and origin or source (e.g., hostile attitude). She recommended that these all be assessed in any study of anger and CHD, noting that these dimensions may vary in terms of their implications for coronary disease. At the very least, more information on the construct validity of the above measures, their behavioral and psychosocial referents, and their relationship with the Type A behavior pattern is needed. The use of these anger/hostility measures in behavioral cardiovascular research is motivated by a need to specify the active ingredients of the Type A pattern: It would be a mistake merely to substitute one set of subjective, globally-defined measures for another.

SUMMARY

This chapter presented the reader with a critical, state-of-the-art appraisal of the methods commonly used to assess the Type A behavior pattern. A number of procedures were reviewed, including various interview techniques, self-report instruments, performance measures, and psychophysiological tasks. The strengths and limitations of each procedure were examined, and specific suggestions were offered. The importance of careful clinical judgment was emphasized, along with the development of more precise methods for assessing those specific aspects of the Type A behavior pattern that may be especially pathogenic. The concurrent assessment of the behavioral, psychological, and psychophysiological domains may be the most effective strategy for identifying individuals at risk for the premature development of coronary heart disease.

James A. Blumenthal, PhD, is an Associate Professor of Medical Psychology in the Department of Psychiatry, an Associate in the Department of Medicine, and Director of the Behavioral Physiology Laboratory at Duke University Medical Center. Dr. Blumenthal completed his PhD in clinical psychology at the University of Washington in 1975 and was a postdoctoral Fellow at Duke University's Center for the Study of Aging and Human Development from 1977 to 1979. Dr. Blumenthal has published extensively in the area of behavioral cardiology, has edited two books, and published more than 50 papers. His main interests are in the areas of behavioral approaches to the primary and secondary prevention of coronary heart disease and age-related changes in cardiovascular and psychological functioning. Dr. Blumenthal may be contacted at the Behavioral Physiology Laboratory, Box 3926, Duke University Medical Center, Durham, NC 27710.

Thomas Kamarck, PhD, recently completed his clinical internship in medical psychology in the Department of Psychiatry at Duke University Medical Center and is presently a post-doctoral Fellow in Behavioral Medicine at the University of Pittsburgh. He received his PhD in clinical psychology in 1986 from the University of Oregon. Dr. Kamarck's dissertation examined the coping styles associated with successful smoking cessation and maintenance. His research interests include psychosocial predictors of health status and health intervention outcomes, smoking cessation, and coronary-prone behavior. Dr. Kamarck can be contacted at the Department of Psychiatry, University of Pittsburgh, Pittsburgh, PA 15260.

RESOURCES

Anderson, J. R., & Waldron, I. (1983). Behavioral and content components of the Structured Interview assessment of the Type A behavior pattern in women. *Journal of Behavioral Medicine, 6,* 123-134.

Barefoot, J. C., Dahlstrom, W. G., & Williams, R. B. (1983). Hostility, CHD incidence and total mortality: A 25-year follow-up study of 255 physicians. *Psychosomatic Medicine, 45,* 59-63.

Belgian-French Pooling Project. (1984). Assessment of Type A behaviour by the Bortner scale and ischaemic heart disease. *European Heart Journal, 5,* 440-446.

Bendig, A. W. (1962). Factor analytic scales of covert and overt hostility. *Journal of Consulting Psychology, 26,* 200.

Biaggio, K. K., Supplee, K., & Curtis, N. (1981). Reliability and validity of four anger scales. *Journal of Personality Assessment, 45,* 639-648.

Blumenthal, J. A., Herman, S., O'Toole, L. C., Haney, T. L., Williams, R. B., & Barefoot, J. C. (1985). Development of a brief self-report measure of the Type A (coronary prone) behavior pattern. *Journal of Psychosomatic Research, 29,* 265-274.

Blumenthal, J. A., O'Toole, L. C., & Haney, T. (1984). Behavioral assessment of the Type A behavior pattern. *Psychosomatic Medicine, 46,* 415-423.

Blumenthal, J. A., Thompson, L. W., Williams, R. B., & Kong, Y. (1979). Anxiety-proneness and coronary heart disease. *Journal of Psychosomatic Research, 23,* 17-21.

Blumenthal, J. A., Williams, R. B., Kong, Y., Schanberg, S. M., & Thompson, L. W. (1978). Type A behavior and coronary atherosclerosis. *Circulation, 58,* 634-639.

Bortner, R. W. (1969). A short rating scale as a potential measure of pattern A behavior. *Journal of Chronic Diseases, 22,* 87-91.

Bortner, R. W., & Rosenman, R. H. (1967). The measurement of pattern A behavior. *Journal of Chronic Diseases, 20,* 525-533.

Buss, A. H., & Durkee, A. (1957). An inventory for assessing different kinds of hostility. *Journal of Consulting Psychology, 21,* 343-349.

Butensky, A., Faralli, V., Heebner, H., & Waldron, I. (1976). Elements of the coronary-prone behavior pattern in children and teenagers. *Journal of Psychosomatic Research, 20,* 439-444.

Byrne, D. G., Rosenman, R. H., Schiller, E., & Chesney, M. A. (1985). Consistency and variation among instruments purporting to measure the Type A behavior pattern. *Psychosomatic Medicine, 47,* 242-261.

Caffrey, B. (1978). Psychometric procedures applied to the assessment of the coronary-prone behavior pattern. In T. M. Dembroski, S. M. Weiss, J. L. Shields, S. G. Haynes, & M. Feinleib (Eds.), *Coronary Prone Behavior* (pp. 89-94). New York: Springer-Verlag.

Case, R. B., Heller, S. S., Case, N. B., Moss, A. J., & Multicenter Post-Infarction Research Group. (1985). Type A behavior and survival after acute myocardial infarction. *The New England Journal of Medicine, 312,* 737-741.

Chesney, M. A., Black, G. W., Chadwick, J. H., & Rosenman, R. H. (1981). Psychological correlates of the Type A behavior pattern. *Journal of Behavioral Medicine, 4,* 217-224.

Cook, W. W., & Medley, D. M. (1954). Proposed hostility and pharisaic-virtue scores for the MMPI. *Journal of Applied Psychology, 38,* 414-418.

Costa, P. T., Zonderman, A. B., Engel, B. T., Baile, W. F., Brimlow, D. L., & Brinker, J. (1985). The relation of chest pain symptoms to angiographic findings of coronary artery stenosis and neuroticism. *Psychosomatic Medicine, 47,* 285-293.

Dembroski, T. M., MacDougall, J. M., Williams, R. B., Haney, T. L., & Blumenthal, J. A. (1985). Components of Type A, hostility, and anger-in: Relationship to angiographic findings. *Psychosomatic Medicine, 47,* 219-233.

Dembroski, T. M., Weiss, S. M., Shields, J. L., Haynes, S. G., & Feinleib, M. (Eds.). (1978). *Coronary-Prone Behavior.* New York: Springer-Verlag.

Diamond, E. L., Schneiderman, N., Schwartz, D., Smith, J. C., Vorp, R., & Pasin, R. D. (1984). Harassment, hostility, and Type A as determinants of cardiovascular reactivity during competition. *Journal of Behavioral Medicine, 7,* 171-189.

Dimsdale, J. E., Hackett, T. P., Hutter, A. M., Block, P. C., & Catanzano, D. M. (1978). Type A personality and extent of coronary atherosclerosis. *The American Journal of Cardiology, 42,* 583-586.

Esler, M., Julius, S., Zweifler, A., Randall, O., Harburg, E., Gardiner, H., & DeQuattro, V. (1977). Mild high-renin essential hypertension: Neurogenic human hypertension? *New England Journal of Medicine, 296,* 405-411.

Feldstein, S., Siegman, A. W., Simpson, S., Barkley, S., & Kobren, R. (1984, April). *Assessing Coronary-Prone Behavior from the Temporal Structure of Speech.* Paper presented at the meeting of the Eastern Psychological Association, Baltimore.

French-Belgian Collaborative Group. (1982). Ischemic heart disease and psychological patterns. Prevalence and incidence studies in Belgium and France. *Advances in Cardiology, 29,* 25-31.

Friedman, M. (1971). The Type A behavior pattern: Its association with coronary heart disease. *Annals of Clinical Research, 3,* 300-312.

Friedman, M., Brown, A. E., & Rosenman, R. H. (1969). Voice analysis test for detection of behavior pattern. *Journal of the American Medical Association, 208,* 828-836.

Friedman, M., & Powell, L. H. (1984). The diagnosis and quantitative assessment of Type A behavior: Introduction and description of the videotaped structured interview. *Integrative Psychiatry, 2,* 123-136.

Friedman, M., & Rosenman, R. H. (1959). Association of specific overt behavior pattern with blood and cardiovascular findings. *Journal of the American Medical Association, 96,* 1286-1296.

Friedman, M., & Rosenman, R. H. (1974). *Type A Behavior and Your Heart.* New York: Alfred A. Knopf.

Friedman, M., Thoresen, C. E., Gill, J. J., Ulmer, D., Thompson, L., Powell, L. H., Price, V. A., Elck, S. R., Rabin, D. D., Breall, W. S., Piaget, G., Dixon, T., Bourg, E., Levy, R. A., & Tasto, D. L. (1982). Feasibility of altering Type A behavior pattern. Recurrent Coronary Prevention Project Study: Methods, baseline results and preliminary findings. *Circulation, 66,* 83-92.

Glass, D. C. (1977). *Behavior Patterns, Stress and Coronary Disease.* Hillsdale, NJ: Lawrence Erlbaum.

Haynes, S. G., & Feinleib, M. (1982). Type A behavior and the incidence of coronary heart disease in the Framingham Heart Study. *Advances in Cardiology, 29,* 85-95.

Haynes, S. G., Feinleib, M., & Kannel, W. B. (1980). The relationship of psychosocial factors to coronary heart disease in the Framingham Study: III. Eight-year incidence of coronary heart disease. *American Journal of Epidemiology, 111,* 37-58.

Haynes, S. G., Levine, S., Scotch, N., Feinleib, M., & Kannel, W. (1978). The relationship of psychosocial factors to coronary heart disease in the Framingham study: I. Methods and risk factors. *American Journal of Epidemiology, 107,* 362-383.

Heller, R. F. (1979). Type A behavior and coronary heart disease. *British Medical Journal, 2,* 368.

Hicks, R., & Hodgson, J. (1981). Type A-B behavior and the overt and covert hostility levels of college students. *Psychological Reports, 49,* 317-318.

Howland, E. W., & Siegman, A. W. (1982). Toward the automated measurement of the Type A behavior pattern. *Journal of Behavioral Medicine, 5,* 37-54.

Jenkins, C. D., Rosenman, R. H., & Friedman, M. (1966). Components of the coronary-prone behavior pattern: Their relation to silent myocardial infarction and blood lipids. *Journal of Chronic Diseases, 19,* 599-609.

Jenkins, C. D., Rosenman, R. H., & Friedman, M. (1967). Development of an objective psychological test for the determination of the coronary prone behavior pattern in employed men. *Journal of Chronic Diseases, 20,* 371-379.

Jenkins, C. D., Rosenman, R. H., & Friedman, M. (1968). Replicability of rating the coronary-prone behaviour pattern. *British Journal of Preventive Social Medicine, 22,* 16-22.

Jenkins, C. D., Rosenman, R. H., & Zyzanski, S. J. (1974). Prediction of clinical coronary heart disease by a test for the coronary-prone behavior pattern. *New England Journal of Medicine, 290,* 1271-1275.

Jenkins, C. D., Zyzanski, S. J., & Rosenman, R. H. (1971). Progress toward validation of a computer-scored test for the Type A coronary-prone behavior pattern. *Psychosomatic Medicine, 33,* 193-202.

Jenkins, C. D., Zyzanski, S. J., & Rosenman, R. H. (1976). Risk of new myocardial infarction in middle-aged men with manifest coronary heart disease. *Circulation,* *53,* 342-347.

Jenkins, C. D., Zyzanski, S. J., & Rosenman, R. H. (1979). *The Jenkins Activity Survey for Health Prediction.* New York: The Psychological Corp.

Jenkins, C. D., Zyzanski, S. J., Rosenman, R. H., & Cleveland, G. L. (1971). Association of coronary-prone behavior scores with recurrence of coronary heart disease. *Journal of Chronic Diseases, 24,* 601-611.

Kornitzer, M., Magotteau, V., Degre, C., Kittel, F., Struyven, J., & Van Thiel, E. (1982). Angiographic findings and the Type A pattern assessed by means of the Bortner Scale. *Journal of Behavioral Medicine, 5,* 313-320.

Koskenvuo, M., Kaprio, J., Langinvainio, H., & Romo, M. (1983). Mortality in relation to coronary-prone behavior: A six-year follow-up of the Bortner Scale in middle-aged Finnish men. *Activitas Nervosa Superior,* *25,* 107-109.

Krantz, D. S., & Manuck, S. B. (1984). Acute psycho-physiologic reactivity and risk of cardiovascular disease: A review and methodologic critique. *Psychological Bulletin, 96,* 435-464.

Krantz, D. S., Sanmarco, M. I., Selvester, R. H., & Matthews, K. A. (1979). Psychological correlates of progression of atherosclerosis in men. *Psychosomatic Medicine, 41,* 467-475.

Matthews, K. A. (1978). Assessment and developmental antecedents of the coronary prone behavior pattern in children. In T. M. Dembroski, S. M. Weiss, J. L. Shields, S. G. Haynes, & M. Feinleib (Eds.), *Coronary-Prone Behavior* (pp. 71-88). New York: Springer-Verlag.

Matthews, K. A. (1979). Efforts to control children and adults with the Type A coronary prone behavior pattern. *Child Development, 50,* 842-847.

Matthews, K. A. (1982). Psychological perspectives on the Type A behavior pattern. *Psychological Bulletin, 91,* 293-323.

Matthews, K. A. (1985). Assessment of Type A behavior, anger, and hostility in epidemiological studies of cardiovascular disease. In A. M. Ostfeld & E. D. Eaker (Eds.), *Measuring Psychosocial Variables in Epidemiologic Studies of Cardiovascular Disease: Proceedings of a Workshop* (NIH Publication No. 85-

2270, pp. 153-184). Washington, DC: U.S. Department of Health and Human Services.

Matthews, K. A., & Angulo, J. (1980). Measurement of the Type A behavior pattern in children: Assessment of children's competitiveness, impatience-anger, and aggression. *Child Development, 51,* 466-475.

Matthews, K. A., Glass, D. C., Rosenman, R. H., & Bortner, R. W. (1977). Competitive drive, pattern A, and coronary heart disease: A further analysis of some data from the Western Collaborative Group Study. *Journal of Chronic Diseases, 30,* 489-498.

Matthews, K. A., Jamison, J. W., & Cotlington, E. M. (1985). Appendix: Assessment of Type A, anger, and hostility: A review of scales through 1982. In A. M. Ostfeld & E. D. Eaker (Eds.), *Measuring Psychosocial Variables in Epidemiologic Studies of Cardiovascular Disease: Proceedings of a Workshop* (NIH Publication No. 85-2270, pp. 207-312). Washington, DC: U.S. Department of Health and Human Services.

Matthews, K. A., Krantz, D. S., Dembroski, T. M., & MacDougall, J. M. (1982). Unique and common variance in Structured Interview and Jenkins Activity Survey measures of the Type A behavior pattern. *Journal of Personality and Social Psychology, 42,* 303-313.

Novaco, R. W. (1975). *Anger Control: The Development and Evaluation of an Experimental Treatment.* Lexington, MA: Lexington Books.

Price, V. A. (1982). *Type A Behavior Pattern: A Model for Research and Practice.* New York: Academic Press.

Review Panel on Coronary-Prone Behavior and Coronary Heart Disease. (1981). Coronary-prone behavior and coronary heart disease: A critical review. *Circulation, 63,* 1199-1215.

Rosenman, R. H. (1978). The interview method of assessment of the coronary-prone behavior pattern. In T. M. Dembroski, S. M. Weiss, J. L. Shields, S. G. Haynes, & M. Feinleib (Eds.), *Coronary-Prone Behavior* (pp. 55-69). New York: Springer-Verlag.

Rosenman, R. H., Brand, R. J., Jenkins, C. D., Friedman, M., Straus, R., & Wurm, M. (1975). Coronary heart disease in the Western Collaborative Group Study: Final follow-up experience of 8 1/2 years. *Journal of the American Medical Association, 23,* 872-877.

Rosenman, R. H., & Friedman, M. (1961). Association of specific behavior pattern in women with blood and cardiovascular findings. *Circulation, 24,* 1173-1184.

Rosenman, R. H., Friedman, M., Straus, R., Wurm, M., Kositchek, R., Hahn, W., & Werthessen, N. T. (1964). A predictive study of coronary heart disease. *Journal of the American Medical Association, 189,* 113-124.

Scherwitz, L., Berton, K., & Leventhal, H. (1977). Type A assessment and interaction in the Behavior Pattern Interview. *Psychosomatic Medicine, 39,* 229-240.

Scherwitz, L., Graham, L. E., Grandits, G., & Billings, J. (1985). *Behavior Type Assessment in the Multiple Risk Factor Intervention Trial Structured Interview.* Manuscript submitted for publication.

Schucker, B., & Jacobs, D. R. (1977). Assessment of behavioral risk for coronary disease by voice characteristics. *Psychosomatic Medicine, 39,* 219-228.

Shekelle, R. B., Gayle, M., Ostfeld, A. M., & Paul, O. (1983). Hostility, risk of coronary heart disease, and mortality. *Psychosomatic Medicine, 45,* 109-114.

Siegel, J. M., & Leitch, C. J. (1981). Assessment of the Type A behavior pattern in adolescents. *Psychosomatic Medicine, 43,* 45-56.

Siegel, J. M., Matthews, K. A., & Leitch, C. J. (1981). Validation of the Type A interview assessment of adolescents: A multidimensional approach. *Psychosomatic Medicine, 43,* 311-321.

Siegman, A. W., & Feldstein, S. (1985, March). *The Relationship of Expressive Vocal Behavior to Severity of Coronary Artery Disease.* Paper presented at the meeting of the Society of Behavioral Medicine, New Orleans.

Siegman, A. W., Feldstein, S., Barkley, S., & Simpson, S. W. (1985). *Content and Style in the Structured Interview Method for the Assessment of the Type A Behavior Pattern.* Manuscript submitted for publication.

Smith, T. W., & Frohm, K. D. (1985). What's so unhealthy about hostility? Construct validity and psychosocial correlates of the Cook and Medley Ho scales. *Health Psychology, 4,* 503-520.

van Dijl, H. (1978). The A/B typology according to Friedman and Rosenan (sic) and an effort to test some of the characteristics by means of a psychological test (RSL or BUL). *Journal of Psychosomatic Medicine, 22,* 101-109.

Vickers, R. (1973). *A Short Measure of Type A Personality.* Unpublished manuscript, University of Michigan, Institute for Social Research, Ann Arbor, MI.

Williams, R. B., Barefoot, J. C., & Shekelle, R. B. (1984). The health consequences of hostility. In M. A. Chesney, S. E. Goldsten, & R. H. Rosenman (Eds.), *Anger, Hostility and Behavioral Medicine* (pp. 173-186). New York: Hemisphere McGraw/Hill.

Williams, R. B., Haney, T. L., Lee, K. L., Kong, Y., Blumenthal, J. A., & Whalen, R. E. (1980). Type A behavior, hostility, and atherosclerosis. *Psychosomatic Medicine, 42,* 539-549.

Wolf, T. M., Hunter, S., & Webber, L. (1979). Psychosocial measures and cardiovascular risk factors in children and adolescents. *Journal of Psychology, 101,* 139-146.

Wolf, T. M., Sklov, M. C., Wenzl, P. A., Hunter, S. M., & Berenson, G. S. (1982). Validation of a measure of Type A behavior pattern in children: Bogalusa Heart Study. *Child Development, 53,* 126-135.

Young, L. D., & Barboriak, J. J. (1982). Reliability of a brief scale for assessment of coronary-prone behavior and standard measures of Type A behavior. *Perceptual and Motor Skills, 55,* 1039-1042.

ASSESSMENT OF HEADACHES*

Frank Andrasik and Edmund J. Burke

INTRODUCTION

In 1962, a distinguished panel of medical experts met to summarize what was then known about headache and to develop a classification scheme for headache (Ad Hoc Committee on the Classification of Headache, 1962). Fifteen separate types of headache were identified (see Table 1, page 40). Each type was assumed to represent an etiologically distinct pain syndrome, and some were suspected of having multiple causes. The first three headache types--migraine, muscle-contraction, and the two combined--have become a focus for behavioral medicine practitioners because of their demonstrated responsiveness to behaviorally based treatments and their high frequency of occurrence. For example, 94% of patients seeking treatment at a well-known headache specialty clinic received one of these diagnoses (Lance, Curran, & Anthony, 1965).

The prototypical migraine (or vascular) headache is sudden in its onset, affects only one side of the head, builds quickly to an intense throbbing, pounding, or pulsating sensation at its peak, and lasts approximately 8 hours, although it can range from a few hours to several

*Preparation of this chapter was supported by Research Career Development Award 1 K04 NS00818 and grant 1 R01 NS16891, both from the National Institute of Neurological and Communicative Disorders and Stroke and awarded to the senior author.

TABLE 1:   CLASSIFICATION OF HEADACHE

---

1. Vascular Headache of Migraine Type
    A.   "Classic" Migraine
    B.   "Common" Migraine
    C.   "Cluster" Headache
    D.   "Hemiplegic" and "Ophthalmoplegic" Migraine
    E.   "Lower-Half" Headache
2. Muscle-Contraction Headache
3. Combined Headache: Vascular and Muscle-Contraction
4. Headache of Nasal Vasomotor Reaction
5. Headache of Delusional, Conversion, or Hypochondriacal States
6. Nonmigrainous Vascular Headaches
7. Traction Headache
8. Headache Due to Overt Cranial Inflammation
9-13. Headache Due to Disease of Ocular, Aural, Nasal and Sinusal,
      Dental, or Other Cranial or Neck Structures
14. Cranial Neuritides
15. Cranial Neuralgias

Note: From "Classification of Headache" by Ad Hoc Committee on the Classification of Headache, 1962, Journal of the American Medical Association, 179, p. 718.

---

continuous days. Anorexia, nausea, and fatigue frequently accompany migraine; vomiting, pallor, diarrhea, dizziness, paresthesia, hypersensitivity to sound and light, and cold in the extremities are less frequent. Approximately 10% or so migraineurs experience conspicuous neurological symptoms, most commonly visual in nature, during a prodromal phase. These migraines are termed "classic," whereas migraines occurring in the absence of prodromes are termed "common" (Diamond & Dalessio, 1982). This distinction is of questionable value when planning behavioral treatment, so most investigators ignore it.

Migraine is attributed to a two-phase cerebrovascular process; intra- and extra-cranial vasoconstriction prior to headache, which in its severe form produces the neurological prodromes, followed by a reactive vasodilation, which produces the throbbing headache pain. A number of biochemical events accompany these changes in peripheral vascular tone and contribute to the experience of pain (Kudrow, 1983).

In contrast to migraine, the typical muscle-contraction (or tension, psychogenic, or depressive) headache has a more insidious onset and resolution and is experienced as a dull, steady bilateral or band-like pain or ache. The pain is less intense than that of a migraine, but many individuals experience this type of headache on a daily or near daily basis. Pain is believed to result from "...sustained contractions of skeletal muscles in the absence of permanent structural changes, usually as part of the individual's reaction during life stress" (Ad Hoc Committee on the Classification of Headache, 1962, p. 128). Pain is attributed to stimulation of pain receptors in the contracted muscles and ischemia produced by compression of intramuscular arterioles (Haynes, 1981).

The third type of headache identified by the Ad Hoc Committee is not really a separate entity, for it consists of elements of both of the two previously described headache types "predominantly co-existing in an attack" (1962, p. 128). As many as 1/5 to 1/3 of all headache sufferers experience significant symptoms of both types of headache. These combined or mixed headache types are assumed to result from both cerebrovascular and musculoskeletal aberrations.

There is a fourth headache type presumed to have a significant psychological component--delusional, conversion, or hypochondriacal--but exceedingly little is known about this type of headache. Some (Adams, Brantley, & Thompson, 1982) suspect that a sizable portion of individuals classified as muscle-contraction headache may be more appropriately categorized as conversion headache, but data supporting this alternative view and suggesting strategies for treatment are sparse.

Assessment of the headache patient begins with a careful interview, to ascertain specific headache type and to identify factors that might complicate or contraindicate behavioral treatment, and a thorough medical evaluation, to rule out organic causes or contributing factors.

HEADACHE INTERVIEW

The Ad Hoc Committee carefully specified various headache types, but it stopped short of providing specific sets of diagnostic criteria for each type of headache. Most researchers and practitioners use criteria similar to those presented in Table 2 (pages 42-43) to diagnose headache type. The diagnosis is based almost exclusively on information obtained during interviewing because there are no definitive laboratory tests for distinguishing between headache types. Alternative multimodal

TABLE 2: CRITERIA FOR DIAGNOSING HEADACHE

Headache Type	Key Symptoms	Number Required for Definite Diagnosis
Common Migraine	1. headache onset usually unilateral 2. headache usually accompanied by nausea and vomiting 3. headache usually described as throbbing or pulsating 4. photophobia during headache 5. one or more first-degree relatives diagnosed as migraine 6. independent diagnosis of migraine	presence of 3 of the 6

Classic Migraine	above plus
	7. headache usually preceded by
	  a. visual changes
	  b. hemiparesthesias
	  c. transient hemiparesis, or
	  d. noticeable speech difficulty
		presence of item 7 plus 2 of the above 6 for common migraine

Cluster	1. headaches occur in bouts that last several weeks and are separated by 3 or more months 2. during a bout headaches are of brief duration (less than 2 hours) and are present at least once every 2 days	presence of 3 of the above 6 for common migraine plus presence of both items 1 and 2
Muscle-Contraction	1. headache usually described as bilateral and beginning in the occipital, suboccipital, or back of the neck region 2. headache described as usually feeling like a tightness or external pressure on head and/or like a "cap" or "band" around the head 3. headache usually described as a continuing "dull ache" 4. independent diagnosis of muscle-contraction headache	presence of 2 of the 4

42

Headache Type	Key Symptoms	Number Required for Definite Diagnosis
Combined Migraine and Muscle-Contraction	1. patient clearly identifies two distinct types of headache 2. subject meets criteria for both migraine and muscle-contraction headache	presence of both items

Note: From "Psychological Functioning in Headache Sufferers" by F. Andrasik, E. B. Blanchard, J. G. Arena, S. J. Teders, R. C. Teevan, and L. D. Rodichok, 1982, Psychosomatic Medicine, 44, pp. 172-173. Copyright © 1982 by the American Psychosomatic Society, Inc. Reprinted and adapted by permission of Elsevier Science Publishing Co., Inc.

classification schemes have been proposed, but their utility is uncertain. A potentially useful approach developed by Thompson (1982) is summarized in the Appendix (see page 61).

During the initial contact with a patient, we have found it useful to employ a semi-structured interview format which assesses for each key symptom of the major headache types (Blanchard & Andrasik, 1985). In a study conducted in our laboratory (Blanchard, O'Keefe, Neff, Jurish, & Andrasik, 1981), it was found that two independent assessors (a doctoral student in Clinical Psychology and a Board Certified Neurologist) arrived at perfect agreement about diagnosis of headache type 86% of the time using the criteria listed in Table 2. Examination of cases of diagnostic disagreement suggested that just over 1/2 of the disagreements were attributable to patients either giving very different information to the two interviewers, or placing different emphasis on the same information when interviewed. It may be that the professional orientation of the interviewer influences what material the patient reports as important. Clinicians should keep this in mind when seeking to determine a patient's headache type and associated symptomatology.

Accurate diagnosis of headache type is important because of the assumed etiological differences between vascular and muscle-contraction headache and the resultant necessity for different approaches when using certain treatments (i.e., EMG biofeedback for tension headache versus temperature biofeedback for migraine). We need to mention, however, that some investigators are beginning to question whether migraine and muscle-contraction headache are all that different in their etiology (e.g., Bakal, 1982; Raskin & Appenzeller, 1980). An alternative view is the "severity model," which posits that migraine and muscle-contraction are due to similar causes and that muscle contraction headache is simply a less severe form of headache than migraine. If research confirms this notion then there will be little need to continue distinguishing muscle-contraction from migraine headache.

Regardless how this etiological debate turns out, it remains important to distinguish two migraine subtypes-- cluster and menstrual migraine--as both are quite resilient to behavioral treatment.

Cluster headache is extremely rare. It is the only nonorganic headache with a greater prevalence among males who outnumber females by approximately 4 to 1. With other forms of headache the ratio is 2-3 to 1 in favor of females. Cluster headache typically presents in bouts that last from a few weeks to a month or so, during which the patient experiences a series of frequent, excruciating headaches of brief duration (30-90 minutes). Cluster cycles are usually separated by long periods of remission, but it is possible for a patient to experience "chronic" cluster headache with bouts lasting up to a full year or longer. There is disagreement among medical authorities whether cluster is in fact a variant of migraine or whether it represents an independent headache disorder (Kudrow, 1980).

We treated 11 episodic cluster patients by a combination of relaxation and thermal biofeedback (Blanchard, Andrasik, Jurish, & Teders, 1982). Of the seven patients completing treatment, only three reported slight improvement. No patient reported significant improvement, and one was observed to deteriorate during the course of study. Until our treatment technologies and understanding of cluster headache improve, the practitioner is advised to have cluster headache ruled out and to refer these patients to a physician for planning the first line of treatment. The nonmedical practitioner may be able, however, to fill an adjunctive role by helping the cluster patient cope better with headache-related distress, and possibly by administering relaxation-based therapy for palliative purposes.

The remaining migraine subtype that needs to be ruled out is menstrual migraine, defined as migraine headache occurring any time during the menstrual flow or within 3 days prior to or following menstruation. A carefully controlled, large-scale outcome analysis of biofeedback and relaxation showed none of these behavioral treatments surpassed benefits resulting from participating in a no-treatment control condition (Solbach, Sargent, & Coyne, 1984). Solbach et al. argue that menstrual migraine, just like cluster headache, should be recognized and treated as a distinct migraine entity. Again, medical practitioners should have the responsibility for designing the treatment of choice in these cases.

Recent evidence suggests that certain headache medications can actually serve to maintain or induce headaches if taken in sufficient doses for extended periods of time. This is termed "rebound headache." Uncontrolled use of analgesics can even compromise the outcome of what would otherwise have been an effective treatment (Kudrow, 1982). Patients who end up abusing their medications typically start out having infrequent but very intense migraine headaches. Over time, they begin to anticipate headache onset and self-administer medications in an attempt to abort the expected headache. Soon, many of these individuals are consuming high levels of medication on a daily basis which helps perpetuate headache.

Kudrow (1982) speculates that frequent use of analgesics sustains pain by suppressing central serotonergic pathways concerned with the regulation of dull pain. For such cases, it would be wise to have the patient eliminate or significantly reduce analgesics prior to initiating treatment. In considering analgesic withdrawal, it is important to inform the patient that this may temporarily intensify headaches. It is often difficult, however, to convince patients to try this approach. The analgesic abuser has generally exhausted all other medical treatments and may be reluctant to give up the current medication, although aware that it is not adequate to control his or her headache pain. One approach is to ask the patient to eliminate the medication gradually, while following a course of behavioral treatment (Andrasik, 1985). Some patients require a brief hospitalization to be detoxified. Whatever approach is tried, it should be done in concert with the patient's physician. Preliminary data provided by Kudrow (1982) suggest that a sizable number of patients found that their headaches improved markedly following withdrawal from analgesics alone.

Ala-Hurula, Myllyla, and Hokkanen (1982) report that overuse of ergotamine tartrate (the abortive treatment of choice for migraine) can likewise serve to maintain headache. These authors found that ergotamine rebound headache occurred in patients taking dosages as low as .5 to 1.0 mg per day and that patients experienced relatively severe withdrawal symptoms, similar to migraine, upon discontinuation of daily use.

There is also preliminary evidence which suggests that two other medications commonly administered to headache patients can be disruptive to biofeedback therapy. Jay, Renelli, and Mead (1984) have reported that regular use of propranolol impeded the progress of patients undergoing thermal biofeedback, while amitriptyline impeded the progress of patients undergoing EMG biofeedback. These patients were able to reach desired biofeedback training criteria, but with greater difficulty and resulting frustration. Informing patients about the potential interference effects of these medications prior to treatment may serve to minimize patient frustration and lapses in motivation.

Depression and headache are strongly associated. Not only are chronic headache sufferers frequently depressed, but headache is the most common somatic symptom of patients presenting for the treatment of depression, occurring in over 50% of depressed patients (Diamond, 1983; Kudrow, 1976). An important assessment task for the practitioner is to determine whether the depressive symptomatology preceded the headache and thus may be causing or increasing the patient's vulnerability to headache (Luborsky, Docherty, & Penick, 1973) or is more a reaction to living with recurrent pain. We routinely conduct a mental status examination with headache patients to rule out pre-existing psychopathology which may compromise behavioral self-regulatory treatments, and delay or adjust the behavioral treatment as necessary. Preliminary evidence suggests that behavioral treatments for headache can result in decreases in depression (Cox & Thomas, 1981). Increased scores on measures of depression have also been prognostic of a poor response (in terms of reductions in headache activity) to behavioral treatment (Andrasik, 1986). The practitioner is advised to proceed cautiously with patients experiencing significant depression or other major psychopathology.

MEDICAL EVALUATION

Nonmedical practitioners treating individuals with chronic headache need to be assured that physical/neurological factors are not responsible for the individual's symptomatology. We require that patients undergo evaluation by a physician experienced with headache prior to treatment and in many cases have found it necessary to maintain close collaboration with the physician throughout treatment.

A neurologist collaborating in our research (Lawrence D. Rodichok, of the Albany Medical College) has prepared a list of danger signs for the nonmedical clinician which may require immediate referral to a physician. These are summarized in Table 3 (page 48). It is useful, during the initial assessment of a headache patient, to determine whether any of these signs and symptoms are present. Even in their apparent absence, pre-treatment referral to a physician is warranted. While only 1% to 2% of the patients presenting to our research program have been found to have serious medical conditions which would contraindicate behavioral treatment, those who have been identified possessed serious ailments (e.g., brain tumor). This argues strongly for medical evaluation in all cases. Further, the nonmedical professional needs to remain alert to any dramatic change in a patient's headache and treat this as cause for a repeat medical examination.

MEASUREMENT OF HEADACHE PAIN

With all treatment approaches, the clinician should have the patient provide some continuous record of headache activity to gauge severity of the problem, to detect meaningful changes in symptom report (intensification as well as improvement), and to decide when to terminate treatment. Further, it is important that the type of measure used not be altered over time. Research has shown that measures of headache activity determined by interview differ substantially from what is obtained when these same measures are determined from diary records kept by the patient.

47

TABLE 3: **"DANGER SIGNS" FOR HEADACHE PATIENTS WHICH MAY REQUIRE IMME-DIATE REFERRAL TO A PHYSICIAN**

1. Headache is a new symptom for the individual for the past 3 months or the nature of the headache has changed markedly in the past 3 months.
2. Presence of any sensory or motor deficits preceding or accompanying headache other than the typical visual prodromata of classic migraine. Examples include weakness or numbness in an extremity, twitching of the hands or feet, aphasia, or slurred speech.
3. Headache is one-sided and has always been on the same side of the head.
4. Headache is due to trauma, especially if it followed a period of unconsciousness (even if only momentary).
5. Headache that is constant and unremitting.
6. For a patient reporting tension headache-like symptoms:
   a. Pain intensity has been steadily increasing over a period of weeks to months with little or no relief.
   b. Headache is worse in the morning and becomes less severe during the day.
   c. Headache is accompanied by vomiting.
7. Patient has been treated for any kind of cancer and now has a complaint of headache.
8. Patient or significant other reports a noticeable change in personality or behavior or a notable decrease in memory or other intellectual functioning.
9. The patient is over 60 years of age and the headache is a relatively new complaint.
10. Pain onset is sudden and occurs during conditions of exertion (such as lifting heavy objects), sexual intercourse, or "heated" interpersonal situations.
11. Patient's family has a history of cerebral aneurysm, other vascular anomalies, or polycystic kidneys.

Note: List developed by Lawrence D. Rodichok, MD, Department of Neurology, Albany Medical College, Albany, NY. From Management of Chronic Headaches: A Psychological Approach (pp. 21-22) by E. B. Blanchard and F. Andrasik, 1985, New York: Pergamon Press. Copyright © 1985 by Pergamon Press. Reprinted by permission.

The Headache Diary. Pain is a private event, and there is no method yet available for obtaining hard measures of it. By default, subjective ratings of pain, sampled throughout the day, serve as the standard. An example of the commonly used Headache Diary, the notion for which was introduced by Budzynski, Stoyva, Adler, and Mullaney (1973), is shown in Figure 1 (pages 49-50). The front side of the 3" x 5" index card contains a grid upon which patients are asked to make hourly determinations of pain level. The back side of the diary record contains definitions for the pain intensity values and a space for the patient to indicate what medications were taken for ameliorating headache.

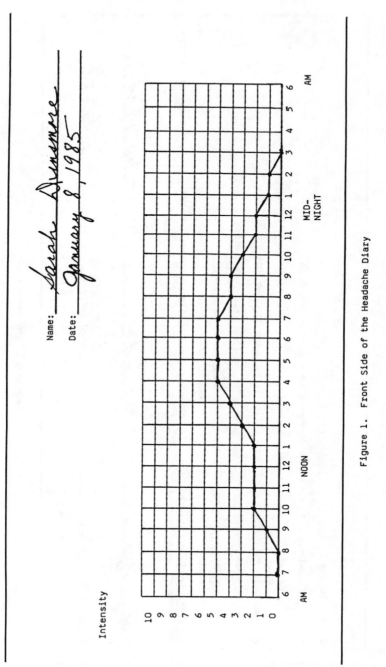

Figure 1. Front Side of the Headache Diary

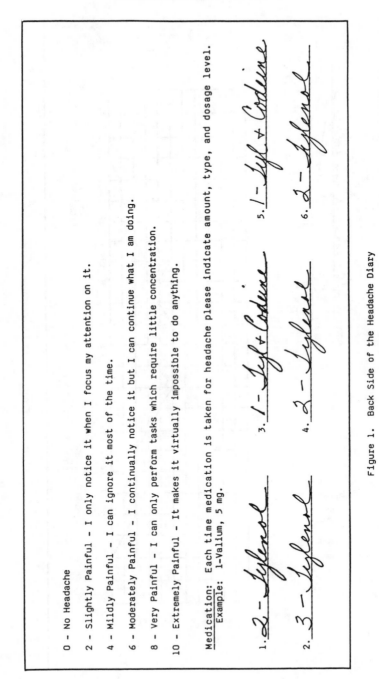

0 - No Headache

2 - Slightly Painful - I only notice it when I focus my attention on it.

4 - Mildly Painful - I can ignore it most of the time.

6 - Moderately Painful - I continually notice it but I can continue what I am doing.

8 - Very Painful - I can only perform tasks which require little concentration.

10 - Extremely Painful - It makes it virtually impossible to do anything.

Medication: Each time medication is taken for headache please indicate amount, type, and dosage level.
Example: 1-Valium, 5 mg.

1. 2 - Tylenol
2. 3 - Tylenol
3. 1 - Tyl + Codeine
4. 2 - Tylenol
5. 1 - Tyl + Codeine
6. 2 - Tylenol

Figure 1. Back Side of the Headache Diary

Data collected in the Headache Diary can be summarized over a specific interval, typically 1 week, to yield a variety of measures. The most useful measures seem to be: (a) Headache Index--sum of intensity values for each hourly rating (which would yield a value of 53 for the single record shown in Figure 1); (b) Frequency--number of discrete headaches; (c) Duration--length of time, to the nearest hour for the chart shown in Figure 1, between headache onset and offset; and (d) Peak Intensity--the highest intensity value for a given period. Peak intensity data allow the therapist to determine whether the "edge" is being taken off the headaches. Graphing the data at periodic intervals can be especially useful. It may be used to demonstrate a patient's progress at times when lack of motivation threatens to undermine treatment effectiveness.

Quantifying changes in medication consumption is difficult when the patient takes several medications concurrently or switches from one medication to another because of possible differences in the potency of the respective medications. Coyne, Sargent, Segerson, and Obourn (1976) had physicians experienced with headache management provide potency ratings for various analgesic preparations most often used to control migraine. We have made additions to their original list and have grouped the medications by potency, ranging in values from 1 to 7 (see Table 4, page 52). A medication index is obtained by multiplying the number of pills taken by the potency value and summing across all medications taken.

Tracking changes in medication consumption is important for several reasons. First, there is the possibility of certain medications exacerbating headache (analgesic rebound phenomenon) or complicating treatment. Second, many patients request behavioral treatment because of a desire to reduce or eliminate need for medication. Systematic measures are necessary to evaluate progress towards this goal. Finally, concurrent measurement of pain and medication will allow the therapist to determine if observed improvements in pain report are due in part to increased use of medications or enhanced compliance with a prophylactic regimen.

Several investigators have attempted to make improvements in the assessment methods suggested by Budzynski and his colleagues (1973). These modifications have primarily been concerned with simplifying the recording procedure, so as to achieve better patient

TABLE 4: POTENCY VALUES FOR MEDICATIONS USED TO TREAT HEADACHE

1	2	3	4	5	6	7
Actifed	Darvocet N	Cafergot	Codeine	Demerol	Dilaudid	Morphine
Alka-Seltzer	Darvon	(Cafregon)	Empirin Compound			Nuvaine
Anacin	Dolene	Dilantin	(with Codeine #3)			
A.P.C.	Fiorinal	Elavil	Empracet			
Arthritic Ascription	Soma	Endep	Leratine			
Aspirin		Ergomar	Percodan			
Bufferin		Ergostat	Ponstel			
Cope		Flexeril	Talwin			
Coricidin D		Gynergen	Tylenol III or IV			
Corincider		Inderal	(with Codeine)			
Dimetapp		Librium				
Empirin		Propranolol				
Excedrin		Sansert				
Idenal		Seconal				
Midrin		Sinequan				
Motrin		Tofranil				
Nervine		Tranxene				
Norgesic		Triavil				
Parafon		Valium				
Percogesic		Zomax				
Persistin						
Phenaphen						
Phenilin						
Robaxisal						
Rondec						
Sinutab						
Sudafed						
Tylenol						
Vanquish						

Note: From Management of Chronic Headaches: A Psychological Approach (p. 52) by E. B. Blanchard and F. Andrasik, 1985, New York: Pergamon Press. Copyright © 1985 by Pergamon Press. Reprinted by permission.

52

compliance and accuracy of self-monitoring. Epstein and Abel (1977), for example, modified the number of times recordings were made. Instead of hourly ratings, patients were asked to make ratings four times per day, at breakfast, lunch, dinner, and bedtime. These tend to occur at fairly regular times during a patient's day, and are times which are easily discriminated. Further, recording in this manner circumvents a problem originally observed with inpatients when using the hourly recording procedure. Epstein and Abel observed some of their patients did not record for several hours and then filled in these recordings later by recall. The recording procedure used by these authors also afforded patients the opportunity to record the situation in which a headache occurred, and methods used to manage pain (e.g., medication, lying down, etc.). This was an important addition to the continuing and careful assessment which is characteristic of behavioral treatments with individual patients (Hersen & Barlow, 1976). The intensity values used by Epstein and Abel ranged from 0 to 5, rather than 0 to 10 as shown in Figure 1. Intensity values were labeled in a manner similar to the sample in Figure 1.

Collins and Martin (1980) compared intensive diary recording to the reduced demand, four times per day self-monitoring procedure in nine pain patients. The reduced demand procedure produced data that were very closely representative of pain fluctuations indicated in the more intensive, bihourly recordings. Therefore, the reduced demand procedure would appear to be preferable for clinicians, who need to be concerned about ease of the recording procedure.

Although the four times per day format is less demanding for patients and likely to yield more reliable and valid data, it does have one shortcoming. By using a time sampling procedure it is not possible to obtain true measures for frequency and duration of headache. If either of these are the prime interest to the therapist, then the four times per day diary recording format will have to be altered. Chronic or near daily headache lends itself quite nicely to either format, but the clinician might want to make alterations for individuals with infrequent, but intense, prolonged migraine headache. In the latter case the patient could make ratings repeatedly throughout an attack or, alternatively, could note the time of onset and offset and then perform a single rating of peak headache intensity. This would allow the therapist to keep track of frequency as well as duration and to monitor headache intensity as well. We are using this latter procedure successfully in an investigation of self-regulatory treatments for children who have migraine (Andrasik, Burke, Attanasio, & Rosenblum, 1985).

It may be adequate for the practitioner to have the patient record only one rating of headache intensity per day. The question then becomes, when is the best time for collecting this measure? Intuitively it may seem that the end of the day would be the best. However, pilot data collected in our laboratory revealed that ratings to be made at bedtime were the ones most often forgotten, while ratings made upon awakening were performed most consistently.

Epstein and Abel (1977) also attempted to evaluate possible extra-laboratory indications of headache by conducting clinical interviews or engaging in telephone conversations with persons in the patient's natural environment (e.g., the patient's spouse, personal physician, etc.). This social validation of the patient's headache pain experience is important clinically in identifying operant contingencies which may be operating, and in promoting generalization of treatment effects beyond the consulting room.

In their presentation of another adaptation and extension of the Budzynski et al. (1973) self-monitoring procedure, Bakal and Kaganov (1976) noted that many patients show symptoms associated with both migraine and muscle-contraction headache, and that there is also variability in the site of head and neck pain symptoms among patients. Thus, their recording format requests that the patient provide information relative to the location and duration of head and neck pain, as well as the intensity of pain. Also, like the procedure advocated by Epstein and Abel (1977), their post-card format permits a daily quantification of situations, and statement of type and amount of medication consumed. Patients are asked to record these parameters at bihourly intervals, and mail in their completed diary cards daily. Daily mailing of the post cards is highly desirable from a validity standpoint, but it serves to increase the costs associated with treatment.

The most important contribution of the Bakal and Kaganov (1976) procedure would seem to be the addition of pain location information which might, as the authors point out, yield useful information about the pathophysiology of headache. For example (and as noted earlier), migraine headache tends to be located unilaterally over the eye and/or in the temporal region; while patients with muscle-contraction headache typically report pain in the neck region, radiating over the scalp and sometimes band-like. Changes in reports of headache location over the course of treatment may indicate a need to alter treatment methods.

The value of the Headache Diary depends in large part upon the degree of recording compliance displayed by the patient. Collins and Thompson (1979) found that approximately 40% of their analog sample of college students (both with and without significant headache activity) were to some degree noncompliant with instructions to record headache activity. The most common type of noncompliance appeared to involve subjects trying to recall pain ratings at a later time, rather than recording at the specified time intervals; this is consistent with Epstein and Abel's (1977) observations with inpatient headache sufferers. Not only must clinicians be alert to this bias when assessing and later treating headache patients, they must also remember that this effect may be operating to bias the extant treatment literature. Of course, it is impossible at this point to assess the extent and direction of such a bias, or even if one exists to a large degree. Reviewing headache records regularly, socially praising efforts to comply (yet refraining from punishing noncompliance), and having the patient mail records to the office when gaps between successive appointments are large may help emphasize to the patient the importance of accurate diary keeping.

Finally, a study reported by Cahn and Cram (1980), comparing headache activity information collected by interviews to information collected through systematic self-observation (the diary format) points to the importance of supplanting interview data with diary recordings, wherever possible. In one sample of patients, Cahn and Cram collected telephone interview data and daily diary records prior to treatment and at follow-up. This same basic procedure was replicated in a second sample except that the follow-up interview was done in person rather than via the telephone.

Several interesting findings emerged from this study (see Figure 2, page 56). First, interview-based measures and diary-based measures differed considerably in the quantities of headache activity they revealed. Compared

55

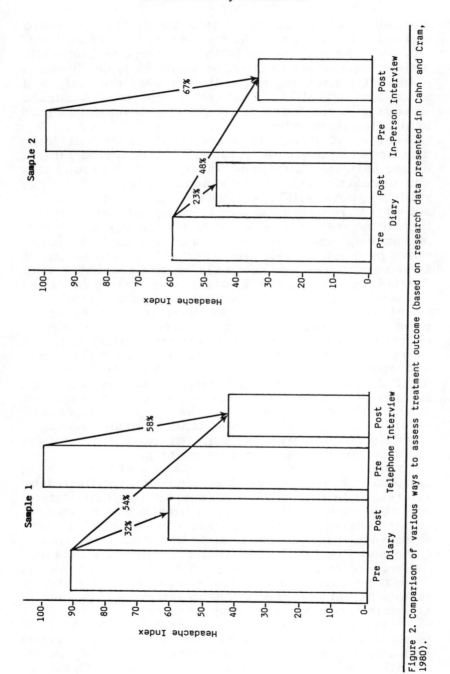

Figure 2. Comparison of various ways to assess treatment outcome (based on research data presented in Cahn and Cram, 1980).

to diary measures, interview measures *overstated* headache activity before treatment and *understated* headache activity after treatment. Calculating percent symptom reduction from pre-treatment to follow-up for each set of data reveals improvement rates vary quite markedly depending on which measure is used. For Sample 1, diary measures show the group as a whole improved by 32%, while interview measures reveal the sample to be improved by an amount nearly twice that of the diary-generated improvement (58%). An even greater discrepancy occurs for Sample 2 (23% rate of improvement versus 67% rate of improvement). The in-person interview led to the lowest estimate of headache activity suggesting it may be the most biased measure of all (if one accepts the diary records as the standard).

It is not unusual for clinicians to have their patients monitor headache on a regular basis during treatment but to conduct follow-up evaluations by interview. Determining percentage improvement utilizing the diary for the pre-treatment value and the interview for the follow-up value (switching the measures) yields a percentage improvement rate of 54% for Sample 1 and 48% for Sample 2, compared to improvement rates of 32% and 23%, respectively, when diaries are consistently kept during follow-up. The clinician needs to be aware of these problems when it is necessary to alter measures midstream and not be lulled into total acceptance of biased reports of benefit.

Alternative and Supplementary Procedures. A number of supplementary and/or alternative measurement procedures are being pilot tested in the experimental literature at present, and three may be easily adopted by the practitioner: (a) social validation of patient improvement, (b) measurement of multiple aspects of experience of pain, and (c) measurement of pain behavior.

In our clinic, we use an easily administered and scored method for socially validating treatment effects. Patients who reside with someone else (e.g., parent, spouse, child, or roommate) are given a brief questionnaire to take home to this person. One part of the questionnaire asks the significant other to rate the degree of change in the patient's headaches since he or she entered treatment and to do so without conferring with the patient. Ratings of improvement are made on a 100 mm visual analog scale, which is anchored by "unchanged" on the left side

57

and "extremely improved or completely cured" on the right side. Measuring the distance between the left-most end of the scale to the point indicated by the significant other yields a percentage improvement score ranging from 0 to 100. In addition to providing a way to verify the accuracy of the patient's headache diary data, this method also serves as a way to assess the social significance and importance of treatment outcome, as advocated by Wolf (1978) and Kazdin (1977).

Data obtained from the social validation rating forms correlate modestly ($r = .44$) with actual diary measures, suggesting some usefulness to this procedure. When the line of best fit was plotted for data collected from 62 patients, it was noted to intercept the y-axis somewhat above the 0 value (Blanchard, Andrasik, Neff, Jurish, & O'Keefe, 1981). We interpreted this to indicate that the report provided by the significant other has a slight positive bias or tends to overestimate patient improvement, and this overestimation may be as much as 30%. Practitioners using this type of assessment device need to be mindful of this point.

The pain experience is complex and includes at least two interacting components (Beecher, 1959). One of these involves a sensory component, which includes stimulus attributes such as intensity, location, and quality of pain; while the other involves the reactive component of pain, or a patient's emotional reaction to the pain, fears about what the pain may signal, and concerns about ability to cope with the pain in a socially acceptable manner.

Available evidence suggests the Headache Diary is sensitive primarily to the sensory dimension and may not be useful for measuring the reactive or affective dimension of pain (Andrasik, Blanchard, Ahles, Pallmeyer, & Barron, 1981). Our clinical experience suggests it is important to consider both aspects of pain. It is not an uncommon experience for a patient to complete treatment with no appreciable change occurring in diary recordings but upon interview to report a marked decrease in level of distress. We submit that in such cases a significant change may have occurred in the reactivity dimension. In support, patients often report, "even though my head hurts just as much, now I don't let it bother me so."

We adapted Tursky's (1976) idiographic multidimensional measurement technique and piloted it with headache patients in the aforementioned study (Andrasik et al., 1981), but Tursky's procedure requires considerable patient time for administration and therapist time for scoring, and these will limit its utility to the busy practitioner. Items contained in the McGill Pain Questionnaire (Melzack, 1975) are similarly designed to access varied components of pain and these items may be more practical for clinicians. In research with chronic pain patients, Price, McGrath, Rafii, and Buckingham (1983) successfully piloted a visual analog scale (VAS) procedure for assessing the two aspects of pain. Their approach could be adapted to headache patients, and it should not ask too much of patients to complete the two separate VASs even at various times during the day. In this procedure the two VASs are anchored as follows: "no sensation" and "the most intense sensation imaginable" for assessing the sensory aspect of pain, and "not bad at all" and "the most intense bad feeling possible for me" for measuring the affective dimension of pain.

Philips and Hunter (1981) recently developed a checklist to assess "behaviors motivated by pain." These investigators constructed items (summarized in Table 5, page 60) on a prima facie basis and divided these into two major categories (avoidance items and complaint items), along with a miscellaneous category, which included medication consumption behaviors and dietary changes. The data obtained from this measure (presence versus absence of a particular behavior) are summed into a grand total (maximum of 19 items) and into two subscores: complaint and avoidance behaviors (both of which contain a maximum of eight items). Philips and Hunter note that this scoring procedure permits a separate examination of two separate aspects of pain behavior, as well as an overall level. Administration of this scale could be helpful for selecting behaviors to target during treatment, as well as for documenting problem severity.

SUMMARY

In summarizing the major points of our discussion, it may be useful to lay out the steps that the clinician should take in assessing a patient who presents for the treatment of headache.

The first step in assessing this patient involves extensive interviewing to establish the particular type of headache the patient is suffering from, using established diagnostic criteria. This will allow an initial gauging of

Assessment of Headaches

TABLE 5: BEHAVIOUR CHECKLIST ITEMS

Avoidance Items
1. Take time off work, housework, occupational therapy, and so on
2. Avoid or minimize physical exertions/activity
3. Avoid or reduce bright lights (turn off or down, wear dark glasses, etc.)
4. Avoid or reduce loud noise
5. Avoid or reduce social contacts
6. Close eyes
7. Lie down and rest
8. Sleep

Complaint Items
1. Tell at least one person that I have a headache
2. Tell more than three people that I have a headache
3. Tell any one person more than once that I have a headache
4. Slump, slouch, or find it hard to stand up as usual
5. Hold, press head, neck, temples
6. Try to reduce pain by massage, rub pain location, apply cold compresses, and so forth
7. Grimace, squint, frown
8. Moan, cry out, sigh

Miscellaneous Items
1. Take a tablet(s) prescribed by my doctor
2. Take a tablet(s) not prescribed by my doctor
3. Avoid certain foods, drinks

Note: From "Pain Behaviour in Headache Sufferers" by C. Philips and M. Hunter, 1981, Behavioural Analysis and Modification, 4, p. 259. Copyright © 1981. Reprinted by permission.

---

the appropriateness of the patient for behavioral treatment. Another function of the initial interview is to identify factors which may be influencing the patient's report of headache pain, including medication abuse and psychological factors which may be a part of the patient's pain experience.

Second, a medical evaluation is warranted to rule out a physical cause for the patient's headaches. An initial evaluation is indicated for all patients, and some might require repeated medical consultations (e.g., in the case of a dramatic change in headache symptomatology).

Following these steps, the clinician must decide on a method of systematic diary recording of principle headache parameters (including frequency, duration, and intensity). Finally, the clinician should be aware of and consider additional methods of assessment (i.e., social validation, behavior checklists) which may serve to enhance understanding of the patient's pain experience.

APPENDIX: MULTIMODAL HEADACHE ASSESSMENT APPROACH

Headache Type	Assessment Procedure		
	Subjective	Behavioral	Physiological
Migraine	1. Usually unilateral onset or pain one side of head 2. Prodromes (may be more evident in classic migraine) 3. Nausea	1. Emergency room treatment may be required 2. Bed rest may be required 3. Avoidance of light and sound	1. Cephalic vascular lability 2. Positive response to vasoconstrictive medication
Muscle-Contraction	1. Dull, aching pain 2. Pain attacks less severe than migraines	1. Rarely requires bed rest or interruption of ongoing activities 2. Stressful situations elicit head pain	1. Elevated EMG in cephalic and neck areas during development of the pain
Combined	1. Characteristics of both migraine and MCH exist in the same attack or in separate episodes	1. Disability is a function of the type of headache	1. Physiology may vary as a function of the type of headache 2. Vascular and musculoskeletal physiological changes may accompany the combined type in which migraine and MCH occur in the same attack
Psychogenic	1. Pattern of pain report does not typically fit the migraine or MCH symptomatology 2. Possible iatrogenic effects	1. Possible presence of secondary gain (reinforcement of pain behavior) 2. Possible precipitating events (such as an accident)	1. Lack of a physiological basis for pain report

Note: From "Diagnosis of Head Pain: An Idiographic Approach to Assessment and Classification" by J. K. Thompson, 1982, Headache, 22, p. 229. Copyright ⊙ 1982 by the American Association for the Study of Headache. Reprinted by permission.

Frank Andrasik, PhD, received his doctorate in clinical psychology from Ohio University after completing an internship at the University of Pittsburgh School of Medicine. From 1979 through early 1986 he held a faculty appointment in the Department of Psychology at the State University of New York at Albany. He recently moved to Greenville, South Carolina to assume the position of Associate Director at Pain Therapy Centers of the Greenville Hospital System. He has published extensively in a number of areas (with most of this work being concentrated in assessment and treatment of pain, stress, biofeedback, and organizational behavior management), and has been the recipient of several federal research grants to investigate recurrent headache. Dr. Andrasik may be contacted at Pain Therapy Centers, Greenville General Hospital, 100 Mallard Street, Greenville, SC 29601.

Edmund J. Burke, PhD, is a staff psychologist at Sunnyview Hospital and Rehabilitation Center in Schenectady, New York. He received his PhD at the State University of New York at Albany, following completion of his internship at Temple University Hospital. His research interests include assessment and treatment of chronic pain. Dr. Burke can be contacted at the Department of Psychology, Sunnyview Hospital and Rehabilitation Center, 1270 Belmont Avenue, Schenectady, NY 12308.

RESOURCES

Ad Hoc Committee on the Classification of Headache. (1962). Classification of headache. *Journal of the American Medical Association, 179,* 127-128.

Adams, H. E., Brantley, P. J., & Thompson, J. K. (1982). Biofeedback and headache: Methodological issues. In L. White & B. Tursky (Eds.), *Clinical Biofeedback: Efficacy and Mechanisms* (pp. 358-367). New York: Guilford Press.

Ala-Hurula, V., Myllyla, V., & Hokkanen, E. (1982). Ergotamine abuse: Results of ergotamine discontinuation, with special reference to the plasma concentration. *Cephalalgia, 2*, 189-195.

Andrasik, F. (1985). Tension headache. In M. Hersen & C. J. Last (Eds.), *Behavior Therapy Casebook* (pp. 118-131). New York: Springer.

Andrasik, F. (1986). Relaxation and biofeedback for chronic headaches. In A. D. Holzman & D. C. Turk (Eds.), *Pain Management: A Handbook of Treatment Approaches* (pp. 213-239). New York: Pergamon.

Andrasik, F., Blanchard, E. B., Ahles, T. A., Pallmeyer, T., & Barron, K. D. (1981). Assessing the reactive as well as the sensory component of headache pain. *Headache, 21*, 218-221.

Andrasik, F., Blanchard, E. B., Arena, J. G., Teders, S. J., Teevan, R. C., & Rodichok, L. D. (1982). Psychological functioning in headache sufferers. *Psychosomatic Medicine, 44*, 171-182.

Andrasik, F., Burke, E. J., Attanasio, V., & Rosenblum, E. L. (1985). Child, parent, and physician reports of a child's headache pain: Relationships prior to and following treatment. *Headache, 25*, 421-425.

Bakal, D. A. (1982). *The Psychobiology of Chronic Headache*. New York: Springer.

Bakal, D. A., & Kaganov, J. A. (1976). A simple method for self-observation of headache frequency, intensity, and location. *Headache, 16*, 123-124.

Beecher, H. K. (1959). *Measurement of Subjective Responses*. New York: Oxford University Press.

Blanchard, E. B., & Andrasik, F. (1985). *Management of Chronic Headaches: A Psychological Approach*. New York: Pergamon.

Blanchard, E. B., Andrasik, F., Jurish, S. E., & Teders, S. J. (1982). The treatment of cluster headache with relaxation and thermal biofeedback. *Biofeedback and Self-Regulation, 7*, 185-191.

Blanchard, E. B., Andrasik, F., Neff, D. F., Jurish, S. E., & O'Keefe, D. M. (1981). Social validation of the headache diary. *Behavior Therapy, 12*, 711-715.

Blanchard, E. B., O'Keefe, D. M., Neff, D., Jurish, S., & Andrasik, F. (1981). Interdisciplinary agreement in the diagnosis of headache types. *Journal of Behavioral Assessment, 3*, 5-9.

Budzynski, T. H., Stoyva, J. M., Adler, C. S., & Mullaney, D. J. (1973). EMG biofeedback and tension headache: A controlled outcome study. *Psychosomatic Medicine, 35*, 484-496.

Cahn, T., & Cram, J. R. (1980). Changing measurement instrument at follow-up: A potential source of error. *Biofeedback and Self-Regulation, 5,* 265-273.

Collins, F. L., & Martin, J. E. (1980). Assessing self-report of pain: A comparison of two recording procedures. *Journal of Behavioral Assessment, 2,* 55-63.

Collins, F. L., & Thompson, J. K. (1979). Reliability and standardization in the assessment of self-reported headache pain. *Journal of Behavioral Assessment, 1,* 73-86.

Cox, D., & Thomas, D. (1981). Relationship between headaches and depression. *Headache, 21,* 261-263.

Coyne, L., Sargent, J., Segerson, J., & Obourn, R. (1976). Relative potency scale for analgesic drugs: Use of psychophysical procedures with clinical judgments. *Headache, 16,* 70-71.

Diamond, S. (1983). Depression and headache. *Headache, 23,* 123-126.

Diamond, S., & Dalessio, D. J. (1982). *The Practicing Physician's Approach to Headache* (3rd ed.). Baltimore: Williams & Wilkins.

Epstein, L. H., & Abel, G. G. (1977). An analysis of biofeedback training effects for tension headache patients. *Behavior Therapy, 8,* 37-47.

Haynes, S. N. (1981). Muscle contraction headache: A psychophysiological perspective of etiology and treatment. In S. N. Haynes & L. R. Gannon (Eds.), *Psychosomatic Disorders: A Psychophysiological Approach to Etiology and Treatment* (pp. 447-484). New York: Gardner.

Hersen, M., & Barlow, D. H. (1976). *Single Case Experimental Designs: Strategies for Studying Behavior Change.* New York: Pergamon.

Jay, G. W., Renelli, D., & Mead, T. (1984). The effects of propranolol and amitriptyline on vascular and EMG biofeedback training. *Headache, 24,* 59-69.

Kazdin, A. E. (1977). Assessing the clinical or applied importance of behavior change through social validation. *Behavior Modification, 1,* 427-452.

Kudrow, L. (1976). Tension headache (scalp muscle contraction headache). In O. Appenzeller (Ed.), *Pathogenesis and Treatment of Headache* (pp. 81-91). New York: Spectrum Publications.

Kudrow, L. (1980). *Cluster Headache: Mechanisms and Management.* New York: Oxford University Press.

Kudrow, L. (1982). Paradoxical effects of frequent analgesic use. In M. Critchley, A. Friedman, S. Gorini, & F. Sicuteri (Eds.), *Advances in Neurology: Vol. 33. Headache: Physiopathological and Clinical Concepts* (pp. 335-341). New York: Raven Press.

Kudrow, L. (1983). Pathogenesis of vascular headache. In W. H. Rickles, J. H. Sandweiss, D., Jacobs, & R. N. Grove (Eds.), *Biofeedback and Family Practice Medicine* (pp. 41-59). New York: Plenum.

Lance, J. W., Curran, D. A., & Anthony, M. (1965). Investigation into the mechanism and treatment of chronic headache. *Medical Journal of Australia, 2,* 909-914.

Luborsky, L., Docherty, J. P., & Penick, S. (1973). Onset conditions for psychosomatic symptoms: A comparative review of immediate observation with retrospective research. *Psychosomatic Medicine, 35,* 187-204.

Melzack, R. (1975). The McGill Pain Questionnaire: Major properties and scoring methods. *Pain, 7,* 277-299.

Philips, C., & Hunter, M. (1981). Pain behaviour in headache sufferers. *Behavioural Analysis and Modification, 4,* 257-266.

Price, D. D., McGrath, P. A., Rafii, A., & Buckingham, B. (1983). The validation of visual analog scale as ratio scale measures for chronic and experimental pain. *Pain, 17,* 45-56.

Raskin, N. H., & Appenzeller, O. (1980). *Headache.* Philadelphia: W. B. Saunders Company.

Solbach, P., Sargent, J., & Coyne, L. (1984). Menstrual migraine headache: Results of a controlled, experimental, outcome study of non-drug treatments. *Headache, 24,* 75-78.

Thompson, J. K. (1982). Diagnosis of head pain: An idiographic approach to assessment and classification. *Headache, 22,* 221-232.

Tursky, B. (1976). The development of a pain perception profile: A psychophysical approach. In M. Weisenberg & B. Tursky (Eds.), *Pain: New Perspectives in Therapy and Research* (pp. 171-194). New York: Plenum.

Wolf, M. M. (1978). Social validity: The case for subjective measurement or how applied behavior analysis is finding its heart. *Journal of Applied Behavior Analysis, 11,* 203-214.

OBSERVATIONAL METHODS FOR ASSESSING PAIN: A PRACTICAL GUIDE

Francis J. Keefe, James E. Crisson,
and Mary Trainor

This chapter describes methods useful for observing pain behavior patterns in patients suffering from chronic pain. We begin by discussing the concept of pain behavior and then describe observational methods that can be used to sample pain behavior in a standard situation and in an inpatient pain unit. Throughout the chapter, we refer to our previous laboratory and clinical studies in this area that have examined the reliability and validity of the observation methods. We conclude with a discussion of how these methods can be extended to a variety of clinical practice settings.

THE CONCEPT OF PAIN BEHAVIOR

Pain behavior is a term introduced by Wilbert Fordyce (1976) to describe those behaviors that patients engage in that communicate the fact that they are having pain. These behaviors include verbal complaints of pain, physical inactivity, taking medication, avoiding work or home responsibilities, and certain motor behaviors such as body posturing or certain facial expressions. These behaviors probably originate in the acute pain stage when they have a functional value. For example, patients having back pain quickly learn that their pain is lessened if they move in a cautious and guarded fashion. Rubbing the painful area may also decrease pain by activating nerve fibers that inhibit pain via a gate control mechanism (Melzack & Wall, 1965). When pain becomes chronic, however, the variables that can control pain behavior are much more complex (Keefe, 1982). Some chronic pain patients show pain behavior that is inappropriate to the physical findings evident.

The study of pain behavior is important from a clinical perspective. Pain behaviors are viewed as significant by examining physicians. Almost every text on low back pain maintains that the examining physician should carefully attend to the way that the patient moves and expresses pain facially. In fact, physicians are encouraged to check these responses unobtrusively when the patient walks into or leaves the examining room. While viewed as important, these behaviors are not assessed systematically. Typically pain behavior is considered a clinical sign and judged either to be excessive or not. Patients who display exaggerated or inconsistent pain behaviors to examining physicians represent a diagnostic dilemma. These patients are considered poor candidates for invasive diagnostic tests such as myelography or for surgical interventions such as laminectomies (Waddell, McCulloch, Kimmel, & Venner, 1980). They are often given repeated trials of conservative treatments such as bed rest, traction, analgesics or narcotics and when these efforts fail, are referred to psychologists and psychiatrists for evaluation.

The study of pain behavior is also significant from a theoretical perspective. Almost all theorists who have written about chronic pain have emphasized the importance of understanding pain behavior patterns. Theories that emphasize the neurophysiological aspects of pain, such as the specificity theory, maintain that pain reactions are an important index of underlying pathology. Overt behaviors controlled by motor mechanisms in the brain are also an important element in the gate control of pain (Melzack & Wall, 1965). This theory emphasizes that pain behaviors are affected not only by sensory-discriminative aspects of pain experience but also by motivational and affective responses.

Psychiatric theorists such as Engel (1959) and Szasz (1957) maintain that in many chronic pain patients, pain behavior provides a means of communication of emotional distress and unmet needs. They believe that depression, anger, loss, repressed hostility, anxiety, and unmet dependency needs greatly influence pain behavior in chronic pain patients.

Behavioral theorists such as Fordyce (1976) maintain that for chronic pain patients a thorough analysis of pain behavior may be just as important as a thorough medical work-up. The reason a behavioral analysis is important is that when pain persists, there are many opportunities for conditioning and learning influences to affect pain behavior. In these circumstances, both respondent and operant conditioning can affect pain behavior.

RESPONDENT CONDITIONING AND PAIN BEHAVIOR

In respondent conditioning, environmental stimuli that were previously neutral acquire the ability to elicit responses. Pavlov (1927) observed this phenomenon in his studies of salivation. He found that stimuli (e.g., sight of an attendant) that signaled to dogs that food would be delivered (an unconditioned stimulus) would eventually themselves elicit a conditioned response of salivation. This basic form of learning is evident in many species, and research suggests that classically conditioned physiological responses play a role in disease and illness. Lown, Verrier, and Rabinowitz (1977), for example, have found that animals who develop classically conditioned emotional reactions are more prone to ventricular fibrillation. Surwit and colleagues (personal communication, 1985) have recently found that mice genetically susceptible to diabetes will show classically conditioned hyperglycemia while normal mice do not show this pattern. These data suggest that learning may play a role in the development and clinical manifestations of a variety of pathological conditions.

Whenever noxious or painful stimulation occurs, there is the possibility that respondent conditioning can affect pain behavior. For example, following an injury such as a burn, pain receptors are barraged with sensory stimulation. This noxious stimulation in turn elicits certain reflexive autonomic responses and voluntary responses (pain behaviors) such as withdrawal of the limb, or complaining about pain, or seeking medical attention. If the burn injury is not a serious or long-lasting one, noxious stimulation ceases after a matter of days or weeks and as this stimulation decreases, the reflexive autonomic as well as voluntary responses soon disappear. The patient is able to resume normal function with a minimum of interference.

Some injuries, however, require a prolonged healing time, and the patient is exposed to repetitive noxious stimulation for months. A patient who has extensive burns, for example, experiences a significant amount of pain in the course of the rehabilitation. Under these circumstances, *conditioned fear reactions* can develop. Previously, neutral stimuli (sight of the rehabilitation therapist, smell of the room in which therapy is carried out) are frequently paired with increased pain. Over time, the patient may experience significant anxiety and arousal whenever these stimuli are present. Avoidance behaviors such as refusal to go to therapy or unwillingness to do mobilization exercises can develop. These behaviors are quite reinforcing because they reduce pain and anxiety.

Avoidance behaviors developed in response to painful stimuli can be very strong habits that are quite resistant to extinction. They also, of course, interfere with treatment goals such as mobilizing the patient and keep the patient from regaining effective functioning.

To summarize, patients who have a clear-cut organic basis for their pain often display pain behavior. This behavior is consistent and clearly relates to events or activities that increase noxious stimulation. Conditioning and learning are apt to influence pain behavior in these settings if prolonged healing time is required, or if patients are exposed to repeated administration of painful medical procedures in the course of their treatment or rehabilitation (e.g., lumbar punctures in children having leukemia). Because conditioned fear reactions can occur under these circumstances, treatment should be structured so as to minimize anxiety and emotional distress. Effective methods to prevent the development of conditioned fear responses include setting realistic goals in treatment, gradually increasing activity, and encouraging patients to use relaxation and distraction techniques (Fordyce, 1976). Jay and her colleagues (Jay, Ozolins, Elliott, & Caldwell, 1983) have recently demonstrated that these techniques can significantly reduce pain, anxiety, and distress behaviors in children undergoing repeated lumbar punctures.

Fortunately, the course of most pain problems is short, and the opportunities for pain behavior to become conditioned are few. For most individuals, once tissue pathology is healed, normal behaviors in the social, occupational, and recreational spheres are quickly resumed.

OPERANT CONDITIONING AND PAIN BEHAVIOR

Some patients continue to display pain behavior long after the normal healing time for tissue pathology. One possible explanation for this, is that pain behaviors have become operantly conditioned responses.

B. F. Skinner (1953) was among the first to systematically investigate operant conditioning. This research emphasized the importance that the consequences of behavior have in controlling behavior. For example, Skinner observed that when a pigeon emitted a simple behavior (key pecking) and received a positive consequence (reward) this behavior was much more likely to be repeated in the future. Delivery of an aversive consequence (punishment) or the withholding of anticipated reinforcement (extinction) decreased the likelihood of responding. This simple form of conditioning has been studied extensively, and recent evidence suggests that biological changes occur when learning takes place. While these principles may seem simple, they have been extended to the analysis of complex behaviors in humans. Much of the behavior therapy and behavior modification literature consists of descriptions of applications of operant conditioning principles in the treatment of maladaptive behavior.

Fordyce (1976) was one of the first to argue that operant conditioning principles could explain the persistence of pain behavior in some chronic pain patients. Patients with protracted histories of pain have many opportunities to learn about the consequences of pain behavior. Patients may find that when they improve, they are expected to return to an unrewarding job, to resume stressful responsibilities as a spouse or family member, or to deal with emotional crises that they could avoid when they had pain. Patients who have limited formal education, few job skills, cognitive impairment due to disease or injury, and long-standing emotional problems often find their return to "well behavior" to be a frustrating and punishing experience. At the same time, the continuation of pain behavior may result in reinforcing consequences such as receiving medications that reduce pain and emotional distress, financial

71

compensation payments, opportunities to rest, and solicitous responses from spouse and friends.

Patients who were deprived of attention as children or who had frequent illness or exposure to adults who had pain or illness, may be especially prone to develop operantly conditioned pain behavior patterns. Another group of patients likely to develop this pattern are those having a history of responding to life stresses with the development of illness, disease, or pain (Sternbach, 1974). Patients with this pattern often are unaware of the relationship between major stresses and their symptomatology. While the major problem is one of emotional distress, it is often mislabeled both by the patient and by medical professionals as a pain problem. When these patients are given drugs and other pain-relieving procedures that provide relief for both the pain and emotional distress, it tends to confirm their view that pain is the central problem. For these patients, medical interventions for pain are not effective over the long run because they do not address the underlying problem of emotional distress (Fordyce, 1976).

Pain behaviors that are operantly conditioned have several features. First, these behaviors are inconsistently related to factors that might be expected to increase or decrease nociception (Fordyce, 1976). Patients with operant pain behavior may fail to show increases in pain behavior when they move affected body areas. They also frequently fail to show decreases in pain behaviors when given nerve blocks or other procedures known to decrease nociception. Second, patients displaying operant pain behavior often display exaggerated responses when asked to carry out simple tasks (Waddell et al., 1980). Patients may flinch in an exaggerated manner when touched by the examining physician or over-react during physical therapy. Third, operant pain behaviors tend to be quite responsive to the social environment. We have seen patients whose pain behavior increases dramatically in the presence of a visiting spouse or a new physician. There may be little evidence of pain or discomfort when others are not present.

DEVELOPMENT OF A PAIN
BEHAVIOR OBSERVATION SYSTEM

Behavior therapy researchers have attempted to develop objective methods for assessing pain behaviors in chronic pain patients. Overt behaviors such as activity level and medication intake that can be easily observed have received the most attention. Fordyce (1976) developed a daily activity diary measure that is widely used. This diary consists of a standard data form on which patients keep hourly records of medication intake and time spent in three categories (sitting, reclining, and standing or walking). Electromechanical devices to automatically record time spent out of bed and time walking or standing have also been described (Keefe, 1982). Objective methods for assessing motor pain behaviors such as body posturing, guarded movement, and painful facial expressions have not received as much research attention. Spouse observation and physician rating scales for recording such motor pain behaviors are briefly mentioned in the literature, but their reliability and validity are untested.

We have recently developed a direct observation method for recording motor pain behaviors in chronic low back pain patients. We started this research with preliminary observations carried out on inpatients units where these patients were being treated.

PRELIMINARY OBSERVATIONS

We began our research on pain behavior by interviewing chronic pain patients, their families, and nurses and physicians. We asked these individuals a simple question: What does the patient do that signals to you that he or she is having an increase in pain? A list of 20 different behaviors was generated. The next step was to carry out preliminary observations of these behaviors on an inpatient unit where pain patients were undergoing treatment. Nurses carried out the observations on a time-sampling basis. Patients were checked every 30 minutes and a notation made as to whether any of the 20 pain behaviors identified were observed. These observations were quite revealing. First, it became evident that many of the pain behaviors such as complaining about pain, requesting medication, or crying occurred at a very low rate. For most patients, these behaviors were never noted. Second, it became apparent that patients did not display pain behavior when they were in a stationary position such as reclining or sitting. Pain behaviors occurred much more frequently when patients changed position or walked. Finally, the nurses noticed that certain pain

73

behaviors were likely to elicit a sympathetic reaction from others or to interrupt the ongoing activity of other individuals. These pain behaviors were considered to be quite salient and did appear to occur at a higher frequency. The behaviors included guarded movement, bracing, rubbing of the painful area, grimacing, and pronounced sighing. Because these behaviors were both frequent and salient, we decided to develop a standardized observation procedure for sampling them.

SAMPLING PAIN BEHAVIOR
IN A STANDARDIZED SITUATION

A series of four studies was carried out to develop and evaluate a standard procedure for sampling motor pain behavior patterns commonly displayed by chronic low back pain patients (Keefe & Block, 1982). In each of the studies, chronic low back pain patients were observed in a 10-minute standard situation that involves static (sitting, standing, and reclining) and dynamic activities (walking or moving from one static position to another).

The first study examined the reliability and validity of the observation system. Twenty-seven chronic low back pain patients served as subjects. Patients rated the intensity of their pain prior to observation on a 0 to 10 scale on which 0 indicated no pain and 10 was pain as bad as it can be. During the 10-minute observation session, the patient was asked to sit, stand, walk, and recline for 1 to 2 minutes each. The sessions were videotaped. To evaluate reliability, the videotapes were scored independently by two trained observers. The position of the patient, movement, and five motor pain behaviors were recorded. (Observations were made using 30-second intervals broken down into 20-second observe, 10-second record phases. Using this interval recording procedure, observers recorded the occurrence or non-occurrence of each behavior category at the end of each 20-second observe phase.) The behaviors recorded were defined as follows:

1. *Guarding*--Abnormally stiff, interrupted, or rigid movement while moving from one position to another.
2. *Bracing*--A stationary position in which a fully extended limb supports and maintains an abnormal

distribution of weight. This must be held for at least three seconds.

3. *Rubbing*--Touching, rubbing, or holding the affected area of pain for a minimum of three seconds. For all of these patients, the affected area was defined to include the low back, hips, and outer aspects of the thigh. Rubbing does not include "hands folded in lap."

4. *Grimacing*--Obvious facial expression of pain that may include furrowed brow, narrowed eyes, tightened lips, corners of mouth pulled back, and clenched teeth.

5. *Sighing*--Obvious exhalation of air, usually accompanied by shoulders first rising and then falling; cheeks may be expanded.

The results of our first experiment demonstrated that the *reliability* of the observation system was quite high. The percentage agreement for independent observers recording the various categories of behaviors ranged from 93% to 99%. A strong positive correlation was also found between the frequency of pain behaviors and self-reported pain intensity ($r = 0.71$, $p < 0.01$) supporting the validity of the observation method. This study also found that pain behaviors were much more likely to occur when patients were moving than when they were in static sitting, standing, or reclining positions.

A second experiment examined the *sensitivity* of the pain behavior observations to treatment effects. In this experiment, standard behavioral observations of 15 patients were conducted before and after treatment in a multidisciplinary, behaviorally oriented pain management program. Significant reductions in guarded movement, rubbing, and total pain behaviors were noted pre-to-post treatment. Further support for the validity of the observation system also came from the finding that change in observed pain behaviors correlated quite well with changes in pain reports ($r = .56$, $p < .01$).

A third experiment examined the *construct validity* of the observation system. If the pain behaviors are indeed communicating to others that the patient is having pain, then the level of these behaviors should correlate with untrained observers' estimates of the intensity of pain that patients were experiencing. In this study, 9 undergraduate observers who had no training in our observation method, viewed and rated 22 videotaped behavior samples of low back pain patients. These naïve observers were asked to rate the amount of pain the patient was experiencing using a numerical scale, a visual analog scale, and a set of pain intensity descriptors. Correlations of the naïve observer's pain ratings with the frequency of specific pain behaviors were then carried out. A significant correlation was obtained between total pain behavior and ratings of pain made by the naïve observers (r = .67 to .69, p < .01). Certain behaviors such as guarded movement appeared to serve as more salient signals that an individual was experiencing pain. Patients who showed high levels of guarding were considered to be having more pain whereas those who showed low levels of guarding were viewed as having little pain.

A final experiment examined the *discriminant validity* of the observation system. This study investigated the extent to which the behaviors adequately differentiated chronic low back pain patients from pain-free, normal, and depressed controls. Statistical comparisons using *t*-test revealed that the levels of guarding, rubbing, grimacing, and sighing were significantly higher (p < .05) in low back pain patients than in normal or depressed controls.

Taken together, these results suggest that the pain behavior observation system we developed is both reliable and valid. We currently use this observation system routinely to evaluate patients before and after treatment in our pain program. We have also modified the observation procedure for clinical use, such as during physical examinations (Keefe, Wilkins, & Cook, 1984).

PRACTICAL METHODS FOR
RECORDING PAIN BEHAVIOR

In this section, we describe observation procedures for sampling pain behavior in a standardized situation and on a pain unit. Methods used for training observers and procedures for the actual observations are described as are practical techniques for checking observer reliability and analyzing data.

SAMPLING PAIN BEHAVIOR
IN STANDARD SITUATIONS

The first method we shall describe is a straight-forward application of methods described in our initial research report (Keefe & Block, 1982). Patients admitted to our pain management program have a standard behavior sample taken within three days of admission and once again prior to discharge.

Observation Procedure. During their initial evaluation, all patients are informed that an observation will be carried out to evaluate their pain problem. On the day of the observation, a research assistant comes to the patient's room and once again explains that the observation is part of their pain management evaluation. Patients are told that they will be asked to sit, walk, stand, and recline. Patients who are unable because of physical limitations to engage in the required activities or who are unwilling to go through the observation are given the option not to participate. This rarely occurs. Patients are told that they will be videotaped and that other than requesting position changes, the assistant will not be conversing with them during the 10-minute observation session.

We have been using a standard (VHS format), commercially available video recorder and camera. This equipment is light and portable, permitting us to carry out observations throughout the hospital and if necessary, in the patient's home. The observations are typically conducted with patients in their hospital rooms. An examining room is used for observations of outpatients. The camera is positioned at the doorway to the room approximately 15 feet from the patient. Shades and curtains are closed and available overhead lighting is used to insure consistency in lighting on the tape.

Prior to starting the observation, patients are asked to rate their pain on a 0 to 10 scale, in which 0 is no pain and 10 is pain as bad as it can be. The research assistant then shows the patient where to sit, recline, stand, and walk in the room so that the behavior can be recorded most easily. In order to standardize the observations, we have made several rules. Patients who are in a room with a bed are asked to sit on the bed. If the patient is in a room that does not have a bed (e.g., an examining room) then sitting should be in a chair that does not have arms. Patients are asked to recline on a bed or examining table. We avoid asking patients to recline in a recliner since this task is much easier and does not provide a valid index of the patient's ability to move from a completely reclining to standing position. Walking is carried out at the farthest end of the room from the camera, and patients are told to walk the width of the room back and forth until told to move on to the next activity. Patients are asked to stand next to the bed or examining table on which they were reclining.

Prior to recording, the assistant shuffles a set of card on which are listed the various activities that patients will be asked to do in order to randomize the order of the activities. The activities include a 1- and 2-minute sitting period, both a 1- and 2-minute standing period, two 1-minute reclining periods, and two 1-minute walking periods.

To start the observation, the assistant instructs the patient to carry out the activity listed on the first card. Unless the patient is moving from one position to another or walking, the assistant does not look through the camera eye-piece but rather turns from the patient and watches a stopwatch. The assistant is specifically instructed not to talk, smile, joke, or interact with the patient, and if the patient makes eye contact, to look away. When the patient is involved in movement, the assistant observes the patient through a view finder to insure that the entire movement is recorded. The patient is requested to perform each of the activities listed on the cards until the entire 10-minute sequence is completed. At the end of the session, the patient is asked for a second pain rating using the 0 to 10 scale.

After the observation, the patient's name, date, history number, and medical status variables such as number of prior surgeries, current narcotic intake, duration of pain, and disability status are recorded from the medical chart.

Training Observers. We have relied on the use of undergraduate observers who are hired for one or two semesters. The observers are trained in four stages. First, they study a sheet that lists the definitions of the behavioral categories. They then discuss with a trained observer examples of situations in which it would be inappropriate or appropriate to score a behavior a certain way. The observers are quizzed to insure that they understand the definitions. The definitions for each of the coding categories are shown in Table 1 (pages 79-80). As can be seen, coding categories for position, movement, and pain behavior are included.

TABLE 1:   OBSERVATION SCORING CATEGORIES FOR USE WITH STANDARD TASKS

Position:

    Standing (Std):   Patient in upright position with one or both feet on the floor for at least 3 seconds.

    Sitting (Sit):   Patient resting upon buttocks for at least 3 seconds. If patient is in process of moving to a reclining position, do not score a sit.

    Reclining (Rec):   Patient in horizontal position for at least 3 seconds.

Movement:

    Pacing (Pce):   Walking two or more steps in any direction within 3 seconds.

    Shifting (Sft):   Change in position upward or downward that is, patient moves from one position to another except stand-pace or pace-stand.

Pain Behaviors:

    Guarding (Gd):   Abnormally stiff, interrupted, or rigid movement while changing from one position to another (i.e., when recording sft) or during pacing. It includes patients using canes or walkers, and cannot occur during a stationary position (i.e., sit, std, rec). The movement must be hesitant or interrupted, not merely slow.

    Bracing (Brc):   Position in which an almost fully extended limb supports and maintains an abnormal distribution of weight. It cannot occur during movement (i.e., pacing, shifting), and must be held for at least 3 seconds. It most frequently is the gripping of the edge of a bed while sitting, but can also be grasping a table, cane, or walker while standing. What appears to be bracing during movement is termed guarding. It can occur with a leg if patient leans against wall using no other support, but is not simply the shifting of weight when standing.

    Rubbing (Rb):   Touching, rubbing, or holding the affected area which includes low back, hips, and legs for a minimum of 3 seconds. It includes patients' hands in pockets or behind the back, but not the hands folded in lap. It can occur during an interval of movement or nonmovement. Patients' palm(s) must be touching the affected area to be considered rubbing during a "sit." If a clear view is not available, a rub is recorded if touching can be reasonably inferred from the patient's position.

Pain Behaviors (Continued):

Grimacing (Gr):   Obvious facial expression of pain which may include furrowed brow, narrowed eyes, tightened lips, corners of mouth pulled back, clenched teeth. It often resembles wincing. Observer must be alert to catch this. It often occurs during a shift.

Sighing (Si):   Obvious exaggerated exhalation of air, usually accompanied by shoulders first rising and then falling. Cheeks may be expanded.

The second step in training is for observers to practice coding observations by watching 30-second segments of videotapes of chronic low back pain patients and recording the behaviors observed. Each segment chosen is divided into a 20-second observe, 10-second record phase. The segments chosen illustrate the range of behaviors to be coded. The observers first score five 30-second segments and then progress to scoring 10, 15, and eventually a full set of 20, 30-second segments. The scoring sheet used by observers is displayed in Table 2 (page 81). As can be seen in this example, the occurrence of a coding category is denoted by simply circling the appropriate member on the scoring sheet. Following each viewing, the observers are given immediate feedback as to the accuracy of their coding. The third stage in training is for the observers to watch and score a series of five 10-minute videotapes of patients. Observers are required to reach a criterion of 90% or greater agreement with the correct recordings before they are allowed to score tapes for clinical work or research purposes. Most observers are able to reach this criterion in 4 to 8 hours of training.

Checking Reliability. In order to insure that observers adhere to the correct use of the observation coding system, reliability checks are carried out on every third to fifth patient observed. These checks are made by having two trained observers independently and simultaneously view and score a particular patient's videotape. To insure consistency in the intervals, an observe and record signal is dubbed onto each videotape. The scoring sheet used by observers is displayed in Table 2. To establish the reliability of observers, percentage agreement is calculated by dividing the number of instances in which observers agreed on the behaviors observed by the number of instances in which agreements plus disagreements

TABLE 2: BEHAVIORAL OBSERVATION SCORING SHEET

	POSITION			MOVEMENT		P BEHAVIOR				
1	std	sit	rec	pce	sft	gd	brc	rb		gr	si
2	std	sit	rec	pce	sft	gd	brc	rb		gr	si
3	std	sit	rec	pce	sft	gd	brc	rb		gr	si
4	std	sit	rec	pce	sft	gd	brc	rb		gr	si
5	std	sit	rec	pce	sft	gd	brc	rb		gr	si
6	std	sit	rec	pce	sft	gd	brc	rb		gr	si
7	std	sit	rec	pce	sft	gd	brc	rb		gr	si
8	std	sit	rec	pce	sft	gd	brc	rb		gr	si
9	std	sit	rec	pce	sft	gd	brc	rb		gr	si
10	std	sit	rec	pce	sft	gd	brc	rb		gr	si
11	std	sit	rec	pce	sft	gd	brc	rb		gr	si
12	std	sit	rec	pce	sft	gd	brc	rb		gr	si
13	std	sit	rec	pce	sft	gd	brc	rb		gr	si
14	std	sit	rec	pce	sft	gd	brc	rb		gr	si
15	std	sit	rec	pce	sft	gd	brc	rb		gr	si
16	std	sit	rec	pce	sft	gd	brc	rb		gr	si
17	std	sit	rec	pce	sft	gd	brc	rb		gr	si
18	std	sit	rec	pce	sft	gd	brc	rb		gr	si
19	std	sit	rec	pce	sft	gd	brc	rb		gr	si
20	std	sit	rec	pce	sft	gd	brc	rb		gr	si
21	std	sit	rec	pce	sft	gd	brc	rb		gr	si
22	std	sit	rec	pce	sft	gd	brc	rb		gr	si
23	std	sit	rec	pce	sft	gd	brc	rb		gr	si
24	std	sit	rec	pce	sft	gd	brc	rb		gr	si
25	std	sit	rec	pce	sft	gd	brc	rb		gr	si
26	std	sit	rec	pce	sft	gd	brc	rb		gr	si
27	std	sit	rec	pce	sft	gd	brc	rb		gr	si
28	std	sit	rec	pce	sft	gd	brc	rb		gr	si
29	std	sit	rec	pce	sft	gd	brc	rb		gr	si
30	std	sit	rec	pce	sft	gd	brc	rb		gr	si
31	std	sit	rec	pce	sft	gd	brc	rb		gr	si
32	std	sit	rec	pce	sft	gd	brc	rb		gr	si
33	std	sit	rec	pce	sft	gd	brc	rb		gr	si
34	std	sit	rec	pce	sft	gd	brc	rb		gr	si
35	std	sit	rec	pce	sft	gd	brc	rb		gr	si

occurred. Percentage agreement should be high, averaging greater than 90%. Disagreements may occur, however, and percentage agreement may drop to 80% in some patients.

Retraining sessions are carried out monthly. During these retraining sessions, we typically have four or five observers present, with the most experienced designated as the calibrating observer. Reliability for each observer is then calculated using the calibrating observer's responses as the correct ones. This retraining procedure is crucial since it prevents observer drift and helps identify potential problems in the definition of categories.

Data Analysis. Scores are derived from the observation for each category by adding the total number of occurrences of each coding category over the observation session. A total pain behavior score consisting of the sum of occurrences of all the coding categories is also computed. Table 3 displays data on the mean and standard deviation for each pain behavior category for a sample of 141 chronic low back pain patients admitted to our management program. As can be seen, guarding, bracing, and rubbing are the most frequent pain behavior categories recorded. Grimacing and sighing, while less frequent, are still commonly observed.

TABLE 3: MEAN (SD) PAIN BEHAVIOR

Pain Behavior	M	SD
Guarding	5.18	3.15
Bracing	3.25	3.60
Rubbing	3.87	3.86
Grimacing	0.99	1.80
Sighing	0.63	1.12
Total Pain Behavior	14.13	8.38
Total Pain Behavior Recorded During Movement Intervals	20.36	12.99
Total Pain Behavior Recorded During Nonmovement Intervals	9.75	7.29

N = 141

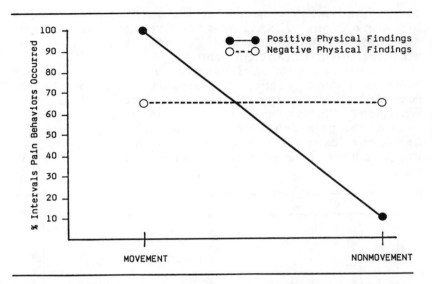

Figure 1. Percentage of movement versus nonmovement intervals in which a pain behavior was observed in two patients: one having positive physical findings (solid line) and one having negative physical findings (dashed line).

The data recorded from a particular patient can be examined in several ways. First, the *level of pain behavior* can be examined. This can be accomplished by comparing an individual patient's score on the pain behavior coding categories to those for the large sample described in Table 3. In some patients, pain behavior levels are quite high. Patients with these extreme responses also often show inconsistencies in pain behavior when observed in other settings. A second use of the observation is to examine the *effects of movement.* If pain behavior is occurring as a respondent behavior, one would expect that the patient will consistently show pain behavior on movement. Figure 1 displays data recorded from two patients, one who had clear evidence of organic pathology responsible for back pain and another who did not. As can be seen, the first patient showed high levels of pain behavior during movement. During nearly 100% of intervals in which movement occurred, a pain behavior was noted. In contrast, very few pain behaviors were recorded during non-movement intervals. The second pain patient, however, showed about the same amount of pain behavior during movement and non-movement intervals. This patient had many elements of the operant pain pattern including strong reliance on addictive medications, over-dependence on spouse and friends, and a law suit regarding his pain problem pending.

A third use of observation data is to *evaluate treatment effects.* Figure 2 displays data on pain behavior recorded from group of 11 patients before and after treatment. As can be seen, reductions were obtained in each of the pain behavior categories. These patients also had significant reductions in their pain intensity and improvements in a variety of functional or well behaviors.

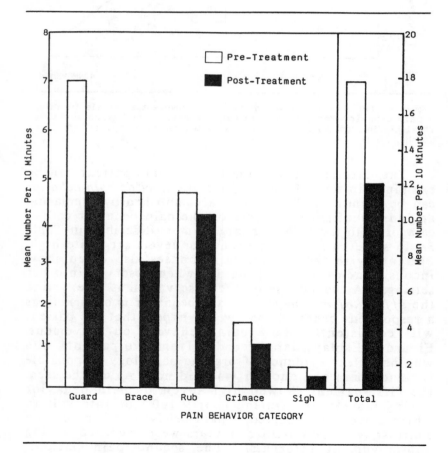

Figure 2. Pain behavior levels pre- and post-treatment on a pain unit.

COMMENTS

The observation system we have described has many advantages. It is relatively simple and provides objective and reliable measures of pain behavior. One potential weakness of this method is that the demand characteristics of the observation session may alter the patient's normal behavior. One could argue that in the observation session, patients change their pain behavior because of the obtrusiveness of the videocamera and research assistant. One way to examine this potential bias is to compare measures of pain behavior taken during the observation session to other measures of pain taken independently. We have done this in a number of different ways and found that total pain behavior scores routinely correlate with pain ratings collected independently from patients within 24 hours of the time of observation (Keefe & Block, 1982). It should be noted that the observation situation is probably not much different in terms of demand characteristics from an evaluation performed by a physician. Despite the potential problems with this method, we feel that its advantages are clear.

SAMPLING PAIN BEHAVIOR IN THE INPATIENT ENVIRONMENT

We have recently extended our observation procedures to record pain behaviors displayed by our patients on our Pain Management Unit. The application of these procedures to this setting has involved active collaboration between the nursing staff on the unit and our own research group.

Observer Training. Hospital policy required that the nursing staff observe patients every 30 minutes to confirm their well-being and presence on the unit. In order to coordinate this function with the pain behavior observation, several modifications to the scoring categories were made. Nurses on the unit were trained in small groups using the methods described for the standard observation session. They then carried out preliminary observations of patients on the unit. Revised coding categories were formulated, and these categories and their definitions are displayed in Table 4 (pages 86-87).

**TABLE 4: OBSERVATION SCORING CATEGORIES
FOR USE ON THE CLINICAL SPECIALTY UNIT**

Location

    1. On unit - out of room
    2. On unit - in room
    3. Off unit - appropriate for category
    4. Unaccounted for

Interaction

    5. No
    6. Yes - with staff
    7. Yes - with family/visitor(s)
    8. Yes - with other patient(s)

Body Position

A. Reclining - Patient reclining or sitting in position with feet off floor for at least 3 seconds.

B. Sitting Upright - Patient in upright position with one or both feet on the floor for at least 3 seconds.

C. Standing - Patient in upright position with one or both feet on the floor at least 3 seconds.

D. Walking - Walking two or more steps in any direction within 3 seconds.

E. Shifting - Change from one position to another (e.g., sit to stand or recline to walk) position.

Pain Behaviors

G. Guarding - Abnormally stiff, interrupted, rigid, or slow **movement** while changing from one position to another (i.e., when recording shifting or during pacing).

B. Bracing - Position in which an almost **fully** extended limb supports and maintains an abnormal distribution of weight. It **cannot occur during movement** (i.e., walking, shifting), must be held for at least 3 seconds. It most frequently is the gripping of the edge of a bed while sitting, but can also be grasping a table, **cane, or walker** while standing. **What appears to be bracing during movement is termed guarding.**

R. Rubbing - Touching, rubbing, or holding the affected area. It can occur during any interval of movement or nonmovement.

F. Facial Grimacing - Obvious facial expressions of pain which may include: furrowed brow, narrowed eyes, tightened lips, corners of mouth pulled back, clenched teeth. It often resembles wincing. Observer must be alert.

Pain Behaviors (Continued):

V.   Verbal Pain Statement - Groan, moan, crying, or direct observation
                             of or description of pain.

A.   Assistance/Support - Use of cervical pillow, body aligner,
                           traction, heating pad, cane, walker, or human
                           help when in static or moving position.

O.   No pain behaviors
     observed.

As can be seen, categories included in the unit observation system allow one to record the patient's location, the occurrence of social interactions, and the patient's body positions. Pain behaviors added include verbal pain behaviors and a record of patients' use of supportive devices such as pillows, heating pads, canes, or walkers. These pain behaviors were included because they are readily observed in the unit and provide a clear signal to others that the patient is having pain. Nurses practiced using these coding categories to record behavior from videotapes generated by our previous research. The nurses then used the observations on the unit. In the early stages, two nurses would observe the patient and then compare their recordings. As better reliability was achieved, individual nurses carried out the observations.

Observation Procedure. Nurses observe patients at half hour intervals beginning at 7:00 am and ending at 11:00 pm. Though 30-minute checks are continued throughout the night shift to evaluate sleep patterns, pain behaviors are not recorded. The patients are told these observations are to check on their status. The procedure is quite simple. The nurse will enter the patient's room, directly observe behavior for 20 seconds, and if the patient initiates a conversation, will then respond but will not engage in a prolonged conversation. After the observation is completed, the nurse records the occurrence or non-occurrence of each of the behavior codes noted in Table 4. The data sheet used for recording is shown in Table 5 (page 88). The table also includes data from a series of 30-minute checks on one patient illustrating how the form is filled out. The example shown in Table 5 is only a partial data sheet covering checks made between 7:30 am and 2:00 pm. However, the reader should note

TABLE 5: NURSE OBSERVATION SCORING SHEET

Name	Room	7:30am	8 & 8:30 BKE	9am MEDS	10am	10:30am	11:00am	11:30am	12 & 12:30 LUNCH	1 & 1:30 MEDS	2pm
	3501										
	3502										
	3503										
	3504										
	3505										
	3506										
	3507										
	3508										
	3509										
	3510	25B / V	26B / O	16C / A	3	18A / O	18B / O	25B / O	3	15D / A-G	3
	3511										
	3512										
	3513										
	3514										
	3515										

*Note: Items in the upper half of each box represent the patient's location, interaction, and body posture. Items in the lower half represent the patient's pain behaviors.

that a complete form would apply to all checks made during the data collection period of 7:00 am to 11:00 pm.

Checking Reliability. Reliability checks are made by having a research assistant accompany a nurse so that simultaneous observations can be made of patients. Percentage agreement is then calculated by comparing recordings made by the research assistant and by the nursing staff. (Reliability is checked using the percentage agreement method. Percentage agreement = number of instances in which agreement of the two observers occurred divided by number of instances in which agreements *plus* disagreement occurred.) Reliability checks have been carried out on several occasions, and percent agreement is in the 90 to 95 percent range. This appears quite acceptable for a clinical instrument.

Data Analysis. Data on patients' behavior on the unit are tabulated and graphed by nursing staff working during the night. The data are entered in each patient's chart. Two summary scores are currently being examined. First, *percentage uptime* is calculated by dividing the total number of intervals that the patient was observed to be standing, walking, or sitting by the total number of intervals in which they were observed. Second, *percentage of time pain behavior observed* is calculated by dividing the number of intervals in which any of the pain behavior codes were scored by the total number of intervals in which patients were observed.

Figure 3 (page 90) displays a typical graph obtained from a patient on the unit. As can be seen, over the course of treatment, time up and out of bed increased and pain decreased.

Data from the nurse observations are available to the treatment team during staffings and rounds. It is a tool that is useful in objectively evaluating patient progress. Treatment decisions are often based on the level of pain behavior observed. Discrepancies between patient reports of activity and nurse observations are discussed with the patient. This is often helpful to the patients in giving them a more accurate appraisal of their activity and pain levels.

One behavior pattern we commonly observe on the unit is for the patient to rapidly increase time out of bed (uptime) until their pain becomes intolerable. At this point, pain behaviors increase dramatically and activity

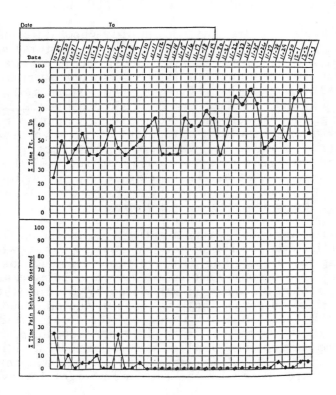

Figure 3. Percentage of observations in which patient was observed to be up and out of a reclining position (top half of figure) and to display pain behavior (bottom half of figure). Data displayed are those collected over the course of an admission (10-29 to 12-3) on an inpatient pain unit.

subsequently decreases to a very low level. We call this pattern a "pain cycle" and it is frequently observed during the early stages of admission. Patients and their families report that similar pain cycles occur frequently in the home setting prior to admission. One of the best methods to modify this pattern is to place patients on a strict temporal cycle of activity and rest. Activity level is initially set at an intentionally low level (e.g., 20 minutes uptime per hour) and rest is also prescribed (40 minutes per hour). Each day the activity level is increased by 1 to 2 minutes and rest correspondingly decreased. The results achieved with this type of program are encouraging in that patients are able to increase their activity levels while at the same time their pain ratings and pain behaviors actually decrease. Figure 3 illustrates progress achieved by one patient who was placed on such a schedule.

COMMENT

Systematic observations of pain behavior by nursing staff have many advantages. In inpatient settings, nurses are usually responsible for administering treatments for pain and evaluating their effectiveness. On pain units where behavioral and psychological techniques are used, it is particularly important that nurses be able to objectively identify pain behaviors and respond in a consistent fashion when they do occur. On a unit where many nurses are working with patients, problems can occur when there is a lack of agreement as to how to respond to the display of both well and pain behaviors.

The observation system that we have described was developed with the active collaboration and participation of the nurses on the pain unit. The process of developing this system has been useful for the entire treatment team. It has helped the nurses and other staff to be more precise in their description of pain behaviors, and the different pain behavior categories have provided a common language with which to describe frequently observed behavioral responses. A second major advantage is that the observation system enables us to more readily monitor a patient's responses to particular treatments. For example, a patient's response to initial nerve blocks often is predictive of later response to repeated blocks. By using the observation system, changes in pain behavior occurring over a 24-hour period after a nerve block can be objectively documented and used to guide decisions about further treatment.

One problem with observation systems such as this is the time required to carry out and score the observations. On our own unit, checks of the patient every 30 minutes are a hospital requirement, and this procedure was in place before the pain behavior observation system was introduced. Thus, little extra time or effort was required on the part of the nursing staff. In our view, even on large or very busy units, observation procedures such as these can be adapted or modified to make them practical. One approach is to use these observations on only selected patients. A second modification would be to take observations at less frequent intervals.

One of the major advantages of any inpatient hospital unit is that it provides many opportunities to observe patient behavior. Typically, these observations are made in an anecdotal fashion. The observation method we have described is simple, objective, and reliable. We believe this observation system is potentially useful in many clinical settings where pain management is the goal. On our unit we are beginning to examine the data we gather from each patient in more detail. The relationship of pain behavior and social interaction patterns is being studied. In particular, changes in pain behavior that occur when spouse and family members visit the patient are being studied. Some patients show marked increases in pain behavior when their spouses visit on the weekend whereas other patients show a very consistent pattern of behavior. The relationship between sleep patterns and pain behavior is also being studied to help us determine whether psychotropic medications used to improve sleep reduce observed pain behavior as well. Individual pain behavior coding categories can also be graphed and studied longitudinally. This can help us identify which pain behaviors respond quickly and which persist, suggesting a need for further intervention. Finally, we are interested in studying how changes in pain behavior that we observe relate to the perceptions of the spouse and family regarding how the patient has changed during treatment.

OTHER CLINICAL APPLICATIONS

Assessment procedures for analyzing pain behavior need not be restricted to use with chronic low back pain patients. We have extended our observation methods to the analysis of pain behavior in patients suffering from temporomandibular joint pain (Keefe & Dolan, 1986), head and neck cancer pain (Keefe, Brantley, Manuel, & Crisson, 1985), and pain secondary to osteoarthritis. A collaborative study carried out with Dr. Laurence Bradley of Bowman Gray Medical Center has also demonstrated the utility of pain behavior observation with rheumatoid arthritis patients (McDaniel et al., 1986). We encourage clinicians and researchers to consider adapting these procedures to specific populations of pain patients. We believe that the information gleaned from this type of research will contribute significantly to our understanding of clinical pain phenomena.

Francis J. Keefe, PhD, is currently Director of the Pain Management Program and is an Associate Professor of Medical Psychology in the Department of Psychiatry at Duke University Medical School. Prior to his present position, he was a post-doctoral fellow at the Psychophysiology Laboratory, Massachusetts Mental Health Center. His training is in clinical psychology. He has published numerous articles on behavioral assessment and treatment of chronic pain. Dr. Keefe may be contacted at Box 3926, Duke University Medical Center, Durham, NC 27720.

James E. Crisson, MA, is employed as a research analyst for the Pain Management Program at Duke University Medical Center and is currently working on his PhD dissertation in social psychology at the University of North Carolina at Greensboro. His areas of interest include pain assessment and the application of social psychological concepts, particularly attributional processes, to this assessment. Mr. Crisson can be contacted at Box 3926, Duke University Medical Center, Durham, NC 27720.

Mary Trainor, RN, is currently Head Nurse on the Clinical Specialty Unit, the inpatient chronic pain unit at Duke University Medical Center in Durham, North Carolina. Her past experience includes nursing positions in both inpatient and outpatient psychiatric settings. Her interests include milieu therapy in an inpatient chronic pain setting and family history profiles and their relationship to specific pain syndromes. Ms. Trainor may be contacted at P. O. Box 3478, Duke University Medical Center, Durham, NC 27710.

RESOURCES

Engel, G. L. (1959). "Psychogenic" pain and the pain prone patient. *Medical Clinics of North America, 42,* 1481.

Fordyce, W. E. (1976). *Behavioral Methods for Chronic Pain and Illness.* St. Louis, MO: C. V. Mosby.

Jay, S. M., Ozolins, M., Elliott, C., & Caldwell, S. (1983). Assessment of children's distress during painful medical procedures. *Journal of Health Psychology, 2,* 133-147.

Keefe, F. J. (1982). Behavioral assessment and treatment of chronic pain: Current status and future directions. *Journal of Consulting and Clinical Psychology, 50,* 896-911.

Keefe, F. J., & Block, A. R. (1982). Development of an observation method for assessing pain behavior in chronic low back pain patients. *Behavior Therapy, 13,* 363-375.

Keefe, F. J., Brantley, A., Manuel, G., & Crisson, J. E. (1985). Behavioral assessment of head and neck cancer pain. *Pain, 23,* 327-336.

Keefe, F. J., Wilkins, R. H., & Cook, W. A. (1984). Direct observation of pain behavior in low back pain patients during physical examination. *Pain, 20,* 59-68.

Lown, B., Verrier, L. R. C., & Rabinowitz, S. H. (1977). Neural and psychological mechanisms and the problem of sudden cardiac death. *The American Journal of Cardiology, 39,* 890-902.

McDaniel, L. K., Anderson, K. O., Bradley, L. A., Young, L. D., Turner, R. A., Agudelo, C. A., & Keefe, F. J. (1986). Development of an observation method for assessing pain behavior in rheumatoid arthritis patients. *Pain, 24,* 165-184.

Melzack, R., & Wall, P. D. (1965). Pain mechanisms: A new theory. *Science, 150,* 971-979.

Pavlov, I. P. (1927). *Conditioned Reflexes.* New York: Oxford University Press.

Skinner, B. F. (1953). *Science in Human Behavior.* New York: Macmillan.

Sternbach, R. A. (1974). *Pain Patients: Traits and Treatment.* New York: Academic Press.

Szasz, T. S. (1957). *Pain and Pleasures: A Study of Bodily Feelings.* London: Tavistock.

Waddell, G., McCulloch, J. A., Kimmel, E., & Venner, R. M. (1980). Non organic physical signs in low back pain. *Spine, 5,* 117-125.

NEUROPSYCHOLOGICAL ASSESSMENT OF COGNITIVE IMPAIRMENT IN THE ELDERLY

Albert S. Aniskiewicz

Clinical neuropsychological assessment can provide a valuable contribution to the differential diagnosis and treatment planning of elderly patients who present with cognitive impairment. And neuropsychological studies conducted with the perspective of viewing brain dysfunction as a dynamic rather than static process (Smith, 1975) provide the additional understanding of the changing nature and extent of impairment associated with evolving or resolving neurological processes. Such a dynamic conceptual approach is especially important when one considers the question of reversible and irreversible dementia in the aged. Despite this and other conceptual and methodological advances which have supplanted the unitary concept of organicity and its psychometric equivalent, the single best test approach, caution still has been advanced concerning the efficacy of psychological testing as a diagnostic tool with the elderly (Wells, 1980). Among the most compelling arguments presented is the problem of false-positive signs found in attempts to differentiate functional and organic disorders. Too frequently, evidence of cognitive impairment is interpreted erroneously as reflecting an organic disease when actually cognitive abilities have been compromised by a functional psychiatric disorder. Similarly, evidence of cognitive decline can be misinterpreted as reflecting a primary and irreversible dementia when instead an exogenous and treatable factor may be the causative agent.

Neuropsychological assessment methods can address such critiques if they are guided by interpretive strategies that consider more than quantitative test scores. Such approaches may rely more heavily on considered clinical judgment than on automated decision making. Thus, a grounding in the neuropsychology of aging and in the specific neurological and psychiatric syndromes commonly associated with aging is essential. Even though an extensive treatment of these areas is beyond the scope of this chapter, they will provide the foundation from which we will highlight some of the clinical issues and assessment strategies involved in evaluating elderly patients who present with cognitive impairment. And since dementia versus depressive pseudodementia is a common differential diagnosis with elderly patients, particular attention will be directed to the practical application of clinical methods that may be helpful in differentiating the two disorders.

CONCEPTUAL AND METHODOLOGICAL ISSUES

An awareness of the conceptual and methodological problems involved in the neuropsychological evaluation of the aged is the essential starting point in the development of an assessment strategy. One major conceptual issue concerns the different patterns of cognitive decline associated with normal and pathological aging. There is extensive literature that contradicts the notion of global deterioration of cognitive abilities with age and, instead, documents a selective and variable decline in specific functions (Bak & Greene, 1980; Benton, Eslinger, & Damasio, 1981; Lezak, 1983). Generally, verbal abilities withstand the effects of age, whereas certain memory functions and problem-solving abilities decline. Some researchers (Goldstein & Shelly, 1981; Klisz, 1978) have suggested that specific patterns of cognitive decline indicate that the process of aging in the right hemisphere differs from that in the left. Specificity in cognitive decline also applies to pathological aging as exemplified by the progressive dementia associated with Alzheimer's disease. Despite the prevalent definition of dementia as a global and general deterioration in mental functioning, which indeed may reflect its end stage, it is well known that the early stages and course of the disease are accompanied by a variable decline in specific neuropsychological functions (Lishman, 1980).

At the methodological level, the clinician encounters the problem of inadequate test norms for use with the aged, since the norms for many commonly used test instruments were developed on younger populations (Albert, 1981). The unqualified comparison of the test performance of an elderly patient with standard but age-inappropriate norms runs the serious risk of false-positive misdiagnosis. The clinician also must be sensitive to factors within the test situation itself that can exacerbate the cognitive changes associated with aging. Solving novel problems, changing response sets, working with time pressures, and the attendant anxiety and fatigue involved in an evaluation can make the cognitive changes of normal aging "be seen at their worst in the very setting where the label of dementia is considered to explain these behaviors" (Gurland & Toner, 1983, p. 3).

ASSESSMENT STRATEGY

A comprehensive neuropsychological evaluation of the elderly patient does not necessarily require a lengthy test protocol. It should include a systematic review of cognitive functioning, a review of the history and course of the patient's complaints, and a consideration of the patient's clinical presentation and test-taking posture. Given that a reliable history is an important element, an interview with the patient's spouse or relatives is a helpful adjunct to the evaluation procedure.

The efficacy of a neuropsychological assessment is enhanced when test results are considered within the context of the patient's current life situation, and this attitude is especially important to work with elderly patients. Therefore, the approach being suggested here does not rely exclusively on quantitative test scores. Instead, a more broad-based strategy is proposed in which the patient's clinical presentation and the history and course of complaints are considered equally important to the evaluation. Furthermore, the qualitative aspects of test performance are noted because we are concerned not only with what patients can or cannot do but also *how* they perform on particular tasks.

Given this framework, we first will review a function-oriented assessment approach. We then will consider the

97

major causes of cognitive impairment in the elderly, emphasizing the clinical features of dementia associated with Alzheimer's disease and the pseudodementia associated with depressive disorders. Through the course of the presentation, those features that are helpful in differentiating the two disorders will be highlighted.

ASSESSMENT METHOD

The time required for the administration of standard neuropsychological test batteries (e.g., Halstead-Reitan) can be prohibitive with the elderly due to their increased fatigability and their difficulties with maintaining sustained attention. The issue of age-appropriate norms also is a problem with some of the widely used standardized batteries. An alternative is to use one of several mini-mental status or dementia rating scales that have been designed specifically for use with the aged to assess degree of dementia (Blessed, Tomlinson, & Roth, 1968; Coblentz et al., 1973; M. F. Folstein, S. E. Folstein, & McHugh, 1975). These scales are efficient and can provide a valid index of overall severity of cognitive decline, but specific patterns of preservation and loss of cognitive abilities can be obscured by a reliance on summary scores alone.

The assessment method suggested here is function-oriented rather than test-oriented. It offers the advantage of a systematic review of specific neuropsychological functions while permitting the flexibility of using a variety of measures as the exigencies of the test situation may determine. It can be less time-consuming than some standardized batteries, yet it permits the analysis of specific patterns of cognitive decline not as readily obtained from brief rating scales. In using such an assessment approach, it is recommended that the following areas be reviewed; (a) orientation and attention, (b) language, (c) memory, (d) visual-spatial abilities, and (e) cognitive flexibility and abstraction.

Orientation and Attention. Orientation for person, place, and time is the traditional starting point for the mental status examination and for several dementia rating scales. Disorientation for time often is observed with dementia, and the traditional mental status review may be supplemented with the Temporal Orientation Test (Benton, Hamsher, Varney, & Spreen, 1983) for a more systematic evaluation of orientation in the temporal sphere.

Immediate auditory verbal attention span can easily be assessed with the Digits Forward test. A score of 6±1 is generally considered to fall within the normal range. Sustained attention can be assessed through various letter cancellation tasks (Lezak, 1983).

Language. A preliminary assessment of language functioning should include an evaluation of comprehension, repetition, articulation, object-naming, writing, and reading. The Reitan-Indiana Aphasia Screening Test (Wheeler & Reitan, 1962) provides a brief review of these areas. A word-generating test such as the Controlled Word Association Test (Benton & Hamsher, 1978) also is suggested because it is sensitive to impaired verbal fluency which is a frequent finding in dementia.

Memory. Although memory impairment is one of the more common features of brain dysfunction, memory itself should not be considered as a unitary factor. An evaluation of memory functioning at least should include a review of remote memory, immediate memory span, and recent memory.

Recent memory should be assessed in the verbal and nonverbal visual modalities. The Revised Wechsler Memory Scale (Russell, 1975) provides an assessment of immediate and delayed recall of verbal material and nonverbal figural material, and it has been demonstrated to discriminate between the normal aging process and dementia (Logue & Wyrick, 1979). The Rey Auditory-Verbal Learning Test (Lezak, 1983) is another measure of new verbal learning ability which affords the additional advantage of examining the effects of practice and interference on learning. The Benton Visual Retention Test (Benton, 1974) is a measure of nonverbal visual memory and can be used to assess immediate and delayed recall. Its format of 10 stimulus figures provides a more extensive review than the figural recall portion of the Revised Wechsler Memory Scale. Age-corrected norms up to age 64 are available for the immediate recall administration, and methods are provided for a qualitative analysis of error patterns.

Immediate auditory verbal memory span can be assessed with Digits Forward, and a comparison of the best Digits Forward performance with the first recall trial of the Rey Auditory-Verbal Learning Test is helpful in evaluating the effects of overstimulation on concentration and memory. For example, a difference of two or more points, favoring Digits Forward, between the best Digits Forward performance and the first recall trial of the Rey word list suggests that new verbal learning abilities may be compromised by overstimulation (Lezak, 1983).

Remote memory traditionally has been assessed through reviewing biographical and historical information. Items from the Information subtest of the Wechsler Adult Intelligence Scale (WAIS) battery are useful in this regard. When referring to the Wechsler Intelligence Scales we will adopt a system used by Lezak (1983). We will refer to the WAIS when specific reference is made to the 1955 version of the test, and we will refer to the WAIS-R when reference is made to the 1981 version. When both versions are discussed together the term WAIS battery will be used. More detailed methods for assessing remote memory also are provided in Lezak (1983).

Visual-Spatial Abilities. In addition to standardized tests of visual-spatial analysis such as the WAIS battery Block Design test and the Hooper Visual Organization Test (Hooper, 1958), visual-spatial functioning can be examined through various constructional drawing tasks. The copying of two-dimensional figures is a part of the Reitan-Indiana Aphasia Screening Test. These tasks can be supplemented by the copying of three-dimensional figures such as a cube or the freehand drawing of a house in perspective, because constructional impairment not readily apparent on two-dimensional figures can be more easily revealed on a more complex task. Another very useful and easily administered task is the freehand drawing of the face of a clock and the setting of the hands for "10 after 11" (Albert & Kaplan, 1980). Visual-spatial distortions may be detected in the overall configuration of the clock and in the placement of the numbers. Stimulus-bound thinking may be revealed through the hand-setting procedure.

Cognitive Flexibility and Abstract Reasoning. A simple test of verbal abstract reasoning is proverb interpretation, and the items from the WAIS battery Comprehension subtest may be used. Standardized measures of complex reasoning such as the Wisconsin Card Sort

100

(Berg, 1948) or Raven's Standard Progressive Matrices (Raven, 1960) provide a more extensive examination of cognitive flexibility and abstract reasoning. If the Raven is selected, it is recommended that the short form developed in Aaron Smith's laboratory (Berker et al., 1979) be used because this briefer version may be more easily tolerated by elderly patients.

Supplementary Measures. The areas of functioning just presented are considered as a minimum for review and can be supplemented with additional investigations. If the demands of the testing situation do not permit the administration of the full WAIS battery, it is recommended that at least the Vocabulary and Block-Design subtests be given. The Vocabulary performance can be used as an estimate of pre-morbid intellectual ability, and the comparison of the Block-Design score with the Vocabulary score can be used as an index of dementia.

The assessment of motor functioning by tests of manual motor speed may be of little help in differentiating between the effects of normal and pathological aging (Boller et al., 1984). However, the evaluation of sequential motor programming through tests of alternating motor sequences (Albert & Kaplan, 1980; Rosen, 1983) can be helpful in assessing tendencies toward disinhibition and perseveration often seen with dementia.

DEMENTIA

Conceptualizing dementia as a global deterioration in intellectual functioning obscures the fact that dementias are evidenced by specific patterns of cognitive decline, the variability of which may reflect different etiologies. For our purposes, dementia will be viewed as a progressive deterioration in mental abilities characterized by specific pattern of relative cognitive preservation and cognitive loss.

Of critical importance clinically is the differentiation between treatable and untreatable dementias; therefore, an awareness of specific etiological factors is an important prerequisite to an evaluation. Our primary focus will be the differentiation between the dementia of Alzheimer's disease and the pseudodementia associated with depressive disorders of the aged. Nevertheless, it should be noted that diagnostic differentiation does not occur solely on the organic-functional dimension. There are a number of intracranial and exogenous factors that can cause severe cognitive impairment in the aged and which are treatable. Although the evaluation of these conditions is the province of the physician, an awareness of their association with cognitive impairment is important for neuropsychological investigations. The principal exogenous factors that can impair cognitive functioning are: drug intoxication, metabolic imbalance and nutritional deficiencies, cardiovascular disorders, and infectious processes (see Albert, 1981 for a more extensive review). The main intracranial conditions that can produce a reversible dementia are: obstructive hydrocephalus, subdural hematoma, and intracranial tumors (see Cummings, 1983 for a more extensive review). The nomenclature used to describe the cognitive impairment associated with these disorders has varied (reversible dementia, delirium, acute brain syndrome, acute confusional state), but the terminology generally reflects the more acute and transient nature of these conditions.

ALZHEIMER'S DISEASE

Alzheimer's disease is one variant of progressive neuronal degeneration that produces dementia. It affects twice as many females as males, and its etiology is unknown. Onset may occur after age 40, and although there is some suggestion that a pre-senile variant (onset before age 65) may differ from the senile variant (onset after age 65), it is more widely accepted that both processes represent a common disease entity. As yet, there is no known cure for the disease, and the course is one of progressive decline with death following approximately 5 years after onset. Alzheimer's disease accounts for approximately 50% of individuals suffering from dementia (Boller et al., 1984), with cerebrovascular multi-infarct disease accounting for approximately 10-20% of the dementias (Hachinski, Lassen, & Marshall, 1974). Estimates vary, however. Other forms of dementia, such as Pick's disease and Creutzfeldt-Jakob disease, are rarer.

It is generally accepted that Alzheimer's disease progresses through three stages and involves changes in cognitive function, mood, and efficiency in the activities of daily living. Diagnosis at the mid and later stages may not be problematic. However, since cognitive changes may precede the emergence of focal signs and structural neurological change in the initial phase of the disease, neuropsychological assessments done at the early stages can be most helpful.

History, Course, and Clinical Presentation. Alzheimer's disease is an insidious and slowly evolving process. Therefore, it may be difficult to document a specific onset. Often, memory problems and inefficiency in the activities of daily living are noticed initially by family members. Other features of early cognitive decline may include word-finding difficulties and spatial disorientation, the latter being noticed when the patient begins to get lost in familiar surroundings. The constellation of symptoms that includes memory dysfunction, word-finding difficulty, and visual-spatial dysfunction is frequently evident in the initial stages of the disease, although they are not always observed concurrently. Social behavior initially may appear generally appropriate, but disturbances in mood and affect may emerge. A loss of initiative and interest in past pleasurable activities may herald the onset of a more pervasive apathy. Mood changes may include depression, agitation, and restlessness, which are especially prominent at night.

The second stage involves a worsening deterioration. Spontaneous speech may decline, and focal signs of neuropsychological dysfunction such as aphasia, apraxia, and agnosia may emerge. Patients become increasingly unable to attend to personal and household responsibilities, insight regarding their own condition becomes impaired, and disorientation for time and place may extend to their own person. Personality disturbances are accentuated, and restlessness may take the form of wandering at night.

In the final stages of the disease, evidence of decline is pervasive; double incontinence may ensue and the patient becomes increasingly apathetic and unable to maintain self-care.

Neuropsychological Findings. During the initial stages of the disease, a systematic review of neuropsychological functioning may reveal that orientation for time is impaired, even though orientation for place and person may be spared. Immediate auditory verbal attention span, as assessed with Digits Forward, may be relatively preserved; but concentration deficits become apparent in impaired performances on Digits Backward.

Dysnomia and verbal dysfluency are the most common early signs of language impairment. Word-finding difficulties are evident in spontaneous speech and in confrontation object-naming. Verbal dysfluency may be revealed in poor performances on the Controlled Word Association Test.

Within the memory sphere, recent short-term and long-term memory in the verbal and nonverbal visual modalities are likely to show significant impairment. Remote memory traditionally has been thought to be relatively better preserved in the initial stages of the disease, but several investigators (Boller et al., 1984) suggest that remote memory also is impaired. This finding is consistent with the patchy quality of remote memory often reported in clinical evaluations.

Visual-spatial impairment may be evidenced by poor performances on the Block Design test. And even if reproductions of the square and triangle on the Reitan-Indiana Aphasia Screening Test are marginally acceptable, evidence of impairment may be seen on the Greek cross and in drawings of three-dimensional figures. Configural distortions and placement errors may be seen in the drawing of the face of a clock, and stimulus-bound thinking may be demonstrated by errors in setting the clock's hands (placing the hands on the *11* and *10* instead of the *2* and *11*). Albert and Kaplan (1980) provide an excellent review of the qualitative analysis of these error patterns.

Patients with dementia do poorly on tasks of cognitive flexibility and abstraction. Proverb interpretation may be characterized by concrete thinking. Evidence of perseveration may be obtained on the Wisconsin Card Sort, and the decline of abilities for abstract reasoning can be revealed by poor performances on Raven's Progressive Matrices.

Although demented patients perform more poorly than normal controls on the WAIS battery, they do show evidence of subtest variability. Information, Vocabulary, Digits Forward, and some Comprehension and Similarities items may be performed relatively well, but poor performances are obtained on Block Design, Digit Symbol, and Digits Backward (Lezak, 1983).

PSEUDODEMENTIA

Pseudodementia is broadly defined as a syndrome in which the symptoms of dementia are mimicked by a functional psychiatric disorder. Although it has been identified with several psychiatric disorders (Kiloh, 1961; Wells, 1979), it is usually associated with depression (Gurland & Toner, 1983; Post, 1975) and occurs most commonly in elderly depressed patients (Caine, 1981). Accordingly, the syndrome of depressive pseudodementia has been delimited. Such a delineation, however, is not without controversy, as some investigators suggest that depressive pseudodementia itself may be a misnomer because "the condition may be produced by some interaction between biochemical alterations associated with depression and the various sources of neuronal depletion associated with aging" (M. F. Folstein & P. R. McHugh, cited in Goldstein, 1984, p. 75). As such, the term "dementia syndrome of depression" has been sug-gested.

It has been estimated that reversible cognitive impairment may occur in 15-20% of elderly depressed patients (Roth, 1980) and that 25% of patients with dementia may be depressed (Boller et al., 1984). Consider-ing this overlap and the implications of failure to recognize a treatable condition, the practicing clinician has the task of careful differentiation.

DEPRESSIVE PSEUDODEMENTIA

Whereas relatively specific patterns of neuropsycholog-ical impairment occur with the irreversible dementia of Alzheimer's disease, such specificity has yet to be consistently identified with depressive pseudodementia. In fact, inconsistent patterns of deficit and variability of performance on neuropsychological measures by elderly depressed patients have in themselves been considered distinguishing features of depressive pseudodementia. Therefore, the clinician should be aware of the pattern of impaired functioning seen in dementia because it can serve as a first level differentiating feature. Further-more, given that the depressed elderly patient may perform in the cognitively impaired range on a number of quantitative neuropsychological indices (most notably, memory), the clinician should consider the qualitative aspects of the patient's performance and the history and course of the illness as equally essential elements in the differential diagnosis.

History, Course and Clinical Presentation. Collective clinical experience (Caine, 1981; Gurland & Toner, 1983; Post, 1975; Wells, 1979) has led to the identification of several features in the history, course of illness, and clinical presentation of patients that are helpful in differentiating dementia and depressive pseudodementia.

Complaints of cognitive impairment and depression may be a common presentation of elderly demented and elderly depressed patients, but the onset and nature of the complaints often are qualitatively different. The onset of depressive symptoms generally precedes those of cognitive impairment in depressive disorders, and the reverse sequence is more likely with dementia. With depressive disorders, the onset of symptoms may be more easily dated, of shorter duration, and associated with a specific precipitant, in contrast to the insidious onset observed in dementia. A personal and familial history of affective disorder favors a diagnosis of depression, whereas a familial history of dementia is more suggestive of dementia.

Both patient groups may present evidence of depressed mood, agitation, and loss of interest in once pleasurable activities. The affective quality of the depressed patient may be more pervasively dysphoric, whereas the affect of the demented patient may be more shallow and labile. For example, it has been suggested that laughter and crying may be elicited from the demented patient by suggesting cheerful or sad themes, but that truly depressed affect may not be so easily influenced by such attempts (Post, 1975).

Vegetative signs of depression, including sleep disturbance, appetite disturbance, and constipation, are less likely to be seen in dementia, and they may be the predominant manifestation of "masked" or "silent" depression in the elderly (Gurland & Toner, 1983). However, the variations in eating and sleeping patterns associated with aging should be considered when applying these signs. For example, sleep disorders may occur for a variety of reasons with the elderly, but "evidence of unpleasant brooding thoughts occurring during episodes of nighttime wakefulness is highly suggestive of depression" (Gurland & Toner, 1983, p. 11). It also should be noted that nocturnal accentuation of general dysfunction in terms of agitation, confusion, and disorientation is more consistent with dementia.

Upon examination, depressed patients may emphasize their disability and give a more detailed account of their dysfunction than demented patients are likely to provide. Likewise, relatives of depressed patients are more likely to be concerned with specific dysfunctions, such as the patient's memory impairment, whereas relatives of the demented patient are more likely to be concerned about changes in the patient's performance of daily activities, such as an inability to perform household tasks or an inability to interpret familiar surroundings. Finally, depressed patients are more likely to exaggerate their memory problems, and generally, their subjective complaints outweigh the objective evidence of cognitive impairment.

Neuropsychological Findings. Despite the marked variability of performance on neuropsychological tests associated with depressive pseudodementia, there are some distinct features of test behavior and performance that are helpful with a differential diagnosis.

Performances on tests involving attention, concentration, and memory often are affected by a patient's motivation. In contrast to demented patients who make attempts to respond to questions of orientation and memory and who try to complete required tasks, depressed patients are more inclined to respond with "I don't know" and their written work may be cursorily performed and sloppy. Encouragement may elicit a better performance from the depressed patient, whereas it is unlikely to have a significant effect on the performance of the demented patient.

Although it has long been thought that specific patterns of neuropsychological impairment are not associated with pseudodementia, the recent work of Caine (1981) shows promise in providing more specificity. He suggests that depressive pseudodementia may be associated with selective deficits in attention, mental processing speed, spontaneous elaboration, and analysis of detail. Specific language functions, delayed verbal recall and recognition, mathematics, finger tapping, and motor praxis evidently are spared.

Traditionally, evidence of focal signs such as aphasia, agnosia, and apraxia is seen as more consistent with dementia, particularly in the later stages, and is uncommon with depression. Even before the appearance of specific aphasic deficits, the language of the demented patient is characterized by dysnomia and dysfluency. Therefore, test evidence of word-finding and object-naming deficits and poor performances on word-generating tests (Controlled Word Association Test) are more likely with dementia than depression.

Complaints of memory impairment often are associated with depression, and memory deficits are among the most common findings in dementia. Thompson (1980) suggested a framework for examining the relationship among memory complaints, memory test performance, and depression. For example, he suggests that a pattern which includes a high level of memory complaints, a normal test performance, and a high level of depression is consistent with a depressive disorder. Following his schema, a pattern of low memory complaints, poor test performance, and a low level of depression would be consistent with severe brain impairment. A pattern that includes high memory complaints, relatively normal test performance, and low depression may reflect an anxious pre-occupation with age-related changes in cognitive functioning. More difficult is the pattern that includes high memory complaints, poor test performance, and high depression. In this instance, a detailed analysis of memory test performance is required to rule out dementia. Both depressed and demented patients may show impairment on tests of immediate recall, such as the first recall of the paragraph on the Revised Wechsler Memory Scale; however, depressed patients demonstrate a capacity to learn and show adequate delayed verbal recall (Caine, 1981). Impairment in new learning ability is likely to be more pervasive with dementia.

Visual-spatial dysfunction is a frequent finding with dementia, as evidenced by impaired performances on the Block Design test and on constructional drawing tasks. Motivational and concentration difficulties affect the performances of depressed patients on these tasks. Test pattern and qualitative analyses are helpful in this regard. Coolidge and associates found that a pattern in which the Vocabulary subtest score of the WAIS is at least twice as large as the Block Design subtest score is more consistent with dementia than depression (cited in Lezak, 1983). The drawings of depressed patients may be sloppy and hastily executed, and encouragement may improve their quality; but, they are unlikely to show the evidence of configural distortion found in the drawings of demented patients.

Dementia is characterized by significant impairment in abstract reasoning and cognitive flexibility. However, depressed patients also may show some degree of impairment on tests of verbal abstract reasoning, such as proverb interpretation (Caine, 1981). While demented patients may be expected to perform poorly on standardized tests such as Raven's Progressive Matrices and the Wisconsin Card Sort, additional research is needed to determine whether there are quantitative and qualitative differences between their performances and those of depressed patients.

CONCLUSION

The contributions of neuropsychological procedures in evaluating the nature and extent of cognitive impairment in the elderly can be significant. The efficacy of these methods is buttressed when careful consideration is given to the special needs of elderly patients. To this end, an assessment method has been proposed which attempts to be comprehensive yet sufficiently flexible for use with elderly patients.

The interpretive strategy underlying the method is guided by a quantitative and qualitative analysis of test findings. Equally essential to this procedure is the interpretation of test results within the context of the patient's clinical presentation and the history and course of the illness. This approach requires a working familiarity with the neuropsychological findings associated with normal and pathological aging; but the meaningfulness of such findings is enhanced when the clinician also has a foundation in general behavioral neurology and in the psychopathology and neuropathology of aging. More extensive treatments of these areas are suggested in the Resource section.

Albert S. Aniskiewicz, PhD, is currently a Professor in the Counseling Center and Department of Psychology at Michigan State University. He also has an adjunct appointment in the Department of Psychiatry. He received his doctorate in clinical psychology in 1973 from Purdue University and is a diplomate in clinical psychology, American Board of Professional Psychology. Dr. Aniskiewicz may be contacted at 347 Olin Health Center, Michigan State University, East Lansing, MI 48824.

RESOURCES

TEST RESOURCES

Benton Revised Visual Retention Test. Available through The Psychological Corporation, 757 Third Avenue, New York, NY 10017.

Controlled Word Association Test. Part of the Multilingual Aphasia Examination (Benton & Hamsher, 1978), University of Iowa, Iowa City, IA.

Hooper Visual Organization Test. Available through Western Psychological Services, 12031 Wilshire Boulevard, Los Angeles, CA 90025.

Raven Standard Progressive Matrices. Available through The Psychological Corporation, 757 Third Avenue, New York, NY 10017. Description of the Short Form is available through Aaron Smith, Neuropsychological Laboratory, The University of Michigan, 1111 East Catherine Street, Ann Arbor, MI 48109.

Reitan-Indiana Aphasia Screening Test. Available through R. M. Reitan, Department of Psychology, University of Arizona, Tucson, AZ 85721.

Rey Auditory-Verbal Learning Test. Description and normative data are provided in Lezak, 1983.

Temporal Orientation Test. Available in Benton et al., 1983.

Wechsler Adult Intelligence Scale (WAIS and WAIS-R). Available through The Psychological Corporation, 757 Third Avenue, New York, NY 10017.

Wechsler Memory Scale. Available through The Psychological Corporation, 757 Third Avenue, New York, NY 10017. See Russell (1975) for a description of the Revised Wechsler Memory Scale.

Wisconsin Card Sorting Test. A test kit and new manual developed by Robert K. Heaton are available through Psychological Assessment Resources, P. O. Box 98, Odessa, FL 33556.

PUBLICATIONS

Albert, M. S. (1981). Geriatric neuropsychology. *Journal of Consulting and Clinical Psychology, 49,* 835-850.

Albert, M. S. & Kaplan, E. (1980). Organic implications of neuropsychological deficits in the elderly. In L. W. Poon, J. L. Fozard, L. S. Cermack, D. Arenberg, & L. W. Thompson (Eds.), *New Directions in Memory and Aging* (pp. 403-432). Hillsdale, NJ: Lawrence Erlbaum Associates, Inc.

Bak, J. S., & Greene, R. L. (1980). Changes in neuropsychological functioning in an aging population. *Journal of Consulting and Clinical Psychology, 48,* 395-399.

Benton, A. L. (1974). *The Revised Visual Retention Test* (4th ed.). New York: Psychological Corporation.

Benton, A. L., Eslinger, P. J., & Damasio, A. R. (1981). Normative observations on neuropsychological test performances in old age. *Journal of Clinical Neuropsychology, 3,* 33-42.

Benton, A. L., & Hamsher, K. (1978). *Multilingual Aphasia Exam.* Iowa City: University of Iowa.

Benton, A. L., Hamsher, K., Varney, N. R., & Spreen, O. (1983). *Contributions to Clinical Neuropsychological Assessment.* New York: Oxford University Press.

Berg, E. A. (1948). A simple objective test for measuring flexibility in thinking. *Journal of General Psychology, 39,* 15-22.

Berker, E., Zubreck, S., Javornisky, G., Whelan, T., Witten, M., & Smith, A. (1979). *Short Form of Raven's Progressive Matrices: A Preliminary Report.* Unpublished manuscript, University of Michigan, Neuropsychological Laboratory, 1111 East Catherine, Ann Arbor, MI.

Blessed, G., Tomlinson, B. E., & Roth, M. (1968). The association between quantitative measures of dementia and of senile change in the cerebral grey matter of elderly subjects. *British Journal of Psychiatry, 114,* 797-811.

Boller, F., Goldstein, G., Dorr, C., Kim, Y., Moossy, J., Richey, E., Wagener, D., & Wolfson, S. K. (1984).

Alzheimer and related dementias: A review of current knowledge. In G. Goldstein (Ed.), *Advances in Clinical Neuropsychology* (Vol. 1, pp. 89-126). New York: Plenum Press.

Caine, E. D. (1981). Pseudodementia: Current concepts and future directions. *Archives of General Psychiatry, 38,* 1359-1364.

Coblentz, J. M., Mattis, S., Zingesser, C. H., Kasott, S. S., Wisniewski, J. M., & Katzman, R. (1973). Presenile dementia: Clinical aspects and evaluation of cerebrospinal fluid dynamics. *Archives of Neurology, 29,* 299-308.

Cummings, J. L. (1983). Treatable dementias. In R. Mayeux & W. G. Rosen (Eds.), *The Dementias: Advances in Neurology* (Vol. 38, pp. 165-183). New York: Raven Press.

Folstein, M. F., Folstein, S. E., & McHugh, P. R. (1975). Mini-mental state: A practical method for grading the cognitive state of patients for the clinician. *Journal of Psychiatric Research, 12,* 189-198.

Goldstein, G. (1984). Neuropsychological assessment of psychiatric patients. In G. Goldstein (Ed.), *Advances in Clinical Neuropsychology* (Vol. 1, pp. 55-87). New York: Plenum Press.

Goldstein, G., & Shelly, C. (1981). Does the right hemisphere age more rapidly than the left? *Journal of Clinical Neuropsychology, 3,* 65-78.

Gurland, B., & Toner, J. (1983). Differentiating dementia from nondementing conditions. In R. Mayeux & W. G. Rosen (Eds.), *The Dementias: Advances in Neurology* (Vol. 38, pp. 1-17). New York: Raven Press.

Hachinski, V. C., Lassen, N. A., & Marshall, J. (1974). Multi-infarct dementia: A course of mental deterioration in the elderly. *Lancet, 2,* 207-209.

Hooper, H. E. (1958). *The Hooper Visual Organization Test.* Los Angeles: Western Psychological Services.

Kiloh, L. G. (1961). Pseudo-dementia. *Acta Psychiatrica Scandinavica, 37,* 336-351.

Klisz, D. (1978). Neuropsychological evaluation in older persons. In M. Storandt, I. C. Seigler, & M. F. Elias (Eds.), *The Clinical Psychology of Aging* (pp. 71-95). New York: Plenum Press.

Lezak, M. D. (1983). *Neuropsychological Assessment.* New York: Oxford University Press.

Lishman, W. A. (1980). *Organic Psychiatry.* Oxford: Blackwell Scientific Publications.

Logue, P., & Wyrick, L. (1979). Initial validation of Russell's Revised Wechsler Memory Scale: A comparison of normal aging versus dementia. *Journal of Consulting and Clinical Psychology, 47*, 176-178.

Post, F. (1975). Dementia, depression, and pseudodementia. In D. F. Benson & D. Blumer (Eds.), *Psychiatric Aspects of Neurologic Disease* (pp. 99-120). New York: Grune & Stratton.

Raven, J. C. (1960). *Guide to the Standard Progressive Matrices.* London: H. K. Lewis.

Rosen, W. G. (1983). Clinical and neuropsychological assessment of Alzheimer's disease. In R. Mayeux & W. G. Rosen (Eds.), *The Dementias: Advances in Neurology* (Vol. 38, pp. 51-64). New York: Raven Press.

Roth, M. (1980). Senile dementias and its borderlands. In J. O. Cole & J. E. Barrett (Eds.), *Psychopathology in the Aged.* (pp. 205-232). New York: Raven Press.

Russell, E. W. (1975). A multiple scoring method for the assessment of complex memory functions. *Journal of Consulting and Clinical Psychology, 43*, 800-809.

Smith, A. (1975). Neuropsychological testing in neurological disorders. In W. J. Freidlander (Ed.), *Advances in Neurology* (Vol. 7, pp. 49-109). New York: Raven Press.

Thompson, L. W. (1980). Testing and mnemonic strategies. In L. W. Poon, J. L. Fozard, L. S. Cermack, D. Arenberg, & L. W. Thompson (Eds.), *New Directions in Memory and Aging* (pp. 367-377). Hillsdale, NJ: Lawrence Erlbaum Associates, Inc.

Wells, C. E. (1979). Pseudodementia. *American Journal of Psychiatry, 136*, 895-900.

Wells, C. E. (1980). The differential diagnosis of psychiatric disorders in the elderly. In J. O. Cole & J. E. Barrett (Eds.), *Psychopathology in the Aged* (pp. 19-31). New York: Raven Press.

Wheeler, L., & Reitan, R. M. (1962). The presence and laterality of brain damage predicted from responses to a short aphasia screening test. *Perceptual and Motor Skills, 15*, 783-799.

INITIAL ASSESSMENT OF MEN WITH SEXUAL COMPLAINTS: THE MALE SEXUAL DYSFUNCTION PROTOCOL

Steve Herman

There are few problems men encounter which hold greater potential for pure psychic misery than impotence.

For many years, male sexual problems were attributed almost exclusively to inner psychosexual conflicts, and believed to be either transient and self-correcting, or deep-seated and essentially untreatable. A number of dramatic developments in recent years have radically altered this view. Advances in medical assessment procedures have yielded a much greater awareness of common physical factors contributing to male sexual dysfunctions (Kaplan, 1983; Krane, Siroky, & Goldstein, 1983; Wagner & Green, 1981), and it is now recognized that a substantial portion-- perhaps a majority--of patients with chronic impotence have some identifiable organic basis for their problem (Jacobs, Fishkin, Cohen, Goldman, & Mulholland, 1983; Montague, James, DeWolfe, & Martin, 1979; Shrom, Lief, & Wein, 1979). At the same time, the field of sex therapy has grown enormously in the decade-and-a-half since the publication of Masters and Johnson's *Human Sexual Inadequacy* (1970). With these developments has come a greater understanding of the more immediate, situational determinants of sexual dysfunction such as performance anxiety, skill deficits, and dyadic factors (Kaplan, 1974). This expanded understanding of both the physical and psychological causes of male sexual dysfunction has yielded a new and highly effective set of treatment options. These range from surgical approaches including penile prosthesis implantation (Sotile, 1979) and vascular surgery (Zorgniotti & Rossi, 1980) to specific behaviorally-based sex therapy techniques such as the "stop-start" method for treatment of premature ejaculation (J. LoPiccolo & L. LoPiccolo, 1978).

As a result of these developments, men suffering from sexual dysfunction who several years ago would have been advised by their physicians to either "give it time," or "learn to live with it," are now regularly referred to specialized programs for multidisciplinary assessment and treatment of sexual problems. Increasing mass-media attention (Ann Landers, *Donahue*, *20/20*, etc.) to the problem of impotence and its new remedies has brought this information to the general public directly, resulting in a dramatic increase in the number of sexually dysfunctional men now taking their first step to obtain professional help.

For a number of years I have been affiliated with the Division of Urology in the Department of Surgery at Duke Medical Center, where my activities have focused on the assessment of men presenting with sexual complaints, most often involving erectile inadequacy. As a psychologist working within a traditional medical setting, I have direct access to a patient population substantially different from that encountered in a psychiatric clinic or a clearly labeled sex therapy program. Most of the patients I work with have never considered consulting a mental health practitioner about their problem, and many are quite resistant to the idea that psychological factors may be involved. Seagraves and his associates (Seagraves, Schoenberg, Zarins, Camic, & Knopf, 1981; Seagraves, Schoenberg, Zarins, Knopf, & Camic, 1982) have provided excellent documentation of the distinctive characteristics of urology clinic, as opposed to psychiatry clinic, patients with impotence. Suffice it to say that such patients present a significant challenge to the clinician seeking a detailed assessment of behavioral, cognitive, emotional, and interpersonal factors bearing on the presenting symptom.

In response to this challenge I have developed and refined an initial assessment questionnaire which is both acceptable to most patients and quite useful in providing me with an overview of the patient and his problem. The centerpiece of this questionnaire is the Male Sexual Dysfunction Protocol (MSDP), the contents of which will provide the primary focus for the remainder of this chapter. Initial sections of the questionnaire include Personal History, Medical History, Family History, and

Dating and Marriage units. Following the MSDP in the battery is a 20-item depression inventory (Center for Epidemiological Studies--Depression Scale; Radloff, 1977) and the Locke-Wallace Marital Adjustment Scale (Locke & Wallace, 1959). Where there is reason to suspect the presence of significant psychopathology, these are supplemented with an MMPI (Hathaway & McKinley, 1943).

These procedures, together with a clinical interview and an interview with the spouse or partner (where possible), constitute the psychological side of the initial assessment. Most patients are also seen on the same day by a urologist, who reviews the medical history, completes a physical and urogenital exam, and carries out penile blood flow (Doppler) studies where indicated. Routine laboratory tests as well as hormonal levels (testosterone, prolactin, luteinizing hormone [LH], and follicle-stimulating hormone [FSH]) are also obtained at this time. In some cases this initial data base is supplemented with nocturnal penile tumescence studies (Fisher et al., 1979; Karacan, 1982) to aid in the differentiation of organic from psychogenic impotence. The analysis and integration of these diverse data are fully described in Helen Singer Kaplan's (1983) book, *The Evaluation of Sexual Disorders: Psychological and Medical Aspects.*

THE MALE SEXUAL DYSFUNCTION PROTOCOL (MSDP)

The MSDP was developed to obtain part of the initial data base for clinical assessment of male sexual dysfunction. In our clinic, patients are asked to fill out the MSDP along with other questionnaires upon their arrival, and these are reviewed by the psychologist prior to the interview. The MSDP is designed to be a *guide* rather than an alternative to interviewing the patient. It focuses primarily on sexual symptomatology and current sexual behavior patterns, the understanding of which are essential for proper diagnosis of the patient's problem. In the pages which follow we will use the 26 items of the MSDP as a framework for discussion of key issues in assessment of male sexual complaints as these are typically pursued in the interview. A complete copy of the MSDP is included in the Appendix (pages 134-138) to this chapter. Permission to reproduce and use the MSDP may be obtained by writing the author with a description of the intended use.

---

1. In your own words, describe as best you can the sexual problem
   for which you are seeking help._____
   _____

Men differ greatly in their knowledge about normal and abnormal sexual functioning, and perhaps even more in their ability to verbalize about sexual problems. This open-ended item provides the appropriate starting point to any inquiry: The patient's immediate formulation of what is wrong. By asking the patient to describe the problem in his own words you learn not only the content of concern but also the manner in which it is conceptualized and the language with which it is expressed. The patient's problem description will provide indications of his sexual sophistication and his working vocabulary of sex, and thereby provide guidelines for the interviewer's appropriate communication level. I generally try to employ the patient's own sexual vocabulary whenever possible, asking for clarification of any terms or phrases which may be ambiguous. This is an important point. The use of terminology which, though technically precise, is unfamiliar to the patient may cause misunderstandings and impede development of rapport. On the other hand, unquestioned acceptance of the patient's usual sexual vocabulary risks significant semantic confusion. It is best to listen to the patient's language, have him clarify any terms which might be unclear, and then stay with this terminology for the remainder of the dialogue.

The patient's natural sexual language may also reveal implicit personal attitudes and assumptions about sex which could be diagnostically relevant. The patient who tells me "I can't get a piece anymore," and another patient who states "I can't get the job done right" may both be describing the same physiological limitation, but each by his expressive style conveys a distinct sense of what sex means to him and how he is reacting to the dysfunction.

---

2. How long have you had this problem?_____

   Did it seem to come on all of a sudden, or did it develop
   gradually?_____
   _____

   Were there any **special circumstances** which **coincided** with the
   start of the problem? (Examples might be illnesses, medications,
   problems at home or work, etc.)_____
   _____

A clear understanding of the temporal parameters of a sexual symptom is often the single most important clue to its etiology. Mere coincidence of symptom onset and particular internal or external circumstances does not in itself prove causality, but it may generate hypotheses to be either supported or refuted by additional evidence. It is always useful to have the patient think back carefully and try to pinpoint when he first became aware of "something being wrong." What was going on in his life at that time: Was there anything unusual or new? And what form did the symptom take when it first appeared? Did it stay essentially the same or did it change over time? How? Although most patients will describe symptom onset as having been either gradual or abrupt, there are others who describe an inconsistent pattern involving sudden decline or improvement perhaps superimposed on a background of gradually increasing impairment. In such cases it is important to identify if possible the circumstances associated with shifts in symptomatic status, whether these be positive or negative. The dimensions of stable versus fluctuating, or global versus situational (Schover, Friedman, Weiler, Heiman, & J. LoPiccolo, 1982), may provide a useful descriptive framework in addition to the temporal dimension of sudden versus gradual onset.

With regard to erection problems it is often generalized that psychogenic impotence is of sudden onset and may fluctuate, while organically based impotence develops gradually and is stable or global. While there is a certain legitimacy to this principle, exceptions abound. Acute organic conditions including illnesses, trauma, surgery, or administration of certain medications can result in abrupt onset of erectile problems, while some common conditions such as prostatitis or poorly controlled diabetes may be associated with a fluctuating course of dysfunction. On the psychogenic side, there are instances where symptoms develop gradually, in step with a progressively deteriorating marital situation, or as a result of repeated frustration and embarrassment such as occurs with severe premature ejaculation. While these exceptions tend to undercut the applicability of any simple formula, they nevertheless highlight the diagnostic importance of obtaining a clear outline of the temporal parameters of sexual symptoms.

3. **Before** this problem developed, did you have a satisfactory sex life?_____

4. **Before** the current problem developed, did you ever have a sexual problem of **any kind**? If so, describe this and indicate when it occurred._____

These two items seek to establish whether the patient's dysfunction is primary (i.e., lifelong) or secondary. At issue is whether there had been any previous experience of adequate, satisfactory sexual functioning. This distinction carries important diagnostic and treatment indications. In erectile dysfunction, the absence of any prior effective sexual functioning, assuming the occurrence of sufficient and repeated opportunity, suggests the presence of either a significant congenital deficit or, more likely, profound and deeply rooted psychosexual conflicts which may be quite difficult to treat effectively. Most often, however, erectile problems are found to be secondary, with the penis and psyche of the patient having been fully operational at some point in the past. In such cases the focus of assessment may safely shift from consideration of early psychosexual development to more current etiological factors including present physical, psychological, and dyadic conditions and the interactions among these.

The situation is somewhat reversed with respect to ejaculatory disorders, which most often do manifest as primary or lifelong patterns of impairment. Here, however, the lifelong nature of the problem does not carry the implication of major psychosexual conflict as it does in erectile disorders. The most common of male sexual complaints, premature ejaculation, is typically primary and yet appears unrelated to neurotic conflict, and is rapidly and easily treated. In the less common cases where premature ejaculation develops as a secondary disorder it is usually attributable to a physical condition, or else is a consequence of erectile difficulties, diminished frequency of sex, or other behavioral changes.

5. Do **you** have any ideas or beliefs about what might be causing your sexual problem?_____

In my experience, most men experiencing difficulties with sexual functioning, particularly those suffering erection problems, are pretty certain that their condition is caused by some sort of *physical* malfunction. To a certain extent this may reflect wishful thinking that the doctor may be able to provide a quick fix. No doubt there is also a large defensive component, holding at bay some highly threatening alternative explanations (emotional weakness, lack of masculinity, being over-the-hill, etc.). I believe, however, that there is more to it than this. In listening to patients explain their basis for believing that their problem is physical rather than psychological, I have been repeatedly struck by a common logic which apparently derives from the phenomenology of impotence itself. A typical explanation might be: "Look, it's not that I don't have the desire for sex--I'm dying for it! And there I am, all excited, and my wife is all excited and ready, *and the damn thing just doesn't get hard!* It's like the fuse is blown or something--that's what it feels like."

The point I wish to make here is that patients do tend to develop beliefs, and draw conclusions about their problem and its causes, which may be firmly rooted in subjective experience and interpretations of subjective experience. These beliefs and observations should be sought out, considered, and thoughtfully addressed when the time comes for interpretive feedback to the patient. The man who believes he has a "blown fuse" may thus be brought to an understanding that he does in fact have a "sexual fuse box," but what is blowing fuses is an overload of performance anxiety. The accuracy of a patient's beliefs about his problem is relatively unimportant. However, such beliefs can provide an experientially relevant basis for enhancing or changing the patient's understanding of his problem.

---

6. Aside from coming here, what have you done to try to help solve your sexual problem? (Check any that apply.)

____Consulted Family Doctor	____Talked with Minister
____Consulted Urologist or Medical Specialist	____Hormone Pills or Injection
____Consulted Psychologist or Psychiatrist	____Other Prescription Drugs
____Sex or Marital Therapy	____Vitamins or Tonics
____Tried New Sexual Techniques	____Used Sex Aids or Devices
____Sought New Sex Partners	____Other (Describe)_____

This is a shopping list of the most common remedies turned to by men troubled with sexual concerns. It is always a good idea to ascertain what the patient has tried in the past, if only to avoid the unfortunate mistake of offering a recommendation which has already proven unhelpful. A patient's answer to this item also provides an indication of his resourcefulness and the degree of activity, or passivity, with which he has approached the problem.

The "sought new sexual partners" item is of particular interest, as it is the only point in the questionnaire where extramarital or outside sexual activities are alluded to. This is a sensitive topic to many patients, but must be inquired about at some point in the interview. It is not uncommon for men with sexual problems to try a different woman to see if perhaps the problem is dissatisfaction or boredom with their usual partner. More often, however, such an experiment is the last thing the sexually dysfunctional man would venture, for fear of failure, embarrassment, and ridicule. Another situation which comes up regularly is the patient who maintains ongoing sexual involvements with more than one partner. Where this is the case it is essential to identify and account for commonalities and differences in the patient's sexual response with the various partners. Such information is not only important diagnostically, but can also identify significant limitations in the range of feasible intervention strategies. For example, it would hardly be appropriate to refer for conjoint sex therapy a man who is dysfunctional with his wife yet fully potent with a mistress.

7. How has your spouse (partner) reacted to your sexual problem? (Check any of the following that are **true**.)

___ She has felt sexually deprived or frustrated.
___ She has been understanding, patient, and supportive.
___ She has been critical, impatient, or angry.
___ She doesn't seem to be concerned about it, or doesn't mention it.
___ She has felt hurt. She thinks it means I don't care for her.
___ Other (Describe)_____

8. How does your spouse (partner) feel about your coming to get help with your sexual problem? (Check any of the following that are **true**.)

___ She is eager for me to get help.
___ She is opposed to my getting help.
___ She doesn't seem to care one way or the other.
___ Other (Describe)_____

```
9.  Do you think your spouse (partner) would be willing to cooperate
    in your treatment, if necessary?  ____Yes  ____No  ____Not Sure

    Would you be willing to have your wife (partner) participate?

    ____Yes    ____No    ____Not Sure
```

In a sense, the term male sexual dysfunction is a misnomer, insofar as virtually all sexual dysfunctions affect and involve both partners to a significant extent. Where the problem is absence of erection, however, there is a decided tendency for men--and to a lesser extent their partners--to view the problem as clearly belonging to the male. Thus, it is not inappropriate to ask men how the partner has *reacted* to *their* problem. The multiple choice options offered in questions 7 and 8 represent the most common reactions cited by patients in response to earlier, open-ended versions of the same questions. The issue of partner response is usually quite complex, and should be carefully reviewed during the interview. Patients may describe a sequence of reactions changing over time, or a situation where the partner's overt reactions are believed to be a cover-up of her true feelings. It should be kept in mind that the answers to these questions represent the *patient's* interpretation of the partner's reaction. Whenever possible, independent verification with the partner herself should be obtained.

From a treatment standpoint the optimum partner would be: (a) understanding, patient, and supportive; (b) eager for the patient to get help; and (c) willing to cooperate. Partners who are angry and critical may represent a significant *part* of the problem, while partners who are unconcerned or indifferent may view the dysfunction as a welcomed opportunity to withdraw from sexual obligations.

```
10.  The following questions concern erections:

     a.  When you are having (or attempting to have) sexual relations,
         does your penis get stiff enough to permit you to penetrate
         and begin intercourse?  (Check One):

     Always     Most of     About half     Rarely     Never     Not sure
                the time    the time

     b.  Does your penis become stiff enough at first, but then become
         soft during intercourse, before you have climaxed?  (Check
         One):

     Always     Most of     About half     Rarely     Never     Not sure
                the time    the time
```

123

The MSDP is slanted towards assessment of erectile dysfunction, which represents the primary presenting complaint in the majority of patients who come to us in the Urology Clinic. The symptomatology of erectile dysfunction varies across several dimensions including (a) difficulty *achieving* versus difficulty *maintaining* penile rigidity, (b) the degree of maximal erection attainable, and (c) situational differences in erectile adequacy. The items above seek to differentiate problems of achieving from problems of maintaining erection, as well as estimate the *pervasiveness* of the problems encountered. Often patients will tend to overemphasize the occasions of erectile failure (which are of more concern to them) and neglect or minimize episodes of successful functioning. The first question is worded in such a way as to extract acknowledgment of even occasional moments of potency, which may be a diagnostically salient bit of data. The second question describes an extremely common pattern of erectile dysfunction, which in many organic conditions will represent the first stages of a problem which may progress to a point where the patient is unable to obtain sufficient erections to penetrate at all.

---

11. At the present time, what is the **best** erection (from 0% = no erection to 100% = stiff erection) you can **ACHIEVE** in **each** of the following situations:

   Intercourse (or attempting intercourse) ____%

   Other sexual activities (kissing, petting, "messing around," oral sex, caressing, etc.) ____%

   Masturbation (self-stimulation) ____%

This item asks that patients attempt to quantify the maximum degree of erection they can obtain in different situations. Some patients have difficulty using percentages to rate their erections, and of course the numbers arrived at are arbitrary. Of more importance than the absolute numbers are the *relative* values assigned to the three situations. Where the values vary significantly it is likely that the dysfunction contains a situational component, probably (though not necessarily) reflecting psychogenic factors. The interpretation of these erection rating figures may be enhanced by asking patients to estimate what percent of full erection is the minimum necessary for them to be able to accomplish vaginal penetration with their partners. This estimate can then provide an anchoring point for evaluating degree of erectile inadequacy.

---

12. Do you sometimes wake up at night or in the morning with an erection? ____Yes ____No

If **so**, how often does this occur?_____

Are these full (stiff) erections? ____Yes ____No ____Sometimes

If **not**, how long has it been since you've awakened with an erection?_____

The relationship between REM sleep and regularly occurring periods of penile erection in men (nocturnal penile tumescence, or NPT) has been well documented in studies encompassing the entire life span. Although the exact mechanisms responsible for NPT remain undetermined, its ubiquity among physiologically normal men provides a reliable measure of erectile capacity largely independent of psychologically inhibiting factors (Fisher et al., 1979). Although nocturnal erections occur periodically throughout the night, they typically come and go without notice during sleep. NPT episodes are frequent toward the end of the sleep cycle, and it is common to awaken with an erection (usually accompanied by a full bladder, leading to an erroneous assumption of a causal connection, and the common labeling of these as "piss-hard-ons"). Patients with erection problems should be carefully questioned as to the presence and rigidity of early morning erections. Where such erections are reported to be present and of adequate rigidity, it is almost certain that the patient's problems are psychogenic. Should a patient report absent or partial nocturnal erections, however, there is by no means the same degree of certainty that this problem is organic. Absence of nocturnal erections is *consistent* with an organic etiology, but formal NPT laboratory studies should be obtained for confirmation. Some men who are unaware of having nocturnal erections are found to have very normal erection patterns when observed in the NPT lab. A comprehensive presentation of current NPT laboratory practices can be found in Karacan (1982).

13. Are **you** able to reach an orgasm ("climax," "come," "go off") during sexual activity? (Check One)

| Always | Most of the time | About half the time | Rarely | Never | Not sure |

14. Is **your spouse (partner)** able to reach an orgasm ("climax," "come," "go off") during sexual activity? (Check One)

| Always | Most of the time | About half the time | Rarely | Never | Not sure |

In healthy men the ability to achieve orgasm during sexual activity is virtually universal, but it may be significantly impaired in sexually dysfunctional patients. In some instances the absence of orgasm represents the focal complaint, while in others it is secondary to erectile failure, diminished sexual desire, or inadequate physical stimulation. More often, however, men suffering erectile failure find, much to their surprise, that ejaculation and orgasm continue to occur with a partially erect or even completely flaccid penis, provided that sufficient physical stimulation occurs. Generally speaking, a patient with erectile problems who also reports an inability to achieve orgasm is experiencing either diminished sexual desire, avoidance of sexual activity, inadequate stimulation, or some combination of these.

The question regarding the partner's orgasmic responsiveness is somewhat ambiguous, as it is not clear whether it refers to present or previous (before the problem) status. This should be clarified during the interview. Women differ greatly in orgasmic frequency, and in the quality and duration of stimulation required to bring it about. The partner's characteristics in this regard may have a very significant bearing on the overall dissatisfaction resulting from a given decrement in the man's sexual functioning. A consideration of equal importance is the value or significance placed on orgasm by the partner, as well as the man's own view of the necessity of his partner's orgasm to the success of the sexual experience. Where a couple's sexual communication has been less than open, there is much potential for misunderstanding along these lines. Often men believe that sex without orgasm is completely aversive to the partner, or that the only acceptable means of helping the partner achieve orgasmic release is through intercourse. On the other hand, when I hear from a patient with erectile dysfunction that he and his partner continue to engage in enjoyable alternative sexual activities, including orgasm for both when desired, I am inclined to characterize their approach to sex as mutually supportive, resourceful, and openly communicative. I have found that in such relationships performance anxiety is rarely a factor, and deficits tend to be organic in nature.

---

15. Do you have any problem with ejaculating ("climaxing," "coming," "going off") **too soon**? (Check One)

    ____Yes ____No ____At times

16. Do you have any problem with being **unable** to ejaculate ("come," "climax," "go off") when having intercourse? (Check One)

    ____Yes ____No ____At times

Ejaculatory problems are extremely common among men. Recent surveys have estimated that almost half of all men claim such difficulties, most frequently involving difficulty with overly rapid ejaculation (Frank, Anderson, & Rubinstein, 1978). The items above provide an initial screening for such problems, which in some instances may represent the primary reason the patient has sought help. Premature ejaculation, and its counterpart "inhibited male orgasm" (previously termed "retarded ejaculation"), vary greatly in degree of severity, and further inquiry is necessary to determine whether the rapidity, or slowness, of response is within reasonable limits or is truly dysfunctional. Estimates of the duration of stimulation should be obtained, as well as detailed description of the sexual activities engaged in. Relationships between ejaculatory latency and frequency of ejaculation (or time since last ejaculation) should be explored, as this is often a primary factor with problems of premature ejaculation. In cases of delayed or absent ejaculation the patient should be questioned about ejaculatory ability with masturbation, as ejaculation is usually facilitated for such patients when they are alone and self-stimulating.

As mentioned earlier, ejaculatory disorders are most often lifelong or primary, although we do see many patients who report recent or secondary onset of rapid ejaculation in conjunction with erectile dysfunction.

Several possible explanations present themselves. First, where erections have become unreliable, patients often find themselves working hard to maximize stimulation so as to generate and maintain erection. The added intensity of stimulation may serve to trigger ejaculation more rapidly than usual. Second, when erection problems occur the frequency of sex almost always declines markedly, either through sexual avoidance or as a deliberate attempt to "save it up." Less frequent sex usually brings shortened ejaculatory latency. Third, erection problems generate anxiety, which may affect ejaculatory threshold psychophysiologically and/or impair the patient's ability to attend to and perceive proprioceptive cues signaling the approach of ejaculation. Finally, there is some evidence suggesting that the skin of the penis is more sensitive to tactile stimulation in the flaccid than the erect state.

When patients report a recent onset of absent ejaculation, care must be taken to determine whether they might actually be experiencing anterograde or dry ejaculation. This condition, caused by certain medications and urogenital surgical procedures, results in the ejaculate being propelled backward into the bladder. In contrast to inhibited male orgasm, there is a (usually diminished) sensation of orgasm, followed by detumescence, though no ejaculate is dispelled through the urethra. Diagnosis can be confirmed by testing the urine for sperm cells post-coitally.

---

17. **At the present time,** how often do you and your spouse (partner) have, or attempt to have, sexual intercourse? (Check One)

Not at all	Less than once a month	1-3 times per month	Once a week	2 or 3 times per week	4-6 times per week	Once a day or more

18. **Before the present problem** developed, how often did you and your spouse (partner) have sexual intercourse? (Check One)

Not at all	Less than once a month	1-3 times per month	Once a week	2 or 3 times per week	4-6 times per week	Once a day or more

19. How often would you **prefer** to have intercourse? (Check One)

Not at all	Less than once a month	1-3 times per month	Once a week	2 or 3 times per week	4-6 times per week	Once a day or more

20. How often do you think your **spouse (partner)** would **prefer** to have intercourse? (Check One)

Not at all	Less than once a month	1-3 times per month	Once a week	2 or 3 times per week	4-6 times per week	Once a day or more

21. How often do you masturbate? (Check One)

Not at all	Less than once a month	1-3 times per month	Once a week	2 or 3 times per week	4-6 times per week	Once a day or more

These items all deal with the frequency, or preferred frequency, of sexual activity. Of particular interest here are the relationships between answers to items 17 and 18, and items 19 and 20. The former pair contrasts current with premorbid levels of sexual activity, and indicates the impact the problem has had on the couple's willingness to engage sexually. A large discrepancy suggests the presence of avoidance tendencies. The latter pair of items reflects the patient's perception of his own versus his partner's desire for sex. Often this sexual balance is seen by the patient as shifting over time in significant ways. Where discrepancies are major, and in all cases where the partner's desires are viewed as larger than the patient's own, this factor is very likely to adversely affect the patient's sexual functioning.

The question on masturbation is of particular value in, (a) identifying the presence of excessive or compulsive masturbatory practices, and (b) assessment of low sexual desire.

22. **When you and your spouse or partner have sex,** how often are each of the following activities included in your love-making? (Check One)

	Always	Most of the time	About half the time	Sometimes	Never
a. Kissing on the lips					
b. The man caressing the woman's breasts					
c. The man kissing the woman's breasts					

129

22. (Continued)	Always	Most of the time	About half the time	Sometimes	Never
d. The man caressing the woman's vagina with his hand	_____	_____	_____	_____	_____
e. The man using his lips and tongue to stimulate the vagina	_____	_____	_____	_____	_____
f. The woman caressing or rubbing the man's penis with her hand	_____	_____	_____	_____	_____
g. The woman using her lips and tongue to stimulate the penis	_____	_____	_____	_____	_____
h. Intercourse, with the man on top	_____	_____	_____	_____	_____
i. Intercourse, with the woman on top	_____	_____	_____	_____	_____
j. Intercourse in other positions (sitting, side-by-side, man behind, etc.)	_____	_____	_____	_____	_____
k. Other activities	_____				

This is a brief and simply-worded inventory of heterosexual behaviors, which may indicate the breadth or narrowness of the couple's usual sexual repertoire. When assessing middle aged or older men with erectile problems, I pay particular attention to items (f) and (g) dealing with the partner's active stimulation of the penis. With many of our older patients we find that direct penile stimulation by the partner prior to intercourse has rarely or never been practiced. The usual explanations offered are that "she is kind of old-fashioned," or "it just never used to be necessary." Such avoidance of direct stimulation may be a significant factor contributing to erectile inadequacy in older men, who typically require more intense and prolonged physical stimulation in order to achieve and maintain erection (Brecher, 1984).

During the assessment interview it is always useful to obtain a description of how the couple usually goes about making love. Particular attention should be paid to their typical responses to dysfunction when it arises, including both emotional reactions and compensatory behaviors, if any. For many couples sex and intercourse are one and the same, and the loss of erection invariably signals the end of the sexual interaction. Others maintain a broader conception of sex, and respond to the same circumstance by engaging in alternative forms of sexual gratification. In my experience, couples with a more narrow, intercourse-focused approach to sex are more prone to psychogenic impotence, probably because of the greater performance pressures placed on the man who must keep an erection for any sexual interaction to occur. I usually recommend to such patients that they read Bernie Zilbergeld's (1978) excellent book, *Male Sexuality: A Guide to Sexual Fulfillment*, which persuasively challenges such assumptions.

---

23. Has your interest in sex, or your desire for sex, changed much over the past 5 years or so? (Check One)

____ Much more interested in sex now
____ A little more interested now
____ About the same; no change
____ A little less interested now
____ A lot less interested now

Diminished libido, or a decline in the appetitive component of sexual behavior, has generally been a much more frequent complaint among women than among men. There is some recent evidence that this trend may be shifting, with an increasing number of men seeking counseling for low sexual desire, perhaps prompted by wives or partners less content to accept a life devoid of sexual fulfillment. With men it is often quite difficult to assess diminished sexual desire, and to differentiate it from diminished sexual performance, with which it is often paired. Some men have much difficulty distinguishing desire from psychological arousal. Others are aware of this distinction but are uncertain whether they have low desire for sex because they have been dysfunctional, or are dysfunctional because they have low desire. Often this can be determined by close analysis of the sequence of symptomatic behavior over time. Asking the patient about current sexual fantasies, dreams about sex, masturbation frequency, use of erotic pictures and literature, and related topics may provide additional guidelines in assessing low sexual desire. It is also important to consider the relative desire level of the partner, as this is often the crucial factor in determining the degree to which low sexual desire constitutes a real problem. An authoritative reference is Helen Singer Kaplan's *Disorders of Sexual Desire* (1979).

---

24. When it comes to sex, are you: (Check One)

    ____ Interested in **women only**
    ____ Interested in **women mostly** (but also men to some extent)
    ____ Interested in **women and men equally**
    ____ Interested in **men mostly** (but also women to some extent)
    ____ Interested in **men only**

This is a direct and unambiguous item assessing self-described sexual orientation which avoids the use of labels that may be unfamiliar or objectionable to some patients. It is helpful to be aware of a patient's sexual orientation at the onset of an interview, if for no other reason than to avoid the awkwardness of inappropriately assuming heterosexuality. The patient's sexual orientation may or may not prove to be a factor affecting the presenting sexual complaint, but where there is a basic discrepancy between the actual and the desired sexual object there exists fertile ground for the development of dysfunction. Such possibilities must be explored in depth during the interview.

---

25. Taking everything into consideration, how would you rate your sexual relationship **AT THE PRESENT TIME**:

           ( ) 8 Could not be better
           ( ) 7 Excellent
           ( ) 6 Good
           ( ) 5 Above average
           ( ) 4 Adequate
           ( ) 3 Somewhat inadequate
           ( ) 2 Poor
           ( ) 1 Highly inadequate
           ( ) 0 Could not be worse

    Using the same scale, how would you rate your sexual relationship as it was **BEFORE THE PRESENT PROBLEM**:

           ( ) 8 Could not be better
           ( ) 7 Excellent
           ( ) 6 Good
           ( ) 5 Above average
           ( ) 4 Adequate
           ( ) 3 Somewhat inadequate
           ( ) 2 Poor
           ( ) 1 Highly inadequate
           ( ) 0 Could not be worse

These two parallel items seek global ratings of overall sexual satisfaction before and after the problem arose (this item assumes the problem is secondary rather than primary). The first item provides a view of how dissatisfied the patient is with the current state of affairs, and generally how desperate he is for a cure. The second item indicates the degree of sexual gratification the patient is accustomed to, and, more importantly, the patient's prior view of himself as a sexual being. In our experience, patients checking off a 7 or 8 on item #25 have tended to place extreme importance on sex, and have always taken pride in their sexual capabilities. When such men become dysfunctional they usually come down hard, and tend to rate their current condition as "could not be worse." In this sense the *relative* ratings given to the two items is particularly revealing, providing an index of perceived disruptiveness of the sexual problem. It is by no means always the case that symptom severity correlates with degree of disruption in the sexual sphere. Much depends on the prior level of satisfaction, the importance attached to sexual performance, adaptational capacities, and other factors.

---

26. If there is anything else about your sexual experiences or your sexual problem which might be helpful for us to know, please include this below._____

_____

This final, open-ended item invites disclosure of other facts or concerns not specifically mentioned in the previous sections. Obvious areas of omission include the paraphilias, concern over size or appearance of the genitals, sexually traumatic experiences, pain, or other physical symptoms associated with sex, and religious or ethical conflicts. Future versions of the MSDP will no doubt contain items addressing these issues as our ongoing clinical experience determines their relevance. Comments and suggestions from interested readers would be most welcome.

An exhaustive review of other available scales and instruments for assessment of sexual and marital issues can be found in Volume 5, Number 3 of the *Journal of Sex and Marital Therapy* (Schiavi, Derogatis, Kuriansky, O'Connor, & Sharpe, 1979).

APPENDIX: MALE SEXUAL
DYSFUNCTION PROTOCOL*
Division of Urology
Department of Surgery
Duke University Medical Center

1. In your own words, describe as best you can the sexual problem for which you are seeking help._____
_____

2. How long have you had this problem?_____

   Did it seem to come on all of a sudden, or did it develop gradually?_____

   Were there any **special circumstances** which **coincided** with the start of the problem? (Examples might be illnesses, medications, problems at home or work, etc.)_____
_____

3. **Before** this problem developed, did you have a satisfactory sex life?_____
_____

4. **Before** the current problem developed, did you ever have a sexual problem of **any kind**? If so, describe this and indicate when it occurred._____
_____

5. Do **you** have any ideas or beliefs about what might be causing your sexual problem?_____
_____

6. Aside from coming here, what have you done to try to help solve your sexual problem? (Check any that apply.)

   ____Consulted Family Doctor   ____Talked with Minister
   ____Consulted Urologist or   ____Hormone Pills or Injection
        Medical Specialist
   ____Consulted Psychologist or   ____Other Prescription Drugs
        Psychiatrist
   ____Sex or Marital Therapy   ____Vitamins or Tonics
   ____Tried New Sexual Techniques   ____Used Sex Aids or Devices
   ____Sought New Sex Partners   ____Other (Describe)_____
                                          _____

7. How has your spouse (partner) reacted to your sexual problem? (Check any of the following that are **true**.)

   ____She has felt sexually deprived or frustrated.
   ____She has been understanding, patient, and supportive.
   ____She has been critical, impatient, or angry.
   ____She doesn't seem to be concerned about it, or doesn't mention it.
   ____She has felt hurt. She thinks it means I don't care for her.
   ____Other (Describe)_____

---

8. How does your spouse (partner) feel about your coming to get help with your sexual problem? (Check any of the following that are **true.**)

    ____She is eager for me to get help.
    ____She is opposed to my getting help.
    ____She doesn't seem to care one way or the other.
    ____Other (Describe)_____

9. Do you think your spouse (partner) would be willing to cooperate in your treatment, if necessary? ____Yes ____No ____Not Sure

    Would you be willing to have your wife (partner) participate?

    ____Yes ____No ____Not Sure

10. The following questions concern erections:

    a. When you are having (or attempting to have) sexual relations, does your penis get stiff enough to permit you to penetrate and begin intercourse? (Check One):

Always	Most of the time	About half the time	Rarely	Never	Not sure

    b. Does your penis become stiff enough **at first**, but then become soft during intercourse, before you have climaxed? (Check One):

Always	Most of the time	About half the time	Rarely	Never	Not sure

11. At the present time, what is the **best** erection (from 0% = no erection to 100% = stiff erection) you can **ACHIEVE** in **each** of the following situations:

    Intercourse (or attempting intercourse) ____%

    Other sexual activities (kissing, petting, "messing around," oral sex, caressing, etc.) ____%

    Masturbation (self-stimulation) ____%

12. Do you sometimes wake up at night or in the morning with an erection? ____Yes ____No

    If so, how often does this occur?_____

    Are these full (stiff) erections? ____Yes ____No ____Sometimes

    If not, how long has it been since you've awakened with an erection?_____

13. Are **you** able to reach an orgasm ("climax," "come," "go off") during sexual activity? (Check One)

Always	Most of the time	About half the time	Rarely	Never	Not sure

14. Is **your spouse (partner)** able to reach an orgasm ("climax," "come," "go off") during sexual activity? (Check One)

| _____ | _____ | _____ | _____ | _____ | _____ |
| Always | Most of
the time | About half
the time | Rarely | Never | Not sure |

15. Do you have any problem with ejaculating ("climaxing," "coming," "going off") **too soon**? (Check One)

____Yes ____No ____At times

16. Do you have any problem with being **unable** to ejaculate ("come," "climax," "go off") when having intercourse? (Check One)

____Yes ____No ____At times

17. **At the present time**, how often do you and your spouse (partner) have, or attempt to have, sexual intercourse? (Check One)

| _____ | _____ | _____ | _____ | _____ | _____ | _____ |
| Not at
all | Less than
once a
month | 1-3 times
per month | Once a
week | 2 or 3
times
per week | 4-6 times
per week | Once a
day or
more |

18. **Before the present problem** developed, how often did you and your spouse (partner) have sexual intercourse? (Check One)

| _____ | _____ | _____ | _____ | _____ | _____ | _____ |
| Not at
all | Less than
once a
month | 1-3 times
per month | Once a
week | 2 or 3
times
per week | 4-6 times
per week | Once a
day or
more |

19. How often would you **prefer** to have intercourse? (Check One)

| _____ | _____ | _____ | _____ | _____ | _____ | _____ |
| Not at
all | Less than
once a
month | 1-3 times
per month | Once a
week | 2 or 3
times
per week | 4-6 times
per week | Once a
day or
more |

20. How often do you think your **spouse (partner)** would **prefer** to have intercourse? (Check One)

| _____ | _____ | _____ | _____ | _____ | _____ | _____ |
| Not at
all | Less than
once a
month | 1-3 times
per month | Once a
week | 2 or 3
times
per week | 4-6 times
per week | Once a
day or
more |

21. How often do you masturbate? (Check One)

| _____ | _____ | _____ | _____ | _____ | _____ | _____ |
| Not at
all | Less than
once a
month | 1-3 times
per month | Once a
week | 2 or 3
times
per week | 4-6 times
per week | Once a
day or
more |

136

22. **When you and your spouse or partner have sex,** how often are each of the following activities included in your love-making? (Check One)

	Always	Most of the time	About half the time	Sometimes	Never
a. Kissing on the lips	___	___	___	___	___
b. The man caressing the woman's breasts	___	___	___	___	___
c. The man kissing the woman's breasts	___	___	___	___	___
d. The man caressing the woman's vagina with his hand	___	___	___	___	___
e. The man using his lips and tongue to stimulate the vagina	___	___	___	___	___
f. The woman caressing or rubbing the man's penis with her hand	___	___	___	___	___
g. The woman using her lips and tongue to stimulate the penis	___	___	___	___	___
h. Intercourse, with the man on top	___	___	___	___	___
i. Intercourse, with the woman on top	___	___	___	___	___
j. Intercourse in other positions (sitting, side-by-side, man behind, etc.)	___	___	___	___	___
k. Other activities					

137

23. Has your interest in sex, or your desire for sex, changed much over the past 5 years or so? (Check One)

    ____Much more interested in sex now
    ____A little more interested now
    ____About the same; no change
    ____A little less interested now
    ____A lot less interested now

24. When it comes to sex, are you: (Check One)

    ____Interested in women only
    ____Interested in women mostly (but also men to some extent)
    ____Interested in women and men equally
    ____Interested in men mostly (but also women to some extent)
    ____Interested in men only

25. Taking everything into consideration, how would you rate your sexual relationship AT THE PRESENT TIME:

    ( ) 8 Could not be better
    ( ) 7 Excellent
    ( ) 6 Good
    ( ) 5 Above average
    ( ) 4 Adequate
    ( ) 3 Somewhat inadequate
    ( ) 2 Poor
    ( ) 1 Highly inadequate
    ( ) 0 Could not be worse

    Using the same scale, how would you rate your sexual relationship as it was BEFORE THE PRESENT PROBLEM:

    ( ) 8 Could not be better
    ( ) 7 Excellent
    ( ) 6 Good
    ( ) 5 Above average
    ( ) 4 Adequate
    ( ) 3 Somewhat inadequate
    ( ) 2 Poor
    ( ) 1 Highly inadequate
    ( ) 0 Could not be worse

26. If there is anything else about your sexual experiences or your sexual problem which might be helpful for us to know, please include this below._____
    _____

Steve Herman, PhD, is currently Assistant Professor of Medical Psychology and Associate in Urology at Duke University Medical Center in Durham, North Carolina. He is Co-Director of the Male Sexual Dysfunctions Laboratory at Duke, and also directs the Smoking Cessation Consultation Service in the Department of Psychiatry. Dr. Herman has written articles and chapters in the areas of psychogeriatrics, dream recall, and assessment of Type-A behavior. He also has a deep involvement with the psychology of golf. Dr. Herman may be contacted at Box 2984, Duke University Medical Center, Durham, NC 27710.

RESOURCES

Brecher, E. M. (1984). *Love, Sex and Aging: A Consumers Union Report*. Boston: Little, Brown & Co.

Fisher, C., Schiavi, R. C., Edwards, A., Davis, D. M., Reitman, M., & Fine, M. (1979). Evaluation of nocturnal penile tumescence in the differential diagnosis of sexual impotence: A quantitative study. *Archives of General Psychiatry, 36,* 431-437.

Frank, E., Anderson, C., & Rubinstein, D. (1978). Frequency of sexual dysfunction in "normal" couples. *New England Journal of Medicine, 299,* 111-115.

Hathaway, S. R., & McKinley, J. C. (1943). *The Minnesota Multiphasic Personality Inventory Manual*. Minneapolis: University of Minnesota Press.

Jacobs, J. A., Fishkin, R., Cohen, S., Goldman, A., & Mulholland, S. G. (1983). A multidisciplinary approach to the evaluation and management of male sexual dysfunction. *Journal of Urology, 129,* 35-38.

Kaplan, H. S. (1974). *The New Sex Therapy*. New York: Brunner/Mazel.

Kaplan, H. S. (1979). *Disorders of Sexual Desire*. New York: Brunner/Mazel.

Kaplan, H. S. (1983). *The Evaluation of Sexual Disorders: Psychological and Medical Aspects*. New York: Brunner/Mazel.

Karacan, I. (1982). Evaluation of nocturnal penile tumescence and impotence. In C. Guilleminault (Ed.), *Sleeping and Waking Disorders: Indications and Techniques*. Menlo Park, CA: Addison-Wesley.

Krane, R. J., Siroky, M. B., & Goldstein, I. (1983). *Male Sexual Dysfunction*. Boston: Little, Brown & Co.

Locke, H. J., & Wallace, K. (1959). Short marital adjustment and prediction tests: Their reliability and prediction. *Marriage and Family Living, 21,* 251-255.

LoPiccolo, J., & LoPiccolo, L. (Eds.). (1978). *Handbook of Sex Therapy.* New York: Plenum Press.

Masters, W. H., & Johnson, V. (1970). *Human Sexual Inadequacy.* Boston: Little, Brown & Co.

Montague, D. K., James, R. E., DeWolfe, V. G., & Martin, L. M. (1979). Diagnostic evaluation, classification, and treatment of men with sexual dysfunction. *Urology, 14,* 545-548.

Radloff, L. S. (1977). The CES-D Scale: A self-report depression scale for research in the general population. *Applied Psychological Measurement, 1,* 385-401.

Schiavi, R. C., Derogatis, L. R., Kuriansky, J., O'Connor, D., & Sharpe, L. (1979). The assessment of sexual function and marital interaction. *Journal of Sex and Marital Therapy, 5,* 169-224.

Schover, L. R., Friedman, J. M., Weiler, S. J., Heiman, J. R., & LoPiccolo, J. (1982). Multiaxial problem-oriented system for sexual dysfunctions: An alternative to DSM-III. *Archives of General Psychiatry, 39,* 614-619.

Seagraves, R. T., Schoenberg, H. W., Zarins, C. K., Camic, P., & Knopf, J. (1981). Characteristics of erectile dysfunction as a function of medical care system entry point. *Psychosomatic Medicine, 43,* 227-234.

Seagraves, R. T., Schoenberg, H. W., Zarins, C. K., Knopf, J., & Camic, P. (1982). Referral of impotent patients to a sexual dysfunction clinic. *Archives of Sexual Behavior, 11,* 521-528.

Shrom, S. H., Lief, H. I., & Wein, A. J. (1979). Clinical profile of experience with 130 consecutive cases of impotent men. *Urology, 13,* 511-515.

Sotile, W. M. (1979). The penile prosthesis: A review. *Journal of Sex and Marital Therapy, 5,* 90-102.

Wagner, G., & Green, R. (1981). *Impotence: Physiological, Psychological, Surgical Diagnosis and Treatment.* New York: Plenum Press.

Zilbergeld, B. (1978). *Male Sexuality: A Guide to Sexual Fulfillment.* Boston: Little, Brown & Co. (Also available in paperback from Bantam Books.)

Zorgniotti, A. W., & Rossi, G. (Eds.). (1980). Vasculogenic impotence. *Proceedings of the First International Conference on Corpus Cavernosa Revascularization.* Springfield, IL: Charles C. Thomas.

SECTION II:

TREATMENT

A BEHAVIORAL PERSPECTIVE ON COMPREHENSIVE TREATMENT PLANNING FOR OBESITY PROBLEMS *

Linda Wilcoxon Craighead

Converging evidence from a number of research areas has lead professionals to question traditional notions about the etiology and treatment of obesity and has laid the groundwork for a decision-making perspective (Bennett & Gurin, 1982; Polivy & Herman, 1983). These findings suggest that the potentially negative medical consequences of obesity are highly variable, particularly for the mildly (under 30%) overweight. Weight loss is clearly desirable but may result in substantial health benefits for some individuals and only minimal benefits for others. On the other hand, increased recognition has been given to the potentially negative medical and psychological effects of certain weight loss and weight maintenance strategies (e.g., chronic restraint, purging techniques, and continual weight loss and regain cycles). Furthermore, preliminary evidence regarding set points and as yet unspecified regulatory disorders suggests that socially desirable goal weights may even be inappropriate for some individuals.

Because several distinctively different treatment options are now available, the professional plays a significant role in helping the client evaluate these alternatives. Unfortunately, very few predictors of treatment

---

*Some material contained in this chapter was taken from "A Problem Solving Approach to the Treatment of Obesity" by L. W. Craighead in Handbook of Clinical Behavior Therapy with Adults (pp. 229-268) by M. Hersen and A. Bellack (Eds.), 1985, New York: Plenum. Copyright © 1985 by Plenum.

143

success have been identified so the professional can give the client only rough estimates of the amount of weight he or she is likely to lose with a particular strategy and whether such a loss, if achieved, will actually produce physiological or psychological benefits. The ambiguous and contradictory research findings, the presence of pervasive cultural stereotypes, maladaptive individual beliefs and the high pressure commercial marketing of "miracle" cures and fad diets make rational choices nearly impossible for the client (consumer). The decision-making perspective that is being suggested offers a flexible framework within which the professional and the client can make more realistic, rational, and humane decisions. The client must be educated in the decision-making process and become an active participant in treatment decisions.

A particular individual's treatment must be approached in a trial and error fashion. An initial treatment decision is made but it is followed by a series of critical redecision points based on the individual's response to the treatment. The client must be actively involved in this process which is a continuous re-evaluation of the benefits of the current strategy. Essentially, the client is asking himself or herself, "At what personal cost am I willing to lose (or maintain) weight?"

Weight loss is only one of several acceptable solutions for a client's obesity problem. Within the decision-making framework, a client may come to a different but satisfactory resolution of the problem. Deciding that a certain weight loss is not a viable alternative or that the personal costs are higher than the personal benefits is, at least psychologically, an entirely different outcome from concluding one is a failure at yet another weight loss effort. In a sense, the only unacceptable solution to an obesity problem is for the client to decide that he or she cannot or chooses not to do what it takes to lose weight but that he or she will continue to be miserable about being overweight and will continue to subject himself or herself to repeated failures with whatever fad diet comes out next.

The essence of a decision-making approach is fairly simple and straightforward. The five basic steps of problem solving (Goldfried & Davidson, 1976) have been applied to many clinical concerns and can be adapted to use as a framework for obesity treatment. The success of obesity treatment depends largely on the client's willingness to make lifestyle changes and his or her ability to maintain these changes. Thus, the decision-making model is used initially to focus attention on the need for the client to make an active decision to lose weight and to do so via certain specific strategies. The decision-making approach is not used to persuade an individual either to diet or not to diet but to help the individual initially make a more informed treatment decision and to help the individual revise the decision on the basis of personal experience. Most individuals initially choose fairly short-term diet-oriented approaches but if they are not successful they are often willing to reconsider alternative, more long-term oriented strategies.

PROBLEM-SOLVING APPROACH

STEP 1: DEFINE THE PROBLEM

Assessment of the client's current state of obesity is relatively straightforward. The clinician will be interested first in determining how much the client would like to weigh. Then a simple measure of actual body weight is sufficient for most clinical purposes since weight is fairly highly correlated with the more precise measures of body fat which are often expensive and impractical. Skinfold calipering is the most viable measure of body fat and could be useful feedback for clients in programs that emphasize exercise. However, it is not very sensitive to change. Physical measurements (waist, hips, etc.) are likely to be more personally meaningful to the client and can be useful as yet another way to focus the client's attention on progress rather than the slow rate of change. Using the recently revised Metropolitan height-weight charts (1983) the clinician can determine the general weight range that would be considered appropriate for that client. An initial determination regarding the degree of obesity is made since different treatments may need to be considered depending on how much the client wants to lose. At some point, the client's specific personal goal may need to be challenged but this can easily be done later within the decision-making framework.

The client's goal would need to be challenged at this point only if the client were already near or below the lowest recommended weight for his or her height and wished to lose more. Such clients may have excessive concern over potential weight gain and need to be treated differently from clients who actually need to lose weight. The possibility of bulimia or previous anorectic episodes should always be assessed since the client, especially if currently overweight, may not mention these problems. Bulimic clients who are not overweight need to be treated differently and the reader is referred to Hawkins, Fremouw, and Clement (1984). Bulimic clients who are overweight may need a combination of procedures relevant to obesity and bulimia. Depending on the severity of the bingeing and/or purging, a decision must be made regarding where to start with that client. The presence of bingeing by itself does not preclude behavioral treatment since Dubbert and Wilson (1983) reported no correlation between binge scores and weight loss. Currently overweight clients with a history of anorexia or anorectic episodes will need to be treated with special care since attempts to lose weight may exacerbate their problems. The professional may elicit information regarding these issues as the weight history is taken or use one of the standardized questionnaires that are available (Garner, Olmsted, & Polivy, 1982).

Weight History. Several guidelines are available for obtaining information about a client's weight history (Ferguson, 1975), success or failure of previous attempts to lose and/or maintain weight, family weight history, and medical conditions. However, few of these variables have been demonstrated to predict response to treatment. Gormally, Rardin, and Black (1980) presented data indicating that success in losing weight on previous diets was the best predictor of weight loss in a behavioral program. Initial amount of overweight was not a significant predictor. Their data identified certain clients with a history of chronic dieting and weight regain and they found that a majority of these clients also demonstrated weight regain after the behavioral program. Thus, clients so identified may need special emphasis on relapse prevention procedures and continued support during maintenance.

Current Energy Balance. An initial assessment of daily caloric intake and activity levels is important to clearly define the client's obesity problem. Self-monitoring for a period of 1 or 2 weeks before any treatment is started is

146

strongly recommended. In fact, given the critical role of self-monitoring during behavioral treatment, many professionals recommend using such a requirement as an initial screening device. Clients who are not initially willing to monitor are poor risks.

The client's records will help establish whether the problem is primarily overeating or an underactive lifestyle although it is most typically some combination of the two. Katahn (1982) suggests the following guidelines. Average daily intake of approximately 2000 calories for a 128 pound woman and 2700 calories for a 154 pound man are considered normal eating levels. Intake over these amounts suggests an overeating problem. Obesity in individuals with intake at or below these levels suggests that lack of adequate exercise may have upset the natural energy balance. An active woman of 128 pounds will stay slim eating 2000 calories while an inactive woman of 200 pounds will remain obese eating 2000 calories.

Physiological Functioning. Since obese patients typically state they are losing weight for cosmetic and/or social reasons (Dubbert & Wilson, 1983), assessment of physiological functioning may not be warranted in all cases. However, when a client has been referred by a physician and/or states that better health is a primary motivation, physiological assessment may be quite useful. Changes in various indices such as blood pressure and cholesterol levels may be more important feedback than weight change. Decreased need for insulin injections or blood pressure medication can be very powerful factors in a client's decision to continue weight control efforts. Whatever factor is relevant for the individual client can be assessed through self-monitoring and/or periodic physical assessments. Data collection is important since the client's own improvement is a far more salient piece of information to consider at subsequent decision points than a general statement such as weight loss is likely to decrease blood pressure.

Similarly, measures of physical fitness are perhaps most useful in terms of sustaining adherence to exercise. While the more sophisticated measures of fitness (e.g., stress tests) may not be very practical, clients can monitor exercise and recovery pulse rates, chart distances or times, and carry out other assessments such as the 12 minute walk-run. A client who sees clear evidence of improved physical fitness may choose to continue this strategy (for

147

its own health benefits) even though he or she may not be losing that much weight.

Psychological/Social Functioning. The relationship between psychological functioning and weight reduction has not been extensively evaluated despite the fact that the majority of clients seek treatment because they expect that weight loss will make them feel better about themselves and improve their interpersonal relationships. Several research studies have demonstrated improvements in depression, self-esteem, marital relationships, and so forth, associated with weight loss achieved through behavior therapy. However, research also suggests that depression and anxiety may increase with some types of dieting.

For the practicing clinician, assessment of psychological functioning might include measures of depression, anxiety, daily mood, general psychopathology, self-esteem, marital adjustment, social interaction, and body image. Since these measures have not been shown to predict differential treatment response, however, they would only be useful in the following ways. Clinicians doing treatment in groups might choose to exclude certain clients as they may be disruptive to the group. Evidence of pathology, severe depression, or marital discord may be important information to consider in initial or subsequent treatment decisions. These problems may need to be resolved before the client can benefit from participation in an educationally oriented, structured weight loss program.

Assessment of mood on a daily or weekly basis may be useful as an indicator of client response. If clients can see that their mood clearly improves as they exercise or control their eating, this is again powerful information to utilize at subsequent decision points. In the absence of clearly recorded data, clients are typically not aware of small changes and if a relapse occurs they often find it difficult to remember that they had felt better. On the other hand, if the client's mood deteriorates, this may be evidence of the need to re-evaluate the method of weight loss chosen. Interventions may be needed to counteract the negative emotional effects that may accompany dieting efforts.

Eating Habits and Thoughts. Several self-report measures have been developed to assess client eating habits and thoughts related to eating. At this point, they have been used primarily as research tools rather than treatment guides since the measures correlate only modestly with weight loss during treatment and have not predicted differential response to treatments. Careful self-monitoring of the individual's actual eating problems and/or idiosyncratic negative thoughts will be more useful from a clinical perspective. Many examples of possible formats for self-monitoring are provided in self-help texts.

Identifying High Risk Clients. Research (see Dubbert & Wilson, 1983) suggests that the following initial indicators are fairly strongly related to failure to reduce in behaviorally oriented programs. Clients who are older (over 50), who have a high percent body fat (over 45%), or who have high pre-treatment marital satisfaction scores and/or an obese spouse should be considered high risk. In addition, response during the first month of treatment is a strong indicator of subsequent success or failure. Clients who fail to self-monitor calories or those who demonstrate minimal (less than 2 pounds) losses during this first month will need to reappraise their efforts using the decision-making framework.

STEP 2: GENERATE ALTERNATIVES

While taking the weight history, the clinician has already elicited information about strategies the client has used before or is currently using and how effective they have been. The clinician provides information regarding other types of strategies and assesses the client's initial assumptions regarding various strategies. Often the clinician must deal with misconceptions regarding the etiology of obesity and/or the potential utility of various treatments (e.g., there are no data to support the use of hypnosis, acupuncture, etc.).

STEP 3: EVALUATE ALTERNATIVES

The professional's role at this point is to alert the client to the typical advantages and disadvantages of each strategy. The professional also makes it clear that response to these strategies is highly variable and that the

149

individual client may or may not respond like the average. The professional clarifies how the client's subsequent experiences will be used to modify the initial decision-making matrix. It is explained that clients will need to come back to this step at several points as they get more information about how their own bodies respond to various procedures and as their awareness of their own values and priorities increases.

Initial treatment recommendations reflect the state of the art and currently may be summarized as follows (Stunkard, 1983). For the mild to moderately (less than 40%) overweight, which includes 90.5% of obese women, *cognitive-behavior therapy plus exercise plus moderate calorie restriction* is considered the treatment of choice. Weight loss for such clients is often primarily a cosmetic matter as medical consequences are quite variable and uncertain. Research on cognitive-behavior therapy by itself demonstrates consistent average losses of 1/2 to 2 pounds a week while clients continue in treatment. This rate of weight loss is very similar across programs that vary widely in content, location, types of clients (volunteers vs. medical referrals), fees, levels of therapist training, and client demographics. Thus, lay-led self-help groups and bibliotherapy with minimal therapist contact are the most cost-efficient alternatives. Some people do well in self-help groups such as Weight Watchers where, in essence, they can remain in treatment indefinitely. Similarly, reports on self-help bibliotherapy indicate a few people respond well, losing as much as 25 pounds. However, dropout rates are quite high and clearly these approaches are not for everyone. Professionally led, structured, behaviorally oriented group programs report somewhat higher average weight losses and lower dropout rates. Outpatient programs are often quite reasonably priced and appear to be as effective as the more intensive, live-in programs which are more expensive.

The most effective programs reported in the literature have been longer, professionally led programs that include exercise and diet components. The average weight loss reported is 24 pounds in 24 weeks but losses have varied from slight gains to over 80 pound losses. Thus, clients who have over 30 pounds to lose and those who have been unsuccessful with previous self-help efforts may do best to consider professional help. Individual therapy or going to a live-in treatment center may be necessary if an appropriate group program is not available or if the client has not been successful in an outpatient group program.

Clients should be advised that few (about 25%) clients continue to lose after treatment is terminated so they should plan to stay in some type of treatment until a satisfactory weight is achieved. Weight lost in behaviorally oriented programs is typically fairly well maintained (especially when exercise has been continued) for at least a year after treatment. Variability of response increases the longer the period of follow-up. It is appropriate to encourage clients to try a new behavioral program even if they have previously not been successful with other behavioral (or nonbehavioral) programs, especially if they indicate that they are in some way motivated differently this time. For unknown reasons, past efforts failures do not reliably predict the outcome of subsequent efforts.

Recommendations for the moderately to severely obese (40-100% overweight), which includes 9% of obese women, are more complex. There is a greater likelihood of medical complications to consider and greater possibility of pathological physiology that might limit weight loss. Many such individuals have done well in long-term, comprehensive behavioral treatment programs and this is still the best recommendation if clients are willing to persevere in a long-term commitment. A combination of *severe calorie restriction* (under medical supervision) *plus behavioral treatment plus exercise* may, however, be a more realistic alternative in that a large weight loss can be achieved in a more reasonable period of time. Preliminary evidence suggests that maintenance may be adequate but the possibility of relapse suggests caution and careful attention to follow-up. Exercise must be started slowly and increased very gradually; consultation with medical and/or exercise specialists may be necessary to prevent or reduce risk. Extensive lifestyle change is likely to be critical to maintaining new exercise and eating habits.

The very severely (over 100% overweight) obese constitute only a very small proportion, approximately .5%, of the obese but their treatment is by far the most problematic. Severe medical complications are almost always present and pathological physiology is a likely hypothesis. Clients who do not respond positively to the most effective combination of behavioral treatment and severe calorie restriction may (for medical reasons) need to consider the possibility of surgical measures, but this alternative is not discussed in this chapter. Such a person should be referred to a medical specialist in obesity.

STEP 4: RANK ORDER
ALTERNATIVES AND IMPLEMENT

At this point, the professsional can be a resource person, providing information about alternatives that are available locally plus other, live-in programs if the client is interested. If the decision-making framework is being used within an already pre-determined program, this is simply the time to insure that the client understands the program. Some clients may need to be counseled out of a program at this point if it is not at least close to what they want. If you are working with a client individually, the client may decide to start with a single strategy such as behavioral techniques. At a future redecision point the client may decide either to add a second procedure or to switch to a second procedure.

A decision must be made regarding when to implement the procedure. It is helpful for a client to de-termine the time to start a particular program since many of these programs necessitate a considerable investment of time and energy. The client's life need not be free from stress or other problems in order to undertake a program but those additional variables should be explicitly assessed. The client may be best advised to postpone some types of programs until he or she is able to make weight loss a high priority. Clients may need to consider psycho-therapy or the "undiet" approach until they are more ready to focus on weight loss.

Since obesity occurs in a gradual manner and typical-ly represents a constant, low level (not crisis) personal issue, most individuals have been dealing with it in one of two ways. One way is to ignore the problem most of the time and then make periodic, frantic, short-term efforts such as crash diets. The second way is to make very modest continual efforts (always dieting) which do not amount to much. Within the decision-making framework, when clients choose one of the potentially more effective weight loss strategies (e.g., behavioral techniques and exercise), they make a very different kind of commitment. The commitment is to a fairly long-term period of sustained effort. A person overweight by 20 pounds must think in terms of a 6-month commitment and a 40-pound loss typically means a year commitment.

152

STEP 5: MONITOR PROGRESS AND RE-EVALUATE

This re-evaluation step is the most critical part of the model. The client continues with the chosen strategy as long as progress is satisfactory. If progress appears to have stopped or the client becomes discouraged over a slower than expected rate of loss, going back through the decision-making steps is the best way to reconfirm and restore the client's commitment to the particular strategy or to re-evaluate the pros and cons based on the new experiential evidence. In many treatment programs, a client who does not do well either concludes the program is not for him or her or that he or she is once again a failure. In either case, they typically drop out and continue their search for yet another "cure." A client who has been given a decision-making framework is more likely to see lack of progress as a cue to re-evaluate and to seek help from the professional to modify his or her strategies. In a sense, lack of progress or feeling discouraged is reconstrued for clients as important new information about themselves and their bodies rather than something terrible and awful. Thus, the client may begin to cope with his or her weight problem more rationally and may be more likely to ultimately find a satisfactory resolution. Hopefully, this resolution will include at least some weight loss since for most people there are associated physical and mental health benefits. However, even if it does not, the client is less likely to add further psychological complications to whatever negative consequences are already associated with the obesity.

COGNITIVE/BEHAVIOR THERAPY

Although there are many variations of what is frequently referred to as a standard behavioral program, considerable agreement exists about the major components. The reader is also referred to the numerous self-help manuals available that describe the clinical application of these techniques in greater detail: Ferguson, 1975; Jeffrey and Katz, 1977; Johnson and Stalonas, 1981; Jordan, Levitz, and Kimbrell, 1976; Katahn, 1982; M. J. Mahoney and K. Mahoney, 1976; Stuart, 1977; and Stuart and Davis, 1972.

The following elements, each of which consists of several specific techniques, currently characterize standard behavioral programs: self-control model, analyzing and modifying eating behaviors, stimulus control, and cognitive restructuring. The individual contribution of any particular technique or even of each element is still in question. No one technique (except self-monitoring) seems indispensable nor does any one technique appear to account for a significant proportion of the variance. That so many techniques work and that researchers cannot yet explain how or why they work is quite puzzling, but behavior therapy is clearly more effective than placebo or other comparison therapies. Stalonas, Johnson, and Christ (1978) have suggested the following hypothesis. Most behavioral programs demand an extremely large amount of out-of-therapy time (e.g., to record, graph, monitor) compared to other weight-reduction regimens. Thus, the procedures may be effective because they continually prompt the client's (and others) attention to weight loss.

SELF-CONTROL MODEL

Self-control is a complex process in which the individual learns to manage his or her own behavior. The three basic steps involved are self-monitoring, self-evaluation, and self-reinforcement. Self-monitoring appears to be the most indispensable component of behavioral programs, even though by itself it is not sufficient. Evidence suggests that pre-monitoring (recording immediately before eating) is slightly more effective than post-monitoring (after eating) and that self-monitoring of caloric intake is more effective than monitoring eating habits (Green, 1978). The second step, self-evaluation, is often considered an implicit part of the self-reinforcement procedure. General self-evaluative style is important, however, because people must be willing to set attainable goals and evaluate reaching them in a positive manner. The person who is overly critical and down plays the significance of completing small steps will not be an effective self-reinforcer.

Specific self-reward procedures enhance the effects of self-monitoring. There seems to be little difference whether money or more symbolic rewards are used or whether subjects self-reinforce or self-punish. Any procedure that serves as feedback to the person who wants to lose weight appears to be sufficient. Evidence indicates that self-reinforcement based on eating habit change is more effective than if based on weight loss. Current programs rely primarily on self-reinforcement since the effects of external reinforcement (e.g., earning back money deposited with the therapist) have typically been short-lived. Contracts with significant others, however, have been fairly effective.

ANALYZING AND MODIFYING EATING BEHAVIORS

The following procedures are utilized to modify undesirable eating patterns so that the overweight person develops an appropriate, controlled eating style. There is conflicting evidence regarding whether an obese eating style is truly characteristic of overweight persons and to what extent this causes their weight problem. Nonetheless, most programs have assumed this to be the case, and there is a wealth of clinical evidence that clients find such procedures useful.

1. The pace of eating is slowed by asking clients to put down their forks between bites and to introduce short (2 minute) delays during which they socialize. The extra time allows sensations of fullness to be recognized and reduces the temptation to nibble as others are finishing.
2. Regular, planned meals and snacks are advised so clients do not eat when starved since they are more likely to eat too much too fast at such times.
3. Clients learn to discriminate between internally and externally cued urges to eat and to redefine satiety as the absence of hunger rather than the feeling of fullness in the stomach.
4. Clients are asked to eat only in response to internal cues; thus they are only allowed to eat food they have specifically requested. Rehearsal is used to teach them to refuse assertively all food offered by others. Clients practice leaving food on their plates to remind themselves they do not have to eat all food placed in front of them.
5. Clients learn to substitute noneating responses for externally cued eating urges. The urges tend to diminish if a 10-minute delay is introduced or if an alternative distracting (e.g., bubble bath) or incompatible (e.g., exercise) activity is substituted.
6. Clients learn to analyze behavioral patterns and to intervene early in a chain to avoid situations likely to lead to eating. A better alternative to

155

eating when tired is a brief nap. Meditation, imagery, or other experiential techniques can be used to help clients tolerate negative affect without relying on eating. Clients are also encouraged to deal directly with their negative feelings by figuring out what the problems are and doing something about them (e.g., assertive training, interpersonal problem solving).

STIMULUS-CONTROL MODIFICATION

Stimulus control refers to modifying environmental cues so that a particular, desirable response will be more likely to occur. Used in a self-control framework, it refers to something that a person does ahead of time to alter the probability of subsequent events. The use of these procedures in controlling obesity is based on the still controversial assumption that the obese person is overly responsive to environmental cues. The procedures are designed to eliminate cues for impulsive, uncontrolled eating and to introduce new cues for controlled eating.

1. All extraneous visual food cues are eliminated. Tempting foods are not brought into the house or left in plain sight.
2. Clients eliminate any unnecessary exposure to food cues (shopping, cooking, and cleanup) especially when they are already hungry. Leftover food or tempting food gifts are thrown out or given away.
3. Clients narrow the range of cues associated with eating by eating only in designated eating areas and not eating while doing other activities (e.g., watching TV).
4. Clients introduce cues to eat less (e.g., graphs, signs, special dishes, or place mats); small dishes also make small portions look larger.
5. Clients pre-plan (in writing) their meals and snacks the day before so they will be more likely to stick to a plan. Handling parties or eating out is enhanced when the person is committed to a plan ahead of time. Snacks bought (or pre-prepared) in small packaged amounts also enhance controlled eating.

COGNITIVE RESTRUCTURING

Cognitive restructuring techniques, widely used in many areas of behavioral treatment (Goldfried & Davidson, 1976), have been specifically adapted to the treatment of obesity. Clinical reports indicate that overweight clients think about food a great deal and their subsequent internal monologues are frequently maladaptive since they do not reliably lead to controlled eating. Little data is available to suggest that cognitive factors are casually related to obesity but evidence suggests that adaptive cognitions are related to success in treatment (Sjoberg & Person, 1979; M. K. Straw et. al., 1984). M. J. Mahoney and K. Mahoney (1976) have identified five general categories of problematic thoughts: rigid, unrealistic goals; negative evaluations of personal capability to lose weight; justifications (excuses) for eating; inability to distract from food thoughts; and impatience with slow rates of loss. Clients self-monitor their thoughts and replace the negative self-defeating thoughts with more adaptive, encouraging self-talk.

Example: (from M. J. Mahoney & K. Mahoney, 1976, p. 62)

Negative Self-Talk	Appropriate Self-Talk
If it weren't for my wife and the kids, I could lose weight.	My schedule isn't any worse than anyone else's. What I need to do is be a bit more creative in how to improve my eating.

RELAPSE PREVENTION

Behavioral programs have demonstrated by far the best maintenance, but successful maintenance varies considerably across individuals and researchers are just beginning to understand some of the reasons for relapse. Reviews of the effect of periodic booster sessions has revealed inconsistent results and clearly their contribution, if any, is quite modest and inadequate. A significant problem in the literature has been a failure to differentiate between those who have lost significant amounts and have relapsed and those who were never very successful. Intervention appears to be needed very early in the relapse process to help clients cope with their own reactions to a "slip" and to restore their disrupted self-regulation. At this point, the best clinical suggestion that can be made is to teach clients relapse prevention strategies *before* treatment is terminated and then provide immediate access to assistance as needed. Scheduling frequent checkups on clients may even be needed since some reports show that clients frequently are reluctant to initiate contact once they "slip" even when access is available.

Currently available research suggests that the following factors are most strongly related to successful maintenance of weight loss: exercise, continued self-monitoring of progress (mentally self-monitoring is not sufficient), setting a specific weight regain (3-5 pounds) as a danger cue, continued use of specific strategies that had been identified as being useful during initial weight loss, spouse support in weight loss efforts, making more general lifestyle changes, absence of disruptive life events, and/or ability to cope effectively with emotional states. The data suggesting a link between relapse and emotional states seem particularly compelling given the frequency of clinical reports of emotionally related eating and the relative lack of emphasis on coping with emotions characteristic of traditional behavioral programs. Retrospective client reports indicate that unsuccessful maintainers report they eat in response to emotional states such as depression and stress (Gormally et al., 1980). Analyses of reported initial dieting "slip-ups" suggests that positive emotional states associated with social situations (e.g., enjoying a party, taking a vacation) are as significant a factor as negative emotional states (e.g., reaction to divorce, bereavement) and negative physical states (illness, fatigue) (Dubbert & Wilson, 1983).

The relapse prevention model developed by Marlatt (1982) is the most fully articulated specific maintenance strategy that is available. The model has received considerable support in the treatment of alcohol abuse but evaluation of its effectiveness in weight maintenance is still in the preliminary stages. A "slip" or lapse in the relapse prevention model is typically defined as the first cigarette or the first drink after a period of abstinence. This abstinence model must be adapted to some degree for eating problems since total abstinence from eating is not possible. However, many clients do tend to think about certain problem foods in an abstinence-oriented manner. The psychological consequences of this type of dichotomous thinking are part of the reason that in most behaviorally oriented programs abstinence from specific "problem" foods is not advised. Carefully structured, limited eating of problem foods seems to reduce the power that certain foods appear to have to trigger uncontrolled eating.

The skills of controlled eating are critical during maintenance as the client is now likely to feel it is safe to indulge to some degree. For some people true binge or a party weekend may serve as clear evidence of a slip. The first doughnut, cookie, or second helping, however, is not likely to be a salient cue. A slow, almost imperceptible increase in amounts eaten may not trigger the use of the appropriate relapse prevention mechanisms. Thus, it is critical to set up a specific early warning signal that will serve to define an initial lapse. Data from Stuart and Guire (1978) indicated that successful maintainers weighed weekly and set an upper limit of a 3-pound gain.

Identifying High-Risk Situations. The client first learns to identify situations that are likely to be a problem. Descriptions involve both a specific environmental situation (such as being at a party) and an emotional state (such as anxiety). Self-monitoring is the most useful technique since the situations are typically quite idiosyncratic. If the client is currently eating appropriately, it may be useful to review his or her initial eating records to draw up a list of potential problem situations. The client can also monitor current urges or impulses to identify temptation situations. Relapse fantasies can be used to help the client become more aware of possible problem situations. The client then learns to respond to these high-risk situations as danger cues (i.e., discriminative stimuli). They signal the client to avoid or to leave the situation if possible or, if not, to institute specific coping responses to get through the situation. The notion is that the earlier the client can identify potential trouble and prepare for it the more successful he or she will be. Once a client finds himself or herself already "in the act" it is more difficult to stop.

Developing Coping Skills for High-Risk Situations. General problem-solving skills (Goldfried & Davidson, 1976) plus specific response skills (a combination of instruction, modeling, rehearsal, coaching, feedback, and self-instructions) are taught so the client will have

159

numerous alternative responses for potential problem situations. For example, a person facing free doughnuts being provided every morning at coffee break might develop the following alternative coping skills: take an orange to eat instead, walk around the block or meditate instead of eating, assertively refuse the doughnuts, contract to limit doughnuts to once a week, and so on.

Cognitive decision-making techniques are also used to help clients overcome the tendency to focus only on the pleasant short-term effects of the indulgent behavior. Marlatt has labeled this the "Problem of Immediate Gratification or PIG phenomenon" (1982). Clients are taught to use a decision matrix to force themselves to look at the total picture. If clients become aware that they will tend to exaggerate the positive aspects, especially if they have been avoiding that food for some time, they will be less likely to give in to their perceived need for immediate indulgence. For example, the person who has avoided the doughnuts for a month may begin to focus on how great one would taste and this builds up until there is an intense need to have just one. The person can remind himself or herself that the doughnut probably would taste good but would not live up to exaggerated expectations. In addition, the 2 minutes of pleasure may not be worth the long-term weight problem.

Marlatt also recommends the use of a "programmed relapse" in which the client who feels compelled to resume an old habit agrees to come in and have the first cigarette or drink under the direct supervision of a therapist. The client who resumes the habit as a response to stressful conditions is likely to attribute his or her ability to cope to the substance and be more likely to turn to it again when under stress. Also, the client who resumes the habit under particularly pleasant circumstances (a birthday celebration) is likely to exaggerate his or her own positive response (the ice cream tastes absolutely wonderful) which will make subsequent abstinence more difficult. Clients need to experience the behavior apart from its usual negative (or positive) circumstances so they can more objectively evaluate their own responses. For example, a person who has been avoiding chocolate bars may sit down under neutral conditions and very carefully note his or her reactions while slowly eating a candy bar. Often, he or she can begin to identify that the real pleasure is in the first few bites and that it rapidly diminishes. In many cases even the initial taste is not quite as wonderful as the person had been anticipating. Such experiences may help the clients avoid unrealistic expectations about the effects of food, encourage them to eat moderate amounts rather than binge, and help them understand how strongly the social context effects their pleasure with food.

Coping with an Initial Lapse. Once the client has identified that a lapse has occurred, behavioral and cognitive techniques are applied to prevent a full-blown relapse. A behavioral contract is typically set up ahead of time to limit the extent of use should a lapse occur. For example, a client may contract that even if he or she exceeds the pizza limit one night, he or she will eat a regular breakfast the next morning. He or she will not eat doughnuts or skip breakfast or fast the next day. Clients are also prepared to cope with the negative emotional reactions they are likely to experience. Marlatt and his colleagues (1982) have described a phenomenon called the Abstinence Violation Effect (AVE), a combination of cognitive dissonance (conflict and guilt) and personal attribution (blaming self), which is frequently sufficient to trigger a more serious relapse. To the extent that a person holds a dichotomous view that he or she is either in control or out of control, any perceived violation is likely to result in a shift to a period of indulgence during which it is difficult to restore a sense of control.

Cognitive techniques are used to teach the client to reconceptualize the violation as a single, independent event that can be corrected rather than a sign of failure. Clients will tend to *overgeneralize*, to make the slip more catastrophic than it really is. An external attribution (explaining the slip in terms of an interaction of a high-risk situation and a lack of coping responses) is more adaptive than an internal attribution of lack of will power or control. The lapse is viewed as a potential learning experience. The client is not to punish himself or herself but to analyze the situation to figure out what happened and what he or she needs to learn in order to handle such a situation better in the future. Clients are also taught that conflict/guilt feelings are to be expected after a lapse and that this negative affect will tend to trigger additional eating. Clients are reassured that such feelings will subside over time if they do not give in to them (reinforce them by eating) but simply wait them out. Meditation is often used as a technique to tolerate or

detach oneself from the negative affect until it passes.
The client may even carry a small reminder card with his
or her AVE instructions including: the appropriate self-
statements, a list of what to do next generated from the
relapse contract, and a person or hot line number to call
if more assistance is needed.

Promoting a Balanced Lifestyle. Research by Marlatt
and his colleagues (1982) suggests that an unbalanced
lifestyle, one characterized largely by "shoulds" (activities
perceived as external demands) rather than "wants"
(activities for pleasure or self-fulfillment) tends to set the
stage for a relapse. The more a person feels deprived, the
greater the desire for self-indulgence and immediate
gratification and the more easily it can be justified or
rationalized. Frequently, the person manages to get into a
high-risk situation and feels overwhelmed. The person
then feels he or she just couldn't help himself or herself;
it just happened. One of the goals of relapse prevention
is to help clients become aware of lifestyle problems and
the way decisions they make contribute to putting them in
temptation situations that they are not able to resist.
Lifestyle changes must be quite individualized but may
focus on rescheduling to avoid the stress of a constant,
hectic pace; setting aside some type of personal time;
modifying interactions with significant others; and
making changes in type of employment or living situations. A more generally positive lifestyle appears to
reduce the desire for self-indulgence; the client learns to
substitute other, more adaptive forms of self-indulgence
(i.e., "positive addictions").

CALORIE RESTRICTION

Traditional behavioral programs focus on modifying
eating habits, not counting calories. Clients are strongly
advised to follow a nutritionally sound diet, not to
exclude any specific foods or food groups, and not to skip
meals. The message is to cut down, not out, and to
substitute low calorie foods for high calorie snacks.
Special diets such as the Scarsdale diet or setting rigid
calorie goals are not typically recommended. People do
not usually follow such diets for more than a few weeks
and research indicates there is no difference in the long
run, even for those individuals who lose a little faster in
the first few weeks of following a particular diet. The

most effective behavioral programs have included nutrition information and flexible, exchange-type diets that are used as general guidelines, but the specific contribution of this component cannot be isolated from the overall program effect.

A number of severe calorie restriction diets have become popular in recent years as initial weight loss is quite rapid. Previously, the serious problems with relapse made such approaches ill-advised. The first reports are just now coming out that indicate the substantial weight losses achieved through severe calorie restriction can be maintained by including behavioral techniques in the training program and by providing a period of modest calorie restriction during which relapse prevention strategies can be learned (Wadden, Stunkard, Brownell, & Day, 1984).

EXERCISE

The appropriateness of increasing energy expenditure as well as decreasing caloric intake in order to balance the energy equation has long been acknowledged within the behavioral model of treating obesity. However, the relative weight put on these two strategies varies considerably among programs. Initial assessment of the client helps to indicate the extent to which the obesity appears to be due to low activity levels rather than overeating. Research provides very strong support for the inclusion of exercise in any weight control program. The effects on initial weight loss are quite modest, but evidence suggests that people who continue to be regular exercisers are more likely to maintain their initial weight loss successfully (Katahn, Please, Thackrey, & Wallston, 1982).

Since many overweight clients are at least initially reluctant to exercise it is helpful to consider exercise as a separate decision within the decision-making approach. Often it is best to start with behavioral techniques and have clients add in exercise at a later point as they become more aware that they can only go so far with reducing their food consumption and that exercise may in fact be more palatable in the long run than chronic restraint.

Behavioral programs have typically included exercise in one of three ways. Suggestions are made to increase routine exercise such as using stairs, walking part of the way to work, and so on. Clients are likely to adhere to such recommendations but there is only modest payoff in terms of fitness and weight loss. Exercise contracts are used to set up more intensive, individualized exercise programs that fit into the client's lifestyle. However, it is difficult to monitor adherence and to provide the support that is often needed to sustain initial exercise efforts. Blum and Craighead (1982) found the initial use of a formal, supervised group exercise program was more effective in the long run than relying entirely on exercise contracts.

Katahn et al. (1982) recommend an integrated exercise program for group-based obesity programs which includes both group-based and individual exercise. Katahn (1982) describes in detail a gradual walk/run program suitable for even the severely overweight. Katahn makes a very significant point which needs to be highlighted within the decision-making approach. The value of exercise is directly related to the frequency, duration, and intensity of the effort. Occasional or sporadic attempts are probably not even worth the effort, at least from a weight loss perspective. It is Katahn's contention that one must make a serious commitment to a lifestyle change due to the amount of exercise needed to have a serious impact on an obesity problem. He suggests that clients must plan to expend at least 200 calories a day on exercise; this translates into walking an extra 3 miles a day, approximately 45 minutes.

Although the primary effect of exercise on weight appears to be in long-term maintenance, there are several additional payoffs that may be evident much more quickly. Focusing client attention on these factors may be helpful in the short run in establishing and maintaining regular exercise. Considerable research is available to document the physiological changes associated with exercise and the accompanying improvements in cardiovascular risk (Brownell, 1982). Exercise improves the ratio of lean to fat tissue, resulting in a better physical appearance than when weight is lost without exercise. Evidence is also rapidly accumulating that exercise is associated with general improvements in psychological functioning (e.g., less depression and anxiety) in both normal and clinical populations (Folkins & Sime, 1981; Fremont & Craighead, in press). Such psychological improvements are clearly worthwhile even if the client does not lose weight but they may also serve an important indirect function in weight loss. Polivy and Herman

(1983) have noted that continual efforts to diet appear to be quite stressful and may increase emotionality. Furthermore, stress tends to disinhibit cognitive restraint, disrupting diet efforts. Foreyt, Goodrich, and Gotto (1981) have suggested that exercise may reduce stress (whether from dieting or other sources) and thus may allow many people to comply with weight loss programs more effectively. This may be particularly critical for clients identified as "emotional" eaters.

UNDIET

Polivy and Herman (1983) have suggested a "natural weight undiet" program as a rather dramatic alternative to other approaches to obesity. At the current time, there are no experimental studies evaluating this program or its relative effectiveness compared to other approaches. The theoretical premise of such an approach is based on the still controversial hypothesis that people have a "natural weight" and that deprivation (dieting) sufficient to alter this natural weight can be accomplished only by learning to ignore normal hunger cues. Chronic dieters eventually lose their ability to regulate weight naturally and may, in fact, end up at weights even higher than their initial "natural weight." The undiet program is designed to reinstate normal regulatory processes and allow the person to assume his or her natural weight. The authors contend that many people will be pleasantly surprised to find they may in fact lose weight although they may well never reach their hypothetical ideal.

From a decision-making perspective, this alternative is worth cautious consideration as we await further validation. It may be useful as a first choice in situations when clients decide it is not a good time to put the time and resources into a demanding program. For others, it may be useful as a secondary strategy. Their initial experiences with other techniques may tell them they are not willing to pay the personal price of constant deprivation. The undiet is an alternative to giving up and it is distinctly different from saying "I just don't care and I'll eat all I want."

Persons choosing the undiet are working to restore natural biological and psychological functioning so that their weight reflects their biological needs rather than their psychological needs. The undiet is not incompatible with behavioral techniques; however, techniques are used only to regulate and restore normal eating patterns and are not to be used to set up feelings of deprivation. The primary emphasis is on learning the difference between natural hunger (the physiological cue to eat) and appetite (the psychological desire for taste or sensation) and learning to stop eating as soon as one's hunger is satisfied. Thus, one is to eat as much as he or she *needs,* not as much as he or she *wants.* As in behavioral programs, there are no forbidden foods and alternative ways are sought to fill the psychological functions that food has been serving. The major difference is the deliberate de-emphasis on calories and weight loss and the strong emphasis on accepting one's "natural weight." Thus, even if one's "natural weight" is higher than what is socially desirable, the negative psychological consequences of chronic, severe restraint or feeling like a failure may be avoided.

A program focusing on natural regulation and stable weights may also turn out to have fewer risks from a medical point of view. Evidence is accumulating which suggests that overeating may be a more serious culprit than overweight and that large weight fluctuations may be more stressful to one's physiology than just staying overweight.

PHARMACOTHERAPY

Pharmacological treatments for obesity have typically not been recommended because of the negative side effects, rapid relapse, and abuse potential of many of the appetite suppressants that have been evaluated. Recent efforts to utilize some of the weaker (but safer) appetite suppressants within behavioral programs as a way to enhance the slow and often discouraging rate of loss have also not turned out to be particularly promising (Craighead, 1984). While most clients initially responded extremely positively to the use of medication, providing only behavior therapy was equivalent in the long run. Thus, the use of medication appears to be superfluous. It is interesting to note this is the same effect that is shown when a specific diet is added to behavior therapy. A more intensive period of relapse prevention (as was provided in the Wadden et al. (1984) study on severe calorie restriction) may allow the effects of medication to be sustained but this has not yet been demonstrated. If so, pharmacotherapy may become a viable alternative for those who do not initially respond to behavior therapy by itself and/or those clients who cannot or will not tolerate severe calorie restriction.

SUMMARY

A problem-solving approach to the treatment of obesity has been presented as a flexible framework within which professionals and clients can make more realistic, rational, and humane treatment decisions regarding a disorder that is still poorly understood. The initial assessment is used to clarify the client's obesity problem and to educate the client about the important role that physiology may play in weight regulation. Since many people do lose weight fairly easily and maintain with modest effort, the notion persists that obesity is a fairly simple matter of eating too much and/or exercising too little. Lack of knowledge concerning physiological factors may, however, lead to maladaptive dieting patterns. Dieters want weight loss to be fast, steady, easy, and permanent when in fact it is likely to be slow, inconsistent, costly in terms of time and personal effort, temporary, and perhaps nearly impossible for certain individuals. The person with a weight problem typically continues to seek out new, promising methods but ditches them when they do not show quick results, or when it becomes clear they require effort. If dieters do lose weight, they are likely to regain it fairly quickly, setting up a yo-yo pattern of feast or famine. It usually takes many such unsuccessful efforts before dieters are willing to revise their beliefs and accept the notion of slow, effortful weight loss plus continued lifestyle change to insure maintenance.

In the decision-making approach, difficulty in either weight loss or weight maintenance is reconstrued as important new information about one's body, values, and priorities. Thus, in re-evaluating their efforts, clients may eliminate or incorporate additional techniques. Clients who are not successful and who have no additional compelling medical reasons to lose weight may need to re-evaluate their goals. Some clients may need to focus on exercise or undieting rather than emphasizing restraint to such a degree. In a sense, the only unacceptable solution to an obesity problem is for the client to decide that he or she cannot or chooses not to do what it takes to maintain an acceptable weight. Such a client may continue to be miserable about being overweight and subject himself or herself to repeated failure with whatever fad diet comes out next.

Linda Wilcoxon Craighead, PhD, is currently an Associate Professor in the Division of Counseling and Educational Psychology at the Pennsylvania State University. Her training was in clinical psychology and her research has focused primarily on the evaluation of cognitive/behavioral therapies. She has published several articles on the treatment of obesity and in her other interest areas which include assertion training, depression, and the role of physical exercise in the treatment of psychological problems. Dr. Craighead may be contacted at 229 Cedar Building, University Park, PA 16802.

RESOURCES

Bennett, W., & Gurin, J. (1982). *The Dieter's Dilemma: Eating Less and Weighing More.* New York: Basic Books.

Blum, M., & Craighead, L. W. (1982). *Evaluation of a Supervised Exercise Component in Behavioral Treatment of Obesity.* Unpublished manuscript.

Brownell, K. D. (1982). Obesity: Understanding and treating a serious, prevalent and refractory disorder. *Journal of Consulting and Clinical Psychology, 50,* 820-840.

Craighead, L. W. (1984). Sequencing of behavior therapy and pharmacotherapy for obesity. *Journal of Consulting and Clinical Psychology, 52,* 190-199.

Dubbert, P. M., & Wilson, T. (1983). Treatment failures in behavior therapy for obesity: Causes, correlates, and consequences. In E. Foa & P. M. G. Emmelkamp (Eds.), *Failures in Behavior Therapy* (pp. 263-288). New York: Wiley.

Ferguson, J. M. (1975). *Learning to Eat: Behavior Modification for Weight Control.* Palo Alto, CA: Ball.

Folkins, C. H., & Sime, W. E. (1981). Physical fitness training and mental health. *American Psychologist, 36,* 373-389.

Foreyt, J. P., Goodrich, G. K., & Gotto, A. M. (1981). Limitations of behavioral treatment of obesity: Review and analysis. *Journal of Behavioral Medicine, 4,* 159-174.

Fremont, J., & Craighead, L. W. (in press). Aerobic exercise and cognitive therapy in the treatment of dysphoric moods. *Cognitive Research and Therapy.*

Garner, D. M., Olmsted, M. P., & Polivy, J. (1982). Development and validation of a multidimensional eating disorder inventory for anorexia nervosa and bulimia. *International Journal of Eating Disorders, 2,* 15-34.

Goldfried, M. R., & Davidson, G. C. (1976). *Clinical Behavior Therapy.* New York: Holt, Rinehart, & Winston.

Gormally, J., Rardin, D., & Black, S. (1980). Correlates of successful response to a behavioral weight control clinic. *Journal of Counseling Psychology, 27,* 179-191.

Green, L. (1978). Temporal and stimulus factors in self-monitoring by obese persons. *Behavior Therapy, 9,* 328-341.

Hawkins, R. C., Fremouw, W. F., & Clement, P. F. (1984). *Binge Eating: Theory, Research, and Treatment.* New York: Springer Publishing Co.

Jeffrey, D. B., & Katz, R. C. (1977). *Take It Off and Keep It Off.* Englewood Cliffs, NJ: Prentice-Hall.

Johnson, W. G., & Stalonas, P. M. (1981). *Weight No Longer.* Gretna, LA: Pelican Publishing Co.

Jordan, H. A., Levitz, L. S., & Kimbrell, G. M. (1976). *Eating Is Okay!* New York: Rawson, Wade Publishers.

Katahn, M. (1982). *The 200 Calorie Solution.* New York: W. W. Norton.

Katahn, M., Please, J., Thackrey, M., & Wallston, K. A. (1982). Relationship of eating and activity self-reports to follow-up maintenance in the massively obese. *Behavior Therapy, 13,* 521-528.

Mahoney, M. J., & Mahoney, K. (1976). *Permanent Weight Loss.* New York: Norton.

Marlatt, G. A. (1982). Relapse prevention: A self-control program for the treatment of addictive behaviors. In R. B. Stuart (Ed.), *Adherence, Compliance and Generalization in Behavioral Medicine* (pp. 329-378). New York: Brunner/Mazel.

Metropolitan height and weight tables for men and women. (1983). *Statistical Bulletin, 1,* 2-9.

Polivy, J., & Herman, C. P. (1983). *Breaking the Diet Habit.* New York: Basic Books.

Sjoberg, L., & Person, L. (1979). A study of attempts by obese patients to regulate eating. *Addictive Behaviors, 4,* 349-359.

Stalonas, P. M., Johnson, W. G., & Christ, M. (1978). Behavior modification for obesity: The evaluation of exercise, contingency management and program adherence. *Journal of Consulting and Clinical Psychology, 46,* 463-469.

Straw, M. K., Straw, R. B., Mahoney, M. J., Rogers, T., Mahoney, B. K., Craighead, L. W., & Stunkard, A. J. (1984). The Master Questionnaire: Preliminary reports of an obesity assessment device. *Addictive Behavior, 9,* 1-10.

Stuart, R. B. (1977). *Act Thin, Stay Thin.* New York: W. W. Norton Co.

Stuart, R. B., & Davis, B. (1972). *Slim Chance in a Fat World.* Champaign, IL: Research Press Company.

Stuart, R. B., & Guire, K. (1978). Some correlates of the maintenance of weight loss through behavior modification. *International Journal of Obesity, 2,* 225-235.

Stunkard, A. J. (1983). The current status of treatment for obesity in adults. *Psychiatric Annals, 13,* 862-867.

Wadden, T. A., Stunkard, A. J., Brownell, K. D., & Day, S. C. (1984). Treatment of obesity by behavior therapy and very-low-calorie diet: A pilot investigation. *Journal of Consulting and Clinical Psychology, 52,* 692-694.

MODIFYING THE TYPE A BEHAVIOR PATTERN: A SMALL GROUP TREATMENT APPROACH

Lynda H. Powell and Carl E. Thoresen

> In the worry and strain of modern life, arterial degeneration is not only very common but develops often at a relatively early age. For this, I believe that the high pressure at which men live and the habit of working the machine to its maximum capacity are responsible rather than excesses in eating and drinking. (Osler, 1892, p. 14)

Sir William Osler's observation reflects the views of a few others down through the centuries: How people think, feel, and behave in their daily life plays a role in processes linked to chronic disease. Strong and intimate connections among emotional factors, health, and disease have long been suspected, dating back at least three centuries to Harvey, Heberden, and Hunter in the case of ischemic disease (Weiner, 1977). Despite the prevalence of such clinical observations over the years, difficulties in measuring social and emotional habits and specifying the mechanisms by which they contribute to disease have limited empirical validation of the relationship and its incorporation into medical practice (Friedman, 1969; Friedman, Thoresen, & Gill, 1981).

Building on the psychosocial or personality perspectives of early investigators concerned with heart disease (Dunbar, 1943; K. A. Menninger & W. C. Menninger, 1936),

171

Meyer Friedman and Ray Rosenman, laboratory researchers as well as practicing cardiologists, identified a set of behaviors and characteristics which they repeatedly observed in their coronary patients. They articulated a constellation of observable behaviors and characteristics which became known as the Type A behavior pattern (TABP) (Friedman & Rosenman, 1974). They noted the ubiquitous sense of impatience and time urgency, the pervasive pattern of competitive striving, and the quickness with which angry behavior and hostile feelings were aroused in their patients and identified the major components of the syndrome as impatience/time urgency and anger/hostility. To them, the term "struggle" captured the essence of the Type A syndrome--the seemingly incessant struggle to overcome real (or imagined) obstacles imposed by events, time, and the actions of other people.

Friedman and Rosenman (1974) speculated that this persistent struggle was accompanied by a persistent state of hyperarousal in the person which could be observed in how individuals acted (e.g., rapid, abrupt speech), what they said (e.g., critical comments about others), what they thought (e.g., perceiving others as challenging one's control of situations), how they felt (e.g., irritation, impatience), and how they responded physiologically (e.g., elevations in heart rate, blood pressure). They believed that the Type A pattern was not a personality trait (a person's style regardless of the particular situation) but instead was evoked in response to certain demands.

Feelings of insecurity and pervasive self-doubt about personal worth were theorized to be at the heart of the Type A pattern (Friedman & Rosenman, 1974). This insecurity seemed to be linked to a fear of inadequacy and of inability to gain others' respect and admiration, fears that perhaps went back to early childhood experiences. Striving to seek symbols of recognition and reward conceivably acted to reduce these fears. Thus, the TABP was strongly reinforcing to the person.

Despite the assertion by Friedman and Rosenman (1974) that the TABP was a complex behavioral syndrome occurring only in certain situations (i.e., an interaction of person-environment factors), the notion of the TABP as a fixed personality trait became popularized. For example, the common use of the term "Type A personality" contributed to a fixed trait orientation. ("Once an A, always an A....") The idea of Type B, routinely defined as the absence of Type A behaviors and characteristics, tended to encourage a highly oversimplified and confusing trait conception of the TABP.

The consequences of a trait orientation to the TABP has seriously restricted the quality of conceptual, empirical, and especially intervention, research (Suinn, 1982; Thoresen & Ohman, in press). Too often people have been labeled as Type A or Type B and their thoughts, feelings, and actions have been explained by these labels. Such homogeneity, however, rarely exists in the individual case. Instead, individuals have a certain number and intensity of Type A behaviors, thoughts, and feelings. The task of intervention is not to change a Type A personality into a Type B personality, but instead to help people reduce the number and intensity of their Type A behaviors across situations. A clear need exists to expand well beyond simplistic global classifications of Type A, particularly for those concerned with helping persons to alter their TABP.

Despite these conceptual and assessment problems, the TABP has been related to clinical coronary heart disease (CHD) in a variety of laboratory (Carruthers, 1969; Friedman, Byers, & Rosenman, 1965; Friedman, Rosenman & Byers, 1964), clinical (Blumenthal, Williams, Kong, Schonberg, & Thompson, 1978; Caffrey, 1969; Friedman et al., 1973; Glass, 1977), and epidemiologic (Haynes, Feinleib, & Kannel, 1980; Rosenman et al., 1975) studies. An expert panel of behavioral and medical scientists, convened by the National Heart, Lung, and Blood Institute, concluded that substantial evidence exists for an association between the TABP and CHD, a relationship of the same magnitude as that found for cigarette smoking, elevated serum cholesterol, and hypertension (The Review Panel on Coronary-Prone Behavior and Coronary Heart Disease, 1981).

Recently, however, some investigators have failed to find a relationship between the TABP and CHD criteria (R. B. Case, Heller, N. B. Case, Moss, & the Multicenter Post-Infarction Research Group, 1985; Dimsdale, Gilbert, Hutter, Hackett, & Block, 1981; Ruberman, Weinblatt, Goldberg, & Chaudhary, 1984; Shekelle et al., 1985). But these studies can be criticized from a methodological standpoint. Some of the investigations used an unvalidated Type A questionnaire (Ruberman et al., 1984), or a questionnaire that was not validated for the population on which it was used (R. B. Case et al., 1985). One problem with the Multiple Risk Factor Intervention Trial (MRFIT) study (Shekelle et al., 1985) is that the interviewers who made the structured interview assessments of behavior type appeared to have been inconsistent in their judgments (Scherwitz, 1985). Finally, failure of *any* risk factor to predict health outcomes in *high-risk* populations (e.g., coronary patients [R. B. Case et al., 1985], patients referred for angiography [Dimsdale et al., 1981], or patients at high risk on other risk factors [Shekelle et al., 1985]) could be explained by design limitations. High-risk subjects, by definition, are elevated on risk factors. Thus the risk factor of interest tends also to be elevated. The implication of this is that risk factor scores tend to be loaded on the high end of the distribution, their scale attenuated, and correlations with health outcomes reduced. (By analogy, consider the problem of trying to predict achievement using the IQ scores of a group of students all of whom have scored above 140.)

Following these recent failures, some have concluded that the TABP is not predictive of significant CHD endpoints. But considering these assessment and design limitations, such a conclusion may be premature. Cognizance of these methodologic limitations is important not only for the researcher, who is in danger of replicating mistakes, but also for the clinician, who may be faced with explaining these studies to challenging, if not hostile, Type A patients.

Intervention studies offer an alternative approach to predictions in high-risk populations. Rather than trying to predict recurrent events with a population that is homogeneous on the risk factor of interest, the aim of intervention is to make the population more heterogeneous by promoting *change* on the risk factor of interest, and then determining whether risk reduction has taken place. Intervention studies are ambitious because the change produced must last long enough to influence CHD criteria. They are especially ambitious in the case of the Type A risk factor since the TABP appears to rest on a foundation of firmly entrenched beliefs and attitudes. Nevertheless, there is some basis for cautious optimism. The TABP has been shown to be substantially reduced in both healthy and post-infarction patients with positive effects on CHD indicators (Friedman et al., 1984; Gill et al., 1985; Roskies, 1985). Less is known about the stability of such behavioral reductions over several years.

THE RECURRENT CORONARY
PREVENTION PROJECT

The treatment program we will describe was developed by the staff of the Recurrent Coronary Prevention Project (RCPP), under the direction of Meyer Friedman. This San Francisco-based clinical trial investigated the feasibility of altering the TABP in post-infarction patients, and the influence of such alteration on recurrence of cardiovascular disease.

The study was unique for two reasons. First, it was a large-scale, long-term lifestyle intervention. The way a change in lifestyle was promoted was to target the beliefs and attitudes that underlie Type A behavior.

Second, its success was evaluated using a "hard" CHD endpoint. The hard endpoint in this trial was total recurrent cardiac events, defined as fatal and nonfatal myocardial infarction. After exposure to 3 years of treatment, experimental subjects exposed to a combination of Type A behavioral counseling and cardiac information had 45% fewer recurrent cardiac events (7.2%) than control subjects who were exposed to cardiac information alone (13.2%) (chi-square: $p<0.01$). Figure 1 (page 176) presents the "survival without cardiac recurrence" curves for these two treatment groups. Those subjects randomized to the experimental treatment had a significantly greater survival without recurrence rate (94%) after 3 years of treatment than subjects randomized to the control treatment (87%) (logrank: $p<0.01$) (Friedman et al., 1984). The trend toward a reduction in cardiovascular recurrence was evident after 2 years (L. H. Powell, Friedman, Thoresen, Gill, & Ulmer, 1984). The 4.5 year results showed that the observations at 3 years were maintained (Thoresen, 1985).

The substantial success of the RCPP, coupled with promising results from other intervention studies (Suinn, 1982; Thoresen, Telch, & Eagleston, 1981), suggests that behavior change is a viable goal in the secondary prevention of CHD. Replication of these findings is needed, especially replications of treatment variations that may prove to be more cost-efficient.

To encourage controlled intervention studies and to assist clinicians in their work, this paper will describe the Type A group treatment used in the RCPP. In so doing, we acknowledge that the program must be tailored to its

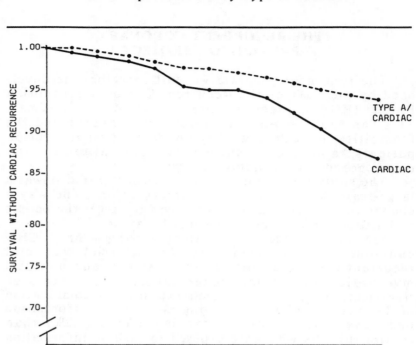

Figure 1. Survival without cardiac recurrence curves for RCPP subjects receiving Type A and cardiac counseling and cardiac counseling alone. The subjects receiving Type A/cardiac counseling had a significantly greater survival (94%) than subjects receiving cardiac counseling alone (87%) (logrank: $p < 0.01$).

From: "Alteration of Type A Behavior and Reduction in Cardiac Recurrences in Post-Myocardial Infraction Patients" by M. Friedman, C. E. Thoresen, J. J. Gill, L. H. Powell, D. Ulmer, L. Thompson, V. A. Price, D. D. Rabin, W. S. Breall, T. Dixon, R. Levy, and E. Bourg, 1984, *American Heart Journal*, 108, pp. 237-248. Copyright © 1984 by The C. V. Mosby Co. Reprinted by permission.

specific patient population. Further, the original RCPP program was a seminal effort. As such, it may not have provided the best possible treatment. Much was learned in the process of designing and implementing small group treatment for hundreds of post-infarction patients. Thus, where appropriate, suggestions will be offered for treatment variations or new procedures, based upon the RCPP experience and that of other investigators.

OVERVIEW OF TYPE A COUNSELING

The aim of this treatment program is to produce a sustained reduction in the emotional and behavioral hyperarousal associated with the TABP. To accomplish this, a shift in the attitudes and beliefs that underlie the overt behavior pattern is needed. These beliefs and attitudes are believed to emerge from feelings of low self-esteem and insecurity (Friedman & Rosenman, 1974). Thus, reducing the TABP is closely tied to enhancing self-esteem.

Early treatment targets are directed at the identification of overt Type A behaviors, such as irritation while driving a car, impatience while waiting in lines, interruptions during group sessions, and annoyance at the trivial errors of friends and family members. During the course of discussions about these more superficial characteristics, latent Type A beliefs and attitudes emerge. The patient must be made aware of these cognitions and helped to explore their possible relationship to self-esteem. Recognizing a connection between certain attitudes (e.g., distrust of others, hypersensitivity to criticism) and low self-esteem stimulates interest in alternative attitudes. Here treatment targets shift to an exploration of attitudes and beliefs associated with greater self-esteem (e.g., genuine respect for others, tolerance of their errors and mistakes).

The role of group leaders is multidimensional (Thoresen, Friedman, Gill, & Ulmer, 1982). They must be teachers in presenting information on pathophysiology of heart disease; supportive facilitators in helping patients explore sensitive issues such as fears, insecurity, and hostility; respected professionals in providing positive (and often coping) social models; and good friends in offering the unconditional positive regard that is essential in fostering positive self-esteem.

Patients move through treatment at different rates. In general, as they progress, there is an evolution of patient concerns. This evolution is outlined in Figure 2 (page 178). Initially, patients tend to have difficulty believing that Type A exists as a distinct syndrome of behavior or that it is significant in CHD. When they start to recognize the Type A syndrome, their observations tend to be impersonal. They typically see it in other drivers, co-workers, spouse, children, and other group members. A

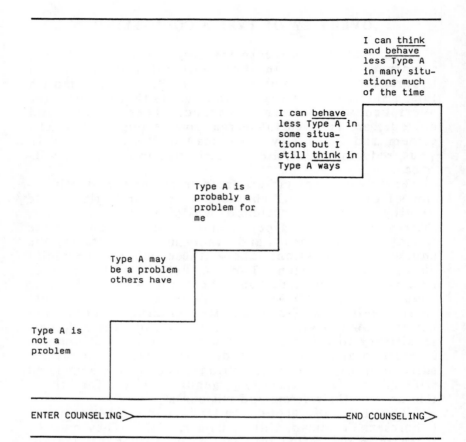

Figure 2.   Some emerging issues as patients progress through Type A counseling.

sign of progress is when patients begin to observe the TABP in themselves, despite the fact that these initial observations are often accompanied by rationalizations for its importance or necessity. Early attempts at change tend to result in rather modest, superficial changes (e.g., not wearing a watch, speaking more slowly in the group). Patients may talk in less Type A ways, but continue to think like Type As. With persistence and patience some begin to undergo a shift in attitudes and beliefs. A sign of an attitude shift in patients is the habitual use of self-monitoring to prompt and encourage new behaviors and to

178

notice reversions to old Type A habits of thinking, feeling, or acting.

The foregoing description may suggest that there is a fixed progression that all patients follow in reducing the intensity of their TABP. Rarely, however, is this true in the individual case. Some patients plunge forward making great strides early on. This excerpt from a letter written by an RCPP participant who had undergone only 4 months of Type A counseling indicates rapid and genuine progress:

> You may escape prison only if you know that you are bound. Fortunately I knew how limited I was making my life, but until I came to your group I did not know the way out. With your help the impossible has become only difficult. I wish you to know that every small freedom is thrilling.

Others become stuck at an early stage. For example, it was common during the RCPP to observe some patients with 3 or 4 years of counseling protesting, in an obvious Type A fashion, that they no longer had a problem with the TABP. This kind of denial is well illustrated in this quote from a patient in treatment.

> I do not believe that I have excess hostility; this is due in part to the fact that my intellectual, physical, cultural, and hereditary attributes surpass those of 98 percent of the bastards I have to deal with. Furthermore those dome-head, fitness freak, goody-goody types that make up the alleged 2 percent are no doubt faggots anyway, whom I could beat out in a second if I weren't so damn busy fighting every minute to keep that 98 percent from trying to walk over me. (Friedman & Ulmer, 1984, p. 203)

It is important for the group leader to acknowledge individual differences in commitment to change and rate of progress. It is particularly important to realize that some patients have such an extreme TABP that they are hopeless. We have often observed leaders persist in "banging their heads against the wall" in their attempt to help certain patients change. Many group leaders, especially those who themselves manifest considerable Type A behavior, appear to resist clear and converging evidence of intransigence on the part of their patients.

FOUR KEY FEATURES OF TYPE A COUNSELING

If we were to isolate *one* element that was most critical to the success of the RCPP treatment program, it would be the group leader--the professional who conducted treatment sessions. Characteristics and qualities of the leader will be discussed later. Beyond this, four key features of this program deserve special mention.

THE SMALL GROUP

The RCPP treatment was conducted in small groups of approximately 10 patients each. There were many advantages of using the small group context. In contrast to the therapeutic dyad, information that comes from more than one source tends to be perceived as more credible. In the small group, other members can be enlisted as aids in making observations about Type A behavior.

A small group can become a supportive setting for interpersonal learning (Thoresen et al., 1982). Patients can learn about the TABP vicariously by listening to others discuss their problems and observing the similarities between those problems and their own struggles. In addition, the group offers valuable opportunities for patients to sharpen their typically dull listening skills. Too often, the Type A patient suffers from a woefully inadequate ability to listen (rather than just hear words).

The small group also offers an excellent opportunity to experience the benefits of ongoing social support. Friendships can develop and the experience of intimate sharing can take place. An atmosphere of mutual trust and support, however, seldom characterizes a newly formed group of Type A coronary patients. Rather, this type of atmosphere must be cultivated. Initially, members relate to each other in the same competitive, impatient, and hostile style in which they relate to others in their lives. For example, in the beginning, patients triumphantly, rather than gently, point out Type A behaviors in other group members. Commonly, when one patient begins to describe a personal situation, others fail to listen, resent the time taken up, and/or interrupt, rendering their own accounts in an "I can top yours" fashion.

The group leader must strive patiently, yet persistently, to create an atmosphere of trust, respect, and caring by consistently modeling desired actions and reactions. Positive reinforcement by the leader for any indication in patients of more trusting, supportive, empathic attitudes, however slight, is important.

DRILLS

William James (1890), in writing about changing habits in *The Principles of Psychology*, observed, "If we wish to conquer undesirable emotional tendencies in ourselves, we must assiduously, and in the first instance cold-bloodedly, go through the outward movements of those contrary dispositions which we prefer to cultivate." Changing habits associated with the TABP requires practicing alternative behaviors until they become incorporated into the patient's repertoire. In the RCPP, we called this practice drilling.

A book of drills was developed for patients that was composed of a series of daily actions to teach patients to act in a less Type A fashion and a series of quotes from famous people that served as an object of reflection over the time between groups. Table 1 (page 182) presents a page from this Drill Book.

In the beginning of treatment, drills were aimed at practicing simple, overt, non-Type A behaviors, such as purposely driving in the slow lane on the highway. To help remind patients to practice this behavior, we gave them a small red dot which served as a cueing device and asked them to stick it on their steering wheel. To encourage a more relaxed driving attitude, we instructed them to listen to classical music on the car radio or tape deck. As treatment progressed, drills focused on more subtle attitudes. For example, to bring attention to opinionated and inflexible attitudes, we asked participants to practice saying "Maybe I'm wrong" during conversations involving differences of opinion.

Regular drilling takes considerable self-control. Patients need help to continue. The group leader can play an important role in reinforcing practice by requiring that patients bring the Drill Book to each session. Having patients place check marks beside each drill after it is practiced is also helpful. Treatment sessions can be

TABLE 1:	EXAMPLE FROM RCPP DRILL BOOK USED IN THE TYPE A BEHAVIORAL GROUP TREATMENT

OCTOBER

MONDAY:	Set aside 30 minutes for yourself
TUESDAY:	Practice smiling
WEDNESDAY:	Practice removing your grimaces
THURSDAY:	Eat more slowly
FRIDAY:	Recall memories for 10 minutes
SATURDAY:	Verbalize affection to spouse/children
SUNDAY:	Linger at table

1. "The only future we can conceive is built upon the forward shadow of our past."--Proust

2. "If you make the organization your life, you are defenseless against the inevitable disappointments."--Peter Drucker

3. "The moment numeration ceases to be your servant, it becomes your tyrant."

4. "Habit is the hardiest of all the plants in human growth."

structured so that time is always reserved for group discussion of experiences during drills, including asking group members how often they did drills. Table 2 (page 183) presents a typical group session format, illustrating how drills can be incorporated into a group session.

THE AVAILABILITY OF THERAPEUTIC TOOLS

In the RCPP, a variety of therapeutic tools were assembled to assist group leaders in promoting change. These tools were particularly effective at stimulating discussions and helping patients translate abstract concepts into concrete actions. Some are presented in this

182

section and others are used elsewhere in this chapter to serve as illustrations.

Acronoyms. The most successful acronym used was AIAI (Anger, Irritation, Aggravation, Impatience), representing the main features of the TABP. The AIAI acronym was useful because it diminished any glamour or prestige associated with Type A, instead depicting it as a constellation of negative emotions. Another acronym was used to convey the goal of treatment: ASAS (Acceptance of the trivial errors of others, Serenity, Affiliation, and Self-Esteem).

Metaphors. Becoming "hooked" provided a well established and highly useful metaphor among RCPP patients. Patients were taught that trivial, unexpected situations which arouse anger, irritation, or impatience are hooks. We, as fish, begin our swim for the day in clear water. Suddenly, a hook drops before us with attractive bait and we make the decision to bite (get angry, irritated, annoyed) or to let the hook float by. Whatever is done

---

TABLE 2: TYPICAL GROUP SESSION FORMAT (Time: 1-1/2 to 2 hours)

---

1. Physiological and/or psychological information and relaxation practice (5-10 minutes)

   Leader or participant led, using physical and cognitive methods (e.g., progressive muscle relaxation, deep breathing, autogenic suggestions, positive imagery); leader presents information on particular physiologic or psychologic factor (e.g., role of norepinephrine in arousal; different ways in which hostility is expressed).

2. Review of drills

   Open Drill Book to appropriate page. Ask each participant if he or she has checked behaviors as they were practiced. Inquire about problems, reactions, and consequences of practicing behavior and reflections on weekly quotes.

3. Group discussion/problem solving

   Focus on experience of participants. What is working well in reducing AIAI (Anger, Irritation, Aggravation, Impatience)? What are the current obstacles (spouse, co-worker, personal ambitions)?

4. Assignments, reminders

5. Closing benediction

---

with any particular hook is relatively unimportant because inevitably another one will follow and we must again make the choice about taking the bait. Perhaps as many as 30 hooks drop in front of us each day. Sometimes they come close together; other times they are spaced widely apart. What is important is to consider the actual number of hooks we swallow as we go through each and every day, how many we have remaining in our mouths when we go to sleep, and how many we have ignored or taken but then successfully spit out.

Audiotapes and Videotapes. Over the years, Meyer Friedman has assembled a set of audiotapes and videotapes that are rich in the information they convey about a variety of topics associated with the TABP. Audiotapes of leaders of America were available, some of whom have extreme versions of the TABP and others of whom are relatively free of the pattern. One powerful audiotape is that of a famous heart surgeon who possessed few Type A behaviors and, despite a very full and demanding schedule on the day ahead, appears on tape to be calm, relaxed, confident, and comfortably in control. Audiotapes of widows describing the lifestyles of their dead husbands serve to educate patients about the powerful personal and familial repercussions of the TABP. Probably the most poignant tape we had was that of an extremely severe Type A male describing his driving habits. The tape, in a few minutes, illustrates a variety of Type A speech and psychomotor behaviors, and presents a type of harried driving that is both humorous and disturbing. One way this tape was used was as negative reinforcement. When a group member reported having become irritated on the road, a tape recorder was put in front of him or her, the tape was played through, and it was followed up with an alternative--a tape of soothing classical music.

Diagrams. RCPP group leaders devised a variety of graphic representations of complex concepts. Figures 2 and 3 (pages 178 and 185) are examples of diagrams used in group sessions. Another example is a three-dimensional pyramid to demonstrate the reciprocal influences of cognitive, behavioral, environmental, and physiologic factors in determining Type A behavior. All group sessions were conducted in rooms where a chalkboard or flip chart was available.

184

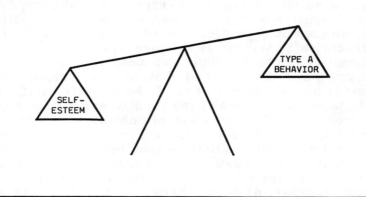

Figure 3.   The relationship between self-esteem and Type A behavior.

Books. Only a small portion of the richness of the TABP and alternatives to it can be transmitted during group sessions. Thus, readings were assigned to provide background.   These books included, among others: Friedman and Rosenman (1974), a detailed description of the nature of the TABP and its association to CHD; J. Powell (1976), a profile of individuals with high self-esteem; Layden (1977), a discussion of ways to identify and alter hostility; Manchester (1978), a biography of General Douglas MacArthur useful in discussions of the possible origins of Type A, especially related to insecurity and need for power; Kearns (1976), a biography of Lyndon Johnson, an example of the familial roots of the TABP; Terkel (1974), to illustrate the many ways people relate their working life to their private life; and Stroebel (1982), a presentation of a technique for incorporating quick physical and mental relaxation into one's daily life. Specific page assignments were made for the time between group sessions and discussion time was reserved during group meetings for questions and reactions. Compliance is enhanced significantly if patients realize that they will be asked about reading assignments during group sessions.

THE TYPE A SELF-MONITOR

The formation of an internal Type A self-monitor is one of the most important outcomes of Type A counseling.

The notion of a self-monitor was derived from behavioral research on self-monitoring (Thoresen & Mahoney, 1974) involving persons observing and recording their actions (e.g., number of cigarettes smoked). It applies to Type A intervention by serving as a device whereby patients can systematically observe their own behavior. The monitor de-emphasizes the *object* of distress and instead makes observations of the presence of the distress itself. For example, when a person is impatiently waiting for a slow elevator, the self may start grumbling about archaic technology in the building (i.e., the *object* of the distress), but the self-monitor quietly makes the observation that the self is acting impatiently and that remaining calm is in order (i.e., the occurrence of the distress itself). In effect, the patient is taught to use an observing and impartial third person--someone who has first person intimacy, including candid knowledge of fears, foibles, and rationalizations.

The overall objective of the self-monitor is to keep manifestations of the TABP salient to patients as they go through their day. In a treatment group, the group leader and other group members serve the role of monitor. In a sense, the patient's self-monitor is the internalization of these messages.

Patients with effective self-monitors are made aware of their Type A reactions *at the time they occur.* By contrast, some patients develop retrospective self-monitors and have difficulty converting them into prospective self-monitors. These patients make a habit of reflecting on "Type A" days with hindsight about their undesired reactions to various situations. Although this type of monitor is better than no monitor at all, it should be clearly labeled as a *step* in the process of developing a complete self-monitor. Retrospective monitors are ineffective in the long-run; deposition on the atherosclerotic plaques is uninfluenced by regrets.

It is overly optimistic to expect that therapy can eradicate all Type A behavior. A more realistic goal is that patients develop an ongoing commitment to altering Type A behavior. This ongoing commitment is embodied in an active Type A self-monitor.

THE PROCESS OF TYPE A COUNSELING

Group counseling can be divided into two major stages: (a) identifying the TABP; and (b) modifying the

TABP by raising self-esteem. In the first stage, the patient gains a clear understanding of the various maladaptive behaviors, attitudes, and beliefs associated with the TABP. In the second stage, emphasis shifts to reducing the frequency of Type A behaviors and attitudes and practicing those behaviors and attitudes associated with high self-esteem.

IDENTIFYING THE TYPE A BEHAVIOR PATTERN

The goal of this phase of counseling is to help each patient become sensitive to his or her personal version of the TABP. This self-knowledge is crucial to the successful replacement of these behaviors with more desired alternatives.

The early sessions are important because patients often make snap judgments about the usefulness of treatment. If they judge it to be useless, irrelevant, or too critical of them, they often drop out or attend sporadically. To keep early interest high, simple and impersonal topics are discussed. These evoke little defensiveness and are likely to result in an early sense of mastery. One topic well suited to the early phase of treatment is the TABP while driving a car. Driving is a situation where the TABP is extremely prevalent and obvious. A columnist for the *San Francisco Chronicle* observed this phenomenon.

> Why do people drive the way they do? Not because they're in such a hurry to get from Point A to Point B, obviously. Even a dolt knows that in city driving, the tortoise beats the hare every time. No it's rage, frustration and hate. You have seen their faces as you lumber along in your law-abiding fashion - the bulging eyes, the white-knuckled death grip on the wheel, the flipped finger. These are the choleric signs of the times and it's a wonder more of these sad and highly dangerous people don't die of heart attacks while trying to pass a cable car on the wrong side. (Herb Caen, *San Francisco Chronicle*, September 23, 1979)

We elicit from patients stories of their experiences while driving (all patients have poignant stories to tell!), and ask them to systematically examine all Type A

187

characteristics involved. It is important to emphasize these characteristics by writing them on the board, repeating them, and continually eliciting them from the group to insure that all patients understand. We have found that it is unwise to assume comprehension has occurred without repeated exposure and review.

Another good starting point is lectures and discussion on the physiologic implications of chronic TABP. Simple, short lectures on the relationship between behavior and physiologic variables (e.g., heart rate, blood pressure, norepinephrine, cortisol, platelet aggregation, and endogenous cholesterol) can provide patients with an intellectual understanding of why they need to reduce their TABP. They can also observe directly the relationship between behavior and physiology by practicing physical and cognitive relaxation using simple biofeedback devices. Our most successful device was the biodot, a temperature sensitive dot that sticks to the wrist (Medical Device Corporation, 1555 Bellefontaine Street N. Drive, Indianapolis, IN 46202).

It is wise to confine these early discussions to observation of the TABP in *other people*, since defensiveness and denial at this stage tend to be high. Lyndon Johnson provides an excellent example of the TABP and its familial roots. In her biography of Johnson, Kearns (1976) describes Johnson's perceptions of inadequate maternal love and his use of repression as a defense against it.

> It was then that he began to talk more and more about his childhood...A painful story of an unhappy boy trapped in a divided home, relentlessly tumbled among the impossible demands of an unyielding mother, love offered and then denied in seeming punishment; contempt for a father who had failed, admiration for a father who was a model for Texas manhood; commanded to be what he could not be, forced to become what he was not. How different from his earlier public descriptions--the rags-to-riches rise from a happy childhood, guided by an adoring mother and the example of a manly, principled father. (p. 17)

To illustrate the connection between overt Type A manifestations and low self-esteem, various character sketches were used, such as this one of Peter Sellers, as related by David Niven at the time of Sellers' death.

> Peter Sellers was expensive, difficult, ungracious, despotic; a man who would fire directors and turn scripts upside down; bitter, depressed, lonely, in a constant state of turmoil; vexatious, quarrelsome, distrustful, self-destructive, neurotic, and arrogant...Even when he was right on top of the mountain, Peter's advisers were constantly trying to restrain him from leaping at the very next film presented to him because he was genuinely afraid that he would not be offered another...Niven recalled that a few years ago he and Sellers attended a memorial service for Noel Coward. "As we walked out into the sunshine, Peter said: 'I do hope no one will ever arrange that sort of thing for me.' I asked him why. He looked a little sad and said 'Because I don't think anyone will show up.'" (*London Times*, September 8, 1980)

A description of track star, Mary Decker, makes the same point about the connection between the TABP and low self-esteem. Says a former coach,

> What you've got to understand about Mary is that she judges her worth as a person solely by what she accomplishes on the track. It is scary to contemplate, but the competitive nature that we so admire in this woman is actually a huge personality flaw. (*Newsweek*, August 5, 1983)

As treatment progresses and an atmosphere of supportive trust is established, patients begin to identify aspects of their own TABP. Therapists should capitalize on these opportunities by helping patients to explore and clarify these observations. They should draw others in by asking for reports of similar feelings, keeping in mind that group members will be at different levels of openness and receptivity. As more and more patients acknowledge their Type A tendencies, group leaders can increasingly direct discussions toward these topics.

Intimate discussions about personal versions of the TABP ensued when patients were asked to write their own obituaries and read them to the group. One RCPP group leader habitually asked patients to "Listen to others' angry comments and, instead of listening with regard to the *object*, listen to what it says about the persons themselves. You think that every time you tear someone else down you build your own self-esteem. In actuality, you tear yourself down." Another strategy is to make a habit of following discussions with the question "Have you noticed any Type A behaviors in yourself during this group?" Table 3 (page 191) presents a list of some Type A behaviors likely to occur during group discussions. Therapists would do well to memorize this list to enable them to make on-the-spot observations.

MODIFYING THE TYPE A BEHAVIOR PATTERN BY RAISING SELF-ESTEEM

The psychological precursors of the TABP are not well understood. One hypothesis, based upon observations of Type A college students, suggests that the TABP is motivated by an exaggerated need for control (Glass, 1977). Another view argues that hostility is at the heart of the TABP (Williams et al., 1980). Our observations of coronary patients have led us to propose that both need for control and hostility are motivated by low self-esteem. To the extent that self-esteem is low, Type A manifestations are high (Figure 3). Accordingly, to produce a sustained reduction in the TABP, one must raise self-esteem.

In contrast to the focus in the early stages of treatment on the undesired behavior (Type A), in the latter stages of treatment the focus is shifted to the desired behavior (high self-esteem). Self-esteem has two components (Branden, 1969). One is the perception of some degree of control (Glass, 1977) or self-efficacy (Bandura, 1982) in one's life. That is, the feeling that one's actions result in desired outcomes. The other is a positive perception of one's worth as a person.

Increasing Perceptions of Control. Type As commonly struggle for control as a way to ward off feelings of having little control. These feelings are a logical outcome of a narrow view of the nature of control. Type As believe that being in control is synonymous with controlling the environment (i.e., other people, situations). This works well in situations where such control is possible, but breaks down in situations where it is not. An alternative belief is that control has two components--

TABLE 3: A SELECTED LIST OF COMMON TYPE A BEHAVIORS, ATTITUDES, AND
ENVIRONMENTAL DETERMINANTS LIKELY TO EMERGE DURING GROUP
DISCUSSIONS

OVERT BEHAVIOR	Hostility
	Relives anger about past incidents
	Hypersensitive to criticism: is defensive, rationalizes own actions
	Argues tenaciously to win small points
	Becomes annoyed at trivial errors of others
	Expresses strong opinions
	Challenges validity of other's statements
	Is short-tempered
	Appears edgy
	Time Urgency
	Interrupts others
	Listens poorly
	Engages in polyphasic behavior, thoughts
	Speaks rapidly, with acceleration of terminal words
ENVIRONMENTAL DETERMINANTS	Trivial situations which are uncontrollable, unexpected
	Driving a car
	Waiting for someone who is late
	Waiting in line
	Interpersonal challenge
	People who talk too much with nothing to say
	"Incompetent" telephone operators, clerks in stores, waitresses/waiters, bank tellers
	Busy signals on the phone
	Ongoing struggle with family member, work associate
SIGNS AND SYMPTOMS OF PHYSIOLOGICAL REACTIVITY	Tense body posture
	Fast, jerky movements
	Repetitive movements: knee jiggling, finger tapping
	Expiratory sighing
	Tic-like grimaces
COVERT ATTI-TUDES AND BELIEFS	Egocentrism: dominates conversations; is interested in self only; narcissistic
	Suspiciousness: distrusts others' motives
	Competitiveness: belittles achievements of others, perceives other group members as adversaries
	Resentment: harbors feelings of ill will toward others
	Prejudice: has stereotyped generalizations about groups
	Deterministic world view: believes self to be a pawn of the environment rather than active determiner of fate
	Short-term perspective: deals with problems from immediate consequences
	Belief in inherent injustice: acts like the policeman of the world

control over others *and* control over one's reactions to others (Weisz, Rothbaum, & Blackburn, 1984). This belief has more pragmatic value since in reality one can *seldom* control others, but can *always* control one's reactions to others. Thus if both methods of control are in one's repertoire, the perception of being in control is maximized.

From a therapeutic point of view, Type A patients need to adopt better skills at exerting direct control over others. Far more importantly, they need to develop an appreciation of the power of indirect control where others are influenced by assuming control, not over them, but over one's reactions to them. The first skill we will present is aimed at improving direct control; the latter two are aimed at improving indirect or self-control.

Assertiveness. When it is necessary to stand up for one's rights, to make reasonable requests or demands of others, or to refuse to comply with unreasonable demands, assertiveness is needed. Characteristically, Type As respond to such situations with anger and aggression and/or passive resentment and avoidance. Both reactions are counter-productive: they result in strong and/or sustained physiologic and cognitive arousal with little chance for accomplishing one's goals.

Type As justify their anger and aggression because it gets results. But this position fails to make a distinction between short-term and long-term gains. Short-term compliance may be achieved, but in the long term forced compliance tends not to last. Furthermore, aggression can be viewed as a sign of weakness. Gandhi made this connection when he observed "Violence of any kind, no matter how justified at times, is, in itself, demeaning."

To turn an aggressive response into an assertive one, the emotional intensity of the statement must be reduced. In contrast to an explosive demand, an assertive statement is a rational declaration. One way to reduce the emotional intensity of a response is to learn the importance of the timing of a declaration. Emotional reactivity is a function of time (Folkman & Lazarus, 1985). The immediate response to a conflict tends to be emotional, but over time, it tends to be replaced by a more rational appraisal. To make this time trend work to the patients' advantage, they should be taught to buy time. That is, to introduce some filler comments (e.g., "Let me see if I understand what you are saying..."; "Let me think about this for a day/hour/few minutes") that permit a more rational appraisal and response.

Assertive responses also require attention to the psychomotor phenomena that accompany the responses. Characteristics of assertive responses include appropriate volume, emphasis, eye contact, and a complete elaboration of the problems/feelings so that the request can be adequately understood. The interested reader might see G. Bower and S. Bower (1976) for an excellent discussion of these issues. Drilling in the psychomotor phenomena accompanying assertive responses is a central component of most assertiveness training programs.

Group sessions can be used to practice assertive responses. Table 4 presents some hypothetical situations in which assertiveness skills can be role played. It is generally more effective, however, for role-play exercises to be based on actual patient problems.

TABLE 4: HYPOTHETICAL SITUATIONS WITH WHICH
TO ROLE PLAY ASSERTIVE SKILLS

SITUATION 1

NARRATOR: In this scene, picture yourself standing in a ticket line outside of a theater. You've been in line now for at least 10 minutes, and it's getting pretty close to show time. You're still pretty far from the front of the line, and you're starting to wonder whether there will be enough tickets left. There you are, waiting patiently, when two people walk up to someone in front of you and begin talking. They're obviously all friends, and they're going to the same movie. You look quickly at your watch and notice that the show starts in just 2 minutes. Just then, one of the newcomers says to his friend, "Hey, the line's a mile long...How about if we cut in here with you?"

PERSON IN LINE: "Sure, come on, a couple more won't make any difference."

NARRATOR: And as the two people squeeze in line between you and their friend, one of them looks at you and says: "Excuse me. You don't mind if we cut in, do you?"

SITUATION 2

You have just come home from a hard day's work, dead tired. Your wife informs you that she has accepted an invitation for you both to visit some friends that evening. You are definitely not in the mood to go out.

WIFE: "I'm looking forward to seeing these folks tonight. Let's go right after we eat."

Physical Relaxation. An ability to physically relax in the face of daily stressors is the cornerstone of most stress reduction programs. Patients who learn to switch from arousal to relaxation develop feelings of control from having the ability to calm down while in the midst of demands.

Many Type A patients have become habituated to the feeling of arousal ("anger junkies"). Initial attempts to switch from a familiar feeling of arousal to an unfamiliar feeling of relaxation evoke fears of being out of control, and are often accompanied by resistance. Practice at home, between group sessions, helps patients to become more familiar with the relaxed state. To sensitize patients to the difference between the relaxed and aroused states we use biodots (as described earlier).

Demonstration of skill at relaxation during the group sessions is not the final goal. More important, and much more difficult, is to learn to incorporate moments of relaxation into a daily schedule. Once patients become sensitive to the feeling of relaxation, they can use any of a variety of strategies on a daily basis, including deep muscle relaxation, meditation, prayer, passing the time of day with a stranger, and enjoying a brisk walk or a humorous exchange with a co-worker. Stroebel (1982) has written about quick relaxation, an accelerated relaxation strategy that takes less than a minute to perform in response to unexpected stressors.

Cognitive Restructuring. Cognitive restructuring is based upon the principle that an individual is an active construer of experience (Bandura, 1977). That is, an emotional reaction is produced by demands in the environment *and* one's perceptions of those demands. Since perceptions play a role in determining an emotional response, they can be used as a target for the purpose of altering that response. William James (1890) was among the first to make this observation. He stated, "The greatest discovery of our generation is that human beings, by changing the inner attitudes of their minds, can change the outer aspects of their lives."

An example can serve to illustrate a practical application of cognitive restructuring. An individual with a well developed TABP arrives at a concert early to insure that he gets a good seat. Just before it begins, his view is blocked by latecomers who, because of the large crowd, have not been able to find seats. The Type A becomes irritated at the unfairness of the situation and the rudeness of the latecomers. He stews throughout the concert, abruptly leaves it, or angrily insists that the latecomers move.

The Type A's ability to achieve his goal (to enjoy the concert) was blocked by the environment (the latecomers standing in his way). If the environment is (or is expected to be) intransigent (the latecomers refuse to move), he is left with excess physical and emotional reactivity and nagging fears of having limited control.

Cognitive restructuring in this situation might follow this chain of thought: "Certainly this situation is unfair. But, in addition, it is a hook--no different from the scare I had with the reckless driver on the highway, the problems I had finding a parking space, the delay at the grocery store, or the parking ticket I received yesterday. These trivial annoyances happen all of the time. I've waited a long time to enjoy this concert and I am not going to fail to do so by letting myself get hooked by this one."

The point here is that the situation has a variety of descriptors. If the choice is made to perceive the situation as a hook, instead of a transgression, irritation is reduced and the perception of control (in this case of self-control) is increased. With reactivity low, it is easier to change a potentially aggressive response into an assertive one and at the same time increase one's influence over others. Patients often report amusement at recognizing hooks. Feeling humor in the face of adversity may be a response to being freed from the prison of fixed perceptions.

The hook analogy is one way to restructure experience. But a variety of alternative perceptions can be developed. For example, patients may be asked to practice a drill where they must substitute pity, understanding, and forgiveness for anger and irritation. We also quote observations of famous people. For example, Winston Churchill might discuss the concert incident by observing "When a man cannot distinguish a great from a small event, he is of no use." Alternatively, we might respond to the concert situation by saying "five dollars worth of physiology for five cents worth of irritation."

Cognitive restructuring is not appropriate for all situations, as this would encourage passivity in the face of clear moral and ethical transgressions. The point here is not to replace, but to expand, response repertoires. By so doing, choice expands and, at the same time, the feeling of freedom and control increases.

Increasing Feelings of Self-Worth. The private estimate of one's own worth is an important component of self-esteem. It is unalterable to the extent that the criteria used to judge it remain unaltered. In the case of the Type A patient, these criteria tend to be narrow, transitory, and conditional. A narcissistic pre-occupation with the self and individual achievement takes precedence over more enduring sources of self-worth such as intimacy, altruism, and commitment. Because self-worth for most Type As is tied directly to achievement, the intensity of competition to achieve rewards is great and the cost of failure is high.

In contrast, persons with high self-worth make self-appraisals using a variety of sources. When setbacks occur in one area of their lives, other areas can be relied upon for continued affirmation. Thus, the self-perception remains relatively stable.

Persons with high self-worth often have a long-term perspective on life. This comes from having an overall sense of purpose which may take a variety of forms, such as commitment to their work, to family, or to a religious group. Because this purpose is enduring, it provides direction to help in weathering the vicissitudes of daily life.

Persons with high self-worth commonly have a broad perspective on life. They see themselves as small units within a larger context. This provides them with a humility that counteracts egocentrism and the tendency to take oneself too seriously.

Probably the most important quality associated with high self-worth is the ability to give and receive love (J. Powell, 1976). Intimate relationships can raise feelings of self-worth if they are unconditional. They provide support and perspective during shifts in transitory environmental circumstances, and provide a sense of being needed when that support and perspective is offered to another. The less personal version of this quality is altruism. Positive expectations of others generate good will and produce security in the knowledge that others wish one well.

This sketch of an individual with high self-worth provides directions for helping patients to raise their own levels. One approach, we call general personality enhancement, is based upon the idea that patients should be reinforced for expanding the criteria upon which they base their estimates of self-worth. They have many eggs, but they have put all of them into only one basket. The task in therapy is to help patients rediscover (or discover) their aesthetic sides. They are encouraged to bring hobbies to the group and are assigned readings from the classics. We announce aesthetic offerings in the community, discuss quotes of famous people, and have patients practice such drills as "stop to observe the leaves on the trees and the songs of birds."

Discovery of the importance of aesthetic appreciation is perhaps more delicate than it first appears. Type A patients tend to have a short-range perspective and to be overly pragmatic. When things are reduced to short-term cost-benefit ratios, the benefits of broadening interests are much less apparent than the costs of cutting down work time. Drilling can be particularly useful as a way to promote initial interest. Table 5 (pages 198-199) presents a list of drills and aphorisms that we have used to foster personality enhancement.

Another approach to increasing self-worth is to encourage self-acceptance. In Friedman and Rosenman's first book on Type A behavior (1974), they presented a description of an individual who had achieved self-acceptance, despite past limitations and failures. They report,

> When asked how a charming and relaxed doctor avoided Type A behavior, he smiled and said, "A few years ago, I faced up to the truth that I always had been and always will be a second-rate physician. After I realized this, it was quite easy to begin to relax." (p. 175)

At some point, most everyone who is engaged in a struggle quits it. Some, like this physician, quit by accepting what they are and enjoying what they have. Others quit but deny any limitations and indulge in bitterness and resentment about what could have been. Still others quit by destroying themselves physically, financially, legally, or socially (Friedman & Ulmer, 1984).

One way to increase acceptance of oneself is to lower expectations. William James (1890) observed that self-esteem is the result of achievements divided by expecta-

---

TABLE 5:   QUOTES, APHORISMS, AND DRILLS USEFUL
           IN THE PROMOTION ON PERSONALITY ENHANCEMENT

Quotes and Aphorisms

"Up to the age of thirty or beyond it, poetry of many kinds gave me great pleasure; and even as a schoolboy I took intense delight in Shakespeare, especially in the historical plays. I have also said that pictures formerly gave me considerable, and music very great, delight. But now for many years I cannot endure to read a line of poetry. I have tried lately to read Shakespeare, and found it so intolerably dull that it nauseated me. I have also almost lost my taste for pictures or music...My mind seems to have become a kind of machine for grinding general laws out of large collections of facts; but why this should have caused the atrophy of that part of the brain alone on which the higher tastes depend, I cannot conceive...If I had to live my life again, I would have made a rule to read some poetry and listen to some music at least once every week; for perhaps the parts of my brain now atrophied would thus have been kept alive through use. The loss of these tastes is a loss of happiness and may possibly be injurious to the intellect, and more probably to the moral character, by enfeebling the emotional part of our nature."--Charles Darwin

"It is only with the heart that one can see rightly. What is essential is invisible to the eye."--St. Exupery

"Culture is acquainting ourselves with the best that has ever been known and said in the World."--Matthew Arnold

"To let friendship die away by negligence and silence is to voluntarily throw away one of the greatest comforts of this weary pilgrimage."--Samuel Johnson

"The next thing most like living one's life over again seems to be a recollection of that life."--Benjamin Franklin

"Human felicity is produced not so much by the great pieces of good fortune that seldom happen, as by the little advantages that occur every day."--Benjamin Franklin

"On the average, a man having no avocations on retiring receives only 13 Social Security checks before he dies."--Unknown

"The chief ornament of a house is the friends who frequent it."--Unknown

"Success is getting what you want; happiness is wanting what you get."--Unknown

"There are reasons of the heart about which reason knows nothing."--Pascal

Drills

Ask a member of the family about their day's activities.
Verbalize your affection to spouse/children.
Practice smiling and look at your face carefully to see if you detect
     hostility or tension.

198

Drills (Continued):

Recall memories for 10 minutes.
Note carefully tree, plant, bush.
Listen to music and do nothing else for 15 minutes.
Visit an art museum, aquarium, or park.
Invite someone to lunch and keep your friend talking about his/her
    interests--not yours.
Take time out to plan a new hobby.
Look at old photographs in albums. If they are in disorder, put them in
    order.
Say "good morning" or "good afternoon" with a soft voice.

---

tions (Self-Esteem = Achievements/Expectations). One way to raise self-esteem, then, is to lower expectations (by accepting what one is).

Another aid in helping patients to accept themselves as they are is the experience of unconditional positive regard from someone they respect. The group leader can serve this role, but it can come from other sources as well. For example, during the RCPP, an unintended development occurred. Under the direction of a warm and very caring field director who was a nurse, the office staff assumed a primary responsibility in giving care, concern, and consideration to each of the 1000 participants. The field director herself assumed the crucial role of mother surrogate to these patients, always making time to talk, provide information, and offering support as needed. She knew almost all participants by first name and could recount details of their situations and physical conditions.

Programs aimed at altering the TABP often present rich and sophisticated content, but fail to acknowledge the importance of caring. When treatment goals involve such delicate issues as raising self-esteem and reducing hostility, caring is critical.

DETERMINING WHEN TO END

Type A counseling is likely to result in diverse outcomes for individual patients. In the RCPP, we observed considerable differences in response to treatment. After 3 years, 21% of those who entered treatment presented no evidence of change, 27% presented some evidence of change, 18% presented clear evidence of change, and 34% had dropped out (Friedman et al., 1984).

We do not know if 3 years of treatment is necessary or just sufficient. In the RCPP, significant reductions in cardiac incidence were observed after 3 years. But in a subsequent study of Type A alteration in healthy middle-aged men, 42% of the 62 subjects randomized to receive the same Type A counseling achieved, in 20 sessions, the same level of behavior change as that observed in the RCPP after 44 sessions (Gill et al., 1985). Similar levels of behavior change were observed following a 10-week treatment in the Montreal Type A intervention project (Roskies, 1985). Since these latter two studies failed to evaluate change using hard CHD endpoints, the exact meaning of these findings is difficult to determine. They do, however, raise questions about the optimum number of sessions necessary to reduce cardiovascular risk.

Ideally, decisions about ending counseling should be made on a case-by-case basis. The development of an internal Type A self-monitor (mentioned earlier) is an important sign of meaningful change. Patients could be terminated when it was demonstrated that they achieved this level of change. However, since this approach may prove costly, decisions about number of group sessions are often made before treatment begins. In lieu of empirical guidelines for the optimum number of treatment sessions, it is important to keep in mind that Type A counseling is justifiable only if it can produce *sustained* behavior change, for such change is necessary to promote CHD risk reduction. This is an ambitious undertaking and the possibility of erring on the side of too few sessions is great, especially when considerations of cost weigh heavily. It is our opinion that investigators and clinicians restricted to short-term treatment approaches would be well-advised against conducting interventions designed to alter the TABP.

GROUP LEADER CHARACTERISTICS

Group leaders in the RCPP came from a variety of theoretical orientations. Although any orientation can be used to convey the content of the message, the process by which the message is conveyed must incorporate an understanding of the principles of behavior change. A solid basic knowledge of the pathological and clinical aspects of CHD enables leaders to teach patients about the connection between behavior and CHD. An awareness of some of the spiritual wisdom and psychological insights found in the classics and humanities also provides a basis to help patients reclaim their atrophied personalities.

Therapists in the RCPP were experienced clinicians. They looked and acted like mature, sensible, respectable, and successful professionals. Thus, recommendations made for change, which at first glance appear to be ridiculous to some patients, were often followed in good faith. The leaders were effective communicators who had the ability to inspire others. Use of psychological jargon spells disaster when counseling Type As because their difficulties in listening to simple English are multiplied when jargon is used. Successful leaders were sincere and believed in what they said. Very importantly, they had a good sense of humor and could laugh at their own foibles and silliness as easily as they could laugh at those of others.

Although all of the foregoing characteristics are desirable in a Type A leader, there are perhaps two that are most important. The first is a thorough understanding of the TABP. The greatest advances in alteration of beliefs and attitudes came during "teachable moments"-- the times patients struggle in the group with a personal problem. If leaders are quick to recognize the underlying Type A attitude that creates the problem, they can help the patient to gain a similar perspective. This helps the patient to attach great personal meaning to the principles of Type A alteration. If the leader does not have a thorough understanding of the cognitive aspects of the TABP, these unexpected opportunities pass unnoticed.

To gain this in-depth understanding of the TABP, leaders should be actively involved in altering their own TABP. For this reason, it is perhaps the case that coping Type A group leaders (those who are in the process of altering their own TABP) may be especially effective. This excerpt is from a letter sent to the RCPP by one of the group leaders who, along with his group members, became actively involved in altering his own TABP.

> Type A has become for me a living reality from the abstract concept of my first contact with you. It has become a metaphor which at times assumes transcendental proportion. In the process of getting to know my group members and helping them to transform their own Type A personalities, I have become profoundly influenced myself. My wife, the final arbiter of changes in my personality, has already given me an A minus (she grades easily) for changes in my approach. My

former vesuvian temperament has mellowed considerably.

Leaders can bring their patients only to a level that is as high as the highest level at which they themselves are functioning. If they do not have insight into their own behavior, are not willing to freely admit to it in the group, and are not actively attempting to modify it, their effectiveness may be lessened.

The second key leader characteristic is the element of caring. Type A counseling is, at one level, counseling to help individuals improve self-esteem. Perhaps more than any other thing a leader can do for these patients is to provide them with what many did not adequately secure in childhood--unconditional love and affection from a respected parent figure. Caring is a necessary, but not sufficient, characteristic. The caring must be rendered along with expertise about the TABP and the principles of behavior change. This caring and competent leader must at times be tough on certain patients. But if the tough approach is blended with respect and genuine caring, growth can emerge.

A FINAL WORD

Type A patients present a difficult clinical challenge. They are locked in a struggle and feel that if they simply persist long enough they will win. At some level, the leader represents a threat to the attainment of this goal. Thus, it is not uncommon for free-floating hostility to be vented directly at the leader. What patients do not realize is that this struggle may be slowly killing them. The very best outcome that can be aspired to by the conclusion of counseling is that they get to the point where they begin to ask themselves "Is this worth dying for?"

Lynda H. Powell, PhD, is an Assistant Professor of Epidemiology and Public Health at the Yale Medical School. Prior to this appointment, she served as research psychologist and biostatistician for the Recurrent Coronary Prevention Project, a clinical trial aimed at studying the secondary prevention of CHD by reducing Type A behavior. She received a PhD in counseling psychology from Stanford University and has published articles on adolescent stress, assessment of Type A behavior, and intervention with Type A patients. General interests include the relationship between patterns of psychosocial stress and chronic disease, and lifestyle intervention. Dr. Powell may be contacted at the Department of Epidemiology and Public Health, School of Medicine, Yale University, P. O. Box 3333, 60 College Street, New Haven, CT 06510.

Carl E. Thoresen, PhD, is a Professor of Education and Psychology at Stanford University and is currently the principal investigator of a 3-year follow-up study of the RCPP and the principal investigator of a multi-year study of chronic stress in children. Dr. Thoresen has published several books on subjects such as behavioral counseling, sleep, and self-control, and has authored or co-authored over 60 journal articles and 20 book chapters. He has also served as Series Editor of over eight books on the topic of health behavior and self-management. He is the founder of Learning House, a residential treatment facility for emotionally disturbed children in Palo Alto. He has twice received the Outstanding Research Award of the American Personnel and Guidance Association. He currently serves on the governing Council of Representatives of the American Psychological Association as well as its Education and Training Board. Dr. Thoresen can be contacted at the School of Education, Stanford University, Stanford, CA 94305.

RESOURCES

Bandura, A. (1977). *Social Learning Theory.* Englewood Cliffs, NJ: Prentice-Hall.
Bandura, A. (1982). Self-efficacy mechanism in human agency. *The American Psychologist, 37,* 122-147.
Blumenthal, J. A., Williams, R. B., Jr., Kong, Y., Schonberg, S. M., & Thompson, L. W. (1978). Type A behavior pattern and coronary atherosclerosis. *Circulation, 58,* 634-639.
Bower, G., & Bower, S. (1976). *Asserting Yourself: A Practical Guide for Positive Change.* Boston: Addison-Wesley.

Branden, N. (1969). *The Psychology of Self-Esteem.* New York: Bantam.

Caffrey, B. (1969). Behaviour patterns and personality characteristics related to prevalence rates of coronary heart disease in American monks. *Journal of Chronic Diseases, 22,* 93-103.

Carruthers, M. E. (1969). Aggression and atheroma. *Lancet, 2,* 1170-1171.

Case, R. B., Heller, S. S., Case, N. B., Moss, A. J., & the Multicenter Post-Infarction Research Group. (1985). Type A behavior and survival after acute myocardial infarction. *New England Journal of Medicine, 312,* 737-741.

Dimsdale, J. F., Gilbert, J., Hutter, A. M., Hackett, T. P., & Block, P. C. (1981). Predicting cardiac morbidity based on risk factors and coronary angiographic findings. *American Journal of Cardiology, 47,* 73-76.

Dunbar, H. F. (1943). *Psychosomatic Diagnosis.* New York: Hoeber.

Folkman, S., & Lazarus, R. S. (1985). If it changes it must be a process: A study of emotion and coping during three stages of a college examination. *Journal of Personality and Social Psychology, 48,* 150-170.

Friedman, M. (1969). *Pathogenesis of Coronary Artery Disease.* New York: McGraw-Hill.

Friedman, M., Byers, S. O., & Rosenman, R. H. (1965). Effect of unsaturated fats upon lipemia and conjunctival circulation. *Journal of the American Medical Association, 193,* 882-886.

Friedman, M., Manwaring, J. H., Rosenman, R. H., Donlon, G., Ortega, D., & Grube, S. M. (1973). Instantaneous and sudden death: Clinical and pathological differentiation in coronary artery disease. *Journal of the American Medical Association, 225,* 1319-1328.

Friedman, M., & Rosenman, R. H. (1974). *Type A Behavior and Your Heart.* New York: Alfred A. Knopf.

Friedman, M., Rosenman, R. H., & Byers, S. O. (1964). Serum lipids and conjunctival circulation after fat ingestion in men exhibiting Type A behavior pattern. *Circulation, 29,* 874-886.

Friedman, M., Thoresen, C. E., & Gill, J. J. (1981). Type A behavior: Its role, detection and alteration in patients with ischemic heart disease. In J. W. Hurst (Ed.), *Update V: The Heart* (pp. 81-100). New York: McGraw-Hill.

Friedman, M., Thoresen, C. E., Gill, J. J., Powell, L. H., Ulmer, D., Thompson, L., Price, V. A., Rabin, D. D., Breall, W. S., Dixon, T., Levy, R., & Bourg, E. (1984). Alteration of Type A behavior and reduction in cardiac recurrences in post-myocardial infarction patients. *American Heart Journal, 108,* 237-248.

Friedman, M., Thoresen, C. E., Gill, J. J., Ulmer, D., Thompson, L., Powell, L., Price, V., Elek, S. R., Rabin, D. D., Breall, W. S., Piaget, G., Dixon, T., Bourg, E., Levy, R. A., & Tasto, D. L. (1982). Feasibility of altering Type A behavior pattern after myocardial infarction. Recurrent Coronary Prevention Project Study: Methods, baseline results, and preliminary findings. *Circulation, 66,* 83-92.

Friedman, M., & Ulmer, D. K. (1984). *Treating Type A Behavior and Your Heart.* New York: Alfred A. Knopf.

Gill, J. J., Price, V. A., Friedman, M., Thoresen, C. E., Powell, L. H., Ulmer, D., Brown, B., & Drews, F. R. (1985). Reduction in Type A behavior in healthy middle-aged American military officers. *American Heart Journal, 110,* 503-514.

Glass, D. C. (1977). *Behavior Patterns, Stress, and Coronary Disease.* Hillsdale, NJ: John Wiley & Sons.

Haynes, S. G., Feinleib, M., & Kannel, W. B. (1980). The relationship of psychosocial factors to coronary heart disease in the Framingham study. III. Eight-year incidence of coronary heart disease. *American Journal of Epidemiology, 111,* 37-58.

James, W. (1890). *The Principles of Psychology* (Vols. I & II). New York: Dover Publications, Inc.

Kearns, D. (1976). *Lyndon Johnson and the American Dream.* New York: Harper & Row.

Layden, M. (1977). *Escaping the Hostility Trap.* Englewood Cliffs, NJ: Prentice-Hall.

Manchester, W. (1978). *American Caesar: Douglas MacArthur, 1880-1964.* New York: Little.

Menninger, K. A., & Menninger, W. C. (1936). Psychoanalytic observations in cardiac disorders. *American Heart Journal, 11,* 10-21.

Osler, W. (1892). *Lectures on Angina Pectoris and Allied States.* New York: Appleton.

Powell, J. (1976). *Fully Human, Fully Alive.* Niles, IL: Argus.

Powell, L. H., Friedman, M., Thoresen, C. E., Gill, J. J., & Ulmer, D. K. (1984). Can the Type A behavior pattern be altered after myocardial infarction? A second year report from the Recurrent Coronary Prevention Project. *Psychosomatic Medicine, 46,* 293-313.

Powell, L. H., Thoresen, C. E., & Friedman, M. (1985). Modification of the Type A behavior pattern after myocardial infarction. In H. Hofmann (Ed.), *Primary and Secondary Prevention of Coronary Heart Disease. Results of New Trials* (pp. 119-131). New York: Springer-Verlag.

The Review Panel on Coronary-Prone Behavior and Coronary Heart Disease. (1981). Coronary-prone behavior and coronary heart disease: A critical review. *Circulation, 63,* 1199-1215.

Rosenman, R. H., Brand, R. J., Jenkins, C. D., Friedman, M., Straus, R., & Wurm, M. (1975). Coronary heart disease in the Western Collaborative Group Study: Final follow-up experience of 8 1/2 years. *Journal of the American Medical Association, 233,* 872-877.

Roskies, E. (1985). *Intervention with Healthy Men: Results of the Montreal Type A Intervention Project.* Paper presented at the Society of Behavioral Medicine Sixth Annual Meeting, New Orleans, LA.

Ruberman, W., Weinblatt, E., Goldberg, J. D., & Chaudhary, B. S. (1984). Psychosocial influences on mortality after myocardial infarction. *New England Journal of Medicine, 311,* 552-594.

Scherwitz, L. (1985). *The Type A Behavior Pattern and Coronary Heart Disease: Issues and Problems* Paper presented at the Society of Behavioral Medicine Sixth Annual Meeting, New Orleans, LA.

Shekelle, R. B., Hulley, S. B., Neaton, J. D., Billings, J. H., Borhani, N. O., Gerace, T. A., Jacobs, D. R., Lasser, N. L., Mittlemark, M. B., & Stamler, J. for the Multiple Risk Factor Intervention Trial Research Group. (1985). The MRFIT behavior pattern study. II. Type A behavior and incidence of coronary heart disease. *American Journal of Epidemiology, 122,* 559-570.

Stroebel, C. F. (1982). *QR: The Quieting Reflex.* New York: G. P. Putnam's Sons.

Suinn, R. M. (1982). Intervention with Type A behavior. *Journal of Consulting and Clinical Psychology, 50,* 933-949.

Terkel, S. (1974). *Working.* New York: Pantheon.

Thoresen, C. E. (1985). *Reducing the Type A Behavior Pattern in Post-Infarct Patients.* Paper presented at the

Society of Behavioral Medicine Sixth Annual Meeting, New Orleans, LA.

Thoresen, C. E., Friedman, M., Gill, J. J., & Ulmer, D. K. (1982). The Recurrent Coronary Prevention Project. Some preliminary findings. *Acta Med Scandinavia (Suppl.), 660,* 172-192.

Thoresen, C. E., Friedman, M., Powell, L. H., Gill, J. J., & Ulmer, D. (1985). Altering the Type A behavior pattern in postinfarction patients. *Journal of Cardiopulmonary Rehabilitation, 5,* 258-266.

Thoresen, C. E., & Mahoney, M. J. (1974). *Behavioral Self-Control.* New York: Holt, Rinehart, and Winston, Inc.

Thoresen, C. E., & Ohman, A. (in press). The Type A behavior pattern: A person-environment interaction perspective. In D. Magnusson & A. Ohman (Eds.), *Psychopathology: An Interaction Perspective.* New York: Academic Press.

Thoresen, C. E., Telch, M. J., & Eagleston, J. R. (1981). Approaches to altering the Type A behavior pattern. *Psychosomatics, 22,* 474-481.

Weiner, H. (1977). *Psychobiology and Human Disease.* New York: Elsevier North-Holland.

Weisz, J. R., Rothbaum, F. M., & Blackburn, T. C. (1984). Standing out and standing in. The Psychology of control in America and Japan. *The American Psychologist, 39,* 955-969.

Williams, R. B., Jr., Haney, T. L., Lee, K. L., Kong, Y. H., Blumenthal, J. A., & Whalen, R. E. (1980). Type A behavior, hostility, and coronary atherosclerosis. *Psychosomatic Medicine, 42,* 539-549.

PERSPECTIVES ON MEMORY RETRAINING OF PERSONS WITH COGNITIVE DEFICITS

Frederick A. Schmitt and Jonathan Farber

Cognitive rehabilitation is an activity that has emerged as clinicians working with neurologically impaired populations have broadened their objectives to include interventions as well as assessment. Many of the techniques used in cognitive rehabilitation are borrowed from the experimental literature on cognitive processes. The systematic study of applied interventions with brain-injured persons has only recently become a focus of some programs (Gianustos, 1980; Goldstein & Ruthven, 1983; Wilson, 1984). Candidates for cognitive rehabilitation are, for example, patients with a history of head trauma or cerebrovascular lesions (stroke), or who are in the early stages of a degenerative disease. Particularly for the former two groups of patients, cognitive rehabilitation is a component of a multidisciplinary treatment program that might include psychotherapy; speech, physical, and occupational therapy; and vocational rehabilitation, along with traditional medical interventions.

Theories concerning the physiological substrates of recovery of cognitive function are at present only speculative and controversial (see Craine, 1982 for a review). Some recovery of brain function does follow central nervous system (CNS) insult and this recovery may be enhanced through behavioral interventions (Luria, 1948/1963, 1963/1966). Due to the lack of a comprehensive empirical research base in this new field, however, clinicians must function flexibly and imaginatively in treating the brain-injured patient.

This chapter is intended as a brief summary of techniques and guidelines in one area of cognitive rehabilitation. Therapeutic efforts may be directed at dysfunctions in memory, attention, language, abstract reasoning, and social cognition. This chapter will focus on the rehabilitation of memory functions because (a) memory disturbances accompany a large proportion of localized and diffuse CNS disorders as well as a wide range of emotional problems; (b) even mild memory disturbances can have a profound impact on a person's vocational status, capacity for independent living, interpersonal relations, and psychological well-being; and (c) a wide range of therapeutic procedures can improve memory performance.

The following review will discuss: (a) assessment of memory disordered patients, (b) treatment strategies, (c) supportive or auxiliary psychological treatment, and (d) principles for program integration and implementation, adapted from mainstream behavior therapy.

MEMORY ASSESSMENT

Memory performance in almost any situation is theoretically determined by four factors. As described by Flavell and Wellman (1977) the difficulty of a given memory situation is determined by the type of information that a person is attempting to remember (e.g., names and faces vs. phone number) and by the situational (task) demands placed on the individual (e.g., immediate recall vs. recall at the end of the day). These two factors combine to determine the difficulty of the memory situation. Memory performance is also determined by person variables (e.g., mood, intellect) and available memory strategies. Performance may be less than optimal because of diminished cognitive resources, changes in mood or overwhelming difficulty in the type of material that the person is trying to remember. Rehabilitation of memory may be targeted at any of these areas. For instance, if a person has no concept of visual mnemonics and has problems remembering where a car was parked, training in visual imagery techniques may prove to be beneficial. Or, if anxiety tends to interfere with remembering, then providing relaxation therapy as a coping resource may improve remembering (Yesavage, Rose, & D. Spiegel, 1982). In the diagnosis and treatment of a memory disorder the therapist would ideally (Poon, 1980, 1984):

210

(a) determine the client's subjective complaints, (b) conduct an objective psychometric evaluation, (c) integrate emotional and psychosocial data, (d) determine relevant treatment, and (e) assess treatment effects at various intervals during therapy.

In evaluating the client's memory complaints, it is important to identify which information is not remembered and to evaluate person variables, cognitive abilities, and coping styles evidenced in day to day performance. Depending on the underlying nature of the memory disturbance, complaints may be vague and global or they may refer to specific instances. Often, it will be the client's family that provides this information. Regardless of the source and nature of a memory complaint, it is worthwhile to document these complaints as an initial step in remediation. It may be useful to corroborate these memory failures with significant others (e.g., spouse or family) and to obtain an estimate of the degree of disruption of the client's daily activities (Crovitz, Cordoni, Daniel, & Perlman, 1984).

The memory literature abounds with questionnaires designed to describe the subjective elements of memory functioning (Bennett-Levy & Powell, 1980; Sunderland, Harris, & Baddeley, 1983; Zelinski, Gilewski, & Thompson, 1980). Questionnaires can supplement the clinical interview by isolating and rank ordering individual memory strengths and weaknesses. They also provide useful therapeutic information when memory disturbances are secondary to emotional problems. An alternative approach involves the use of forgetting notebooks or diaries (Cavanaugh, Grady, & Perlmutter, 1983). Here memory abilities are assessed through the use of a daily log of times when the client's memory failed (e.g., when they realized or were reminded that they forgot).

Because many therapists are proficient in personality assessment techniques, a detailed discussion of these methods is not warranted. While it is helpful to relate problems such as depression to memory functioning (Popkin, Gallagher, Thompson, & Moore, 1982), assessment of situationally specific anxiety is useful as well. Often, clients who have experienced repeated memory difficulties become anxious when confronted with the task of remembering. They may be quite capable of recall in a nonanxious state. Finally, an analysis of potential reinforcement contingencies for forgetting should be conducted. Positive reinforcement may take the form of real or perceived attention or nurturance from significant others. Negative reinforcement may also be present in the form of onerous responsibilities that are avoided by convenient forgetting.

Equally important as the assessment of personal memory ability is the assessment of cognitive and neuropsychological status. Many clients seen for memory therapy are referred following various types of organic injuries. Neuropsychological assessment provides an index of the patient's cognitive resources as well as insights into brain behavioral relationships that may underlie specific memory problems. For example, a patient who has suffered a stroke might present with a test profile on neuropsychological assessment implicating a right hemisphere dysfunction. If this patient's complaints involve the inability to recall verbal information, then the use of visual imagery mnemonics (generally presumed to be mediated by right brain functioning) may not prove beneficial until much later in the patient's recovery of function. Objective testing, therefore, provides clues as to the causes of memory failure and can suggest treatment strategies. Brain injury does not only have lateralized effects on cognitive function, there are also the general effects of OBS (organic brain syndrome) as well. These are often manifested as a loss of problem solving skills and flexibility of thinking. We, therefore, urge that prior to memory rehabilitation a good neuropsychological evaluation or screening be obtained (Filskov, 1983), if a more complete battery of tests is not feasible.

MEMORY TESTS

Standardized tests of memory are useful in documenting memory complaints. They also provide insights into the functioning of the various hypothesized memory systems and can be used to monitor the effectiveness of training. Nevertheless, there are many problems inherent in the various memory tests available today. A discussion of these is beyond the scope of this overview. Instead, the reader is referred to reviews by Erikson and Scott (1977) and Erikson, Poon, and Walsh-Sweeney (1980). In our neuropsychological assessments we generally use the Russell Revision of the Wechsler Memory Scale (McCarty, Logue, Power, Ziesat, & Rosenthiel, 1980; Russell, 1975), and/or the Randt Memory Test (Randt, E. R. Brown, & Osborne, 1980). The Revised

Wechsler Memory Scale allows for semantic and figural memory comparisons while providing an impairment score comparable to the Halstead-Reitan impairment index. The Randt Memory Test provides for the assessment of a wide variety of memory abilities as well as five alternate forms that are useful for reassessment during therapy.

The mental status exam is an additional area of formal assessment relevant to the initiation of effective memory therapy. In many cases, a brief mental status exam provides an excellent screening of the patient's memory function (R. A. Kane & R. L. Kane, 1981). These measures provide a brief assessment of a person's basic knowledge store, orientation, and language skills. If mental status is severely compromised, much of the formal assessment of intellectual and memory functioning may be irrelevant and the appropriate therapeutic interventions may involve medical care or referral to reality orientation sessions (Greene, Nicol, & Jamieson, 1979).

Finally, as Baddeley (1984) suggested, knowledge of the general memory literature will provide the clinician with: "a general orientation and understanding, suggestions as to particular therapeutic techniques and finally, methodological help in evaluating such techniques" (p. 6). Maintaining contact with the memory literature can provide useful information regarding new diagnostic tools as well.

STRATEGIES FOR MEMORY IMPROVEMENT

Memory can be inefficient as a result of changes in medical, pharmacological, biochemical, and/or emotional variables. Regardless of the underlying cause(s) of a memory disturbance, the therapist's task is to evaluate the patient's existing strengths and weaknesses before determining the therapeutic goals and relevant mnemonic techniques. One useful conceptual framework described by A. L. Brown (1975) delineates three types of memory knowledge relevant to remediation of memory problems. These three categories are: (a) "Knowing," (b) "Knowing about Knowing," and (c) "Knowing How to Know."

First, knowing refers to an individual's dynamic knowledge system, internalized since birth through experience and education (another term might be Tulving's [1972] "semantic memory"). This mental encyclopedia includes the rules, definitions, and general knowledge that serve as a basis for cognitive behavior. Obviously, organic brain dysfunction disrupts this system. For example, an amnestic (e.g., with Korsakoff's disease) may not have access to information once stored in memory, while patients with progressive lesions may be losing whole sections of their mental library. Access to this knowledge base determines, in part, how efficiently memory works (Chi, 1978). Weingartner et al. (1982) have shown that the memory performance of depressed patients is reduced when they are required to remember material that is relatively unorganized (therefore requiring mental effort). Yet, when the material is organized for them by category, performance is essentially normal. Many internal and external mnemonics rely on organizing and fitting information with the individual's knowledge to make things more memorable.

Knowing about knowing is more commonly called "metamemory" (Flavell & Wellman, 1977). This refers to the introspective information that is available regarding the working's of one's own memory. While this is often elusive knowledge (even for adequate memorizers) it appears to be critical to the success of and continued usefulness of memory training. Patients who deny or are unaware of memory dysfunctions may be experiencing a metamemory problem. Similarly, metamemory may be malfunctioning when a memory strategy is not used in appropriate situations as is the case for many patients with frontal lobe disorders.

Knowing how to know encompasses the skills used to remember information. This category includes such diverse systems as writing notes to oneself, repetition, or even visualization of what is to be remembered. In general, these techniques are the crux of memory retraining. These categories are helpful when considered in the context of therapy. Often, it is the therapist who not only provides information on how to remember but also helps patients learn how their memory works. The following sections will focus on the more common techniques used to help patients know how to know.

EXTERNAL MNEMONIC STRATEGIES

Perhaps the most familiar methods of remembering involve some external device or aid for keeping track of what we wish to remember. These methods generally include lists, notebooks, schedules, calendars, filing systems, computers, and other persons. Use of a particular strategy is usually determined by the importance, amount, accuracy which is required, or distance in time of the information to be remembered. While the use of memory strategies increases with age (Hagen, Jongeward, & Kail, 1975), the efficient use of these methods depends on the individual's needs, ability, and assessment of the memory situation.

External memory storage can be an efficient and flexible form of memory rehabilitation. Lists, calendars, and schedules can be tailored to include the minimal amount of information (memory cues) necessary for adequate remembering. Or, they can be more detailed (step by step instructions) depending on the nature and degree of memory deficit (e.g., Crovitz et al., 1984). Often, the repeated use of these aids can also serve to internalize information so that reliance on extensive detail in these aids can be reduced.

Problems exist with these techniques, however. Foremost among these are the client's beliefs about using memory aids and the possible negative effect on self-image. Second, the degree of effort required to develop and maintain a schedule or memory notebook may lead persons to forget or simply refuse to use the aid. Third, patients may not use an external cueing system because of a lack of overall cognitive ability. Finally, memory impaired persons may have a conviction that there is nothing wrong with their memory. For example, one 72 year old gentleman who was seen after multiple small strokes felt that his memory was fine even though his wife described many incidents of memory failure. He had (for many years) maintained a notebook listing important events or information that was readily accessible in his shirt pocket. Although he repeatedly pointed to this memory aid, stating that what he needed to remember was written on the pad, he experienced problems even in remembering the topic of conversation or much of his past history. As we later discovered on closer inspection of his lists, even though he referred to them quite often, they were 3 to 4 weeks out of date and quite disorganized.

The predominant function of external memory aids is to provide cues. In other words, they provide external reminders for information that was stored internally. Cues increase the accuracy of remembering and reduce the risk of forgetting over time. Harris (1978, 1984) has suggested a number of criteria for useful external cues and cueing devices. For a cue to be an effective reminder, it must first *be close to the to-be-remembered (TBR) event in time.* Contiguous cues and memory information increase the chances that once cued, the TBR information is not forgotten. Another requirement is that *the cue be an active reminder.* A passive note, for example, on a calendar may or may not be consulted. However, an active reminder to consult the calendar is more likely to help a person remember. Therefore, a person who reminds you to check your schedule or a computer that draws your attention by signaling both help to assure that your memory has been jogged. The final criterion is that the reminder *be specific to the desired memory.* For example, the classic piece of yarn tied around a finger or moving a ring to another finger may provide a cue to remember. But the specifics associated with the cue may not necessarily be recalled.

Additional criteria for external memory aids suggested by Harris (1984) apply to mechanical aids used to supplement external memory cues. These criteria, which are summarized in Table 1 (page 217), are potentially met by a well-programmed portable computer. Restrictions in terms of cost and portability of a computer tend to limit its usefulness at this time. Further, remembering how to use a computer or watch with a memory bank can add an additional memory load for most patients (Harris, 1984).

The structured use of a diary or written reminder appears most useful, especially when it is combined with inexpensive active reminders (e.g., watches set to chime periodically). Attaching the diary to the person's belt or clothing can be helpful as well. This prevents accidental forgetting or misplacement of the memory aid and the attached notebook serves as a reminder when seen (or felt) by the wearer. Active cues to consult external aids can also come from significant others. This helps to establish a pattern of regular use but more important, can be structured to reduce negative feelings associated with using a memory crutch and/or reminders about less efficient memory.

INTERNAL MEMORY STRATEGIES

There are a great number of memory strategies that can be used in therapy. In addition to the external aids discussed above, there are mental or internal aids. These

---

TABLE 1:   EXTERNAL CUEING CRITERIA

Cues in General

   1.   Active reminder

   2.   Contiguous to memory event

   3.   Specific to memory event

Cueing Devices

   4.   Portable

   5.   Wide range of applications

   6.   Large capacity of cues/reminders

   7.   Wide time range (minutes to months)

   8.   Cues are reviewable

   9.   Actual and elapsed time settings

  10.   Easy to use (low memory demand on patient)

Note.   From "Methods of Improving Memory" by J. E. Harris in Clinical Management of Memory Problems (pp. 53-57) by B. Wilson and N. Moffat (Eds.), 1984, Rockville, MD: Aspen. Copyright © 1984 by Aspen Systems Corporation. Adapted by permission.

---

mnemonics can loosely be grouped into those using visual imagery and those using verbal association. Once again, the clinical literature is filled with case examples using these mnemonic aids for different patient groups. Perhaps the most popular ones in use are based on visual imagery techniques (Crovitz, Harvey, & Horn, 1979; Glasgow, Zeiss, Barrera, & Lewinsohn, 1977; Malec & Questad, 1983; Wilson, 1982). Mnemonics structure information in various ways (e.g., categories, rhyming, imagery), provide organization of the TBR information, and help fit this information into the client's knowledge systems.

Many books are available that describe these techniques (Cermak, 1975; Higbee, 1977; Lorayne, 1985; Lorayne & Lucas, 1974; Young & Gibson, 1978) and include exercises as well. The use of these skills requires a clear understanding of, and practice with the technique before more efficient remembering is achieved (Bellezza, 1982). Many patients feel that better remembering is the result of exercising mental muscle. In fact, memory skill development is very much like problem solving as the individual must learn to choose appropriate techniques to achieve the goal of accurate remembering (A. L. Brown & DeLoache, 1978).

There are a variety of visual imagery techniques. The best known are the Method of Loci and the Rhyming Peg Method. These two methods rely on the learning of a standard set of familiar locations or peg words to which TBR items are subsequently associated. In the case of the Method of Loci, familiar locations are visualized (e.g., locations around the patient's house or parts of their body) and then visual images of what the person wishes to remember are visualized in (and linked to) these locations. Although this method is often difficult, the use of these familiar scenes is very efficient in cueing recall. On the other hand, use of the peg method combines a learned list of words and images of those words which are in turn associated to what is to-be-remembered (TBR). This method uses over learned rhyming sequences such as one-bun, two-shoe, three-tree, and so forth as the basis for forming interactive visual images with the TBR material. For example, a person wishing to remember appointments at the dentist, a luncheon, and automobile repair shop, might use this method. The resultant mental images might be: (a) a large bun with a tooth inside, (b) a giant shoe sitting on top of a particular restaurant, and (c) a wrecked car hanging from a tree limb. An added benefit of the rhyming peg method is that it may be employed to help remind the patient of future activities and sequences for carrying out these activities (Moffat, 1984).

Related techniques use imagery to remember names and faces by constructing mental images linking distinctive personal features of an individual with aspects of their name. Another peg method relies on a phonetic system linking consonant sounds to numbers. Although this system is quite difficult initially, Patten (1972) reported success with patients trained to use this strategy. A final imagery strategy involves mental reconstruction of an event or sequence of events to aid recall. This technique involves logical search behavior and can be used to locate lost objects. This method is a good supplement to the imagery techniques mentioned earlier.

Verbal mnemonics also rely on linking and associating information in a meaningful fashion. Examples of these techniques include organizing by category (e.g., fruits and meats in a grocery list), creating a verbal link between words, or making up a story to link words together. Two other methods are rhymes and first letter(s) of words as cues (e.g., vac = veins, arteries, capillaries).

Perhaps the most useful method for remembering prose material is the PQRST (or PQRST-v) technique (see Case #1, page 226). This method prompts the review of prose in distinct steps (Glasgow et al., 1977). First, the person must preview (P) the material and discern the general outline and organization of the prose. Then the person thinks about the questions (Q) raised by the major points of the text followed by a careful reading (R) of the material. Having read the material, the person states (S) the information contained in the text. Finally, the person self-tests (T) to confirm that the text material has been understood and the issues raised in step (Q) were answered. This method is quite successful as a study technique for memory impaired persons. It not only focuses attention on what is to be learned but builds in a review of the material. Another rehearsal opportunity can be created by expanding the test (T) section to include a verification (V) or visual review, stressing the information gathered in steps (Q) and (S).

With both internal and external strategies, added techniques derived from behavioral psychology such as modeling, prompting, and chaining often prove helpful. Some of these methods are incorporated into mnemonic strategies and can be extremely helpful in training. For example, Schmitt, Murphy, and Sanders (1981) successfully used a modeling technique in training older adults in a verbal categorization strategy. Schacter, Rich, and Stampp (1985) showed improved learning ability in four patients with organic dysfunctions with a spaced retrieval method. Wilson (1984) used the chaining method (where each behavior becomes a cue for the next) to teach patients how to remember the steps involved in moving from wheelchairs to normal chairs.

The success of any of the techniques mentioned above is dependent on the patient-task interaction. For example, right hemisphere injured patients may not benefit from imagery training but may successfully use verbal strategies. The reverse may be the case for left hemisphere injured people. Also, as the most general effect of an organic injury is the loss of cognitive flexibility, knowing when and where to remember and knowing how to know may be impaired. Thus trials with both verbal and visual mnemonics may be needed. Finally, the nature of the deficit may prove to be modality specific (e.g., auditory or visual scanning defect), requiring additional interventions such as speech therapy.

AUXILIARY THERAPIES

Theoretically, psychological responses to brain damage may be divided into direct consequences of neurological damage, emotional responses to the challenges of living with CNS impairment (e.g., perceptual, cognitive, or motor dysfunction), and emotional responses to other concurrent changes such as disfigurement or loss of economic independence. In practice, these distinctions are often difficult to draw, but some appreciation by both patient and therapist of the possible interactions and causal loops is essential to the maintenance of an optimal affective and motivational climate for rehabilitation.

For example, extreme psychological reactivity (so-called catastrophic reactions of intense anxiety and frustration) seems most prevalent among patients with lesions to the left hemisphere, even when controlling for IQ and motoric functioning (Valenstein & Heilman, 1979). Some right hemisphere injured patients may have difficulty acknowledging their disabilities, while their emotional reactions may appear inappropriately muted and they may be difficult to motivate for memory retraining. Persons with frontal lobe pathology may present with labile but superficial affect and behavioral disinhibition. Yet these emotional reactions may also reflect a response to impaired cognitive and perceptual faculties. For example, catastrophic reactions can be a response to restricted capacity for communication, attentional deficits may be partly responsible for apparent indifference, and a breakdown of automatic self-monitoring processes may result in inappropriate affect and behavior. Depression, anxiety, frustration, or apathy need not be seen simply as responses to cognitive impairment, but can in turn disrupt new learning and derail the rehabilitative process. This can occur both in and out of formal retraining situations, thereby sustaining or exacerbating functional impairment. The objective of auxiliary therapies in a memory retraining program is to interrupt such cognitive-affective-cognitive impairment loops at the affective phase.

Among the functional disorders having impact on memory performance, anxiety, particularly task-specific anxiety, is probably the most treatable with behavioral methods. Assessment of anxiety includes evaluation of self-report of somatic symptoms (increased sweating, tachycardia, chronic muscle tension), and delineating the situations (e.g., demands on memory) that elicit anxiety. The more precisely the cognitive-behavioral sequence is understood, the more precisely either that sequence can be bypassed, or the anxiety can be treated directly.

For instance, one patient with suspected early Alzheimer's disease became extremely anxious in the study phase of most learning situations, especially when it was identified as such and when material was presented auditorily. In contrast, at retrieval this patient experienced minimal anxiety; his attitude seemed to be "either I know it or I don't." In treatment he was told that his concentrating and studying did not help his performance (in fact, his anxiety made matters worse). He was then encouraged to simply listen to the material once and if he felt that he was becoming anxious anyway, to write the material down on a slip of paper so that he could process it visually. This served to distract him from his own mounting anxiety, as it bypassed the threatening activity and modality.

A second patient's anxiety could not be bypassed. He was an intelligent insurance executive, eager to resume work, and extremely sensitive to any dysfunction which might interfere with his work. Any memory task involving numbers, even immediate recall tasks such as Digit Span, swiftly generated intense anxiety that in turn confirmed his worst fears about his rehabilitative prospects. His anxiety thus took on the self-sustaining properties of a phobic dynamism. In this case, systematic desensitization using an abridged form of progressive muscle relaxation was helpful in reducing anxiety and improving memory performance. The relationship of anxiety to memory impairment can be complex, however (see Case #2 on page 227 for a similar discussion with objective assessment data included). For instance, one study has shown that while highly anxious older adults show memory improvement with relaxation training, subjects with initially low levels of anxiety may actually show memory decrements after relaxation training (Yesavage et al., 1982).

Biofeedback, typically EMG feedback from the frontalis muscle, can be useful in the early stages of desensitization with patients whose anxiety is so pervasive or whose cognitive functioning is so impaired that they have difficulty following relaxation instructions even in low stress situations. Autohypnotic procedures can be at least as effective as muscle relaxation, especially with more cognitively intact patients. Autohypnotic procedures also lend themselves more readily to rapid and frequent utilization throughout the day, which is advantageous as anxiety is much easier to prevent than to reduce.

One three-stage rapid self-induction technique (adapted from H. Spiegel, 1976) is particularly attractive because of a self-contained mnemonic structure. This technique is as follows: "First, do one thing; second, do two things; and third, do three things...First roll the eyes up; second, slowly close the eyes while inhaling; third, relax the eyes, exhale, and imagine that you are floating gently downward." Of course, preparation for hypnosis, deepening techniques, development of imagery, and plans for integration of self-hypnosis into daily life must be highly individualized. It should be kept in mind that hypnosis can be as inappropriate for brain-injured patients who are subject to impaired reality testing or confusional states as it would be in psychiatric cases where such difficulties appear functional in origin.

Depressive affect can hamper rehabilitative efforts, and the experienced clinician will recognize the need to intervene directly, rather than hoping that eventual rehabilitation and adjustment over time will resolve matters. The reader is referred to Carson and Adams (1981) for a concise summary of behavioral perspectives on depression, several of which may be useful in case formulation with depressive neurological patients. Activity schedules, contingency management, and social skills training are often appropriate with patients whose lives have been severely disrupted.

Pharmacological treatment for depression should be undertaken with caution because of the potential for increased sensitivity to drug side effects in brain-injured individuals (Branconnier, DeVitt, Cole, & Spera, 1982; Winograd & Jarvik, 1986). Further, negative effects on cognitive abilities might be misattributed to the underlying neurological deficiency. Ideally, the initiation of a psychopharmacological regimen would always be accompanied by repeated testing on a sensitive memory measure with multiple equivalent forms, such as the Randt Memory Test (see Case #3, page 228).

Denial of manifest cognitive difficulties, and apathy in response to acknowledged impairment, are also common obstacles to cognitive retraining. Denial is perhaps most frequently encountered in early degenerative dementia, though of course it is found to varying degrees in most kinds of neurological patients. Some denial can be adaptive in a patient trying to cope with brain damage and considerable clinical sensitivity is warranted. Nevertheless, overcoming denial can be the decisive success in rehabilitation efforts, as no memory strategy will prove effective if the patient is not motivated to learn to employ it. In fact, patients who do overcome denial may spontaneously begin using their own strategies (most often external mnemonics) and require no additional intervention.

Therapy groups are potentially very powerful in overcoming denial, not necessarily through confrontation but more productively through suggestion, modeling, and direct support (see Chapter 10 in this book). Groups also provide a vehicle for helping patients deal with expectations, stereotyping, and stigmatization associated with memory loss (Zarit, Cole, & Guider, 1981; Zarit, Gallagher, & Kramer, 1981). Family interaction patterns around the issue of denied memory problems can be extremely negative (e.g., overprotectiveness, hostility, mistrust) and so entrenched that family meetings may also be indicated to reduce acute tensions. Experienced therapists seem to find ways to work with the complaints that patients and families report whether these are explicitly focused on memory or on something quite far afield. These therapists also manage to make memory strategies relevant to the explicit concerns of the patients. For example, patients who experience the memory losses and denial of early degenerative dementia usually appear physically healthy. Yet, their memory dysfunction is both debilitating and insidious. The slow progression of forgetting and confusion is therefore often interpreted by other family members as secondary to some personality change or malicious intent as family members are often unaware of the nature of the memory disturbance. For example, one patient a few months post-closed head injury, complained that his family had forgotten that "there was something wrong with how I think and remember" as family and friends only saw an outward appearance of physical health. This patient's inability to think and remember was misinterpreted as an attention/sympathy getting device.

Profound apathy in the brain-injured patient can be extremely difficult to accept, for therapist and family alike, particularly when cognitive functions appear relatively intact at those sporadic times when the patient really tries. It is sometimes productive to treat apathetic patients as if they were depressed, for example, with psychoactive medication, or a schedule of rewarding activities. If there is success with these approaches and a broad return of affect and motivation, one might even make a retroactive inference of depression. Barring such a success, a highly structured environment will probably be necessary for the long-term. Hypothetically, though, the patient might ultimately be trained in self-reward procedures and thereby to some degree undertake his or her own management.

PROGRAMMATIC CONSIDERATIONS

Several principles should always be considered in program implementation. It is important that the difficulty of memory exercises be maintained at a moderate level so that frustration and self-esteem problems are not exacerbated. Often a brief and relatively successful remembering experience with something akin to the "airplane list" described by Crovitz (1979) is helpful. Target percentages of correct responses must of course be adjusted on an individual basis, but a target figure of 50% correct may be rather high for a brain-injured population, at least in initial stages of training. Superficial similarities between some clinical memory exercises on the one hand and learning experiments with undergraduate subjects on the other, should not mislead the clinician into the relatively passive role of providing massive quantities of practice material ("let them rehearse for better or worse"). Brain-injured patients are coping with biological and psychosocial trauma, and meaningful rehabilitation depends on integrating cognitive functioning into the ecology of the individual's personality and circumstances. Effective memory retraining, which hinges on knowing how to know, requires not simply providing practice opportunities while allowing patients to discover strategies for themselves. Nor does providing strategies and allowing patients to apply them on their own appear adequate. Knowing how to know for a given patient means knowing when and how to select the appropriate (and efficient) memory strategy, while managing concurrent affective and interpersonal situations. Program design, therefore, must include continuous feedback. This feedback should be qualitative (i.e., identifying the weak link in the chain of processes required for adequate memory performance) as well as quantitative.

Cognitive rehabilitation thus needs to be longitudinal, consultative, and holistic (Logue, Harkey, Horn, & Wang, 1984). Every opportunity for rehabilitation of functions that support effective remembering (e.g., attention, language) should continually be explored. Cognitive rehabilitation as an applied field is at a very early developmental stage. There are no established predictors for individual response to cognitive interventions, and patients should only be excluded from retraining efforts if they are too cognitively impaired, or too physically ill to participate (Delisa, Miller, Melnick, & Mikulic, 1982). To give one extreme example, one Vietnam veteran was seen more than 10 years after a head trauma. He had been comatose for 9 months, aphasic for 2 years, hemiparetic, and deaf. Ten years after the original injury, he was still making significant gains, on a monthly basis, with memory exercises, social skills retraining, supportive therapy, and occupational therapy.

CASE EXAMPLE #1: DR. J

Dr. J, a 33-year old male, was referred for neuropsychological testing for estimates of recovery 1 year after a left hemisphere cerebrovascular accident (CVA). He had completed medical school and was a resident at the time of the CVA. Initially, he presented with global aphasia and right hemiplegia. At the time of the assessment, he had been receiving speech therapy for approximately 1 year.

WAIS:	VIQ = 91	**Digit Span:**	6 forward 5 backward	
	PIQ = 110	**Aphasia Screening:**	mild impairment	
	FSIQ = 99	**Category Test:**	no impairment	

Revised Wechsler Memory Scale:

Short-term semantic (STS): severe impairment
Long-term semantic (LTS): mild impairment
1/2 hour retention (%S): no impairment
Short-term figural (STF): minimal impairment
Long-term figural (LTF): mild impairment
1/2 hour retention (%F): moderate impairment

Memory retraining was requested by Dr. J one year after his injury as he was experiencing problems in remembering written material along with names and faces. His verbal skills were clearly affected by his brain-injury but his right hemisphere abilities appeared reasonably intact. Therefore, visual imagery techniques were selected as strategies for names and faces, as well as other lists of to-be-remembered information. The PQRST technique was incorporated into his speech therapy sessions in an effort to improve recall of text material. Dr. J experienced difficulties in using imagery at first but gradually incorporated imagery mnemonics over time. His scores on the Randt Memory Test are listed below. His initial improvement was seen in story (text) recall with later improvement in list learning. Of course, the improvement due separately to memory and speech therapy cannot be disentangled nor can the effects of therapy be distinguished from a natural recovery process.

Randt Memory Test Data:

	Time Since Injury		
Standard Score	12 Months	15 Months	24 Months
Acquisition	66	62	88
Delayed Recall	51	72	96
Memory Index	52	62	91

CASE EXAMPLE #2: MS. B

Ms. B was a 58-year old female who referred herself for assessment and therapy because she believed that her memory abilities were declining. She had a BS degree and was an active writer. On a questionnaire, Ms. B indicated that she was experiencing a "major" memory dysfunction. She stated that her memory had been declining for roughly 6 years. Information that proved most difficult to remember involved: (a) names and faces, (b) phone numbers, (c) text material, and (d) locations of objects. Memory strengths were remembering appointments, directions, and meaningful events and dates. Ms. B did not appear depressed or anxious although her husband was recovering from "heart problems" and they were both "going through retirement."

Revised Wechsler Memory Scale:

STS:	no impairment	STF:	no impairment
LTS:	minimal impairment	LTF:	no impairment
%S:	minimal impairment	%F:	no impairment

Randt Memory Test (standard scores):

Acquisition: 130   Delayed Recall: 135   Memory Index: 137

Ms. B's performance was well above normal on memory testing Although she may have lost some of her earlier skills, she appeared to be overly anxious about a failure to recognize a casual acquaintance from 30 years in the past. This anxiety evidently also derived from a belief that significant memory loss inevitably accompanied aging ("there is no future without my memory"). Over the course of three sessions, she was given various techniques in memory enhancement, such as visual mnemonics, and was asked to keep a forgetting notebook. Interestingly, she made no entries in the notebook over a 2-week period. When given feedback and reassurance about her test performance which she felt would be "awful," Ms. B was relieved. Based on the objective data, she felt better about not becoming "senile" and returned to her daily activities and enrolled in a college course as well.

CASE EXAMPLE #3: MR. H

Mr. H was a 54-year old male who was referred for an evaluation of memory loss. He had been experiencing problems at work and was forgetting information that had always been "at my fingertips." Mr. H had a 12th grade education and managed the supply division of a large electronics firm. He had always been known for his ability to provide the names and associated codes and procedures for hundreds of electronic parts. Cognitive testing revealed average performance on the WAIS, while affective testing and interview revealed depressive symptomatology.

WAIS:		MMPI:	
VIQ	= 93	Scale 2	= 93T
PIQ	= 97	Scale 3	= 87T
FSIQ	= 95	Scale 1	= 85T

Zung Scale: SDS Index = 79 (severe depression)

Russell Revised Wechsler Memory Scale:

STS:	mild impairment	STF:	moderate impairment
LTS:	mild impairment	LTF:	moderate impairment
%S:	minimal impairment	%F:	no impairment

Mr. H was given antidepressant medication and monthly therapy using verbal and visual strategies and followed over an 8 month period. His Randt Memory Test standard scores reflect his change in functioning.

Randt Memory Test Scores:

	Initial Testing	8-Month Follow up
Acquisition	84	103
Delayed Recall	90	122
Memory Index	85	114

Frederick A. Schmitt, PhD, currently is Director of the Neuropsychology Service at the University of Kentucky Medical Center and an Assistant Research Professor in Neurology and at the Sanders-Brown Research Center on Aging. He is also a Senior Fellow in the Center for the Study of Aging and Human Development at Duke Medical Center. His research interests include developmental changes in cognition, and relating neuropsychological data to changes associated with disease (dementia, stroke, cancer), aging and to medical interventions. Dr. Schmitt may be contacted at the Department of Neurology, Albert B. Chandler Medical Center, University of Kentucky, Lexington, KY 40536-0084.

Jonathan Farber, PhD, is a Clinical Assistant Professor in the Psychology Department at the University of North Carolina in Chapel Hill, and Staff Psychologist at John Umstead Hospital. His neuropsychological interests include behavioral toxicology, learning disabilities, and the cognitive effects of ECT. Dr. Farber can be contacted at the Department of Psychology, UNC-Chapel Hill, NC 27514.

RESOURCES

MEMORY THEORY AND RESEARCH

Baddeley, A. D. (1984). Memory theory and memory therapy. In B. Wilson & N. Moffat (Eds.), *Clinical Management of Memory Problems* (pp. 5-27). Rockville, MD: Aspen.

Brown, A. L. (1975). The development of memory: Knowing, knowing about knowing, and knowing how to know. In H. W. Reese (Ed.), *Advances in Child Development and Behavior* (Vol. 10, pp. 103-151). New York: Academic Press.

Brown, A. L., & DeLoache, J. S. (1978). Skills, plans, and self-regulation. In R. S. Siegler (Ed.), *Children's Thinking: What Develops?* (pp. 3-35). Hillsdale, NJ: Lawrence Erlbaum Associates.

Cavanaugh, J. C., Grady, J. G., & Perlmutter, M. (1983). Forgetting and use of memory aids in 20 to 70 year-olds' everyday life. *International Journal of Aging and Human Development, 17,* 113-122.

Chi, M. T. H. (1978). Knowledge structures and memory development. In R. S. Siegler (Ed.), *Children's Thinking: What Develops?* (pp. 73-96). Hillsdale, NJ: Lawrence Erlbaum Associates.

Flavell, J. H., & Wellman, H. M. (1977). Metamemory. In R. V. Kail, Jr., & J. W. Hagen (Eds.), *Perspectives on the Development of Memory and Cognition* (pp. 3-33). Hillsdale, NJ: Lawrence Erlbaum Associates.

Hagen, J. W., Jongeward, R. H., & Kail, R. V. (1975). Cognitive perspectives on the development of memory. In H. W. Reese (Ed.), *Advances in Child Development and Behavior* (Vol. 10, pp. 57-101). New York: Academic Press.

Sunderland, A., Harris, J., & Baddeley, A. D. (1983). Do laboratory tests predict everyday memory? A neuro-psychological study. *Journal of Verbal Learning and Verbal Behavior, 22,* 341-357.

Tulving, E. (1972). Episodic and semantic memory. In E. Tulving & W. Donaldson (Eds.), *Organization of Memory* (pp. 381-403). New York: Academic Press.

Zarit, S. H., Gallagher, D., & Kramer, N. (1981). Memory training in the community aged: Effects on depression, memory complaint, and memory performance. *Educational Gerontology, 6,* 11-27.

MEMORY ASSESSMENT

Bennett-Levy, J., & Powell, G. E. (1980). The subjective memory questionnaire (SMQ): An investigation into the self-reporting of "real-life" memory skills. *British Journal of Social and Clinical Psychology, 19,* 177-183.

Erikson, R. C., Poon, L. W., & Walsh-Sweeney, L. (1980). Clinical memory testing of the elderly. In L. W. Poon, J. L. Fozard, L. S. Cermak, D. Arenberg, & L. W. Thompson (Eds.), *New Directions in Memory and Aging* (pp. 379-402). Hillsdale, NJ: Lawrence Erlbaum Associates.

Erikson, R. C., & Scott, M. I. (1977). Clinical memory testing: A review. *Psychological Bulletin, 84,* 1130-1149.

Kane, R. A., & Kane, R. L. (1981). *Assessing the Elderly: A Practical Guide to Measurement.* Lexington, MA: D. C. Heath.

McCarty, S. M., Logue, P. E., Power, D. G., Ziesat, H. A., & Rosenthiel, A. K. (1980). Alternate-form reliability and age-related scores for Russell's Revised Wechsler Memory Scale. *Journal of Consulting and Clinical Psychology, 48,* 296-298.

Poon, L. W. (1980). A systems approach for the assessment and treatment of memory problems. In J. Ferguson & C. Taylor (Eds.), *Handbook of Behavioral Medicine: 1, Systems Intervention* (pp. 191-212). New York: Spectrum.

Randt, C. T., Brown, E. R., & Osborne, D. P., Jr. (1980). A memory test for longitudinal measurement of mild to moderate deficits. *Clinical Neuropsychology, 2,* 184-194.

Russell, E. W. (1975). A multiple scoring method for the assessment of complex memory functions. *Journal of Consulting and Clinical Psychology, 43,* 800-809.

Zelinski, E. M., Gilewski, M. J., & Thompson, L. W. (1980). Do laboratory tests relate to self-assessment of memory ability in the young and old? In L. W. Poon, J. L. Fozard, L. S. Cermak, D. Arenberg, & L. W. Thompson (Eds.), *New Directions in Memory and Aging* (pp. 519-544). Hillsdale, NJ: Lawrence Erlbaum Associates.

MEMORY TRAINING TECHNIQUES

Bellezza, F. (1982). *Improve Your Memory Skills.* Englewood Cliffs, NJ: Prentice Hall.

Cermak, L. S. (1975). *Improving Your Memory.* New York: McGraw-Hill.

Crovitz, H. F. (1979). Memory retraining in brain-damaged patients: The airplane list. *Cortex, 15,* 131-134.

Crovitz, H. F., Cordoni, C. N., Daniel, W. F., & Perlman, J. (1984). Everyday forgetting experiences: Real-time investigations with implications for the study of memory management in brain-damaged patients. *Cortex, 20,* 349-359.

Crovitz, H. F., Harvey, M. T., & Horn, R. W. (1979). Problems in the acquisition of imagery mnemonics: Three brain-damaged cases. *Cortex, 15,* 225-234.

Glasgow, R. E., Zeiss, R. A., Barrera, M., Jr., & Lewinsohn, P. M. (1977). Case studies on remediating memory deficits in brain-damaged individuals. *Journal of Clinical Psychology, 33,* 1049-1054.

Harris, J. E. (1978). External memory aids. In M. M. Gruneberg, P. Morris, & R. Sykes (Eds.), *Practical Aspects of Memory* (pp. 172-179). London: Academic Press.

Harris, J. E. (1984). Methods of improving memory. In B. Wilson & N. Moffat (Eds.), *Clinical Management of Memory Problems* (pp. 46-62). Rockville, MD: Aspen.

Higbee, K. L. (1977). *Your Memory: How it Works and How to Improve it.* Englewood Cliffs, NJ: Prentice-Hall.

Lorayne, H. (1985). *Page a Minute Memory Book.* New York: Holt, Rinehart, & Winston.

Lorayne, H. & Lucas, J. (1974). *The Memory Book.* New York: Ballantine.

Malec, J., & Questad, K. (1983). Rehabilitation of memory after craniocerebral trauma: Case report. *Archives of Physiological Medical Rehabilitation, 64,* 436-438.

Moffat, N. (1984). Strategies of memory therapy. In B. Wilson & N. Moffat (Eds.), *Clinical Management of Memory Problems* (pp. 63-88). Rockville, MD: Aspen.

Patten, B. M. (1972). The ancient art of memory: Usefulness in treatment. *Archives of Neurology, 26,* 25-31.

Poon, L. W. (1984). Memory training for older adults. In J. P. Abrahams & V. Crooks (Eds.), *Geriatric Mental Health* (pp. 135-151). New York: Grune & Stratton.

Schacter, D. L., Rich, S. A., & Stampp, M. S. (1985). Remediation of memory disorders: Experimental evaluation of the spaced-retrieval technique. *Journal of Clinical and Experimental Neuropsychology, 7,* 79-96.

Schmitt, F. A., Murphy, M. D., & Sanders, R. E. (1981). Training older adult free recall rehearsal strategies. *Journal of Gerontology, 36,* 329-337.

Wilson, B. (1982). Success and failure in memory training following a cerebral vascular accident. *Cortex, 18,* 581-594.

Wilson, B. (1984). Memory therapy in practice. In B. Wilson & N. Moffat (Eds.), *Clinical Management of Memory Problems* (pp. 89-111). Rockville, MD: Aspen.

Young, M. N., & Gibson, W. B. (1978). *How to Develop an Exceptional Memory.* North Hollywood, CA: Wilshire Book Company.

Zarit, S. H., Cole, K. D., & Guider, R. L. (1981). Memory training strategies and subjective complaints of memory in the aged. *Gerontologist, 21,* 158-164.

GENERAL RESOURCES

Branconnier, R. J., DeVitt, D. R., Cole, J. O., & Spera, K. F. (1982). Amitriptyline selectively disrupts verbal recall from secondary memory of the normal aged. *Neurobiology of Aging, 3,* 55-59.

Carson, T. P., & Adams, H. E. (1981). Affective disorders: Behavioral perspectives. In S. M. Turner, S. K. Calhoun, & H. E. Adams (Eds.), *Handbook of Clinical Behavior Therapy* (pp. 125-161). New York: Wiley & Sons.

Craine, J. F. (1982). Principles of cognitive rehabilitation. In L. E. Trexler (Ed.), *Cognitive Rehabilitation: Conceptualization and Intervention* (pp. 83-98). New York: Plenum Press.

Delisa, J. A., Miller, R. M., Melnick, R. R., & Mikulic, M. A. (1982). Stroke rehabilitation: Part 1. Cognitive deficits and prediction of outcome. *American Family Physicians, 26,* 207-214.

Filskov, S. B. (1983). Neuropsychological screening. In P. A. Keller & L. G. Ritt (Eds.), *Innovations in Clinical Practice: A Source Book* (Vol. 2, pp. 17-25). Sarasota, FL: Professional Resource Exchange, Inc..

Gianustos, R. (1980). What is cognitive rehabilitation? *Journal of Rehabilitation, 46,* 36-40.

Goldstein, G., & Ruthven, L. (1983). *Rehabilitation of the Brain-Damaged Adult.* New York: Plenum Press.

Greene, J. G., Nicol, R., & Jamieson, H. (1979). Reality orientation with psychogeriatric patients. *Behavioral Research and Therapy, 17,* 615-618.

Logue, P. E., Harkey, C. A., Horn, R., & Wang, H. S. (1984). Multidisciplinary approaches to rehabilitation: A case study. In P. E. Logue & J. M. Shear (Eds.), *Clinical Neuropsychology: A Multidisciplinary Approach* (pp. 386-424). Springfield, IL: Charles C. Thomas.

Luria, A. R. (1963). *Restoration of Brain Function After Brain Injury* (O. L. Zangwill, Trans.). New York: Pergamon Press. (Original work published 1948)

Luria, A. R. (1966). *Human Brain and Psychological Processes* (B. Hargh, Trans.). New York: Harper & Row. (Original work published 1963)

Popkin, S. J., Gallagher, D., Thompson, L. W., & Moore, M. (1982). Memory complaint and performance in normal and depressed older adults. *Experimental Aging Research, 8,* 141-145.

Spiegel, H. (1976). A single-treatment method to stop smoking using ancillary self-hypnosis. In I. Wickramasckera (Ed.), *Biofeedback, Behavior Therapy, and Hypnosis* (pp. 535-549). Chicago: Nelson-Hall.

Valenstein, E., & Heilman, K. (1979). Emotional disorders resulting from lesions of the central nervous system. In K. Heilman & E. Valenstein (Eds.), *Clinical Neuropsychology* (pp. 413-438). New York: Oxford University Press.

Weingartner, H., Kaye, W., Smallberg, S., Cohen, R., Ebert, M. H., Gillin, J. C., & Gold, P. (1982). Determinants of memory failures in dementia. In S. Corkin, K. L. Davis, J. H. Growdon, E. Usdin, & R. J. Wurtman (Eds.), *Alzheimer's Disease: A Report of Progress in Research* (pp. 171-176). New York: Raven Press.

Wilson, B., & Moffat, N. (Eds.). (1984). *Clinical Management of Memory Problems.* Rockville, MD: Aspen.

Winograd, C. H., & Jarvik, L. F. (1986). Physician management of the demented patient. *Journal of the American Geriatrics Society, 34,* 295-308.

Yesavage, J. A., Rose, T. L., & Spiegel, D. (1982). Relaxation training and memory improvement in elderly normals: Correlation of anxiety ratings and recall improvement. *Experimental Aging Research, 8,* 195-198.

RESOURCE AND SUPPORT GROUPS

Alzheimer's Disease and Related Disorders Association (ADRDA), National Headquarters, 360 North Michigan Avenue, Suite 601, Chicago, IL 60601.

American Academy of Neurology - "Neurologists Handbook for Patient Information." Available from: American Academy of Neurology, 2221 University Avenue, S. W., Suite 335, Minneapolis, MN 55414.

American Heart Association (Stroke Council), 7320 Greenville Avenue, Dallas, TX 75231.

American Rehabilitation Foundation, Kenny Rehabilitation Institute, 1800 Chicago Avenue, Minneapolis, MN 55404.

Chenoweth, B., Snearline, P., Stevens, L., & Wooley, B. (1980, November). *Didactic/Experimental Program for Memory Strengthening.* Paper presented at the 33rd annual meeting of the Gerontological Society of America, San Diego, CA. Information available from:

Turner Geriatric Clinic, University of Michigan Hospital, 1010 Wall Street, Ann Arbor, MI 48109.

Family Survival Project for Brain Damaged Adults, 1736 Divisidero Street, San Francisco, CA 94115.

National Head Injury Foundation, 280 Singletary Lane, Framingham, MA 01701.

National Huntington's Disease Association, 128A East 74th Street, New York, NY 10021.

National Multiple Sclerosis Society, 205 East 42nd Street, New York, NY 10017.

National Parkinson Foundation, 1501 N. W. 9th Avenue, Miami, FL 33136-9990.

National Rehabilitation Association, 1522 K. Street, N. W., Suite 1120, Washington, DC 20005.

Research and Training Center on Head Trauma and Stroke, New York University Medical Center, 400 East 34th Street, New York, NY 10006.

Stroke Club International, 805 12th Street, Galveston, TX 77550.

BEHAVIORAL TREATMENT OF CHRONIC PAIN

Michael J. Follick, David K. Ahern,
and Edward W. Aberger

Chronic pain is one of the most prevalent, difficult, and expensive problems in medicine. An estimated 50 million Americans are partially or totally disabled by chronic pain at an annual projected cost of over 40 billion dollars in health services, drugs, compensation payments, and days out of work ("Management of Chronic Pain," 1976). Even more significant is the cost of chronic pain in terms of human suffering. In addition to the subjective experience of pain, these patients frequently develop a host of other inter-related problems, referred to as the Chronic Pain Syndrome (Follick, Aberger, Ahern, & McCartney, 1984). It includes marked limitations in functional capabilities; depression and emotional distress; chemical dependency; marital and family disruption; and vocational and financial difficulties.

Despite medical and surgical advances, it is estimated that only 30% to 40% of chronic pain patients obtain satisfactory long-term relief from pharmacologic or surgical treatments (Loesser, 1974; White, 1969). Many pain experts contend that pharmacologic and surgical treatments have a poor success rate because they address only one element of the chronic pain problem, the pathophysiology. They argue that pain is a much more complex phenomenon than a simple and linear relationship between the amount of organic pathology and the experience of pain. Instead it involves an interaction of psychological and environmental variables as well as biological factors (Fordyce, 1976; Melzack, 1974). This biopsychosocial model helps explain the limited success of procedures designed to correct the physical pathology or block the so-called pain pathway, and has led directly to the development of interdisciplinary efforts in both the study and treatment of chronic pain.

A learning theory model of chronic pain, as proposed originally by Fordyce (1974, 1976), emphasizes the role and importance of environmental factors in chronic pain. This model does not focus on the private, subjective experience of pain, but instead emphasizes the pre-eminent role of pain behaviors, or the objective, observable manifestations of the patient's pain experience. Examples of pain behaviors include verbal complaints, grimacing, guarded movements, lying down, medication use, and avoidance of routine activities. According to Fordyce, there are two types of pain behaviors--respondent and operant. Whereas respondent pain behaviors occur reflexively to antecedent stimuli arising from the site of tissue damage, operant pain behaviors are controlled directly by environmental consequences. Fordyce (1976) contends that in chronic pain, behaviors that were originally respondents can become operants through the process of learning. He further postulates that three sets of conditions can influence the frequency and maintenance of pain behaviors: (a) positive reinforcement, such as attention, sympathy and concern, compensation payments, or medications; (b) negative reinforcement, or the removal of noxious stimulation; such as anxiety invoking situations; or the avoidance of work or other unpleasant responsibilities; and (c) extinction or nonreinforcement of "well" behavior.

The learning theory model of chronic pain has direct implications for the treatment of chronic pain. In those instances where pain behaviors are considered operants, the reinforcement for those behaviors should be withdrawn and reinforcement must be provided for activity or well behaviors. Pain behaviors will decrease in frequency and will ultimately extinguish if reinforcement no longer follows those behaviors. Thus, the behavioral approach does not attempt to modify pain directly but rather to modify maladaptive pain *behaviors*. It is important to note that this is a rehabilitative rather than a curative approach and the ultimate goal of a behaviorally oriented program is to reduce a patient's disability through a reduction in the frequency of pain behaviors and increases in activity or functional behaviors.

238

Since the goal is to modify the patient's behavior, which is believed to be in large part a function of the environment, it is necessary to involve the spouse and perhaps other family members in the retraining process. This requirement is important to insure that the pain behavior no longer receives sustaining reinforcement and that activity or well behavior is reinforced.

This chapter describes a behaviorally oriented, outpatient-based chronic pain treatment program. While it is based on a learning theory model of chronic pain similar to those of inpatient programs, this outpatient program offers several advantages: It is less costly, reduces hospital bed utilization, and is adaptable to smaller, less extensive facilities. The cost per patient is substantially less than that of inpatient programs. In addition, it directly promotes generalization because it is an outpatient-based program and treats the patient in the natural environment. Furthermore, this program should be better able to address the problem of maintenance, because the protocol includes the patient's private physician as a member of the treatment team, and employs a structured follow-up component. Finally, this program does not require extensive facilities or personnel and can serve as a structure for the treatment of an individual patient with chronic pain in the absence of a formal pain treatment program.

PROGRAM OVERVIEW

The program adheres to a cognitive-behavioral model and is designed to retrain patients and their families in the management of chronic pain and associated problems. The treatment team is interdisciplinary and includes the patient's private physician (usually an orthopedic surgeon, a neurosurgeon, or a psychiatrist), a psychologist, a physical therapist, and a vocational rehabilitative counselor. The protocol is conceptualized as a "private practice model" because it employs the private physician who has been treating the patient and who intends to continue to treat the patient medically. This is in opposition to the more conventional model which requires that a patient travel, often long distances, to a chronic pain treatment facility for a brief period of time, and then return to the local physician.

The goals of the program are to: (a) reduce the frequency of pain behaviors, (b) increase the patient's physical capabilities and activities to a level considered normal for his or her age and sex, (c) eliminate the patient's reliance on pain relieving medications, and (d) reduce the patient's utilization of medical care resources for purposes of pain relief.

Major treatment components include:

1. *Behavior Modification.* These procedures are employed for the systematic modification of maladaptive pain behavior and the promotion of activity or well behavior.

2. *Physical Therapy.* In physical therapy, muscles that are weakened by pain and disuse are progressively strengthened in the daily treatment program. The patient's activity level is gradually increased to the point where the patient is doing things considered normal for his or her age, sex, and level of physical impairment.

3. *Conjoint Marital Therapy.* In marital or family therapy, the patient and spouse are taught to identify pain behaviors and alter their responses to them. They are also trained to identify appropriate or well behaviors and to reinforce those behaviors systematically. In addition, other psychological and marital difficulties that exist are dealt with in these sessions by various cognitive-behavioral procedures (Jacobsen & Margolin, 1979).

4. *Cognitive Restructuring and Attributional Changes.* This is probably one of the more important elements of the program and involves helping patients to realize that in order to return to a normal and satisfying way of life, they must assume some of the responsibility for these changes. This is done by challenging directly their irrational cognitions--for example, "I should not have pain" or "once you eliminate my pain all of the other problems in my life will automatically be resolved" (Ellis & Greiger, 1977). Patients who expect total pain relief or believe that health care professionals should provide that total relief will engage in a relentless search for the "magic treatment" that will eliminate their pain. If patients come to expect that total relief may not be possible and assume the responsibility of learning to control the influence of pain on their lives, they

will no longer search for someone who can provide a cure but instead will engage in the process of rehabilitating themselves.

This program necessarily restricts itself to the specific treatment strategies outlined above since the primary focus is on rehabilitation rather than pain relief. The inclusion of pain relieving strategies (e.g., biofeedback, massage, nerve blocks) tends to reinforce the patient's expectation that it is necessary to achieve pain relief prior to engaging in functional activities and therefore deters the achievement of the primary goal: *learning to live a normal life despite pain.*

ASSESSMENT

Comprehensive assessment is a critical component in the treatment process. Data gathered during the assessment phase provide the clinician with direction in choosing appropriate treatment modalities, help develop an individualized treatment program, and are also necessary for evaluating treatment effectiveness.

A patient is first evaluated by the primary physician who, often with consultations from other medical specialists, assesses the extent of organic pathology and determines if rehabilitation is indicated. The psychologist then evaluates the patient and focuses on the role of psychological and environmental variables in the patient's chronic pain problem. Also, the psychologist evaluates other information (presence of measurable pain behavior, motivation for change, vocational limitations) that will help determine whether or not the patient is an appropriate candidate for the pain treatment program. This evaluation includes the patient's spouse or significant other so that marital difficulties can be assessed and to provide additional data on the social/environmental factors involved in the patient's chronic pain condition. Our assessment battery includes the following:

1. *Videotaped Ratings.* The patient's functional limitations are determined and recorded in physical therapy (limping, inability to climb stairs, exercise limitations, etc.). These tapes are later used to document changes in the patient's pain behaviors and level of physical capabilities, thus

241

providing objective measurement of change. The tapes can be rated on the frequency of pain behaviors displayed by the patient. Several pain behavior rating systems have been developed and the interested reader is referred to Follick, Ahern, and Aberger (1985) and Keefe, Crisson, and Francis's chapter (Chapter 3) on assessment in this volume. However, if the program has been successful, the viewing of the pre-/post-treatment tapes should provide the clinician and patient with clear-cut evidence of increases in functional activity and decreases in observable pain behavior.

2. *Daily Activity Diary.* The patient completes a Daily Activity Diary for each day during the week prior to evaluation week. This diary records the type and amount of the patient's activities; the frequency and types of medication used; and self-reported ratings of pain, tension, and mood each day. These measurements are important because they provide a means of documenting changes in a person's behavior outside of the hospital environment (see Appendix A, pages 258-265). Follick, Ahern, and Laser-Wolston (1984) have established the reliability and validity of this activity measure.

3. *Sickness Impact Profile.* The Sickness Impact Profile (Bergner, Bobbitt, Cater, & Gilson, 1981) is employed as a behaviorally based measure of pain-related disability. In addition to yielding an overall percentage of disability score, this measure provides quantitative indices of the patient's impairment in physical functioning (e.g., ambulation, mobility), psychosocial functioning (e.g., social interaction, emotional behavior), and work, social, and recreational functioning. Follick, Smith, and Ahern (1985) have also established the reliability and validity of this measure and present normative data for a large sample of chronic low back pain patients.

4. *Family and Marital Inventories.* Since marital and family distress can be related to chronic pain syndromes, and marital therapy often is an integral component of treatment, the Marital Adjustment Test (Locke & Wallace, 1959) and the Areas of Change Questionnaire (Weiss, Hops, & Patterson, 1973) are administered.

5. *Minnesota Multiphasic Personality Inventory.* The patient completes an MMPI before and after treatment so that appropriate interventions can be developed and to document changes in emotional distress and psychological functioning.
6. *Cognitive Error Questionnaire.* This questionnaire (Lefebvre, 1981) assesses the occurrence of maladaptive thinking styles as conceptualized by Beck (Beck, Rush, Shaw, & Emery, 1979) in relation to both general and pain themes. This measure provides useful information regarding the extent to which cognitive factors may be contributing to the patient's disability and maladaptive behavior and is useful in formulating the cognitive restructuring component of treatment.
7. *Health Care Utilization Questionnaire.* This questionnaire measures the patient's total number of contacts with the health care system (e.g., physician visits, diagnostic and treatment procedures, hospitalizations, emergency room visits) during a 1 year period. Patients complete this questionnaire prior to treatment and at 1 year follow-up. This instrument can provide a quantifiable measure of the pain program's impact on the patient's utilization of health care services for the purpose of pain relief.

It is important to note that this assessment battery is used not only to develop an individualized treatment plan but also to evaluate treatment outcome. Thus, these measures should be administered both before and after treatment.

Data gathered in the physical and psychological assessments are first used to determine the patient's appropriateness for the pain treatment program. This is a very important step in the assessment process because not all chronic pain patients are appropriate for a behaviorally oriented pain program. As the relative contribution of biological, psychological, and social/environmental factors vary in each patient's condition, so do the treatment requirements. These assessments allow the physician and the psychologist to determine whether the patient satisfies the following list of inclusion and exclusion criteria which have been found to be useful clinical screening criteria.

INCLUSION CRITERIA

1. The patient's physician must judge further medical/surgical intervention impractical or of no additional value. In cases where medical/surgical procedures may offer a limited probability of pain relief, *both* the patient and physician must agree that a pain rehabilitation program focusing on the restoration of functional capabilities is the preferred treatment approach.
2. The physician must indicate that there are no contraindications to an extensive physical exercise program (e.g., unstable cardiac condition), and the patient should be medically capable of restoration of normal levels of physical functioning.
3. The patient must exhibit observable and measurable pain behaviors, and these behaviors must have identifiable environmental consequences that are potentially modifiable.
4. The patient's pain must be interfering with his or her life and preventing him or her from engaging in desired physical activities.
5. The patient should be able to identify specific goals which are observable and measurable, and which are achievable within the time constraints of the program.
6. The patient must be motivated to participate in the program and indicate explicitly that he or she is willing to learn to live with pain.
7. The family members must be motivated and willing to change their behaviors and help the patient learn to change.

EXCLUSION CRITERIA

1. The patient should have no litigation pending related to his or her pain injury unless the litigation is judged not to be important in the maintenance and promotion of a continued disability.
2. There should be no severe psychopathology that would prevent progression through the program. That is, the patient should not be suffering from a psychosis or an organic brain syndrome.
3. The patient should *not* be severely addicted to pain medications. In those instances where chemical dependency is judged to be primary rather than

secondary to the pain condition, the patient should be referred to a chemical dependency treatment center for detoxification.

Perhaps the most important criterion is the patient's motivation. A major goal of the initial psychological evaluation is to assess whether the patient is willing to alter the chronic pain lifestyle and attempt to lead as normal a life as possible despite pain. During the initial interview, the patient is challenged directly to reflect upon his or her current lifestyle and the futility of seeking repeated medical interventions in order to obtain a magical cure. The patient is then presented with the alternatives of continuing to seek pain relief in an effort to control the pain per se or of assuming the responsibility for controlling the influence that pain has on his or her life and begin the process of rehabilitation. This confrontation frequently has therapeutic as well as diagnostic value, and it has not been unusual for patients to alter their daily activities and medication intake patterns subsequent to the initial assessment.

After determining that the patient satisfies the screening criteria and has had time to consider and discuss the program with his or her physician, the patient and spouse return for a follow-up interview. The purpose of this interview is to discuss the details of the treatment program, to further assess the couple's expectations regarding treatment, and to review the Treatment Program Agreement (see Appendix B, pages 266-267). If the couple still indicates a desire to participate after detailed discussion of the treatment goals and procedures, the patient is formally enrolled in the treatment program.

TREATMENT

EVALUATION WEEK

To this point, the assessment process has been primarily directed at determining the patient's appropriateness for the treatment program. The first week of the treatment program is utilized as an evaluation week and is used to gather additional, specific information through extensive outpatient physical therapy and marital/family functioning evaluations. This additional information, in conjunction with the data from the assessment battery, is used to tailor an individualized treatment program.

The patient attends physical therapy a minimum of three times during the first week of the program. The physical therapist employs standard procedures to determine the patient's current physical capabilities and limitations (e.g., deficits in range of motion, strength in upper and lower extremities, gait disturbance). In addition, the physical therapist observes the patient's *pain behaviors* and identifies *potential reinforcers*. The patient is videotaped while performing exercises at the end of this week to document the pre-treatment level of physical functioning.

The purposes of the family evaluation sessions are threefold. First, assisted by the treatment team, the couple identifies pain behaviors (i.e., how the patient communicates pain to others) and environmental contingencies that maintain those behaviors (i.e., how others respond to the pain behaviors). Second, marital difficulties and maladaptive communication patterns are targeted. Third, the patient is assisted in listing specific individualized treatment goals to be accomplished by the end of treatment.

EVALUATION CONFERENCE

At the end of the evaluation week, all members of the treatment team participate in an evaluation conference. Problem areas, generally encompassing physical functioning, psychological adjustment, marital functioning, drug usage, and vocational rehabilitation are operationalized so that specific treatment plans can be formulated. The structure of physical therapy, individual therapy, and conjoint marital therapy are determined for each patient during the evaluation conference. In addition, a list of pain behaviors is constructed from the observations of the treatment team and family members.

To improve the patient's functional capabilities, a specific physical therapy regimen is developed that includes the starting and goal levels of each of a set of specific exercises tailored to the individual's strengths, weaknesses, and vocational needs. Although all team members provide input into the physical therapy program, the physical therapist holds primary responsibility for its development, implementation, and documentation (see Table 1, page 247).

Following the evaluation conference, the patient and his or her spouse sign the Treatment Program Agreement (see Appendix B). During the remaining seven weeks of

TABLE 1:   CASE EXAMPLE--PHYSICAL EXERCISE PROGRAM

Exercise	Beginning Level	Final Level
Straight leg raises	4 repetitions	21 repetitions
Knees to chest	4 repetitions	21 repetitions
Bridges	4 repetitions	21 repetitions
Leg crossovers	4 repetitions	21 repetitions
Upper back extension	4 repetitions	21 repetitions
Cat and camel	4 repetitions	21 repetitions
Alternate arm and leg extension	4 repetitions	21 repetitions
Windmills	4 repetitions	21 repetitions
Side bends with pole	4 repetitions	21 repetitions
Twists with pole	4 repetitions	21 repetitions
Toe touches with extension	4 repetitions	21 repetitions
Shoulder squeezes	4 repetitions	21 repetitions
Wall push-ups	4 repetitions	21 repetitions
Step-ups	4 repetitions	21 repetitions
Walking	10 minutes	20 minutes
Sit-ups	0	13 repetitions
Side leg raises	0	13 repetitions
Knee push-ups	0	13 repetitions
Bicycling	0	25 minutes

treatment, the patient attends physical therapy sessions at least three times per week and exercises at the assigned level on remaining days at home. Attendance at all scheduled appointments is required and pain is not an acceptable excuse for nonattendance. The physical therapist constructs a set of graphs based on the patient's evaluation conference. The graph for each exercise includes the beginning number of repetitions, the number of repetitions to be performed on each day of the program, and the final goal. The patient typically begins each exercise at approximately one-half of his or her maximum performance level during the evaluation week and gradually increases to a level considered normal for the patient's age, sex, and degree of physical impairment.

It should be emphasized that the role of the physical therapist goes much beyond that of exercise management. The physical therapist provides differential reinforcement to shape functional behavior and extinguish pain behaviors. Through this process, the physical therapist also serves as a role model and active teacher of the skills necessary to develop satisfying relationships that are not based upon pain and disability. The structured progressive physical therapy regimen minimizes patient frustration and promotes the patient's sense of accomplishment and self-efficacy. Members of the treatment team, who regularly observe the patient in physical therapy and review the exercise charts, also provide reinforcement for improvements in physical functioning. A concentrated effort is made by all staff members to ignore, in nonpunitive ways, all pain behaviors, and to reinforce adaptive efforts.

When applicable, a pain medication withdrawal program is established. In conjunction with the physician, the psychologist constructs a schedule that gradually reduces medication intake during treatment. A target date for total elimination of medication may be set. As noted above, however, the presence of severe chemical dependency is a contraindication to this outpatient approach. If the patient is severely addicted, an inpatient pain program is required or, at the very least, the patient should be detoxified prior to beginning this program.

The patient and his or her spouse are also seen in conjoint therapy sessions once per week. When indicated, these sessions include other family members. The initial goal of these sessions is to train the couple to identify pain behaviors, to alter the maintaining consequences, and to reinforce well behavior. The second goal of these sessions is to assist the couple in recognizing how pain has become a way of life. Learning to live a normal life despite pain is continuously emphasized. Patients are helped to see that, rather than being regulated by pain, they can control their pain by altering influences on their behavior. Patients are encouraged to employ activity and exercise as a way of coping with pain, to reinforce themselves for engaging in these coping strategies, and to set attainable functional goals. The third purpose of conjoint therapy is to address difficulties in the relationship that were targeted during the evaluation conference. Role-playing exercises are used to test deficits in communication and problem-solving skills. These sessions assist the couple in learning new ways of interacting that do not center around pain and to return to activities that were formerly satisfying and reinforcing to both of them.

Individual therapy with the psychologist is also arranged when necessary. These sessions can focus on a wide range of problem areas that may be limiting the patient's functioning and thereby contributing to disability. Typically, a behaviorally oriented skills training approach is utilized. Examples include training in relaxation, assertiveness, and problem-solving skills. Cognitive restructuring techniques are concurrently em-

248

ployed to modify the presumed cognitive substrates of maladaptive behavior.

The ultimate goal of treatment is to assist the patient in returning to work or some other productive activity. This often necessitates the involvement of community-based vocational rehabilitation programs. In some cases, private vocational rehabilitation specialists representing the insurance carrier are included to serve as a liaison between the treatment program and the patient's former employer if a return is feasible.

This treatment approach is generally conducted within an 8 week time frame. However, slight modifications may be necessary, depending upon the particular needs and deficits of the individual patient. The treatment program is arranged so that the patient achieves all exercise and functional goals 1 week prior to the end of treatment, leaving the last week as maintenance. During the final week, the patient is reinforced for accomplishments made over the past 6 weeks. In addition, the patient is able to challenge members of the treatment team to complete his or her exercise program on a designated day. The challenge allows the patient to compare his or her current level of functioning to that of others considered normal and serves to reinforce the patient's progress. The patient's exercise performance and functional capabilities are again recorded on videotape and the patient, along with family members and the treatment team, view both the before and the after treatment tapes. The viewing allows the patient to observe former and present behavior and usually reinforces a sense of accomplishment. On the last day of the program, the patient is presented with a certificate indicating that he or she is a "Pain Expert" and has successfully completed the program and is, therefore, entitled to the "greatest admiration and respect."

Following treatment, the patient again completes all of the pre-treatment assessment measures. In addition, the physician re-evaluates the patient's physical condition at the end of treatment and a determination about the patient's ability to return to work or enter a retraining program is made.

FOLLOW-UP

The structure of the follow-up program is decided during the discharge conference. The follow-up program, typically lasting 6 months, is designed to maintain treatment gains and to continue to treat unresolved problems. Physical therapy as well as couples and individual sessions are gradually tapered off to approximately once every 6 to 8 weeks.

In the event of a setback during the follow-up component, both physical therapy and conjoint sessions are arranged. Counseling and emotional support are provided during this time, and if there is a loss in physical functioning, the patient is asked to construct a set of exercise graphs to assist in regaining his or her prior level of physical functioning.

The following case example illustrates the application of these assessment and treatment procedures.

CASE EXAMPLE

Mrs. S was referred to the Miriam Hospital Chronic Pain Treatment Program by her orthopedist because of a protracted period of pain and disability. Her physician determined that surgery was not likely to be beneficial and that her disability was disproportionate to the degree of detectable physical pathology.

The patient had a 9 year history of low back and neck pain subsequent to an injury incurred while working as a secretary. Mrs. S complained of constant pain in her low back and in her right leg from the knee to the toes. She also reported intermittent neck pain radiating into the right shoulder, periodic stabbing pain in her chest, and frequent bilateral, frontal headaches.

Over the course of her pain problem, Mrs. S had been hospitalized seven times. Extensive diagnostic testing, including two myelograms, a venogram, discogram, electromyelogram (EMG), and CAT scan had been essentially within normal limits. She had received multiple nonsurgical treatments, including traction, hydrocollator, transcutaneous electrical nerve stimulation (TNS), back brace, chiropractic manipulation, and extended bed rest, but none of these procedures had provided sustained pain relief or resulted in a significant reduction in her level of disability.

Mrs. S noted that her pain was exacerbated by extended walking, sitting, and standing; lifting; twisting; and damp, inclement weather. She also reported increased pain associated with sexual intercourse. Activities routinely employed by the patient to help her pain were lying down several hours per day, chiropractic manipulation two times per week, hot baths and hot showers, massages by her husband, and medication. At the time of her pre-treatment evaluation, Mrs. S was reportedly taking Fiorinal #3, four times per day, and Extra-Strength Tylenol, twice per day.

As a result of her chronic pain, Mrs. S had become markedly restricted in her functioning and performance of routine activities. She was unable to work, could not drive as she feared that pain might cause her to lose control of the car, and had abandoned social and recreational activities that she previously enjoyed. While the patient had remained intermittently active in a local social organization, she described a pattern of requiring pain medication prior to participating in social events, and paying the price for increased activity by being totally incapacitated and bedridden for several days afterwards. Moreover, she was not completing household chores and tasks on a routine basis.

The patient's pain problem had also adversely affected her marriage. While she and her husband denied marital discord and increased arguments since her injury, they acknowledged her chronic pain and disability had detrimentally affected their relationship by preventing and limiting their involvement in previously shared, reinforcing activities. Both partners reported strong displeasure with this change in their relationship, because prior to the patient's injury they had been very active together. Additionally, Mrs. S's pain problem had significantly curtailed their sexual activity. The patient refrained from sex because of its association with worsened pain, and she reported requiring pain medication prior to attempting intercourse. Her spouse, on the other hand, indicated that his enjoyment of sex was greatly diminished by his consciousness of his wife's pain.

Perhaps the greatest effect of the patient's pain problem was on her self-esteem and emotional functioning. Whereas the patient denied any psychiatric history or difficulties prior to her pain problem, she acknowledged that since her injury she had become increasingly depressed. During her evaluation, Mrs. S complained of pervasive dysphoria and anxiety, loss of self-confidence, and feelings of helplessness and hopelessness. She reported feeling useless and angry at herself because of her inability to work or freely engage in activities with her husband.

Mrs. S met the criteria for admission to the chronic pain program and was enrolled. During the evaluation week, the staff identified a number of marital and environmental factors that apparently were influencing the patient's chronic pain and disability. These variables included both direct reinforcement of pain behavior provided by her husband (i.e., massages), as well as indirect reinforcement in the form of avoidance of various unpleasant household and family responsibilities. Weekly conjoint marital sessions were arranged in order to assess the marital relationship and develop new patterns of interaction that would promote increased functioning rather than pain behavior and disability. These sessions focused on improving communication patterns as well as restructuring those components of the relationship which centered around the patient's pain and disability. In addition, Mrs. S, in conjunction with her spouse and the staff, established a number of marital activity goals, including golfing with her husband two times and taking an overnight vacation to Cape Cod. She also set individual goals such as driving a car again, taking golf lessons, increased involvement in social activities, and performance of more household chores (see Appendix B). Furthermore, the patient agreed to graduated time-contingent programs aimed at reducing and then eliminating her use of medication, chiropractic visits, hot baths and showers, and lying down for pain relief. Finally, Mrs. S participated in a physical therapy exercise regimen specifically tailored to overcome the physical limitations associated with her many years of inactivity and disability (see Table 1).

Mrs. S did extremely well over the course of treatment and met all of her goals by the specified time. The patient gradually increased her activity level, while simultaneously decreasing and eliminating her medication usage and other pain-relief activities. As marital therapy progressed, the patient's spouse quickly learned to ignore pain behaviors and instead reinforce and encourage appropriate well behaviors. The couple increasingly engaged in shared activities, including more frequent sexual activity, and by the end of treatment both partners reported substantially improved marital satisfaction.

With increased participation in pleasant activities and an improved marital situation, Mrs. S exhibited more positive affect in the initial stages of treatment. However, in the fifth week of treatment she began to complain of heightened anxiety with lightheadedness, difficulty breathing, and tightness in her chest. She indicated that these symptoms tended to be elicited by many of the activities that she recently resumed.

These symptoms were conceptualized by the staff as an anxiety/phobic reaction to activities that she had avoided for several years but were now within her functional capabilities. Individual psychotherapy sessions were arranged to train the patient in systematic relaxation techniques and to provide her with extensive instruction in the use of various cognitive coping strategies. Mrs. S reliably practiced these techniques and was soon able to utilize them to diminish her anxiety and successfully function in these situations. By the end of treatment, she reported markedly improved affect and increased self-confidence attributable at least in part to her mastery of activities that she had formerly avoided because of pain or anxiety.

The patient's successful completion of treatment is illustrated in her pre-/post-treatment measures (see Table 2, page 254). Her post-treatment daily activity diaries revealed a substantial improvement in her functional capabilities, reduction in time spent lying down or engaged in pain-relief activities, and decreased ratings of pain intensity. Her overall disability index on the Sickness Impact Profile decreased from a pre-treatment level of 23.6% to 5% at post-treatment. Although Mr. and Mrs. S's pre-treatment scores on the marital questionnaires were within the low end of the range obtained by maritally satisfied couples, their post-treatment scores on these measures reflected a substantial increase in the level of their satisfaction. Mrs. S's scores on the post-treatment Cognitive Error Questionnaire indicated substantially reduced cognitive distortion relative to pre-treatment. Additionally, the patient's post-treatment MMPI profile was within normal limits, compared to her pre-treatment MMPI which had indicated significant levels of depression and emotional distress.

Follow-up sessions over the next 6 months indicated that Mrs. S maintained her daily exercise regimen, continued to be functionally active, and abstained from routine use of medications and other pain-relief activities. Monitoring of the patient's marital situation and her emotional status, via regularly scheduled marital and individual therapy sessions, has confirmed maintenance of treatment gains in these areas.

TABLE 2: CASE EXAMPLE - EVALUATION INSTRUMENTS

	Pre-Treatment	Post-Treatment
Activity Diaries		
Percent lying down[1]	20	4
Percent sitting[1]	60	70
Percent standing/walking[1]	20	26
Hours in pain-relief activities	2.3	0
Minutes in physical exercise	0	60
Pain-rating (0-10 scale)	5.0	3.7
Sickness Impact Profile		
Physical impairment	2	0
Psychosocial impairment	19.9	0
"Other" impairment (work, recreation, social)	27.8	17.8
Overall impairment[2]	23.6	5.0
Marital Measures		
Locke-Wallace Marital Adjustment Test[3] (patient)	109	142
Locke-Wallace Marital Adjustment Test[3] (spouse)	116	145
Areas of Change Questionnaire[4]	14	2
Cognitive Error Questionnaire		
General distortion	23	3
Low-back specific distortion	47	1
MMPI		
L	50	50
F	48	46
K	57	62
Hypochondriasis	68	58
Depression	74	63
Hysteria	70	63
Psychopathic deviance	52	62
Masculinity/femininity	49	56
Paranoia	58	57
Psychasthenia	60	55
Schizophrenia	54	54
Mania	58	43
Social introversion	64	55

[1]Percentage of waking hours.
[2]Follick, Aberger, Ahern, and McCartney (1984): M = 23.8 for chronic pain patients; M = 3.6 for general population.
[3]Locke and Wallace (1959): M = 135 for well-adjusted couples.
[4]Weiss, Hops, and Patterson (1973): M = 6.9 for nondistressed couples.

254

During her involvement in the 8 week intensive phase of the pain program, Mrs. S was referred to a vocational specialist in her community. She met regularly with the vocational specialist to identify realistic vocational options that would interest her. Approximately 3 months post-treatment, she decided to become a paralegal professional. She has now entered school to become a paralegal and expects to begin full-time work in this capacity in the near future.

While Mrs. S is somewhat atypical in that she had no prior surgeries, she is fairly representative of the majority of chronic pain patients in that her pain behaviors appear to have been influenced by a number of psychological and environmental factors. It was felt that her chronic pain and disability were influenced not only by the positive reinforcement provided by her spouse, but also through negative reinforcement in the form of avoidance of anxiety-provoking activities and situations. As a result of the interactive nature of these influences on her chronic pain behavior, individualized treatment plans were necessary in addition to the routine structure provided by the program.

PROGRAM EFFECTIVENESS

Several chronic pain treatment programs employing the operant approach have reported their results. In a study which followed patients for periods ranging from 5 to 175 weeks after treatment, Fordyce et al. (1973) found reports of significantly less pain, less interference with daily activities, reductions in the utilization of pain medications, and less time spent in bed as a result of pain. Anderson, Cole, Gullickson, Hudgens, and Roberts (1977) reported that 75% of the 34 patients who completed their 8 week inpatient program were leading normal lives without medication when followed between 6 months and 7 years after treatment. In a long-term follow-up of the effectiveness of the same program, Roberts and Reinhardt (1980) compared the group that completed treatment to a group of 20 individuals rejected for treatment, and a group of 12 individuals accepted for treatment who refused to participate. Of all of the comparison subjects, only one individual from the latter group was leading a normal life without medication at long-term follow-up. Cairns, Thomas, Mooney, and Pace (1976) found that at 10 month follow-up, 75% of their patients reported either a

255

significant decrease in pain or an increase in activity level. Fifty-eight percent reported that they no longer required narcotic pain medications, and 74% sought no further medical advice.

Preliminary outcome data on the efficacy of this outpatient-based program indicate that, compared to a waiting list control group, patients completing treatment evidence statistically and clinically significant increases in functional capacity, reductions in the use of pain medications and pain-relief activities, and marked improvements in psychological and marital functioning. Twenty randomly selected admissions to our Chronic Pain Program were compared with a waiting list group of 18 subjects matched on age, sex, duration of pain, and number of surgeries. These 38 subjects had a mean age of 38 years, an average duration of pain of 40.5 months, and an average of one pain-related surgery. Subjects in the treated group were measured immediately before and after treatment, whereas waiting list control subjects completed a full set of measures at the time of their initial evaluation and again 2 months later. Patients in the treated group had a mean total SIP impairment index of 28.9% prior to treatment. At post-treatment, the mean SIP score decreased to 11.6% representing a 60% reduction in disability, compared to no change in the waiting list control group (M SIP score = 27.3% at initial assessment compared to 27.5% 2 months after initial evaluation). Similarly, treated patients reduced their lying down time from 5.1 hours per day prior to treatment to less than 2 hours per day post-treatment, and increased their standing/walking time from 4.3 hours per day to 5.7 hours per day. In contrast, waiting list control patients did not evidence significant changes in either time spent lying down (M = 3.9 to 5.0) or standing/walking (M = 4.1 to 4.3). The average number of hours per day spent in pain-relief activities for treated patients was reduced 80% from 6.2 hours per day pre-treatment to 1.1 hours per day post-treatment, compared to no change in the waiting list control group (M = 7.9 to 7.3). While no attempt is made to directly modify pain, the treated group's self-report of pain decreased from a pre-treatment mean of 6.3 on a scale of 0-10 to 3.8 post-treatment, and most of these patients were not using pain medications at discharge. Patients in the treated group also showed significant reductions in emotional distress as measured by the Depression, Psychasthenia, and Schizophrenia scales of the

MMPI. The waiting list comparison group evidenced no significant changes on pain intensity ratings, medication usage, and emotional or marital distress. Perhaps of greatest significance was the fact that 80% of the patients treated either returned to their former occupation or entered a vocational retraining program. Although more extensive outcome research is required to fully confirm the utility of this approach, our preliminary data suggest that this outpatient-based treatment program is effective in modifying the disability and pain behaviors of patients suffering from chronic pain.

APPENDIX A: DAILY ACTIVITY DIARY

Name: _____

Date: _____

Time	POSITION Lying 1	Sitting 2	Standing-Walking 3	Asleep for the night 4	Major Activity	For pain relief 5	Alone 6	With family 7	With others 8	At home 9	Medications	Other Pain Relief Activities or Devices
A.M. 6:00–6:30	1	2	3	4		5	6	7	8	9	1. 2. 3.	
6:30–7:00	1	2	3	4		5	6	7	8	9	1. 2. 3.	
7:00–7:30	1	2	3	4		5	6	7	8	9	1. 2. 3.	
7:30–8:00	1	2	3	4		5	6	7	8	9	1. 2. 3.	
8:00–8:30	1	2	3	4		5	6	7	8	9	1. 2. 3.	
8:30–9:00	1	2	3	4		5	6	7	8	9	1. 2. 3.	
9:00–9:30	1	2	3	4		5	6	7	8	9	1. 2. 3.	

FOR EACH HALF HOUR CIRCLE ONE POSITION ONLY

PAGE 1

DAILY ACTIVITY DIARY (Continued)

Name: _____

Date: _____

Time	POSITION				Major Activity	For pain relief 5	Alone 6	With Family 7	With others 8	At home 9	Medications	Other Pain Relief Activities or Devices
	Lying 1	Sitting 2	Standing-Walking 3	Asleep for the night 4								
A.M. 9:30–10:00	1	2	3	4		5	6	7	8	9	1. 2. 3.	
10:00–10:30	1	2	3	4		5	6	7	8	9	1. 2. 3.	
10:30–11:00	1	2	3	4		5	6	7	8	9	1. 2. 3.	
11:00–11:30	1	2	3	4		5	6	7	8	9	1. 2. 3.	
11:30–12:00	1	2	3	4		5	6	7	8	9	1. 2. 3.	
P.M. 12:00–12:30	1	2	3	4		5	6	7	8	9	1. 2. 3.	
12:30–1:00	1	2	3	4		5	6	7	8	9	1. 2. 3.	

FOR EACH HALF HOUR CIRCLE ONE POSITION ONLY

PAGE 2

259

Name: _____

Date: _____

DAILY ACTIVITY DIARY (Continued)

Time	POSITION				Major Activity	For pain relief 5	Alone 6	With family 7	With others 8	At home 9	Medications	Other Pain Relief Activities or Devices
	Lying 1	Sitting 2	Standing-Walking 3	Asleep for the night 4							1. 2. 3.	
P.M. 1:00-1:30	1	2	3	4		5	6	7	8	9	1. 2. 3.	
1:30-2:00	1	2	3	4		5	6	7	8	9	1. 2. 3.	
2:00-2:30	1	2	3	4		5	6	7	8	9	1. 2. 3.	
2:30-3:00	1	2	3	4		5	6	7	8	9	1. 2. 3.	
3:00-3:30	1	2	3	4		5	6	7	8	9	1. 2. 3.	
3:30-4:00	1	2	3	4		5	6	7	8	9	1. 2. 3.	
4:00-4:30	1	2	3	4		5	6	7	8	9	1. 2. 3.	

FOR EACH HALF HOUR CIRCLE ONE POSITION ONLY

Name: _____

Date: _____

DAILY ACTIVITY DIARY (Continued)

Time	POSITION Lying 1	Sitting 2	Standing-Walking 3	Asleep for the night 4	Major Activity	For pain relief 5	Alone 6	With family 7	With others 8	At home 9	Medications	Other Pain Relief Activities or Devices
P.M. 4:30-5:00	1	2	3	4		5	6	7	8	9	1. 2. 3.	
5:00-5:30	1	2	3	4		5	6	7	8	9	1. 2. 3.	
5:30-6:00	1	2	3	4		5	6	7	8	9	1. 2. 3.	
6:00-6:30	1	2	3	4		5	6	7	8	9	1. 2. 3.	
6:30-7:00	1	2	3	4		5	6	7	8	9	1. 2. 3.	
7:00-7:30	1	2	3	4		5	6	7	8	9	1. 2. 3.	
7:30-8:00	1	2	3	4		5	6	7	8	9	1. 2. 3.	

FOR EACH HALF HOUR CIRCLE ONE POSITION ONLY

PAGE 4

261

Name:

Date:

DAILY ACTIVITY DIARY (Continued)

Time	POSITION				Major Activity	For pain relief 5	Alone 6	With family 7	With others 8	At home 9	Medications	Other Pain Relief Activities or Devices
	Lying 1	Sitting 2	Standing-Walking 3	Asleep for the night 4								
P.M. 8:00– 8:30	1	2	3	4		5	6	7	8	9	1. 2. 3.	
8:30– 9:00	1	2	3	4		5	6	7	8	9	1. 2. 3.	
9:00– 9:30	1	2	3	4		5	6	7	8	9	1. 2. 3.	
9:30– 10:00	1	2	3	4		5	6	7	8	9	1. 2. 3.	
10:00– 10:30	1	2	3	4		5	6	7	8	9	1. 2. 3.	
10:30– 11:00	1	2	3	4		5	6	7	8	9	1. 2. 3.	
11:00– 11:30	1	2	3	4		5	6	7	8	9	1. 2. 3.	

FOR EACH HALF HOUR CIRCLE ONE POSITION ONLY

PAGE 5

DAILY ACTIVITY DIARY (Continued)

Name: _____

Date: _____

Time	POSITION				Major Activity	For pain relief 5	Alone 6	With family 7	With others 8	At home 9	Medications	Other Pain Relief Activities or Devices
	Lying 1	Sitting 2	Standing-Walking 3	Asleep for the night 4								
P.M. 11:30-12:00	1	2	3	4		5	6	7	8	9	1. __ 2. __ 3. __	
A.M. 12:00-12:30	1	2	3	4		5	6	7	8	9	1. __ 2. __ 3. __	
12:30-1:00	1	2	3	4		5	6	7	8	9	1. __ 2. __ 3. __	
1:00-1:30	1	2	3	4		5	6	7	8	9	1. __ 2. __ 3. __	
1:30-2:00	1	2	3	4		5	6	7	8	9	1. __ 2. __ 3. __	
2:00-2:30	1	2	3	4		5	6	7	8	9	1. __ 2. __ 3. __	
2:30-3:00	1	2	3	4		5	6	7	8	9	1. __ 2. __ 3. __	

FOR EACH HALF HOUR CIRCLE ONE POSITION ONLY

PAGE 6

263

DAILY ACTIVITY DIARY (Continued)

Name: _____

Date: _____

Time	POSITION				Major Activity	For pain relief	Alone	With family	With others	At home	Medications	Other Pain Relief Activities or Devices
	Lying 1	Sitting 2	Standing-Walking 3	Asleep for the night 4		5	6	7	8	9	1. 2. 3.	
A.M. 3:00-3:30	1	2	3	4		5	6	7	8	9	1. 2. 3.	
3:30-4:00	1	2	3	4		5	6	7	8	9	1. 2. 3.	
4:00-4:30	1	2	3	4		5	6	7	8	9	1. 2. 3.	
4:30-5:00	1	2	3	4		5	6	7	8	9	1. 2. 3.	
5:00-5:30	1	2	3	4		5	6	7	8	9	1. 2. 3.	
5:30-6:00	1	2	3	4		5	6	7	8	9	1. 2. 3.	

FOR EACH HALF HOUR CIRCLE ONE POSITION ONLY

PAIN RELIEF ACTIVITIES OR DEVICES

1. Corset/Brace	3. Home traction	5. Ice packs	7. Whirlpool	9. TENS/Stimulator	11. Pillow/Pad
2. Collar	4. Heating pad	6. Massages	8. Hot baths/Showers	10. Vibrator	12. Other_____

PAGE 7

264

DAILY ACTIVITY DIARY (Continued)

DAILY RATINGS

PAIN

Indicate the level of pain which you feel represents the average for the day:

(Circle one)

0	1	2	3	4	5	6	7	8	9	10
None										Worst Possible

TENSION

Indicate the amount of tension which you feel represents the average for the day:

(Circle one)

0	1	2	3	4	5	6	7	8	9	10
None										Very tense

MOOD

Indicate the mood which you feel represents the average for the day:

(Circle one)

-5	-4	-3	-2	-1	0	1	2	3	4	5
Sad					Neutral					Happy

PAGE 8

265

APPENDIX B: THE MIRIAM HOSPITAL
OUTPATIENT PAIN TREATMENT PROGRAM AGREEMENT

The purpose of this agreement is for me:_____

the patient, to understand and agree with _____

representing the treatment team, and_____

a member of my family or someone else who is significant to me ("significant other"), on the following:

1. The program is mainly designed to recondition me physically and will also be directed toward my learning to live with pain, and changing those of my actions and attitudes ("behaviors") which are associated with the pain. During the evaluation week the staff, my significant others, and I have identified my pains as well as the behaviors that communicate to other people that I am in pain. Some of these behaviors include the following:

   _____

   _____

   _____

   _____

   I understand that my pains, and all my behaviors relating to pain will be completely ignored by the treatment team.

2. I give my permission to my significant others, including _____

   _____

   to ignore my pains, complaints of pain, and behaviors related to pain while I am in the program and after its completion in order to help me manage my life in ways that will be more satisfying to all of us.

3. Our goal is to increase my activities in kind and amount to the point at which I can do things considered normal for a person my age and sex. More specifically, I have the following goals:

   _____

   _____

   _____

   _____

4. Pain medications will be gradually eliminated as my activity level increases. Once my program begins, I agree to dispose of any other pain relieving medications or devices that I have at home.

5. I will keep graphs showing my progress. I understand that I alone am responsible for these graphs and with help from the treatment team I will keep them up to date and available for inspection **at all times.**

6. Members of my family or others significant to me will be considered essential, active participants in this program: They will work with me, breaking my old habits and learning new ways I can live with my pain, without being disabled by it. The following persons agree to participate when requested:

_____

_____

    In addition, I understand that you may talk with me or meet with other members of my family if that will improve the chances of maintaining my gains after the program is completed. I understand that I will be informed about this before they are contacted.

7. This is an outpatient based treatment program, and I will be required to come to the hospital on a regular basis, as determined by the treatment team. I understand that I am expected to attend **all** scheduled sessions as well as perform all activities to be conducted at home. Pain is no excuse. I further understand that if I am absent from two (2) successive sessions, or a total of three (3), this program will automatically terminate.

8. If, for three (3) consecutive days, I do not improve on any or all of my activities (as demonstrated in the graphs), my activity schedule goal for those exercises will be lowered one step. In the event that I do not improve during the next three (3) days, this program will be terminated. This procedure will be employed twice and on the third occasion that I fail to meet any or all of my scheduled goals, the program will automatically terminate.

9. The treatment program will continue until I have maintained all activity and work goals for one (1) full week. After that, I will participate in any follow-up program that the treatment team feels is necessary for me, even though I have improved considerably by that time.

10. Based on my treatment needs, members of the treatment team will decide what the follow-up components of the program will consist of and how long it will continue.

I understand and agree to the above program, which has now been explained to my satisfaction.

_____   _____
(Patient)   (Date)

_____   _____
(Team Representative)   (Significant Other)

267

Michael J. Follick, PhD, is currently Director of the Miriam Hospital Chronic Pain Treatment Program and the Division of Behavioral Medicine, Miriam Hospital. He is also an Associate Professor of Psychiatry in the Department of Psychiatry and Human Behavior at Brown University and is the Director of the Brown University Psychology Internship and Fellowship training programs. His training is in clinical psychology with a specialty in health psychology. He received his PhD from the University of Iowa and completed his internship training at the University of Minnesota. He has published numerous articles and book chapters in the area of chronic pain and his other interests include worksite health promotion and the relationship between stress, cardiovascular reactivity, and arrhythmias. Dr. Follick may be contacted at the Division of Behavioral Medicine, Miriam Hospital, 164 Summit Avenue, Providence, RI 02906.

David K. Ahern, PhD, is currently Program Coordinator of the Miriam Hospital Chronic Pain Treatment Program. He is also an Assistant Professor of Psychiatry in the Department of Psychiatry and Human Behavior at Brown University. Dr. Ahern received his PhD from Nova University and completed his clinical internship training at the Brown University Internship Consortium. He has published numerous articles in the area of chronic pain. His other interests include psychophysiology and computer applications. Dr. Ahern can be contacted at the Division of Behavioral Medicine, Miriam Hospital, 164 Summit Avenue, Providence, RI 02906.

Edward W. Aberger, PhD, is currently Clinical Coordinator of the Miriam Hospital Chronic Pain Treatment Program. He is also an Assistant Clinical Professor of Psychiatry in the Department of Psychiatry and Human Behavior at Brown University. His primary clinical and research interests are the behavioral assessment and treatment of chronic pain. Dr. Aberger may be contacted at the Division of Behavioral Medicine, Miriam Hospital, 164 Summit Avenue, Providence, RI 02906.

RESOURCES

Anderson, T. P., Cole, T. M., Gullickson, G., Hudgens, A., & Roberts, A. H. (1977). Modification of chronic pain: A treatment program by a multidisciplinary team. *Clinical Orthopedics and Related Research, 129,* 96-100.

Beck, A. T., Rush, A. J., Shaw, B. P., & Emery, G. (1979). *Cognitive Therapy of Depression.* New York: Guilford Press.

Bergner, M., Bobbitt, R. A., Cater, W. B., & Gilson, B. S. (1983). The Sickness Impact Profile: Development and final revision of a health status measure. *Medical Care,* 787-805.

Cairns, D., Thomas, L., Mooney, V., & Pace, J. B. (1976). A comprehensive treatment approach to chronic low back pain. *Pain, 2,* 301.

Ellis, A., & Greiger, R. (Eds.). (1977). *Handbook of Rational-Emotive Therapy.* New York: Springer.

Follick, M. J., Aberger, E. W., Ahern, D. K., & McCartney, J. R. (1984). The chronic low back pain syndrome: Identification and management. *Rhode Island Medical Journal, 67,* 219-224.

Follick, M. J., Ahern, D. K., & Aberger, E. W. (1985). Development of an audiovisual taxonomy of pain behavior: Reliability and discriminant validity. *Pain, 4,* 555-568.

Follick, M. J., Ahern, D. K., & Laser-Wolston, N. (1984). Evaluation of a daily activity diary for chronic pain patients. *Pain, 19,* 75-79.

Follick, M. J., Smith, T. W., & Ahern, D. K. (1985). The Sickness Impact Profile: A global measure of disability in chronic low back pain. *Pain, 21,* 67-76.

Fordyce, W. E. (1974). Pain viewed as learned behavior. In J. J. Bonica (Ed.), *Advances in Neurology* (Vol. 4, pp. 415-422). New York: Raven Press.

Fordyce, W. E. (1976). *Behavioral Methods for Chronic Pain and Illness.* St. Louis: Mosby.

Fordyce, W. E., Fowler, R. S., Lehmann, J. F., Delateur, B. J., Sand, P. L., & Trieschmann, R. B. (1973). Operant conditioning in the treatment of chronic pain. *Archives of Physical Medicine and Rehabilitation, 54,* 399-408.

Jacobsen, N. S., & Margolin, G. (1979). *Marital Therapy: Strategies Based on Social Learning and Behavior Exchange Principles.* New York: Brunner/Mazel.

269

Lefebrve, J. J. (1981). Cognitive distortion and cognitive errors in depressed psychiatric and low back pain patients. *Journal of Consulting and Clinical Psychology, 49*, 517-525.

Locke, H. J., & Wallace, K. M. (1959). Short marital adjustment and prediction tests: Their reliability and validity. *Marriage and Family Living,* 251-255.

Loesser, J. D. (1974). Dorsal rhizotomy: Indications and results. In J. J. Bonica (Ed.), *Advances in Neurology* (Vol. 4, pp. 375-380). New York: Raven Press.

Management of chronic pain: Medicine's new growth industry. (1976, October). *Medical World News.*

Melzack, R. (1974). Psychological concepts and methods for the control of pain. In J. J. Bonica (Ed.), *Advances in Neurology* (Vol. 4, pp. 275-280). New York: Raven Press.

Roberts, A. H., & Reinhardt, L. (1980). The behavioral management of chronic pain: Long-term follow-up with comparison groups. *Pain, 8,* 151-162.

Weiss, R. L., Hops, H., & Patterson, G. R. (1973). A framework for conceptualizing marital conflict, a technology for altering it, some data for evaluating it. In S. W. Clark & L. A. Hamerlynck (Eds.), *Proceedings of the Fourth Banff International Conference on Behavior Modification* (pp. 309-342). Champaign, IL: Research Press.

White, A. W. (1969). Low back pain in men receiving Workmen's Compensation: A follow-up study. *Canadian Medical Association Journal, 101,* 61-67.

LONG TERM REMEDIATION OF HEAD INJURED PATIENTS*

*Ronald M. Ruff, Randall W. Evans,
and Richard Green*

INTRODUCTION

In a single year, 4900 patients were hospitalized
following head injury in San Diego County (Klauber,
Barrett-Conner, Marshall, & Bowers, 1981). Nationwide,
head injuries have reached epidemic proportions and the
number of victims continues to escalate (Caveness, 1979).
Air evacuation, paramedical services, and advances in
medical management have allowed many more patients to
survive each year. In contrast to these advances in acute
treatment, long-term rehabilitation efforts have lagged far
behind. Lack of hard data supporting the effectiveness
of such efforts and a general failure to recognize the
needs of this population have contributed to this gap in
services. A number of researchers have illustrated that
patients with traumatic brain damage represent a neglected group from the perspective of long-term rehabilitation (Rusk, Block, & Lowman, 1969; Timming et al., 1980).
Head injured patients are in need of advanced reme-

*The authors would like to acknowledge with appreciation the helpful
comments of Igor Grant, MD, Martha Minteer, MD, Lawrence F. Marshall,
MD, and Sharon A. Bowers, BSN, of the University of California at San
Diego in reviewing this article. This work was supported by contracts
(NOI-NS-9-2309 and NOI-NS-9-2312) with the U. S. National Institute of
Neurological and Communicative Disorders and Stroke. We are grateful
for their assistance.

diation programs which focus not only on the physical but also on the emotional and psychosocial residual impairments.

More and more studies are beginning to document in detail the extent of the neuropsychological sequelae resulting from brain trauma (Bond, 1975, 1976; Jennett & Bond, 1975; Eson, Yen, & Borke, 1978; Levin, Benton, & Grossman, 1982). The senior author is a participant in a multicenter research project for the traumatically head injured and, in that capacity, has followed this patient population for 2 years post-injury. Follow-up protocol consists of a neuropsychological test battery administered at baseline, 6, 12, and 24 months post-injury. To assure compliance with the follow-up protocol, family consultations were held to delineate the levels of performance. It was common during these consultations for both patients and family members to ask the examiners many complex questions concerning such issues as marriage, mood changes, driving, independence, memory, attention, and vocational potential. Initial attempts to find adequate referral placements in our community failed. Frequently, the patients and their families were isolated because they felt their experience was a unique one. The aim of this chapter is to report the efforts taken to establish support groups in response to the clinical needs of the head injured and their families.

To date, only one study has addressed the advantages of group psychotherapy for the head injured (Rosenbaum, Lipsitz, Abraham, & Najenson, 1978). In that study, 13 severely head injured veterans were engaged in a therapeutic workshop. The authors particularly emphasized the supportive aspect of the group experience. Despite the sparse findings in the literature, group psychotherapy has achieved recognition with a host of other populations including stroke patients (Evans & Northwood, 1983), spinal injured patients (Roessler, Milligan, & Ohlson, 1979), individuals with cancer (Blanford, 1979), the terminally ill (Yalom, 1983), and persons with multiple sclerosis (Hartings, Pavlou, & Davis, 1976).

The question arises as to why group psychotherapy is seldom employed with head injured patients. The answer may be based on the assumption that patients with severe head injuries lack the necessary cognitive skills, such as adequate attentional and memory capacities, to profit from group interactions. No doubt, cognitive deficiencies can interfere with psychological treatments, but is the interference with treatment substantially different in a group setting compared to individual therapy? The present study addresses this question.

All the patients who were referred for individual therapy were extended an invitation to participate in the group therapy, regardless of cognitive deficits or degree of psychological difficulties. Since the residual deficits of the head injured are rarely confined to cognitive impairments, emotional as well as psychosocial problems need to be treated concurrently. Emotional sequelae which often occur following a significant head injury include apathy, diminished motivation, and interpersonal difficulties, that is, decreased verbal communication and diminished sexual satisfaction (Brooks & McKinlay, 1983; Kinsella & Duffy, 1979; Stern, 1978). The point that needs to be emphasized is that maladjustments extend beyond the intrapersonal domain to the interpersonal spheres. This raises a key question: What are the pros and cons of group psychotherapy compared to individual psychotherapy? More specifically, can group psychotherapy become the treatment of choice for effectively dealing with emotional, mental, or intrapersonal disorders and the psychosocial or interpersonal problems which result?

To facilitate both the intra- and interpersonal adjustments, group psychotherapy for the head injured was established with the following aims: (a) to create a specialized service for an escalating patient population whose adjustment difficulties have been sadly neglected in the past, (b) to provide supportive care and information to family members who have suddenly been thrust into the caretaking role, (c) to develop a therapy mode in which the various disciplines can orchestrate their efforts, and (d) to provide a service which extends beyond the period of acute recovery and facilitate a sensitivity towards long-term recovery phases, all of which have their unique problems.

The *client characteristics* of the head injured patients included in our groups were as follows:

1. Self-reported history of residual cognitive and/or emotional impairments secondary to brain injury.
2. Expressed interest in group participation aimed at addressing impairments.

3. Head injury severe enough to result in a period of coma of at least 4 hours duration or a period of post-traumatic amnesia of at least 48 hours. (According to the Galveston Orientation and Amnesia Test; Levin et al., 1982.)
4. Absence of a pre-existing neurological disorder or chronic psychiatric illness.

A total of 12 patients were selected for each group and paired with an approximately equal number of their family members. No patients were excluded because of length of recovery, locus of lesion, age, ethnic background, or sex, although the male to female ratio was about 5:1. (This statistic approximates the sex incidence ratio of closed head injury.)

The *procedure* for the sessions followed this format: Group meetings, which lasted 1.5 to 2 hours, were held weekly for 12 consecutive months for both the patient groups and the family groups. Two different groups of approximately equal size met 1 year each. Participation was voluntary and at no cost. The group work was structured according to the following three phases:

PHASE I: INFORMATION

The major purpose of Phase I was to provide the patients and their significant others with information about the effects of a head injury as viewed by clinicians from various disciplines. These sessions were held weekly. Each patient was sent a questionnaire and an outline of a lecture series with the dates and titles of the various presentations (see Table 1, page 275). The content of these multidisciplinary presentations was representative of the interests expressed in response to a pre-treatment questionnaire. The speakers were encouraged to provide audiovisual aids and handouts, utilize mnemonic devices, be repetitive, and use cues and reviews. We felt it was important not to force group participation but to allow ample time for spontaneous discussions, to relate topics to everyday experiences, and to avoid the use of professional jargon. In summary, Phase I served the purpose of providing a nonthreatening exchange of relevant and interesting information within a social setting. Phase I lasted approximately 8-10 weeks.

TABLE 1:   LECTURE SERIES – PHASE I

Presenter	Topic
Driving Specialist	Defensive Driving Skills Learning to Drive Again with Handicaps
Neuropsychologist	Brain-Behavior Relationships Cognitive Rehabilitation
Nutritionist	Diet Planning--Positive Effects on Recovery
Occupational Therapist	Vocational Skills Training Vocational Counseling
Physical Therapist	Physical Rehabilitation Daily Exercising Skills
Psychologist	Systematic Desensitization Relaxation Training Problem Solving Skills
Social Worker	Family Therapy Referrals and Placement Opportunities
Speech Therapist	Language and the Brain Speech Therapy
Recreational Therapist	Creative Relaxation Planning Leisure Time Alternatives Community Resources for the Handicapped

PHASE II: PERSONAL EXCHANGE AND ACCEPTANCE OF PROBLEM

Patients and family members met separately in subgroups during Phase II; however, every other week participants would have a brief joint session. A team of three experienced therapists and one pre-doctoral psychology intern served as subgroup leaders. The same two co-therapists always worked with the same subgroup.

Unlike Phase I, the majority of the time in Phase II was spent on group discussions. The aim was to stimulate individuals to recognize changes that had taken place as a result of the accident. In the patient subgroup, the therapists generally presented a central theme for the discussion; examples of these themes are listed in Table 2 (page 276). In the family subgroups, discussions were less structured and involved exchanges of past experiences, sharing of resources, and updating one another about recent developments. Phase II lasted approximately 4 months.

TABLE 2: GROUP THERAPY DISCUSSION TOPICS – PHASE II	
Topic	Sample Inquiry by Therapists
Memory Functioning	Have you noticed if you've been forgetful since the injury? Are you having unusual difficulties remembering faces, names, dates?
Physiological Changes	Have your sleeping patterns or eating habits changed since the injury?
Self-Disclosure	Have you noticed any changes in the way you talk to others about personal matters?
Sexuality	Has your desire for sexual activity changed at all since the injury? Have your sexual habits changed?
Socialization	Do you visit with your friends or go out as much as you used to prior to the injury?
Body Image	Have you noticed any changes in the way you view yourself physically since the injury?
Motivation	Have you noticed any changes in your ability in starting to do a job or task?
Alcohol	Have your drinking habits changed since the injury? Has your tolerance for alcohol changed since the injury?
Employment	Has the injury affected your job performance? If so, how?
Suicide/Depression	Have you had thoughts of harming yourself since the injury? Have you noticed any changes in your mood since the injury?
Role Changes	Has your wife/husband/father/mother had to take over any of your duties?

PHASE III: PROBLEM SOLVING

During Phase III, the work in the subgroups was intensified by meeting 3 weeks in a row, with joint group sessions only once a month. In this phase, instead of the co-therapists introducing topics, the patients talked about their own needs and problems and, as a result, these sessions were less structured. In the family sessions, participants began to address their own needs and became less pre-occupied with the patients' needs. Phase III lasted approximately 6 months.

OUTCOME AND DISCUSSION

Summarized in Table 3 (page 278) are clinical observations gathered after observing and treating approximately 24 head injured patients and their family members. Specific areas highlighted included residual deficits observed in both the intra- and interpersonal dimensions. Presented below are discussions emphasizing the (a) patient's response to treatment, (b) family members' responses to treatment, (c) role of the therapist, and (d) importance of establishing specific treatment goals as exemplified by three case study presentations.

PATIENT'S RESPONSE

Self-Determination. The lecture series of Phase I contrasted subtly but significantly with the patient's prior experience in the standard rehabilitation program. Unlike the given structure of other forms of therapy, the patients were now actively solicited for their interests. Based on *their* responses to topics, the content of the lecture series was determined. Prior to this point the patients had usually participated in various therapies as determined by their physician. Another contrast was that group participation was totally voluntary and at no cost. Attendance was not based on the usual referral mechanisms. The lectures of Phase I were well received and usually generated lively discussions. A group cohesion emerged. One of the reasons for this may have been that the group itself remained unchanged but the different speakers were faced with having to adjust to the patient group. The group members were genuinely thankful for information as well as for the time and effort given to answer their questions in detail. Group participation in Phases II and III was completely voluntary and absences from sessions were not negatively commented upon. The participants' schedules and decisions to attend or not were respected in order to facilitate their self-determination.

Acceptance. Head injured patients do not have a reputation for being congenial. These patients are known to regress in their social skills and commonly exhibit irritable, aggressive, and egocentric behavior. It was

TABLE 3: AREAS OF PROBLEMS FOLLOWING HEAD INJURY

Intrapersonal			Interpersonal		
Physical	Emotional	Mental	Family/Spouse	Acquaintances	Employment
gross and fine motor movements (hemiparesis, slowing of dexterity)	mood swings (lability)	recent memory disturbance	financial changes (loss of income, applying for social security, litigation)	initial support (separate between curious and supportive friends)	loss of prestige
	loss of impulse control (irritability)	attentional disorder		lack of understanding	insecurity
		word finding difficulties	accepting caretaker role		false hope
vision (diplopia, reduced visual field)	depression (suicidal thought)	problems in abstract thinking (locking into an idea without properly considering alternatives)	dependency issues	isolation	reduced to nonproductive level, now what
	identity crisis		altered relationship (loss of spouse and sexual partner)	risk of making new friends	
	denial				lack of resources for retraining
smell/taste	lack of motivation (apathy)				
fatigue					

therefore surprising and impressive that the patients interacted in a courteous and tolerant manner with each other.

Finding the Common Denominator. During Phase I of their treatment, patients were observed to ask questions which related exclusively to themselves. In Phases II and III, however, patients started to show an interest in others. For example, one patient would start by asking a question such as "Does anyone else have problems with tasting food?" This would lead to other comparative questions and eventually some questions were directly posed to others. Individuals were not only interested in the extent and severity of their own symptoms but were curious to determine what residual impairments follow head injury *per se*. The realization emerged and was frequently expressed that although no two head injuries resulted in identical deficits, there was a clustering of similar impairments. Frequently, the psychosocial and emotional sequelae were also similar. In fact, individuals from drastically different socioeconomic backgrounds bonded together in their effort to understand more about each other as individuals and as victims of head injury.

Resocialization. For the majority of patients, interacting with old acquaintances or meeting new people was drastically reduced. Head injured patients, in general, are fearful of revealing weaknesses or are anxious that others will judge them as abnormal or brain damaged. As a result, these patients have a tendency to shy away from social affairs and isolation becomes a more comfortable alternative. The group therapy allowed for a resocialization process since it provided a unique absence of these concerns. Patients would spontaneously express how comfortable they felt about being among "equals." Role playing exercises in meeting strangers were utilized and patients would explain to someone that they were head injured or would share with one another how social isolation can be overcome.

FAMILY MEMBER RESPONSE

Grieving. Since head injury occurs without warning, the family with a head injured member faces a catastrophe it knows nothing about. The initial reactions are typically mixed between those of gratitude for the victim's survival and fear about what to expect in the future. Family members often described the acute phase as an emotional roller coaster comprised of very intense feelings of hostility, gratefulness, denial, religious experiences, and depression. Although the acute phase of head injury had passed by the time the patients had joined the group, family members still showed a need to readdress or complete their grieving process. Anger directed at professionals was a common topic in the initial group meetings during Phase II. Specifically, anger at acute hospital and rehabilitation personnel was generally worked through, but the lack of post-rehabilitation resources in the community was an ongoing complaint, particularly in the area of social and vocational concerns. New resources were shared and eagerly explored.

Caretaker Role. When head injuries occur, some family member is typically thrust into the role of caretaker without any real choice. Reactions to this role, which requires physical, financial, social, and emotional adjustments, vary extensively. Some caretakers view it as a unique challenge, quitting their jobs to attend to the victim's needs on a 24-hour basis. Other family members question their personal involvement, preferring that someone else face the responsibilities. Nonetheless, the latter mentioned group typically has no alternative since the cost of full time professional care is usually prohibitively high.

Becoming a caretaker causes far reaching changes in a family member's short term and long term life goals. Independent of their intentions, feelings of loss, frustration, and resentment were common. The focus of the group was directed at helping to encourage the caretakers meet their own needs. The burden of responsibility fell heavily on the family members as the patients' old friends lost interest and professional support gradually tapered off. As a substitute, some families sought out rather unusual forms of "treatment." Group consensus helped to distinguish between reasonable and totally useless procedures. In general, individual families were relieved to discover that another family was faced with similar problems. Often, caretakers were more ready to accept statements made by head injured patients they were taking care of once they were validated by other families. Some of these exchanges between families provided great emotional relief and, subsequently, friendships were quickly cemented.

Mood Swings. Patients' mood swings were a common topic of concern. The focus of constructive discussion usually was on the need for predictability of the mood swings. Possible predictors of emotional lability were subsequently identified. Caretakers are particularly vulnerable to these swings since their dedication and the efforts they expend do not necessarily correspond with the rate of mood fluctuations. The therapists emphasized that a neurochemical imbalance, as well as intrapersonal factors, could play a role and, when necessary, individual patients were referred to the appropriate health care professionals. Patients typically tended to blame the caretakers for their problems, while family members complained that patients showed a very different and more cooperative front to professionals than they presented in the home setting.

Specific Parental Issues. Frequently, the parents of those young adults who had functioned more or less independently or had already left the home were forced back into the parental role, causing far-reaching changes in their lives. Parents had difficulty gauging the degree of independence to allow their brain injured child. Some of the parents had a tendency to adopt a martyr role, subjecting their own needs to those of the patient. These parents were assisted in differentiating the needs of the patient and their own identity. Support was provided to assist them in reseparating and reindividuating from their child. A more detailed discussion of this will follow. An additional concern that was frequently raised was: What will happen when we are not able to take care of the patient anymore? With this, as with nearly all issues addressed in the group, the sharing of experience had a strong effect on the process of building group identity.

Specific Spouse/Partner Issues. Frequently concern focused on role changes involving the overwhelming dependency of the patient on his or her spouse. Resentment of these changes by both partners was common. The loss of their former partner and readjusting to a "new person" were central concerns of the spouse.

Compared to spouses, parents adapted better to the situation. Since they had known the patient from birth, they were able to say, "He is sort of like he was when he was 10." In contrast, the spouse felt, "How can I deal with a 10 year old partner?" The character changes were, therefore, of major significance to the spouses. The egocentricity, shallowness of affect, and the childlike qualities which are common in these patients proved extremely difficult for them.

The resumption of sexual activities caused major conflicts. Complaints of feeling incestuous or being with a child were expressed. The patients tended to be concrete in thinking and felt that sex was a required function of marriage. This, when coupled with pressure from the patient's parents to normalize this area of their relationship, accentuated the pressure on the spouses. Generally, the spouses found themselves dealing with a different and difficult marital relationship and, as a result, were confused about their feelings. Separation and/or divorce was nearly always considered as an option. Tremendous guilt was always present in these considerations; the idea of standing by a husband in his hour of need and adhering to marital vows was counterbalanced by a sense of being cheated. Some wives felt this was not "the deal" they had made. It is important to note that the parents in the support group were surprisingly sympathetic to spousal needs.

ROLE OF THERAPIST

Information Exchange. Great care was taken to facilitate effective communication between the therapist and the head injured patients and their families. Technical jargon was avoided and when medical terminology was introduced it was carefully defined and explained. Therapists maintained and expressed the attitude that there was still more to learn about head injuries and that it was helpful to listen to the experiences of both the patients and the family members. As a rule, statements like, "this is just a simplified version" or "it is, of course, much more complicated than I can explain to you" were omitted.

On this basis trust gradually emerged, and patients and family members found the courage to ask long overdue questions and to explore the validity of some of their reasoning. In some instances, the therapist would review the medical histories with the patients in order to gain a more thorough understanding of the patient's specific circumstances. This unrestricted flow of information facilitated an openness to the sharing of feelings. Initially, the families' reactions towards the treating personnel fell into two rather polarized opinions. On the one side, there were those families who were extremely thankful and positive about the people who "saved the patient's life." These positive feelings towards the group were usually extended to the group leaders who became transference objects. On the other hand, there were those families who displayed an inordinate amount of anger and frustration towards the individuals responsible for medical care. Literally no services were good enough and they highlighted the errors that had been made. For both groups, time was needed to readjust expectations or to air grievances.

Multidisciplinary Approach. Particularly in Phase I there was an active interchange between the various disciplines such as language pathologists, physical and occupational therapists, recreational therapists, social workers, clinical and neuropsychologists, physiatrists and psychiatrists. This in itself necessitated a simplification of terms used. Numerous therapists attended meetings regularly and, with the interchange of ideas, the potential for future collaborative efforts was sparked. From these interactions we successfully launched the creation of the San Diego Head Injury Foundation. Moreover, the support groups have continued and currently meet on a weekly basis.

SPECIFIC TREATMENT GOALS
EXEMPLIFIED BY CASE STUDIES

Denial. When faced with a major illness it is all too common that the initial reaction is denial. Patients who suffer brain traumas are possibly even more susceptible to this defense mechanism because the event is, as a rule, erased from memory. The moderate to severely head injured patient is without memory as to how the head was struck, how transportation to the hospital occurred, and what the initial pain or treatments were like. Instead he or she can barely recall waking up from coma hours if not days after the accident. The aftermath typically includes a prolonged state of disorientation and confusion (post-traumatic amnesia). This reduction in mental capacity also contributes to a difficulty in the patient's comprehending the difference between his or her post-injury status and the pre-morbid level of functioning. In order to accept assistance and to be motivated for therapy, it is essential that the patient realize the severity of his or her residual impairments. In fact, denial is frequently a major hurdle. The following case illustrates the complexities and long range aspects of denial.

Case Study A: Mr. A was a 36 year old boiler maker who slipped and fell off a ladder while running a pipe along a 10' high ceiling. His head hit a concrete floor with considerable force rendering him unconscious at the scene of the accident. He was initially transported by ambulance to the nearest hospital and a few hours later was taken to a major medical clinic where his head injury was rated as moderate to severe. Neurosurgery was required for the evacuation of a left epidural hematoma and a facial nerve palsy was decompressed. After Mr. A emerged from coma his management during the acute phase was problematic due to sudden outbursts of anger.

Four months after the accident Mr. A was referred for his first neuropsychological evaluation. At that time it was noted that the patient had partial return of facial nerve functioning of the left side but he continued to complain of cramping in his face. He also complained of general unsteadiness of his gait, but otherwise did not recognize any other residual impairments. He focused exclusively on physical deficits and when he was asked specific questions about cognitive and emotional changes, he always denied any difficulties.

The neuropsychological evaluation documented a cluster of impairments with the most severe being in the areas of (a) sustained attention, (b) verbal learning, and (c) fine motor speed and eye-hand coordination, primarily with the left hand. A personality evaluation revealed that the patient was very concerned with his somatic problems. There were also some signs of depression but these were neither severe nor debilitating.

In the post-test consultation, Mr. A's strengths and weaknesses were discussed within the context of his neuropsychological profile. During the consultation the patient strongly objected to the terms "impairment" and "deficiency" and insisted that all his problems could be labeled as "minor inconveniences." He agreed to return for a number of individual sessions, but made no real gains with regard to accepting his post-trauma status.

However, he did agree to attend a few group meetings so that the professionals could learn more about the head injured. He was confident that all his cognitive functions would return to normal within a few months. Since he was self-employed he insisted on returning to work as soon as possible, expecting all along to work at his pre-morbid levels. The therapist's advice to gradually phase himself back into employment was dismissed as not being practical.

At the time of the accident Mr. A was married but separated from his spouse. His developmental milestones had been unremarkable and 3 years after finishing high school he joined the family business. Together with his parents, Mr. A had worked long days as a skilled boiler maker. Efficiency and high quality work were his trademarks. Outside of work he maintained an active social life and his hobbies included rebuilding motorcycles and restoring old guns.

Mr. A's emotional problems emerged when he was no longer able to complete a job to his satisfaction, and when he noticed he was experiencing serious signs of fatigue after only 2 to 3 hours of work. When bidding for a job his estimates were no longer accurate and he had difficulty with business transactions, particularly those held over the telephone or in direct conversation with others.

In Phase I of the group meetings his interests centered primarily around acquisition of legal information, particularly in reference to financial compensation. When addressing possible sequelae of his head injury he frequently made jokes and rationalized at great length that the quality of his work had not changed. Starting with Phase II of the group sessions he attended meetings regularly, but remained primarily silent. Initially when questions were addressed to him he pointed out that he was not really a head injured patient, but rather that he was "less perfect." When other group members would show self-pity he would occasionally call them on it, but always in a humorous manner. As the other head injured patients continually voiced their problems, Mr. A began to realize that he was complaining of similar difficulties when talking about work. From this, the realization grew that his work-related difficulties might be related to underlying cognitive impairments. He admitted that on one occasion when he was tired he slammed the car door on his left leg. He also noted that his eye-hand coordination was no longer trustworthy and he would frequently drop his tools. In general, his fine motor movements were no longer at an expert level and he became increasingly insecure about working around machines. While his final work product resembled what he was able to do prior to the accident, he stated that he was now so much slower at accomplishing a task that there was practically no margin of profit.

As the months passed, Mr. A admitted to feelings of depression, lack of energy, sadness, and inflexibility. Prior to the accident there were no plans of divorce but, since he did not want his wife to take care of a "cripple," divorce proceedings were initiated. Subsequently he became more and more socially isolated, eating infrequently and sleeping in the afternoons. Television became his primary form of entertainment. Only on one or two occasions was he accompanied to the meetings by a companion. As time progressed, he became attached to the group and his attitudes toward the therapists also changed favorably. As a former motorcycle enthusiast he had cultivated strong feelings of loyalty towards other head injured bikers. For example, once he stated that he was a bigot, but would not be bigoted towards a person who was head injured. Identifying himself as a part of the group, he gradually admitted that he was suffering more than "minor inconveniences" and his denial was gradually overcome.

Once Mr. A admitted his difficulties, his role in the group changed considerably. He volunteered help for others, particularly for one group member who had frequently threatened suicide. He encouraged other patients to get over their denials and face reality.

Since he had been active in the martial arts prior to the accident, Mr. A particularly valued the relaxation exercises and started again with an exercise program. In social settings he was able to communicate to others that he had been head injured. He also made some positive adjustments with regard to the family business. A partner was chosen to help with the administrative aspects and help was hired to assist with certain manual tasks.

The difficulty of early fatigue remained despite the fact that Mr. A restructured his working habits to include frequent breaks. The perfectionistic tendencies that would potentially prevent him from continuing his work were discussed in detail and some slight improvements were noted. At the time of termination Mr. A expressed an interest in continuing in further groups.

Independence. Once a patient has accepted his or her deficits the next major treatment goal is to achieve the highest possible level of independence. In the following case, self-sufficiency was drastically changed as a consequence of a head injury leading to the reliance of the patient on his parents. Since most head injured victims are under the age of 30, parental involvement is common. Group therapy must address the problems from the perspective of family members and of the patient in order to assist in the recovery process and facilitate independence.

Case Study B: Mr. B, 21 years of age, was involved in a serious motor vehicle accident in which he sustained multiple broken bones and a severe closed head injury. The patient underwent approximately 3 months of intensive care followed by approximately 2 years of physical rehabilitation, including speech therapy for dysarthria. Prior to the accident the patient had been gainfully employed as a construction worker and had been taking classes at the local community college where he was considered to be an excellent student. He had been living apart from his parents and was economically self-supporting.

Following his release from the hospital, there was little doubt that Mr. B would have to return to the home of his parents. Initially he was confined to a wheel chair and, according to the patient's mother, had little awareness of his physical condition or of the accident itself. It would have been impossible for the patient to live by himself and the parents were the logical choice to become the caretakers. This drastic and sudden reliance upon his parents profoundly altered the parent/child relationship.

Mr. B's mother described her new role by stating "all of a sudden I became a nurse." She emphasized that her son was "like a child all over again...having to learn again how to walk...having to crawl around initially." She described this period as very difficult for her and her family (husband and daughter) in that the patient required continual nursing care and close attention. The patient's mother took a 3 month leave of absence from her job while the husband maintained his full time work schedule.

At the time Mr. B joined the group he suffered a residual dysarthria and was having difficulty walking. While initially resistive in discussing his problems, he soon emerged as one of the more vocal members of the group. At first Mr. B expressed some ambivalence about continuing to live at home. He was torn between feeling grateful to his parents for the care he had received and a desire to re-establish his independence. As time passed Mr. B set the goal for himself of living in an independent setting. However, his parents could not accept this idea because they felt that they had more insight into the difficulties their son would have if he lived alone. For the patient the problem was to balance setting realistic goals and remaining motivated toward change. The key event in the treatment was when Mr. B started to set reasonable conditions for living independently. In this case it was essential that both the patient and his parents agree to the newly formulated goals. Group psychotherapy was a logical mode for the resolution of those goals. Mr. B expressed the insight that the group had helped him to begin to think about the future. He also received comfort in discovering that there were other persons his age with similar adjustment problems to be faced.

Both Mr. B and his mother confirmed that the group experience encouraged the patient to seek his desired autonomy through open and candid discussions. Both parties needed to face the future from a drastically altered standpoint as compared to their pre-accident expectations. The parents had to learn to become "less helpful" as the patient improved.

Approximately 11 months after joining the group and 3 years after the accident, Mr. B was able to move away from his parents' house. At that time he and his older sister rented an apartment together. While offering emotional support, the sister allowed him to function relatively on his own. By then Mr. B had achieved his set goals to walk with the aid of a cane and to drive a car. He also enrolled in a community college on a part-time basis.

The case of Mr. B illustrates a classic reworking of separation-individuation issues which often arise in patients following head injury. Mr. B insisted that each patient must strike out on his own if "they are going to make it." This continual strong message was interpreted by the therapists and the group members as an indication of the patient's intense desire to eventually achieve his pre-morbid level of self-sufficiency. Because Mr. B frequently resisted seeking help from others, he was sometimes perceived as stubborn by other group members.

The therapists observed that Mr. B's reluctance to accept assistance did not extend to all his behaviors and goals. Certainly the continual love and encouragement Mr. B received from his family contributed substantially to his eventual re-establishment of autonomy. It also appeared that the group experience enabled Mr. B and his mother to plan realistically for the future and to take steps toward achieving Mr. B's optimal independency.

Permanent Disability. The long term treatment of brain damage would be incomplete without having the patients and their family members deal with the fact of irreversible damage. The first step in overcoming a nonadaptive level of denial is an acknowledgment of impairments. Some patients find false comfort in the belief that all will miraculously return to normal. This does not mean that they do not accept their impairments, but rather that they have some false hopes about the recovery process. For parents and therapists alike it is essential to develop a realistic estimation of what degree of improvement can be expected.

Frequently there is a misunderstanding with regard to the concept of spontaneous recovery. During the group interaction we stressed that this is a natural healing process which is completed after several years. Effortful learning can, however, take place during and after spontaneous recovery. Nevertheless, despite this hope and the expected gains, irreversible and permanent damage is the rule rather than the exception after moderate to severe brain trauma.

It is important that the patient understand that this is not a personal criticism. On this basis realistic expectations with respect to future employment, financial status, and social relationships can be developed. One of the most difficult problems is that of marital relationships, as illustrated from the spouse's perspective in the following case.

Case Study C: Mrs. C was a 28 year old woman whose husband had been in a car accident 1 year previous to joining the group. He had suffered a right temporal contusion involving generalized brain damage, as well as multiple peripheral injuries. Mr. C was in a coma for 2 months and was respirator-dependent in the ICU for several weeks after his accident. He was in acute and rehabilitation hospitals for a total of 8 months, where the focus for Mrs. C had initially been on supporting his physical recovery. The full impact of her husband's neuropsychological deficits, which included both retrograde and anterograde amnesia, problem solving deficits, and emotional instability, did not appear to affect her until after her husband's discharge.

In the initial sessions, Mrs. C presented herself as being very competent and as having adjusted well to her situation. She tended to say little, but when she made comments she demonstrated good awareness of others' problems, was supportive of her husband and other group members, and was articulate in describing the positive values of the group.

After approximately 2 months in group therapy Mrs. C requested a referral for individual psychotherapy with one of the group therapists. At this point she began to share more personal information with the group. She was at that time only living sporadically with her husband. He was spending longer periods of time living with his parents because of her inability to cope with him. The core issue of Mrs. C's work in individual therapy and in the subgroup involved a resolution of her relationship with her husband.

Mrs. C described herself as having had a good childhood and successful young adulthood. She had completed 2 years of college and never had problems with employment. She continually stressed how independent she had been as a child and as an adult. Her relationships with men she admitted had been unfulfilling. Through lengthy discussion it appeared that her childhood had, in fact, been difficult. For example, she lived with her mother who had lived with a succession of different men; none of them was loving and one was abusive. Mrs. C had a tendency to become involved with immature men who treated her badly and upon whom she became overly dependent.

Her husband had been independent, self-assured, intelligent, and loving--"the answer to her prayers." For the 3 years prior to his accident they had had an excellent relationship, built on mutual trust, support, and caring.

After his accident, as his cognitive and emotional deficits became clearer, she realized how dependent she had been upon the relationship. As a consequence of the injury, their roles were reversed and, despite his physical independence (he was able to drive a car), he was dependent on her for all decision making. He was generally hostile to her in private, irrationally blaming her for all his many problems and manipulating her through guilt. On one occasion he physically abused her and twice he attempted suicide. An attempt to re-establish a sexual relationship proved disastrous. Any discussion of sexual feelings or in-depth conversation was difficult due to his extreme concreteness. He denied the extent of his limitations in this area.

In public, however, the patient was able to compensate quite well for his deficits. He appeared close to normal to his family and friends. This compounded Mrs. C's feelings of guilt and failure as people overtly or unconsciously told her she should be coping better, "hanging in there and standing by her husband in his hour of need."

The family subgroup was able to assist her in her feelings about these issues. Other spouses were able to share their thoughts of separation and divorce, guilt and failure. Everyone in the family subgroup was acutely aware of the ability of some head injured patients to impress others well on the short term while being totally incapable of managing their lives on a 24 hour basis. Through group discussion Mrs. C was helped to grieve the loss of her idealized pre-injury husband, to see the earlier relationship in more realistic terms, and to deal with her husband in a more rational manner rooted in the present. She came to see how well she had handled her situation over the last year and to accept that separation might be a positive outcome for both partners. Through the observations of others she could identify her husband's behaviors which were manipulative and those which were similar to pre-morbid behaviors so that she became less liable to react to them out of feelings of guilt or loss. She had a forum to safely express her feelings of frustration, anger, and sadness and to receive constructive problem-solving input from a group of people who knew her situation well.

By group's end Mrs. C had initiated divorce proceedings, had found a job, and was living alone. She had been able to discuss with her husband each of these steps in detail. They would see each other once a week at group and talk on the phone regularly. He became better able to see her position as he became more open to admitting his own problems. After conclusion of the group, Mrs. C continued in individual treatment for several months and, as her sense of self-worth markedly improved, she began to acknowledge the possibility of other meaningful relationships in her future.

SUMMARY

ADVANTAGES FOR THE GROUP MODEL

We believe that the preceding discussions not only demonstrate the *efficacy of group psychotherapy* for head injured patients and their family members, but also document distinct advantages groups can have over individual treatment. In two groups, each spanning a period of 1 year, a total of 24 patients and 22 family members were helped during the adjustment period following the accident. Against all odds, six severely head injured patients of our groups resumed gainful employment. However, in all cases, the level of employment was significantly below that of their pre-morbid professions. In addition, all of these patients worked at reduced time schedules because of daily signs of fatigue. Note, therefore, that all the successfully selected jobs allowed for a flexible time schedule, for example, selling cosmetics, real estate, or part time work as a security officer. Out of the remaining 14 patients, four won large settlements following court decisions, which left these individuals financially independent. The remaining 10 patients were being supported by the State and/or their families, and 7 of these were encouraged to attend special classes at their local Junior Colleges.

In previous years in which the authors treated similar cases on an individual basis, the *dropout rate* was consistently higher as compared to that for the group. As a rule, head injured patients would discontinue treatments after an average of 5 to 6 sessions. In follow-up conversations it became clear that the reason for this was frequently the patient's denial of mental and psychological problems. As compared to individual treatment, the group offers unique opportunities for dealing with denial. For example, when a patient faces another head injured victim whose recovery period has been 2 or 3 years longer, and this person admits not only to difficulties but also to his or her initial denial, then this can provide decisive insight. Similarly, group therapy can aid patients and their families in reaching optimal independence and facing the irreversible residual deficits of the brain trauma, as described in the cases of Mr. B and Mrs. C. In fact, mutual support among group members turned out to be the driving force behind accepting the long term prospects of brain damage.

Another reason why the group enjoyed this significantly *lower rate of attrition* is that group treatment not only provided help, but also allowed the patients to help themselves by helping others. This, in turn, brought with it a twofold advantage which is unavailable with individual treatments. First, the patient was no longer locked into the role of a recipient, but instead was asked to assist others by sharing experiences. It was frequently observed that with such sharing, the patient's self-image improved because the past experiences of pain and suffering took on a purpose--namely helping others. Secondly, head injured patients and their families received support not only from professionals, but also from those actually experiencing the same types of pain, emotions, and suffering. This, in turn, lead to a unique support system among the group members. As a result, families started to meet socially outside of the group meetings, and long lasting friendships were formed. Indeed, this led to the creation of the San Diego Head Injury Foundation, an organization run by family members of the head injured.

Group therapy is the treatment of choice in dealing with interpersonal difficulties, both from the standpoint of family dynamics and from that of the patients who generally keep themselves socially isolated following head trauma because of a drastic decline of pre-accident friendships. Individual therapy simply cannot match the group setting for practicing new interpersonal relationships. Fellow patients and family members as a rule communicated with each other in a direct and uninhibited manner, in contrast to the more formal interactions that occur between patients and therapists. For example, with little time wasted, group members were able to distinguish problems experienced by all, such as problems with medical treatment, insurance, and legal issues, from those problems specific to particular families, for instance difficulties with spouses, children, or colleagues at work. In short, the group has the capacity to be therapeutic in dealing with intrapersonal matters. As illustrated in Table 3, these include, in addition to emotional and psychological demands, the working through of physical and mental disabilities.

Underlying the impairments and the reactions secondary to the deficits of brain injury is the patient's unique but altered pre-morbid personality. The effects of therapy can be greatly increased by having the family members readily available at different points in time to help tease out the injured patient's underlying pre-morbid personality traits. This, in turn, can lead to an understanding of the individual's reactions that can vary extensively through the different phases of recovery.

A further advantage that group therapy has over individual treatment stems from the *amalgamation of treating disciplines* it can provide. That is, a multidisciplinary approach was provided by professionals representing the disciplines of clinical psychology, neuropsychology, and social work. In addition, during the 14 sessions of Phase I, a wide range of additional disciplines was represented (see Table 1). No single therapist can hope to match the range of specialized information presented. In our opinion, the developed group approach provided a far superior exchange of information than would have been possible in the context of individual treatment.

Finally, if one therapist had worked with a similar case load on an individual basis, then it would have required one full time therapist position for at least 1 year. It is noteworthy, therefore, that our treatment was achieved within a span of 1.5 hours per week for four therapists, which represents a significantly *enhanced cost/benefit ratio.*

INDICATIONS FOR INDIVIDUAL THERAPY

There are specific difficulties, however, which may be more effectively treated on an individual basis. When necessary, individual treatment was arranged. Sexual adjustment difficulties were a primary reason for individual treatment. When these problems arose, the group situation tended to be more inhibiting than were individual discussions with a therapist. Individual psychiatric consultations were also sought to ascertain whether medications would assist in the rehabilitation process. The symptomatology ranged from increased impulsiveness, marked apathy, depression, suicidal thought, extreme emotional lability, and suspiciousness or paranoid ideation.

294

CONCLUSION

We present our observations on the usefulness of group therapy in the rehabilitation of head injured patients. Two groups of 12 patients who had suffered moderate to severe head injuries were accompanied by their family members and treated on a weekly basis over the span of 12 months. Their group treatment was structured into three phases which included multidisciplinary presentations, theme oriented group discussions, and problem oriented psychotherapy. We present case studies to exemplify three major themes that emerged in therapy: denial of residual symptoms versus acceptance, dependent living versus optimal independence, and false expectations versus accepting irreversible damage. Finally, the advantages and limitations of group psychotherapy are discussed vis-à-vis individual psychotherapy.

In the initial period following their accidents, the patients were continuously surrounded by nurses, physicians, therapists, friends, and family members. Physical recovery was the major focus. The patients would often report that they had been showered with attention which climaxed in a heroic welcome home. However, once the patients were living at home their emotional and thinking disorders became the primary concerns. Compared to the recovery of physical abilities, mental recovery proved to be more tedious and psychosocial and emotional adjustments tended to shift; the frequency of visits from friends dropped after a few months. Family members as well as friends were confused by and uncertain about the patient's behavior. We emphasize that treatment not be limited to the initial phases of recovery from head injury but that feasible methods must be developed to help not only the head injured themselves, but also their family members over the long range of the recovery process. In our experience, group psychotherapy is an effective and efficient means for treating both the head injured and family members on a long term basis.

Ronald M. Ruff, PhD, is currently head of the Neuropsychology Unit at the University of California Medical Center at San Diego, and he is the Chief of Psychology Services at the UCSD Gifford Mental Health Clinic. He holds a faculty appointment at the Assistant Professor level in both the Department of Psychiatry and the Division of Neurosurgery. Prior to his present position, he trained at the University of Zurich and at Stanford University. His training is in clinical and experimental neuropsychology, and he has published numerous articles in these areas. He is a participant in the National Head Injury Data Bank. His primary research interests are the neurobehavioral recovery from head injury as well as the potential for neuropsychological rehabilitation. Dr. Ruff may be contacted at the Division of Neurosurgery H-893, UCSD Medical Center, 225 Dickinson Street, San Diego, CA 92103.

Randall W. Evans, PhD, is presently a Post-Doctoral Research Fellow at the Biological Sciences Research Center, University of North Carolina School of Medicine at Chapel Hill. He also holds a faculty appointment at the Clinical Assistant Professor level in the Department of Psychiatry. Prior to his present position Dr. Evans was a staff clinical psychologist at the University of California Medical Center at San Diego. His primary research interests are in the area of adult and child psychopharmacology as they relate to neuropsychological status and the psychopharmacological management of head injury. He has published numerous articles in this area. Dr. Evans may be contacted at the Biological Sciences Research Center, 220-H, University of North Carolina School of Medicine, Chapel Hill, NC 27514.

Richard Green, LCSW, is a Licensed Clinical Social Worker in the Outpatient Department of Sharp Rehabilitation Center in San Diego. In this capacity, he has been responsible for the development of support systems for the brain injury population in San Diego. Previously, he worked in an acute rehabilitation setting. He has extensive experience in group and individual treatment of disabled individuals and their families, and also works as a therapist in Sharp's Employee Assistance Program. He has presented at national conferences on brain injury. Other interests include psychodrama and the treatment of teenagers. Mr. Green may be reached at Sharp Rehabilitation Center, 7901 Frost Street, San Diego, CA 92123.

RESOURCES

Blanford, B. R. (1979). Peer group membership of young women with cancer. In R. G. Lasky & A. E. Orto (Eds.), *Group Counseling and Physical Disability: A Rehabilitation and Health Care Perspective* (pp. 17-25). North Scituate, MA: Duxbury.

Bond, M. R. (1975). Assessment of the psychosocial outcome after severe head injury. In Ciba Foundation Symposium, No. 34, *Outcome of Severe Damage to the Central Nervous System* (pp. 141-157). Amsterdam: Elsevier.

Bond, M. R. (1976). Assessment of the psychosocial outcome of severe head injury. *Acta Neurochirurgica, 34*, 57-70.

Brooks, D. N., & McKinlay, W. (1983). Personality and behavioral change after severe blunt head injury - a relative's view. *Journal of Neurology, Neurosurgery, and Psychiatry, 46*, 336-344.

Caveness, W. F. (1979). Incidence of craniocerebral trauma in the United States in 1976 with trend from 1970 to 1975. In R. A. Thompson & I. R. Green (Eds.), *Advances in Neurology* (pp. 1-4). New York: Raven Press.

Eson, M. E., Yen, J. K., & Borke, R. S. (1978). Assessment of recovery from serious head injury. *Journal of Neurology, Neurosurgery, and Psychiatry, 41*, 1036-1042.

Evans, R. L., & Northwood, L. K. (1983). Social support needs in adjustment to stroke. *Archives of Physical Medicine and Rehabilitation, 64*, 61-64.

Hartings, M. F., Pavlou, N. M., & Davis, F. A. (1976). Group counseling of MS patients in a program of comprehensive care. *Journal of Chronic Disease, 29*, 65-73.

Jennett, B., & Bond, M. (1975, March). Assessment of outcome after severe brain damage. *Lancet, 1*(7905), 480-484.

Kinsella, G. J., & Duffy, F. D. (1979). Psychosocial readjustment in the spouses of aphasic patients. *Scandinavian Journal of Rehabilitation Medicine, 11,* 129-132.

Klauber, M. R., Barrett-Conner, E., Marshall, L. F. & Bowers, S. A. (1981). Epidemiology of head injury: A prospective study of an entire community, San Diego, California, 1978. *American Journal of Epidemiology, 113,* 500-509.

Levin, H. S., Benton, L. A., & Grossman, R. G. (1982). *Neurobehavioral Consequences of Closed Head Injury.* New York: Oxford Press.

Roessler, R., Milligan, T., & Ohlson, A. (1979). Personal adjustment training for the spinal cord injured. In R. G. Lasky & A. E. Orto (Eds.), *Group Counseling and Physical Disability: A Rehabilitation and Health Care Perspective* (pp. 66-72). North Scituate, MA: Duxbury.

Rosenbaum, M., Lipsitz, N., Abraham, J., & Najenson, T. (1978). A description of an intensive treatment project for the rehabilitation of severely brain-injured soldiers. *Scandinavian Journal of Rehabilitation Medicine, 10*(1), 1-6.

Rusk, H. A., Block, J. M., & Lowman, E. W. (1969). Rehabilitation following traumatic brain damage. *Medical Clinics of North America, 53,* 677.

Stern, J. M. (1978). Cranio-cerebral injured patients. *Scandinavian Journal of Rehabilitation Medicine, 10,* 7-10.

Timming, R. C., Cayner, J. J., Grady, S., Grafman, J., Haskin, R., Malec, J., & Thornsen, C. (1980, February). Multidisciplinary rehabilitation in severe head trauma. *Wisconsin Medical Journal, 79,* 49-52.

Yalom, I. D. (1983). *Inpatient Group Psychotherapy.* New York: Basic Books.

SECTION III:

HEALTH PROMOTION

TREATMENT OF CIGARETTE SMOKING*

Sharon M. Hall and Robert G. Hall

Like other risky habits, smoking provides immediate, often intense gratification for the short term. The long-term consequences are remote, difficult to visualize, and uncertain. Therein lies the clinician's task: Helping the client give up an enjoyable, powerful, probably addictive, habit when the long-term consequences may never occur. If they do occur, however, they are often tragic.

In this chapter, we will review the process of treating smokers we have found most useful. Four issues in the treatment process will be described: (a) background information for the therapist treating smokers, (b) enhancing the decision to quit, (c) treatment methods, and (d) relapse prevention techniques.

The treatment techniques described in this chapter are based on a model which assumes that both social learning and pharmacological factors are important in smoking. We accept the premise that, for most smokers, cigarette smoking is adopted in youth because of social pressure. We assume that, over time, smoking comes to serve many purposes in the smokers' life--it is a social bond, a way of handling emotion, and a conditioned response to many different situations. Throughout life it is maintained by

*Work on this chapter was supported in part by ADAMHA Research Scientists Development Award (SMN) (DA00065), and Research Grants DA02538 and DA03082, from the National Institute on Drug Abuse, and by the John D. and Catherine T. MacArthur Foundation Research Network on Health-Promoting and Health-Damaging Behavior.

social pressures and cues. We further assume that some smokers are really addicted to nicotine. They require a dose of it each day to feel normal, and experience physical withdrawal symptoms when they stop its use.

INFORMATION FOR THE
THERAPIST TREATING SMOKERS

EXPECTATIONS ABOUT QUITTING

Public Health messages have generally emphasized the positive: that quitting smoking is possible, and often easy. Quitting smoking may be easy for some smokers. However, we suggest that it is not these smokers who seek the help of a formal treatment program. Clients of smoking clinics and private practitioners may represent the more physically or psychologically dependent smokers. For these clients, quitting smoking is sometimes a difficult process, involving readjustment in physical, intrapsychic, and social domains. If smokers fail to acknowledge these potential problems when quitting smoking they are poorly prepared for the difficulties involved and at higher risk for relapse. Relapse may occur because: (a) Ex-smokers are not aware that the acute discomfort they are experiencing is time-limited, and feel they must endure it indefinitely; (b) they believe that the problems they are experiencing are uncommon, and relapse because they feel alone and helpless to deal with them; and (c) they did not develop appropriate cognitive and behavioral coping strategies.

The difficulties that occur after quitting smoking are many and varied. It is not possible to predict with any certainty who will experience problems, or how difficult the course of quitting will be for a given smoker. We do not discuss all the problems with potential quitters before they begin treatment. However, the client should understand the following points: (a) Cigarette smoking is an ingrained habit that may have become intertwined in many aspects of his or her life; (b) the client may have become addicted to nicotine; (c) the client can expect quitting smoking to be a difficult task that may require readjustment in social, emotional and physical demands; (d) others with the same problems have succeeded; (e) the difficulties that the client experiences are time-limited; and (f) effective tools are available to the client through this period.

We find the ideas of individual responsibility and readiness for a struggle are important. It is the smoker's responsibility not to smoke and to endure the physiological withdrawal and the psychological discomfort that occur. No techniques now available can free the smoker of all the negative side effects of quitting. It is important that the smoker understand this, and not have unrealistic expectations for any treatment technique. Usually, these messages cannot be repeated too frequently, since they are not the most congenial of communications. They should be presented to the client before quitting and during the quitting process if need be.

CHANGING THE SMOKER'S THINKING

Before or immediately after quitting, it is helpful to inoculate the client against thoughts that encourage smoking. Some thoughts may be the result of subtle environmental pressures, for example, the messages communicated by cigarette advertisements. Cigarette companies associate tobacco products with a variety of desired characteristics such as affluence, sensuality, competence, and companionship. The verbal portion of the advertisement may describe a smooth drawing cigarette with mild taste, but the nonverbal portion projects an image of beauty, luxury, and sexuality.

Common problem thoughts are: (a) nostalgia for the old pleasures of smoking, (b) keeping cigarettes around to test oneself, (c) the belief that a crisis is an acceptable excuse for a cigarette, (d) the belief that not smoking brings about unwanted changes, such as weight gain, that can *only* be ameliorated by returning to smoking, and (e) the belief that one is unable to quit (Danaher & Lichtenstein, 1978).

The task of the therapist is to alert clients to these common thought patterns and review the client's progress regularly after the quit day. During follow-up visits it is important to ask clients about regrets, nostalgia, ideas of testing, response to crises, and doubts even if they are not smoking. It is also advisable to address excuses for smoking as they occur. The more common excuse is stress. Complaints about stress usually take the form of "It just isn't a good time for me--I am under too much stress," or "I was doing just fine, and then this horrible thing occurred." There may well be a grain of truth in this. Level of stress probably does interact with motivation to

303

affect quitting. The clinician should explain this to the client, noting that there is probably no good time for quitting, but if motivation is strong enough abstinence will prevail.

After a slip, the client should be encouraged to begin attempts at abstinence anew.

CHRONIC AND ACUTE WITHDRAWAL SYMPTOMS

Withdrawal symptoms occurring immediately after stopping drug use are the acute withdrawal syndrome. It is not clear whether there is a specific acute syndrome that can be ascribed to tobacco dependence. Most smokers report some symptoms, but their nature varies greatly from smoker to smoker. Generally, these are most acute during the first 7-10 days of quitting. Most common complaints are heightened anxiety, irritability, inability to concentrate, fatigue, increased mucous production, and headache. Occasionally, smokers will report mouth sores and mild gastrointestinal upset. A nearly universal symptom is tobacco craving. At first, the ex-smoker may experience withdrawal symptoms as constant, but most of them, except craving, usually subside after the first week to 10 days.

Chronic tobacco withdrawal symptoms are more subtle than acute symptoms. Predominant among these is craving. It can occur in situations in which the individual formerly smoked months or even years after quitting. This is especially so when the situation is encountered unexpectedly, and the smoker has not had the time to prepare for the possibility of temptation.

From a physiological perspective, the occurrence of such symptoms is puzzling. Nicotine has a half-life of 4-5 hours. Its most active metabolite, cotinine, has a half-life of 24-48 hours. Therefore, symptoms continue to occur long after nicotine and its major active metabolites are clearly from the body. Similar phenomena have been described with opiates. Theorists suggest that chronic withdrawal symptoms are classically conditioned reactions to internal and environmental stimuli associated with either smoking or changes in nicotine blood levels. For example, after smoking, the nicotine blood level rises to a peak within minutes, then begins to fall. The fall in blood nicotine may result in mild withdrawal symptoms, which become conditioned to the environment in which they occur (Leventhal & Cleary, 1980).

304

Treatment of Cigarette Smoking

One would expect heavier smokers to experience greater or more withdrawal symptoms. It has been our experience that extremely heavy smokers (more than three packs per day) do experience strong withdrawal symptoms, if only craving. Other than this observation, it is difficult to predict who will be troubled by withdrawal symptoms. Nicotine gum is helpful in alleviating such symptoms, and we suggest that smokers who have experienced strong withdrawal symptoms during quitting attempts may be particularly appropriate candidates for treatment with nicotine gum, a prescription drug.

WEIGHT GAIN

Weight gain is a long lasting physical response to quitting smoking. Most smokers gain some weight after quitting. The average gain, over the period of 1 year in several studies and in the senior author's clinic has been about 10 pounds for both men and women. Most of this gain takes place in the first 3-6 months. It is not known whether it represents decreased energy metabolism, more efficient use of food by the body, decreased activity, increased eating, or some combination of these.

There are at least three approaches to treating weight gain caused by smoking cessation. However, none has been tested in articles appearing in the published literature, so far as we could find. The first is to work with the smoker to develop strategies to prevent the gain, the tactic usually recommended in the public health literature. This is more difficult than it sounds, since most of the gain occurs early, at precisely the time when withdrawal phenomena occur. At that time many do not have the energy to change eating habits or exercise levels as well. A second strategy is to provide the smoker with weight loss techniques after the gain occurs. Many good behaviorally based weight control programs are available (Jeffrey & Katz, 1977; Johnson & Stalonas, 1981; Stuart, 1978; Stuart & Davis, 1978). We recommend that one of these be used if the gain is greater than 10 pounds. If it is not, simple calorie counting or an increase in activity level may be enough. A final strategy is to consider the costs and benefits of the weight gain versus continued smoking. For most people, the health risks of such a gain are small when compared with the risks of continued smoking. Indeed, current thinking is that measurable risks to health owing to obesity may occur when the individual is 30% or more above ideal weight. For a man who is of normal weight at 165 pounds, this is a weight gain of 49.5 pounds, greater than that we have ever observed in the more than 300 smokers we have treated. However, obesity has cosmetic as well as health consequences. If cosmetic concern appears pre-eminent, the smoker can be aided in gaining insight about his or her own reasons for objecting to the weight gain, especially if it is a small one. Often, the insight that the concern emanates from social norms and pressures, not health consequences, changes the clients' perception of the importance of the gain.

It has been our experience that two groups of smokers are especially likely to experience weight gain when they quit smoking. These are smokers who have a history of weight problems and, to a lesser extent, heavy smokers. The former finding is more consistent.

EMOTIONAL READJUSTMENT

Some smokers use cigarettes as a substitute for important, complex coping behaviors. Among the most frequently reported are use of cigarettes to control anger and anxiety or as a device to remove oneself psychologically from a difficult situation. Delineation of such strategies is useful. "The Reasons for Smoking Test" a widely used self-test instrument, facilitates this process for some smokers (Horn, 1972). Others can benefit simply by being given a list of common uses of cigarettes.

Most smokers who do use cigarettes in this way are sufficiently resourceful to develop new coping strategies on their own. Some may need help with the development of new behaviors by role playing or help in labeling their experience. Special help may be needed if the client is highly anxious or experiencing much life stress.

PSYCHOLOGICAL READJUSTMENT

Smoking is an integral part of common social situations. Bars and parties are the most frequently encountered social situations. Such situations are doubly troubling. They provide potent smoking cues, and the disinhibitory effects of alcohol can easily overcome the smoker's resolve. It has been our practice to warn clients about this, and to suggest that they avoid such situations immediately after quitting. Other social cues occur at work. In some worksites, the cigarette break is an opportunity for relaxation and talking with co-workers. Often, smokers congregate. The ex-smoker must be prepared to be the only nonsmoker in the group. The group clearly provides indirect pressure to smoke (Marlatt & Gordon, 1980). Depending on the local attitudes towards smoking, others may also exert direct social pressure, by teasing or tempting the ex-smoker. Again, the recently abstinent smoker may have to avoid such situations until the first strong smoking cravings have passed.

PREPARING THE SOCIAL SUPPORT SYSTEM

The importance of significant others in facilitating and impeding abstinence from cigarettes is well documented in the research literature, but the mechanism by which they exert influence is not clear. Data from several studies indicate that the presence of smokers in the home facilitates relapse. On the other hand, perceived support of others helps the smoker to maintain abstinence. McIntyre, Mermelstein, and Lichtenstein (1982) suggest that partner behaviors can be categorized as helpful or detrimental. These investigators acknowledge that the exact form helpful behaviors take depends, in part, on the couple. However, their research has shown that helpful behaviors are providing rewards, compliments for the decision to quit, as well as for actual quitting, expressing interest in being involved and confidence in the partner, and not smoking in the quitter's presence. Detrimental behaviors including nagging, shunning, and policing. These investigators have prepared a manual for partners of smokers (Lichtenstein & Mermelstein, 1982). In it, they also emphasize the role of nonspecific caring and support and maintaining open lines of communication. A particularly useful strategy they use is preparation of the partner for the difficulties that may be encountered upon quitting. The first of these difficulties is uncertainty about what behaviors will be helpful. These investigators suggest uncertainty can best be removed by acknowledging it and discussing with the partner what would be helpful. A second task for the partner is to cope with withdrawal symptoms. McIntyre and her colleagues suggest reminding the partner that these are not permanent personality changes, but they reflect transient withdrawal symptoms. This warning is probably best offered for the many changes that the smoker may temporarily experience, including difficulties in concentrating, depression, and fatigue. A final problem is the smoking partner who wishes to encourage abstinence in the client. It is heartening to note that the sparse data available indicate no difference in efficacy as a function of smoking status of the support person (Mermelstein, Lichtenstein, & McIntyre, 1983).

If the smoker is not supportive of the client's efforts, a minimal contract still needs to be negotiated. Central to the contract is an agreement not to smoke in the presence of the quitter, and not to leave cigarettes in places where the client might come across them. Our experience indicates one can offer little hope of success if such minimal contracts cannot be negotiated.

Another thorny issue is that of assumption of responsibility by the partner. Clinicians who have treated smokers agree that for successful outcome the smoker must take responsibility for quitting smoking. Overly solicitous, guilty, or controlling partners will attempt to weaken this. It is the therapist's responsibility to clarify this issue.

ENHANCING THE DECISION TO QUIT

Most smokers who come to the clinician's attention are already motivated to quit. During treatment, however, resolve may wane. At different points in treatment, smokers' motivation can be increased by a careful description of the benefits to be received by quitting smoking.

Smokers can be reminded of the general health benefits of quitting. Cigarette smoking is linked to increased incidence of many forms of cancer, as well as morbidity and mortality owing to other diseases, including heart disease and chronic lung disease. Most smokers know that smoking is harmful, but few know the specific diseases it causes, or how it is most likely to affect them personally.

For almost all smoking treatment clients, it is helpful to provide specific information about the health effects of smoking and quitting. Several publications summarize the general consequences of smoking, and the potential benefits of quitting. These are listed under Additional Resources (at the end of this chapter). These publications compare the rates of cancers, heart disease, children's birth defects, and life span for smokers and nonsmokers. For example, 35 year old male smokers can expect to live

8.3 years less than nonsmokers and are more likely to have cancer or heart disease. On the other hand, after 10-15 years of cigarette abstinence a smoker's risk of premature death approaches that of a nonsmoker.

For certain subgroups of smokers, risks are moderated by family history or lifestyle. Such individualized information can be motivating for some smokers. Smokers with a family history of premature parental death from illness, family history of heart disease or of cancer are at higher risk than smokers without such a history. Smokers who consume alcohol excessively, are overweight, or who avoid exercise are at higher risk than those who drink moderately, exercise, and who are of normal weight. This information is also available from books listed in "Additional Resources." Benefits are different for smokers with chronic smoking related illnesses. Smoking cessation for this group may reduce symptoms of the disease and slow its progression. Quitting will not restore the damage already done. However the benefits of quitting for this group may be among the most immediately discernible and can be described to the client. For example, emphysemic smokers can expect their endurance and mobility to improve after quitting. Patients with heart disease reduce their risk of fatal and nonfatal recurrence by 50%.

Other nonhealth benefits are important. Estimating money saved over 10 years in cigarettes, lighters, and cleaning bills can be a positive force for many smokers. Still others quit for social or cosmetic reasons. For example, smokers frequently wish to quit because they have no friends who continue to smoke, or because they wish to avoid the more rapid onset of wrinkles that occurs in smokers. It is also important that the therapist help the client be realistic about such benefits. Stopping smoking is not a panacea for complex social problems, nor does it assure eternal youth. Unrealistic expectations may well lead to relapse.

TECHNIQUES FOR CESSATION

Many techniques have been recommended for quitting smoking, including hypnosis, acupuncture, psychoanalysis, self-management training, relaxation, and several different forms of aversion therapy. Of these, most have been evaluated and two stand out. One is Rapid Smoking and its variants (e.g., smoke holding and rapid smoking, Tori,

309

1978), which can produce 40-60% abstinence at 6 months under optimal treatment conditions (R. G. Hall, Sachs, & S. M. Hall, 1979; R. G. Hall, Sachs, S. M. Hall, & Benowitz, 1984; Schmahl, Lichtenstein, & Harris, 1972). The second is nicotine gum, which produces lower abstinence rates (30-45%). However, the gum is especially useful for heavy smokers, and can produce dramatic long-term abstinence rates (59-67%) when combined with multimodal programs, especially those including aversive smoking (Fagerstrom, 1982; S. M. Hall, Tunstall, Rugg, Jones, & Benowitz, 1985).

Cessation techniques other than these fall into two categories: those which have not been evaluated in rigorously controlled trials, such as hypnosis and acupuncture, and those which have been evaluated, and found to produce abstinence rates of about 20-35% at 1 year. Some therapists may need to use techniques which fall into one or the other of these categories. Even though the general probability for success is lower than with other techniques, they may be the only alternatives possible, because of the client's health, or preferences. Both rapid smoking and nicotine gum are contraindicated for pregnant women, since their effects on the fetus are not known. Some smokers refuse aversive techniques owing to fear, or lack of faith in their efficacy. Many smokers refuse nicotine gum because they do not want to continue to ingest nicotine in any form, or do not like to chew gum.

AVERSIVE SMOKING

Aversive smoking procedures, when properly used, are effective techniques. The best known version is rapid smoking. Rapid smoking requires that a smoker inhale a cigarette of his or her preferred brand every 6 seconds until unable to continue for fear of vomiting or fainting. The client then rests for 5 minutes and completes a checklist of symptoms experienced. A second trial follows and is terminated in the same way with a similar rest and symptom review. A third trial is given if the smoker feels capable of proceeding. To successfully use rapid smoking, the therapist should be knowledgeable about the safe use of rapid smoking and elements important to smoker's success.

Before beginning treatment, the health of the smoker should be carefully assessed. Recent studies have shown that the healthy smokers may rapid smoke without health risk greater than that of normally paced smoking (Sachs, R. G. Hall, & S. M. Hall, 1978). For chronically ill smokers there are important considerations.

Nonphysician clinicians may safely conduct rapid smoking therapy on a patient recovered from myocardial infarction. However, the nonphysician clinician should closely collaborate with the patient's physician in selecting rapid smoking. Potential patients whose heart attack has been complicated by congestive heart failure or the need to take digoxin or diuretics following an infarction should be excluded. Cautious therapists may not wish to carry out rapid smoking on patients with cardiopulmonary disease unless the therapist is in a medical setting. The probability of a recurrent myocardial infarction in this population is greater no matter what the patient's activity. If enough patients with cardiac disease underwent rapid smoking, by chance alone a small percentage would have a heart attack during treatment (Sachs, Benowitz, S. M. Hall, R. G. Hall, & Moir, 1984).

There are a number of elements in rapid smoking that are necessary for success. First, the client cannot smoke between sessions. The first day of rapid smoking is the smoker's quit day. After the first session clients may not feel like smoking for several hours. They are warned that the urges may return and they must ignore them and not smoke. If they want to smoke, they must wait and come to the next session and rapid smoke.

Second, sessions should be directed by a therapist. Rapid smoking is not usually successful without supervision. Smokers have difficulty carrying out the instructions by themselves. Also, a warm, supportive therapist has added value to clients. Evidence also suggests that rapid smoking is more effective when the rapid smoking is administered to clients individually.

Third, sessions should continue until the client reports no more urges to smoke. Typically sessions begin on Monday and continue on Tuesday, Wednesday, Friday, and the following Monday. After the first five meetings the next sessions are held at intervals of the client's choosing. The therapist encourages clients to pick their next appointment time based upon their conviction they can remain abstinent until then. Usually this happens after seven or eight sessions. Most studies have limited the maximum number of sessions to 12. This number is rarely reached. Most participants either quit smoking or quit treatment before then.

Fourth, the nature of aversion and the importance of the client's cooperation must be stressed. The client should understand he or she will smoke to the point of dysphoria and nausea and the procedure will work best if the client accepts the rationale. The client is warned that smoking between sessions can disrupt the aversion process and that they must help the process by trying to intensify the aversion.

Fifth, it is essential that the therapist heighten the client's awareness of the aversion. Smokers have rapid smoked for 20 minutes or longer without nausea and vomiting when they were allowed to distract themselves by looking out the window or engaging in other activities. To maximize the effect of rapid smoking, participants are asked to face a blank wall while they inhale every 6 seconds. At intervals the therapist urges them to concentrate on how badly smoking makes them feel. Before the session begins clients are warned to stop before the symptoms of nausea and lightheadedness become too great. An emesis basin is placed within reach. During the rest period when the client completes a checklist of symptoms, the therapist points out how smoking is causing the burning throat, lightheadedness, nausea, tingling of the extremities, and the like.

Sixth, the aversion is enhanced by the process of revivification. After rapid smoking trials have ended and the client rested, they are asked to close their eyes and recall the unpleasant feelings produced by rapid smoking. They are asked to intensify these feelings as much as possible. Then they are instructed to return home and revivify the rapid smoking when they have the urge to smoke. This technique is presented as the means the client can use to fight off urges until the next rapid smoking session.

Clinical experience has led the second author to advise clients to have someone else drive them home after a session. Some clients have reported feeling "foggy" and not alert after rapid smoking.

OTHER AVERSION TECHNIQUES

Given the concern about the safety and unpleasantness of rapid smoking, therapists have modified the procedure to make it less intense. Regular paced aversive smoking is identical to rapid smoking, but uses a larger interval between puffs (e.g., 30 or 60 seconds). The symptoms of nausea and lightheadedness are far less pronounced and usually a single trial of either three cigarettes or a specified time period is used. The therapist's efforts to focus the smoker's attention on the aversive aspects of smoking is even more important in this version. The efficacy of this variant is less than that of rapid smoking. There are several other aversive smoking methods, including focused smoking (Hackett & Horan, 1978) and taste satiation (Tori, 1978).

NICOTINE GUM

Nicotine gum has been a prescription drug in the United States since early 1984. Use of the gum is based on the premise that smokers smoke, at least in part, to obtain nicotine, and that abrupt withdrawal of nicotine causes withdrawal symptoms which impede quitting. The gum is designed to provide low blood levels of nicotine. Theoretically, this substitution of nicotine should ameliorate withdrawal symptoms and allow the smoker to attend to the psychosocial aspects of quitting. After 3-6 months, the smoker tapers off the gum. Presumably this is easier than quitting cigarettes, for two related reasons. The low constant level of blood nicotine does not produce the highs felt with the sharp peak levels obtained from smoking. Second, these low levels also should reduce the degree of physical dependence, and make tapering easier.

There has been considerable research in both Europe and the United States studying the efficacy of the nicotine gum. The conclusions from this research are threefold. First, most, but not all, studies indicate that nicotine gum is more effective than placebo in aiding quitting. Differences between studies seem to be owing to early inadequate formulations of the gum (now corrected) that did not allow enough nicotine to be absorbed, or to less than optimal instructions or social support.

Second, there is evidence that the gum is especially efficacious for smokers who are highly dependent on nicotine. The best measure of dependence now available is blood cotinine (S. M. Hall, Herning, Jones, Benowitz, & Jacob, 1984). However, cotinine assays are expensive and not widely available. Fagerstrom (1982) has developed a scale which has been shown useful in some studies in differentiating highly dependent subjects from those less dependent. Based on data from these studies, Merrell-Dow, the marketers of the gum in the United States, suggest eight subject characteristics are correlated with need for nicotine replacement: (a) intake of more than 15 cigarettes per day, (b) preference for brands of cigarettes with nicotine levels greater than 0.9 mg, (c) inhaling, rather than puffing, (d) smoking the first cigarette within 30 minutes of arising, (e) finding the first cigarette in the morning the hardest to give up, (f) smoking more frequently during the morning than during the rest of the day, (g) finding it difficult to refrain from smoking in places where it is not allowed, or (h) smoking when ill and in bed. Merrell-Dow implies clients should endorse more than one of these items to be good candidates for nicotine replacement therapy. We suggest that at least four of these items be endorsed. The gum increases abstinence rates among highly dependent subjects, but does not impede quitting among those less dependent. However, the gum is expensive. One month's worth of gum, assuming use of one box per week, may cost the patient up to $88.00 at 1985 retail prices. Currently, there are no satisfactory criteria defining who can best use the gum. Indeed, development of such a criteria may be difficult, since they vary as a function of the other treatment services offered with the gum.

Third, researchers, the Food and Drug Administration, and Merrell-Dow agree that it should only be prescribed in the context of a support program. The exact parameters of such programs have not been spelled out, but would seem to include all the interventions psychologists usually provide. Although physicians must prescribe the gum, it is unlikely that many of them will have the time or the skills to offer the psychosocial interventions that must accompany it. Articles reporting integration of nicotine gum use with psychological techniques have been published (Fagerstrom, 1982; S. M. Hall et al., 1985) and can be used as starting points from which the practitioner can develop individualized treatment programs. Nicotine gum is contraindicated for patients with serious cardiovascular disease, for pregnant women, for individuals with active ulcers, and for those with temporomandibular joint disease.

OTHER TREATMENT CONSIDERATIONS

GROUPS VS. INDIVIDUAL TREATMENT

Most smoking treatment is provided in small groups of 5-10 people. So far as we could find, there is no evidence that groups are superior to individual treatment for smoking. However, many clients who have participated in groups report that the group support was central in achieving and maintaining abstinence. Groups are more cost effective than individual sessions, even though individual sessions may produce higher abstinence rates. On the other hand, there are certain pitfalls in group treatment. First, relapse can sometimes be contagious, especially if those relapsing are vocal or have achieved high informal status in the group. Second, group members sometimes give each other permission to fail. Lastly, if group members are poorly matched or antagonists to one another, attendance rates can poorer than in individual sessions.

ABRUPT VS. GRADUAL QUITTING

We use abrupt cessation, for it is most congenial with the primary treatment methods we use, aversive smoking and nicotine gum. Smokers are asked to set a quit date, and to stop smoking completely on that day. Some smokers gradually cut down before that date, although others prefer to continue to smoke at their usual pace. We have not noted any difference in outcome as a function of which strategy was used.

Many therapists have the smoker set a quit day and spend the preceding period decreasing smoking and preparing to stop. This method has some advantages. It gives the smoker time to experience problems associated with quitting. These experiences are frequently motivators to learn techniques to deal with the problem before they occur in more severe form, as they might during total abstinence. The experience also indicates to the smoker specific problem areas. Therapist and client efforts can be targeted to these areas. This method can be used with aversive smoking. However, it is less sensible with nicotine gum, where standard use is to fade the gum, rather than cigarettes. This practice is based on the assumption that it is easier to taper from the gum than from cigarettes.

MONITORING SMOKING BEHAVIOR

Another commonly used treatment technique that we employ initially is monitoring smoking behavior. Many smoking treatment programs have clients monitor the number of cigarettes smoked or the urges to smoke throughout treatment. We find that monitoring either is incomplete, or is disregarded after the first week or two. However, it is valuable initially as a learning device.

Smoking is such an overlearned activity that many smokers are not aware of the times at which they smoke, nor do they realize the cues that elicit smoking. By recording smoking urges, times, cigarettes smoked, and activities or emotions related to smoking, the client and therapist can identify environmental and internal stimuli that elicit smoking by 1-2 weeks of monitoring smoking.

A monitoring card (attached to the front of the pack of cigarettes or carried in the wallet) includes at least three columns: (a) hours of the day, (b) marks for smoking or urges ("s" or "u") and, (c) a brief description of salient activities or emotions.

SELF-MANAGEMENT TECHNIQUES

Many programs encourage the smoker to use self-management techniques to weaken elements of smoking behavior before the quit day. For example, smokers can smoke low tar and nicotine brands, smoke only half the cigarette, change the time or circumstances they normally smoke, or use the nondominant hand.

Other techniques remove the reinforcers associated with smoking. The smoker can restrict all other activities when smoking. Since smoking is often associated with other pleasurable activities, taking away this pleasure will disrupt and decrease the urge to smoke.

The smoker can also adjust the environment to heighten cues that are reminders not to smoke. Other examples are to change the location where cigarettes are kept each day, or leaving reminders in key smoking places. These techniques and many more are described in several pamphlets published by the American Cancer Society, the American Lung Association, and the Office on Smoking and Health. We use these materials by asking clients to read them, select a few techniques they feel will be most useful to them, and then make a commitment to the therapist, or to the group, to use the techniques as needed. This sequence is important. Without it, clients select too many techniques, and usually fail to use any consistently.

RELAPSE PREVENTION

The relapse prevention program we use has three components: relapse prevention skill training, cost-benefit analyses of smoking and quitting, and brief relaxation training. Although we have no empirical evidence, we suspect that the relaxation training component adds little, and we are omitting it in our current studies.

In the cost-benefit analysis, clients and leader review the costs of smoking and the benefits of quitting. This review involves several worksheets, adapted by us from Hildebrandt and Feldman (1976). Much of the information presented in these sessions is similar to the sort offered as part of antismoking education by public agencies. However, we present this material after clients stop smoking, rather than before. It has been our experience that before quitting such material is too threatening to be assimilated, but is reinforcing after quitting. Rather than attempting to spur smokers to action by arousing their anxiety, we attempt to reinforce their quitting by providing immediate feedback about the positive benefits of this action. Benefits discussed include not only health benefits, but also financial and consumer benefits.

Over the years, we have used variants of relapse prevention skill training. It is an effective technique. However, it takes considerable therapeutic skill to implement effectively. Many people feel uncomfortable in role plays. We use two techniques to reduce this discomfort. The first is to use a party as a first role play. The advantage of this procedure is that most individuals find the situation relevant to their smoking, since almost all smoke at parties. Also, a party scene allows everyone in the group to "jump in," unlike other role plays which may include only two participants. Lastly, for most smokers, a party is not such an emotionally charged situation that the role play elicits resistance. In addition, some of the resistance experienced in role playing probably reflects clients' lack of familiarity with the technique and discomfort in being asked to role play without preparation. Currently, we give preparation for role plays as homework assignments. Smokers are asked to think about situations that have been problems for them in the past, and then to come to sessions ready to role-play alternate ways of handling them.

Other relapse prevention techniques have been suggested, but few have been systematically evaluated. Still, many merit consideration because they are simple, and if successful will be cost effective. These include pre-planned booster sessions and drop-in sessions. Both may be useful for motivated subjects who have recently slipped, or for subjects who feel their resolve is weakening. They are less likely to be useful when the subject has already relapsed and has lost motivation for abstinence. These subjects are likely to avoid coming to groups. In working with such individuals, the clinician is well advised to set up a contact schedule that he or she initiates, rather than to rely on the client to initiate contacts. Telephone follow-ups would seem particularly useful for this.

Buddy systems and groups that evolve into self-help groups are also cost effective. However, buddy systems are difficult in settings where client populations are heterogeneous. Even in groups where clients are similar demographically, differences in client preferences for amount of support and need for privacy make effective buddy systems difficult. For these reasons, we have not used them. Similarly, we have seen little success designing groups so that they ultimately become self-help groups led by a group member. Such groups may require more skill than group members commonly have. Also, continued group attendance after successful quitting may be infrequent and serve more of a social function than a therapeutic one.

Sharon M. Hall, PhD, is Associate Professor of Medical Psychology at the Langley Porter Psychiatric Institute of the University of California, San Francisco. She received her PhD in 1971 from Washington State University in psychology, and completed a clinical internship at the Palo Alto Veterans Administration Hospital. Since then, she has held faculty positions at the University of Wisconsin and at UCSF. Her research interests and publications are in addictions, particularly in tobacco dependence and opiate addiction. She has also published articles on the behavioral treatment of obesity. Dr. Sharon Hall may be contacted at University of California at San Francisco, Center for Social and Behavioral Sciences, 1350 Seventh Avenue, CSBS-204, Box 0844, San Francisco, CA 94143.

Robert G. Hall, PhD, is Chief of the Health Psychology Section and Program Evaluation (Psychiatry) at the Palo Alto Veterans Administration Hospital and a member of the clinical faculty in the Department of Psychiatry at Stanford University. He received his PhD in psychology in 1971 from Washington State University and completed a clinical internship at the Palo Alto Veterans Administration Hospital. His clinical and research interests focus on chronic illness. He has published articles on token economics and treatment of cigarette smoking. Dr. Robert Hall can be contacted at Psychology Service (116B), Veterans Administration Hospital, 3801 Miranda, Palo Alto, CA 94103.

RESOURCES

CITED REFERENCES

Danaher, B. G., & Lichtenstein, E. (1978). *Become an Ex-smoker.* Englewood Cliffs, NJ: Prentice-Hall.

Fagerstrom, K. O. (1982). A comparison of psychological and pharmacological treatments in smoking cessation. *Journal of Behavioral Medicine, 5,* 343-351.

Hackett, G., & Horan, J. J. (1978). Focused smoking: An unequivocally safe alternative to rapid smoking. *Journal of Drug Education, 8,* 216-266.

Hall, R. G., Sachs, D. P. L., & Hall, S. M. (1979). Medical risk and therapeutic effectiveness of rapid smoking. *Behavior Therapy, 10,* 249-259.

Hall, R. G., Sachs, D. P. L., Hall, S. M., & Benowitz, N. L. (1984). Two year efficacy and safety of rapid smoking in patients with cardiac and pulmonary disease. *Journal of Consulting and Clinical Psychology, 52,* 547-581.

Hall, S. M., Herning, R. L., Jones, R. J., Benowitz, N. L., & Jacob, III, P. (1984). Blood cotinine levels as indicators of smoking treatment outcome. *Clinical Pharmacology and Therapeutics, 356,* 810-814.

Hall, S. M., Rugg, D., Tunstall, C. D., & Jones, R. (1984). Preventing relapse to cigarette smoking by behavioral skill training. *Journal of Consulting and Clinical Psychology, 52,* 372-382.

Hall, S. M., Tunstall, C. D., Rugg, D. L., Jones, R. T., & Benowitz, N. L. (1985). Nicotine gum and behavioral treatment in smoking cessation. *Journal of Consulting and Clinical Psychology, 53,* 256-258.

Hildebrandt, D. E., & Feldman, S. E. (1975, December) *The Impact of Commitment and Change Tactics Training on Smoking.* Paper presented at the meeting of the Association for the Advancement of Behavior Therapy, San Francisco, CA.

Horn, D. (1972). *Smoker's Self-Testing Kit* (DHEW Publication No. HSM 72-7506). Washington, DC: U. S. Government Printing Office.

Jeffrey, D. B., & Katz, R. (1977). *Take It Off and Keep It Off: A Behavioral Program for Weight Loss and Healthy Living.* Englewood Cliffs, NJ: Prentice-Hall.

Johnson, W. G., & Stalonas, P. M. (1981). *Weight No Longer.* Gretna, LA: Pelican.

Levanthal, H., & Cleary, P. D. (1980). The smoking problem: A review of the research and theory in behavioral role modification. *Psychological Bulletin, 88,* 370-405.

Lichtenstein, E., & Mermelstein, R. (1982). *Helping Your Partner Quit Smoking: A Manual for the Oregon Smoking Control Program.* Unpublished manuscript, University of Oregon, Psychology Department, Eugene, OR.

Mahoney, M. J., & Mahoney, K. (1976). *Permanent Weight Control.* New York: Norton.

Marlatt, G. A., & Gordon, J. R. (1980). Determinants of relapse: Implications for the maintenance of behavior change. In P. O. Davidson & S. M. Davidson (Eds.), *Behavioral Medicine: Changing Health Lifestyles.* New York: Brunner/Mazel.

McIntyre, K., Mermelstein, R., & Lichtenstein, E. (1982). *Counselor Manual for the Oregon Smoking Control Program.* Unpublished manuscript, University of Oregon, Psychology Department, Eugene, OR.

Mermelstein, R., Lichtenstein, E., & McIntyre, K. (1983). Partner support and relapse in smoking cessation programs. *Journal of Consulting and Clinical Psychology, 51,* 465-466.

Sachs, D. P. L., Benowitz, N. L., Hall, S. M., Hall, R. G., & Moir, T. W. (1984). *Physiologic Effects of Rapid Smoking Therapy in Patients with Cardiovascular Disease.* Manuscript submitted for publication.

Sachs, D. P. L., Hall, R. G., & Hall, S. M. (1978). Effects of rapid smoking: A physiologic analysis. *Annals of Internal Medicine, 88,* 639-641.

Schmahl, D. P., Lichtenstein, E., & Harris, D. E. (1972). Successful treatment of habitual smokers with warm, smoky air and rapid smoking. *Journal of Consulting and Clinical Psychology, 38,* 105-111.

Stuart, R. B. (1978). *Act Thin, Stay Thin.* New York: W. W. Norton.

Stuart, R. B., & Davis, B. (1978). *Slim Chance in a Fat World.* Champaign, IL: Research Press.

Tori, C. D. (1978). A smoking satiation procedure with reduced medical risk. *Journal of Clinical Psychology, 34,* 574-577.

ADDITIONAL RESOURCES

National Institute on Drug Abuse. The National Institute on Drug Abuse has published excellent resource materials on cigarette smoking. Titles, editors or authors, prices, and addresses at which to obtain these are given in the annotated bibliography below. Description of monograph content in quotation marks is taken from National Institute on Drug Abuse publications.

While supplies last, copies of NIDA monographs may be obtained free from the National Clearinghouse for Drug Abuse Information (NCDAI) at Room 10A-43, 5600 Fishers Lane, Rockville, MD 20857.

Copies may also be purchased from the U. S. Government Printing Office (GPO) or the National Technical Information Service (NTIS). NTIS prices are for paper copy. Microfiche copies from NTIS are $4.50. Prices from either source may change.

Grabowski, J., & Bell, C. S. (Eds.). (1984). *Measurement in the Analysis and Treatment of Smoking Behavior.* "An attempt to delineate measures for analysis of smoking behavior in research and treatment settings." The chapter by Benowitz on biochemical verification of abstinence and smoking is an excellent resource.

(GPO Stock #017-0240-01181-9--$4.50. NTIS PB #84-145-184--$14.50.)

Grabowski, J., & Hall, S. M. (Eds.). (1985). *Pharmacological Adjuncts in Smoking Cessation.* A review of smoking treatment and related research issues using pharmacological adjuncts to smoking treatment. Focus is on nicotine replacement therapy. (NIDA Research Monograph #53, DHHS, Washington, DC.)

Jarvik, M. E., Cullen, J. W., Gritz, E. R., Vogt, T. M., & West, L. J. (Eds.). (1977). *Research on Smoking Behavior.* "Includes epidemiology, etiology, consequences of use, and approaches to behavioral change." Useful chapters on smoking and disease (Van Lancker) and sociocultural factors in smoking (Reeder). The treatment section is now a bit outdated. (GPO Stock #017-024-00694-7--$7.50. NTIS PB #276 353/AS--$29.50.)

Krasnegor, N. A. (Ed.). (1979). *Cigarette Smoking as a Dependence Process.* "Discusses factors involved in the onset, maintenance, and cessation of the cigarette smoking habit." Tobacco use from a psychopharmacologic perspective. (GPO Stock #017-024-00895-8--$6.00. NTIS PB #297 721/AS--$19.00.)

The Surgeon General's Report. Each year, the Office on Smoking and Health produces *The Health Consequences of Smoking: A Report of the Surgeon General.* The content depends upon the theme of the report for that year. Topics in recent years have been the health consequences of smoking for women (1980); health consequences related to changes in cigarette constituents, with emphasis on low tar, low nicotine cigarettes (1981); the relationship of cigarette smoking and cancer (1982); and cigarette smoking and cardiovascular disease (1983). The 1980 report is noteworthy for its excellent summary of the etiology, demographics, and descriptive data on smoking in women. It is also a good review of treatment methods to that time. Sound reviews of treatment outcome are also found in the 1982 and 1983 reports. These latter two reports are especially good sources for preparing materials on the health consequences of smoking. These reports are usually out of print within a year or so of their publication. However, most university libraries should be able to obtain back copies.

Treatment of Cigarette Smoking

Pamphlets for Smokers. Several government agencies have produced pamphlets which contain information about the effects of smoking and quitting, or describe self-managed quitting programs. These are listed below. American Lung Association pamphlets can be obtained from local lung association offices. NIH publications can be ordered from the Government Printing Office in Washington, DC or from local branches of the Printing Office.

Cigarette Smoking: The Facts about Your Lungs. (1975). American Lung Association.

Clearing the Air. A Guide to Quitting Smoking (NIH Publication No. 82-1647). (1982). Office of Cancer Communications, National Cancer Institute, Bethesda, MD 20205.

How to Stop Smoking! (1969). American Heart Association.

It's a Matter of Life and Breath. (undated). American Lung Association.

Me Quit Smoking? How? (1970). American Lung Association.

Quitter's Guide: 7 Day Plan to Help You Stop Smoking Cigarettes. (1978). American Cancer Society.

What Everyone Should Know about Smoking and Heart Disease. (1976). American Heart Association, Communications Division.

323

PROMOTING PROHEALTH BEHAVIOR IN YOUNG PEOPLE: SOME REPRESENTATIVE ISSUES

Brian Stabler

INTRODUCTION

Keeping children healthy is perhaps the single best investment adults may make in the future. But, like the weather, everyone seems to talk about it and relatively few people do much about it. Perhaps this is in part because of the mistaken belief that childhood is, almost by definition, the epitome of health as we understand it. Children are naturally healthy, so why should we worry about them? Nothing could be further from the truth. Although research has demonstrated the beneficial effects of health promoting activities such as exercise, smoking cessation, reduction in alcohol consumption, and development of proper dietary habits in adults, the difficulties of modifying well established patterns of behavior in older people has also been recognized. Because of this difficulty the focus of health promotion activities has turned increasingly to younger people. Primary prevention has become the guiding principle, rather than coping with illness; and the most effective way of implementing prevention strategies is to begin as early in the life cycle as possible.

There is much evidence to support the idea that children and adolescents can significantly alter their health behaviors. However, a good deal of the research into child health promotion has been done by nonclinicians: epidemiologists, anthropologists, sociologists, and other social scientists. Converting such research findings into pragmatic clinical interventions is not an easy task, nor is it one which many clinical health psychologists are as yet engaged in (Coates, Petersen, & Perry, 1982). This chapter focuses briefly on some representative areas of health promotion activities for children and adolescents: exercise, obesity, dental health, alcohol abuse, and smoking. Parental effects on the development of health behaviors in children are discussed, as are childrens' own concepts of health and illness. Since the scope of the issues involved is massive and the current research is highly diverse, any attempt at an all-encompassing or even comprehensive treatment of these subjects is clearly beyond the scope of this chapter. To provide a brief synopsis of the current efforts in child health promotion a review of studies which offer practical application in the field is given. Reference and other resource materials are included at the close of the chapter.

PARENTS' EFFECTS ON
CHILD HEALTH BEHAVIOR

It is believed by many child development specialists that there are basically two ways of rearing children, the *developmental* approach which stresses a child's individual needs; and the *disciplinary* approach, which emphasizes the needs and expectations of the parents (L. Pratt, 1973). Child rearing methods have recently received increased attention in light of accelerated rates of teenage pregnancy, juvenile delinquency, school dropout, drug abuse, and other behavioral and social indicators of breakdown in the parent-child transaction. Proponents of developmental child rearing practices stress the recognition of the child's autonomy, reward of behavior, and sharing information about expectations. Disciplinary methods, in contrast, call for punishment of behavior, parental dominance, and little, if any, parent-child dialogue. It is apparent that each of these styles of child rearing could have profoundly different impact on the adoption of health practices by children. The effects of child rearing practices on other aspects of child behavior have been well documented (Eron, Walder, Toigo, & Lefkowitz, 1963; Kagan & Moss, 1962; R. Sears, Whiting, Nowlis, & P. Sears, 1953), but little is known about how child rearing practices influence health behavior in children and adolescents.

326

In 1973 L. Pratt interviewed 510 families in a study of the relationship between child rearing practices and subsequent child health attitudes. She found that the parental use of reasoning and information sharing were highly correlated with individual autonomy and self-directedness, and with greater prohealth attitudes in the children. Earlier studies (Baumrind, 1967; T. E. Smith, 1970) supported the notion that those parents who offer justification for their actions, and who listen to their children, are more likely to have children with social competence. In this case, the argument can be made that a key element of social competence is the ability to assimilate and analyze information bearing on health status. In the L. Pratt (1973) study social competence was found also to be correlated with child rearing styles which focused on the use of reward systems rather than punishment. The specific health practices most highly correlated with such child rearing styles were cleanliness, dental hygiene, and elimination of habits. Less effect was evident on exercise, nutrition, and smoking. Aronfeed (1968) reported that giving specific rewards for initiative was consistently associated with higher child motivation and performance. The use of punishment or coercive pressure, however, tended to correlate with inconsistent and dependent levels of child performance. Thus a developmental child rearing style seems to be best suited for developing long-term health related decision-making skills, while a disciplinary approach appears to effect only short-term conformity to parental standards.

CHILDREN'S CONCEPTIONS OF HEALTH AND ILLNESS

A 4 year old visiting the doctor's office for a checkup resisted the pediatrician's attempt to listen to his chest with a stethoscope. "Why are you afraid?" asked the doctor. "Shall I warm it up with my hand so it won't be cold on your skin?" The resistance continued unabated. What the pediatrician could not realize, nor the child explain under these circumstances, was that his fear was not of the coldness of the instrument but what he thought it might do to him. He believed, as many 4 year olds do, that anything which listens to your heart might also listen to other things, like the sometime bad thoughts one has or the secret feelings one experiences (Bibace & Walsh, 1979).

Psychologists have recognized that the understanding of health and illness is tied, to a large extent, to a child's developmental stage (Brodie, 1974; Campbell, 1975; Palmer & Lewis, 1975; Whitt, 1982). Developmental theories have relied heavily on Piaget's (1926) schema of ontogenic development using the broad stages of pre-operational, concrete operational, and formal operational thought. Bibace and Walsh (1979) have extended Piaget's constructs to add those representing specific content implicit in children's concepts of health and illness. In developmental order they are Phenomenism, Contagion, Contamination, Internalization, Physiological, and Psychophysiological. Phenomenism and contagion are the least mature of childhood constructs to explain health and illness. For example, a child using a phonomenism explanation for a brother's illness might say, "It was a cold day, he got sick," equating a coincidence with a causative relationship. A contagion explanation might be, "He just caught it off somebody else, that's all." Single, concrete factors usually relating to a past experience with illness and a close temporal or proximal relationship to the causative factor or event are typical components of phenomenism and contagion conceptual styles.

At a formal operational level physiological and psychophysiological explanations are likely to be used. Physiological explanations recognize specific body or organ dysfunction even though the organ system is invisible. With these, the child uses abstractions and possibilities to explain an illness event. What causes cancer? A physiological-formal operational response might be: "Cells divide out of control in the blood stream. Caused by different things like air pollution, diet, or your genes." Moving away from concrete or temporal events the child can entertain possibilities which he or she cannot now see and can accept both internal and external causes for illness. At this level, usually around the 7th grade in school, a child can recognize the need for a personal initiative in health maintenance. However, at the preceding stage of concrete operational explanations the child might view illness as an internal event but in a global, less differentiated way, still relying on rather concrete and external causes. Concrete analogies for internal organ functions may be common, as in this explanation of a heart attack, which relies on an Internalization model of cause: "Your heart just stops working. It's like a pump. You just work it too hard that's all."

These views of illness causation are typical of the grade school child and suggest that health education aimed at this group should rely on specific concrete analogies for body functions in formulating the curriculum. In relation to the developmental sequence of cognitive maturity outlined by Piaget (1926) the pre-operational period (age 2-6 years) encompasses Phenomenism, Contagion, and Contamination; the concrete operational period (age 7-11 years) encompasses Internalization and Contamination content; and the formal operational period (age 12 to adulthood), the Psychophysiological and Physiological content.

A child's understanding of health concepts can be determined by asking specific questions, such as "What causes influenza?" A pre-operational-contagion conception would be reflected in the response, "Germs that get in your throat." A formal operational-physiological response might be, "An infection caused by a virus in the respiratory tract." The developmental stage-specific responses are quite different both in content and in quality. Pre-operational concepts of health and illness are couched in very concrete terms of cause and effect, and often with a high degree of egocentrism (e.g., "My head hurts when cold germs bite me"). Children at the pre-operational stage have difficulty separating self from the world, dealing with things which cannot be seen (such as bacteria), and in believing in the concept of reversibility. Thus, for example, a 5 year old might attribute an illness to something he or she had done wrong and fear that nothing, not even the doctor's prescription, can make things change.

Older children are able to deal with abstractions such as illness causation by referring both to their own past experiences and to concepts, such as unseen organ systems, to explain their health status. Thus there may be a progression from explanations based on what is seen and touched to that which may affect health by invasion (i.e., contagion) to the mature conception of illness as a part of the continuum of health, affected by mental and physical events (psychophysiological) (Bibace & Walsh, 1979). For clinicians concerned with enhancing the understanding a child has about illness and health this developmental schema has much to contribute. Specifically, the work of Bibace and Walsh points out the need to pay close attention to the level and type of understanding a child has evolved about his or her own health-illness experi-

329

ence. Contradicting such understandings by giving the "facts" is not necessarily a productive endeavor. More effective cognitive change can be brought about by properly categorizing a child's current level of understanding and by paying attention to the cognitive methods used to explain health (i.e., Phenomenism, Contagion, Contamination, Internalization, Physiological, and Psychophysiological). By pinpointing a child's current conceptual framework along one of these axes, and by recognizing the age-related level of cognitive maturity (i.e., preoperational, concrete, formal operational) related to it, the clinician may achieve a clearer appreciation of a patient's knowledge about personal health-illness status. Such methods will permit more realistic patient education which focuses on achieving the optimal level of understanding and not merely the transmission of factual material. Returning to the example of the small boy who feared the stethoscope, the realization that this child was operating at a concrete operational-phenomenism level would have guided the physician's response. Instead of "Don't be scared, I won't hurt you," the doctor might say, "Did you know your heart makes a noise as it works?" Then, by allowing the child to listen to his own heartbeat, the doctor can give the child sufficient control to understand that neither his body nor his mind is subject to harm from such an interesting device as a stethoscope. Using the approaches outlined by Bibace and Walsh (1979) the clinician involved in educating children on their health status can accomplish more direct and effective outcomes.

EXERCISE

Evidence continues to accumulate indicating that life-threatening conditions such as hypertension, coronary artery disease, and atherosclerosis have their origins during the early years of life (McGill, 1980; Stamler, 1978; Strong, 1978). While the rapid development of medical and surgical technology have aided the care of adult patients with cardiovascular disease, the more appropriate emphasis for care should be placed on preventive measures (Rowland, 1981). Attention has been paid to the benefits of reducing high cholesterol foods in the diet, smoking cessation, alcohol use in moderation, reducing caffeine intake, stress management, and exercise. Preventive educational programs have had some success in teaching youngsters the dangers of smoking and alcohol consumption (see later sections in this chapter), and experimental diet modification programs are now under way at several centers across the country. In adult cardiac rehabilitation programs emphasis has been placed on structured exercise and physical fitness regimens for several years with notable success (Paffenbarger & Hyde, 1980) although there is no corresponding application in children (Rowland, 1981). Again, the question arises: Why should we *prescribe* exercise for children when they seem to exercise so fully in everyday play and games? This view overlooks several important aspects of exercise as it relates to health promotion. First, for children the rate, frequency, and type of play they engage in varies significantly with age, sex, and social status. Second, although great fun can be had in playing the team games which are a large part of most children's play, there is little concentrated physical effort demanded. Third, the use of physical exercise as a prohealth measure requires a level of conscious understanding of its purpose and a commitment to sustained practice which no ordinary childhood play entails. Finally, exercise for better cardiac function requires specific exercise activities which create increased cardiovascular activity, such as running, swimming, bicycling, and aerobic dancing. Clearly if such activities are undertaken seriously the notion of "play" may take a back seat.

EXERCISE AS A CHILD
HEALTH PROMOTION STRATEGY

It is generally well accepted that habits are learned early in life. However to test this belief, and particularly as it may relate to health-promoting habits such as regular exercise, would necessitate a longitudinal study of several years duration. As an alternative, several programs evaluating the short-term effects on cardiovascular health in children have been reported. Project Superheart was begun in 1977 for elementary grade children in New York and targeted both cardiovascular fitness and understanding of what constitutes cardiovascular health (Way, 1981). The program is based in schools and teaches personal responsibility for physical fitness through instruction in jumping rope, hiking, aerobic exercise, and swimming. Teaching children how to measure and record their own heart rate reinforces progress and gives a strong sense of

331

personal responsibility. Although still only a few years old the program evaluation shows significant changes in the knowledge level of youngsters enrolled. As yet the physiological parameters targeted, such as blood pressures, body fat percentages, and serum cholesterol levels do not show such positive effects. The study directors postulated that significant changes in physiological risk factors will not be seen until later in the children's lives. Further follow-up is planned.

Problems associated with measuring long-term effects of physical exercise on cardiovascular health are common to almost all such studies (Rowland, 1981). There are no prospective studies demonstrating effects of risk factors in childhood such as obesity, family history, sedentary lifestyle, with later cardiovascular fitness (Linder, DuRant, & Gray, 1979). As a result most programs emphasizing physical activity for children do so in the belief that active intervention is necessary to modify specific risk factors, regardless of demonstrated effect on health outcomes in adult life. An example of this approach is the "Know Your Body" health education program sponsored in part by the National Cancer Institute (Williams, Carter, & Eng, 1980). A developmental curriculum designed for children in grades 1 through 9, the Know Your Body program, teaches a broad range of skills for health promotion. Again, personal responsibility for health maintenance is stressed, including regular physical exercise regimen. Measurement of effect is by self-report of the students through a 52 item health habits survey carried out after a 3 year trial. No attempt is made to evaluate actual physical changes in body functioning but "reliability checks" of student reports of cigarette smoking (plasma cotinine levels) show a high degree of agreement (better than 95%).

The most objective studies of the effects of exercise in children have measured serum lipid levels of high risk children, that is, those who had two or more high risk factors such as obesity, family history, diabetes mellitus, hypertension, or poor diet. Results have been mixed. Linder and his co-workers reported that serum lipid levels of a group of black youngsters did not appreciably decline after a 4 week program of moderate exercise training (Linder et al., 1979). A more recent study of white teenagers on a longer period of training showed significant increase in vital capacity (Linder, DuRant, & O. M. Mahoney, 1983); however a significant decrease in serum lipid levels was not found. A provocative finding of recent studies is that children who are normally predisposed toward greater physical activity have lower levels of serum triglycerides, even though they may consume more calories (Thorland & Gilliam, 1981).

OBESITY IN CHILDHOOD

Eight out of 10 obese children will become obese adults unless they slim down before the end of adolescence (Brownell & Stunkard, 1978; Stunkard & Burt, 1967). Obesity is among the most difficult health problems to reverse (Stunkard, 1975). National surveys reveal that weight among the population has progressed so rapidly the rate of obesity is now roughly double what it was at the turn of the century (Waxler & Leef, 1969). Data for young people show similar trends (Forbes, 1976). The physical consequences of childhood obesity are many and varied, ranging from hypertension to decreases in growth hormone secretion and diabetes in adult life. However, the psychological consequences may be more immediate and painful. Obese children are frequently isolated from peers (Lerner & Gellert, 1969), viewed as less socially acceptable even at early school years (Lerner & Schroeder, 1971), and have difficulty gaining college entry compared to average weight peers (Canning & Mayer, 1966). Social isolation and rejection have profound effect on the development of body image and self-concept (Sallade, 1973). Contrary to a widely held myth in our culture, "cute chubbiness" only has meaning when applied to infants; after toddlerhood it is anathema. Thus the health-related consequences of childhood obesity are of two types: the medical problems which ensue, usually in young adulthood, and the mental health problems which attend the problem of obesity largely because of social-interpersonal sanctions.

METHOD OF INTERVENTION
FOR WEIGHT REDUCTION

Orthodox methods of treating obesity include caloric restriction, exercise, anorectic medications, and, in the most severe cases, intestinal bypass surgery. Weight loss achieved by these methods is often difficult to sustain, leading to drop out or relapse rates which are often clinically unacceptable (Charney, Goodman, McBride, Lyon, & R. Pratt, 1976). The American Academy of Pediatrics stated over 20 years ago "our ignorance concerning the etiology, pathogenesis and treatment of obesity is remarkable" (Committee on Nutrition, 1964, p. 135). Such observations are still to some extent applicable today, although recent advances in behavioral approaches hold great promise. Behavioral therapies emphasize modification of the behaviors which lead to obesity, not just to losing weight. Obesity is treated as the outcome of dysfunctional patterns of eating behavior, patterns learned, reinforced, modeled, and practiced over periods of years. As a learned response, eating behavior is therefore susceptible to the same learning mechanisms of all human behavior. Here are some of the behavioral principles and mechanisms which have been effective in modifying eating behavior in children.

EATING RATE

A recurring theme in all behavioral therapies for weight control is, "It's not so much how much you eat, it's how fast you eat." Emphasis on slowing down what for many overweight people is an automatic, rapid rate of food ingestion has helped patients gain greater cognitive control over eating behaviors. In addition, slower ingestion rate allows normal physiological satiety mechanisms to operate efficiently and signal the eater to stop. Although used originally with adults, slowing eating rate has had success with children. Epstein and his co-workers used instruction to replace utensils after each bite of food with a group of 7 year old children (Epstein, Parker, & McCoy, 1976). Using trained observers it was noted that rate of eating, expressed as bites per minute, decreased significantly. Interestingly the rate of what the authors call "concurrent activities," such as talking and laughing, also decreased. Although no significant weight loss was noted, it was hypothesized that relative rate of weight gain could be reliably decreased by this simple method. Children learning to slow their rate of eating require positive models and benefit from positive reinforcement. Without sufficient structure and prompting it is unlikely that the technique will be effective (Gaul, Craighead, & M. J. Mahoney, 1975).

REWARDS

While for adults the knowledge that weight loss enhances self-image and contributes to better health often serves to reinforce their efforts, the same principles seldom hold true for children. Positive reinforcers are a necessary element of any treatment program for children, the most common being praise, trinkets, toys, or special activities. Pairing positive comments with secondary tangible reinforcers is also an effective means of encouraging appropriate behavior. M. J. Mahoney (1975) makes the point that reinforcement is given both for weight loss and for change in eating behavior. Of the two, reinforcement for behavior change seems to be most desirable. Prompt rewards achieve greatest effect with children. For this reason token rewards are often paired with more tangible reinforcers (Brownell & Stunkard, 1978). Points, checks, or "stars" are earned for specific behaviors such as calorie counting, chewing slowly, laying down utensils, eating at specified times, and so on. Administration of reinforcers is most efficiently accomplished through an agreement between client and therapist which details what behaviors are expected, what reinforcers are to be delivered contingent on those behaviors, and what response costs ("refunds") are to be paid. Such an agreement is usually in the form of a written contract called a *contingency contract*, and signed by both client and therapist. Many child workers prefer to establish such a contract with parents who then set up a system with their child.

ENVIRONMENTAL PROMPTING

Hunger is a physiological event which may come under control of external stimuli. For children this is particularly true. Mealtimes and snack time may vary from day to day, access to "junk food" is almost unlimited, sweets and chewy candy abound. The constant advertising blitz by television, radio, magazines, billboards, and so on may render children incapable of totally ignoring their appetizing gustatory prompts. Dealing with such environmental prompts requires restriction of their frequency, availability, or intensity. Behavioral approaches to weight reduction have devised a number of strategies under the general rubric of *stimulus control* to deal with external cues or prompts to eat. For example eliminating sweets, high sugar cereals, cakes, cookies, and so on from the pantry at home is an important first step in many programs. Eating only at mealtimes, never while watching television or alone; having all meals at the same table; eating together as a family. Children are not given "pocket money" for school to discourage the impulse to buy snacks or candy. Snacks are of the low calorie type, celery, fruit, or carrot sticks. Stimulus control is eventually gained by reducing the random opportunities to eat that occur each day and providing a set of alternate stimuli which are paired with appropriate eating times, that is, home, family, mealtimes, and appropriate food. For children still under guidance from their parents such methods are part of normal socialization. However, older children and teenagers may find learning new cues for appropriate eating behavior very difficult without much help and support.

INVOLVING PARENTS

Few systematic studies of the effects of employing families as behavioral change agents in obesity exist (Aragona, Cassady, & Drabman, 1975; Kingsley & Shapiro, 1977) even though the family seems to be the single most important element in maintaining childhood eating habits. Aragona and his co-workers (1975) used parents to change the eating behaviors of their obese children using a combination of response-cost contracting and positive reinforcement for weight loss. Parents of a group of elementary grade school children made monetary deposits at the outset of treatment on the understanding that specific refunds could accrue as they achieved treatment goals. Parents were trained to monitor calorie intake, chart daily weights, and count specific eating behaviors. Monetary refunds were given at completion of these tasks and for losing predetermined weight. Treatment consisted of 12 weekly family sessions with a therapist who provided guidance to the parents and controlled refund reinforcers. At follow-up 8 weeks after treatment a group treated with response-cost techniques was found to be gaining weight faster than a group treated with the same technique plus positive reinforcement. A similar study at the University of Pennsylvania involved mothers of obese children in a 10 week program to learn techniques of calorie counting, use of rewards and contracts, and modeling appropriate eating behaviors (Rivinus, Drummond, & Combrinck-Graham, 1976). The parent-child couples attended weekly sessions which included eating a meal. The therapist supervised food selection and reinforced target eating behaviors such as replacing utensils while chewing food and slowing the rate of eating. Weight loss was remarkable, averaging 2.8 kg. Strikingly, the weight loss of children with normal weight mothers was greater than that of children whose mothers were overweight. Both these studies point out the value of modeling appropriate eating behaviors as opposed to simply counting calories or attending to weight loss. Kingsley and Shapiro (1977), although not finding strong support for the importance of parental involvement, came across an unexpected outcome. Mothers who were trained to monitor the eating habits of their children actually lost significant amounts of weight themselves, reportedly not simply from dieting but from changes in their own eating habits. This, and other findings, serve to underscore the need for a better understanding of the family's effect on childhood eating patterns.

SELF-MONITORING

The act of eating may be largely automatic (Aragona et al., 1975; Brownell & Stunkard, 1978; Stunkard, 1975). Because of this the usual first step in any behavior change program is to carefully note and count the target behaviors to be modified (e.g., weight, snacks, calories, activity, etc.). It is also useful to note the time of day, location, and antecedent events of any eating behavior. There are some data which suggest merely by making what otherwise would be automatic behaviors conscious acts, the frequency and intensity of target behaviors, such as eating, actually diminish (Kazdin, 1974). Increasing conscious awareness of a particular problem may serve to motivate or sustain efforts to change (Romanczyk, 1974) and also provides a means to assess the effects of those efforts (M. J. Mahoney, Moura, & Wade, 1973). Observations made in close temporal sequence with specified eating behaviors constitute the most effective method of self-monitoring. Providing a record keeping device, such as a daily log or diary, facilitates the process greatly. Parents may keep a log of their own in addition to the child client's. This check of reliability in the observations is another piece of useful clinical data for the therapist. Finally, it is often equally as important to

337

monitor secondary factors impinging on the target behavior, such as emotional state, time of day, hunger pangs, surroundings, and significant others present. Wider ranges of self-monitoring provide greater possibilities of change in target behavior which may have various antecedent conditions associated with them.

PROMOTING DENTAL HEALTH

Children do not naturally brush their teeth regularly. In fact, the complaints of parents trying to follow the pedodontists' admonition, "have him brush after each meal and floss once a day," suggest that many children would do almost *anything* rather than brush or floss. It appears that it is the dentists, not the general public, and most certainly not children, who recognize that with proper cleaning almost all tooth and gum disease can be eradicated (Evans, 1982). It is estimated that 1 in 4 American children will have dental cavities by age 6 years, and 1 in 5 will have some periodontal disease by teenage years (A. M. Horowitz & H. S. Horowitz, 1980). Clearly, the problem is a significant threat to child health but the means for motivating good dental health behaviors are much less apparent.

As in almost all aspects of child health promotion efforts, the parents have been major targets for dental health education. Dental education programs have sought to motivate dental hygiene through first convincing parents of the issues involved. The most common motivation for promoting good dental health practice has been the threat of long-term negative consequences (i.e., dental cavities, gum disease, expensive procedures, etc.). However, in a review of the literature on fear as a motivator for behavior change, Higbee (1969) concluded that the efficacy of fear as a motivator is far from clear. In a classic study on preventive dentistry techniques Janis and Feshbach (1953) suggested that small amounts of fear produced more toothbrushing than larger amounts of fear. Later, the whole notion of using fear as a motivator for toothbrushing was questioned by a study which found that simply giving clear and precise directions was highly effective in increasing toothbrushing behavior (Leventhal, R. P. Singer, & Jones, 1965). The most elegant studies of this issue have been undertaken by Richard Evans and his group at the University of Houston (Evans, Rozelle, Lasater, Dembroski, & Allen, 1968). They compared the effects of three conditions on reports of toothbrushing in a cohort of junior high school students; oral hygiene instructions with no accompanying emotional component; the same instructions with a strong fear component; and, instruction with a positive appeal by pointing out all the favorable consequences of regular brushing. A control group received no instructions. The findings were interesting for two reasons pertinent to clinical practice. First, it was found that *reported* toothbrushing was misleading as an indicator of oral hygiene. Through a pre-intervention technique which involved photographing each student's teeth it was possible to compare *actual* brushing with *reported* brushing activity. Thus, it behooves both investigators and practitioners to consider using more reliable indices of oral hygiene than self-report. Second, and perhaps of most interest, was that by merely giving one highly specific instruction session, without emotional appeal of any sort, the objective difference in oral hygiene improved significantly. Adding these same oral hygiene instructions to a positive appeal proved to be almost as effective, less so when a negative appeal was operating. In an extended follow-up program Evans' group determined that positive dental hygiene was maintained most effectively when the students were examined at irregular intervals, without further instruction. The effect of intermittent, but expected, examinations appears to have obliged the students to maintain a high level of oral hygiene, presumably in anticipation of the examination.

Drawing on human learning research one concludes the evidence supports an optimal learning event as containing two key elements; clear and specific information about what is expected of the learner, and a performance monitoring schedule which is irregular and unpredictable by the learner. Teaching good dental health is a process in which many professions are involved, including dentists, dental hygienists, and educators. In addition, the primary education for dental health is usually done mainly by parents. Hence, it is entirely likely that mixed or sometimes even incorrect information can be obtained, especially by younger children. To counter this possibility the clinician involved with questions of dental hygiene should follow an investigative protocol emphasizing: (a) parental motivation, (b) developmental stage of the child, (c) previous understanding of both parent and child regarding dental hygiene, and (d) family expectations for outcome (i.e., unrealistic expectations of no cavities simply due to brushing). Only by carefully matching an educational program with individual needs, socioeconomic level, and developmental stage of the child involved can one expect effective learning and behavior change to occur.

THE PROBLEM OF TEENAGE DRINKING

Adolescent drinking is believed to be a major public health problem (Chauncey, 1980). Results of recent polls indicate that as many as 1 in 3 teenage males and 1 in 4 females drink alcohol on a weekly basis (Wechsler, 1980). In another survey 20% of high school seniors said they drank to intoxication at least once a month and 35% reported their friends were drunk at least once a week (Johnston, Bachman, & O'Malley, 1979). Factors related to the onset and maintenance of teenage drinking include socioeconomic status, influence of the media, pressure from peers, religious/ethnic background, and parental influence.

SOCIAL CLASS IMPLICATIONS

Cloward and Ohlin (1960) pointed out that poorer families tend to use alcohol as a means for resolving feelings of helplessness and failure, to block out the impact of poverty, overcrowding, and stress. Youngsters in such families have reportedly greater orientation to the present, what can be seen and touched and experienced, now rather than later. Alcohol use fulfills their needs readily and cheaply. However, in times of economic crisis when jobs are scarce and money less available the middle class youth may also resort to increased alcohol use (Donovan & R. Jessor, 1978). Many middle class families are changing dramatically through divorce, separation, or dual career marriages. Teenagers are often forced to greater independence at earlier ages, thus increasing their detachment from the family and their subsequent need for economic self-reliance. Such changes put teenagers at greater risk for alcohol use by exposing them earlier to the pressures extant in the world at large. However, as a single factor social class is not predictive of drinking behavior.

MEDIA INFLUENCE

Magazines are perhaps the most potent source of material to affect drinking behavior in teenagers. The glossy advertisements picturing physically attractive individuals engrossed in alcohol consumption in glamorous locations is often more than the vulnerable teenager can withstand. Research involving the effects of television on drinking behavior has not been reported for teenagers, although as Esserman (1981) points out there is evidence that commercials on television have strong cognitive impact on pre-teenagers.

PEER PRESSURE

Teenagers are enormously susceptible to influence from their peers as they focus their major point of developmental reference away from the family. Similarities in standards of behavior, recreational pursuits, role models, and the like are characteristic of teenage peer groups (M. Sherif & C. Sherif, 1964). The relationship between belonging to a group of peers who drink and initiating drinking behavior has been demonstrated (R. Jessor & S. I. Jessor, 1975; Riester & R. A. Zucker, 1968). Expectations for drinking behavior undoubtedly have important impact on a teenager's decision to drink or not. However, it has also been shown that teenagers regularly overestimate the frequency of drinking behavior among peers and thus may find themselves unrealistically drawn to exaggerated "drinking norms" (Fishbein, 1980). Interestingly, the teenage peer group standards for drinking behavior and those of the associated adult community have much in common. Barnes (1981) pointed out that community attitudes toward drinking are likely to be reflected directly in the drinking behavior of its teenagers, particularly in reported personal attitudes toward drinking and alcohol consumption patterns. For example, working class communities where adults regularly stop by a bar after work are likely to see similar patterns in their teenagers stopping at a bar on their way home from school. No studies have clarified the question of whether teenagers are pressured to conform to begin drinking or whether their choice of a particular peer group reflects already active interest in alcohol consumption (Barnes, 1977). Hartocollis (1982) points out that the average age for taking the first drink is 13.7 years, a figure which coincides with the early years of attendance at junior high school in most states, and reinforces the notion of incipient temptation occurring in the peer group context.

RELIGIOUS/ETHNIC BACKGROUND

Although there seems to be little difference in incidence of teenage drinking between the sexes there are marked differences according to ethnic and religious background. R. Jessor and S. I. Jessor (1975) reported that their survey showed Catholic-Irish youths report drinking more than Catholic-Italians, although Catholic-Italians begin drinking at an earlier age, as do Jewish teenagers. Black teenagers drink less than whites, and white-protestant teenagers report the highest drinking rate and number of problems related to drinking. Lowest incidence of reported heavy drinking occurs among Catholic-Italians. Several studies have indicated that family religious orientation may not be so important as the extent to which the teenager actively participates in organized religious activities such as youth groups (Donovan & R. Jessor, 1978; Schlegal & Sanborn, 1979). It has also been proposed (Mizruchi & Perrucci, 1970) that religions such as Judaism which prescribe alcohol use as a sacrament in religious observance help regulate teenage attitudes toward drinking. Those fundamentalist religions which ban alcohol consumption in any form may be unwittingly setting up a strong curiosity about alcohol use in their young people which eventually could lead to drinking.

PARENTAL INFLUENCE

Teenagers do not "invent" the idea of drinking; it is provided for them by their parents (Maddox, 1966). It is known that the best indicators of potential for teenage drinking are the attitudes and behaviors of parents toward drinking (Gordon & McAlister, 1982). Favorable parental attitudes toward alcohol consumption have been linked with teenage attitudes toward drinking, to greater likelihood of teenage drinking (Shain, Riddell, & Kilty, 1977), and problem drinking in those teenagers whose parents vigorously oppose drinking (McKechnie, 1976). Abstainers are most likely to have abstaining parents, moderate drinkers moderate drinking parents, although for heavy drinkers there is not such a direct association. Heavy drinkers may be the product of either an abstaining or heavy drinking household (R. A. Zucker, 1976). The drinking behavior of teenagers of an alcoholic family may take on especially charged emotional meaning for youngsters attempting to emulate the role model of an older sibling or parent.

APPROACHES TO ALCOHOL ABUSE PREVENTION

Few alcohol abuse prevention programs have been sufficiently well grounded in psychological theory to incorporate measures of effectiveness. Programs have ranged from peer counseling to family psychotherapy, using school-based educational materials, films, discussion groups, presentations by Alanon, even television celebrities to get the message across. Three major methods for prevention-education are used: education by teaching cognitive material, changing emotional response to drinking behavior, and changing the environment.

Cognitive Education. A major problem with information-based education about alcohol abuse is the dearth of objective data about the effects of teenage drinking on long-term health status (Jacobson & Zinberg, 1975). As a consequence the educational efforts to promote abstinence have relied on provoking fear responses through medical outcome data from the effects of long-term heavy drinking in older adults (Turner, Mezey, & Kimball, 1977). Programs have attempted to reach youngsters through the schools and early in this century specific curricula were developed. Unfortunately, much of the earlier work to teach alcohol abuse prevention was motivated by strong moralistic and religious arguments which did little to bring about cognitive understanding in many of its recipients (Globetti, 1971). White and Biron (1979) reported that prevention programs aimed at informing youngsters of the psychological effects of alcohol use seemed to modify the early experimental drinking of pre-adolescents. There is much less effect with older teenagers. It is apparent from much of the literature on prevention of alcohol abuse that programs of an educational nature may have a stimulating or provocative effect on the drinking behavior of older teenagers. Younger children are still susceptible to adult instruction and role modeling. Teenagers are more likely to see a

343

challenge to their evolving autonomy through such instruction and particularly to pick up on perceived inconsistencies between what many adults preach about alcohol consumption and what they appear to practice in reality. Emphasizing prohibition and abstinence for older teenagers has the effect of a challenge to overcome authority; the outcome is almost certainly undesirable (Gordon & McAlister, 1982). Most effective is an approach which combines several cognitive sources, including but not exclusively, exposure to moderated alcohol use in the family, lack of moral restriction against drinking, the belief in the family that drinking does not connote maturity, and information about the effects of drinking on health presented in a developmentally appropriate fashion. Perhaps the lack of impact many purely cognitive information sharing approaches have had is due to the absence of family involvement and the lack of interactive components in the educational programs. Giving little or no opportunity for questions, dialogue, or discussion leaves teenagers confused and sometimes resentful, paving the way for natural curiosity drives toward experimentation and more emotionally motivated drinking behaviors.

Changing Emotional Responses to Alcohol Use. The decision to begin using alcohol is generally not simply a cognitive one for most teenagers. Whether initial drinking is prompted by stress, peer pressures, chaotic family situations, or just teenage daring, there is a significant element of emotion attached (Meichenbaum, 1979). In the past 10 years the National Institute on Drug Abuse has recognized the need to include affective as well as cognitive components in educating young people about alcohol effects (NIDA, 1975). This initiative has produced program efforts directed toward promoting thoughtful use of alcohol, with full awareness of possible health consequences, rather than emphasizing avoiding abuse through abstinence. One of these programs is the teaching of life skills which would counter the psychological factors which often are associated with drinking: low self-esteem, alienation from family, reckless or impulsive lifestyles (Botvin, Eng, & Williams, 1980). Lifestyle training, as such programs are known, seeks to "inoculate" adolescents against such psychological vulnerability to alcohol abuse. Using group discussion, role playing, behavior rehearsal, and assertion training these programs provide both a supportive and shaping environment for teenagers to learn in. Problem solving and decision making skills are taught, usually by well trained psychological counselors. There is no attempt, however, to bring up alcohol abuse as a direct issue, but rather to foster and build the emotional maturity necessary to deal with teenage drinking in a measured fashion. Little research on outcome has been reported as yet, although descriptive reports suggest that lifestyle skills development holds great promise for prevention of alcohol and other drug abuse.

A second program method relating to this issue is that which seeks to foster better decision making skills in relation to alcohol use (Gordon & McAlister, 1982; Simon, Howe, & Kirschenbaum, 1972). This type of curriculum tries to prepare young people for the decisions they must make in the future by helping clarify life goals, establish criteria for personally acceptable standards of behavior, and recognize the kinds of cognitive input needed to make effective decisions about drinking. As in the life-styles training approach (Botvin et al., 1980) the primary goal is not abstinence but rather the transmission of sufficient emotional support coupled with strategies and problem solving skills to "immunize" young people against social pressures to drink to excess. Drinking in moderation is preferred over excess, if the decision is made to drink at all. Understandably these approaches have not met with complete approval by many parents, especially if the home belief system is proabstinence. Another problem lies in the fact that much of the training going on in these programs has to be done on a purely hypothetical basis since the students are under age to drink. Questions about the possible effect of actually prompting alcohol use in teenagers where otherwise none would have occurred leave much concern among some educators (Freeman & Scott, 1966). What is clear is that most researchers agree that any attempt to prepare teenagers to deal with alcohol is better than none at all.

The most visible method for countering teenage alcohol use is that which involves regulation of access to alcohol through state and local ordinances. Smart (1980) suggests that manipulating the legal drinking age may give confusing results as a short-term measure. Forcing teenagers to buy alcohol covertly by increasing the legal drinking age often leads to informal parties where beer or liquor is supplied either by parents, often unknowingly, or by legal age young people (Wechsler, 1980).

PREVENTION OF SMOKING

Smoking among teenagers in the United States has been called a growing epidemic (Evans & Raines, 1982). A wide range of statistics indicates that over the past 20 years initiation of smoking is at an earlier age, and that both sexes are smoking at about the same rate, a fact which was not the case 10 years ago (Green, 1979; National Clearinghouse for Smoking and Health, 1972). Survey studies suggest that cigarette smoking among teenagers is associated with a number of factors, including developmental, social, behavioral, and personality characteristics (Botvin, 1982). Teenagers today face greater pressures to mature early and to become independent as parental influence declines and peer pressures increase. This can bring about marked changes in the developmental process and render many teenagers susceptible to initiating smoking. The personality characteristics of teenagers who smoke reflect impulsiveness, impatience, rebelliousness, and a tendency to rely on others for decision making. Behaviorally, teenagers who smoke are likely to be poorer students in school and to have discipline problems. From a social standpoint, youngsters who smoke have parents who smoke and friends who smoke. The public media, advertising, and television play a part in provoking cigarette smoking by teenagers by offering desirable smoking models for youngsters to emulate (Botvin & McAlister, 1981).

HOW DOES SMOKING BEGIN?

Cigarette smoking beginning in teenager years is a multidetermined behavior. Two major schools of thought contribute some understanding as to why teenagers take up smoking. One of these, the *social learning theory* model (Bandura, 1977) emphasizes the effects of emulation, imitation, and modeling in combination with social reinforcement for smoking. The other model, described by R. Jessor and S. I. Jessor (1977) as a *problem behavior theory*, suggests that teenagers take up smoking as a means of coping with psychological stress.

Social learning theory explanations for smoking behavior implicate the effects of prosmoking models of high prestige or social desirability. Young people are enormously impressed by the behavior of idealized models such as celebrities, rock musicians, actors, and so on. When the communications industries couple such figures in magazine and television advertising campaigns for cigarettes the impact on teenagers can be irresistible (Olshavsky, 1978). It is still unclear as to exactly how such advertising in the mass media affects teenager's smoking habits, but it seems unlikely that such media are directly responsible for initiation of smoking (Ward, 1971). What seems to happen is that mass media, including billboards, newspaper, and magazine advertisements, play a role in shaping attitudes toward smoking during earlier years of childhood. Actually beginning to smoke in teenage years, especially when personal usage is important among peers, may be more a function of family and peer models (Borland & Rudolph, 1975). Conformity to group standards is widely held to be the reason many teenagers undertake smoking (Newman, 1970) and indeed, the incidence of teenage smoking in families where both parents smoke is roughly twice that where neither parent smokes (NIE, 1979). Having a friend who smokes (Levitt & Edwards, 1970) or a sibling who smokes (Surgeon General, 1980) also seems to correlate with a greater likelihood of taking up smoking.

Although many of the studies report correlational and descriptive statistics there are no well controlled prospective studies of the apparent interaction between social pressures and individual characteristics (Evans & Raines, 1982). Factors which originate within the individual, as opposed to the effects of social-external events, are more difficult to pinpoint as contributors to smoking behavior. Stressors for teenagers take a number of forms from academic to social to familial. Low self-esteem, external locus of control, and academic failure can all contribute to the decision to take up smoking (Tedeschi & Bonoma, 1972). Coping with stress can result in adopting rebellious or antisocial behaviors, including smoking (Bynner, 1969; Stewart & Livson, 1966). Evans and C. K. Smith (1980) reported that teenagers who smoke feel unhappy at home. Clausen (1968) found adolescent smokers to have significantly weaker ties to adult values than nonsmokers and a higher level of noncompliance with parental wishes. A number of risk factors are clear-

347

ly related to initiating smoking (e.g., parental or older sibling models, impulsivity and rebelliousness, academic stress, and social isolation). The problem behavior model described by the Jessors (1977) suggests that the basic trigger for smoking onset is often a combination of stresses and failures which lead the teenager to believe that smoking will offer some form of satisfaction. Unfortunately, the chemical action of nicotine does have a short-term calming effect, and a troubled teenager taking up smoking is also likely to find social-peer reinforcement. The social-reinforcement cycle can be very difficult for concerned adults to interrupt (R. Jessor & S. I. Jessor, 1977).

SMOKING PREVENTION PROGRAMS

It has been suggested that the health issues implicit in smoking prevention in teenagers are so complex and multifactorial that solution by any "one-size-fits-all" methods or programs is unlikely (Rabinowitz & Zimmerli, 1974). Until 1979 many smoking prevention programs were aimed at adult populations, overlooking the potential for preventive approaches with children. Since then a large number of smoking prevention education programs have developed, many under the impetus of the 1980 Surgeon General's report (Coates, Perry, Killen, & Slinkard, 1981). For the most part, smoking prevention programs have been didactic and informational in nature, relying on providing health-related information about the consequences of smoking. The belief is that if teenagers are informed of the health dangers smoking will lose its attractiveness. Using fear as a motivator, these educational programs, largely offered through the schools, showed graphic pictures of diseased lungs, patients with emphysema, mortality and morbidity statistics, and so on. There is no doubt that such efforts have raised the knowledge level and availability of prevention programs. Unfortunately, many teenagers still elect to smoke, despite these dire warnings (NCI, 1977). Apparently, knowledge of consequences and even altered attitudes do not translate readily into changes in behavior.

PLANS FOR THE FUTURE

Orthodox educational antismoking programs are clearly less than successful in combating the rise in

348

smoking by teenagers (NIH, 1976). Recently, there has been increased interest in programs which de-emphasize motivation based on fear, and more attention has been given the complex factors which prompt teenagers to take up smoking in the first place. Particularly important in this effort has been the focus on ways of teaching teenagers how to avoid or resist the sometimes subtle pressures put on them to smoke by peers, siblings, or the mass media. The techniques of building strategies of resistance goes on in group discussions, role playing, behavior rehearsal, and videotapes of self-confrontation sessions. These strategies which are a form of psychological "inoculation," reportedly decrease cigarette smoking by as much as 50% (McAlister, Perry, Killen, Slinkard, & Maccoby, 1980). A model program of this type is the Houston Project (Evans et al., 1978). The strategies employed by Evans and his colleagues draw from social learning theory and utilize rather elegant communication theory methods to present nonsmoking teenager models as both narrative and role playing participants. The idea of minimizing the "fear of illness" issue allowed the insertion of a positive component based on a more "here and now" focus which appeared to meet the temporal orientation of adolescents. Outcome measures and other methodologic problems inherent in earlier studies were carefully controlled. Early findings suggest that youngsters exposed to such training take up smoking at a rate only half that of those not given the training (Evans et al., 1978). Similar findings are reported by studies in New York, the Know Your Body Program (Botvin et al., 1980), in Oregon (Biglan, Severson, Bavry, & McConnell, 1980), and in California at Stanford University (McAlister, Perry, & Maccoby, 1979). The rigor of scientific method and the conceptual elegance of many current studies are providing much needed objective guidance for future efforts in teaching smoking abstinence to children.

SUMMARY

One thing stands out in reviewing some of this work on child and adolescent health promotion. Children are typically not given responsibility for their own health behavior until a significant level of threat to health is identified (i.e., alcohol, drug use, cigarette smoking). Our child rearing methods in health behaviors or health attitudes seem to be oriented toward the notion "...what he don't know can't hurt him." Health problems must assume significant proportions and a marked degree of urgency before adult awareness is raised. To apply yet another old saying "...if it ain't broke, don't fix it." Too often, it seems, we adhere to this adage and through such benign neglect unknowingly reinforce patterns of health-threatening behavior. Our clinical efforts in modifying established patterns of health-threatening behavior such as smoking, overeating, and drinking alcohol in excess are often understandably less than successful. What now seems clear is that more attention must be paid to the modification of antecedents to health-threatening behaviors. The family context seems to be the most obvious focus for such efforts, and the methods of change will surely involve not only the transmission of cognitive information but the modification of beliefs and attitudes about health and illness and the development of new prohealth lifestyles beginning in early childhood. A tall order? Not so if pediatric health psychologists are willing to put their energies into such programs as well as into activities which emphasize direct care of illness.

Brian Stabler, PhD, is Associate Professor of Psychology and Pediatrics at the University of North Carolina School of Medicine, Chapel Hill, North Carolina. He is a member of the editorial boards of *Health Psychology, Journal of Pediatric Psychology, and Journal of Clinical Child Psychology.* His special interests in pediatric health psychology include the coping mechanisms of children with chronic medical conditions, childhood recurrent abdominal pain, and the psychological consequences of growth delay in children. Dr. Stabler may be contacted at the Department of Psychiatry, School of Medicine, University of North Carolina, Chapel Hill, NC 27514.

RESOURCES

Aragona, J., Cassady, J., & Drabman, R. S. (1975). Treating overweight children through parental training and contingency contracting. *Journal of Applied Behavior Analysis, 8,* 269-278.

Aronfeed, J. (1968). *Conduct and Conscience.* New York: Academic Press.

Bandura, A. (1977). *Social Learning Theory.* Englewood Cliffs, NJ: Prentice Hall.

Barnes, G. (1977). The development of adolescent drinking behavior: An evaluation of the impact of the socialization process within the family. *Adolescence, 12,* 571-591.

Barnes, G. (1981). Drinking among adolescents: A subcultural phenomenon or a model of adult behaviors? *Adolescence, 16,* 211-219.

Baumrind, D. (1967). Child care practices anteceding three patterns of preschool behavior. *Genetic Psychology Monographs, 77,* 43-88.

Bibace, R., & Walsh, M. E. (1979). Developmental stages in children's conceptions of illness. In G. Stone, F. Cohen, & N. Adler (Eds.), *Health Psychology: A Handbook* (pp. 285-301). San Francisco, CA: Jossey-Bass.

Biglan, A., Severson, H., Bavry, J., & McConnell, S. (1980). *Social Influence and Adolescent Smoking: A First Look Behind the Barn.* Paper presented at the annual meeting of the American Psychological Association, Montreal, Canada.

Borland, B. L., & Rudolph, J. P. (1975). Relative effects of low socio-economic status, parental smoking and poor scholastic performance on smoking among high school students. *Social Science and Medicine, 9,* 27-30.

Botvin, G. J. (1982). Broadening the focus of smoking prevention strategies. In T. J. Coates, A. C. Petersen, & C. Perry (Eds.), *Promoting Adolescent Health: A Dialogue in Research and Practice* (pp. 137-148). New York: Academic Press.

Botvin, G., Eng, A., & Williams, C. (1980). Preventing the onset of cigarette smoking. *Preventive Medicine, 9,* 135-143.

Botvin, G. J., & McAlister, A. L. (1981). Cigarette smoking among children and adolescents: Causes and Prevention. In C. B. Arnold (Ed.), *Advances in Disease Prevention* (pp. 222-249). New York: Springer.

Brodie, B. (1974). Views of healthy children toward illness. *American Journal of Public Health, 64,* 1156-1159.

Brownell, K. D., & Stunkard, A. J. (1978). Behavioral treatment of obesity in children. *American Journal of Diseases of Childhood, 132,* 403-412.

Bynner, J. M. (1969). *The Young Smoker.* London: Government Social Survey, Her Majesty's Stationary Office.

Campbell, J. D. (1975). Illness is a point of view: The development of children's concepts of illness. *Child Development, 46,* 92-100.

Canning, H., & Mayer, J. (1966). Obesity: Its possible effect on college acceptance. *New England Journal of Medicine, 275,* 1172-1174.

Charney, E., Goodman, H. C., McBride, M., Lyon, B., & Pratt, R. (1976). Childhood antecedents of adult obesity: Do chubby infants become obese adults? *New England Journal of Medicine, 295,* 6-9.

Chauncey, R. (1980). New careers for moral entrepreneurs: Teenage drinking. *Journal of Drug Issues, Winter,* 45-70.

Clausen, J. A. (1968). Adolescent antecedents of cigarette smoking: Data from the Oakland growth study. *Social Service and Medicine, 1,* 357-382.

Cloward, R. A., & Ohlin, L. E. (1960). *Delinquency and Opportunity: A Theory of Delinquent Gangs.* Glencoe, IL: Free Press.

Coates, T., Perry, C., Killen, J., & Slinkard, L. A. (1981). Primary prevention of cardiovascular disease in children and adolescents. In C. Prokop & L. Bradley (Eds.), *Medical Psychology* (pp. 157-197). New York: Academic Press.

Coates, T. J., Petersen, A. C., & Perry, C. (Eds.). (1982). *Promoting Adolescent Health: A Dialogue on Research and Practice.* New York: Academic Press.

Committee on Nutrition, American Academy of Pediatrics. (1964). Factors affecting food intake. *Pediatrics, 33,* 135-143.

Donovan, J., & Jessor, R. (1978). Adolescent problem drinking: Psychosocial correlates in a national sample survey. *Journal of Studies on Alcohol, 39,* 1506-1524.

Epstein, L. H., Parker, L., & McCoy, J. F. (1976). Descriptive analysis of eating regulation in obese and nonobese children. *Journal of Applied Behavior Analysis, 7,* 402-416.

Eron, L. D., Walder, L. O., Toigo, R., & Lefkowitz, M. (1963). Social class, parental punishment for aggression, and child aggression. *Child Development, 34,* 849-867.

Esserman, J. F. (Ed.). (1981). *Television Advertising and Children: Issues, Research and Findings.* New York: Child Research Service.

Evans, R. I. (1982). Modifying health lifestyles in children and adolescents: Development and evaluation of a social psychological intervention. In A. Baum & J. E. Singer (Eds.), *Handbook of Psychology and Health, Vol. 3, Issues in Child Health and Adolescent Health* (pp. 231-245). Hillsdale, NJ: Lawrence Erlbaum Associates.

Evans, R. I., & Raines, B. E. (1982). Control and prevention of smoking in adolescents: A psychosocial perspective. In T. J. Coates, A. C. Petersen, & C. Perry (Eds.), *Promoting Adolescent Health: A Dialogue in Research and Practice*. New York: Academic Press.

Evans, R. I., Rozelle, R. M., Lasater, T. M., Dembroski, T. M., & Allen, B. P. (1968). New measure of effects of persuasive communications: A chemical indicator of toothbrushing behavior. *Psychological Reports, 23,* 731-736.

Evans, R. I., Rozelle, R. M., Mittelmark, M. B., Hansen, W. B., Bane, A. L., & Havis, J. (1978). Deterring the onset of smoking in children: Knowledge of immediate physiological effects and coping with peer pressures, media pressure, and parent modeling. *Journal of Applied and Social Psychology, 8,* 126-136.

Evans, R. I., & Smith, C. K. (1980). *Cigarette Smoking in Teenage Females: A Social-Psychological-Behavioral Analysis and Further Evaluation of a Model Prevention Strategy.* National Cancer Institute Preliminary Report, Washington, DC.

Fishbein, M. (1980). A theory of reasoned action: Some applications and implications. In M. M. Page (Ed.), *Nebraska Symposium on Motivation 1979* (pp. 65-116). Lincoln, NE: University of Nebraska Press.

Forbes, G. B. (1976). Prevalence of obesity in childhood. In G. A. Bray (Ed.), *Obesity in Perspective* (Vol. 2, DHEW Publication No. NIH 76-852, pp. 348-353). Washington, DC: U. S. Department of Health Education and Welfare.

Forman, S. A., & O'Malley, P. L. (1984). School stress and anxiety interventions. *School Psychology Review, 13,* 162-170.

Freeman, H., & Scott, J. (1966). A critical review of alcohol education for adolescents. *Community Mental Health Journal, 2,* 222-230.

Gaul, D. J., Craighead, W. E., & Mahoney, M. J. (1975). Relationship between eating rates and obesity. *Journal of Consulting and Clinical Psychology, 43,* 123-125.

Globetti, G. (1971). Alcohol education in the schools. *Journal of Drug Education, 1,* 241-248.

Gordon, N. P., & McAlister, A. L. (1982). Adolescent drinking: Issues and research. In T. J. Coates, A. C. Petersen, & C. Perry (Eds.), *Promoting Adolescent Health: A Dialog on Research and Practice* (pp. 201-223). New York: Academic Press.

Greene, J. W., & Thompson, W. (1984). A physician/psychologist team approach to children and adolescents with recurrent somatic complaints. *School Psychology Review, 13*, 204-210.

Hartocollis, P. C. (1982). Personality characteristics in adolescent problem drinkers: A comparative study. *Journal of the American Academy of Child Psychiatry, 21*, 348-353.

Higbee, K. L. (1969). Fifteen years of fear arousal: Research on threat appeals: 1953-1968. *Psychological Bulletin, 72*, 426-444.

Horowitz, A. M., & Horowitz, H. S. (1980). School based fluoride programs: A critique. *Journal of Preventive Dentistry, 6*, 89-96.

Jacobson, R., & Zinberg, N. (1975). *The Social Basis of Drug Abuse Prevention*. Washington, DC: Drug Abuse Council, Inc.

Janis, I. L., & Feshbach, S. (1953). Effects of rear-arousing communications. *Journal of Abnormal and Social Psychology, 48*, 78-92.

Jessor, R., & Jessor, S. I. (1975). Adolescent development and the onset of drinking: A longitudinal study. *Journal of Studies on Alcohol, 36*, 27-51.

Jessor, R., & Jessor, S. I. (1977). *Problem Behavior and Psychosocial Development: A Longitudinal Study of Youth*. New York: Academic Press.

Johnston, L., Bachman, J., & O'Malley, P. L. (1979). *Drugs and the Class of '78: Behaviors, Attitudes and Recent National Trends* (DHEW Publication No. ADM 79-877). Washington, DC: U. S. Government Printing Office.

Kagan, J., & Moss, H. A. (1962). *Birth to Maturity: A Study in Psychological Development*. New York: John Wiley.

Kazdin, A. E. (1974). Self monitoring and behavior change. In M. J. Mahoney & C. E. Thoresen (Eds.), *Self Control: Power to the Person* (pp. 21-35). Belmont, CA: Brooks/Cole.

Kingsley, R. G., & Shapiro, J. (1977). A comparison of three behavioral programs for the control of obesity in children. *Behavior Therapy, 8*, 30-36.

Lerner, R. M., & Gellert, E. (1969). Body build identification, preference and aversion in children. *Developmental Psychology, 1,* 456-462.

Lerner, R. M., & Schroeder, C. (1971). Physique identification, preference and aversion in kindergarten children. *Developmental Psychology, 5,* 538.

Leventhal, H., Singer, R. P., & Jones, S. (1965). Effects of fear and specificity of recommendation upon attitudes and behavior. *Journal of Personality and Social Psychology, 2,* 20-29.

Levitt, E. E., & Edwards, J. A. (1970). A multivariate study of correlative factors in youthful cigarette smoking. *Developmental Psychology, 2,* 5-11.

Linder, C. W., DuRant, R. H., & Gray, R. H. (1979). The effects of exercise on serum lipids in children. *Clinical Research, 27,* 797.

Linder, C. W., DuRant, R. H., & Mahoney, O. M. (1983). The effects of exercise on serum lipid levels in white male adolescents. *Medical Science and Sports Exercise, 15,* 1341-1354.

Maddox, G. L. (1966). Teenagers and alcohol: Recent research. *Annals of the New York Academy of Science, 133,* 856-865.

Mahoney, M. J. (1975). Fat fiction. *Behavior Therapy, 6,* 416-418.

Mahoney, M. J., Moura, N. G. M., & Wade, T. C. (1973). The relative efficacy of self reward, self punishment and self monitoring techniques for weight loss. *Journal of Consulting and Clinical Psychology, 40,* 404-407.

McAlister, A. L., Perry, C., Killen, J., Slinkard, L. A., & Maccoby, N. (1980). Pilot study of smoking, alcohol and drug abuse prevention. *American Journal of Public Health, 70,* 719-721.

McAlister, A. L., Perry, C., & Maccoby, N. (1979). Adolescent smoking: Onset and prevention. *Pediatrics, 63,* 650-658.

McGill, H. C. (1980). Morphologic development of the atherosclerotic plaque. In R. M. Lauer & R. B. Shekelle (Eds.), *Childhood Prevention of Atherosclerosis and Hypertension* (pp. 41-49). New York: Raven Press, Inc.

McKechnie, R. J. (1976). Parents, children and learning to drink. In J. S. Madden, R. Walker, & W. H. Kenyon (Eds.), *Alcoholism and Drug Dependence* (pp. 451-456). New York: Plenum.

Meichenbaum, D. (Ed.). (1979, January 4). *Cognitive Behavior Modification Newsletter*, p. 2.

Mizruchi, E., & Perrucci, K. (1970). Prescription, proscription and permissiveness: Aspects of norms and deviant drinking behavior. In G. L. Maddox (Ed.), *The Domesticated Drug: Drinking Among Collegians.* New Haven, CT: College and University Press.

Nader, P., Perry, C., Maccoby, N., Solomon, D., Killen, J., Telch, M., & Alexander, J. (1982). Adolescent perceptions of family health behavior: Tenth grade educational activity to increase family awareness of a common cardiovascular risk reduction program. *Journal of School Health, 4,* 372-377.

National Cancer Institute. (1977, October). *The Smoking Digest. Progress Report on a Nation Kicking the Habit.* Washington, DC: U. S. Department of Health, Education and Welfare, Public Health Service, National Institute of Health, National Cancer Institute.

National Institute of Education. (1979, November). *Teenage Smoking: Immediate and Long-Term Patterns.* Washington, DC: U. S. Department of Health, Education and Welfare, National Institute of Education.

National Institute of Health. (1976). *Teenage Smoking: National Patterns of Cigarette Smoking, Ages 12 through 18, in 1972 and 1974* (DHEW Publication No. NIH 76-391). Washington, DC: U. S. Government Printing Office.

National Institute on Drug Abuse. (1975). *Toward a National Strategy for Primary Drug Abuse Prevention Programs: Final Report Delphi II.* Rockville, MD.

Newman, I. M. (1970). Peer pressure hypothesis for adolescent cigarette smoking. *School Health Review, 1,* 15-18.

Olshavsky, R. W. (1978). Marketing's cigarette scar. *Business Horizons, 21,* 46-51.

Paffenbarger, R. S., & Hyde, R. T. (1980). Exercise as protection against heart attack. *New England Journal of Medicine, 302,* 1026.

Palmer, B. B., & Lewis, C. E. (1975). *Development of Health Attitudes and Behaviors.* Paper presented at the annual meeting of the American School Health Association, Denver, CO.

Piaget, J. (1926). *The Language and Thought of the Child.* New York: Harcourt, Brace & Co., Inc.

Pratt, L. (1973). Child rearing methods and children's health behavior. *Journal of Health and Social Behavior, 14*, 61-69.

Rabinowitz, H. S., & Zimmerli, W. H. (1974). Effects of a health education program on junior high school students' knowledge, attitudes, and behavior concerning tobacco use. *Journal of School Health, 44*(6), 324-330.

Riester, A., & Zucker, R. (1968). Adolescent social structure and drinking behavior. *Personnel and Guidance Journal, 47*, 304-312.

Rivinus, T. M., Drummond, T., & Combrinck-Graham, L. (1976). A group behavior treatment program for overweight children: Results of a pilot study. *Pediatric Adolescent Endocrinology, 1*, 55-61.

Romanczyk, R. G. (1974). Self monitoring in the treatment of obesity: Parameters of reactivity. *Behavior Therapy, 5*, 531-540.

Rowland, T. W. (1981, July). Physical fitness in children: Implications for the prevention of coronary artery disease. *Current Problems in Pediatrics, 11*, 9.

Sallade, J. (1973). A comparison of the psychological adjustment of obese and nonobese children. *Journal of Psychosomatic Research, 17*, 89-96.

Schlegal, R., & Sanborn, M. (1979). Religious affiliation and adolescent drinking. *Journal of Studies on Alcohol, 40*, 693-703.

Sears, R., Whiting, J., Nowlis, V., & Sears, P. (1953). Some child rearing antecedents of aggression and dependency in young children. *Genetic Psychology Monographs, 47*, 135-236.

Shain, M., Riddell, W., & Kilty, H. (1977). *Influence, Choice and Drugs.* Lexington, MA: Lexington Books.

Sherif, M., & Sherif, C. (1964). *Reference Groups: Exploration into Conformity and Deviation of Adolescents.* New York: Harper.

Simon, S., Howe, L., & Kirschenbaum, H. (1972). *Values Clarification: A Handbook of Practical Strategies for Teachers and Students.* New York: Hart.

Smart, R. C. (1980). The impact of changes in legal purchase or drinking age on drinking and admissions to treatment. In H. Wechsler (Ed.), *Minimum Drinking Age Laws: An Evaluation* (pp. 12-28). Lexington, MA: Lexington Books.

Smith, T. E. (1970). Foundations of parental influence on adolescents: An application of social power theory. *American Sociological Review, 35*, 860-873.

Stamler, J. (1978). Lifestyles, major risk factors, proof, and public policy. *Circulation, 58*, 3.

Stewart, L., & Livson, N. (1966). Smoking and rebelliousness: A longitudinal study. *Journal of Consulting and Clinical Psychology, 30*, 225.

Strong, W. B. (1978). Is atherosclerosis a pediatric problem? An overview. In W. B. Strong (Ed.), *Atherosclerosis: Its Pediatric Aspects* (pp. 1-14). New York: Grune & Stratton.

Stunkard, A. J. (1975). From explanation to action in psychosomatic medicine: The case of obesity. *Psychosomatic Medicine, 37*, 195-236.

Stunkard, A. J., & Burt, V. (1967). Obesity and the body image: II Age of onset of disturbances in the body image. *American Journal of Psychiatry, 123*, 1443-1447.

Surgeon General/United States Department of Health, Education, and Welfare. (1980). *Smoking and Health.* Washington, DC: U. S. Government Printing Office.

Tedeschi, J. T., & Bonoma, T. V. (1972). Power and influence: An introduction. In J. T. Tedeschi (Ed.), *The Social Influence Processes.* New York: Aldine-Atherton.

Thorland, W. G., & Gilliam, T. B. (1981). Comparison of serum lipids between habitually high and low active preadolescent males. *Medical Science and Sports Exercise, 13*, 316.

Turner, T. B., Mezey, E., & Kimball, A. W. (1977). Measurement of alcohol related effects in man: Chronic effects of alcohol consumption, Part B. *Johns Hopkins Medical Journal, 141*, 273-286.

Ward, S. (1971). Television advertising and the adolescent. *Clinical Pediatrics, 10*, 462-464.

Waxler, S. H., & Leef, M. F. (1969). Obesity--doctor's dilemma. *Geriatrics, 27*, 98-106.

Way, J. W. (1981). Project Superheart: An evaluation of a heart disease intervention program for children. *Journal of School Health, January*, 16-19.

Wechsler, H. (1980). *Minimum Drinking Age Laws: An Evaluation.* Lexington, MA: Lexington Books.

White, R., & Biron, R. (1979). *A Study of the Psychological and Behavioral Effects of the Decisions About Drinking Curriculum* (Evaluation Report No. 9). National Institute on Alcohol Abuse and Alcoholism.

Whitt, J. K. (1982). Children's understanding of illness: Developmental considerations and pediatric intervention. In D. K. Routh (Ed.), *Advances in Developmental and Behavioral Pediatrics* (pp. 163-201). New York: JAI Press, Inc.

Williams, C. L., Carter, B. J., & Eng, A. (1980). The "Know Your Body" program. *Preventive Medicine, 9,* 371-383.

Zucker, R. A. (1976). Parental influence upon drinking patterns of their children. In M. Greenblatt & M. Schuckit (Eds.), *Alcoholism Problems in Women and Children* (pp. 211-238). New York: Grune & Stratton.

RESOURCE MATERIALS

These reports are a valuable source of information about specific health promotion programs and useful bibliographic resources.

National Cancer Institute. (1977, October). *The Smoking Digest. Progress Report on a Nation Kicking the Habit.* Washington, DC: U. S. Department of Health, Education and Welfare, Public Health Service, National Institute of Health, National Cancer Institute.

National Clearinghouse for Smoking and Health. (1972). *Teenage Self-Test: Cigarette Smoking* (DHEW Publication No. CDC 74-8723). Washington, DC: U. S. Department of Health, Education and Welfare, Public Health Service, Center for Disease Control.

National Institute on Drug Abuse. (1975). *Toward a National Strategy for Primary Drug Abuse Prevention Programs: Final Report Delphi II.* Rockville, MD.

United States Congress/Senate Select Committee on Nutrition and Human Needs (1977). *Dietary Goals for the United States.* Washington, DC: U. S. Government Printing Office.

United States Department of Health and Human Services. (1980, June). *Smoking Programs for Youth* (NIH Publication No. 80-2156). USDHHS, PHS, NIH, National Cancer Institute.

United States Department of Health, Education, and Welfare. (1979, August). *Preventing Disease/Promoting Health. Objectives for the Nation* (Document No. 1979-644-770). Washington, DC: U. S. Government Printing Office.

BOOKS FOR PARENTS

Ferguson, J. M. (1976). *Habits Not Diets.* Palo Alto, CA: Bull.

Lorin, M. I. (1978). *The Parent's Book of Physical Fitness for Children.* New York: Atheneum Press.

Mahoney, M. J., & Mahoney, K. (1976). *Permanent Weight Control.* New York: Norton.

Mahoney, M. J., & Thoresen, C. E. (1976). *Self Control: Power to the Person.* Monterey, CA: Brooks/Cole.

Miller, L. K. (1975). *Principles of Everyday Behavior Analysis.* Monterey, CA: Brooks/Cole.

Stuart, R. B., & Davis, B. (1971). *Slim Chance in a Fat World: Behavioral Control of Obesity.* Champaign, IL: Research Press.

EXERCISE PROMOTION

John E. Martin and Patricia M. Dubbert

As the mental and physical benefits of a regular program of exercise are better documented, so too are the difficulties in establishing and maintaining such a program (Martin & Dubbert, 1982). To receive many of these benefits, such as weight reduction and maintenance, blood pressure lowering, control of depression, and stress management, the exercise must be done regularly. Yet, we know that as many as one-half of those enrolled in some of the best equipped and staffed programs will drop out within the first few months, with the majority ceasing to exercise within 1-2 years (Martin & Dubbert, 1982, 1985). The picture may be even worse for those who undertake a fitness program on their own. Surveys suggest that in spite of the so-called fitness boom, two-thirds of Americans still may not exercise on a regular basis, and between 28% and 45% may not exercise at all (Martin & Dubbert, 1985).

The use of exercise in behavioral medicine and health psychology programs remains a new, though very important, development in disease prevention and health promotion. Psychologists and other health professionals are beginning to look for help in developing and conducting programs that emphasize the behavioral and motivational aspects of initiating and maintaining a physically active and healthful lifestyle. Although we know a great deal about *why* one should exercise regularly, we know relatively little about *how* best to start and continue such a program. This chapter will provide some guidelines, drawing from the research and clinical experience of the authors and others who have been exploring the problem of exercise adherence in a variety of clinical and nonclinical populations.

THE GOALS AND BENEFITS OF EXERCISE

There are many possible goals for exercise. In health-related settings, research has supported the following objectives: (a) cardiovascular/fitness improvement, (b) caloric expenditure/weight management, (c) cardiovascular risk factor modification, (d) cardiac rehabilitation, (e) adjunctive treatment for blood pressure and diabetes control, (f) reduction of anxiety and depression, and (g) rehabilitation of specific joint and muscle functions that are limited by disease or injury. Because various forms of exercise affect the body differently, a program must be tailored to the client's particular needs. For example, weight lifting primarily improves muscle strength, whereas long-distance running improves cardiovascular fitness, endurance, and leg and hip muscle strength. For further discussion of the physiology of exercise, interested readers are referred to texts such as McArdle, F. I. Katch, and V. L. Katch (1981) and Montoye (1978). The exercise program is usually designed by a physician, exercise physiologist, occupational therapist, physical therapist, or other expert; the psychologist is consulted to insure or restore optimal adherence to the prescribed program. (See Chapter 19 by Dr. Schocken for discussion of the exercise prescription.) We will address the screening and assessment phases of an exercise program as they relate to efficacy and safety issues as well as to the procedures associated with higher and lower adherence.

Because there are so many different kinds of exercise, each having specific goals, we will focus on the most commonly prescribed and desired form of noncompetitive exercise--aerobic, endurance exercise. Most of our experience lies in this area, and most of the research on adherence also concerns cardiovascular conditioning programs.

EXERCISE PROGRAM SCREENING

Once it has been determined that an exercise program would benefit a particular individual, we must consider any safety precautions relevant to the client's capacities and limitations. For example, hypertensives should not take up weight lifting because it spikes the blood pressure. Psychologists and others involved in supervising exercise programs therefore should be aware of methods for determining higher risk candidates requiring medical screening and/or assessment, as well as candidates inappropriate for unsupervised exercise programs.

MEDICAL PROBLEMS AND POTENTIAL RISKS

Research and experience have clearly indicated that most varieties of exercise are far less dangerous than previously had been thought. For example, those over 35 years old formerly were advised to undergo a complete physical examination including maximal graded exercise test (e.g., treadmill) before beginning even the mildest form of exercise, and programs such as aerobics classes recommended written physician's consent. More recently, this age cutoff for the apparently healthy exercise candidate has been increased to 50 (USPHS, 1981), and by some, 60 years of age. Because the safety and benefits of regular exercise are so well known, we may soon need our physician's permission to remain sedentary, given the potential risks of that lifestyle!

However, we still recommend precautionary screening for the safety and protection of the prospective participant as well as the psychologist/exercise program provider. We use a screening instrument called the Physical Activity Readiness Questionnaire (PAR-Q+; DNHW, 1978), which combines recommendations of the National Heart, Lung, and Blood Institute (USPHS, 1981) and some of our own precautionary questions. The PAR-Q+ is completed by all our exercise candidates before exercise assessment, prescription, or programming is initiated. We have included the PAR-Q+ in the Appendix (page 395).

MEDICAL EVALUATION

Although the physician must decide whether it is necessary to perform a complete physical and/or graded exercise testing (sometimes referred to as a "stress" test), the nonphysician exercise program prescriber/provider should conduct some type of screening to insure the safety of the client. Physician consultation is strongly recommended prior to any strenuous exercising or fitness

363

testing, or whenever there is any doubt about the appropriateness of exercising particular clients.

THE EXERCISE PHYSIOLOGIST

Exercise physiologists have graduate-level training in exercise science and specialize in screening and assessing individuals at various risk levels. They can prescribe and conduct safe exercise programs for those who range from the apparently healthy (the exercise physiologist's term for those who seem to be without disease or disability), to the higher risk (hypertensives, diabetics, obese), to hospital patients with heart disease. Exercise physiologists work hand-in-hand with cardiologists and other medical specialists in both the clinical side of cardiac rehabilitation and in research on the prevention and control of cardiovascular disease through exercise training. They are also involved in community fitness and recreation programs designed to improve the quality of life in a variety of nonclinical populations.

Exercise physiologists can thereby provide an important resource for help in establishing and conducting safe and appropriate fitness assessment and training, and can also recommend medical referral when relevant. Further, they are becoming more interested in using behavioral psychologists to help them construct effective exercise motivation packages that make use of modern behavioral technology, so as to enhance exercise adherence in their clients (see the *Journal of Cardiac Rehabilitation*, April and May issues, 1984, for some excellent articles on this topic).

EXERCISE/FITNESS ASSESSMENT

Baseline exercise capacity or fitness level should be established prior to initiating any exercise program. Also, regular progress or maintenance checks should be conducted to document fitness improvements and to serve as an adherence incentive. Measures of other dependent variables targeted for change also should be obtained, such as weight/body fat/girth measures, blood pressure assessment, mood or anxiety levels, as well as measures of baseline fitness level and activity, such as resting and exercise heart rates and routine physical activity levels.

A thorough initial assessment with regular follow-up can also help document changes in health status for the client who does not experience changes in his or her primary goal variable (e.g., weight) as soon as expected. Thus, although a client may not achieve desired weight loss in 4 weeks, he or she may be motivated by a significant decrease in resting and exercise heart rate. This type of feedback appears to be extremely important to most individuals who exercise. Also, the failure to show change after a reasonable time can cue the program provider to several possibilities: (a) the client is not adhering well enough to the exercise prescription (exercise mode or type, frequency, intensity, and duration) to produce the desired change; (b) the exercise prescription itself is faulty or inadequate; or (c) the measures are not sensitive enough to the changes, and perhaps they should be altered, replaced, or supplemented by other measures.

In deciding the type of fitness assessment, one should first determine the goals of the exercise program, thus specifying the variables to be measured. If the goal is improved cardiovascular endurance, then some kind of an endurance assessment should be considered. Maximal graded exercise tests last until the exerciser is unable to continue. Submaximal tests continue for either a set period of time (e.g., the 5-minute Harvard Step Test), or until a specific heart rate is achieved (e.g., an Astrand Bicycle Ergometer Test, using 80% or 85% of maximal heart rate as a cutoff) (McArdle et al., 1981; Montoye, 1978). Care should be taken to insure that the fitness test chosen does not negatively affect later exercise adherence. For example, tests that are even partly motivation-dependent, such as Cooper's (Cooper, 1968) Twelve Minute Run/Walk, may encourage performance overstress ("I'll show them just how fit I really am by giving it all I've got!"). We changed from the Twelve Minute Run to the nonmotivation-dependent step test (described below) because so many of our beginners were pushing so hard that it was extremely unenjoyable. The extreme fatigue and later stiffness sometimes even led to early dropout-- exactly the kind of early experience we were trying to avoid!

Thus, for many reasons the choice and performance of an exercise/fitness test can be a complicated task. An individual (such as a psychologist) with no medical or exercise physiology training should never attempt exercise tests on symptomatic/clinical patients without direct supervision by a medical or exercise physiology specialist. Some issues regarding the psychologist's use of exercise testing are discussed in an article by J. K. Thompson and

Martin (1984). The interested reader is also encouraged to consult the American College of Sports Medicine (ACSM) publications on exercise testing and prescription (ACSM, 1978, 1980). Numerous special training courses are provided around the country by ACSM on exercise testing, prescription, and program implementation (contact ACSM, P. O. Box 1440, Indianapolis, IN 46206; 317-637-9200).

THE STEP TEST

One submaximal exercise/fitness test that can provide a generally safe, easily performed, and monitored alternative to a more comprehensive (e.g., treadmill or bicycle ergometer with ECG) assessment is a Step Test (McArdle et al., 1981). It was originally developed to test masses of students. They would step up and down a standard locker room bench once a second for 5 minutes. First the resting heart rate (HR) was determined, followed by post-exercise assessment, and 1, 2, and 5 minute recovery HRs. Its advantages are that it can test a number of subjects at the same time (providing they can accurately take their own pulses), it is relatively safe, can be done almost anywhere in normal street clothes (does not usually entail lots of sweating, or maximal effort), and provides reliable indices of cardiovascular fitness level and relative improvement over time. However, it is disproportionately stressful and potentially less reliable for overweight individuals and others with poor leg strength or orthopedic problems. Since the original development of the test, many adaptations have been added. One such example is provided in Table 1 (see page 367).

We generally conduct this submaximal aerobic fitness step test once every 4 weeks; little or no change is likely to be detected before 3 to 4 weeks after the onset of a regular exercise program. There are several reasons for conducting and repeating this assessment: (a) to document relative fitness level, (b) to assess improvements in cardiovascular fitness/endurance, (c) to serve as an indirect check on adherence to home exercise programs, (d) to serve as a check on the adequacy (efficacy) of the exercise prescription, and (e) to provide regular feedback to the clients on their relative improvements and rate of improvement, and to motivate clients who are influenced by feedback on achievement of personal goals.

TABLE 1: MODIFIED STEP TEST FOR CARDIOVASCULAR FITNESS EVALUATION

Procedure:

1. Find a standard 8" to 12" step or ledge (needs to be same height for subsequent testing of an individual).

2. Take resting pulse after 5 minute sitting (radial/wrist or carotid/neck are usually best). (We find 15 second sample—multiplied by 4—to be best for quick and reliable results.)

3. Conduct paced stepping, one foot/step per 1/2 second, for 3 minutes. (We have used a 1-second beep-timer to pace people; otherwise can call out "step" every .5 seconds while modeling proper pacing.)

4. Take HR again after 1 minute of sitting (1 minute recovery HR).

5. Optional: Take 2, 3, and/or 5 minute recovery HRs. (If time permits we suggest taking at least one more after the 1 minute recovery HR to more precisely document fitness and recovery improvements.)

6. Graph baseline/resting HR, exercise HR, and recovery HRs by date (same line connecting same date HRs). Fitness improvement should be illustrated by lower graph lines (lower HRs) from one testing to another.

EXERCISE ADHERENCE:
THE EFFECTIVENESS PROBLEM

Despite the evidence supporting the many benefits of exercise, the overall effectiveness of the exercise program depends on insuring sufficient adherence to the regimen to produce the desired health benefit (Haynes, 1984). As noted previously, the research to date strongly suggests that the majority of people who begin a systematic exercise program, either on their own or in a structured program, will discontinue the exercise before any lasting benefits are experienced. This is probably due, in large part, to inappropriate, inadequate, or inefficient behavioral programming—both in the all-important habit acquisition stage and during maintenance (i.e., transition from structured program to self-management of exercise). Poor attention to the learning environment and behavioral techniques appears to be responsible for many of the dropouts and burn-outs that are the frequent casualties of so many ambitious exercise programs.

The remainder of the chapter will discuss this problem from the perspective of social learning theory, both in terms of short and long-term adherence as well as appropriate prescription of behavioral and cognitive adherence-promoting strategies. The suggested interventions will apply to proper acquisition and maintenance of habitual exercise, along with special strategies for the problem exercise-adherer. We will suggest a program that combines tested techniques for enhancing exercise adherence and components that may help make exercise a lifetime habit. These simple steps have been drawn from proven behavioral technologies and from predictors and techniques found in exercise physiology and preventive cardiology literature.

ACQUISITION OF THE EXERCISE HABIT

The most important considerations for developing and implementing an exercise treatment program include (a) ample programming of early enjoyability and reinforcement of the exercise habit, (b) very gradual shaping, (c) use of low to moderate exercise intensity, and (d) insuring convenience of the program/facility.

Exercise programmers often view adherence to the program as the natural outcome of initial health education and the motivation provided by improved performance and fitness. In our opinion, more often the opposite is true: Fitness improvement and health education are the inevitable by-products of exercise programs that insure long-term adherence. Reinforcement can come from being with others; from easy, invigorating activity; or from praise by family and program members.

THE EXERCISE PRESCRIPTION

Now that we have discussed some of the important considerations concerning adherence, we will suggest how to select and implement an exercise regimen. Important considerations include the goals of the therapy; the needs, preferences, and convenience of the exerciser; and factors and approaches associated with poor adherence and exercise dropout.

The first consideration is the exercise prescription. Usually, this will be determined by an exercise professional or physician. Many components of the exercise prescription have the potential to significantly influence subsequent adherence to the exercise regimen, including type or mode of exercise, frequency, intensity, and duration.

368

Exercise Mode. The exercise chosen must be appropriate and attractive to the individual. The program director needs to thoroughly assess the client's prior exercise history, home and work situations, and individual goals and preferences before prescribing any exercise regimen. Individual tailoring of the exercise mode to personal goals, history, and lifestyle is supported by C. E. Thompson and Wankel's study (1980), in which participants who believed their program had been specifically designed for them continued longer than those who were not given that impression.

However, in some cases (such as our community exercise program and hypertension/exercise project) the exercise mode is predetermined because of superior efficacy or programmatic constraints. This lack of individual tailoring can be overcome by extra attention to other aspects such as greater flexibility in exercise sites, times, and companions; and more feedback and reinforcement for attending and throughout the session. The rule for us is: When we must cut corners on the ideal program, always bolster other positive features to an equal or greater amount.

Exercise Frequency. The ideal frequency of aerobic exercise for improving cardiovascular fitness is three times per week. Fewer sessions means minimal improvement in cardiovascular fitness, endurance, weight loss, blood pressure reduction, and other goals of exercise. In addition, lower frequency may not be enough to establish and maintain the exercise habit. For example, when we tried to offer a program that met once a week for intermediate (3-month or longer) exercisers, the adherence was atrocious, even in previously faithful exercisers who had persistently requested a continuation of the class. One or two sessions per week with us supplemented by one or two at home was fairly successful in both our community programs and our hypertension project. We were careful, however, to check on adherence to the home program components (see home programs section).

Programmed exercise sessions of more than four times a week, especially when combined with higher exercise intensities, has been associated with significantly increased exercise dropout, nonadherence, and injury. Interestingly, for the vast majority of exercise goals--not including competitive sports training--three to four times per week of exercise is optimal, with very little or no added benefit for additional sessions. One effective frequency regimen is to exercise briskly every other day, resting on the alternate days. Because it is so easy to keep track, this schedule works well for a self-managed exercise program.

However, there are two exceptions to this frequency recommendation:

1. Some individuals find it easier to maintain an exercise habit on a daily basis. The question for them becomes not *whether* they should exercise that day, but *when*. Chaining the exercise response to standard, daily events and stimuli (e.g., riding stationary bicycle immediately upon waking each morning) is one advantage of daily exercise. We recommend, however, that the daily exercise bout be less intense than a three-times-per-week regimen, and that if higher intensities of exercise are desired (see next section on intensity prescription), these be conducted only every other day. In this way, there is always an easier, restful exercise session separating the more ambitious sessions.

2. The second exception to the 3- to 4-day rule has to do with routine exercise programs. Although the section on routine exercise programming is discussed in a special section of the chapter, it should be noted that not all forms of exercise need to be scheduled into special sessions that require dropping everything else. Depending on the goal of exercising, routine periods of exercise might be not only allowable but also highly desirable. For example, if weight loss is an important goal of the exercise, then the individual can increase routine activity on a daily basis. However, this increase should not be so sudden or intense that it becomes taxing or aversive. We are talking about sweatless increases in physical activity that do not require a change of clothes before or after the exercise (moderate walk upstairs, or walking following getting off bus early, etc.). As noted in the home exercise section, a good way to monitor this routine activity is through the use of a pedometer, worn during all waking hours. In this way, any sudden and significant increases in activity can be detected and modulated.

Exercise Intensity. The most convenient and reliable index of overall exercise intensity is HR. As noted earlier, the exercise intensity required for aerobic/cardiovascular benefit is 65% or more of the individual's maximum heart rate. Yet, if the intensity of the exercise exceeds 85% of the HR/aerobic maximum capacity then, as in the football pass, three things can happen and two of them are bad. One possible result is a slight enhancement of the exercise effect, although this has little benefit for the beginning exerciser who is generally unable to maintain over 80%-85% capacity performance for more than a few minutes or even seconds. A second and related potential effect of very intense exercise is the experience of pain and exhaustion for beginning, unfit exercisers who attempt this level of exercise intensity. This diminishes their enjoyment of and subsequent adherence to the regimen. In fact, the dropout rate for beginners in higher intensity programs is twice as high as for those in low to moderate intensity programs. The third consequence of high intensity exercising is that the rate of injuries to the muscles, tendons, and joints doubles. Importantly, these injuries account for the dropout of up to half of the participants in programs that either prescribe, encourage, or passively permit high intensity exercise (Martin & Dubbert, 1985).

In our programs we teach participants to monitor their own HRs, using a 15-second sample similar to that described in the assessment section, or to use electronic HR monitors such as the portable Exersentry (about $150) that can be worn on the belt or chest and display average beats per minute about every 4 seconds (Respironics, Inc., 650 Seco Road, Monroeville, PA 15146). These devices are especially useful for the safe, reliable, and effective testing and training of individuals just beginning an exercise/fitness program who have not yet learned the biological, behavioral, and psychological signals of overstress.

We also train our exercisers to carefully monitor their exercise intensity. For example, once a sample of exercise HR is obtained (e.g., immediately following exercise cessation), participants plot this HR on a graph showing a target/bandwidth zone between 60% and 75% of maximum calculated HR (220-age) (see Figure 1, page 372). We have termed this the Effective Comfort Zone (ECZ), because it depicts the level of exercise intensity within which aerobic benefit can be obtained but is not so intense that

371

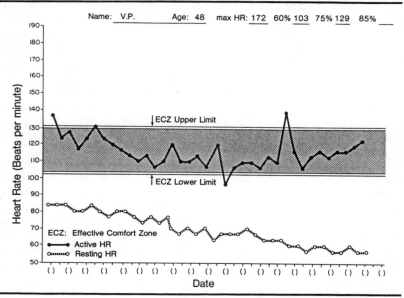

Figure 1. Exercise/ECZ Graph

it is uncomfortable, aversive, or injury-inducing. If portable HR monitors are worn, they can have their alarms set at the upper and lower point of ECZ range, thus providing immediate feedback when these limits are not adhered to. Also, by monitoring individuals' graphs, program therapists can give feedback and praise on adherence to exercise within the ECZ.

Whenever possible, we try to praise and reinforce program attendance and adherence to easy exercising (e.g., "Very nice, you have been coming regularly to class, and by your HRs you are staying right in the zone that is optimal for you...great job"), rather than for exercise performance per se (e.g., "You ran 6 miles today...great"). Interestingly, we even found that graphing HRs within the comfort zone was an extremely useful and effective technique in modulating and maintaining the exercise patterns of some young children who initially insisted on running as fast as they could (and then complained that they did not like this "exercise stuff").

An additional method of determining if the exercise intensity is so high as to compromise adherence is the self-report of the exerciser, and your observation of the physical appearance and behavior of the exerciser. We use three techniques here:

1. First, we suggest that they exercise at an intensity level whereby they can comfortably talk with another without becoming breathless (huffing and puffing while talking, or just exercising) (Cooper, 1977). The simplest method of determining this on site is to go over and ask a question. Our rule is that if someone in the first 4 to 6 weeks of an exercise program cannot talk normally, then the intensity is too high, and we suggest reduction in rate or workload, or a momentary rest. The rest or backing-off period should last until the breathlessness ceases.

2. Another check on this is to take HR, and wait until it returns to the effective comfort zone (i.e., below 75%). Generally, breathlessness does not usually begin until about 80%-85% of maximum HR or aerobic capacity. We usually encourage exercisers to exercise with one another and to talk so that they become immediately aware if the intensity of exercise is excessive (i.e., above the effective comfort zone). Other important reasons for group exercise will be discussed in the section on cognitive behavior during exercise. For those who exercise alone, we suggest setting the proper pace by slowly increasing the pace just to the point where breathlessness first starts, and then backing off slightly until there is little or no breathlessness. We also recommend occasionally monitoring this pacing by talking or singing to oneself, or checking HR.

3. A final method of proper pacing intensity is to use one of the HR monitors that can have alarms set at the minimum and maximum intensity desired. Thus, depending on which alarm goes off, pacing can be appropriately modified. These are especially useful devices with cardiac and higher risk patients for whom monitoring is more critical.

Another self-report measure we use is the Rating of Perceived Exertion (RPE; Borg, 1970). This is used frequently in cardiac rehabilitation programs, and especially with those patients on beta blocker (cardiac modulator) drugs that artificially dampen HR. The RPE, shown in Table 2 (page 374), is especially useful for these individuals because an RPE of 13 correlates highly with 70% aerobic capacity. For adherence-enhancing pur-

---

TABLE 2: RATING OF PERCEIVED EXERTION (RPE)

Rating	Definition
6*	
7	Very, Very Light
8	
9	Very Light
10	
11	Fairly Light
12	
13**	Somewhat Hard
14	
15	Hard
16	
17	Very Hard
18	
19	Very, Very Hard
20***	

```
 *   Corresponds to an average resting HR of 60 beats per minute.
 **  Corresponds to an average work (maximum aerobic) capacity of 70%.
 *** Corresponds to an average maximum HR of 200 beats per minute.
```

Note: From "Perceived Exertion As an Indicator of Somatic Stress" by G. V. Borg, 1970, Scandinavian Journal of Rehabilitative Medicine, 2, pp. 92-98. Copyright © 1970.

---

poses in early exercisers, we like to have them report that they are between a 10 and a 12, with 11 as an ideal. We display the RPE scale on the wall of all our exercise rooms and during each session we ask clients to indicate their RPEs. We also ask them to rate their enjoyment levels on a 1 to 5 scale (1 = very unenjoyable, 3 = neutral, 5 = very enjoyable) during or after each session. If enjoyability of the session falls below 3-4 for several consecutive sessions, we review the program and perform- ance and talk with the individual about programming more enjoyment into the routine. Generally, two factors most control the enjoyment--intensity and socialization during the exercise (more on that later).

A final method of monitoring exercise intensity is to carefully observe the client, or, in the case of the home exerciser, ask specific questions of a significant other who may have observed the client during or shortly after the exercise. Was the individual's face bright red, was there profuse sweating or very heavy breathing? If so, the exercise is probably too intense. (Incidentally, exces- sive sweating, or the cessation of sweating and skin dryness and redness are signs of heat problems--the latter often a result of dehydration.) We tell our clients, especially in the summer months and in humid and hot climates, to drink water throughout the day, and to drink a large glass of cool water before, after, and even during exercise, if possible.

Table 3 (pages 376-377) shows the monitoring form we use for tracking intensity, enjoyability, and other characteristics of the exercise bouts. These forms are routinely checked by our program staff. If we detect signs of excessive intensity, we then ask the exerciser to reduce intensity, and generally offer the choice of slowing down, reducing work load, or resting briefly. We try to be as flexible as possible in suggesting methods to reduce intensity (see goal setting for more on this), but we insist on lower intensity when necessary. Especially with our Type A clients, this is often not an easy task and demands firm but kind persistence; distraction can be useful here ("I'm having trouble understanding you, why don't you slow down a bit and then we can talk"). In some instances, we have even gently grabbed people by the shoulders (in brisk walking and jogging programs) to hold them back, or feigned injury in ourselves to slow them down. In our laboratory we will manipulate the work loads and speeds of the treadmill or ergometer. The client is informed of the change and why, but is given no choice. One superior method for many is to convince *them* to make the reduction in work load or intensity so that they maintain the perception of control and do not feel so coerced. Either way, beginning exercisers should rarely if ever be allowed to overexert themselves. Obviously, one of our major goals is to get them to monitor and appropriately modify their own regimen, while we reinforce and guide their efforts in this direction.

Exercise Duration. This final component of the exercise topography prescription concerns the amount of time devoted to exercising during each session. For aerobic benefit, the minimum exercise duration is 15-20 minutes. However, for proper shaping of the exercise habit in the formerly inactive, we suggest an initial duration of between 5 and 15 minutes, depending on fitness level, preference, exercise setting, and the mode, frequency, and intensity prescription. For example, an

TABLE 3: EXERCISE TREATMENT AND HOME PROGRAM MONITORING FORM

ACTIVITY RECORD

Name _____   Social Security # _____   Exercise Goal _____

Date: _____

	Sun	Mon	Tues	Weds	Thurs	Fri	Sat
Activity							
Type:							
Total Time:							
Distance:							
Heart Rate							
Before Exercise:							
During Exercise: ( ):							
After Exercise:							
Enjoyment:	1 2 3 4 5	1 2 3 4 5	1 2 3 4 5	1 2 3 4 5	1 2 3 4 5	1 2 3 4 5	1 2 3 4 5

1. Very Unenjoyable
2. Somewhat Unenjoyable
3. Neutral
4. Somewhat Enjoyable
5. Very Enjoyable

TABLE 3 (Continued)

Where did you exercise?							
With **whom** did you exercise?							
Perceived Exertion (Scale Below)							

Perceived Exertion Scale

6
7 Very, Very Light
8
9 Very Light
10
11 Fairly Light
12
13 Somewhat Hard
14
15 Hard
16
17 Very Hard
18
19 Very, Very Hard
20

377

individual who chooses to exercise at home riding a stationary bicycle should probably start with around 5-7 minutes, adding 2-3 minutes a week. Conversely, someone in a group, center-based, lower intensity and frequency brisk walking/jogging program with supervision might be able to tolerate an initial duration of 15 minutes. Generally, we try to start exercisers at an easily mastered duration, frequency, and intensity.

Cooper's (1968, 1977) aerobic point system for quantifying exercise levels successfully combines exercise mode, frequency, intensity, and duration into a single quantitative scale. It is especially appropriate for individuals or programs that combine more than one type of exercise and exercise topography. Thus, instead of trying to compare jogging apples with swimming or biking oranges, it converts all of them to strawberries. This quantification system will be discussed further in the section on exercise maintenance.

In summary, selecting and properly implementing the right exercise prescription is exceedingly important to maximizing subsequent adherence. Table 4 can help the reader visualize an appropriate prescription, while Table 5 (page 379) shows initial assessment data with prescription guidelines.

TABLE 4: SAMPLE EXERCISE PROGRAM FOR APPARENTLY HEALTHY/LOWER-RISK DROPOUT

				WEEKS			
	1-2	3-4	5-8	9-12	13-24	25-52	>1yr
MODE	brsk wlk	-	wlk/jg	jg	-	jg/rn	rn/jg
FREQUENCY C	2/wk	2/wk	2/wk	1/wk	1/mo	1/3mo	1/6mo
H	0	1/wk	2/wk	3/wk	4/wk	4/wk	4/wk
T	1		1	1	1	2	n
INTENSITY	60-75%	...	65-80%	70-85%	...	...	...
DURATION (minutes)	5-15	10-20	15-25	20-30	20-40	20-45	...

Key:

C = Center Exercise Program
H = Home Exercise Program
T = number of submaximal tests

TABLE 5: COMPUTERIZED FITNESS FEEDBACK

NAME: V. P.   AGE: 48   SEX: F   DATE: October, 1981

MAXIMUM CALCULATED HEART RATE/HR (220-AGE): 172

RECOMMENDED AEROBIC RANGE/EFFECTIVE COMFORT ZONE (ECZ):

                                 LOWER LIMIT (60% MAX HR): 103 BPM
                                 UPPER LIMIT (75% MAX HR): 129 BPM

SKINFOLD SUM = 58   ESTIMATED % BODY FAT = 33.2
                                 IDEAL % BODY FAT   = 25 (Female)

STEP TEST RESULTS:

POST EXERCISE HR   = 124 BPM   (72.1% OF YOUR MAXIMUM HR)
1 MINUTE RECOVERY HR = 104 BPM   (60.5% OF YOUR MAXIMUM HR)

RECOMMENDATIONS FOR BEGINNING WALKING/JOGGING PROGRAM:

1. Try to keep your HR in your aerobic/effective comfort zone (ECZ) of 103 to 129.
2. For optimal cardiovascular benefits and exercise habit control, we recommend three exercise sessions per week at first. If you miss a session at our program, make it up by doing a home session (but talk to us first).
3. Exercise for 15 to 20 minutes each time.
4. Begin and end each session with 2-5 minutes of moderate to brisk walking, followed by slow jogging, but ONLY IF YOU ARE COMFORTABLE AND NOT BREATHLESS (we recommend an RPE of 10-12 for first 2-6 weeks).
5. Positive changes in fitness can usually be observed within 3 to 6 weeks if you follow your training program faithfully.
6. The first 4 to 6 weeks is a critical time for establishing the exercise habit. Be extra vigilant in following your program during this time (i.e., even if you do not feel like exercising, be sure to show up and DO SOMETHING).
7. Please contact one of the instructors or assistants if you have any problems or questions between sessions (day phone number: _____; night and weekends: _____). Someone will be happy to assist you.
8. Try to exercise with at least one other at an easy pace, talk, enjoy and distract from the exercising per se. Use a portable radio or some other form of distraction if alone.
9. If you know you will be missing a class or out of town, please inform us as soon beforehand as possible so we can accommodate your program. Be sure to call before class if you are sick or cannot attend.

COGNITIVE ASPECTS OF EXERCISE ADHERENCE

The exerciser's mind is as important as the exercise prescription and actual performance. Specifically, the internal goal setting prior to and following exercise, and the thoughts during the exercise bout, may be critical to the eventual maintenance or cessation of the exercise regimen.

Goal Setting. A number of studies illustrate the importance of goal setting to exercise performance and adherence (Martin & Dubbert, 1982, 1985). In general, these investigations indicate that the more flexible, individually tailored, and achievable the goals are, the better the ensuing adherence. For example, a common mistake for many exercisers is to set a goal that requires more persistence with the exercise regimen than anticipated. This may extinguish the exercise behavior before any recognizable progress is experienced. The individual who wants to lose pounds and shape up from exercise alone may be expecting to see noticeable changes within the first few critical weeks. When these changes fail to occur, our impatient, overweight exerciser becomes an exercise dropout. When weight loss is a primary goal for exercise, we advise combining a reasonable weight loss goal with a goal of establishing the exercise habit. We may offer a weight reduction diet to accompany the exercise program, or simply focus on establishing the exercise habit first if we feel it might be too problematic to try to establish both at once. In some cases we have contracted with clients to begin with 8 or 12 weeks of regular exercise, and as a reward for adherence to that program, offer free weight/diet management training. However, for those whose sole desire is to lose weight as fast as possible, combining a very low calorie diet (i.e., liquid protein + diet) with exercise might be most appropriate.

Educating our clients concerning reasonable goals to achieve through exercising and a reasonable timetable for achieving results is one of our most vital tasks in the initial stages of the exercise program. That is why for some the most immediate benefit of exercise (when done properly) is feeling so much better. Though often ignored or de-emphasized, this quality-of-life benefit is the most reliable effect of regular exercise.

Once the overall goals of exercising are determined, our attention turns to the subgoals set by the exerciser, and how the mental aspects of setting and achieving, or failing to achieve, these goals might affect sticking with the exercise program. For example, we found that those beginning exercisers who were given guidelines for setting their own exercise goals, and encouraged to be flexible within and across sessions as to how much they would do, showed better attendance, adherence, and exercise maintenance than those who were provided fixed goals by the exercise therapists (Martin et al., 1984). It may be that the more flexible the individual's exercise goals, both for specific sessions and regarding hoped-for performance across weeks and months (e.g., "I want to run 6 miles without stopping within 3 months," or "I want to do a marathon by next year"), the fewer occurrences of failure to meet rigid or too-ambitious goals. We encourage exercisers to concentrate more on adherence and regularity rather than performance per se. We do this, in part, by (a) not encouraging the sole monitoring of performance, (b) requiring monitoring and graphing of adherence/regularity (e.g., see intensity topography section on plotting sessions within effective comfort zone), and (c) praising attendance at exercise sessions over actual performance. In short, we stress showing up and doing what they feel like doing after a sufficient warm-up (i.e., after the first 5-10 minutes or third of the planned time has elapsed...whichever comes first). It has been said that 80% of success in life is showing up on time. We agree that the most important aspect of the initial (i.e., first 6 to 12 weeks) acquisition of the exercise habit is showing up (somewhere) to exercise, three times a week, *no matter how little is performed*. If the exercise is performed regularly, then improvements will eventually accrue (even if it takes some time for the individual to gradually increase to the minimum exercise dose necessary for a training effect to occur). This approach might be too extreme, however, if progress is so slow that improvements are not readily detectable. On the other hand, fantastic initial training improvements are useless if the exercise habit is not solidly established and the exercise program is eventually discontinued. People too often attempt too much at too ambitious an intensity in too short a time period and this may, in turn, lead to psychological or physical burn-out. We respond to this dilemma by closely monitoring exercise HRs, RPEs, enjoyment levels, and percentage of time exercising within the ECZ, and by encouraging/praising and otherwise reinforcing clients for staying within their ECZ.

As noted earlier, the individual should have a say in the setting and the changing of exercise goals, or at least have the perception that his or her needs, goals, and preferences are considered. We also recommend that programs not only be tailored to the historical background, lifestyle, and individual preference, but also that clients have an important part in establishing and changing the exercise prescription. Obviously, if they choose an inappropriate, impractical, or potentially harmful program, this should be discouraged. But the future exerciser should understand and have input into the overall prescription outline.

One of our studies (Martin et al., 1984) indicated that for nonstationary aerobic activities such as brisk walking and jogging, time-based exercise goals might be superior to distance-based goals--particularly for those who are not in a program that is formally supervised by enthusiastic participant-therapists who provide regular praise and feedback. We found that those beginning exercisers who were assigned distance goals (e.g., jog 1 mile) tended to go too fast, were uncomfortable (e.g., "I've only got two more laps to go...the quicker I do it the quicker I'll get to stop and go do something I like"), had significantly poorer attendance exercise adherence, and much higher program dropout than those assigned time-based goals (e.g., "jog 12 minutes"). The latter tended to go at a more reasonable pace, presumably because a certain distance did not have to be covered.

Cognitive Strategies During Exercise. Several studies and our clinical experience have supported the use of dissociative or distraction-based thoughts during exercise. In one study, we found that those individuals who were taught to dissociate their thoughts from the actual exercise or the bodily sensations connected with the exertion had significantly better class attendance, exercise adherence, and long-term maintenance of their regimen than those who were taught to associate by thinking of the exercise and how it felt, and acting as their own coach (Martin et al., 1984). We termed our dissociational strategy group the "smelling the roses" group, in part because we emphasized concentrating on pleasurable aspects of the environment, and because it was springtime. Other studies reviewed elsewhere (Martin & Dubbert, 1985) suggest that distraction during the exercise enhances performance and increases exercise duration. It has been hypothesized that beginning exercisers, especially if they are very unfit, overweight, smokers, and so forth, receive almost continual feedback from their bodies during even very moderate exercise, most of it resulting from the discomfort of limited cardiopulmonary and muscular capacities. Attending closely to these signals might accentuate these punishing aspects of breaking the sedentary addiction. Conversely, using distracting cognitions can minimize this aversive feedback--a strategy particularly useful when initially establishing and reinforcing the exercise habit. Several of the methods we recommend for inducing distraction in these earlier stages of training include exercising with others and talking, using a small portable radio for exercising alone, reading or watching TV for stationary exercising (e.g., stationary bicycle), or exercising in a pleasant or interesting setting such as a park or gym.

There are two notable exceptions to this distraction/dissociation recommendation:

1. First, these strategies are not recommended for clinical populations such as cardiac patients, asthmatics, diabetics, or those with orthopedic injuries (see the PAR-Q+, for similar precautions regarding screening, testing, and prescribing exercise for these individuals). In fact, by using dissociative strategies we may be teaching them to ignore important biological danger signals, such as impending angina, important blood sugar changes, or orthopedic injuries. For this higher risk exerciser, we recommend a blend of monitoring for danger signals regularly, and using distraction techniques between brief monitoring periods, especially after the first several weeks and the exercise regimen has been safely and comfortably established.

2. The other circumstance that precludes the unbridled use of distraction-based cognitive strategies during exercise is for competitive athletes, both during hard training and in competition. Whenever a maximum or near-maximum effort is pursued, it is important to closely monitor all systems to avoid breakdown while insuring optimal performance. Not surprisingly, studies have suggested that the most successful elite athletes do indeed employ internal-focus, associative cognitive strategies (Morgan, 1978, 1984).

ADHERENCE-PROMOTING PROGRAM STRUCTURE

A final, but exceedingly important consideration in effectively establishing the exercise habit concerns the more general aspects of the exercise program and facility itself. Several considerations and recommendations should be noted here, including (a) the overall convenience of the program/facility and regimen, (b) the use of group exercise formats, (c) supervision by participant-therapists, (d) emphasis on shaping individual responsibility for the exercise program, (e) liberal use of behavioral technologies to prompt and reinforce the exercise habit, (f) early generalization training, and (g) the use of continued contact/feedback and testing.

Program Convenience. One of the most common findings in the exercise adherence research is that the more inconvenient the program facility, the poorer the participation and long-term adherence to the exercise program. Studies show that centralized exercise facilities and health spas show a relatively high dropout rate. The greater the response cost and effort to prepare for the exercise, such as driving to and from the facility, the greater the program dropout. Although a centrally located facility might be used for initiating the exercise regimen, a more convenient exercise location should be used whenever possible (or the central facility should be used only temporarily). If transfer to more decentralized and convenient exercise locations is not possible (such as in cardiac rehabilitation programs, where specialized staff and equipment may be required), then relatively greater amounts of feedback and reinforcement and closer follow-up should be considered for those who live or work farther away, or who seem to have more trouble getting to the facility.

Another suggestion is to make the exercise group-based, not individual, thereby emphasizing social aspects. Also, all participants should be routinely surveyed to assess the more inconvenient and taxing parts of the program, so that these aspects might be modified. For example, in the Ontario Exercise Heart Program, difficulty finding a parking place was reported to be an important inconvenience by many of those who dropped out, although this post-hoc finding may reflect the unrelated rationalizations of individuals speculating on their program dropout.

Convenience may also relate to both time and type of exercise. Some programs, recognizing that schedules and optional exercise times vary, provide multiple sessions at different times of the day--early morning, noon, after working hours, and evenings. Unfortunately, not all programs have the luxury of a large staff and well-equipped facility. The type of exercise may also require more or less preparation, and thus be more or less convenient. The response cost of cross-country skiing or water skiing is very high for most everyone except in certain areas of the country and at certain times of the year. Brisk walking or jogging, on the other hand, has a very low response cost and effort, and, therefore, is highly convenient. Therefore, we recommend that seasonal exercises and exercise modes that require more than a few minutes of preparation be considered only as supplements to the normal regimen. If the exercise mode, time, or place is inconvenient for an individual, then positive aspects of the program, increased feedback and reinforcement, program adaptation, or other programs need to be considered.

Group Exercise. The bulk of the literature indicates that those who exercise in groups are roughly twice as likely to remain in an exercise program as those who attempt to exercise alone. Several factors appear to be operating here, including the social support and reinforcement of the exercise by the group and the distraction from the typical physical and psychological discomforts experienced in the initial acquisition of fitness and the exercise habit (see discussion on cognitive strategies on this point). There should be at least three people in the group, so that if one drops out, the individual still has company for continued motivation. Co-ed exercise groups also highly enhance the social/enjoyment and distraction aspects of the exercise group. In fact, a powerful reinforcer for many is participation in local Fun Runs, group walks, bicycle tours, and so on, with other healthy, happy, and attractive people.

Supervision by Participant Exercise Assistants. We have found that participant models who provide guidance, feedback, and ample praise for beginning exercisers are an especially useful and effective component in our exercise promotion programs. Whenever possible, we try to select individuals from previous groups who are similar to those who typically enter the programs and who have excelled in the program. We offer them free use of the equipment, advanced training in exercise techniques as well as health programs (e.g., weight reduction), and regular contact with the professional supervisors of the program. This system benefits both the participants and the special assistants. Our professional supervisors and nonprofessional assistants exercise along with the participants whenever possible. They praise the participants during the exercise, provide conversational distraction, and pay special attention to beginners and those who are having difficulty.

Shape Individual Responsibility for Exercise Programs. In each of our exercise therapy programs, we stress individual responsibility for the exercise program. For example, at an early stage in most regimens we teach individuals to take their own HR (and blood pressure if they are hypertensive), chart their RPE and enjoyment levels, and be responsible for home and program exercise monitoring and graphing. Exercisers are made aware that they are being trained to establish and maintain their own exercise program, and that we are one resource for assisting them in that endeavor. We systematically praise the taking of responsibility over eventually all phases of their exercise program, as evidenced by the various strategies we use to establish and maintain the exercise habit.

Liberal Use of Behavioral Strategies to Create and Maintain Exercise Habit. A number of learning-based approaches have been suggested or described as effective methods of creating or enhancing exercise behavior and maintenance. Some of these methods, including shaping, reinforcement and stimulus control, contracting, attendance lotteries, self-control, fading, and generalization training, have been described here in the context of creating and maintaining the exercise habit as well as in several recent publications (Martin et al., 1984; Martin & Dubbert, 1984, 1985). We recommend that these behavioral technologies be extensively used in all phases of promoting the fit lifestyle, and particularly in the initial 6 to 12 weeks when the behavior is the weakest and most subject to extinction. In general, generous praise *during* exercise should be paired with very gradual shaping of the response. Given the dropout problem, initial emphasis should be on the regularity of at least some level and form of exercise, and the reinforcing of that habit. Once the exercise habit is solidly established (i.e., the individual has exercised regularly three times per week for 2 to 3 months), we can focus on insuring close adherence to the most effective fitness prescription.

Early Generalization Training. After the second week of the exercise program, we begin to shape generalization of the exercise response through required home sessions. For example, by the third week we usually add a home exercise session to the two-per-week required at our facility. By the fourth and fifth week, a second home session is added to the two on-site sessions (that way, even if they miss one lab session or one home session, they can still achieve the aerobic requirement of three per week). We continually assess problems that might arise in adhering to a home exercise regimen, as opposed to waiting until the formal, on-site program is finished. By this time, in our case after 12 weeks, the home program should be well established. Those who had difficulty adhering to the home program might have been placed on a different exercise (stimulus generalization) that is more compatible with the home environment. We also fade lab sessions while increasing home sessions toward the end of the formal program, and even involve the family in exercising in the lab and at home to enhance generalization of the exercise response further.

Continued Contact and Testing for Those "Graduated" from the Program. Finally, we both encourage clients to stay in touch with us by phone or exercise with us occasionally, and we maintain letter contact on a regular basis (e.g., monthly progress letters, newsletter, yearly Fun Run with awards, etc.) and perform fitness testing every 3 to 6 months. Our yearly VA Heart Health Fun Run (both 1 mile and 5 kilometer) was set up to attract former clients back to the program and to serve as an incentive for those in treatment or maintenance to stay on their fitness program. We have even used special recognition prizes and adherence/performance awards for those who come and run or walk. This is also a good opportunity for socialization with other program clients and special testing of current fitness levels. It is noteworthy that throughout assessment, treatment, and follow-up we keep in close contact with referring physicians, providing regular fitness measure feedback.

PROGRAMMING EXERCISE MAINTENANCE

Despite even the best exercise prescription and program characteristics, individual exercisers must be prepared for a *self*-motivated home or work-based exercise program. We feel it is important to reiterate the procedures and considerations that help insure adequate maintenance of the exercise habit.

GENERALIZATION TRAINING

We begin response generalization training from the beginning of the exercise program by requiring home exercise sessions (see home exercise programming below). Thus, we attempt to insure the transfer of the particular exercise we are shaping in the facility or treatment program to the home environment. We also attempt to program new exercises (stimulus generalization) in both the old (treatment facility) and new (home or work) environments, especially if the individual has problems generalizing the primary response to the new stimulus setting (e.g., they don't own a bicycle ergometer, and, therefore, must also be trained in jogging). In any case, an exercise program first should be thoroughly established in one setting before attempting to shape it in a foreign setting.

Cooper's (1968, 1977) aerobic point system is an excellent exercise prescription and monitoring tool for exercise generalization. Using this system, an individual can switch from one exercise to another and from one topography to another, while maintaining relative parity between the energy output and the benefits. Unfortunately, Cooper's point system and writings do not address the relative adherence-promoting or limiting aspects of these types of multiple-exercise miniprograms. We have commented previously on the potential extinction of the exercise responses that have not been well established before undertaking new exercises or exercise in new settings, and we hope that the present chapter will help to fill this gap.

FADING OF FORMAL PROGRAM SESSIONS

The section on exercise prescription (frequency) discusses the importance of fading on-site sessions prior to program graduation or before entering the maintenance phase of treatment. Indeed, we try to develop a strong resistance to exercise extinction by using a variety of reinforcers that are thinned across time such that while most of the early exercise behaviors are praised/reinforced, feedback is faded across a 2- to 3-month period. At the same time home exercise sessions are increased, we fade treatment program sessions, so that by the time the formal program is completed, only partial treatment program contact is occurring.

HOME EXERCISE PROGRAMMING

Home programming of exercise is a vital part of any adherence-promoting exercise program, and should be actively prepared for, trained, and monitored following formal (on-site) program involvement. In some cases, however, the home program might be the sole program. Though we are not strong proponents of exclusively home exercise programs for beginning exercisers, sometimes formal, supervised sessions are not feasible. In these cases, we recommend very gradual shaping of exercise frequency (e.g., every other day, or twice a week for the first 1-3 weeks), intensity (50% to 70% of aerobic capacity or maximum heart rate, gradually increasing to 70% to 85% over a 12-week period), and duration (5-15 minutes initially, at low intensity, gradually increasing 2-5 minutes per week up to 30-45 minutes). We also encourage a highly convenient exercise mode, such as brisk walking. Routine exercise such as stair climbing as opposed to elevator riding, and parking and walking rather than driving right up to destinations, is also highly recommended for home programs, especially when weight and stress reductions are targeted.

In any home exercise component, whether it be the primary program or secondary to an on-site, supervised program, exercise monitoring must be performed by the client. Table 3 provides a sample monitoring form with information on exercise sessions and topography, HRs achieved, and any routine and programmed exercise (walking/running) distances. One of the most convenient tools for assessing routine walking mileage is the pedometer (approximately $15-$20 at most athletic supply stores). While these measurements of miles traveled may not be highly valid, depending on the care with which the stride length is set, they tend to be reasonably reliable for any individual and can provide a somewhat consistent estimate of daily walking mileage. In addition, there are desirable reactive effects of wearing pedometers in many of our clinical and nonclinical exercisers, who tend to increase their walking mileage as a function of the pedometer feedback. We also recommend that a graph of daily mileages be plotted across time.

Whenever home program monitoring is kept by the individual, there is the possibility of inaccurate or false reports. To help insure accurate and regular monitoring as well as home exercise adherence, we ask clients for permission to contact significant others to "see how you are doing from another's point of view, and to look for potential problems with the exercise regimen that they, but not you, may be aware of...." We have not had any of our clients refuse this permission. We then try to check at least once a month by phone or letter. An additional important check on home adherence is a periodic graded exercise evaluation. For individuals who are active in our combined on-site and home program, we assess fitness every 4 to 6 weeks, while for those in maintenance or follow-up (or on home programs from the start), every 3 months is adequate. Although a step test can be used, we have the luxury of treadmills and stationary bicycle ergometers and can perform submaximal graded exercise tests using several fixed work loads. After assessing 5-10 minutes resting pulse, we check HR at the end of 5-minute periods of exercise at 1/3, 1/2, and 2/3 of maximal work capacity (initially established at beginning of the program using a medically supervised graded exercise test). Following the 15 minutes of graded exercise, we take a recovery HR after 5 minutes of rest. We then plot and connect the five HRs on a graph containing previous test results. Improved fitness, suggesting proper adherence to the home program, is generally reflected across time by decreased HRs at least at some of the exercise or recovery points.

RELAPSE INOCULATION

A final consideration in effectively strengthening the exercise habit focuses on preparing the client for exercise slips or lapses (Marlatt & Gordon, 1985). The importance of cognitive influences on exercise performance and adherence suggests the need to train the individual to cope with the inevitable slip or exercise lapse.

Studies suggest that many breaks in the exercise routine are due to injury or sickness, much of which is due, in turn, to exercising too intensely. Thus, a number of these relapses might be prevented through more careful shaping and monitoring of the exercise topography. The remainder of the slips or relapses are generally related to (a) work and home changes (i.e., transfer) and conflicts, or (b) motivational problems and loss of interest in the exercise. As noted previously, perhaps some of the motivational problems were preceded by failure to achieve goals that may have been inappropriate or overambitious, excessive and aversive program intensity, and/or inadequate reinforcement and social support during and after the exercise.

But, what should be done if a slip or relapse does occur, especially if it is in the maintenance or follow-up period after the formal program has discontinued? Some programs have maintained a crisis phone line for such situations. Also, special booster sessions might be provided for those who have slipped (e.g., allow them back into the program for a brief period of several weeks, or have a special session just for relapsers). We recommend continued contact through the mail or by phone during the critical 3- to 6-month period following formal program cessation. Finally, we have experimented with special relapse inoculation and coping training.

We explain to exercisers that they will probably experience a period in which they stop exercising, for one reason or another. Our concern is not whether they slip, but what they can do when it occurs. In one program we provided special sessions and training on the high risk situations and conditions for a relapse--how to recognize them and what to do to avoid a relapse. We also provided training in how to recover from a relapse, even including a forced, week-long relapse toward the end of our 3-month exercise program. This *in-vivo* practice with a relapse allowed exercisers to practice the strategies under realistic but carefully monitored circumstances. Some helpful strategies include the following:

1. Admit and take responsibility for the exercise slip, which includes letting go of guilt, blame, and so on. Participants are encouraged to call a friend and talk about it in objective (not self-loathing) terms. It happened; it was no one's fault. Now what do I do about it?

2. Plan to exercise the following day, or as soon as possible. This includes when, where, what, for how long, and with whom. Writing these plans down, and/or sharing them with another are encouraged.
3. Arrange to meet another to exercise. Exercising with another of equal fitness level or who will agree to go at a mild intensity enhances reinforcement and distraction aspects the first day back. The individual should not attempt the highest intensity/frequency/duration exercise level previously achieved, especially after an extended layoff--this is courting trouble, burn-out, and injury. The first several weeks of exercise should be especially easy and enjoyable to solidly reshape the exercise habit.
4. Prepare completely for exercise on the planned return day, both cognitively and physically: Get a good night's rest, eat well, mentally go over each step of the return event, lay out proper clothing, clear away competing events, show up early, warm up properly, and give it your best.
5. Reinforce showing up. No matter how little or much is accomplished in the early return to exercise sessions, praise yourself and encourage others to praise you for your positive steps. Plan some reinforcing event following each session, such as going to the movies or a favorite dinner spot, or a nice hot bath.

These techniques have not been empirically validated for exercise populations, but they make sense and are generally well received. The only exception is the planned relapse, which many exercisers rightfully fear as dangerous to their adherence, so close monitoring through this phase is especially important.

PROGRAMMED VS. ROUTINE EXERCISE

Up to this point we have discussed more intensive and systematic exercise programs for which special preparation and performance are required--mainly for cardiovascular benefits to accrue. Another mode of physical activity that does not necessitate special facilities, preparation, equipment, or minimum performance standards has been labeled routine, or regular (as opposed to programmed) physical activity, such as routine walking or stair climbing (Brownell & Stunkard, 1980). One of the chief advantages of this type of exercise is the adherence-enhancing low response effort/cost. Some studies have indicated that even these low-intensity activities can help prevent coronary heart disease (Morris, Everitt, Pollard, Chave, & Semmenence, 1980), and may be associated with superior long-term adherence when compared to programmed aerobic exercises (Epstein, Wing, Koeske, Ossip, & Beck, 1982).

These routine activities may also contribute to the early shaping of the exercise habit, particularly with the very unfit. Once the basic goals and exercise prescription are selected, several related questions arise regarding the desirability of beginning with or blending nonprogrammed exercise in the regimen. Is it possible or desirable to prescribe increases in normal, daily physical activities such as walking and bicycle riding for transportation, stair climbing instead of elevator or escalator riding, using a push lawn mower instead of a riding/power mower, or walking and carrying one's bag instead of riding in a cart during golf? Generally, programmed exercise requires special preparation, dress, or facilities and tends to be more intense than routine exercise, which requires no special preparation, equipment, or facility. Also, routine exercise is not so intense that it requires bathing and change of clothes afterward.

There are additional advantages to using routine activities in the exercise prescription:

1. They are already a part of the individual's repertoire and require only slight changes in behavior and little or no preparation.
2. They are convenient, efficient, and can be shaped up gradually and with few problems.
3. They can serve as an excellent first step in shaping a much more extensive fitness program for the especially unfit.
4. They can be easily monitored by methods sensitive to small but important changes or trends.
5. They can serve as an excellent adjunct to any programmed exercise regimen. They may be especially helpful in weight and stress management, and can provide important, immediately available, alternative behavior for controlling urges to over-

393

eat, smoke, consume alcohol, or engage in some other unhealthy behavior.

6. These kinds of activity, though not generally providing any aerobic benefit, can increase overall work capacity and muscle/tendon and joint flexibility, and decrease fatigue and boredom, especially important goals in elderly populations.

PUTTING IT ALL TOGETHER

The present chapter has outlined our approach to effectively shaping and maintaining the exercise habit. A variety of individual and program needs and exercise goals have been addressed. Although circumstances and goals will vary, exercise should be treated as a new behavior, subject to learning principles. Thus, individual programs can be tailored for both the high and low-risk dropout, using different combinations of exercise prescriptions, program practices, and reinforcement contingencies to maximize adherence over the short and long term. Although much more carefully controlled and larger-N research on the modification of exercise adherence is needed, enough is known to structure and implement an excellent adherence-promoting package using relatively sophisticated and powerful behavioral strategies that have been effective for exercise behavior as well as many other health behaviors. We hope that all these suggestions distilled from our clinical experience and research, and from the research of others, will be helpful in designing the ideal exercise promotion program.

Exercise Promotion

APPENDIX: THE PAR-Q+ EXERCISE SCREENING TEST*

You Should Consult Your Physician Before Exercising If:

_____You are over 50 years old and have been physically inactive.

_____You have been told you have heart trouble, heart disease, a heart murmur, or you have had a heart attack.

_____You frequently have pains or pressure in the left or midchest area, left neck.

_____You often feel faint or have spells of severe dizziness.

_____You experience extreme breathlessness after mild exertion.

_____Your doctor said your blood pressure was too high and is not under control, or you do not know whether your blood pressure is normal.

_____You have bone or joint problems such as arthritis.

_____Your family has a history of early heart attacks or strokes.

_____You have another medical condition, such as diabetes or asthma, that might need special attention in an exercise program.

_____You are significantly overweight.

_____You have an old, serious injury (e.g., knee, back) that might warrant special precautions, a special exercise evaluation or prescription, or which may be worsened by a strenuous exercise program.

* * * * * * * * * *

IF YOU ANSWERED YES TO ANY OF THESE ITEMS, TALK TO YOUR PHYSICIAN BEFORE YOU BEGIN ANY STRENUOUS EXERCISE PROGRAM.

---

*Developed from several sources, Physical Activity Readiness Questionnaire by Department of National Health and Welfare, 1978, Canada: British Columbia Ministry of Health; Exercise and Your Heart (NIH Publication No. 81-1677 by United States Public Health Service, 1981, Washington, DC: U. S. Government Printing Office; and from the Jackson VA Medical Center Heart Health Program in consultation with exercise physiologist Dr. Neil Oldridge, Mt. Sinai Medical Center, Milwaukee, WI.

John E. Martin, PhD, is currently Professor of Clinical Psychology at San Diego State University and Associate Adjunct Professor of Psychiatry, University of California at San Diego. Formerly he was Director of the Behavioral Medicine Program at the Jackson, Mississippi VA Medical Center, Associate Professor of Psychiatry and Human Behavior, and Assistant Professor of Medicine (Preventive Cardiology) at the University of Mississippi Medical Center. He is trained as a clinical psychologist with specialties in behavioral medicine and psychophysiology. He has published numerous articles on exercise and cardiovascular risk factor modification. Dr. Martin may be contacted at the Department of Psychology, San Diego State University, San Diego, CA 92182.

Patricia M. Dubbert, PhD, is currently Acting Chief of Psychology at the Jackson VA Medical Center and Assistant Professor of Psychiatry (Psychology) at the University of Mississippi Medical Center. She received her PhD in psychology from Rutgers University. In addition to training in clinical psychology, she has a masters degree in nursing and has worked as a clinical specialist in psychiatric nursing and nursing instructor. Current clinical and research interests include behavioral medicine, particularly cardiovascular risk factor modification and compliance with medical regimens, and dietary and exercise programs. She has published three books and a number of articles. Dr. Dubbert can be contacted at the VA Medical Center, Jackson, MS 39216.

RESOURCES

American College of Sports Medicine (ACSM). (1978). Position statement on the recommended quantity and quality of exercise for developing and maintaining fitness in healthy adults. *Medicine and Science in Sports and Exercise, 10,* 7-10.
American College of Sports Medicine. (1980). *Guidelines for Graded Exercise Testing and Exercise Prescription.* Philadelphia: Lea & Febiger.

Borg, G. V. (1970). Perceived exertion as an indicator of somatic stress. *Scandinavian Journal of Rehabilitative Medicine, 2*, 92-98.

Brownell, K. D., & Stunkard, A. J. (1980). Physical activity in the development and control of obesity. In A. J. Stunkard (Ed.), *Obesity* (pp. 415-437). Philadelphia: W. B. Saunders.

Cooper, K. H. (1968). *Aerobics*. New York: Bantam Books.

Cooper, K. H. (1977). *The Aerobics Way*. New York: Bantam Books.

Department of National Health and Welfare (DNHW). (1978). *Physical Activity Readiness Questionnaire*. Canada: British Columbia Ministry of Health.

Dubbert, P. M., Martin, J. E., & Epstein, L. H. (1986). *Self-Management of Exercise: Self-Management Approaches to the Prevention and Treatment of Physical Illness*. New York: Academic Press.

Epstein, L. H., Wing, R., R., Koeske, R., Ossip, D., & Beck, S. (1982). A comparison of life-style change and programmed aerobic exercise on weight and fitness changes in obese children. *Behavior Therapy, 13*, 651-665.

Haynes, R. B. (1984). Compliance with health advice: An overview with special reference to exercise programs. *Journal of Cardiac Rehabilitation, 4*, 120-123.

Journal of Cardiac Rehabilitation. (1984, April and May). (Vol. 4 & 5). [Entire issue]

Marlatt, G. A., & Gordon, J. R. (Eds.). (1985). *Relapse Prevention*. New York: The Guilford Press.

Martin, J. E., & Dubbert, P. M. (1982). Exercise applications and promotion in behavioral medicine: Current status and future directions. *Journal of Consulting and Clinical Psychology, 50*, 1004-1017.

Martin, J. E., & Dubbert, P. M. (1984). Behavioral management strategies for improving health and fitness. *Journal of Cardiac Rehabilitation, 4*(5), 200-208.

Martin, J. E., & Dubbert, P. M. (1985). Adherence to exercise. In R. L. Terjung (Ed.), *Exercise and Sport Sciences Reviews* (Vol. 13, pp. 137-167). New York: Macmillan.

Martin, J. E., Dubbert, P. M., Katell, A. O., Thompson, J. K., Raczynski, J. R., Lake, M., Smith, P. O., Webster, J. S., Sikora, T., & Cohen, R. E. (1984). Behavioral control of exercise in sedentary adults. Studies 1 through 6. *Journal of Consulting and Clinical Psychology, 52,* 795-811.

McArdle, W. D., Katch, F. I., & Katch, V. L. (1981). *Exercise Physiology.* Philadelphia: Lea & Febiger.

Montoye, H. J. (1978). *An Introduction to Measurement in Physical Education.* Boston: Allyn and Bacon.

Morgan, W. P. (1978). The mind of the marathoner. *Psychology Today, 4*(April), 10-14.

Morgan, W. P. (1984). Mind over matter. In W. F. Straub & J. M. Williams (Eds.), *Cognitive Sports Psychology* (pp. 85-118). Lansing, NY: Sport Science Associates.

Morris, J. N., Everitt, M. G., Pollard, R., Chave, S. P. W., & Semmenence, A. M. (1980). Vigorous exercise in leisure-time: Protection against coronary heart disease. *Lancet, 2,* 1207-1210.

Thompson, C. E., & Wankel, L. M. (1980). The effects of perceived activity choice upon frequency of exercise behavior. *Journal of Applied Social Psychology, 10,* 436-443.

Thompson, J. K., & Martin, J. E. (1984). Exercise in health modification: Assessment and training guidelines. *The Behavior Therapist, 7,* 5-8.

United States Public Health Service. (1981). *Exercise and Your Heart* (NIH Publication No. 81-1677). Washington, DC: U. S. Government Printing Office.

HEALTH PROMOTION IN THE WORKPLACE: GUIDELINES FOR THE CLINICAL EVALUATOR

Nanette M. Frautschi and Gary E. Swan

INTRODUCTION

In 1981 the national health expenditure was more than $320 billion. This figure represents 9% of the Gross National Product. It is estimated that employers pay from 25% to over 60% of this total (cited in Pelletier, 1984). The skyrocketing costs of health care and heightened consumer interest in disease prevention and self-help groups has prompted executives, government officials, and third party payers to examine the costs and benefits of worksite health promotion as an adjunct to the present delivery system. Businesses have instituted health promotion programs with the reduction of costs incurred with absenteeism, hospitalization, disability, and premature death, and increases in the health and productivity of employees as the main objectives. Because the costs of health care are not limited to employees, but include family members and retirees as well, some programs have been broadened to include these individuals.

The ultimate goal of worksite health promotion is to facilitate behavior leading to higher levels of employee health through a combination of educational, organizational, and environmental approaches (Parkinson et al., 1982). In addition to the potential reduction in health care costs to industry, the worksite offers many advantages as a site for health behavior change. People are accessible in occupational settings, and the stability of the population favors long-term intervention and follow-up. Adherence to health promotion programs is enhanced at the worksite because obstacles to participation such as time lost, transportation problems, and the inconvenience of typical clinic visits are minimized. The clinician's control over environmental conditions that support and maintain both healthy and unhealthy habits is likely to be greater in the work setting.

This chapter is intended as a guide for occupational health professionals engaged in the establishment and evaluation of worksite health promotion programs. This process entails the following steps: (a) review of assumptions underlying health behavior change; (b) identification of needs and existing resources for health promotion efforts, (c) choosing intervention strategies, and (d) program evaluation (Parkinson et al., 1982; Windsor, Baranowski, Clark, & Cutter, 1984).

PLANNING A HEALTH PROMOTION PROGRAM

ASSUMPTIONS UNDERLYING HEALTH BEHAVIOR CHANGE

Any health promotion enterprise should critically examine the assumptions underlying its efforts. Failure to fully appreciate the complexities involved could lead to the establishment of goals that are clearly unrealistic given the current state of knowledge in the area of health promotion. This, in turn, could lead to the premature termination of a health promotion program because it has the appearance of missing its intended objectives.

There are at least four assumptions upon which the clinical practice of health promotion is based (Kaplan, 1984). These are:

1. Behavior increases the risk of certain chronic diseases.
2. Changes in behaviors can reduce the probability of risk of certain diseases.
3. Behavior can be easily changed.
4. Behavioral interventions are cost effective.

Each of these assumptions has implications for the design of a health promotion effort. These are discussed briefly below.

The first two assumptions imply that certain behaviors increase the risk for certain chronic diseases and that

400

modification of these behaviors will reduce the risk for these diseases. These assumptions should be considered very carefully so that the design of a program is consistent with findings from empirical research. For example, the evidence is reasonably clear that smoking and alcohol do, in fact, contribute directly to chronic disease. On the other hand, the relationship of diet and exercise to eventual coronary heart disease (CHD) is much less clear. Yet there is a strong belief that these two behaviors do contribute to CHD (Kaplan, 1984). Thus, a company that sets up a program based on exercise to reduce cardiovascular related health problems is not based on unequivocal evidence. If the main goal is to reduce cardiovascular health-related problems, an empirically based health promotion program would focus on smoking cessation in heavy smokers rather than on exercise per se.

The third assumption is that health behavior can be easily changed. This assumption is especially problematic for the company that supports a health promotion program. The available evidence would suggest that for those individuals who do not drop out of a health promotion effort such as smoking cessation, the behavioral approach can be quite effective in achieving short-term behavior change (Kaplan, 1984; Leventhal & Cleary, 1980). However, long-term (i.e., for greater than 1 year) behavior change is, at present, extremely difficult to achieve across virtually all health behaviors. Generally, about 12% to 13% of those beginning or 25% of those finishing a program are successful in the long term. Thus, it is possible for a company to correctly choose to target its efforts on smoking cessation but to fail in its attempts to reduce chronic obstructive pulmonary disease (COPD)-related disability because, except for a minority, long-term behavior change in employees did not occur. Epidemiological evidence suggests that risk for certain illnesses does lessen after permanent health behavior change. However, smoking cessation, for example, must be maintained 3-5 years before ex-smokers' risk for lung cancer approaches that of nonsmokers. Because of the time factor reflected in the epidemiological results and in the underlying restorative biological processes, companies should view the achievement of health behavior change (smoking cessation, weight loss, exercise) as only a beginning. When planning their budgets, health directors should allocate resources to specifically reduce dropout from programs and maintain and support long-term maintenance of health behavior change. Typically, these are difficult problems to solve and they should get proportionately more attention in terms of funds and resources.

The fourth assumption refers to the cost-effectiveness of health promotion programs. As Kaplan (1984) points out, when the costs of health promotion programs are analyzed in relation to the number of additional years of life they produce, they are generally shown to be cost *in*effective. This could be due mainly to the fact that most health promotion programs are extremely labor intensive. Thus, companies should devote increased attention to the replacement of labor intensive strategies with less costly marketing and advertising approaches. They might also consider a staged approach, using the less intensive advertising approaches for company-wide health promotion while saving the labor intensive approaches for specific individuals at especially high risk (e.g., smoking cessation among obese employees).

IDENTIFICATION OF NEEDS AND EXISTING RESOURCES

After general assumptions and expectations for a health promotion program are clarified, a systematic needs assessment is required. Specifically, the health problems and high risk behaviors of greatest priority for employees and their incidence, prevalence, severity, and duration must be determined. The picture of a company's health status and needs may be obtained through a multitude of techniques. Pre-existing databases provide important information at little additional cost.

Epidemiological Data. Epidemiological data provide information regarding the incidence and prevalence of illness in various segments of the population, including the frequency of illness as a function of age, race, sex, and other demographic information. For example, heart disease, cancer, and stroke are the leading causes of death within the United States at this time, with coronary heart disease found to be particularly frequent among middle-aged men (U. S. DHEW, 1979a). This would suggest that companies employing large numbers of men within this age group could benefit from health promotion programs that focus on the reduction of coronary heart disease.

Existing Company Records. Whenever possible, use should be made of existing company records. Demographic information, including employees' age, sex, race, marital status, educational level, job title, home and office addresses may be available through personnel, and can be useful in defining the extent of health problems. Other important archival records include company reports of the type and frequency of accidents and associated medical records such as the number and reason for visits to the medical dispensary and the number of sick days taken. Insurance and disability claims provide not only a source of data regarding various health problems within the organization, but are necessary in calculations of the average expenses per year for employees, dependents, and retirees.

In addition to the development of an overall view of a company's health status, these data may also stimulate hypotheses regarding the relationship of specific health problems to occupational demands or conditions. For example, illness or injury may be more frequent among certain occupational groups such as laborers and secretaries ("How to Deal," 1978). Seasonal changes in illness or injury may be associated with concurrent changes in work demands. An unusually high incidence of illness in a particular work setting may reflect stressful environmental conditions such as excessive noise, poor lighting, the absence of ventilation, or crowding (Cohen, Evans, Krantz, & Stokols, 1980; Henry, Meehan, & Stephens, 1967; Kryter, 1970; and Poulton, 1978).

Ongoing health programs within a company provide records of attendance and behavior change. Information regarding types of programs offered and the demographic characteristics of the employees served will reduce the likelihood of redundancy in services. Similarly, the percentage of dropouts, participants' ratings of satisfaction with the training, and the documentation of change in the participants' health knowledge, attitudes, habits, or physical status can alert the clinician to approaches that are effective or ineffective.

Collecting Information from Employees. Epidemiological data and existing company records may assist in understanding which problems are widespread and which subgroups are at highest risk. Based on this information, it may also be necessary to gather additional information from employees directly. In particular, it is important to assess employees' (a) *knowledge* regarding the detrimental effects of negative habits and appropriate alternatives; (b) *attitudes and beliefs* regarding practices and their role in maintaining health; (c) *behavior* that may contribute to illness or promote health, including self-reports of diet, exercise, smoking, and alcohol consumption; (d) *clinical indicators of risk* such as body mass index, blood pressure, lipid levels, and smoking status; and (e) *perceptions of health needs,* and *perceived barriers* to behavior change. The self-report data may be collected through surveys, including mailed or telephone questionnaires and face-to-face interviews. Anthropometric information, blood chemistry tests, and blood pressure readings may be obtained through supplementary visits to the medical dispensary. This information can be used as baseline data for evaluation of the program's effectiveness if the initial assessment covers the entire group of prospective recipients of health training.

To be more cost-effective, initial assessments can be conducted on a representative sample of targeted employees. This would be a smaller number of employees who were selected to serve as the basis for conclusions regarding the entire company population. This may be done randomly, with or without regard for special characteristics of specified subgroups.

Observation of Employee Behavior. An alternative, though costly, method of assessing needs is through direct observation of a small number of employees. Observation provides some measure of the accuracy of employee self-report. For example, the adherence of employees to safety procedures or nonsmoking regulations in designated work areas may be observed and recorded using checklists. Event or frequency recording involves simply tallying the number of times that a specified behavior (i.e., lighting a cigarette) occurs during a given period of time, and is particularly useful when the behavior occurs at a low to moderate frequency.

Assessing Available Resources. Concurrent with the needs assessment, it is important to elicit information regarding available resources to be used, and the organizational hierarchy and attitudes of key staff with regard to health promotion programs. Development of a realistic budget consistent with the specifications and scope of the program are important in evaluating whether existing company personnel can implement the program. Internal staffing may include physicians, nurses, and health educators. If staffing internally is a problem, outside resources such as consulting health professionals may be acquired. Outside staffing usually includes psychiatrists, psychologists, and social workers providing services through employee assistance programs, and exercise physiologists in rehabilitation programs. Media staff may be solicited to help promote the program.

The use of existing staff has both advantages and disadvantages. They are readily available, allowing for convenience in scheduling and monitoring of activities, and providing continuity and flexibility to ongoing programs. However, the use of company staff also may require job redefinition, additional training, and limitation of program activities to work hours (Parkinson et al., 1982).

Community resources include private physicians and mental health professionals; academic consultants; health promotion programs offered by hospitals, clinics, and voluntary agencies; and specialized, pre-packaged health programs that may be obtained for presentation at the worksite. Cost varies considerably with these alternatives. While they may offer greater flexibility in scheduling, they may lack the continuity necessary to maintain behavior change (Parkinson et al., 1982).

Pelletier (1984) has argued strongly against the use of pre-packaged, circumscribed interventions. Broad-based approaches that have a variety of linked programs increase the likelihood of successful behavior change in one or more areas of an individual's life. Chadwick (1982) notes that interventions that hold the greatest promise of improving employee health, such as smoking cessation groups, are often the least popular. Interventions with less clearly documented beneficial effects such as exercise groups are normally ranked the most popular. Fortunately, exercise may lead to other positive changes in lifestyle and may stimulate interest in modifying other risk factors (e.g., few regular joggers are heavy smokers). When employers offer a variety of programming, employees have the opportunity to succeed at making lifestyle changes. These small changes can stimulate and enhance further health improvements.

In addition to information regarding internal and external resources, it is important to understand the organizational dynamics and relative authority of various

405

staff members. The role and attitude toward health promotion of the chairman, president, medical director, benefits manager, and union leaders should be taken into account during planning.

IMPLEMENTING A HEALTH PROMOTION PROGRAM

INTERVENTION STRATEGIES

After completion of a systematic needs assessment, the next step toward the establishment of a health promotion program is to implement interventions consistent with the organization's priorities and objectives. Methods of intervention can be quite varied and fall into six broad categories: (a) *education,* (b) *skills training,* (c) *incentive plans,* (d) *environmental restructuring,* (e) *personnel placement,* and (f) *community referral.* Empirical research can help the evaluator determine the likelihood that an intervention will meet its established objectives: whether to increase knowledge, change attitudes or behavior; or reduce risk, illness, or cost. The methods of intervention under consideration should also be consistent with available resources and the organizational climate. For example, aerobic dance classes may be more suitable for a company that has a younger, predominantly female work force. Generally, a combination of approaches are used within a setting.

Educational Approaches. Educational approaches are the treatment of choice when the objective of a health promotion program is to increase awareness and knowledge regarding health risks and health enhancing alternatives. These include media campaigns or large group meetings that intend to reach large segments of the employee population. Materials such as films, videotapes, slides, brochures, newsletters, self-instruction kits, and computer-based, self-instruction programs are available. Governmental and voluntary agencies, insurance companies, professional groups, and private research firms often will provide educational materials at reduced or no cost. Alternatively, materials can be developed so that the approach is tailored to the needs of the work setting. Usually, these materials address the physiological consequences of health-related habits such as smoking, alcoholism, poor nutrition, lack of exercise, stress, or lack of adherence to medical regimens and/or safety regulations.

Effective materials present information that enables individuals to assess their own risk. Diagnostic criteria, tables, and charts that present age and sex norms for risk factors may be included to alert employees to the need for lifestyle change and to assist them to set realistic goals. In addition, educational materials should specify behavior that will achieve positive change in risk factors. For example, in the area of weight reduction, educational materials may include age and sex specific weight tables. Charts that specify average daily caloric intake totals for the maintenance of weight levels, caloric expenditure charts for occupational and recreational tasks, and calorie counters provide the necessary information to make changes in the caloric intake-energy expenditure balance essential to weight loss. While there may be considerable variability in the content and format of educational materials, care must be taken to match the difficulty level to the educational level of the employees. In the event that models are depicted performing health behaviors in pictures or film, their characteristics (e.g., race, income level) should be representative of the targeted population (Bandura, 1969).

Skills Training. Educational approaches maximize the exposure of employees to health information. While they may serve as an excellent introduction or recruitment technique for smaller behaviorally oriented groups, they frequently lack the intensity, specificity or in-depth focus necessary to produce behavior change and, finally, to reduce morbidity and mortality. Skills training for the self-management of health-related behavior typically involves teaching employees to record or monitor a behavior of interest such as smoking, caloric intake, or exercise, along with potential environmental, cognitive, or emotional triggers and consequences of these behaviors. An example of a self-monitoring form for smoking and its eventual cessation appears below (Figure 1, pages 408-409). A functional assessment of this sort provides a pre-training measurement of the behavior. It can also assist the employee to identify the situational, cognitive, or emotional factors which maintain the behavior.

Once identified, these factors can be changed and the impact on the behavior of interest monitored. For

DAILY SMOKING RECORD

Name_____   Date_____

	Time	Intensity of Craving*	Was Cigarette Smoked? (X)	Place	Activity	With Whom	Mood
1.	7:00	2	X	Kitchen	Drinking Coffee	No One	Neutral
2.	8:00	2	X	Office Desk	Drinking Coffee	Co-Worker	Neutral
3.	9:30	1	X	Office Desk	Telephone	No One	Neutral
4.	10:00	3	X	Boss's Office	Meeting	Boss/Co-Worker	Anxious
5.	11:10	3	X	Boss's Office	Meeting	Boss/Co-Workers	Anxious
6.	12:00	2	X	Cafeteria	Finishing Lunch	Co-Workers	Relaxed
7.	1:00	1		Office Desk	None	No One	Bored
8.	1:45	2	X	Office Desk	Telephone	No One	Upset
9.	2:00	3	X	Office Desk	Report Writing	No One	Frustrated
10.	3:15	3	X	Office Desk	Finished Report	No One	Relieved/Pleased
11.	4:00	2	X	Mail Room	Waiting In Line	Co-Workers	Bored

	Time	Intensity of Craving*	Was Cigarette Smoked? (X)	Place	Activity	With Whom	Mood
12.	4:30	1		Conference Room	Listening To Presentation	Acme Employees	Excited
13.	5:00	2	X	Car	Driving-Traffic	No One	Tired
14.	5:30	3	X	Kitchen	Finished Dinner	Husband	Relaxed
15.	6:00	3	X	Living Room	TV And Coffee	Husband	Relaxed
16.	6:45	3	X	Living Room	Arguing	Son	Angry
17.	7:15	3	X	Living Room	Thinking About Son	No One	Angry
18.	8:30	2	X	Living Room	Reading	No One	Sad
19.	9:45	1		Bedroom	Talking	Husband	Relaxed
20.	10:45	1		Bedroom	After Sex	Husband	Relaxed

*Indicate the intensity of your craving on a scale of 1 to 3: 1 = little craving; 2 = moderate craving; 3 = intense craving.

Total number of cigarettes smoked ____15____.

Figure 1. Note. Adapted from Break the Smoking Habit: A Behavioral Program for Giving up Cigarettes (pp. 91-92) by O. F. Pomerleau and C. S. Pomerleau, 1984, Ann Arbor, MI: Behavioral Medicine Press. Copyright o by the Behavioral Medicine Press. Adapted by permission.

example, smoking cessation efforts may change environmental characteristics that reinforce smoking to those that reinforce nonsmoking. Contracts may be established in which reductions in smoking or periods of abstinence are rewarded, and continued or increased smoking not rewarded. Smoking can be made less frequent by requiring the employee to keep his or her smoking paraphernalia in inconvenient locations. Smoking may be restricted to certain places or times, thus breaking associations with other triggers (e.g., coffee breaks). Alternatives to smoking that reduce anxiety, depression, or anger such as exercise, relaxation, assertive behavior, or problem solving skills, may be introduced.

Skills training materials include brochures, pamphlets, films and audio-visual media, self-instruction kits, workbooks, computer programs, and pre-packaged behavioral modules. These materials are readily available through a variety of governmental, voluntary, professional, or private research agencies. They differ from educational materials in that their focus is on teaching of behavior self-management skills in addition to providing information.

Incentive Plans. A number of companies offer incentives to their employees for health behavior changes or maintenance of health either in conjunction with or independently of a skills training program. Increased pay, more vacation time, or time off from work may be used to reward weight loss or smoking cessation. Publicity or awards also reinforce improved health habits. Incentive plans may offset the powerful reinforcers of poor health habits and illness that exist in many companies in the form of sick leave, disability, and insurance payments. However, incentive programs introduce a number of complex issues that need to be considered (Parkinson et al., 1982). Self-reported changes in health habits, such as exercise or smoking cessation may be difficult to document. The prescribed health behaviors may be inappropriate for a subgroup of employees because of age or medical limitations, thereby making these individuals ineligible for incentives. Additionally, the improved habits, may not be maintained by natural reinforcers in the environment after the program has concluded. Thus, it may be necessary to continue the incentive plan to insure the maintenance of health behavior change.

Environmental Restructuring. While incentive plans provide increased motivation for improved health habits, environmental restructuring may affect directly the health status of employees by elimination or modification of noxious conditions. Structural changes can also reduce the likelihood of employees engaging in poor health habits. Environmental interventions include the reduction of employees' exposure to hazardous industrial wastes, the adoption of nonsmoking regulations in office areas, the reduction of crowding by installation of room dividers, and the improvement of lighting and ventilation (Cohen et al., 1980; Henry et al., 1967; Kryter, 1970; Poulton, 1978). Fresh fruit can be substituted for high calorie snacks and decaffeinated coffee for caffeinated brands in vending machines. However, environmental restructuring, in some instances, limits employee choices, and may require policy change or reallocation of resources. Resistance may be reduced by gradually introducing changes. For example, the gradual reduction of the number of areas designated as smoking areas may allow time for relearning of new health habits. A cost analysis regarding structural or procedural changes will shed light on their feasibility.

Personnel Placement. Health-related behavior and risk factors are a function of the interaction between environmental stressors and individual worker characteristics, or the person-environment fit (Chesney et al., 1981; Cooper & Marshall, 1978). The importance of the interactions of employee and worksite characteristics is demonstrated in Type A (coronary-prone) behavior pattern and hypertension research. Type A individuals exhibit competitive, impatient, and aggressive responses to work challenge while Type B individuals show less of these behaviors during challenge. Type A employees who describe their work environment as encouraging autonomy and peer cohesion had lower blood pressure than Type As who perceived their environment as lacking in these characteristics. The reverse was found for Type Bs. Similarly, Type Bs show heightened systolic blood pressure in environments with reduced physical comfort, while Type As do not (Chesney et al., 1981).

This research suggests potential benefits of matching characteristics of employees to their work setting, either at the time of initial placement or at a point when reas-

signment appears imperative. Decisions regarding placement of personnel requires familiarity with empirical
literature documenting interactions between employee and
occupational variables, and thorough assessment of these
variables in the company.

Community Referral. The expense associated with the
provision of skills training groups and the creation and
maintenance of needed facilities may make the utilization
of community resources the approach of choice for many
companies. Information regarding scheduling, cost,
accessibility, and effectiveness of alternative community
services can be gathered during the needs assessment.
This information can be used to increase the appropriateness of subsequent referrals. While community referrals
are usually geographically specific, Pelletier (1984) provides a comprehensive listing of agencies across the
United States that provide services.

EVALUATION OF HEALTH
PROMOTION PROGRAMS

Although program evaluation is an integral component of health promotion, it is frequently not conducted.
Limited time, staff, and resources, and the perceived
complexity of the task are commonly given as reasons for
its omission. However, the investment of considerable
resources in health promotion programs necessitates
demonstration that benefits have accrued. Program evaluation involves measurement of process and outcome.
Process evaluation refers to the method by which quality
and appropriateness of activities are assessed. Outcome
evaluation refers to the methods used to assess whether
program objectives are met (Parkinson et al., 1982;
Windsor et al., 1984). There is a wide range of dependent
measures and of research designs that are commonly used
in industry. While a comprehensive discussion of these
alternatives is beyond the scope of this chapter, a broad
overview of available measures and methodology follows.
Readers are referred to Campbell and Stanley (1966),
Shortell and Richardson (1978), Weiss (1972), and Windsor
et al. (1984) for more in-depth descriptions of available
research designs and methods of statistical analysis.

DEPENDENT MEASURES

It is particularly important in ongoing health promotion programs to conduct quality assurance assessments. The amount of resources or staff time devoted to program activities, as determined through internal audits, the number of program participants and rates of attrition, and the adherence of trainers to program guidelines as measured by observation of actual behavior during a session are just a few of the process measures that yield information about the quality of the services offered.

Outcome measures may include any or all of the variables examined during the initial assessment. Short-term or immediate consequences of health promotion programs include changes in knowledge, attitudes, and health behavior. Increased knowledge of the risk factors for cardiovascular disease or early warning signs of cancer, a stronger belief in personal responsibility in disease prevention, and reduced rates of smoking and exposure to toxic wastes are potential measurable benefits. Intermediate consequences such as lower blood pressure and weight reduction may not be apparent for several months. Long-term consequences such as reduced insurance and disability claims and cardiovascular morbidity and mortality, may not be observed for a period of years. This necessitates an ongoing commitment to research and a willingness on the part of industry to absorb the costs of the program with relatively little in the way of immediate evidence for its effectiveness.

DESIGNS FOR PROGRAM EVALUATION

There are numerous designs that may be selected for program evaluation (Shortell & Richardson, 1978; Weiss, 1972; Windsor et al., 1984). These include experimental, quasi-experimental, and nonexperimental designs. Experimental designs require random assignment of subjects or groups of subjects to control and treatment conditions. Measurements are generally taken prior to and after treatment intervention. Because of random assignment to at least two groups, experimental designs allow for the greatest degree of control over factors that influence the validity of the results, and provide the strongest evidence of a program's effectiveness. Quasi-experimental designs require the establishment of a treatment and comparison group and observation of both groups before and after

413

treatment. However, because these designs do not include random assignment of subjects to groups, findings may only be viewed as strongly suggestive of the program's effectiveness rather than definitive. Nonexperimental designs do not include random assignment of subjects or a control or comparison group. Because nonexperimental designs do not allow for control over major factors that confound interpretation of results, the findings of nonexperimental designs may only be viewed as suggestive in favor of or against conclusions concerning program effects.

Nonexperimental Designs: One Group Pre-Test and Post-Test. The measurement of outcome variables prior and subsequent to application of a treatment intervention with one group of subjects is the simplest design for program evaluation. Because this nonexperimental design does not control for a number of factors that confound interpretation of observed changes, it is not an appropriate design for assessment of a program's effectiveness. Changes in the outcome measure that occur between pre- and post-testing may be attributed to factors other than treatment such as historical events that intercede (e.g., a company-wide reduction in overtime), maturational effects (e.g., age-related changes in health), or the process of testing itself (e.g., becoming more relaxed with repeated blood pressure measurements). However, the design may prove useful in the formative stages of program development, particularly if steps are taken to reduce the impact of historical or maturational factors by minimizing the time period between tests. Choice of testing procedures with high stability over time also reduces the likelihood that change will occur simply as a function of the assessment procedure. Additionally, if this design is utilized, it is important to demonstrate that employees chosen for the program are representative of the organization as a whole. Care must be taken to insure that the treatment group is not selected on the basis of extreme characteristics that would confound treatment impact with so-called regression effects, or the increased probability of moderate values of these characteristics at the second testing.

Quasi-Experimental Design: Nonequivalent Control Group. The addition of a control group to a one group pre- and post-test design increases the likelihood that observed effects are correctly attributed to the health promotion program. The inclusion of a comparison (or control) group helps the evaluator to rule out competing explanations of effects such as historical events, maturational changes in the participants, reactivity to testing, and unreliability of assessment instruments. The failure to assign participants to groups randomly in this quasi-experimental design necessitates close matching of individuals in the two groups to reduce pre-test differences in subject characteristics that might explain later post-test differences. As in the nonexperimental design, neither the treatment nor the control group should be selected on the basis of unusually high or low level characteristics that would confound treatment outcome with regression effects.

Quasi-Experimental Design: Time Series. A time series design is characterized by a sequential series of outcome measurements on one treatment group, in some instances up to 6 months to 1 year before and after treatment. This design is appropriate for interventions that can be administered for a designated period and concluded abruptly. For example, a time series design can be used to evaluate the effectiveness of a company-wide team competition to motivate employees to lose weight. The greater number of observation points, the greater the ability of the evaluator to make causal inferences (in this instance, to attribute the employee's weight loss to the contest). Generally, a minimum of 50 data points is recommended for assessing an effect (Ostrom, 1978), with the measurements occurring at equal intervals within a time frame sufficient to assess pre- and post-intervention variations in outcome measures. As with the one group, pre- and post-test design, the impact of historical events cannot be ruled out as an explanation of observed effects for this design. That is to say, the effects of temporal changes in occupational demands, personnel, or resources that are concurrent with treatment cannot be separated from the effects of treatment, and must be considered as a reasonable alternative interpretation of the findings.

Quasi-Experimental Design: Multiple Time Series. The multiple time series design involves the addition of a comparison group to the time series approach described above. This quasi-experimental design produces greater control over potential historical confounders than the single time series procedure. However, the design also requires a large number of observations for both groups which may make it costly in time and resources.

Experimental Design: Randomized Pre-Test and Post-Test with Control Group. An experimental evaluation of program effectiveness involves random assignment of participants to a treatment and control group with measurement of outcome variables pre- and post-intervention. The objective of this design is to create two groups that are similar if not identical with respect to the outcome variables of major interest at the time of the initial assessment. Randomization allows for greater control over factors that can compromise the validity of the results.

Participants in a study may be assigned randomly to groups at the same time, or be assigned sequentially as they enter the program. Stratified random assignment provides even greater precision by insuring that selected demographic characteristics are represented equally in both groups. This method of assignment initially groups individuals according to relevant demographic characteristics. Then participants are selected randomly from these subgroupings so that these characteristics are equally represented in treatment and control groups.

Improvement of participants in health promotion programs as a function of the training they have received is determined by comparing them to individuals who did not undergo any training (control group) or those who underwent an alternative training (comparison group). An issue that limits the use of control groups in the evaluation of health promotion programs is the appropriateness of withholding treatment from employees. If withholding treatment is inappropriate in a particular setting, a common strategy is to delay training for the control group. In this approach, eligible individuals are assigned randomly to an immediate or delayed training. After baseline observation, those assigned to the treatment interventions are given training while those in the control group are not. At the completion of the program, measurements are made on both groups, and at a pre-determined point in the future, those in the control group are given training.

The establishment of a comparison group is a second alternative when training cannot be withheld. A comparison group can vary the intensity of methods, materials, duration, or frequency of training. Comparison of these modifications in training with the components of the basic program may help identify factors associated with treatment success. Comparison with a standard or pre-existing program is another alternative.

Selection of a design for program evaluation requires review of its strengths and weaknesses with regard to its ability to unequivocally attribute effects to programmatic activities. Time, resource, and staffing constraints that exist within the setting will also guide the evaluator's decision. The designs presented above vary in their ability to provide defensible evidence of a program's effect. The one group pre- and post-test design is the weakest in this respect, with subsequent designs providing progressively more conclusive findings. There is a direct relationship between the strength of a design and its cost; time series analysis, multiple time series analysis, and experimental designs being the most costly.

HEALTH PROMOTION PROGRAM PLANNING, IMPLEMENTATION, AND EVALUATION

AN EXAMPLE

As the needs assessment is conducted, priorities and objectives for the company should emerge. Obvious priorities will undoubtedly include the identification of the prevalence of employee behavior that is the most costly, frequent, and/or disabling. Less obvious priorities will emerge as certain employee characteristics are considered in combination with the characteristics of the environments in which they work. These person-environment interactions could, in turn, lead to inordinately high company costs that are disproportional to the number of employees affected. The detection of these interactions could be a major priority.

After the prevalence of a particular high-risk behavior (high-risk in this case means a behavior leading to potentially high cost illnesses) has been determined along with its environmental interactions, a company is then in a position to specify at what level and at what point in the behavior-illness sequence an intervention should be made. There are at least three entry points into this sequence:

1. Establishing a healthy company culture in order to prevent the increase in frequency of certain high-risk behaviors;
2. Reduction of high risk behavior leading to disease;
3. Early detection of disease before it becomes chronic, disabling, and costly.

After a company decides on which of the three (or what combination of the three) entry points to intervene on, it is in a position to design an appropriate intervention. It is often the case that much cost and energy goes into the design and delivery of a program. Much less attention goes into the selling of the program to employees so that sign up rates can be maximized. The sign-up rate directly influences the per-employee cost and benefit of the program and, for this reason, should be given increased attention.

We will use smoking behavior in order to illustrate the above-mentioned process of priority-setting for a hypothetical company, Acme, Inc. Let us assume that Acme is a company of 4000 employees, 3000 of which are blue collar workers involved in the production of energy conservation products at six different geographically distinct locations. The company president has been watching with alarm the increased health care costs and lost time and productivity due to respiratory-related problems among his 3000 blue collar workers. The needs assessment indicates that while the prevalence of smoking in the American public is roughly 30%, 40% of Acme's blue collar work force currently smokes. Moreover, it appears from an examination of the data that there are clusters of employees determined by their organizational affiliation within the company, that have smoking rates as high as 50%. It is known that smoking interacts with asbestos particles to heighten the risk for lung cancer (e.g., smoking asbestos workers have many times the risk than smoking nonasbestos workers or nonsmoking asbestos workers) (U. S. DHEW, 1979b). An examination of the health data of the blue collar workers at Acme also suggests an interaction between smoking status and work environment. In this case, the odds ratio for diagnosed COPD is much higher for smokers working in production, than for those working in quality assurance, all other factors held constant.

The above findings suggest that a program of intervention could have the following priorities for Acme:

418

1. Because the risk for COPD is excessive for smokers working in production (with the resultant health costs), Acme may decide on a combination of smoking cessation interventions and the establishment of a healthy culture by providing protective masks for the workers and incentives for not smoking;
2. Those involved in health promotion could target specific group smoking cessation efforts for those clusters of employees that have an excessively high rate of smoking;
3. Acme could begin a broad-based but less intensive program aimed at the entire blue-collar force in order to reduce the company-wide smoking rate.

Before Acme embarks on its program of intervention, the company's health promotion manager decides to explore ways to interest smokers in smoking cessation. Marketing and advertising executives at Acme are consulted on this issue. Possible approaches to increase the recruitment rate include the use of brochures, mailings, company newsletters, car windshield announcements, contests, and so on (Brownell, Cohen, Stunkard, Felix, & Cooley, 1984).

Stachnik and Stoffelmayr (1981) present data which indicate that anywhere from .0001% to 4% of the smokers in a given geographic region will actually enroll in a smoking cessation program. If these percentages serve as estimates of enrollee rates, it is fairly straightforward to estimate the final long-term quit rate (ex-smokers who remain abstinent for at least 1 year) as a percentage of the total number of smokers. Table 1 (page 420) presents two scenarios in which the number of smokers who become interested in smoking cessation as a result of two different recruitment programs varies. Fairly common program characteristics are assumed: The dropout rate through the completion of the program is assumed to be 50%; of those who stay in the program a quit rate of 95% is assumed; of those who quit, a long-term abstinence rate of 25% is assumed (Leventhal & Cleary, 1980). Scenario 1 portrays a typical recruitment program in which only 4% of the number of smokers at Acme show up for their first session of smoking cessation training. As shown, this scenario produces a total of six long-term ex-smokers out of a total of 1200 smoking employees. This results in a per employee cost to achieve long-term cessation of $5000.

TABLE 1:   THE EFFECT OF DIFFERENT RECRUITMENT RATES ON THE COST TO
ACHIEVE AN ABSTINENT SMOKER FOR AT LEAST 12 MONTHS ASSUMING A
$10 PER EMPLOYEE COST

	Scenario #1	Scenario #2
Number of employees (3000 blue collar workers)	3000	3000
Number of smoking employees (1200 blue collar workers)	1200	1200
Number of smokers showing interest	192 (16%)	792 (66%)
Number of smokers showing up for first session	48 (4%)	300 (25%)
Number of smokers completing the program	24 (2%)	150 (12.5%)
Number of smokers who quit	23 (1.9%)	144 (12%)
Number of smokers who quit for at least 12 months	6 (.5%)	36 (3%)
Cost per smoking employee who quit for at least 12 months	$5000	$833

Scenario 2, on the other hand, indicates the outcome if a much more effective recruitment program is used at Acme. Four times as many smokers express an interest in smoking cessation as did in the first scenario. This results in 300 smokers showing up for the first session (25% of the total). Working through the cessation and maintenance process, it is shown that a final long-term quit rate of 3% ($N = 36$) is achieved. This is six times larger than that achieved under the first scenario. Consequently, the cost to achieve an ex-smoker abstinent for at least 12 months is only $833.

It is important to note that these numbers were achieved by assuming the worst in terms of dropout and long-term cessation rates. The company certainly can influence both. In other words, the selling of the program should not end once the smoking employee has signed up. Continued participation and abstinence should be acknowledged and reinforced throughout the entire process by the company.

In order to evaluate the effectiveness of its interventions on smoking cessation, Acme's health promotion manager decides to utilize the randomized pre-test, post-test with control group experimental design. This design is selected because the decision makers at Acme want to have unequivocal evidence about the impact of the program. The cost to do this evaluation is justified in their minds because of the potentially even greater costs of not knowing beyond a reasonable doubt how to bring down the smoking rate and associated health costs.

Acme is in the fortunate position of having six different production sites that employ approximately comparable types of employees who have similar rates of illness. These sites are located about 100 miles apart so that the chances of the treatment group affecting the control group are minimal. Sites A, C, and E are randomly selected to receive the smoking cessation and a protective mask intervention while Sites B, D, and F are chosen as the control sites. Employees in this setting are told that they are simply being monitored for smoking rates and COPD (as measured by the forced expiratory maneuver) and that they will be given the opportunity to participate in a health program at some time in the future.

Short-term, intermediate, and long-term dependent measures are chosen for this study. The short-term dependent measure is smoking cessation which is to be corroborated with biochemical measures. Several such measures are available; two reliable and noninvasive measures are selected to provide supporting evidence of cessation, expired carbon monoxide and saliva cotinine. It is expected that changes in these measures, if they occur, will be observable within 2 months of the beginning of the program. The intermediate measure is the repeated test of lung function done at 3 month intervals over a period of 2 years. The long-term outcome variables are the number of sick-days taken for pulmonary-related reasons and long-term disability costs.

In order to assess the effectiveness of the company-wide broad-based educational program to inform employees of the health risks of smoking, the health program evaluator chooses a time-series approach. Because this program included all blue-collar workers at the experimental and control sites, it is decided that the primary goal is the reduction of self-reported smoking behavior as determined by employee responses on pre-coded questionnaires distributed with each paycheck every 2 weeks. The questionnaires are pre-coded to insure adequate follow-up of nonrespondents. Measurement

421

begins approximately 6 to 8 months before the 3 month program. Measurement of self-reported smoking continues thereafter via the paycheck survey for another 8 to 10 months.

It is determined that the randomized trial of smoking cessation intervention described above will not be compromised by the time-series measurement of the concomitant education program. This conclusion relies upon the fact that the education program is common to both the experimental and control sites, and thus has an approximately equal effect.

SUMMARY

Effective health promotion at the worksite requires a commitment on the part of both managers and professionals to the pre-existing empirically derived fund of knowledge that forms the basis for this approach to health care. This chapter has attempted to highlight examples of the use of currently existing epidemiological and clinical trial data to focus health promotion efforts in a coherent fashion. In those instances where relevant data are not available from research conducted previously, methods were proposed by which the health promoter/evaluator can collect the necessary data at the local level. A wide variety of possible interventions were presented, the use of which depend on the severity and cost of the health problems, the number of employees involved, the available resources, and the extent to which multiple causative agents (e.g., airborne particles and smoking) combine to increase risk for illness. Evaluation of health promotion programs is essential to demonstrate their effectiveness in achieving short-term, intermediate, and long-term goals. Evaluation, if done properly, will also contribute generally to the long-term health of this health care approach by providing much needed research-based data to substantiate claims for its viability. The approaches to evaluation presented at the end of this chapter provide an overview of the plans currently available.

Because the emphasis in this chapter has been on the collection and analysis of data gathered from people, issues of confidentiality for the employees involved become extremely important for ethical and legal reasons. The right to privacy of the employees enrolled in health programs should be protected at all costs. More controversial, however, is *how* to protect the right to privacy of involved employees in a way that is consistent both with accepted professional standards and the goals of the organization in which the individuals are employed. Another potential difficulty lies in the identification of person-environment interactions that yield significantly greater levels of risk. Who shoulders the responsibility, ethically and legally, for the consequences of such an interaction that may have gone undetected for many years? The answer to this question may suggest an increased liability on the part of employers. This, in turn, could discourage the targeting of health promotion efforts to high risk groups within the organization. On the other hand, implementing a health surveillance program and evaluation may serve to reduce long-term liability consequences by achieving early identification of the health consequences of both company and employee behaviors. The answers to these issues will be unique to each setting. Consultation with employee and management representatives prior to the implementation of any evaluation efforts will minimize the potential pitfalls described above.

In conclusion, we believe the future of health promotion at the worksite is very promising. However, care must be taken that the benefits of such an approach not be overstated. Unrealistic expectations based on unsubstantiated claims for health promotion's effectiveness can be avoided by a thorough familiarity with the empirical literature currently available. We know that certain health behaviors can be changed in a work setting. Evaluation efforts such as those described in this chapter will identify for whom the efforts are effective or ineffective, for how long the effects endure, and the intermediate and long-term health consequences of these efforts. This remains the challenge for the future which must be confronted by the health promotion clinical evaluator.

Nanette M. Frautschi, PhD, is currently a psychologist with the Outpatient Behavioral Medicine Service at the Kaiser Permanante Health Care Program, Los Angeles, California. Prior to her present position she was Coordinator of Health Psychology at the West Los Angeles Veterans Administration Medical Center, Los Angeles, CA. Her training is in clinical psychology with a Post-doctoral fellowship at the Department of Behavioral Medicine, Stanford Research Institute, Menlo Park, CA. A licensed psychologist, Dr. Frautschi also has served as an Assistant Clinical Professor of Psychiatry at Bio-Behavioral Sciences at UCLA's School of Medicine. Research interests include compliance with antihypertensive medication regimens and Type A (coronary-prone) behavior pattern. Dr. Frautschi may be contacted at Outpatient Behavioral Medicine, Kaiser Permanante Medical Group, 4747 Sunset Boulevard, Los Angeles, CA 90027.

Gary E. Swan, PhD, is currently Senior Health Psychologist in the Department of Behavioral Medicine at Stanford Research Institute in Menlo Park, California. His training is in clinical psychology with a specialty in health psychology. A licensed psychologist, Dr. Swan has also served on the clinical faculty of Stanford University Medical School. He is active in worksite and community-based health intervention and evaluation efforts dealing specifically with hypertension and smoking. Other interests include family health and aging. Dr. Swan can be contacted at BS379, 333 Ravenswood Avenue, Menlo Park, CA 94025.

RESOURCES

Bandura, A. (1969). *Principles of Behavior Modification.* New York: Holt, Rinehart, and Winston, Inc.

Brownell, K. D., Cohen, R. Y., Stunkard, A. J., Felix, M. R. J., & Cooley, N. B. (1984). Weight loss competitions at the worksite: Impact on weight, morale and cost effectiveness. *American Journal of Public Health, 74,* 1283-1285.

424

Campbell, D., & Stanley, J. (1966). *Experimental and Quasi-Experimental Designs for Research.* Chicago: Rand McNally.

Chadwick, J. H. (1982). Health behavior change at the worksite: A problem-oriented analysis. In R. S. Parkinson, R. N. Beck, A. M. McGill, G. H. Collings, C. E. Pearson, M. Eriksen, & B. G. Ware (Eds.), *Managing Health Promotion in the Workplace: Guidelines for Implementation and Evaluation* (pp. 144-161). Palo Alto, CA: Mayfield Publishing Co.

Chesney, M. A., Sevelius, G., Black, G. W., Ward, M. M., Swan, G. E., & Rosenman, R. H. (1981). Work environment, Type A behavior, and coronary heart disease risk factors. *Journal of Occupational Medicine, 23,* 551-555.

Cohen, S., Evans, G. W., Krantz, D. S., & Stokols, D. (1980). Physiological, motivational, and cognitive effects of aircraft noise on children. *American Psychologist, 35,* 231-243.

Cooper, C. L., & Marshall, J. (1978). Sources of managerial and white-collar stress. In C. L. Cooper & R. Payne (Eds.), *Stress at Work* (pp. 82-105). London: John Wiley & Sons.

Henry, J. P., Meehan, J. P., & Stephens, P. M. (1967). The use of psychosocial stimuli to induce prolonged systolic hypertension in mice. *Psychosomatic Medicine, 29,* 408-432.

How to deal with stress on the job. (1978, March 13). *U. S. News & World Report*, pp. 80-81.

Kaplan, R. M. (1984). The connection between clinical health promotion and health status: A critical overview. *American Psychologist, 39,* 755-765.

Kryter, K. D. (1970). *The Effects of Noise on Man.* New York: Academic Press.

Leventhal, H., & Cleary, P. (1980). The smoking problem: A review of research and theory in behavioral risk modification. *Psychological Bulletin, 88,* 370-405.

Ostrom, D. (1978). *Time Series Analysis: Regression Techniques.* Series: Quantitative Applications in the Social Sciences. Beverly Hills: Sage Publications.

Parkinson, R. S., Beck, R. N., McGill, A. M., Collings, G. H., Pearson, C. E., Eriksen, M., & Ware, B. G. (1982). *Managing Health Promotion in the Workplace: Guidelines for Implementation and Evaluation.* Palo Alto, CA: Mayfield Publishing Co.

425

Pelletier, K. R. (1984). *Healthy People in Unhealthy Places.* New York: Delacorte Press/Seymour Lawrence.

Pomerleau, O. F., & Pomerleau, C. S. (1984). *Break the Smoking Habit: A Behavioral Program for Giving Up Cigarettes.* Ann Arbor, MI: Behavioral Medicine Press.

Poulton, E. C. (1978). Blue collar stressors. In C. L. Cooper & R. Payne (Eds.), *Stress at Work* (pp. 52-78). London: John Wiley & Sons.

Shortell, S., & Richardson, W. (1978). *Health Program Evaluation.* St. Louis: Mosby.

Stachnik, T. J., & Stoffelmayr, B. E. (1981). Is there a future for smoking cessation programs? *Journal of Community Health, 7,* 47-56.

U. S. Department of Health, Education and Welfare. (1979a). *Healthy People: The Surgeon General's Report of Health Promotion and Disease Prevention* (DHEW PHS Publication No. 79-55071). Washington, DC: U. S. Government Printing Office.

U. S. Department of Health, Education and Welfare. (1979b). *Report of the Surgeon General.* (DHEW PHS Publication No. 79-50066). Washington, DC: U. S. Government Printing Office.

Weiss, C. (1972). *Evaluation Research: Methods for Assessing Program Effectiveness.* Englewood Cliffs, NJ: Prentice-Hall.

Windsor, R. A., Baranowski, T., Clark, N., & Cutter, G. (1984). *Evaluation of Health Promotion and Education Programs.* Palo Alto, CA: Mayfield Publishing Co.

NUTRITION GUIDELINES IN HEALTH PROMOTION

Priscilla Hastedt

An individual's everyday decisions about food have profound effects on growth, development, long-term health, and in general, overall well-being. Good nutrition is essential to achieving and maintaining optimal health, both physically and mentally. Many of the identified health risk factors are behavioral risk factors over which each individual has a significant amount of control. Food choices and dietary patterns provide a critical tool in health promotion and disease prevention. As such major health problems as coronary heart disease, obesity, hypertension, diabetes, and cancer are diet related, the role of nutrition cannot be underestimated.

Nutrition-related behaviors are complex in nature and causation. Food habits, many of which are established in childhood, are interrelated with psychological, social, cultural, economic, and other forces and facets of daily living. Diet and nutrition-related concerns also change significantly throughout the life cycle.

Gaps exist in our knowledge concerning nutrition and its impact on health and disease. There is, however, a large body of information that continues to grow. The human body requires about 50 different nutrients to stay healthy. These include water, vitamins, minerals, amino acids (from proteins), linoleic acid (an essential fatty acid found in vegetable oils), and sources of energy (calories from carbohydrates, proteins, and fats). No one food provides all of these nutrients. Therefore, the greater the variety of foods consumed, the less likely one is to devel-

427

op either a deficiency or an excess of any single nutrient. A well-balanced diet requires the daily selection of foods from several major groups: fruits and vegetables; cereals, breads, and grains; dairy products; and protein foods such as eggs, dried beans and peas, fish, poultry, and meat. In addition to selecting from a variety of foods, healthy eating should be guided by the principle of moderation. For most individuals, moderation means portion control. Consuming foods in excessive amounts is likely to be the single greatest obstacle to healthy dietary practices.

HOW CAN ONE BE ASSURED OF AN ADEQUATE DIET?

National and international recommendations have been devised for optimal nutrient intakes. In the U. S., the Food and Nutrition Board of the National Research Council has established the Recommended Dietary Allowances (RDAs) (National Research Council, 1980). These recommendations are defined as levels of intake considered adequate to meet the known nutritional needs of most healthy persons. The RDAs should not be confused with nutritional requirements. Individual nutrient requirements vary greatly. The RDAs represent estimates that exceed the requirements of most people. Therefore, they cannot be used by themselves as standards for assessing the nutritional status of individuals. The biggest problem with the RDAs is how to translate the numbers into the actual foods consumed by an individual. Other methods have been devised to help individuals to select foods to insure an adequate diet.

The basic food group concept is a fairly simple method developed to help guide individuals in selecting a nutritious, well-balanced diet. Foods are grouped according to their major nutrient contribution to the diet. These basic food groups, their recommended minimum number of servings per day (for adults), and the major nutrient(s) provided by each group are listed below:

* *Protein Group* (Two servings; one serving = 3-4 ounces): provides protein, iron, B-vitamins (niacin and thiamin).
* *Milk Group* (Two servings; one serving = 1 cup): provides protein, calcium, B-vitamin (riboflavin).

* *Bread and Cereal Group* (Four servings; one serving = 1 slice or 1/2-3/4 cup): provides B-vitamins (niacin and thiamin), iron, trace minerals, fiber.
* *Fruit and Vegetable Group* (Four servings; one serving = 1/2-3/4 cup): provides vitamin A, vitamin C, fiber.
* *Miscellaneous--Fats/Sugars*: provides calories, essential fatty acid.

The recommended minimum number of servings from the first four groups will provide approximately 1200 to 1500 calories. Additional calories needed to meet individual energy requirements are best provided by choosing extra servings from the fruit and vegetable group and the bread and cereal group. Fats and sugars will also contribute some calories to the diet.

An optimally balanced and nutritious diet also requires the adequate intake of water. Water, the most essential of all the nutrients, is often the most frequently forgotten one. An adequate intake of water is necessary for body temperature control, energy production in the body, digestion of other nutrients, and elimination of metabolic waste products.

Thoughtful meal planning organized around the basic food groups achieves several objectives, one being the provision of adequate intakes of the essential nutrients within a reasonable caloric intake. Energy nutrients (protein, carbohydrate, and fat) should be balanced so that adequate protein is supplied (12-18% of the total calories) with the remainder of calories obtained from carbohydrate (approximately 50-60% of the total calories) and fat (30% or less of the total calories) (see Table 1, page 430).

NUTRIENT MEGADOSES OR NECESSARY SUPPLEMENTS: WHAT'S THE DIFFERENCE?

Vitamin and mineral supplements are extremely popular and used widely in the U. S. today. The health benefits and potential harmful effects associated with nutrient "megadoses" is an extremely controversial issue. Presently, for most healthy persons, there are no proven advantages to consuming nutrients in excess amounts (five to 10 times the RDA). Intakes of vitamins and minerals in these amounts may be toxic (National Research Council, 1980).

TABLE 1:   SAMPLE MENU PATTERN FOR A HEALTHIER DIET

The following menu pattern is designed to meet recommended dietary intakes for carbohydrate, protein, and fat, in addition to insuring a selection of foods from the basic food groups. This daily menu provides approximately 2000 calories: 16% from proteins; 55% from carbohydrates (about 8% from refined sugars); 29% from fats; and 270 milligrams of cholesterol.

PATTERN

BREAKFAST	LUNCH	DINNER
Fruit	Fruit	Protein
Protein	Protein	Pasta/Starchy Vegetable
Cereals, grains	Bread	Vegetable
Low fat milk	Vegetable	Bread
Water	Low fat dessert	Fruit
	Low fat beverage	Low fat milk
	Water	Water

SAMPLE MENU

BREAKFAST	LUNCH	DINNER
Orange juice, 4 oz	Apple, 1	Baked chicken, 3-4 oz
Egg, 1	Sliced turkey, 2 oz	Rice, 1/2 cup
Toast, 1 slice	Whole wheat bread,	Snap beans, 1/2 cup
Cereal, 3/4 cup	2 slices	Tomato salad
Milk, 8 oz	Tossed salad with	Corn muffin, 1
	dressing	Fresh fruit
	Sherbet, 1/2 cup	Milk, 8 oz
	Beverage	

*SNACKS: Include one fruit (i.e., peach) and one selection from the bread group (i.e., graham crackers).

*Also included in the daily menu: 2 tablespoons oil (for cooking and salad dressings); 1 teaspoon margarine; and 1-1/2 tablespoons of refined sugars (i.e., jam, honey, syrup).

For many years, many people obtained all the nutrients they needed from the foods they consumed. The use of multivitamin and mineral supplements was not a common practice. However, just as uncommon was the consumption of processed foods and the use of drugs, cigarettes, and alcohol, each of which can interfere with adequate nutrition. As a result, some individuals today are not meeting the recommended intakes for essential nutrients. Studies have shown that adequate intakes of iron, vitamin B_6, magnesium, and zinc are those which may be the most difficult to achieve (King, Cohenour, Corruccini, & Schneeman, 1978). However, eating a variety of foods, with a greater emphasis on consuming such rich sources of these nutrients as dried beans and peas, leafy green vegetables, whole grain cereals, meat, fish, and poultry, will supply the nutrients needed by most healthy persons. In addition, obtaining essential nutrients from natural foods rather than in supplement form will more likely insure better nutrient absorption and utilization as well as the provision of trace nutrients.

There are certain situations where nutrient supplements may be recommended if dietary deficiencies are established. Supplements which meet 100% of the RDA may be indicated in any of the following situations:

1. Pregnant or breast-feeding women (iron, multivitamin).
2. Women in their child-bearing years (iron).
3. Women on oral contraceptives (B_6).
4. Heavy smokers (vitamin C).
5. Heavy drinkers (folic acid, multivitamin).
6. Persons with certain disorders (surgical patients-- Vitamin C).
7. Elderly persons (multivitamin/mineral).
8. Persons on weight-reducing diets (multivitamin).
9. Post-menopausal women (calcium).

ARE AMERICANS CONSUMING ADEQUATE AND HEALTHY DIETS?

Although it is not possible to identify an ideal diet for each individual, a consensus is emerging from the scientific community regarding dietary concerns and specific changes which encourage healthier eating patterns. Health organizations and government agencies alike have released dietary recommendations to be used as a basis for food selection. If employed, these guidelines can promote better health and positively influence prevention or treatment of some disorders (American Cancer Society, 1984; American Diabetes Association, 1979; American Heart Association, 1981; and U. S. Department of Agriculture and U. S. Department of Health and Human Services, 1985). Some of these recommendations are focused upon generally healthy people, and demonstrate a preventive approach. Others can be applied more specifically to individuals with certain health problems, and demonstrate both preventive and therapeutic approaches. All are primarily concerned with the typical American's intake of the following energy foods: *fats* and *cholesterol, complex carbohydrates,* and *fiber, sugar, sodium (salt),* and *alcohol.* This chapter focuses on each of these foods and their relationship to various chronic disorders, and provides guidelines for including appropriate amounts of these foods in the diet.

FAT, SATURATED FAT, AND CHOLESTEROL

Americans have made some significant changes in the last several years in the amount of fat and cholesterol they eat. Whether for reasons of economics, health, or weight control, the average American today consumes less saturated fat, less cholesterol, and more polyunsaturated fat than was consumed a generation ago. In spite of these transitions, however, fat and cholesterol are still far too prominent in the American diet, and they are considered dietary risk factors for several chronic diseases. Although exact recommendations for appropriate intakes are controversial, a reduction in saturated fat and cholesterol is sensible for the population as a whole.

TYPES AND SOURCES OF DIETARY FAT AND CHOLESTEROL

Fat is a necessary component of the diet, supplying the essential nutrient *linoleic acid.* It is also needed to transport the fat-soluble vitamins A, D, E, and K. Fat provides the most concentrated source of energy to the diet, 9 calories per gram. Dietary fat intake in a typical American diet accounts for approximately 40% of the total caloric intake (U. S. Senate Select Committee on Nutrition and Human Needs, 1977). People, on the average, consume about 8 tablespoons of fat per day. However, the body's requirement is equal to only 1 tablespoon per day (National Research Council, 1980).

The three types of dietary fat include saturated fat, monounsaturated fat, and polyunsaturated fat. Saturated fat, usually solid at room temperature, is derived mainly from animal sources. Most vegetable fats are unsaturated (monounsaturated and polyunsaturated) and are liquid at room temperature (see Table 2, page 433).

Cholesterol is a fatty substance which is produced as a part of fat by all animals. It is abundant in brain and

TABLE 2: COMMON SOURCES OF SATURATED AND UNSATURATED FATS

Saturated	Monounsaturated	Polyunsaturated
Coconut and coconut oil	Peanut oil (peanuts)	Vegetable oils:
Palm oil	Olive oil (olives)	corn
Fat in beef	Avocado	cottonseed
lamb	Cashews	safflower
pork	Peanut butter	soybean
chicken		sunflower
Vegetable shortening		Fat in fish
Lard		Margarine (most)
Egg yolks		Almonds
Cream		Pecans
Milk		Walnuts
Butter		
Cheese		
Ice Cream		
Chocolate		

nervous tissue and is a component of cell membranes. More than half is manufactured by body tissue, primarily the liver. The body's production of cholesterol is decreased when dietary cholesterol is consumed (usually from foods of animal origin).

Cholesterol is carried through the bloodstream in the form of lipoproteins. Two main types of lipoproteins formed in the liver are important to cholesterol transport. Low-density lipoproteins (LDLs) are the major cholesterol-carrying lipoproteins. Approximately 70% of blood cholesterol consists of LDL-cholesterol. LDL-cholesterol levels correlate to the total cholesterol level in the blood. High-density lipoproteins (HDLs), contain less than 25% cholesterol. HDLs appear to remove excess cholesterol from the arterial walls and return it to the liver. HDLs may also help the liver excrete unneeded cholesterol through the intestinal tract.

DISORDERS ASSOCIATED WITH EXCESSIVE DIETARY INTAKES OF FAT AND CHOLESTEROL

Although the body requires certain minimal amounts of fat and cholesterol, excessive dietary intakes have been implicated both directly and indirectly as causes of several disorders.

Obesity. A high consumption of fat (including cholesterol) can contribute to an excessive caloric intake which

433

in turn can lead to obesity. In itself, obesity is a major risk factor for hypertension, diabetes, and elevated blood cholesterol and triglyceride levels. All of these problems are associated with increased risks of heart attack and stroke. Obesity may also contribute to the development of certain types of cancer. Those individuals who are 40% above their ideal body weight are considered to be at greatest risk (American Cancer Society, 1984). A simple rule of thumb for determining ideal body weight is: for females, 100 pounds for first 5 feet in height and add 5 pounds for each inch over 5 feet; for males, 106 pounds for first 5 feet in height and add 6 pounds for each inch over 5 feet.

Atherosclerosis. High blood cholesterol levels are the major cause of atherosclerosis, a condition in which fat deposits cause arterial walls to become thick and hard. Cholesterol, the principal component of these fat deposits, can build up over a period of years, eventually narrowing the diameter of the blood vessels and reducing the flow of blood. Atherosclerosis can lead to complete blockage of blood vessels, resulting in death of heart tissue (myocardial infarction) or death of brain tissue (stroke or cerebral infarction). Approximately half the deaths in the U. S. can be attributed to atherosclerosis (McGill & Mott, 1976). For persons with diabetes, it is the major cause of morbidity and mortality (National Diabetes Data Group, 1985). LDL-cholesterol, by keeping cholesterol in circulation, appears to be the most atherogenic. On the other hand, HDL-cholesterol, which removes cholesterol from the circulation, appears to be protective against atherosclerosis. In the U. S. the risk of coronary heart disease (CHD) increases significantly at cholesterol levels greater than 220 mg/dl (Pooling Project Research Group, 1956). A recently completed study, funded by the National Heart, Lung, and Blood Institute and conducted over a 10 year period, clearly indicates that reduced blood cholesterol does reduce the risk of heart attacks and related deaths (Lipid Research Clinics Program, 1984). An optimal cholesterol range for adults has been defined as levels between 120 and 190 mg/dl. This is well below the level seen in many individuals. It is estimated that 50-60% of adult American men have cholesterol levels greater than 200 mg/dl (Heiss, Tamir, & Davis, 1980).

Triglycerides, another major lipid (fat) of the blood, circulate in association with the lipoproteins. Elevation of blood triglyceride levels has also been implicated as a risk factor for coronary heart disease (Hulley, 1980).

The evidence for the relationship between diet and atherosclerosis comes from multiple sources including experimental animal studies, population surveys, and dietary intervention trials. The general principle appears to be that diet contributes to the relatively high blood cholesterol and triglyceride levels in the U. S. population. Hence, the increased health risks associated with these higher levels should be reduced by dietary modifications.

Total blood cholesterol and LDL-cholesterol levels are influenced by dietary cholesterol and fat intakes. However, at present, there are no proven reliable ways to manipulate HDL-cholesterol levels by diet. It appears that saturated fats have the greatest potential for increasing total blood cholesterol levels. On the other hand, polyunsaturated fats, which appear to favor cholesterol transport by HDLs, have the opposite effect by lowering cholesterol levels. Monounsaturated fats appear to have a neutral effect on cholesterol levels (McGill & Mott, 1976). Total caloric intake, as well as alcohol and possibly carbohydrate intake, are the major influences on triglyceride levels.

Cancer. Epidemiologic and laboratory studies have indicated an increased risk of breast, colon, uterus, endometrium, and prostate cancer with excessive dietary fat and cholesterol intakes (Willett & MacMahon, 1984a, 1984b). At present, there are more data available suggesting an association between dietary intake and breast and colon cancer. Several mechanisms have been proposed by which dietary fat may increase the risk of breast cancer. High fat intakes may increase the synthesis of estrogens by intestinal bacteria, thereby increasing estrogen levels in the body. High estrogen levels are in turn likely to be related to breast-cancer risk. Dietary fat may also increase the deconjugation and reabsorption of estrogens excreted by the biliary system. There is some evidence linking high fat and cholesterol diets with increased risks of colon cancer, and it is possible that high fat and low fiber intakes act synergistically. The research suggests that the mechanism may be one of tumor promotion (Willett & MacMahon, 1984a). High levels of dietary fat and cholesterol cause an increase in the excretion of bile acids. Intestinal bacteria may then transform the bile acids to potential carcinogens.

435

REDUCING FAT AND CHOLESTEROL IN THE DIET

As a result of the increasing evidence implicating excessive fat and cholesterol intakes as risk factors for several serious disorders, recommendations to reduce both cholesterol and fat intakes are prudent and applicable to the population in general. (Individuals with moderate to severe hypercholesterolemia require stricter dietary modifications and/or drug therapy.)

The following guidelines can be applied in the daily meal planning and selection of foods in order to reduce the intake of cholesterol and fat, as well as to control caloric intake. (Because cholesterol and saturated fat are usually present in the same foods, cholesterol-restricted diets and saturated fat-restricted diets are similar.)

	Recommendations	Current U. S. Diet
Fat:	≤30% of total calories *10% saturated *10% monounsaturated *10% polyunsaturated	40-45% of total calories
Cholesterol:	≤300milligrams(mg)	500-700mg (males) 300-400mg (females)

Choose these foods......	Instead of these......
* Liquid vegetable oils and margarines that are high in polyunsaturated fats	* Butter, shortening, lard, meat fat
* Fish, poultry, veal, dried beans/peas	* Beef, lamb, pork, bacon, sausage, cold cuts, organ meats
* Skim or low fat milk, buttermilk	* Whole milk
* Skim milk cheeses, uncreamed or low fat cottage cheese	* Whole milk cheeses and creamed cottage cheese
* Ice milk, sherbet	* Ice cream
* Fast-food salad bar	* Fast-food French fries, double-cheeseburger, milkshake

In addition:

* Moderate the intake of eggs and shellfish (three times per week).
* Bake, broil, roast, or stew foods rather than frying them.
* Remember that a serving size of meat, poultry, or other related products is approximately 3-4 ounces.

It is true that the variability existing among individuals makes it difficult to predict the effects of dietary intake on blood cholesterol and triglyceride levels.

436

TABLE 3:   FAT AND CHOLESTEROL CONTENT OF SOME COMMON FOODS*

Foods which provide major sources of fat and cholesterol in the diet include milk products, meat and related products, fats, and oils. This table lists examples of foods from each of these groups. (For a 2000 calorie meal pattern, 67 grams of fat would contribute 30% of the total caloric intake.)

Food	Total Fat grams	Cholesterol milligrams
Whole milk (1 cup)	9.0	34
Skim milk (1 cup)	trace	5
Cottage cheese, creamed (1/2 cup)	5.0	24
Cottage cheese, uncreamed (1/2 cup)	0.5	7
Cream cheese (1 tbsp)	6.0	16
Ice milk (1 cup)	7.0	26
Ice cream (1 cup)	14.0	53
Cheddar cheese	9.1	28
Mozzarella cheese	4.7	18
Ground beef patty, 21% fat (3 oz)	17.0	80
Lean beef (3 oz)	8.4	77
Poultry (3 oz)	5.1	74
Fish (3 oz)	4.5	63
Shrimp (11 large)	1.0	96
Liver, beef (3 oz)	3.4	372
Egg (1 large)	6.0	250 (yolk only)
Beef hot dog (1)	17.0	34
Peanut butter (2 tbsp)	16.0	0
Butter (1 tbsp)	12.0	35
Margarine (1 tbsp)	11.2	0

*Note. Fat and cholesterol content figures are derived from several sources including The Dictonary of Sodium, Fats, and Cholesterol by B. Kraus, 1974, New York: Grosset and Dunlap. Copyright © 1974. Also American Heart Association Cookbook by R. Eshleman, 1979, New York: David McKay, Inc. Copyright © 1979.

Moreover, factors such as genetic predisposition also play an important role and can contribute to the development of atherosclerosis and related disorders. Even so, it is sensible and prudent to make dietary changes designed to control cholesterol and triglyceride levels, for these changes are conducive to good health and are likely to reduce the incidence of a variety of chronic diseases (see Table 3).

COMPLEX CARBOHYDRATES AND FIBER

The American population, in general, is being advised to increase their consumption of carbohydrate up to 50-

60% of total caloric intake (U. S. Senate Select Committee on Nutrition and Human Needs, 1977). Today the carbohydrate content of a typical American diet accounts for about 45% of the total energy intake. Since the early 1900s, the percentage of carbohydrate in the diet has gradually declined, while the percentage of fat has increased. However, the push is specifically to increase the intake of complex carbohydrates (starches) and natural simple sugars, which are high in fiber, and to cut down on the consumption of refined and processed simple carbohydrates. Currently, about 40% of the total carbohydrate intake consists of refined and processed simple carbohydrates (sugars), in sharp contrast to the early 1900s when complex carbohydrates and natural simple sugars (in fruits and vegetables) accounted for a much greater percentage of the carbohydrate intake (U. S. Senate Select Committee on Nutrition and Human Needs, 1977). As a result, fiber content in the U. S. diet has also declined, averaging only about 10-12 grams daily (National Cancer Institute, 1985). Most of the current recommendations for increased consumption of fruits, vegetables, and whole grains translate into a recommended fiber intake ranging from 20-35 grams daily (American Cancer Society, 1984; American Diabetes Association, 1979; National Cancer Institute, 1985; and U. S. Department of Agriculture and U. S. Department of Health and Human Services, 1985). Many of the data which support these recommendations are based on accumulating evidence linking the role of low intake of complex carbohydrate and fiber with a variety of chronic disorders.

TYPES AND SOURCES OF DIETARY CARBOHYDRATE AND FIBER

Carbohydrates are the body's most efficient source of energy, providing approximately 4 calories per gram. Dietary carbohydrates are made up of glucose units and are of two types--complex and simple. The polysaccharides, starch and cellulose (fiber), are complex carbohydrates. The monosaccharides (glucose and fructose) and the disaccharides (sucrose, maltose, and lactose) are simple carbohydrates.

Both types of carbohydrates are found naturally in foods. Sources of complex carbohydrate include breads, cereals, dried beans and peas, and vegetables. Naturally occurring food sources of simple carbohydrate include fruits, vegetables, and milk products. However, much of our carbohydrate intake is in the form of refined, processed foods. Refined foods refer to those that have been processed in order to remove the coarse parts of the food. As a result of this processing, fiber and certain vitamins and minerals are also removed, and create the need for an enrichment process, which reconstitutes those nutrients lost during the refining process. The major difference between unrefined natural carbohydrates and those that have been processed is that the former provide fiber and possible trace nutrients. The major differences between complex carbohydrates (either unrefined or enriched) and processed simple carbohydrates (sugars) is that complex carbohydrates provide vitamins, minerals, protein, and energy; whereas refined sugars are solely a source of energy.

Dietary fiber includes the portions of plants that are not digested in the human small intestine. Most of these fibers are structural components of plant cell walls. Some fibers are manufactured by the plant to serve specialized functions, while others are stored by the plant to meet future energy needs. Most plant fibers are complex carbohydrates that can only be digested or fermented in the colon. The two major types of fiber are the water-soluble fibers, pectins, gums, and mucilages; and the insoluble fibers, cellulose, hemicelluloses, and lignins.

The water-soluble fibers are found mainly in fruits and dried beans and peas. These fibers delay intestinal transit time and decrease the rate of nutrient absorption. Although all plants contain some soluble fibers, the insoluble fibers make up the majority of plant fibers. Found mainly in wheat bran, grains, and vegetables, the insoluble fibers increase intestinal transit time. Because natural foods do contain a variety of fibers, their effects on blood glucose and blood lipid levels are a result of several actions.

DISORDERS ASSOCIATED WITH INADEQUATE DIETARY INTAKE OF COMPLEX CARBOHYDRATES AND FIBER

Epidemiologic evidence indicates a strong association between low fat, high fiber, high complex carbohydrate diets and reduced incidence of coronary heart disease, diabetes, and cancer. Separating the individual effects of these dietary components is not always easy. However, evidence exists which suggests the varying influences these dietary factors have on blood cholesterol, triglyceride, and glucose levels, and thus the role they may play in the disease process.

Carbohydrates. Controversy exists over the effect that carbohydrates have on blood triglyceride levels. It appears that simple carbohydrates tend to raise triglyceride levels, while complex carbohydrates, if high in fiber, tend to lower triglyceride levels (Anderson, 1985). Data are not conclusive on the effect carbohydrates have on cholesterol levels.

Recommendations for amounts and types of carbohydrates appropriate for individuals with diabetes have been debated for many years. The recent focus has been on the influences that different types of carbohydrates have on blood glucose levels. The American Diabetes Association's recommendations for the appropriate amount of carbohydrate in the diabetic diet are consistent with recommendations for the general population (American Diabetes Association, 1979): emphasis has been on a high intake of complex carbohydrates due to their slower rate of digestion and absorption, which results in a slower blood glucose rise. Simple carbohydrates should be avoided because their rapid absorption would supposedly result in the greatest blood glucose rise.

Now, however, researchers are finding that this view is an oversimplification and that carbohydrates are too diverse to be lumped into two categories in terms of their glycemic (blood glucose) responses (Jenkins et al., 1981). Variations in the magnitude of the blood glucose rise occur in both complex and simple carbohydrates. Differences in the glycemic response of carbohydrates depends primarily on the following factors: (a) type of carbohydrate; (b) physical state of food; (c) presence of fiber and other food components (e.g., phytates), and (d) presence of protein and fat (within the food itself and/or in foods consumed simultaneously). In addition to the wide variability among foods in terms of their glycemic response, there is significant individual variability among persons with diabetes. This current research highlights the complexity encountered in defining the optimal diet for individuals with diabetes. However, the general recommendation that unrefined complex carbohydrate containing fiber should be emphasized in the diet remains appropriate.

Fiber. Water-soluble fibers lower blood cholesterol levels, an effect which is thought to be due to fiber's ability to interfere with the reabsorption of bile salts. The only route of cholesterol excretion is by way of the bile salts. Thus, increased excretion of bile salts results in decreased body cholesterol levels. Cholesterol levels are not influenced by insoluble fibers (Jenkins et al., 1980). Triglyceride levels appear to be lowered by both types of dietary fiber (Anderson, 1985).

Different actions of the two types of dietary fiber have varying effects on blood glucose levels. Water-soluble fibers are found to be most effective in reducing post-meal blood glucose rise. Insoluble fibers may have long-term effects on glucose tolerance, but do not have a significant impact on immediate blood glucose response (Anderson, 1985).

Several gastrointestinal disorders, including constipation, gallstones, diverticulosis, and irritable bowel syndrome, are associated with low dietary fiber intakes. Considerable success has been observed in treating these disorders with high fiber diets. The beneficial effects are attributed mainly to the insoluble fibers' ability to increase stool size and thus increase transit time through the intestinal tract and decrease pressure within the large bowels.

High fiber intakes have also been linked to a reduced incidence of colon cancer. Fiber's precise role in cancer prevention, however, is a matter of debate. It is thought that this association may be due in part to the lower fat content of these high fiber diets. However, some suggest that fiber increases transit time and reduces the time that food carcinogens stay in contact with the bowel walls. Fiber may also lower the concentration of such carcinogens by increasing fecal bulk. The rate of formation of mutagens (carcinogens) by the intestinal bacteria may also be reduced by fiber (Adlercreutz, 1984).

Although the available data are not entirely consistent, evidence generally supports the hypothesis that increased dietary intakes of complex carbohydrates and fiber is consistent with good health and may be protective against several disorders.

INCREASING COMPLEX CARBOHYDRATES AND FIBER IN THE DIET

Considering the health benefits associated with increased complex carbohydrate and fiber intakes, the following guidelines should be implemented in the dietary patterns of most individuals:

* Increase unrefined foods in the diet, including whole grain cereals, breads, crackers, and dried beans and peas.
* Increase fruits in the diet, especially fresh fruits with skins (e.g., apples), membranes (e.g., oranges), or seeds (e.g., strawberries) for increased fiber intake.
* Increase vegetables in the diet, especially raw and slightly cooked vegetables. Vegetables with skins (e.g., corn, peas, beans, potatoes) and vegetables with stems and leaves (e.g., salad greens, broccoli) are especially high in fiber. (See Table 4, page 443.)

SUGARS

Sugars, also referred to as simple carbohydrates, come in many different forms. The two basic types are monosaccharides (glucose, fructose, and galactose) and disaccharides (sucrose, lactose, and maltose). Sugar, regardless of its form, provides only calories to the diet (4 calories per gram) and accounts for approximately 24% of the total daily calories consumed by the average American: 14% from refined sugars; 4% from processed sugars like corn syrup, honey, and molasses; and only 6% from natural sources such as fruits, vegetables, and milk products (U. S. Senate Select Committee on Nutrition and Human Needs, 1977). Sucrose, which includes white, refined table sugar, is by far the most widely used sugar, and it is the intake of this particular sugar that is of greatest concern to health professionals.

On the average, each American uses more than 130 pounds of sugars and sweeteners a year. The most obvious forms of sugar in the diet include not just sugar from the sugar bowl, but also the sugar and syrups in jams, jellies, candies, cookies, pies, cakes, ice cream, and soft drinks. The less obvious, but significant, hidden sources of sugar in the diet include the sugars found in processed foods such as cereals, crackers, bread, soups, peanut butter, cured meats, ketchup, salad dressings, and

TABLE 4: SOURCES OF FIBER IN THE DIET*

The following food groups contain the richest sources of dietary fiber. The table indicates the <u>average</u> amount of <u>fiber per serving</u> for foods in each of the groups. Some foods with amounts <u>higher</u> than average are listed.

Food Group	Grams Fiber/Serving
<u>Vegetables</u>, cooked	2.0g - 1/2 cup
raw	3.0-4.0g - 1/2 cup
<u>Starchy Vegetables</u>	3.0g - 1/2 cup
corn, cooked	4.7g - 1/2 cup
peas, cooked	3.8g - 1/2 cup
parsnips, cooked	5.9g - 1/2 cup
<u>Fruits</u>	2.0g - 3/4 cup or 1 piece
blackberries, raw	6.7g - 3/4 cup
raspberries, raw	6.9g - 3/4 cup
strawberries, raw	2.6g - 3/4 cup
prunes, dried	2.4g - 2 medium
<u>Breads</u> and <u>Grains</u> (unrefined)	2.0g - 1/2 cup or 1 slice
<u>Cereals</u>	3.0g - 3/4 cup
All (100%) Bran	17.0g - 3/4 cup
Oat bran, dry	5.3g - 1/4 cup
Bran Chex	6.0g - 3/4 cup
Corn Bran	6.6g - 3/4 cup
<u>Dried Beans</u> and <u>Peas</u>	8.0g - 1/2 cup
<u>Nut</u> and <u>Seeds</u>	3.0g - 1 oz or 1/4 cup

Fiber Comparisons

Food	Fiber	Food	Fiber
Orange, 1 small	1.6g	Orange juice, 1/2 cup	0.0g
Brown rice, 1/2 cup	2.4g	White rice, 1/2 cup	0.8g
Whole wheat bread, 1 slice	2.1g	White bread, 1 slice	0.7g
Bran Chex, 3/4 cup	6.0g	Corn Chex, 3/4 cup	2.4g

*Note. Fiber content figures are derived from several sources including <u>Plant Fiber Source Book</u> by J. Anderson, 1980, Lexington, KY: HCF Diabetes Research Foundation, Inc. Copyright ● 1980.

spaghetti sauce. Several problems arise from the overconsumption of sugar. The American population is being advised to limit the intake of simple carbohydrates to no more than 10% of the total caloric intake (U. S. Senate Select Committee on Nutrition and Human Needs, 1977).

443

DISORDERS ASSOCIATED WITH
EXCESSIVE DIETARY INTAKES OF SUGAR

Sugar's role in tooth decay is probably more widely known among Americans than any other presumed health hazard of sugar. The microorganisms which cause tooth decay depend mainly on sugar as their energy source. The risk of dental caries is not simply a function of how much sugar is eaten. The longer and more frequently sugar is in contact with the teeth, the greater the damage caused by the microorganisms. For example, a chewy candy which sticks to the teeth is far more cariogenic than a sweetened beverage which is consumed more quickly and does not stick to the teeth. Sugar's role as a risk factor for other disorders is less clearly defined.

Sugar contains the same number of calories per gram as do proteins and complex carbohydrates (starches). While obesity is a result of excess calories, regardless of whether the extra calories come from sugar, protein, starch, or fat, there are some important differences in these food sources. Unlike starches and proteins, sugars are devoid of vitamins, minerals, and fiber. Hence, the reason sugary foods are often referred to as "empty calories." Moreover, because sugar-containing foods are high in caloric density and low in nutrient density, it is easy to overconsume sugar calories long before nutrient satiety is reached.

Two popular misconceptions are current about sugar (sucrose) and diabetes: The first contends that overconsumption of sugar causes diabetes; the second, that all persons with diabetes must totally restrict their consumption of sugar. The concept that overconsumption of sugar leads to the development of diabetes is not substantiated by scientific evidence. On the other hand, excess sugar consumption, if associated with obesity, may play an indirect role in the development of diabetes. Excess caloric consumption rather than the intake of sugar itself is the major diabetogenic factor.

Then, the contention that all persons with diabetes must totally avoid sugar has been and continues to inspire heated debate. The recommendation and rationale for an increased carbohydrate intake in the diabetic meal plan has even been discussed. Unrefined complex carbohydrates should make up the majority of the total carbohydrate intake. Simple carbohydrates (sugars) may also be included in the diet. In fact, some foods, such as fruits, which contain naturally occurring sugars, are essential to the diet.

When foods or beverages that contain sucrose or other simple sugars are ingested, the degree of blood glucose response is determined by the amount of sugar consumed, by the nature of the other foods that are consumed simultaneously, and by individual variability. The intake of simple carbohydrates may be acceptable in controlled amounts in the diabetic diet. However, the decision in regard to the type and amount of simple carbohydrates to include in the diabetic meal plan must be made on an individual basis. If weight reduction is necessary, simple carbohydrates must be restricted. In addition, it is recommended that simple carbohydrates be consumed in nutritionally balanced meals that also contain some protein and complex carbohydrate.

Additionally, some researchers claim that a high sugar intake is associated with higher blood levels of triglycerides and cholesterol, but the evidence is far from conclusive. Dietary cholesterol and saturated fat intake as well as total caloric intake are by far the most critical factors. Under certain conditions, carbohydrate intake increases triglyceride levels, but this increase tends to be transient. Simple carbohydrates appear to have the greater influence on triglyceride levels. Complex carbohydrates, which are high in fiber, tend to reduce triglyceride levels (Anderson, 1985).

REDUCING SUGAR IN THE DIET

Considering the possible adverse effects resulting from excessive sugar consumption, it would be prudent for the population in general to consider adhering to the following suggestions:

* Use less of all sugars, including white sugar, brown sugar, raw sugar, honey, and syrups. Raw sugar, nutritionally speaking, is the same as white sugar. The claim that honey is more nutritious than white sugar is misleading; honey is essentially a source of calories only.
* Limit the intake of foods containing sugars such as soft drinks, cakes, cookies, pastries, and ice cream. Instead of buying cakes, pies, and cookies, make them at home using 1/2-3/4 less sugar than stated in the recipe.

  * Select fresh fruits or frozen/canned fruits packed without sugar. Dried fruits--raisins, dates, figs, and apricots--have a fairly high concentration of sugar.
  * Read food labels for information on sugar content; look for the words sucrose, glucose, maltose, dextrose, lactose, fructose, or syrups. Ingredients must be listed in descending order of amount. If one of these sugars is listed as the first or second ingredient, it can be assumed that the product contains a relatively large amount of sugar.

SODIUM (SALT)

Salt (sodium chloride) is the dietary form in which sodium is most often encountered. After sugar, salt is our leading food additive, both in processing and home cooking. The average American consumes 6-18 grams of salt (2-6g sodium) a day (U. S. Senate Select Committee on Nutrition and Human Needs, 1977). This is roughly equivalent to 1-3.5 teaspoons of salt (1 teaspoon is approximately 5g). The Food and Nutrition Board considers a range between 1.1 and 3.3 grams of sodium per day safe and adequate for healthy adults (National Research Council, 1980).

Sodium is primarily involved with maintenance of osmotic equilibrium and extracellular fluid volume. Along with potassium and chloride, sodium regulates the balance of acids and bases in body fluids and cells. Sodium also plays an important role in nerve transmission and muscle contraction. The kidneys regulate the sodium content of body fluids and a normal sodium level is maintained by the kidneys' actions of excreting excess sodium when the level rises, and reabsorbing sodium when the level decreases.

SOURCES OF SODIUM IN THE DIET

Enough sodium is naturally present in foods and water to meet the needs of almost everyone. However, it is estimated that natural foods and water account for only one-third of the total sodium intake. The sodium (salt) used for food processing, food preparation, and at the table accounts for the other two-thirds majority of the total sodium consumption.

It is easy to identify salty foods such as nuts, pretzels, potato chips, pickles, sauerkraut, and soy sauce. Less

446

obvious, but salty as well, are cheeses, cereals, luncheon meats, canned soups, canned vegetables, and tomato juice. These foods are high in salt and other sources of sodium, including leavening agents (baking powder and baking soda) and such additives as sodium nitrate, sodium phosphate, sodium ascorbate, monosodium glutamate (MSG), and sodium saccharin. In addition, some medications, such as antacids, contain a significant amount of sodium (see Table 5, pages 448-449).

DISORDERS ASSOCIATED WITH EXCESSIVE DIETARY INTAKES OF SODIUM

Excessive sodium consumption has been implicated as a contributing factor in the development of hypertension, one of the major risk factors for cardiovascular disease. Approximately 15% to 20% of American adults are afflicted with mild to significant hypertension (Grundy, 1983). Evidence from animal studies, epidemiological studies, and clinical investigations in humans have focused on the potential role of sodium in causing hypertension in susceptible individuals. Further research suggests that other dietary factors may also affect blood pressure. Hypertension has been associated with low calcium and potassium intakes (McCarron, Morris, Henry, & Stanton, 1984). Evidence exists that the ratio of sodium to potassium intake may also be important in determining blood pressure and the occurrence of hypertension (Meneely & Butterbee, 1976).

It is clear that not everyone is equally susceptible to the effects that dietary factors may have on blood pressure. Approximately 15% of the U. S. population is considered to be salt sensitive and thus prone to develop high blood pressure if their diets are high in salt (sodium) (Grundy, 1983). Unfortunately, it is difficult to identify these individuals. Hence, recommendations have been made to the general population that sodium intake be reduced to no more than 2g/day (or 5g salt/day) (U. S. Senate Select Committee on Nutrition and Human Needs, 1977). Considering that most Americans consume over twice the amount of sodium they need, guidelines to reduce sodium intake are applicable to the majority of the population. For those individuals being treated with hypertensive medication, sodium restriction may also minimize body potassium loss and enhance the medication's therapeutic effects.

TABLE 5: SODIUM CONTENT OF POPULAR FOODS*

The following table compares the average amounts of sodium found in foods from the basic food groups to foods classified as processed, convenience, snack, or fast foods.

Food	Sodium, mg
Milk Group	
Milk (1 cup)	120
Fruit and Vegetable Group	
Fruit	5
Fresh vegetables (1/2 cup)	50
Canned vegetables (1/2 cup)	150-250
Protein Group	
Cheeses (most types; 1 oz)	200
Peanut butter (2 tbsp)	200
Poultry, beef, fish (3 oz)	75
Dried bean and peas (1/2 cup)	10
Bread and Cereal Group	
Bread (1 slice)	150
Muffin (1)	250
Cereals: most ready-to eat (3/4 cup)	150-300
- Grits, puffed cereals, shredded wheat (3/4 cup)	<2
- Rice (1/2 cup)	<10
Fast Foods	
Kentucky Fried Chicken Dinner (3 pieces)	2,285
MacDonald's Big Mac (1)	1,510
Snack Items	
Pretzel twist, thin (1)	100
Potato chips (10)	200
Peanuts, salted (1/4 cup)	275
Dill pickle (1 large)	2,000
Tomato juice (4 oz, canned)	250
Convenience Foods	
Meat and vegetable TV dinner (frozen)	1,300
Spaghetti with meatballs (1 cup, canned)	1,220
Tomato soup (1 cup, canned)	1,000
Pork and beans (1/2 cup, canned)	500
Cheese pizza mix (1 slice)	600
Miscellaneous Processed Foods	
Beef hot dog (1)	500
American cheese (1 oz)	350

Condiments
Soy sauce (1 tbsp)	1,300
Tomato catsup (1 tbsp)	200
Olives (2 green)	300
Bouillon cube (1)	900

*Note. Sodium content figures are derived from several sources including The Dictionary of Sodium, Fats, and Cholesterol by B. Kraus, 1974, New York: Grosset and Dunlap. Copyright © 1974. Also Sodium Content of Your Food (Home and Garden Bulletin No. 233) by U. S. Department of Agriculture, 1980, Washington, DC: U. S. Government Printing Office. Copyright © 1980.

REDUCING SALT AND SODIUM IN THE DIET

Significant amounts of sodium are found in processed foods and salt is added to foods during preparation. The following guidelines address ways to reduce total sodium and salt consumption:

* Learn to enjoy the unsalted flavors of foods (this may take a month or so); avoid adding salt at the table and never add salt before tasting the food.
* Gradually reduce the amount of salt used in cooking and baking; start by cutting the salt in a recipe by half.
* Use herbs and spices, lemon, garlic, and onion, in place of salt, soy sauce, MSG, ketchup, mustard, and bouillon cubes.
* Limit the intake of processed foods high in sodium and salt especially canned soups and vegetables, cheeses, luncheon meats, packaged mixes, and ready-to-eat meals.
* Read food labels carefully to determine the amounts of sodium in processed foods and snack items. In July, 1985 food processors and manufacturers that fortify their products or make nutritional claims were required to list sodium content on labels.
* In fast-food restaurants, select low sodium foods, such as salad bar items, rather than French fries and sandwiches which are higher in sodium.
* Check the labels of medications which may contain sodium, such as antacids and cough preparations.

Calcium and Potassium Requirements. The evidence linking low potassium and calcium intake with an increased incidence of hypertension warrants consideration of the adequate consumption of these nutrients. Foods especially rich in potassium and calcium are listed below:

Potassium-Rich Foods	Calcium-Rich Foods
Raisins	Milk and milk products (best
Bananas	sources)
Cantaloupe	Dark, green, leafy vegetables
Avocados	Dried beans and peas
Dried dates and prunes	Tofu (soybean curd)
Peaches	Sardines
Oranges and orange juice	Oysters
White and sweet potatoes	
Tomato juice	
Dried beans and peas	
Milk	
Fish (flounder, salmon, tuna)	

ALCOHOL

Alcohol supplies the body with usable energy, therefore, it must be considered a nutrient. Alcohol, however, is solely a source of calories--7 calories per gram--with no other nutrients provided. Many questions have been raised regarding the healthy and harmful effects of alcohol intake. Can one or two drinks a day be beneficial to health? How much is too much? What is meant by drinking in moderation?

DISORDERS ASSOCIATED WITH EXCESSIVE ALCOHOL INTAKE

Heavy alcohol consumption can compromise nutritional status and can lead to a variety of serious conditions. Although moderate alcohol consumption may not have a significant effect, heavy alcohol consumption has a deleterious impact on nutritional status in the following ways: (a) Alcohol alters nutrient intake by suppressing the appetite and displacing essential nutrients in the diet; (b) alcohol can impair the digestion and absorption of nutrients especially the B-vitamins; and (c) alcohol can affect the storage, mobilization, activation, and metabolism of nutrients.

The only organ that can metabolize alcohol is the liver. If the alcohol is not immediately used for energy,

450

it is used for the synthesis of fatty acids. These fatty acids combine with glycerol to form triglycerides (fat) which are deposited in the liver. Excessive alcohol consumption leads to an increased production of triglycerides. Excess triglycerides, if they accumulate in the liver, create a fatty liver. Continuous heavy alcohol consumption can lead to cirrhosis, a chronic and potentially fatal degeneration of the liver that also increases the risk of liver cancer. Furthermore, as with liver disease, heavy drinkers, especially those who also smoke cigarettes, are at an increased risk for developing cancers of the larynx, esophagus, and oral cavity.

In addition to elevating triglyceride levels, alcohol consumption also increases cholesterol production in the liver and may thereby raise total blood cholesterol levels. Such elevations seem to increase the risk of atherosclerosis. Alcohol consumption has been associated with elevated concentrations of HDL-cholesterol (Glueck, Hogg, Allen, & Gartside, 1980) suggesting that moderate alcohol intake may be protective against heart disease. Recent studies suggest that moderate alcohol intake does not increase the HDL-cholesterol fraction that is thought to be protective against heart disease (Haskell et al., 1984). Furthermore, evidence indicates that heavy alcohol consumption is associated with an increased risk of developing hypertension and related complications. In those individuals with pre-existing heart disease, alcohol may lead to further damage of the heart muscle cells. These patients are usually advised to consume no more than one drink a day.

Excessive alcohol intake should be avoided by individuals with diabetes. However, many diabetologists now feel that alcohol in moderation is not contraindicated in diabetes, if several cautions and precautions are considered. Alcohol potentiates the effect of certain oral hypoglycemic agents, increasing the likelihood of hypoglycemia, so diabetic patients are advised to drink alcohol only when eating. Alcohol intoxication can mask the symptoms of hypoglycemia and delay appropriate treatment. Alcohol intake can also potentiate the problem of elevated triglyceride levels, frequently seen in people with diabetes. Finally, alcohol is a concentrated source of calories and the caloric content of alcohol beverages must be considered in the meal plan if they are to be consumed. For those individuals on calorie-restricted diets, it would be prudent to avoid alcohol consumption.

451

DRINKING IN MODERATION

The measurement of a drink must be based on the absolute alcohol content of the beverage; one drink usually means 0.5 ounce of absolute alcohol. This would be the equivalent of 1.5 ounces of 80 proof distilled spirits (97 calories), 1 ounce of 110 proof distilled spirits (70-115 calories), 12 ounces of beer (150 calories), or 4 to 5 ounces of table wine (100 calories).

Suggestions for safe alcohol consumption include: (a) Consume alcohol with food; (b) dilute alcohol concentration by mixing with water, club soda, and seltzer; (c) drink alcohol slowly; and (d) do not mix drugs with alcohol. Moderate degrees of alcohol consumption, one to two drinks per day, do not appear to affect nutritional status or otherwise compromise health in male and nonpregnant female adults.

SUMMARY

Nutrition plays a vital role in health promotion and disease prevention. Although many questions remain, sufficient data exist to support general dietary recommendations for the majority of our population. These guidelines, acknowledging both individual variability and the concept of health risk factors, represent a consensus among scientific, medical, and public health authorities.

Many factors, in addition to diet, have an impact on an individual's health status. We have a significant amount of control over some of these factors, and our nutrition-related behaviors are among them. The guidelines outlined in this chapter are designed to bring about positive changes in dietary practices. They can serve as a valuable tool in promoting improved health and well-being.

Priscilla Hastedt, MPH, RD, is currently a practicing nutritionist and patient care specialist. She has been involved in diabetes research at Duke University Medical Center and Healthware Corporation in Durham, North Carolina. She is a Registered Dietitian and has a masters degree in Public Health Nutrition from the University of North Carolina in Chapel Hill. Other areas of expertise include nutrition and athletic performance. Ms. Hastedt may be contacted at 5632 11th N. E., Seattle, WA 98105.

RESOURCES

Adlercreutz, H. (1984). Does fiber-rich food containing animal lignin precursors protect against both colon and breast cancer? An extension of the "fiber hypothesis." *Gastroenterology, 86,* 761-766.

American Cancer Society. (1984). *Nutrition, Common Sense and Cancer* (Publication No. 2096-LE). New York: American Cancer Society, Inc.

American Diabetes Association. (1979). Principles of nutrition and dietary recommendations for individuals with diabetes mellitus. *Diabetes Care, 2,* 520-523.

American Heart Association. (1981). *Rationale of the Diet-Heart Statement: Report of the Nutrition Committee* (Publication No. 72202-A). Dallas, TX: American Heart Association.

Anderson, J. (1980). *Plant Fiber Source Book.* Lexington, KY: HCF Diabetes Research Foundation, Inc.

Anderson, J. W. (1985). Dietary fiber in the nutrition management of diabetes. In G. Vahouny & D. Kritchevsky (Eds.), *Basic and Clinical Aspects of Dietary Fiber* (pp. 343-350). New York: Plenum Press.

Eshleman, R. (1979). *American Heart Association Cookbook.* New York: David McKay, Inc.

Glueck, C. J., Hogg, E., Allen, C., & Gartside, P. S. (1980). Effects of alcohol ingestion on lipids and lipoproteins in normal men: Isocaloric metabolic studies. *American Journal of Clinical Nutrition, 33,* 2287-2293.

Grundy, S. M. (1983). Cardiovascular disease. In H. A. Schneider, C. E. Anderson, & D. B. Coursin (Eds.), *Nutritional Support of Medical Practice* (pp. 282-301). Philadelphia, PA: Harper & Row.

Haskell, W. L., Camargo, C., Williams, P. T., Vranizan, K. M., Krauss, R. M., Lindgren, F. T., & Wood, P. D. (1984). The effect of cessation and resumption of moderate alcohol intake on serum high-density-lipoprotein subfractions. *New England Journal of Medicine, 310,* 805-810.

Heiss, G., Tamir, I., Davis, C. E., et al. (1980). Lipoprotein cholesterol distributions in selected North American populations: The Lipid Research Clinics Program Prevalence Study. *Circulation, 61,* 302-315.

Hulley, S. B. (1980). Epidemiology as a guide to clinical decisions: The association between triglycerides and coronary heart disease. *New England Journal of Medicine, 302,* 1383-1389.

Jenkins, D. J. A., Wolever, T. M. S., Taylor, R. H., Barker, H. M., Fielden, H., Baldwin, J. M., Bowling, A. C., Newman, H. C., Jenkins, A. L., & Goff, D. V. (1981). Glycemic index of foods: A physiological basis for carbohydrate exchange. *American Journal of Clinical Nutrition, 34,* 362-366.

Jenkins, D. J. A., et al. (1980). Dietary fibre and blood lipids: Reduction of serum cholesterol in type II hyperlipidemia by quar gum. *American Journal of Clinical Nutrition, 32,* 16-18.

King, J. C., Cohenour, S. H., Corruccini, C. G., & Schneeman, P. (1978). Evaluation and modification of the basic four food guide. *Journal of Nutrition Education, 10,* 27-29.

Kraus, B. (1974). *The Dictionary of Sodium, Fats, and Cholesterol.* New York: Grosset and Dunlap.

Lipid Research Clinics Program. (1984). The lipid research clinics coronary primary prevention trial results: 1. Reduction in incidence of coronary heart disease. *Journal of the American Medical Association, 251,* 351-364.

McCarron, D. A., Morris, C. D., Henry, H. J., & Stanton, J. L. (1984). Blood pressure and nutrient intake in the United States. *Science, 224,* 1392-1398.

McGill, H. C., & Mott, G. E. (1976). Diet and coronary heart disease. In D. M. Hegsted, et al. (Eds.), *Nutrition Reviews' Present Knowledge in Nutrition* (4th ed., pp. 376-391). Washington, DC: Nutrition Foundation.

Meneely, R. L., & Butterbee, H. D. (1976). The high sodium--low potassium environment and hypertension. *American Journal of Cardiology, 38,* 768-774.

National Cancer Institute. (1985). *Diet, Nutrition and Cancer Prevention: A Guide to Food Choices* (National Institutes of Health Publication No. 85-2711). Washington, DC: U. S. Department of Health and Human Services.

National Diabetes Data Group. (1985). *Diabetes in America: Diabetes Data Compiled 1984* (National Institutes of Health Publication No. 85-1468). Washington, DC: U. S. Department of Health and Human Services.

National Research Council, Food and Nutrition Board. (1980). *Recommended Dietary Allowances.* Washington, DC: National Academy of Sciences.

Pooling Project Research Group. (1956). Relationship of blood pressure, serum cholesterol, smoking habit, relative weight and ECG abnormalities to incidence of major coronary events: Final report of the Pooling Project. *Journal of Chronic Diseases, 31,* 201-306.

U. S. Department of Agriculture. (1980). *Sodium Content of Your Food* (Home and Garden Bulletin No. 233). Washington, DC: U. S. Government Printing Office.

U. S. Department of Agriculture and U. S. Department of Health and Human Services. (1985). *Nutrition and Your Health: Dietary Guidelines for Americans* (Home and Garden Bulletin No. 232). Washington, DC: U. S. Government Printing Office.

U. S. Senate Select Committee on Nutrition and Human Needs. (1977). *Dietary Goals for the United States* (Publication No. 052-070-04376-8). Washington, DC: U. S. Government Printing Office.

Willett, W. C., & MacMahon, B. (1984a, March). Diet and cancer--an overview (Part 1). *New England Journal of Medicine, 310,* 633-638.

Willett, W. C., & MacMahon, B. (1984b, March). Diet and cancer--an overview (Part 2). *New England Journal of Medicine, 310,* 697-703.

RECOMMENDED RESOURCES

American Dietetic Association & American Diabetes Association. (1983). *Family Cookbook: Volume II.* Englewood Cliffs, NJ: Prentice-Hall.

Bailey, C. (1984). *The Fit-Or-Fat Target Diet.* Boston: Houghton Mifflin.

Brody, J. E. (1981). *Jane Brody's Nutrition Book.* New York: W. W. Norton and Co.

Feldman, E. B. (Ed.). (1983). *Nutrition in the Middle and Later Years.* Boston: John Wright--PSG, Inc.

Hamilton, E. M., & Whitney, E. (1982). *Nutrition: Concepts and Controversies.* St. Paul, MN: West Publishing Co.

Jordan, H. A. (1976). *Eating Is Okay.* New York: The American Library, Inc.

Robertson, L., Flinders, C., & Godfrey, B. (1976). *Laurel's Kitchen: A Handbook for Vegetarian Cookery and Nutrition.* Petaluma, CA: Nilgiri Press.

ORGANIZATIONS

American Diabetes Association, 1660 Duke Street, Alexandria, VA 22314.

American Dietetic Association, 430 N. Michigan Avenue, Chicago, IL 60611.

American Heart Association, 7320 Greenville Avenue, Dallas, TX 75321.

Food and Nutrition Information and Educational Materials Center, National Agriculture Library, 10301 Baltimore Boulevard, Beltsville, MD 20705.

National Academy of Sciences, National Research Council, Food and Nutrition Board, 2101 Constitution Avenue, Washington, DC 20418.

National Cancer Institute (Cancer Information Clearinghouse), Building 31, Room 10A18, 9000 Rockville Pike, Bethesda, MD 20205.

Nutrition Today Society, 101 Ridgely Avenue, P. O. Box 465, Annapolis, MD 21404.

Society for Nutrition Education, 2140 Shattuck Avenue, Suite 1110, Berkeley, CA 94704.

SECTION IV:

MISCELLANEOUS

RELAXATION TECHNIQUES WITH CANCER PATIENTS

Patricia H. Cotanch

The use of relaxation techniques such as progressive muscle relaxation, autogenic training, hypnosis, diversion, systematic desensitization, and guided mental imagery as interventions for cancer patients may be the newest frontier in behavioral medicine. (The application of behavioral techniques has proved valuable in many areas of neurology and cardiovascular disease, stress-related disorders, and in altering unhealthy habits, both as adjuvant treatment and sometimes in primary treatment.) Success in these areas has prompted interest in using the same techniques to assist cancer patients in coping with the physical discomforts and stress-related concomitants of their disease and its treatments. The advantages of behavioral approaches extend beyond specific symptom management to potentiating the placebo effect of medications, improving patient-provider relationships, transforming the role of the patient from passive recipient into active participant, aiding self-management, and improving patient compliance.

This chapter will present information on the use of relaxation and related techniques as coping strategies for decreasing the distress associated with cancer and various cancer treatments. Special consideration will be given to clinical issues in the application of relaxation techniques in the management of cancer. Hopefully, such discussion will set the stage for health care providers to begin applying such techniques in the treatment of their patients.

USE OF RELAXATION TECHNIQUES
TO DECREASE SYMPTOMS

Relaxation techniques have been successful in the management of symptoms from the disease (pain, anxiety, anorexia, depression) and treatment-related side effects (nausea, vomiting, needle phobias, stomatitis, pain). Recently there have been several published articles on the use of behavioral intervention to successfully treat the condition of pre-treatment or anticipatory nausea and vomiting that occurs in 20-60% of cancer patients receiving chemotherapy (Burish & Redd, 1984).

Clinicians are very aware that patients sometimes become queasy and vomit even before chemotherapy is administered. Needless to say, patient and clinician alike are distressed when the patient, while greeting the clinician, promptly vomits. Patients have reported that they begin to "feel sick" when they are en route to the clinic to receive chemotherapy; often the sight of the hospital or entrance way evokes this anticipatory phenomenon. Health care staff tend to interpret pre-treatment nausea and vomiting as "hysteria" or "anxiety," and often the response pattern is dismissed as "nerves" even by clinicians. Sometimes patients are embarrassed to mention the symptoms for fear they will be labeled "psychologically abnormal" (Cotanch, 1983).

Pre-treatment nausea and vomiting is described as a syndrome (a) developing only after a number of months of treatment; (b) being precipitated by sight, smell, or thought of the clinic; (c) having a gradual onset and becoming more severe over time; and (d) continuing when patients return to the clinic for follow up, nonchemotherapy visits. The patients with pre-treatment symptoms are more likely to have more advanced disease, to have received more chemotherapy, and to have more extensive and severe vomiting after chemotherapy than patients without pre-treatment symptoms. Diagnostic, demographic, and psychological profiles were to date are not predictive as to who is likely to develop pre-treatment symptoms.

The occurrence of pre-treatment symptoms suggests a classically conditioned response. The nausea is analogous to Pavlov's dog's conditioned salivation when it hears a tone that has been repeatedly paired with food. Previously neutral clinical environmental stimuli (visual, olfactory, and tactile) acquire the capacity to elicit

460

anxiety, nausea, and vomiting after the patient has been repeatedly subjected to drug-induced nausea and vomiting in the same or even a similar clinical environment. Reports showed that patients with pre-treatment vomiting were more anxious and depressed and exhibited an inhibitive coping style when compared with the patients without pre-treatment symptoms (Altmaire, Ross, & Moore, 1982). Conditioned aversion is more likely to occur with chemotherapy that is accompanied by a strong taste sensation (e.g., Cytoxan).

Various relaxation interventions have been employed and found effective in helping cancer patients adjust to the trauma and discomfort of their disease. The following is a brief description of the most commonly used relaxation interventions.

PROGRESSIVE MUSCLE RELAXATION

Therapist-directed or taped progressive muscle relaxation (PMR) has been effective in decreasing symptoms in cancer patients. The effects include decreasing drug-related nausea and vomiting, improving oral intake, and decreasing both the intensity and severity of pain. PMR takes approximately 20 minutes, works better in a quiet environment, and requires the patients to practice the skill on their own. While standard procedures can be effective, the clinician needs to be sensitive to the patient's impairment. For example, if the patient has dyspnea (shortness of breath), attention should be directed away from deep breathing or focusing on breath control. The dyspneic patient is probably already struggling for oxygen intake and will experience more comfort if attention is directed away from the source of discomfort. If the patient has limb amputation, tense-relax muscle suggestion should involve only the unaffected limbs. Some patients have experienced immediate relief from the disease-related and/or treatment-related discomfort after the first practice session. Other patients do not seem to be able to concentrate on the intervention for an adequate period of time to experience a relaxation response. Some patients are unable to concentrate because of depression, fatigue, or anxiety. If patients are depressed or overly anxious, they may not have the psychic energy to take on another intervention. Additional information on clinical issues related to this behavioral intervention is on page 470.

USE OF RELAXATION
AND SYSTEMATIC DESENSITIZATION

The use of systematic desensitization to specifically counter the classical conditioning aspect of pre-treatment nausea and vomiting has been reported with very favorable results by Morrow and Morrell (1982). Information on the pre-treatment phenomenon shows that patients typically continue to have the conditioned response during the first several nontreatment follow-up visits. With repeated exposures to the general conditioning stimuli (the clinic environment), in the absence of the particular conditioning stimulus (the medication that induces nausea and vomiting), the conditioned response of nausea and vomiting is gradually extinguished. The study used the behavioral technique of systematic desensitization to decondition the anticipatory nausea and vomiting response. The study sample was made up of 31 patients randomly placed in one of three groups: (a) a behavioral group who were coached in systematic desensitization, a behavioral management technique that uses progressive deep muscle relaxation to counter the conditioned anticipatory nausea and vomiting responses; (b) a therapist-directed counseling group with whom a supportive, problem-solving approach was employed; and (c) a control group who received no intervention.

With the behavioral group, the clinicians applied three basic steps in the desensitization process. The first step was to have the patients rank stimuli in terms of the probability of their eliciting the undesirable response. Based on previous findings, Morrow identified the clinic environment as the conditioning stimulus to nausea and vomiting and he used distance as the underlying basis for construction of a hierarchy of stimuli. Patients were told to imagine their transport to the clinic--for example, getting into the car, being one mile from the clinic, then a half mile, then in the parking lot, then walking to the building, sitting in the waiting room and so forth, until they were in the specific treatment room.

The second step in systematic desensitization was learning a response that could countercondition the undesirable response. Because relaxation is the most commonly used counterconditioning response, the patients in the behavioral group were trained in progressive muscle relaxation.

The third step in the process involved the presentation of the hierarchy of stimuli while the patient was in a deeply relaxed state. The result was that relaxation rather than anxiety was paired with the conditioning stimuli and this systematically deconditioned the undesirable response of anticipatory nausea and vomiting.

Patients in the counseling group were given supportive problem-solving therapy sessions. They spent the same amount of time with the experimenter, kept the same records of food intake and accounts of symptom occurrence, but did not construct the home-to-clinic hierarchy of stimuli, nor were they trained in relaxation. The control group of patients enabled comparisons to be made with the standard procedures used by nursing staff and other treatment personnel. Seven out of 10 patients in the behavioral group had a complete response, defined as no anticipatory nausea or vomiting for the duration of treatments following the intervention. This was a significantly greater rate of response than was seen in either the counseling or control group.

HYPNOSIS

Clinical hypnosis has been reported as an effective intervention for cancer patients. Hypnosis consists of encouraging patients to experience a sense of relaxation by narrowing their focus of concentration and giving increased attention to the suggestion being offered by the therapist (or by the patient in self-hypnosis). Hypnosis for pain control was reported by Milton Erickson as early as 1950 (Erickson, 1980). Recently, Redd and his colleagues have used hypnosis to control drug-related nausea and vomiting in cancer patients (Redd, Andresen, & Minagawa, 1982). It should be mentioned that the term hypnosis can cause concern in patients who may think of this technique as a theatrical device. One patient stated his perception of hypnosis was a mad scientist who made people make animal sounds. The patient actually expressed disappointment when he realized he was not going to be made to bark like a dog. He was assured he could bark if he wanted to in his fantasy, but the therapists had no ability to cause him to do so.

Hypnosis with Children. Hypnosis is the behavioral intervention used with children more commonly than other behavioral intervention as children sometimes get

bored with structured progressive muscle relaxation procedures. However, using hypnosis with children requires
careful instruction and explanation to prevent unfounded
anxiety about its meaning. Time should be spent assuring
the child and family that hypnosis is a self-relaxation
technique to assist in gaining control over a situation. It
should be stressed that the hypnotized individual does not
relinquish control to another but becomes more skilled in
self-control. Hypnosis with children should be done only
by a trained therapist capable of dealing with the child's
fears and frightening recollections.

During the hypnotic session the following suggestions
are given in an age-appropriate manner for the child:
feelings of safety and comfort, thoughts of restful sleep
from the antiemetics, impressions of chemotherapy
working effectively, and thoughts of a short hospital stay
with the child soon returning home. It is suggested that
the child will awaken following completion of chemotherapy feeling thirsty without nausea. Children are
encouraged to picture a safe place or a favorite activity
where they can escape, becoming relaxed and unaware of
the hospital surroundings. Emphasis is placed upon each
child's own ability to command his or her own behavior
and attain control of chemotherapy side effects.

Children undergoing hypnosis differ drastically from
adults utilizing hypnosis. Unlike adults, children require
little or no relaxation induction. Most children become
involved in fantasy readily, whereas adults require a
prolonged relaxation period where they attempt to set
aside inhibitions and concentrate on a pleasant thought.
Fantasy is a daily activity for the child and occurs easily
and without hesitation. We have observed children and
adolescents becoming bored with structured progressive
muscle relaxation used frequently and successfully
(Hockenberry & Cotanch, 1985) with adults. A shortened
attention span may create this boredom or children simply
may not require this 10-20 minute period of relaxation to
achieve an altered state of consciousness. Authorities in
hypnosis agree that work must be done quickly for the
child to achieve a hypnotic state (Zeltzer & LeBaron,
1984).

Adults undergoing hypnosis may select a sedentary
relaxing imagery scene such as sitting on the beach, lying
in a meadow, or soaking in a hot tub. In comparison,
children focus on an action imagery scene such as riding
a bicycle, roller skating, running, or swimming. Children

prefer imagery themes based on life experience, requiring unique individualized induction sessions. Attempts at hypnosis induction using a standardized tape recording have frequently been unsuccessful with children who express a need to use their own life experiences to create an atmosphere for relaxation.

Age-appropriate vocabulary is essential to provide understanding of the imagery scenes being described by the therapist. Children and adolescents frequently regress and use imagery scenes that are several years behind their stage of development. One 10-year-old recalled a funny experience from his past. As he began to describe this experience he opened his eyes and spoke in a noticeably less mature manner. After the hypnosis session was finished the child stated he was five years old when the event occurred. It is probable that he experienced spontaneous age regression during hypnosis and was actually communicating as a 5-year-old.

Children seem to be more trusting than adults and have natural ability to fantasize and imagine. They more easily obtain a somnolent state, which may occur even during the initial hypnotic session. Children the ages of 10-14 commonly appear to be in deep sleep, yet immediately respond to suggestions such as wiggling their toes or raising a hand. While children appear to achieve deep trance quickly, they are noticeably slower in awakening. Adults awaken within 5-15 seconds in comparison to most of our younger patients who require as long as 2-4 minutes to become fully awake. During hypnosis, most adolescents and adults keep their eyes closed as compared to most of our younger children who obtain relaxation and even deep trance with their eyes open (Zeltzer & LeBaron, 1984).

Hypnosis as a relaxation technique to reduce anxiety, pain, and drug-related nausea and vomiting in children is a new treatment modality that may prove to be of major benefit. Its effectiveness in adults with cancer has paved the way for establishing itself as a therapeutic modality in pediatric oncology patients.

BIOFEEDBACK AND RELAXATION

Biofeedback has been described as the single most significant development in psychophysiological research since Pavlov's methods were first developed early in the

20th century. In clinical and experimental biofeedback procedures, the patient is placed in a controlled environment in which certain physiological responses are identified, recorded, and measured. When the desired response occurs in the patient, for example change in heart rate, muscle tension, blood pressure, or breathing, a reinforcer in the form of visual and/or auditory feedback is presented to the patient. The reinforcer (a flashing light, tone, or digital read out) has both informational and reinforcing properties, in indicating to the patient that the desired response has occurred. The effects of the reinforcers in eliciting the desired responses are evaluated by measuring changes in the desired response over time. Of course, for biofeedback to be effective, the patient needs a thorough explanation of the procedure. The nature of the psychophysiological information to be measured and modified, and the contingencies of reinforcement used need to be explicitly defined and completely understood by the patient.

Three clinical studies have used a combination of relaxation training and biofeedback monitoring to help patients deal with the stress of cancer and its related treatments. All three studies used a form of relaxation training as an intervention to alter the stress response experienced by patients with cancer, and used biofeedback to measure patients' ability to learn the relaxation skill. Burish, Shartner, and Lyles (1981) reported on the effectiveness of PMR multiple muscle-site electromyographic (EMG) biofeedback in reducing the aversiveness of cancer chemotherapy. The patient was followed during three chemotherapy sessions and then instructed in PMR and biofeedback for four consecutive chemotherapy treatments. The patient was told to practice relaxation skills daily while in the hospital and at home. Once the patient had learned to relax, the relaxation and biofeedback training were terminated and the patient received three more courses of chemotherapy. Following relaxation and biofeedback training, the patient reported feeling less anxious and nauseated during chemotherapy sessions and experienced a reduction of physiological arousal (EMG, pulse rate, and blood pressure). The reductions were maintained during the follow-up chemotherapy sessions. These results support the view that behavioral techniques may be helpful in ameliorating some undesirable effects of cancer chemotherapy.

Pelletier (1979) used a combination of EMG biofeedback, autogenic training, and meditation with restful imagery for stress management in 12 patients who were receiving cancer treatments. Autogenic training is a relaxation technique in which the patient is given verbal instructions which are supposed to produce a physiological deactivation of the sympathetic branch of the autonomic nervous system. For example, the verbal instruction may be to feel heaviness and warmth in the arms and legs. The sensation of relaxation is mediated via reduction of sympathetic input to the smooth muscles regulating the arterioles. The arterioles then dilate and the patient experiences increasing blood flow to the extremities. The report states that the use of autogenic training was an effective technique to help patients cope with the stress related to cancer and its treatments.

Much remains to be learned about the clinical application of specific techniques of biofeedback. This is specifically true for cancer patients. For example, frequently cancer patients have low blood counts, exhibit suppressed immune responses, and consequently require protective isolation. It is therefore impossible for the patient to go to a biofeedback laboratory. Fortunately, with the increased availability of portable equipment, the laboratory can be brought to the patient's room. Some of the general questions regarding biofeedback that need to be answered are: (a) Does auditory, visual, or tactile feedback make a difference? (b) Is continuous (moment-to-moment) feedback more advantageous than discrete intermittent information? (c) Is immediate feedback better or worse than delayed feedback? (d) How many sessions are necessary to test the utility of biofeedback? (e) What is the optimal spacing of sessions? (f) How important is it to have the patient focus on internal cues, and does this correlate with the specific response to be changed? (g) What patients are most likely to respond to biofeedback training?

INCREASING EFFECTIVENESS OF RELAXATION INTERVENTIONS

The potential usefulness of relaxation and related techniques has yet to be fully established. In addition to circumventing clinical issues such as noisy environment, interruptions, skeptical physicians and patients, the primary limitation of the intervention may be the clinician's skill or lack of skill. The following information may help clinicians increase their skill and perceptiveness in being able to suggest and teach the most appropriate relaxation technique for a specific cancer patient.

ESTABLISHING RAPPORT

As with most clinical interventions rapport needs to be established between clinicians and client(s). Developing rapport or therapeutic alliance is considered a lynch pin in psychotherapy; this is especially true in relaxation therapy.

The ground rules of establishing rapport with a patient are *no* different from the elements that are the foundation of good human relations and interpersonal communication. The elements of a successful therapeutic relationship are respect, awareness, acceptance, concern, objectivity, and flexibility. There are countless textbooks published on establishing rapport and effective communication, however, a classic book on the subject is *Helping Relationships: Basic Concepts for the Helping Professions* by Combs, Avilla, and Purkey (1971). The text discusses the humanistic essentials common to any people-oriented profession. Writings of Milton Erickson (1980) explain the concepts of establishing a relationship with patients focusing more specifically on psychotherapeutic and psychophysiologic situations.

Erickson explains the importance of the therapist using what the patient brings to the therapeutic encounter. He stresses the need to listen to patients' selection of words and to observe body position. In our American culture there are three common modalities for accessing and processing information. These are visual, auditory, and kinesthetic (Bandler & Grinder, 1976). Most people favor one mode even though they use all three. The selection of words (predicates) people use to explain or describe a situation gives us clues as to what modality they prefer. People who are highly visual will tend to process information using internal pictures. These people will use words such as see, view, imagine, and look when they converse. People who are highly auditory will use words like hear, take in, listen, and sounds like when they describe their world. Kinesthetic people use words like feel, stir, sharpen, and soften when they converse. By listening to the words people use we can employ similar language and increase the possibility of building rapport.

We need to be aware of our own predominant mode of perceiving and processing information so we can recognize others' predominant mode and switch to other modes to more effectively communicate with patients. Brockopp (1983) gives the following example of how the same thought can be expressed using different predicates.

1. Visual: "Yes, I can see that you are much better. You look good, your eyes are clear, your appearance has certainly changed."
2. Auditory: "Yes, I can hear from the sound of your voice that you are better. Talking with you today is quite different from yesterday. You sound really good today."
3. Kinesthetic: "Yes, you do seem to be feeling much better today, you're holding your head up, and your grasp is certainly firmer than yesterday. You have a good hold on things."

When people hear these three statements they often react with complete comfort to one, moderate comfort to another, and actual discomfort to the third.

Once you are aware of your own predominant mode of predicate selection you can practice speech using other modes. Thus, you will improve and expand methods of effective communication. Developing clear, individualized communication patterns with each patient increases the probability of establishing client-clinician rapport. More important, by using the patient's major representational system, the therapist can tailor a specific relaxation procedure to better fit the patient's manner of taking in information.

PACING AND LEADING

Once you have successfully matched the clients' verbal and nonverbal behaviors you can attempt to "pace and lead" the client. You can induce patients to follow your leads by gradually changing (pacing) aspects of your own behavior.

For example, you are interviewing a person who has a sad, flat facial expression, shoulders slumped, head hung down. The person is quiet and responds to a question in a slow, low voice with long pauses between phrases. You could first attempt to subtly match the client's position and speech pattern (matching). Then, in a slow, smooth

469

fashion, you can attempt to change your posture and see if the client follows you (pacing). If not, go back to matching and in a little time attempt another behavior change. Try speaking with a slightly quicker cadence and see if the client follows (leading). Thus, the pacing *leads* the client from a withdrawn depressed state to a more open, communicative state. The process of gaining attention, establishing rapport, arriving at an appropriate relaxation technique, and offering therapeutic suggestions can take place in a relatively short time period.

The clinical skill of pacing and leading is profoundly important in approaching cancer patients with behavioral intervention. The therapist has to be sensitive and respect the affective state of the cancer patients. If the therapist enthusiastically approaches a depressed, withdrawn cancer patient with a relaxation technique then the chances of achieving a successful intervention are almost nil (Cotanch, 1984).

CLINICAL ISSUES

Although there is evidence that behavioral techniques can help remedy cancer-related psychophysiological aversiveness, once thought treatable only by somatic interventions, further research is needed before these techniques can be advocated as standard treatment for the general cancer patient population. In addition to questions of efficacy and questions of the comparative (or additive) effects of behavioral techniques and standard forms of treatment, a host of practical issues need to be addressed in considering the role of behavioral medicine in treating cancer patients.

Perhaps the most obvious issue is patient acceptance, or motivation. Relaxation and related techniques are skills that need to be learned and can only be learned with practice. The common prescription is to practice relaxation training for 15 or 20 minutes twice a day, but no studies exist to indicate how much practice is most effective. Patients being trained in relaxation may have concerns about fatigue and about their ability to handle another demand on their time and their physical and emotional resources. The idea that relaxation can be tiring seems paradoxical until one realizes that training and practice require sustained mental concentration. Progressive muscle relaxation entails tensing and relaxing of various muscle groups and can be physically taxing to the chronically ill patient. Patients' emotional resources may be taxed also because the techniques require them to get in touch with their own bodies, focusing on each part separately, in order to recognize and then release muscle tension. Cancer patients are often already pre-occupied with bodily sensations and functions as a result of their illness and treatments. The increased conscious focus on the body that is designed to reduce tension may actually result in increased anxiety and stress.

One female patient was trained in deep muscle relaxation but although the relaxation significantly lowered her post-training physiological measurements (e.g., pulse, respiration, blood pressure, and muscle tension), she adamantly refused to continue training. The patient said she did not mind being a patient while she was in the hospital but between hospital visits she wanted to forget about cancer. Daily relaxation practice would interfere with her ability to forget that she had cancer. Interestingly, this same patient eventually refused to continue with prescribed chemotherapy. It is possible that her need to deny may have ultimately contributed to her decision to terminate treatment. Perhaps if relaxation training had been instituted earlier, the patient would have accepted it more readily. Also, behavioral therapy designed to treat a disorder sometimes ignores the subtleties of the patient's gestalt. Perhaps this patient would have benefited from traditional insight-oriented psychotherapy aimed at maintaining more appropriate defenses.

Patient motivation may be influenced by the attitudes of family and significant other individuals towards the benefits of relaxation. Family members often consider the patient to be very anxious and think he or she needs to relax, but this concern may be a projection of the stress being experienced by family members themselves. Clinicians are well aware of the feelings of helplessness and hopelessness that family members endure while their loved one is experiencing the wretched side effects of treatment. Perhaps these family members are also appropriate candidates for some type of behavioral interventions.

In addition to a better understanding of patient motivation, we need more information on those patient characteristics which might be associated with the success of behavioral treatments. Most clinical and experimental work has been done with highly educated, motivated individuals. It is still unclear how intelligence, socioeconomic status, and overall psychological adjustment are related to the outcome of behavioral treatment. Studies of other diseases indicate that certain personality variables can predict success in behavioral treatment.

The ratio of cost to benefit is of special concern in the clinical application of behavioral techniques. Can we justify the time and effort they require on the part of the patient and clinician? Even if behavioral techniques were clearly shown to be effective, would the patient opt for time-consuming (and thus costly) relaxation training if the same therapeutic benefit could be obtained with antiemetics, analgesics, tranquilizers, and mood elevators? Would the side effects of drug treatment justify the difficulties associated with behavioral intervention? Whether behavioral approaches are superior to pharmacological interventions remains to be seen.

There is a strong and growing conviction that the management of medical disorders should be largely under the control of the patient with health care personnel providing appropriate input. It is premature to conclude that human self-regulation is understood or that the most powerful techniques for accomplishing self-management have been identified. However, it is safe to say that certain self-management techniques, such as relaxation training, have begun to show therapeutic promise. Further research may help to identify those patient characteristics that will predict success in specific clinical applications of behavioral techniques.

A significant feature of behavioral intervention is that it gives that patient the opportunity to do something for him or herself other than being a passive recipient of a therapeutic procedure performed by a health care provider. Learning a coping response actually reduces the patient's feelings of helplessness and anxiety. This has an important general therapeutic effect in addition to the specific effect of the learned control (decreasing nausea and vomiting) and improved coping (experiencing less stress and anxiety). This general effect is somewhat analogous to the placebo phenomenon. It is important to distinguish the specific effects of a treatment from its general, nonspecific placebo effects. This is the final pervading question that needs to be addressed in the clinical application of behavioral techniques. It would be a waste of time and effort to mount a research program to evaluate the effectiveness of a technique on the assumption that the technique is producing specific effects, if in fact nothing more than a general placebo effect is involved. The ubiquity and potency of placebo effects have been discussed by Shapiro (1978). It is the very power of this nonspecific placebo phenomenon that makes it a nuisance in behavioral medicine research and yet medically important. Much remains to be learned about how variables interrelate to produce therapeutic change.

Patricia H. Cotanch, RN, PhD, is currently an Associate Professor of Nursing and Assistant Professor of Psychiatry at Duke University Medical Center. She is also a faculty member at the Duke University Comprehensive Cancer Center. Prior to her present position she was on the faculty at the University of Pittsburgh. She has training in behavioral medicine and oncology nursing with a special interest in clinical hypnosis for adult and pediatric oncology patients. Dr. Cotanch may be contacted at 1055 School of Nursing, Duke University Medical Center, Durham, NC 27710.

RESOURCES

Altmaire, E., Ross W., & Moore, K. (1982). A pilot investigation of the psychologic function of patients with anticipatory vomiting. *Cancer, 19,* 201-203.

Bandler, R., & Grinder, J. (1976). *Frogs into Princes: Neuro-Linguistic Programming.* Moab, UT: Real People Press.

Brockopp, D. (1983). What is NLP? *American Journal of Nursing, 83,* 1012-1013.

Burish, T., & Redd, W. (1984). Behavioral approaches to reducing conditioned responses to chemotherapy in adult cancer patients. *Behavioral Medicine Update, 5,* 12-16.

Burish, T., Shartner, C., & Lyles, J. (1981). Effectiveness of multiple muscle-site EMG biofeedback and relaxation training in reducing aversiveness of cancer chemotherapy. *Biofeedback and Self-Regulation, 6,* 523-535.

Combs, A., Avilla, R., & Purkey, R. (1971). *Helping Relationships: Basic Concepts for the Helping Professions.* Boston, MA: Allyn and Bacon.

Cotanch, P. (1983). Relaxation techniques as antiemetic therapy. In J. Laszlo (Ed.), *Antiemetics and Cancer*

Chemotherapy (pp. 164-176). Baltimore: Williams and Wilkins.

Cotanch, P. (1984). Diversion therapy. *Proceedings of the Fourth National Cancer Conference, American Cancer Society* (pp. 110-113). Anaheim, CA.

Erickson, M. (1980). Hypnosis in terminal illness. In E. Rossi (Ed.), *Innovative Hypnotherapy. The Collected Papers of Milton Erickson on Hypnosis* (Vol. IV, pp. 255-261). New York: Irvington Publishers, Inc.

Hockenberry, M., & Cotanch, P. (1985). Hypnosis in children with cancer. *Nursing Clinics of North America, 20,* 105-107.

Morrow, G., & Morrell, C. (1982). Behavioral treatment for the anticipatory nausea and vomiting induced by cancer chemotherapy. *New England Journal of Medicine, 307,* 1476-1480.

Pelletier, K. (1979). Adjunctive biofeedback with cancer patients: A case presentation. In C. A. Garfield (Ed.), *Stress and Survival* (pp. 86-92). St. Louis: C. V. Mosby.

Redd, W., Andresen, G., & Minagawa, R. (1982). Hypnotic control of anticipatory emesis in patients receiving cancer chemotherapy. *Journal of Consulting and Clinical Psychology, 50,* 14-19.

Shapiro, A. (1979). Placebo effects in medicine, psychotherapy, and psychoanalysis. In A. Bergin & S. Garfield (Eds.), *Handbook of Psychotherapy and Behavior Change: Empirical Analysis* (pp. 369-410). New York: Wiley Company.

Zeltzer, L., & LeBaron, S. (1984). Behavioral intervention for children and adolescents with cancer. *Behavioral Medicine Update, 5,* 17-21.

AMBULATORY MONITORING OF CARDIOVASCULAR FUNCTION*

Paul A. Obrist

INTRODUCTION

The ambulatory monitoring of cardiovascular activity serves two functions. First, it permits one to determine whether laboratory evoked cardiovascular reactivity is a stable characteristic indicative of an individual's response to the challenges faced in everyday life. Because there are appreciable individual differences in cardiovascular reactivity observed with laboratory stressors, the question arises, particularly in regard to the more reactive subjects, as to whether they react cardiovascularly to the same quantitative degree to the life stress of daily life. If so, it is one line of evidence implicating the individual-environment interaction in the etiology of cardiovascular disease. Second, ambulatory monitoring has the potential to provide valuable diagnostic information, particularly in regard to the blood pressure (BP). It has now been shown that customary clinical evaluation of the BP (casual measurement) provides an imprecise estimate of typical waking values. This is particularly the case in individuals who are considered to have a marginally elevated BP (borderline hypertension) and for whom the decision of whether to treat is difficult to make.

*Preparation of this article was supported in part by National Institute of Health Grant HL18976. Appreciation is expressed to Dr. Michael T. Allen for critical appraisal of this manuscript and editorial assistance, and to Andrew Sherwood for his help editorially with this manuscript.

475

Since this volume is primarily concerned with practical applications in behavioral medicine, and an elevated BP is by far one of the more commonly encountered conditions, this chapter will focus on the ambulatory monitoring of BP. The discussion of BP monitoring will focus on the auscultatory technique, which uses cuff inflation and some means to detect Korotkoff (K) sounds (see Geddes, 1970 for a detailed discussion of the techniques). In clinical practice and research, the stethoscope has been the most commonly used instrument for detection of K sounds. In more current research applications, K sounds are usually transduced with a microphone. A brief description of the technology for the ambulatory monitoring of heart rate (HR) will also be offered since some may find this information of practical value. It should be noted that no other aspects of cardiovascular function are currently subject to ambulatory monitoring. Finally, a brief description of the ambulatory monitoring of plasma neurohumoral substances, particularly catecholamines, will also be provided since these provide one means to assess the influence of naturalistic stress on critical neuroendocrine substances that can influence cardiovascular function and may play an important role in the development of coronary heart disease.

AMBULATORY MONITORING OF BP--THE NECESSITY

Blood pressure is not static. This statement is no better documented than when one compares resting (particularly sleeping) values to those obtained during exercise in normotensive individuals. The difference in systolic blood pressure (SBP) can reach 50 mmHg or more and the diastolic blood pressure (DBP) difference can reach 15 mmHg (Holmgren, 1956) with the absolute levels reached during exercise clearly in the hypertensive range, for example, 176/87 (see Table 1, page 477; and Holmgren, 1956). Such data make the point that increases in BP, even to levels customarily considered hypertensive, may serve a very important metabolic function. The increased pressure is one means the cardiovascular system adjusts to insure an adequate perfusion of blood to the working muscles, usually with no pathophysiological consequences, at least with a healthy cardiovascular system. Thus, an

TABLE 1: M SBP AND DBP DURING REST (SUPINE AND SITTING) AND FOUR LEVELS OF EXERCISE (N = 20) - Holmgren, 1956

Condition	Rest Supine	Rest[1] Sit	600	Exercise 900	kpm/min 1200	1500[2]
SBP M	126	136	157	162	168	176
SD	15	14	15	17	17	17
DBP M	73	82	85	84	84	87
SD	12	9	9	11	10	11

[1] Rest sit refers to sitting on the ergometer.
[2] Values given are the means for minutes one and six of exercise.

elevation of the BP per se does not make a *prima facie* case that we are dealing with a pathological process.

However, one might propose that the elevation of the BP during exercise is not typical of the elevation of BP observed during the physically less demanding conditions of everyday life. But even under these circumstances, the BP can reach hypertensive values in clinical normotensives. This is best illustrated when the BP is measured invasively via a catheter in the radial or brachial artery. Thus during their normal daily activities (Table 2, page 478) (Bevan, Honour, & Stott, 1969; Littler, Honour, Carter, Sleight, 1975) or in controlled laboratory conditions (Table 3, page 479), individuals can be continuously measured on every cardiac cycle. Table 2 presents the mean values and range for both the waking and sleeping state, while Table 3 is derived from resting values and then the combination of resting values and stress evoked values, again presenting the mean and range. The data in Table 2 are derived primarily from middle aged males, while those in Table 3 are from medical and graduate students all less than 25 years of age. The range of values is appreciable with almost every individual evidencing hypertensive values at some time. The range was so large in eight normotensive subjects (including the first four of Table 1) that the authors concluded that

> The most illuminating results relate to the range of variation and the effects of common activities. The range in each subject was huge, despite the

TABLE 2: AVERAGE WAKING AND SLEEPING VALUES AND RANGE OF VARIABILITY (± 2 SD) IN EACH OF 10 NORMOTENSIVES - (Derived from Bevan et al., 1969 and Littler et al., 1975)[1]

S #	Waking				Sleep			
	M SBP	±2 SD	M DBP	±2 SD	M SBP	±2 SD	M DBP	±2 SD
1	110	74–146	77	41–113	79	61–97	55	47–63
2	153[2]	109–197	92	58–126	126	108–144	77	63–91
3	109	73–145	54	38–70	72	50–94	39	23–55
4	118	90–146	67	47–87	91	25–157	55	11–99
5	108	80–136	60	44–86	86	70–102	45	33–57
6	136	100–172	73	47–99	102	88–116	53	41–65
7	123	101–145	92	64–120	100	84–116	78	62–94
8	123	97–149	72	54–90	99	87–111	56	48–64
9	132	102–162	78	56–100	110	92–128	63	53–73
10	132	112–152	84	90–98	111	103–119	75	67–83
M	124	±30	75	±24	98	±20	60	±16

[1]Subjects 1-4 are from Bevan et al., 1969 and 6-10 from Littler et al., 1975.

[2]While the average waking BP in this subject was in the usually accepted hypertensive range, this subject was reported to be clinically normotensive.

absence of activity that was in any way out of the ordinary...Considering 150 mmHg systolic pressure as a popular division, every subject was hypertensive at some time. (Bevan et al., 1969, p. 343)

The important point of these data is that the reactivity of the BP is appreciable even among normotensive individuals, and like the reactivity of the BP during exercise, can be uninformative as to whether we are dealing with hypertension (see Obrist, 1981; Obrist et al., 1986 for a discussion of some working hypotheses concerning stress-induced cardiovascular reactivity and the etiology of hypertension).

However, even these data, like those derived from exercise, could be considered atypical since they were not obtained under the customary conditions used for clinical

478

evaluation. There are data, however, indicating that the casual clinical pressure may overestimate the more customary pressure that some individuals encounter in everyday life, and that it is a reflection of the conditions of measurement. There is a long history of such studies but their significance is only beginning to have an impact, particularly with the advent of ambulatory monitoring. The following reviews highlights from just a few of the numerous studies.

TABLE 3: **LABORATORY SYSTOLIC AND DIASTOLIC BLOOD PRESSURES OBTAINED WITH A RADIAL ARTERY CATHETER DURING REST AND SEVERAL TYPES OF STRESSORS**

Note: Subjects are young adult males, all but one considered normotensive by casual evaluation. (Unpublished data)

		Rest				Rest and Stress			
		SBP		DBP		SBP		DBP	
		M	±2SD	M	±2SD	M	±2SD	M	±2SD
Study 1 S#									
	1	129	117-141	70	74-76	141	116-166	75	60-90
	2	97	86-108	54	48-60	116	84-148	72	43-101
	3	126	118-134	74	65-83	126	116-136	77	67-87
	4	117	104-130	65	55-75	125	103-147	72	55-89
	5	142	131-153	85	75-95	153	133-173	90	77-103
	6	140	127-153	80	69-91	135	117-153	78	66-90
	7	121	116-126	67	62-72	133	102-164	73	51-95
	8	145	137-153	75	65-85	140*	131-149	82*	71-93
	9	123*	111-135	69	61-77	129*	115-143	72*	63-81
	10	124	117-131	70	64-76	131*	122-140	77*	69-85
	11	133	125-141	62	54-70	135*	121-149	72*	60-84
	12	125	118-132	65	59-71	132*	101-163	78*	55-101
Study 2 S#									
	1	137	118-156	70	60-80	148	118-178	73	51-95
	2	130	123-137	64	58-70	146	113-179	70	47-93
	3	146	126-166	72	60-84	153	107-199	73	57-89
	4	156	146-166	78	68-88	165	129-201	78	58-98
	5	155	138-172	74	62-86	172	137-207	81	59-103
	6	122	107-137	50	52-66	143	104-182	62	44-78
	7	131	110-152	63	47-79	141	115-167	68	50-86
	8	133	118-148	75	68-82	158	126-190	84	65-103
	9	129	119-139	75	69-81	138	115-161	77	60-94
Median range		22		16		49		35	

*Recorded following beta-adrenergic blockade.

First, situational influences on casual or resting BP can be appreciable in normotensive populations. For example, medical students who were requested to come to a laboratory for a blood pressure determination without explanation and who lacked familiarity with the physical surroundings had an average resting value of 129/78 mmHg (vs. 117/70 mmHg in their student health records). On the other hand, those first invited to come to the laboratory for a tour (acclimated to the surroundings) and then given a blood pressure evaluation, averaged 112/67 mmHg (vs. 119/71 mmHg in their student health records) (Ostfeld & Shekelle, 1967). We (Light & Obrist, 1980; Obrist, 1981; Obrist et al., 1983; Obrist & Light, in press) have seen an influence of both familiarity and expectation on baseline values in the "normotensive" young (18- to 20-year old) study subjects used in our studies. For the past several years, we have been obtaining two types of baselines. One is taken while subjects rest on their first visit to the laboratory and just before they are exposed to some procedure, such as a shock-avoidance task. The second is obtained usually 1 to 2 weeks later, when the subjects come to the lab on two occasions to rest for 15 to 30 minutes. The subjects are explicitly informed that they will not be exposed to any other laboratory procedure. In two studies involving 138 subjects, the resting values for SBP averaged 8 mmHg higher on the stress day than on the no-stress days (M = 132 vs. 124 mmHg), but the magnitude of the difference varied among subjects. A total of 21 subjects (15%) demonstrated an elevation of 20 mmHg or more in SBP while resting on the stress day, as compared to their resting values on the no-stress day. On the other hand, 24 with low initial pressures (17%) showed no difference between these resting conditions. It might be noted that these two extreme groups show comparable levels of SBP on the follow-up or the no-stress baseline, indicating that the effects of the novelty of the situation and the anticipation of the procedures on the stress day baseline elevates the SBP in the one subgroup but not the other. Thus, not only does the social milieu have an influence on resting values for SBP, but it varies among individuals, being very appreciable in some and almost nonexistent in others.

Recently we (Obrist, Light, James, & Strogatz, in press) attempted to duplicate the manner the casual blood pressure is taken clinically when young adult volunteers first come to the lab. Blood pressures were based on chart

480

recordings of cuff pressure and K-sounds while simultaneously a technician went through the gestures of measuring the BP with a stethoscope for a total of three readings. Then, resting measures were taken in the manner just described where no person is present; that is, a resting value was obtained just before exposure to the laboratory procedures and again several days later when no stressors were anticipated. Subjects who had the highest initial stethoscopic values (i.e., >135 mmHg SBP and >75 mmHg DBP) evidenced decreases of 11 mmHg SBP and 9 mmHg DBP by the second day. Those subjects with stethoscopic values less than 135 and 75 evidenced either no change or slight increases in BP on the second day. If we had used a SBP of 140 mmHg or greater as a cutoff, a value commonly used to designate borderline hypertension, 27 of 183 volunteers would have been considered borderline hypertensive from the stethoscopic evaluation, but only 13 by the second day baseline (resting) value.

The lability of blood pressure and its sensitivity to individuals' surroundings is not unique to normotensives but is evidenced by hypertensives as well. For example, Surwit and Shapiro (1977) recruited 24 individuals for a behavioral treatment study who, on the basis of their clinical records, would have been considered hypertensive. Prior to any treatment, they were given a physical exam and then 2 days of no-treatment baseline sessions, apparently to acclimate them to conditions. It was observed that the mean BP from their clinical records was 156/94 mmHg, and from the physical exam, 165/103 mmHg. However, by the beginning of the second baseline session, the mean BP values had dropped to 142/87 mmHg. By the end of the second baseline session, the subjects' SBP averaged 134 mmHg. Diastolic values were not reported at this time, but such a systolic value indicates that half the subjects would no longer be considered hypertensive, using the 140 mmHg value as a cutoff. Thus, in comparison with the data from their clinical records and the pre-experimental physical exam, the decrease in the subjects' BP was appreciable, but it must be considered to reflect almost exclusively an acclimatization effect.

Somewhat comparable effects have been observed in young adult borderline hypertensives (M = 25 years) in comparison with normotensives (Julius et al., 1974). In the Julius et al. study BP was evaluated against home, self-administered values. Individuals were considered borderline hypertensives (N = 112) if they had one of the three casual readings either above 140 mmHg SBP or 90 mmHg DBP, as well as one SBP and DBP below these two values. They were considered normotensive (N = 49) if all three casual readings were below these levels. All subjects took home readings twice each day (once in the morning and once before supper) on each of 7 days for a total of 14 readings in all. The normotensives evidence little difference in mean pressure (122/73 casual vs. 121/76 home). The borderline hypertensives evidenced an appreciable reduction in home pressures particularly for SBP (146/88 casual vs. 131/84 home). In comparison to normotensives, 28% of the borderline hypertensives had home readings not exceeding one standard deviation of the mean of the normotensive group. These individuals were considered normal. Another 42% had average home values within one to two standard deviations of the normotensive mean. These values were considered "marginally" elevated pressures. The remaining 30% had home readings greater than two standard deviations above the normotensive mean and were considered to have "high" pressure. Thus, there is considerable overlap among groups, particularly in regard to home readings, with only approximately one-third of the individuals initially considered as borderline hypertensives demonstrating elevated average values at home.

Using a technique developed by Smirk (1973) to acclimate individuals to the taking of the BP, Caldwell (Caldwell, Schork, & Aiken, 1978) in a large sample (N = 471) reported a casual value of 192/111 but an acclimated value of 146/89. Similar effects were observed when the casual BP was compared to direct (invasive) recordings in hypertensive patients when hospitalized but carrying on normal hospital routines. One study (Watson, Stallard, Flinn, & Littler, 1980), for example, found an average casual value in 24 hypertensives of 164/103, but an average hospitalized value of 143/90. Likewise, Rowlands (Rowlands et al., 1982) reported a casual average of 160/101 but a hospitalized average of 136/86 in 32 diagnosed hypertensives. Finally, the variability of the BP appears to increase as its level increases. This was most definitely ascertained with continuous invasive 24 hour measurement of BP in hospitalized normotensives (N = 22), mild hypertensives (N = 26), and severe hypertensives (N = 41) (Mancia, 1983; Mancia et al., 1983). Based upon readings during each half hour of the 24 hour recording period, the standard deviations for SBP were ±9.5 for normotensives, 11.3 for mild hypertensives, and 12.2 for severe hypertensives. They were somewhat less for DBP. This amount of variability suggests that single determinations of the BP could be as much as 20 mmHg too high or too low.

Another problem one faces when using the auscultatory (cuff) method is that inflation of the cuff itself is a very discernible signal and could act either to increase or decrease the BP depending on the circumstances and strategies an individual uses during the measurement. That is, the BP might be expected to decrease in those individuals trained to relax (Patel, 1977) but increase in those who are made apprehensive by the measurement. There is only one study I am aware of (Mancia, 1983; Mancia & Zanchetti, 1983) that directly examined this possibility. In 48 hospitalized normotensives and hypertensives with indwelling catheters, the BP was evaluated by the auscultatory technique after a stable baseline was achieved. The initial determination increased the SBP by an average of 27 mmHg and the DBP by 15 mmHg, with the magnitude of the increase unrelated to baseline. A second determination taken some hours later resulted in comparable increases. However, repeated determinations of the BP taken 5 minutes apart resulted in an appreciable attenuation of the BP change but significant increases that were still appreciable in some individuals. Interestingly, permitting a nurse instead of a physician to take the BP resulted in a smaller increase on the initial determination.

Another line of evidence that questions the validity of the usual casual measurement of the BP for diagnostic purposes originates from some recent treatment studies with mild hypertensives. One such study (Reader, 1983) used a placebo control and selected patients who evidenced a DBP of 95-110 derived from two readings on each of two occasions. Over 3000 individuals were evaluated for a period of up to 6 years. Of the 1548 controls for which there were follow-up data covering at least a 2.4 year period, the average DBP upon the last assessment was <85 mmHg in 128 (8%), between 85-89 mmHg in 383 (25%), and between 90-94 mmHg in 474 (31%). Keep in mind that all subjects had a DBP of 95 mmHg or greater upon initial screening. These data led the investigators to conclude with respect to the diagnosis of mild hypertension that when the diagnosis was made on the mean of four readings over two visits [this was the screening], half of the patients so diagnosed had DBP below 95 mmHg 3 years later. Clearly, patients suspected of having mild hypertension require repeated evaluation before beginning drug therapy. (Management Committee, 1982, p. 190)

Engel and colleagues (Engel, Gaarder, & Glasgow, 1981) used an extensive baseline period (4-5 weeks) with patients taking their own pressure (three readings three times a day) while their pressure was taken professionally once a week. They noted a small but progressive decrease in BP with respect to the initial casual values. While this procedure provides an adequate number of BP readings to achieve a baseline, the use of self-measurement precludes determining whether BP was elevated or decreased at other times. In addition, any effects of the behavioral treatment, which were significant (Glasgow, Gaarder, & Engel, 1982) may have been unique to having patients taking their own pressure. As will be seen, ambulatory monitoring can minimize this problem to some extent since the individual does neither initiate nor actually take a reading.

AMBULATORY MONITORING-- BACKGROUND AND CURRENT USAGE

One of the first of the ambulatory monitoring evaluations was carried out by Sokolow and colleagues (Sokolow, Werdegar, Perloff, Cowan, & Brenenstuhl, 1970). Later Werdegar, Sokolow, and Perloff (1968) evaluated casual BP values in diagnosed hypertensives against values obtained during everyday life events (field values). The latter study involved using a semiautomated portable device where blood pressure was evaluated every 30 minutes for up to 48 hours during everyday waking activities. While the individual initiated each measurement by inflating an occlusion cuff, cuff pressure and K sounds were automatically recorded for later quantification. Such a procedure minimizes patients' underestimation of their actual blood pressure values in the reading of the sphygmomanometer or detection of K sounds. In the 124 individuals evaluated in this matter, the average casual pressure was 170/104, while the field values averaged 156/94. More pointedly, Sokolow notes that "these findings are the more impressive when one considers that the casual readings were taken while the patients were at rest; the recorder pressures [referring to the non-clinical readings] were taken during the course of ordinary activity" (Sokolow et al., 1970, p. 16). Nonetheless, these field values still characterize the sample of subjects as hypertensive. However, two other aspects of the field data should be considered which are more informative than these average values. First, an evaluation of the five lowest and five highest blood pressure values obtained on each individual indicates a great variability among readings and a substantial number that are in the normotensive range. The five highest values averaged 180/110, the five lowest averaged 134/80. Second, it is noted (Werdegar et al., 1968) that a substantial number of subjects had average field BP values that would be considered normotensive, or at most, mildly elevated. For example, 28 of the subjects had average SBP values <140 mmHg, with 11 of these averaging 130 mmHg or less. Forty-four individuals had average DBP values less than 90 mmHg with 19 averaging less than 80 mmHg. If one uses a 140/90 mmHg criterion as a dividing line between normotension and hypertension, then upwards of 25% of this sample of individuals demonstrate average normotensive BP values under naturalistic conditions. Sokolow et al. (1970) also noted that the DBP values derived from field monitoring were better predictors of hypertensive complications than casual values, that is, the lower the field values, regardless of the casual value, the fewer the complications. Subsequently, Sokolow and his co-workers (Perloff, Sokolow, & Cowan, 1983) evaluated clinical status on over 1000 patients on whom they obtained ambulatory pressures between 1962-1976 and found that ambulatory values, particularly in younger individuals who were considered mild hypertensives, were the best predictors of mortality and morbidity.

There is a striking parallel between the Sokolow studies and a recent series of studies reported by a team of investigators at the Cornell Medical School. These studies also compared casual BP values to those obtained under field conditions but used a completely automated system to record field pressures. At fixed time intervals, commonly every 15 minutes, the occlusion cuff automatically inflated then deflated, with cuff pressures and K sounds processed and recorded on a microcomputer. After the recording session, the data were analyzed. These studies represent an improvement on the Sokolow studies in several respects. In addition to using a completely automated BP monitor, field values were evaluated both at work and in the confines of the home, while subjects were awake and while they slept. Also, hypertensives were identified, on the basis of casual BP, as presenting borderline hypertension (marginally elevated BP) or established hypertension. Individuals considered clinically normotensives were also evaluated.

In one study, Pickering, Harshfield, Kleinert, Blank, and Laragh (1982) found that casual BP values were comparable to those observed in the working environment, but usually higher than those observed in subjects while awake at home regardless of diagnostic classification. However, field values were more appreciably correlated with casual pressure in normotensives and fixed hypertensives than borderline hypertensives, indicating that the casual BP was a poorer predictor of BP values observed under naturalistic conditions in the borderline group. This conclusion was further reinforced in two additional studies. Harshfield, Pickering, Kleinert, Blank, and Laragh (1982) evaluated 60 borderline (mild) hypertensives and found that 25% had SBP less than 140 mmHg both at work and home even though all had casual values greater than 140 mmHg. Focusing specifically on 22 of 60 subjects with a casual DBP between 90-104, Harshfield et al. (1982) also reported that 13 had averaged field values <90, and seven averaged <85. In a third study (Pickering, Harshfield, Kleinert, & Laragh, 1982) 30 hypertensives were subdivided into two subgroups, borderline and established hypertensives, on the basis of having a casual DBP of 95 mmHg or more (established) or less than 95 (borderline). Each individual then had 30 awake home determinations of blood pressure taken. The borderline group (N = 17) showed an appreciable reduction of pressure at home (i.e., from an average of 150/92) to approximately 130/85. Little difference between casual and home values was found among the 13 established hypertensives. Reductions of BP between home and clinic using the automated BP monitor were found in most borderline hypertensives (14 of 17 SBP, 16 of 17 DBP). Many fewer established hypertensives evidenced significant reductions between these conditions (5 of 13 SBP, 8 of 13 DBP).

The Cornell investigators (Devereux et al., 1983) also evaluated the relationship between left ventricular hypertrophy (LVH) (a potential consequence of hypertension) and casual and field BP values. They observed in a sample of 81 diagnosed hypertensives that the most appreciable degree of co-variation (correlation) between BP and LVH was obtained from the BP values observed in the working environment, in contrast to either casual or home values. One can conclude that the stress of the working environment and its influence on BP control was of paramount importance with respect to one hypertensive complication.

In summary, the casual pressure as obtained clinically has been found to be appreciably influenced by situational factors and may or may not be predictive of more commonly encountered BP values observed in everyday life, and most importantly be related in hypertensive populations to one potential complication of hypertension.

It should be noted that the casual BP has been found to be related to hypertensive consequences. Some have even recommended that efforts to achieve a true basal BP be dropped because the casual BP is as effective a predictor (Caldwell et al., 1978). Also, the casual DBP (mean of three readings) has been found to be related to succeeding levels of the casual BP over an 8 year span, suggesting that the casual BP is a fairly stable event (Soucheck, Stamler, Dyer, Paul, & Lepper, 1979). Finally, all treatment evaluation projects, including the recent NIH Hypertension Detection and Follow-Up Program (HDFP) (Langford, 1983) have used the casual pressure, usually basing their diagnostic classification on the mean of two or more readings taken on two occasions. These studies typically report some benefit of pharmacological intervention in terms of end points like death or morbidity associated with known hypertension complications even in individuals considered to be mild hypertensive (e.g., DBP 95-110). While these various observations testify to the prognostic value of the casual BP, I do not consider them to contraindicate the use of BP values derived from field sampling (ambulatory monitoring) for a number of reasons. The data already reviewed concerning the instability of the casual pressure in mild hypertensives (Devereux et al., 1983; Harshfield et al., 1982; Pickering, Harshfield, Kleinert, Blank, & Laragh, 1982; Pickering, Harshfield, Kleinert, & Laragh, 1982), and the placebo effects noted in the Australian therapeutic trial in mild hypertension (Reader, 1983), are two considerations. In addition, the casual pressure is not a very powerful predictor of hypertensive complications. In the HDFP clinical trial, for example, mortality over a 25-year span was approximately 7%, with a significant, but small difference between those receiving aggressive treatment (6.4%) compared to those receiving regular treatment (7.7%). No nontreatment control was used. The Australian trials (see Management Committee, 1980, 1982) reported the incidence of clinical end points (expressed as percent of rates per 1000 person years) as 1.8% for treated versus 2.6% for untreated. While it is likely that continuation of the trials would have increased the number of end points, one can not help but wonder whether the accuracy of prediction would improve if ambulatory monitoring had been utilized. Perhaps most important is a recommendation from the HDFP trial that it "demonstrated unequivocally that effective treatment could prolong life in both mild and borderline hypertension and...sufficient data have been accumulated to justify reduction of blood pressure in all patients with diastolic pressures above 80 mmHg" (Fries, 1982, p. 306). The implications of this conclusion, as Fries has pointed out, are quantitatively enormous. At least 40 million Americans would meet the criterion for mild hypertension. Costs for pharmacologic intervention would be very high, and the potential side effects and their costs could be significant.

It is likely these clinical trials are not the last word, as Fries (1982, p. 309) suggested in a critique of the HDFP trial where he concluded:

> In view of the uncertainties [referring to the design of the study and the less than robust effects or even negative results of other clinical trials] we may be doing more harm than good by giving lifelong drug treatment to patients with borderline or mild hypertension. However, because of the possibility of benefit, even though it is unproved, a compromise position...may be most appropriate. Patients with diastolic pressures of 90-99 mmHg...are treated or not according to the number of risk factors present.

These risks include smoking, left ventricular hypertrophy, hypercholesterolemia, and glucose intolerance (see Kannel, 1977 for data from the Framingham study which involved an 18 year follow-up). Fries also cited the number of untreated (control) mild hypertensives in the Australian clinical trial whose DBP fell below 95 mmHg (data previously cited in this chapter) and concluded, "This experience demonstrates the wisdom of waiting for an extended period before initiating antihypertensive-drug treatment in mild hypertension" (1982, p. 309). Might I suggest that data from ambulatory monitoring, as in the Cornell studies, should be a factor in the diagnostic decision. Although the use of ambulatory monitoring of the BP as a diagnostic and prognostic tool is not as extensive as the casual BP, such information would not go unheeded if an individual consistently demonstrated elevated BP in the course of everyday life or on the contrary evidenced consistently normotensive levels under such conditions.

This point is reinforced, particularly the use of ambulatory monitoring of mild hypertensives, by Sokolow's recent follow-up study (Perloff et al., 1983). In response to the recommendation that mild hypertensives be treated pharmacologically, these investigators conclude that

> drug treatment is neither harmless nor inexpensive, and the cost of medical manpower necessary for continued and regular supervision of the millions of mild hypertensive patients in this country is considerable. From a public health and economic point of view, therefore, a means for discriminating among patients with mild hypertension, those who are at increased risk, and those who require aggressive treatment to prevent morbidity and mortality from patients at low risks, in whom immediate drug treatment is not clearly beneficial, provides a useful tool for the clinician in the treatment of the individual patient. Our results suggest that ABP [ambulatory blood pressure monitoring] measurements may be such a tool. (pp. 2797-2798)

Three other points need to be made. First, although the clinical trial data cited in this chapter relied primarily on the DBP, the SBP should not be ignored. According to Kannel (1977, p. 909),

> Examination of the association of clinical cardiovascular events with systolic versus diastolic

pressure reveals little to suggest a greater role for diastolic pressure. Both systolic and diastolic together, the mean arterial pressure, the pulse pressure and tension-time index discriminate cardiovascular disease no better than systolic pressure alone.

Second, ambulatory monitoring has not only the potential for facilitating the diagnostic process, but offers a means to evaluate the effectiveness of any form of treatment. For example, it would be particularly well suited to determine whether the influence of any form of occupational or interpersonal stress on the BP is attenuated by whatever form of treatment is used.

Third, the primary data cited in this discussion is derived from hypertension research, especially studies on pharmacological intervention. However, ambulatory monitoring of BP has equal potential for more behaviorally oriented research such as we are performing (see Obrist & Light, in press) as well as the diagnosis and behavioral interventions in the treatment of hypertension. A recent critical review of this work has been prepared by D. Johnston (in press).

AMBULATORY MONITORING OF BP--THE TECHNOLOGY

The earlier device used by Sokolow (Sokolow et al., 1970) was semiautomated in that the individual had to inflate the cuff at designated times. One potential disadvantage to this technique was allowing the subject to initiate the reading. This requires the individual to stop all ongoing activities and permits latitude as to when a reading will be taken. The latter presents a problem in that individuals concerned about their BP may select periods when they feel their BP is low, that is, when minimally stressed or they prepare themselves in other ways for the measurement, all of which could act to underestimate their BP. For example, we (Light & Obrist, 1980) had subjects take their BP at home during periods of high or low stress. The average at home pressures were found to correspond to those obtained in the laboratory once acclimated to conditions and expecting no stressful experiences. These low BP values obtained from self-administered measurements led us to conclude that these subjects, in spite of instructions, took their BP when minimally stressed. However, a recently published study by Kleinert (Kleinert et al., 1984) found a good correspondence between home self-administered and ambulatory BP values in a hypertensive population. Thus, self-administered values may have some merit depending on the population and circumstances. Since completely automated ambulatory monitors provide measurements at investigator-designated intervals, potential problems of self-administered measurements are avoided. In the remainder of this section, I shall briefly describe three of the completely automated commercial units now available, their accuracy, problems encountered, and close with a description of the unit we have developed which will be available commercially by 1985 from Eutectics Electronics, Raleigh, NC.

All commercially available units have in common a battery operated inflation system and a deflation mode which is pre-set as to bleed the cuff at between 2-4 mmHg per second. They differ somewhat in the manner the BP is determined. Del-Mar Avionics (Irvine, California) developed the first system and now has available two models (Harshfield, Pickering, Blank, & Laragh, 1983). The first model stores K sound and cuff pressure on a self-contained Holter tape. After the recording session the tape is read by an Avionics trend analyzer which among other things provides a digital read out of the BP. A second and newer model obviates the need for a trend analyzer, which is expensive, and uses a solid state memory which can be interfaced with a number of different computers and printers. This provides an appreciable monetary saving. A second system, also evaluated by Harshfield and colleagues (Harshfield et al., 1983) and Dembroski (Dembroski & MacDougall, 1984) was developed by Instruments for Cardiac Research (The VitaStat, Terra-Verde, Florida) and apparently does not differ in principle from the second Avionics unit except that if K sounds are not detectable, it switches from the auscultatory method to the oscillometric method. The latter is of questionable value. While providing reasonably accurate estimates of mean arterial pressure (the average arterial pressure on any given cardiac cycle), the systolic and diastolic pressures must be derived (Geddes, 1984) and are imprecise. While the mean pressure carries significant physiological information, it is not a commonly used index of pressure, at least clinically. A third system referred to as the BP-24 (Clinical Data Brookline, Massachusetts) (Stein, Peterson, & Lee, 1983) is similar to the previous systems except that K sounds and cuff pressure are recorded on an FM cassette tape then played back on an optical oscillograph. BP is read by visual analysis of the oscillographic record. This system has the disadvantage that the BP values are not automatically derived from a microprocessor or Holter tape. However, it does have the distinct advantage of providing the user with the ability to edit each measurement of the BP, accepting those with an obvious onset (SBP) and offset (DBP) of K sounds. The other units rely on the hardware and software of the systems to detect onset and offset of K sounds which can lead to appreciable errors. The Avionics unit does have some built-in software features that reject artifactual readings, but this is at best limited and the criteria for rejecting or accepting a given measurement appear a bit arbitrary.

All systems have been evaluated with respect to accuracy against the auscultatory method using a stethoscope to detect appearance and disappearance of K sounds and in one instance intra-arterial BP records (Harshfield, Pickering, & Laragh, 1979). In all instances, the ambulatory monitors provide quite accurate estimates of the BP-- both SBP and DBP. But a note of caution is warranted. With the Avionics system, and presumably other systems, it has been noted that K sounds were not detectable (and hence no BP measures) in 20% of individuals evaluated, and that in 10% to 20% of readings where K sounds are detectable, the readings are artifactual (Harshfield et al., 1983). The latter could be due in part to arm movements during cuff deflation, thus requiring the individual to immobilize the arm during cuff deflation. This is not a significant problem except during physical exertion or activities requiring use of the arm (nondominant) such as automobile driving. The loss of BP data during such occasions is likely unimportant, at least during physical exertion.

The loss of BP data due to the inability to detect K sounds is a more significant problem. It can be due to such factors as obesity, weak brachial pulses, and large biceps muscles. One recent development that may minimize this problem is the development of a foil electric transducer, in contrast to the typical piezoelectric microphone (West, Busch-Vishniac, Harshfield, & Pickering, 1983). This one published study indicates that the foil transducer detected K sounds in 11 of 12 subjects on whom a piezoelectric microphone failed, using the

Avionics system. More extensive evaluation of this foil transducer is needed but it represents a potential methodological breakthrough since the weakest link in the measurement of the BP with the auscultatory method is the detection of the onset and offset of K sounds, even when using a stethoscope.

There is one other manner in which the detection of K sounds can be improved and in turn improve the accuracy of BP readings. This is to record on tape the K sounds and cuff pressure such as used in the BP-24 (Stein et al., 1983). This is a feature we have incorporated in our own laboratory developed, automated-portable monitor. We also use a microprocessor to detect onset and offset of K sounds and the cuff pressure at each point. The taped signal is a back-up system and the K sounds and cuff pressure are recorded independently of the microprocessor. There are several advantages of the tape system. First, we routinely check the quality of the K sounds when initially preparing a subject for field recording. This can be done by taking BP measurements in the laboratory and observing the amplitudes of the K sounds on a polygraph or oscilloscope. If the amplitude is small and hard to discern from any background noise, we reposition the microphone (piezoelectric) until the signal is clearly detectable. We have rarely found a subject in whom we could not detect a reasonable quality K sound, although our subjects are typically young adults. This procedure assures us that the tape will record a usable K sound even should the microprocessor fail, which is a more common problem. Even if development of the foil electrode minimizes the problem of K sound detection, it would still seem advisable to evaluate the quality of the signal.

The back-up tape system also provides us a means to obtain BP values should the microprocessor fail either completely or on occasions where artifact is a problem. Movement artifact that will cause the microprocessor to fail will also show up as noise on the tape system, but K sounds can still be discerned on some occasions. The disadvantage of the tape system is that it requires visual (manual) reading of the BP measures. But if these agree with microprocessor values upon initial scanning of the record, we then use the microprocessor values.

Our system has been evaluated on two separate samples of subjects ($N = 39$) on each of whom 16-20 readings were taken. I would like to summarize these results since they provide a means to illustrate the accuracy of monitoring BP with these ambulatory devices. These data were collected under laboratory conditions although this does not contraindicate their use under field conditions providing the quality of K sounds is adequate.

Our monitor is lightweight (2.3 kg) using a battery operated pump for cuff inflation, and a piezoelectric microphone to detect K sounds. Both cuff pressure and K sounds are recorded on a precision microcassette tape recorder for playback on the polygraph as well as being processed and stored in memory of a microprocessor. The BP values can be played back on a video terminal, a printer, or any serial ASC11 device. Cuff inflation and deflation as well as the timing between measurements are controlled by the microprocessor. Peak inflation pressure is initially manually set and then automatically adjusts to exceed each previous SBP value by 20 mmHg, which to our knowledge is a feature not available on commercial units. This feature minimizes over- or underinflating the cuff. Deflation rate is also adjustable but usually set at between 2-3 mmHg per second. Inflation is rapid ranging from 4-6 seconds depending on peak inflation pressure. During deflation, once cuff pressure reaches a designated point, like 50 mmHg, cuff pressure then rapidly deflates to zero so as to minimize the deflation time. Diastolic pressure below such values are likely of little clinical consequence. The time between measurements can be set at fixed intervals ranging from 1 minute to 1 hour. This interval can be set to be variable averaging any time between 2 minutes to an hour, thus minimizing when the individual expects a measurement. Up until now, we have used intervals in field studies averaging either 10 or 15 minutes which provide in the course of a 16 hour waking day between 64-80 BP readings. We see little necessity to record BP during night sleep because it provides little additional information.

The cuff and microphone are placed on the nondominant arm. During each measurement, the individual is requested to relax the arm but can continue using the other arm. When standing, the individual drops the arm to his or her side. If sitting or lying, the individual is asked to position his or her arm at the level of the heart which is usually not a problem. The arm can be supported by such things as a chair arm or pillow. In case the arm can not be relaxed, such as when driving a car or during physical activity, we usually are unable to obtain an artifact-free reading. However, this should not prove to be a common problem except with very active people.

The individual is asked to keep an activity log. This involves indicating at the end of each measurement period the time, postural position, and type of activity engaged in using one to three words such as "working at desk," omitting any information considered too personal. They are also asked to judge the stressfulness of the activity.

To determine the accuracy of SBP readings, four validation procedures were used: (a) a pulse wave transducer was placed over the radial artery to detect the presence of the first pulse wave once cuff pressure falls below SBP, a method which provides the most accurate means to evaluate SBP short of direct (invasive) measurement; (b) a stethoscope was used to detect the first K sound during deflation, the examiner being blind to microphone outputs and BP values; (c) unfiltered signals from the microphone were also recorded to insure that the filtering system was not overly attenuating the low frequency component of the K sounds; and (d) processed K sounds were displayed on the polygraph and fed into the self-contained microprocessor for automatic readings. The accuracy of DBP was evaluated by comparing both direct and filtered (microprocessor) microphone outputs with stethoscopic determinations of K sound disappearance. In previous work where BP was measured directly, we found that DBP was associated with disappearance of the high frequency component from the direct output of the microphone as judged visually.

In this evaluation, one estimate of accuracy was based on the difference for any simultaneous pair of BP measurements derived from any two methods of BP measurement. We then examined the percentage of differences that fell into three ranges. One was ±5 mmHg, a range we consider quite accurate since small calibration errors and errors in reading the polygraph records could generate differences of this magnitude (processing error). The second was the percentage within ±6 mmHg, a range which includes both processing error and small differences between methods. The third was the percentage of readings where the difference between methods equaled or exceeded 10 mmHg. Blood pressure differences between methods in this case involve a greater error due to the method of K sound detection.

A second way accuracy was evaluated was to obtain correlations between BP readings using any two techniques to evaluate K sounds. For both SBP and DBP, the correlations were obtained in two ways. One used every measurement across all subjects where the maximal potential N is the number of subjects times the number of readings taken on each individual. The second used the mean of all SBP and DBP for each subject as derived by each method of K sound detection. In this case the maximum potential N is the number of subjects used in each evaluation.

The evaluation of each system with respect to magnitude of differences with both SBP and DBP, when derived with any two methods of K sound evaluation, reveals reasonably good agreement among methods. SBP derived from the detection of the presence of the first pulse at the radial artery corresponded closely with values derived from the output of the piezoelectric microphone. The direct unfiltered microphone output was within ±5 mmHg 88% and within ±9 mmHg 95% of the time. Comparable degrees of accuracy were found with the microprocessor processed values. Stethoscopic detection of K sounds as compared to either of the other three methods slightly underestimated SBP, but with reference to SBP values derived from the detection of the first radial pulse, 77% of all comparisons were within ±5 mmHg and 90% within ±9 mmHg. Stethoscopically derived DBP values corresponded with microphone direct and processed DBP within ±5 mmHg on 77% and ±9 mmHg on 90% of all readings.

The correlations between SBP derived with any of the four methods of SBP derivation are all +.90 or higher, either using all data points or the subject means. Mean BP values correspond quite closely although the stethoscopically derived values read 2-5 mmHg below SBP values derived by the other methods. With DBP, the correlations with stethoscopic as compared to microphone derived values (direct or processed) tend to be slightly lower, but reveal a reasonable degree of reliability, particularly when using average data from each individual (r = +.88). Mean DBP readings derived from each of the three methods of K sound detection correspond quite closely although stethoscopic values tended to be slightly higher than microphone-derived values. In comparisons between direct and processed K sounds, the BP values all co-vary appreciably, with all r values greater than +.90, indicating that the processed values correspond quite well with visual inspection of K sound offset and onset. Therefore, this system provides reasonably consistent estimates of SBP and DBP, regardless of the method used to derive the BP.

When the stethoscopic SBP values exceeded values derived by other techniques by 9 mmHg, the stethoscope values tended to be lower, an effect Geddes (1970) reported with respect to stethoscopic versus direct recording of SBP. Stethoscopically derived values (disappearance) of DBP tended to read slightly higher than microphone-derived values and automatic processed values which evidenced similar levels. Geddes (1970) has also reported a similar discrepancy with stethoscopic versus direct DBP values. In our earlier unpublished study of eight subjects (335 readings) comparing direct radial DBP against cuff pressures derived from visual inspection of microphone detected K sounds, 77% of the two readings were within ±5 mmHg and 94% within ±9 mmHg. An inspection of individual differences with regard to the magnitude of the error reveals that the largest discrepancies were usually confined to certain subjects. Such individuals usually had either faint K sounds when evaluated stethoscopically or weak microphone outputs. The latter can usually be corrected by moving the microphone nearer to the brachial artery.

In the light of the discrepancy we find in some subjects, particularly with DBP, we have decided to evaluate the portable BP monitor against direct readings of radial pressure. Data from this and previous studies should provide us a means to express our expected accuracy or error of measurement (based on the quality of K sounds) for a given individual.

Another two features of this automated system should be emphasized. The software for the detection of K sounds has been developed which is far more sophisticated than anything else available. Also built into the software is a means to summarize the data. However, I can not recommend this unit until such time as the validating studies are completed which we hope will be within 1-2 months and written up for all potential users.

Finally, it should be underscored that all portable-automated devices rely on cuff inflation, a most discernible signal. We do not know the extent the BP is influenced by each measurement either because the measurement has a startle value and associated effects which could momentarily elevate the BP or because measurement may result in cessation of ongoing activities which might decrease the BP. It is our hope that most individuals acclimate to the procedure but the only way to ascertain the significance of this problem is to take cuff pressures under laboratory conditions while simultaneously and continuously measuring intra-arterial pressure.

Even if cuff pressures accurately depict the BP at the point of measurement we are only sampling the BP on a limited number of cardiac cycles. For example, even if we sample every 10 minutes, there are only six measurements per hour during a period where the heart has beat between 3000-7200 times, depending on the heart rate. There is one study (diRienzo, Grassi, Pedotti, & Mancia, 1983) that indicates that such infrequent sampling does provide a fairly good estimate of existing levels of BP; however, these investigators did not use a cuff system. Rather they measured BP invasively and continuously over a 24 hour period in 20 nonbedridden hospitalized hypertensives. They then sampled the BP on one cardiac cycle every 5, 10, 15, 30, and 60 minutes and then compared the mean values and standard deviations derived from each sampling period against the mean and standard deviation for the entire 24 hour period using all cardiac cycles. Mean BP and the standard deviations derived from sampling at 5, 10, and 15 minute intervals closely approximated those obtained from all 24 hours. At longer intervals, the mean values did not deviate appreciably from the 24 hour continuous mean (except for sampling every 60 minutes) but the standard deviations began to deviate appreciably, particularly in some individuals. Thus sampling in the range of every 5-15 minutes would appear to provide reasonably accurate estimates of the BP variations over the course of a day. Since these investigators did not use a cuff system, one can not ascertain any influence of cuff inflation on BP during each measurement. Finally, Drayer (Drayer, Weber, & DeYoung, 1983) compared ambulatory BP values obtained every 7.5 minutes for a 2 hour period and then for a 24 hour period and found very good correspondence between 2 and 24 hour determinations. This suggests that ambulatory monitoring need not encompass a 24 hour time span.

In summary, there are now available several portable fully automatic BP monitoring systems. All have proven accurate, when evaluated under laboratory conditions though an appreciable amount of data is lost. We have had fewer problems with lost data with our system where we have back-up facilities to monitor K sounds. Also, precautions are used in placing the K sound transducer. With the recent advent of the foil electric transducer, data loss may be minimized. While there are still unresolved problems, these systems are to be recommended providing the user is aware of their limitations.

AMBULATORY HEART RATE MONITORING

Ambulatory monitoring of the electrocardiogram (EKG) has a long history particularly for the assessment of electrical instability in damaged hearts. This use is largely unimportant in behavioral medicine unless one is dealing with cardiac patients and evaluating situational influences on the EKG. Ambulatory monitoring of heart rate (HR), on the other hand, has potential in behavioral research endeavors. There are two applications. One is assessing the degree HR reactivity generalizes from laboratory to naturalistic stressors. We have had a limited experience with this use (Obrist & Light, in press). In one pilot study for example, subjects who had been first evaluated in the laboratory were then evaluated under two field conditions--attending class (low stress) and taking an exam (high stress). Individuals who evidenced greater HR reactivity in the laboratory, also evidenced higher levels of HR during the exam than did individuals who evidence lesser degrees of HR reactivity in the laboratory. The two subgroups on the other hand evidenced comparable levels of HR while attending class. Another potential and more clinical application is to monitor HR under field conditions to index possible changes in emotional state (Fowles, 1982) to realistic stressors like public speaking or phobias, particularly to assess the effectiveness of any kind of therapeutic intervention. I am somewhat cautious at recommending this application because HR in our experience does not seem to bear a very robust relationship to affective states (Obrist, 1981). Some individuals regardless of the nature of stressor and even though apparently experiencing the stress as determined by behavioral evaluations, hardly change their HR while others evidence very appreciable changes (also see Elliott, 1974; Obrist, Light, & Hastrup, 1982). One might get around these inexplicable individual differences by using each subject as its own control (an

499

intraindividual analyses) and assess pre-post treatment changes, providing they evidence some HR change pre-treatment.

HEART RATE MONITORING--TECHNOLOGY

The technology for ambulatory monitoring is readily available and accurate but does involve some costs, particularly for computer processing of the data. We use an Oxford Series 4.24 (Oxford Electronic Instruments Limited, Abingdon Oxon OX14 1BZ England) recorder. It is lightweight (1 lb), can be worn on the belt, and can continuously monitor HR for up to 24 hours. There are four channels, one of which is used as an event or timing channel, which provides a mean to time lock HR to events of the day. A problem is that an enormous amount of data can be generated (depending on how long one records) since every cardiac cycle is recorded. We have handled this through our Digital Equipment Corporation PDP 11/34 laboratory computer. The tape is first processed by playing it back through the Oxford PB-2 replay unit which presents the computer a voltage with each R-wave of the EKG. The computer is programmed to time the interval between succeeding R-waves and then over any number of designated cardiac cycles or time periods to provide an average HR. A time or event signal is presented along with the output of the average HR. There are likely less expensive ways to process such data. In any case the technology is available and should not in principal provide any obstacle for the ambulatory monitoring of HR. One note of caution--EKG electrode placement is important particularly if the individual is to be monitored during physical activity. An electrode placement between the upper sternum and left rib cage, with a ground placed midline near the diaphragm, we find minimizes movement artifact.

Finally, it might be noted that most of the commercially available ambulatory BP monitors either provide HR directly or derived HR from the K sounds. In either case, the HR is sampled during deflation and when K sounds are present. Thus, HR is derived over a time span of approximately 10-25 seconds depending on how rapidly the cuff deflates, and the SBP and DBP levels. We do not consider this sampling procedure a problem.

AMBULATORY MONITORING OF BLOOD PLASMA

Venous blood provides a means to monitor a variety of hormones (and neurotransmitters) which are held to be involved in cardiovascular regulation. Two in particular have been most exhaustively studied, the adrenal hormone, epinephrine, and the adrenergic neurotransmitter, norepinephrine. Until recently the sampling of blood has usually been restricted to discrete periods representing relatively long time periods between samples. In the light of the short life of these catecholamines (2-3) minutes, it is possible that any one blood sample will have missed peak values and in effect underestimate their plasma concentration. This problem has been partially obviated by the development of the continuous withdrawal pump (Dimsdale, 1983) where new blood samples can be taken every 2-3 minutes. It has been developed for ambulatory use, being worn like a Holter monitor, but requires a technician to change blood sampling tubes (vacutainers). The advantage of such a sampling procedure is illustrated by Dimsdale (1983) where blood samples were taken at the start and 15 minutes into the course of a public speech. Plasma epinephrine peaked immediately but had returned to baseline within 15 minutes (also see Ward et al., 1983). Plasma norepinephrine on the other hand was also initially elevated but remained elevated at 15 minutes. This discrepancy between the sequence of plasma values of these two catecholamines likely reflects the fact that epinephrine is a hormone secreted by the adrenal and is particularly sensitive to the onset of stressful events such as we find with HR and BP. Plasma-norepinephrine is primarily a neurotransmitter and is significantly influenced by adrenergic activity in the musculature which involves postural influences as well as any physical exertion involved in public speaking (Folkow, DiBona, Hjemdahl, Taren, & Wallin, 1983). A final precaution one might note in the use of plasma catecholamines is that they likely have their greatest validity for intraindividual evaluation (see Obrist et al., in press). Nonetheless, catecholamines, particularly plasma epinephrine, provide the clinical investigator another means to assess adrenergic (sympathetic) activity under naturalistic conditions and in conjunction with either ambulatory BP and/or HR, provide a more complete picture of cardiovascular functioning.

SUMMARY

Ambulatory monitoring of cardiovascular activity, particularly BP and HR are now viable methods for assessing these aspects of cardiovascular activity under field (naturalistic) conditions. This chapter focused primarily on BP since it currently has the greatest clinical relevance. A case is made that ambulatory monitoring of BP, particularly in people considered mild hypertensives, will provide valuable diagnostic information as well as a means to follow the efficacy of any treatment regiment.

Paul A. Obrist, PhD, is currently a Professor in the Department of Psychiatry and Director of the Psychophysiology Research Laboratory, University of North Carolina. Dr. Obrist received his doctorate from the University of Rochester. He became an NIMH Post-doctoral fellow at Fels Research Institute. He has been awarded several NIMH and NIH research grants related to stress on blood pressure control. SPR presented him an award for Outstanding Contributions to Psychophysiology in 1985. He has published a book, edited another, and has authored approximately 100 publications. Dr. Obrist may be contacted at Medical Research Building A-218H, University of North Carolina, Chapel Hill, NC 27514.

RESOURCES

Bevan, A. T., Honour, A. J., & Stott, F. H. (1969). Direct arterial pressure recording in unrestricted man. *Clinical Science, 36*, 329-344.

Caldwell, J. R., Schork, M. A., & Aiken, R. D. (1978). Is near basal blood pressure a more accurate predictor of cardiorenal manifestations of hypertension than casual blood pressure? *Journal of Chronic Disorders, 31*, 507-512.

Dembroski, T. M., & MacDougall, J. M. (1984). Validation of the vita-stat automated noninvasive ambulatory blood pressure recording device. In J. A. Herd, A. M. Gotto, P. G. Kaufmann, & S. M. Weiss (Eds.), *Cardiovascular Instrumentation: Proceedings of the Working Conference on Applicability of New Technology to Biobehavioral Research* (NIH Publication No. 84-

1654, pp. 55-77). U. S. Department of Health and Human Services.

Devereux, R. B., Pickering, T. G., Harshfield, G. A., Kleinert, H. D., Denby, C., Clark, L., Pregibon, D., Jason, M., Sachs, I., Borer, J. S., & Laragh, J. H. (1983). Left ventricular hypertrophy in patients with hypertension: Importance of blood pressure response to regularly recurring stress. *Circulation, 63,* 470-476.

Dimsdale, J. E. (1983). Wet holder monitoring: Techniques for studying plasma responses to stress in ambulatory subjects. In T. M. Dembroski & T. H. Schmidt (Eds.), *Biobehavioral Bases of Coronary Heart Disease* (pp. 173-184). New York: Karger.

diRienzo, M., Grassi, G., Pedotti, A., & Mancia, G. (1983). Continuous vs. intermittent blood pressure measurements in estimating 24-hour average blood pressure. *Hypertension, 5,* 264-269.

Drayer, J. I. M., Weber, M. A., & DeYoung, J. L. (1983). The use of short-term ambulatory blood pressure monitoring in differing forms of hypertension. *Clinical and Experimental Hypertension - Theory and Practice, A-5,* 1597-1610.

Elliott, R. (1974). The motivational significance of heart rate. In P. A. Obrist, A. H. Black, J. Brener, & L. V. DiCara (Eds.), *Cardiovascular Psychophysiology: Current Issues in Response Mechanisms, Biofeedback, and Methodology* (pp. 505-537). Chicago: Aldine Publishing Company.

Engel, B. T., Gaarder, K. R., & Glasgow, M. S. (1981). Behavioral treatment of high blood pressure: 1. Analyses of intra- and interdaily variations of blood pressure during a one-month baseline period. *Psychosomatic Medicine, 43,* 255-270.

Engel, B. T., Glasgow, M. S., & Gaarder, K. R. (1983). Behavioral treatment of high blood pressure: III. Follow-up results and treatment recommendations. *Psychosomatic Medicine, 45,* 23-29.

Folkow, B., DiBona, G. F., Hjemdahl, P., Taren, P. H., & Wallin, B. G. (1983). Measurements of plasma norepinephrine concentrations in human primary hypertension. *Hypertension, 5,* 399-402.

Fowles, D. C. (1982). Heart rate as an index of anxiety: Failure of a hypothesis. In J. T. Cacioppo & R. E. Petty (Eds.), *Perspectives in Cardiovascular Psychophysiology* (pp. 93-126). New York: The Guilford Press.

503

Fries, F. R. (1982). Should mild hypertension be treated? *The New England Journal of Medicine, 307*, 306-309.

Geddes, L. A. (1970). *The Direct and Indirect Measurement of Blood Pressure.* Chicago: Year Book Medical Publishers, Inc.

Geddes, L. A. (1984). The indirect measurement of blood pressure. In J. A. Herd, A. M. Gotto, P. G. Kaufmann, & S. M. Weiss (Eds.), *Cardiovascular Instrumentation: Proceedings of the Working Conference on Applicability of New Technology to Biobehavioral Research* (NIH Publication No. 84-1654, pp. 5-19).

Glasgow, M. S., Gaarder, K. R., & Engel, B. T. (1982). Behavioral treatment of high blood pressure: II. Acute and sustained effects of relaxation and systolic blood pressure biofeedback. *Psychosomatic Medicine, 44*, 155-170.

Harshfield, G. A., Pickering, T. G., Blank, S., & Laragh, J. H. (1983). Ambulatory blood pressure monitoring: Recorders, applications and analyses. In M. E. Weber & J. Drayer (Eds.), *Ambulatory BP Monitoring* (pp. 1-7). New York: Springer Verlag.

Harshfield, G. A., Pickering, T. G., Kleinert, H. D., Blank, S., & Laragh, J. H. (1982). Situational variations of blood pressure in ambulatory hypertensive patients. *Psychosomatic Medicine, 44*, 237-245.

Harshfield, G. A., Pickering, T. G., & Laragh, J. H. (1979). A validation study of the Delmar Avionics ambulatory blood pressure system. *Ambulatory Electrocardiology, 1*, 7-12.

Holmgren, A. (1956). Circulatory changes during muscular work in man. *Scandinavian Journal of Clinical Laboratory Investigation, 8*(Suppl. 24), 1-97.

Hypertension Detection and Follow-Up Program Cooperative Group. (1979). Five-year findings of the hypertension detection and follow-up program. *Journal of the American Medical Association, 242*, 2562-2571.

Johnston, D. W. (in press). How does relaxation training reduce blood pressure in primary hypertension. In T. M. Dembroski, T. H. Schmidt, & C. Blumchen (Eds.), *Biobehavioral Factors in Coronary Heart Disease.* New York: Karger.

Julius, S., Ellis, C. N., Pascual, A. V., Matice, M., Hansson, L., Hunyor, S. N., & Sandler, L. N. (1974). Home blood pressure determination: Value in borderline ("labile") hypertension. *Journal of the American Medical Association, 229*, 663-666.

504

Kannel, W. B. (1977). Importance of hypertension as a major risk factor in cardiovascular disease. In J. Genest, E. Koiw, & O. Kuchel (Eds.), *Hypertension: Physiopathology and Treatment* (pp. 888-910). New York: McGraw-Hill Book Company.

Kleinert, H. D., Harshfield, G. A., Pickering, T. G., Devereux, R. B., Sullivan, P. A., Marion, R. M., Mallory, W. K., & Laragh, J. H. (1984). What is the value of home blood pressure measurement in patients with mild hypertension? *Hypertension, 6,* 574-578.

Langford, H. G. (1983). Further analyses of the hypertension detection and follow-up program. In F. Gross & T. Strasser (Eds.), *Mild Hypertension: Recent Advances* (pp. 307-313). New York: Raven Press.

Light, K. C., & Obrist, P. A. (1980). Cardiovascular reactivity to behavioral stress in young males with and without marginally elevated casual systolic pressures: A comparison of clinic, home and laboratory measures. *Hypertension, 2,* 802-808.

Littler, W. A., Honour, A. J., Carter, R. D., & Sleight, P. (1975). Sleep and blood pressure. *British Medical Journal, 3,* 346-348.

Management Committee. (1980). The Australian therapeutic trial in mild hypertension. *The Lancet,* June, 1261-1267.

Management Committee. (1982). The Australian therapeutic trial in mild hypertension. Untreated mild hypertension. *The Lancet,* January, 185-191.

Mancia, G. (1983). Methods for assessing blood pressure values in humans. *Hypertension, 5*(Supp. III), 5-13.

Mancia, G., Ferrari, A., Gregroini, L. Parati, G., Pomidossi, G., Bertinieri, G., Grassi, G., diRienzo, M. Pedotti, A., & Zanchetti, A. (1983). Blood pressure and heart rate variabilities in normotensive and hypertensive human beings. *Circulation Research, 53,* 96-104.

Mancia, G., & Zanchetti, A. (1983). Blood pressure variability and the assessment of blood pressure: Implications for epidemiologic research and for treatment. In F. Gross & T. Strasser (Eds.), *Mild Hypertension: Recent Advances* (pp. 251-262). New York: Raven Press.

Obrist, P. A. (1981). *Cardiovascular Psychophysiology: A Perspective.* New York: Plenum.

Obrist, P. A. (1982). Cardiac-behavioral interactions: A critical appraisal. In J. T. Cacioppo & R. E. Petty

(Eds.), *Perspectives in Cardiovascular Psychophysiology* (pp. 265-295). New York: The Guilford Press.

Obrist, P. A., Grignolo, A., Hastrup, J. L., Koepke, J. P., Langer, A. W., Light, K. C., McCubbin, J. A., & Pollak, M. H. (1983). Behavioral cardiovascular interaction in hypertension. In D. Krantz, A. Baum, & J. E. Singer (Eds.), *Handbook of Psychology and Health: Vol. III. Cardiovascular Disorders* (pp. 199-230). New York: Lawrence Erlbaum.

Obrist, P. A., & Light, K. C. (in press). Active-passive coping and cardiovascular reactivity: Interaction with individual differences and types of baseline. In A. Baum, W. Gordon, & J. A. Herd (Eds.), *Proceedings of the Academy of Behavioral Medicine Research* (1981-1982). New York: Academic Press.

Obrist, P. A., Light, K. C., & Hastrup, J. L. (1982). Emotion and the cardiovascular system: A critical perspective. In C. E. Izard (Ed.), *Measuring Emotions in Infants and Children* (pp. 299-316). New York: Cambridge University Press.

Obrist, P. A., Light, K. C., James, S. A., & Strogatz, D. S. (in press). Cardiovascular responses to stress: I. Measures of myocardial response and relationships to high resting systolic pressure and parental hypertension. *Psychophysiology.*

Obrist, P. A., Light, K. C., Sherwood, A., Allen, M. T., Langer, A. W., & Koepke, J. P. (1986). Some working hypothesis on the significance of behavioral-evoked cardiovascular reactivity to pathophysiology. In T. M. Dembroski, T. H. Schmidt, & C. Blumchen (Eds.), *Biobehavioral Factors in Coronary Heart Disease* (pp. 406-417). New York: Karger.

Ostfeld, A. M., & Shekelle, R. B. (1967). Psychological variables and blood pressure. In J. Stamler & T. N. Pullman (Eds.), *The Epidemiology of Hypertension* (pp. 321-331). New York: Grune & Stratton.

Patel, C. H. (1977). Biofeedback-aided relaxation and meditation in the management of hypertension. *Biofeedback and Self-Regulation, 2,* 1-41.

Perloff, D., Sokolow, M., & Cowan, R. (1983). The prognostic value of ambulatory blood pressures. *Journal of the American Medical Association, 249,* 2792-2798.

Pickering, T. G., Harshfield, G. A., Kleinert, H. D., Blank, S., & Laragh, J. H. (1982). Blood pressure during normal daily activities, sleep, and exercise: Comparson of values in normal and hypertensive subjects.

Journal of the American Medical Association, 247, 992-996.

Pickering, T. G., Harshfield, G. A., Kleinert, H. D., & Laragh, J. H. (1982). Ambulatory monitoring in the evaluation of blood pressure in patients with borderline hypertension and the role of the defense reflex. *Clinical and Experimental Hypertension, A4*(4 & 5), 675-693.

Reader, R. (1983). The natural history of mild hypertension. In F. Gross & T. Strasser (Eds.), *Mild Hypertension: Recent Advances* (pp. 147-162). New York: Raven Press.

Rowlands, D. B., DeGiovanni, J., McLeay, R. A. B., Watson, R. D. S., Stallard, T. J., & Littler, W. A. (1982). Cardiovascular response in black and white hypertensives. *Hypertension, 4,* 817-820.

Smirk, F. H. (1973). Casual, basal, and supplemental blood pressures. In G. Onesti, K. E. Kim, & J. H. Moyer (Eds.), *Hypertension: Mechanisms and Management* (pp. 13-20). New York: Grune & Stratton.

Sokolow, M., Werdegar, D., Perloff, D. B., Cowan, R. M., & Brenenstuhl, H. (1970). Preliminary studies relating portably recorded blood pressure to daily life events in patients with essential hypertension. In M. Koster, H. Musaph, & P. Visser (Eds.), *Psychosomatics in Essential Hypertension* (Bibliothecapsychiatica No. 144, pp. 164-189). White Plains, NY: Karger.

Soucheck, J., Stamler, J., Dyer, A. R., Paul, O., & Lepper, M. H. (1979). The value of two or three versus a single reading of blood pressure at a first visit. *Journal of Chronic Disorders, 32,* 197-210.

Stein, I. M., Peterson, R., & Lee, A. (1983). Ambulatory blood pressure recorder. *Medical Instrumentation, 17,* 352-354.

Surwit, R. S., & Shapiro, D. (1977). Biofeedback and meditation in the treatment of borderline hypertension. In J. Beatty & H. Legewie (Eds.), *Biofeedback and Behavior* (pp. 403-413). New York: Plenum.

Ward, M. M., Mefford, I. N., Parker, S. D., Chesney, M. A., Taylor, C. B., Keegan, D. L., & Barchas, J. D. (1983). Epinephrine and norepinephrine responses in continuously collected human plasma to a series of stressors. *Psychosomatic Medicine, 45,* 471-486.

Watson, R. D. S., Stallard, T. J., Flinn, R. M., & Littler, W. A. (1980). Factors determining direct arterial pressure and its variability in hypertensive men. *Hypertension, 2,* 333-341.

Werdegar, D., Sokolow, M., & Perloff, D. B. (1968). Portable recording of blood pressure: A new approach to assessments of the severity and prognosis of hypertension. In S. R. Moore (Ed.), *Transactions of the Association of Life Insurance Medical Directors of America* (76th Annual Meeting, pp. 43-115). New York: Sperry Rand.

West, J. E., Busch-Vishniac, I. J., Harshfield, G. A., & Pickering, T. G. (1983). Foil electret transducer for blood pressure monitoring. *Journal of the Acoustical Society of America, 74,* 680-686.

CAFFEINE ABUSE
AND CAFFEINE REDUCTION

James D. Lane

Caffeine is widely accepted as the most commonly used drug in contemporary society. It occurs naturally in a wide range of foods and beverages including coffee, tea, cocoa, and chocolate and is added to many soft drinks. Caffeine is present in many over-the-counter medications, both by itself and in combination with other drugs. Brecher and The Editors of *Consumer Reports* (1972) comments that caffeine use is so widespread and so much a part of the culture that, like nicotine and alcohol, caffeine is seldom thought of as a drug.

Recently, concern has been developing over the potential hazards associated with caffeine use. Although caffeine is generally considered to be beneficial or at least benign in its effects, some studies have created suspicion that excessive caffeine use may be harmful. Concern has focused on the toxic effects of caffeine which may produce significant psychiatric symptoms and on the possibility that caffeine use may be a risk factor for the development of cardiovascular and other diseases.

This chapter begins with acceptance of the likelihood that excessive caffeine use is potentially harmful. Reduction in caffeine intake is for many people an important means of reducing disease and enhancing health. The chapter begins with a brief review of the literature on the effects of caffeine. This provides the foundation for the later discussion of the deleterious effects which caffeine can produce. The chapter concludes with a review of the techniques which can be used to create a program of caffeine reduction for patients or clients who are suffering from the effects of excessive caffeine consumption.

CAFFEINE PHARMACOLOGY

Effective treatment of caffeine-related problems requires some understanding of the actions of caffeine as a drug. This section is not intended as a complete review of the literature on caffeine, but it will focus on those aspects of caffeine pharmacology which are most important for appreciating the risks of excessive caffeine use and for reducing caffeine intake. A more extensive discussion of caffeine's effects can be found in Rall (1980) or Gilbert (1976).

ABSORPTION AND METABOLISM OF CAFFEINE

When caffeine is ingested in foods, beverages, or drugs it enters rapidly into the bloodstream. It begins to appear in tissues within about 5 minutes and will reach maximum levels in the blood after from 30-60 minutes. Once in the blood it is removed only after it has been metabolized by the liver to other compounds which are then excreted by the kidneys. On the average, the elimination of half of the caffeine present in the blood at any time will require 5 to 6 hours (metabolic half-life). However, there are wide individual variations in the rate of absorption and metabolism (Neims & von Borstel, 1983) that can be due to a variety of factors. Fetal and newborn humans have a severely limited capacity to metabolize caffeine, due to the immaturity of their liver function, which extends the half-life period to 3-4 days. When women take oral contraceptive drugs the half-life of caffeine is increased to 10.7 hours. Pregnancy will increase it even more, to 18 hours. Cigarette smoking, on the other hand, speeds the metabolism of caffeine and decreases the half-life to 3-4 hours.

It should be very apparent that, given the time required to eliminate caffeine from the system, regular ingestion of even small amounts throughout the day can result in the accumulation of high levels of caffeine which can produce toxic effects. The accumulation of caffeine is a special problem for children. Although they usually do not consume large amounts of caffeine at any one time (generally avoiding coffee, the most concentrated dietary source) the slow accumulation from the consumption of caffeinated soft drinks and chocolate throughout the day could lead to significant side effects. This is especially true given that, due to their much lower body weight, a smaller total amount of caffeine is needed to produce significant effects in children. The slowed elimination of caffeine in women on contraceptive pills could also put them at increased risk for toxic caffeine effects, even at low levels of ingestion, and coffee drinking during periods of breast-feeding may lead to disturbing caffeine side effects in both mother and infant.

THE BEHAVIORAL AND PHYSIOLOGICAL EFFECTS OF CAFFEINE

Caffeine is a potent stimulator of the central nervous system, thereby producing the experience of reduced drowsiness and fatigue and a clearer flow of thoughts. These are the drug effects which are most likely sought by people who consume caffeine. It can produce an increased capacity for sustained intellectual and physical effort and an improvement in well-practiced tasks, such as typing, although the learning of new tasks or performance of those requiring delicate coordination may suffer (Goldstein, Kaizer, & Warren, 1965; Weiss & Laties, 1962). It can also produce an improvement in mood. Results from a survey of 183 coffee-drinking housewives (Goldstein & Kaizer, 1969) showed that they drank coffee in the morning because they felt that it helped them wake up, gave them energy, and got them ready to start the day. Respondents reported that drinking coffee made them "perk up," made them more alert and active, and able to work more efficiently, effects which were stronger in those who regularly drank more coffee. However, coffee was also associated with a general feeling of well-being, again especially for the heavier coffee drinkers.

Caffeine is widely recognized as a potent stimulator of the cardiovascular system as well (Gilbert, 1976; Rall, 1980). One of its most consistent effects is to elevate blood pressure, an average of about 10 mmHg for both systolic and diastolic values, within 30 to 60 minutes after even low to moderate doses (150-250 mg; Robertson et al., 1978; Whitsett, Manion, & Christensen, 1984). This blood pressure elevation is probably due to an overall increase in the resistance of the blood vessels (Smits, Hoffman,

Thien, Houben, & van't Laar, 1983) rather than an increase in cardiac output.

Caffeine also produces changes in a number of neuroendocrine and hormonal systems. Caffeine will apparently increase the levels of a number of hormones in the blood. The best-established effect is to elevate the blood levels of the two catecholamines, epinephrine and norepinephrine, which are important to the control of the sympathetic nervous system and the expression of the well-known "fight-flight" response to stress (e.g., Robertson et al., 1978).

Caffeine has other noticeable effects as well. It acts as a diuretic, directly leading to an increase in the production of urine. The drug will also increase the rate of metabolism, which can lead to an elevation in body temperature.

Despite all that is known about the physiological effects of caffeine, the actual mechanism through which the drug exerts its effects is still unknown. The explanatory model receiving the most attention at the present time is based upon caffeine's apparent inhibition of the actions of adenosine, a biological compound which affects the activity of a wide variety of organ systems (Fredholm, 1980). This explanation is supported by evidence that the relative effectiveness of caffeine and a variety of caffeine-like compounds is related to how well they bind to adenosine receptors (Snyder, Katims, Annau, Bruns, & Daly, 1981). Furthermore, the actions of adenosine generally are the opposite of the effects of caffeine. Though not yet complete, the evidence suggests that caffeine produces its stimulatory actions by blocking the normal inhibitory actions of adenosine. Other studies based on this model provide potential explanations for both habituation to the effects of caffeine and the withdrawal symptoms which are known to occur when intake ceases abruptly.

TOLERANCE TO CAFFEINE

Not all of the effects of caffeine occur consistently in all subjects. An important potential modulator of these effects is the process of tolerance. Some of the effects may diminish as caffeine is ingested chronically. Whether this is true has not yet been decided. To date, research and clinical evidence both affirming and denying the existence of tolerance has been reported. Human studies have generally compared the effects of caffeine in regular caffeine users to those seen in nonusers. Stronger effects in nonusers suggest that regular use leads to tolerance, but it is also possible that those who are regular users are inherently less sensitive to the effects of caffeine than are those who consume only a little (Goldstein, Kaizer, & Whitby, 1969).

The evidence for tolerance in the cardiovascular system is inconclusive. Studies of caffeine's effects on blood pressure demonstrate this clearly. The ability of caffeine to elevate blood pressure, epinephrine, and norepinephrine (Robertson et al., 1978) was originally found in subjects who had abstained from caffeine for several weeks. When the same tests were applied after the regular administration of 250 mg of caffeine with each meal for several days, the caffeine-related elevations of blood pressure and the stress hormones disappeared (Robertson, Wade, Workman, Woolsey, & Oates, 1981), strong evidence of tolerance. However, a recent study (Whitsett et al., 1984) found that the significant elevation of blood pressure after moderate amounts of caffeine (9/10 mmHg) was the same for subjects who seldom drank coffee, for those who drank two to five cups per day, and even for subjects who drank over 10 cups per day. Caffeine also produced significant blood pressure increases in a group of elderly men (Conrad, Blanchard, & Trang, 1982) who were light to moderate coffee or tea drinkers even though they presumably had a long history of caffeine use.

Research on tolerance to the behavioral effects of caffeine is also inconclusive. Colton, Gosselin, and Smith (1968) reported that caffeine delayed sleep onset and altered the sleep pattern only in subjects who did not regularly drink coffee or tea. Goldstein, Warren, and Kaizer (1965) on the other hand found that caffeine disturbed the sleep of subjects regardless of the number of cups of coffee they consumed daily. Another study (Goldstein et al., 1969) found that coffee drinking produced different effects on mood depending on whether subjects were nonusers or regular coffee drinkers. Caffeine produced jitteriness, nervousness, and gastrointestinal complaints in nonusers but made regular users more alert, talkative, and less sleepy. On the other hand, the existence of a distinct pattern of symptoms associated with chronic excessive use of caffeine, which will be discussed in the next section of the chapter, argues strongly against tolerance to all of caffeine's affect.

It is possible that tolerance to caffeine's cardiovascular effects may develop with continued use but disappears after a relatively brief period of abstinence. Robertson, Wade, Workman, Woolsey, and Oates (1981) reported some return of caffeine's blood pressure effects after less than 24 hours of abstinence. The effects reported by Whitsett et al. (1984) and Conrad et al. (1982) were seen after abstinence periods of 24 hours and 72 hours respectively. Only further research will clarify which of caffeine's effects diminish with chronic use and determine the time course both for the development of tolerance and for the loss of tolerance following abstinence.

PATTERNS OF CAFFEINE USE

Now that it is clear that caffeine can have significant effects on both physiology and behavior, it is worthwhile to review the characteristics of caffeine use, that is, how many people ingest how much caffeine and in what form. Data from several sources support the notion that caffeine may be the most widely used drug in the Western world. Based on the amount of coffee and tea sold, the average daily consumption of caffeine by adults in the U. S. is 200 mg which corresponds roughly to a level of 3 mg/kg of body weight, above the concentration needed to elicit caffeine effects (Roberts & Barone, 1983). Surveys of caffeine use yield a similar average value. If only those adults who consume some caffeinated products are considered, the average rises to 4 mg/kg (250-300 mg of caffeine per day in a person of average weight). Those people in the highest 10% of consumption ingest an average daily dose of 7 mg/kg which corresponds to 400-500 mg of caffeine. Caffeine use tends to increase with age, both in terms of the percentage of people who drink coffee or tea and in the average daily caffeine level, although the latter measure peaks in the middle-aged group.

Surveys of caffeine use and coffee and tea drinking suggest that the vast majority of people consume some caffeine daily. Goldstein and Kaizer (1969) found that only 23% of a group of young housewives abstained from coffee while nearly half 'drank from one to four cups daily. Over one-quarter of the women drank five or more cups everyday. Here too there was a tendency for caf-

514

feine intake to increase with age. Brecher et al. (1972, pp. 476-477) reports a survey of 2500 people done in the early 1970s which found that only 9% of adults aged 18-74 abstained from caffeine completely. Sixty percent drank from two to five cups of coffee or tea daily and over 25% drank more than five cups. Caffeine use is consistently lower in young adults than in the general population. A survey of college students (R. A. Hicks, G. J. Hicks, Reyes, & Cheers, 1983) did not assess complete abstinence but found that about one-third of students drank one serving or less of coffee, tea, or cola per day. However, 13% reported drinking more than five servings each day. A different survey of college students which also investigated the use of caffeine pills (Vener & Krupka, 1982) found similar levels of use. Three-quarters of the students ingested less than 250 mg of caffeine per day. Moderate use (250-500 mg) was reported by 17% and heavy use (500+ mg) by only 7%.

Large-scale epidemiological surveys report consistent results, despite the variety of cut-points used to define the different levels of consumption. Bertrand, Pomper, Hillman, Duffy, and Michell (1978) surveyed the coffee-drinking habits of over 70,000 IBM employees and found that only 10% drank no coffee, almost half drank between one and three cups daily, 38% drank four to eight cups per day, and 4% drank more than eight cups of coffee everyday. Results from the Framingham study (Dawber, Kannel, & Gordon, 1974) reported that 10% of that population drank over six cups of coffee per day. A study of 10,000 males in their forties (Hrubec, 1973) found that only 9% drank no coffee, but 24% drank more than five cups everyday. In a survey of 111,000 people, Klatsky, Friedman, and Siegelaub (1973) found that 20% of males and females reported drinking more than six cups of coffee per day.

Young children generally do not consume as much caffeine as adults but do still ingest significant amounts of caffeine on a daily basis. Caffeine use surveys (Roberts & Barone, 1983) have shown that, in children aged 5-18 years, the average caffeine consumption was 1 mg/kg per day, roughly one-third the level of adults. However, the 10% of children who consumed the most caffeine ingested an average of 3-5 mg/kg daily, the average level for adults.

The principal dietary source of caffeine for adults is coffee, which accounts for 75% of the total on the average and 94% of the total for the heaviest caffeine users. Tea consumption contributes an additional 15% and soft drinks most of the remainder. For the children aged 5-18 years, tea is the source of half of the caffeine intake, although about 20% comes from coffee and from soft drinks and over 10% from chocolate products (Roberts & Barone, 1983).

These results clearly demonstrate that a majority of the population lives daily life under the influence of caffeine, since many of the physiological and behavioral effects begin to appear after only 100 mg or one cup of coffee. Furthermore, as will be shown in the next section of this chapter, a significant proportion of adults consume caffeine in coffee or tea at or above levels which may be associated with deleterious side effects and a potential increased risk of disease.

THE DETRIMENTAL EFFECTS OF CAFFEINE ABUSE

Some of the effects of caffeine are beneficial and, when used in moderation, the drug can be useful for the reduction of fatigue and for the improvement of alertness. Excessive use, however, can lead to consequences which are deleterious to health. James and Stirling (1983) suggested the term "caffeine abuse" for all of the different kinds of chronic or habitual caffeine use at levels which can potentially cause damage to health. The deleterious effects produced by caffeine abuse can be divided into four classes: the toxic effects directly associated with excessive caffeine; the withdrawal effects associated with periods of abstinence after chronic caffeine use; the potential increase in risks for other diseases associated with heavy caffeine use; and the potential aggravation by caffeine of the health-damaging effects of stress. Each of these deleterious effects may have significant clinical consequences and could provide sufficient cause for a program of treatment to reduce caffeine intake.

CAFFEINISM

Caffeinism is the name which has been used for the collection of symptoms caused by caffeine toxicity following the acute or chronic ingestion of high doses of caffeine. In the *DSM-III* (American Psychiatric Association, 1980) the disorder is called "caffeine organic mental disorder." Brecher et al. (1972, pp. 195-198) note that illnesses have been ascribed to caffeine use throughout history. However, only recently have these symptoms received much attention in this century. In one of the earliest of the recent studies, Reimann (1967) reported a case of long-term, low-grade fever accompanied by insomnia, anorexia, and irritability in a woman who drank 15-18 cups of coffee during the day. Her symptoms disappeared soon after she began to severely restrict her intake of caffeine and did not return. Reimann noted that excessive caffeine consumption might be the cause of many unexplained illnesses.

Certainly, the ingestion of large amounts of caffeine can produce a variety of symptoms. Those most characteristic (American Psychiatric Association, 1980) include "restlessness, nervousness, excitement, insomnia, flushed face, diuresis, and gastrointestinal complaints" (p. 161). These symptoms generally appear after consumption of more than 500 mg of caffeine (4-7 cups of coffee) but have been reported to occur after consumption of as little as 250 mg daily. Higher doses (above 1000 mg per day) can produce "muscle twitching, rambling flow of thought and speech, cardiac arrhythmia, periods of inexhaustibility, and psychomotor agitation" (p. 160). These symptoms are essentially exaggerations of the normal effects of caffeine described earlier.

These symptoms are of clinical importance because, as Greden (1974) pointed out, the syndrome is frequently indistinguishable from "anxiety neurosis." Caffeinism can cause a clinical picture similar to manic episodes, panic disorder, or generalized anxiety disorder in which only the temporal relationship of the symptoms to the consumption of large amounts of caffeine can provide the differential diagnosis. A question about regular caffeine intake should be part of every patient history for anxiety disorders, and caffeinism should be ruled out as a possible cause before treatment for anxiety is begun. The incidence of caffeinism has not been studied. However, if a level of 500 mg per day is taken as a "danger level" for the appearance of symptoms, then roughly 20% of the adult population of the U. S. would qualify as being at risk.

In order to provide a clearer picture of the variety of symptoms that can be presented by patients, it is worthwhile to briefly summarize some of the case studies

517

of caffeinism which have been described in the literature. Complete details can be found in each reference.

Greden (1974) provided three case studies to illustrate his report on the symptoms of caffeinism and their similarity to anxiety. A 27-year-old nurse reported light-headedness, tremulousness, breathlessness, headache, and irregular heartbeat which occurred two to three times a day. She reported some general feelings of apprehension which she related to her symptoms. She was diagnosed as having an anxiety reaction but on her own began to associate her symptoms with coffee use. Symptom onset had begun after she bought a new coffee maker and began drinking 10 to 12 cups per day (over 1000 mg) because the coffee was "so much better." All symptoms disappeared within 36 hours after she stopped drinking coffee, although she reported fatigue lasting 1 week.

A 37-year-old man was referred to a psychiatric outpatient clinic for "chronic anxiety" with daily symptoms of "dizziness, tremulousness, apprehension about job performance, 'butterflies in the stomach,' restless-ness," loose stools, and difficulty in falling asleep. He noted that symptoms were increased with the arrival of a difficult new boss. He reported drinking 8-14 cups of coffee a day, saying "My coffeepot is a permanent fixture on my desk" (p. 1091). Total daily caffeine intake was estimated at over 1200 mg. A reduction in caffeine intake led to a partial improvement of many of his symptoms, although his apprehension remained. Increased levels of caffeine for several days led to a return of these symptoms.

The final case involved repeated tension headaches in a 34-year-old man. He was a very hard-working person who drank 10-15 cups of coffee a day at work and often drank tea and cola. He averaged three to four headaches a week, often on weekends, which he treated with remedies that all contained caffeine. Total intake of caffeine exceeded 1500 mg per day. His headaches disappeared several weeks after he followed instructions to avoid all caffeine. In this case, the headaches may have been caused by brief periods of abstinence from caffeine when away from work, a withdrawal symptom which will be discussed in the following section.

MacCallum (1979) described a 28-year-old housewife who suddenly developed palpitations and panic one evening. An anxiety, fluctuating in intensity and associ-ated with attacks of cold sweat, shortness of breath, and tingling in the extremities, persisted through the following weeks. No psychological or psychiatric origin could be found for the symptoms, which were managed by benzodiazepine tranquilizers. When diet was investigated, the woman reported drinking 20 cups of ground coffee per day for the last 4 to 6 months. On the night of the initial panic attack she had brewed coffee continuously while waiting for her husband to return and had consumed excessive amounts. After coffee intake was abruptly stopped the panic disappeared within 10 days. During withdrawal the woman suffered occasional headaches and lethargy but after 3 weeks she was symptom free. Drinking 20 cups of ground coffee could provide 2 grams of caffeine per day, an amount twice that which will produce the extreme symptoms of caffeine toxicity including insomnia, restlessness, delirium, and sensory disturbances (Rall, 1980).

Sours (1983) described how caffeinism can be an important clinical aspect of anorexia nervosa. Commonly, anorectic patients will drink large quantities of coffee, tea, or diet colas which dampen hunger and reduce fatigue. One 16-year-old patient drank 4 to 6 quarts of diet cola each day (roughly 400-600 mg of caffeine), much of it in the mornings, to restore energy and reduce fatigue after her 6-mile run. A 34-year-old female anorectic drank as much as 12 cups of black coffee (over 1000 mg of caffeine) and a gallon of diet cola (400 mg) a day in order to eliminate hunger and because she believed that she needed the extra energy. At these levels of caffeine abuse she experienced "restlessness, jumpy legs, muscle tension, twitchings, anxiety, palpitations, fast speech, diarrhea, heartburn, and onset insomnia," (p. 236) all due to her consumption of excessive amounts of caffeine. Sours (1983) comments that caffeinated diet soft drinks are especially favored by anorectics because these provide for unlimited quantities of a sweet-tasting but low-calorie drink for the "self-starving" individual.

A number of investigators have described symptoms similar to caffeinism, although less intense than those above, in comparisons of heavy caffeine users and nonusers. Higher levels of caffeine use have been associated with increased levels of anxiety and depression in several studies of psychiatric patients (Greden, Fontaine, Lubetsky, & Chamberlin, 1978; Winstead, 1976). In a sample of 83 hospitalized psychiatric patients, Greden et al. (1978) found that high consumers (750 mg per day or more) and moderate consumers (250-749 mg per day) scored higher on a trait anxiety measure than low consumers (less than 250 mg per day). High consumers also had a greater proportion of scores reflecting severe depression. In general, the higher the total caffeine intake from all sources, the more likely it was that patients would report a mixture of symptoms including anxiety and depression, fatigue, tension, feeling blue, worrying, feeling like crying, or feeling upset. Winstead found similar results in 135 other psychiatric patients, specifically that heavy caffeine users had a higher incidence of psychotic diagnoses and reported higher state anxiety.

Two studies also suggest the possibility that people suffering from anxiety or panic disorder may be more susceptible to the anxiogenic effects of caffeine. Boulenger and Uhde (1982) found that daily caffeine intake was positively correlated with trait anxiety in a group of patients suffering from phobic disorders associated with either panic or generalized anxiety symptoms, but not in a normal control group. Charney, Heninger, and Jatlow (1985) found that experimental administrations of high doses of caffeine (700-750 mg) produced greater increases in anxiety and a variety of anxiety-related symptoms in a group of patients suffering from agoraphobia or panic disorder than in normal controls. In the patient group, the intensity of symptoms was correlated with plasma caffeine levels and 71% of patients reported that the behavioral effects of caffeine were similar to those experienced during a panic attack. Thus, patients with anxiety or panic disorders may especially benefit from reduction of caffeine intake or complete avoidance of the drug.

Generalizations from these studies of hospitalized psychiatric patients may be questionable; however, similar findings have emerged from studies of caffeine use in college students. Gilliland and Andress (1981) found that students who consumed caffeine at a level greater than one cup of coffee per day had higher trait anxiety and depression scores than those who abstained from caffeine. Subjects who consumed more than 5 cups per day also reported more symptoms of caffeinism and more psychosomatic disturbances, and had poorer grades. A study by Diamond and Pfifferling ("Cola," 1974) found similar results in students who got caffeine only from cola drinks. The "colaholics" who drank between 48 and 111 oz of cola per day (160-370 mg of caffeine) were more likely to report feeling "sometimes jittery," and having frequent mood changes and sleeping problems.

These mood changes associated with caffeine abuse were experimentally manipulated by De Frietas and Schwartz (1979). The coffee which was freely available to the patients on a closed ward in a psychiatric hospital was secretly switched to decaffeinated coffee for a 3-week period. This switch produced significant decreases in ratings of suspiciousness, somatic concern, anxiety, tension, hostility, and excitement. Nurses' ratings of patient irritability, manifest psychosis, and retardation declined. When regular coffee was returned, the improvements disappeared and ratings returned to pre-decaffeinated levels.

The evidence is strong that caffeine abuse can be associated with detrimental physical and psychological changes. These side effects are apparently reversible and will disappear if excessive caffeine use is reduced to more moderate levels.

CAFFEINE WITHDRAWAL HEADACHE AND OTHER SYMPTOMS

Although there is no strong evidence that caffeine can produce a real physical addiction (Gilbert, 1976), chronic caffeine consumption does evidently produce a change in physiological functioning, perhaps as the different biological systems adapt to the continuing presence of the drug. When caffeine intake is abruptly stopped, a distinct pattern of withdrawal symptoms usually emerges. In some individuals these symptoms will occur if the normal pattern of caffeine intake is interrupted for only a few hours. For this reason, the symptoms of withdrawal deserve consideration as a second deleterious consequence of chronic caffeine abuse.

The most distinct of these symptoms associated with caffeine withdrawal is headache. Dreisbach and Pfeiffer (1943) clearly demonstrated the link between headache and caffeine withdrawal in a study in which subjects were first given daily doses of caffeine which increased over 1 week and then were given placebos. In almost half of the cases, subjects reported a headache which was as bad as any they had ever had. In one-third more, the headache was definite but did not require treatment. Only a few subjects did not get a headache with this experimental regimen. The symptomatology of the headache was consistent. On the day that withdrawal began, subjects noticed lethargy in the morning, while a "feeling of cerebral fullness" developed about noon. Actual headache usually began in the early afternoon and reached a peak 3 to 6 hours later. The headache was initially localized but became generalized and throbbing. Sometimes it was accompanied by nausea and rhinorrhea. Subjects complained of "mental depression, drowsiness, yawning, and disinclination to work" (p. 1214). Bending over or straining intensified the pain, as did relaxation and exercise. The most effective treatment for relief of the headache was more caffeine.

Studies of regular caffeine users have found similar results. Goldstein and Kaizer (1969) obtained survey information from 239 young housewives. Those women who drank five or more cups of coffee per day described a set of dysphoric symptoms which they attributed to missing their morning coffee. These symptoms include headache, irritability, inability to work effectively, nervousness, restlessness, and lethargy. Light coffee drinkers did not report these symptoms. Those women who sometimes experienced withdrawal were more likely than average to drink coffee for its stimulatory effects and the sense of well-being it created. They felt a stronger need for coffee and reported that coffee in the morning made them feel more alert and active, an effect which could have been due to the reversal of incipient withdrawal symptoms. When, in a follow-up study to the survey (Goldstein et al., 1969), some of the heavy coffee drinkers were given placebo in the morning instead of caffeine, these women reported being more jittery, nervous, irritable, and shaky and less alert and content than regular abstainers who got placebo. Symptoms were reported roughly 12 to 16 hours after the last cup of coffee the day before, consistent with the time required for elimination of caffeine (given a half-life of roughly 4 hours). Coffee made them feel better and was apparently necessary to prepare them to face the day.

The essential elements for the development of caffeine-withdrawal headache and the other symptoms are the regular consumption of high levels of caffeine (perhaps 500-600 mg daily), a general adaptation to the effects of such a dose, and the abrupt discontinuation of the drug (Greden, Victor, Fontaine, & Lubetsky, 1980). Headaches will frequently occur on weekends or vacations when coffee consumption may be greatly reduced from the levels consumed at work. The diagnosis should not rely too heavily on the actual caffeine intake level, since the syndrome can occur with moderate consumption as well, but rather on the development of headache when caffeine is absent. Successful treatment requires a reduction in caffeine intake. This is made more difficult by patient disbelief that caffeine could be the cause of the headache. Even though the headaches will disappear if caffeine intake is reduced, Greden et al. (1980) note that after treatment these patients will often begin to slowly increase caffeine intake, leading to another cycle of caffeine abuse and withdrawal headache.

Although it is generally unrecognized, this type of headache, and the other attendant symptoms, may be very widespread. As discussed in an earlier section of this chapter, an estimated 20-25% of all adults have a daily intake of caffeine that is at or above the level thought to be associated with the threat of withdrawal symptoms. Assessment of caffeine intake might provide important diagnostic insight into any otherwise unexplained headache.

CAFFEINE AS A RISK FACTOR FOR DISEASE

Much concern has been expressed over the role which chronic, excessive caffeine use (or coffee drinking) plays in the development of disease. Although suspicions continue with regard to several diseases, clear evidence one way or the other is still lacking. For the most part, the indecision stems from the nature of epidemiological research and the absence of direct experimental studies.

The most extensively studied relationship is that between caffeine (or coffee drinking) and the development of heart disease. Although an early study (Walker & Gregoratos, 1967) found no differences in coffee consumption (assessed as the percentage drinking more than four cups per day) between patients in the hospital with a myocardial infarction and other patients, several other studies found an association. One of the early reports came from the Boston Collaborative Drug Surveillance Program (Vessey, 1972), which compared the coffee and tea intake of 276 patients diagnosed with acute myocardial infarction (MI) to that of 1104 matched control patients with other diseases. The two groups did not differ in tea drinking but the MI patients drank appreciably more coffee. Results suggested that the risk of MI was doubled for persons drinking more than five cups of coffee per day. A more detailed study (Jick et al., 1973) confirmed this finding in a survey of 12,750 patients including 440 with acute MI. After controlling for a number of demographic variables, including smoking, the increase in risk for MI for patients who drank one to five cups of coffee per day was 60%, and for those who drank six or more cups, 120%. Once again, tea drinking was unrelated to cardiovascular disease.

Although these results provided strong evidence in favor of an association, other studies have failed to support this conclusion. The analysis of coffee consumption data taken from routine health examinations of 111,000 people (Klatsky et al., 1973) showed no relationship between the level of consumption and the subsequent occurrence of an MI in 464 of them, once smoking had been controlled for. Hrubec (1973) found a relationship between excessive coffee drinking and angina pectoris in a sample of over 10,000 males, but only in subjects who also smoked more than 31 cigarettes per day. Data from the Framingham study (Dawber, Kannel, & Gordon, 1974) revealed no association of coffee and cardiovascular disease at all. Hennekens, Drolette, Jesse, Davies, and Hutchison (1976) also found no association in a carefully controlled study of MI patients and controls. However, they did find that the association between coffee drinking and MI could be increased or decreased depending on which variables were controlled for. Controlling for variables positively predictive of the outcome but negatively predictive of coffee use would increase the relative risk, while controlling for variables, such as smoking, which are positively related to both the outcome and coffee use will reduce the estimated risk of coffee drinking. A further possible source of the confusion of results was suggested by Rosenberg et al. (1980), who found no significant relationship of coffee and MI when 487 women with an MI were compared to 980 controls. In this study, the controls were patients admitted for an acute emergency and their level of coffee drinking was generally higher than that reported for the control patients of the Boston study (Vessey, 1972) and the Jick et al. (1973) study who were hospitalized for chronic diseases. Apparently, the low coffee consumption of patients in the Vessey, 1972 and Jick et al., 1973 studies were also below normal levels for healthy individuals. Rosenberg et al. (1980) suggested that they may have been avoiding coffee for health reasons. This abnormally low consumption in the control group would have exaggerated the difference from the MI patient group and overestimated the risk.

Although the question of the link between coffee drinking and heart disease remains to be answered, it is important to emphasize that none of the studies has found a similar relationship for tea consumption. This suggests that caffeine may not be the crucial factor in the relationships that have been found so far. Such findings have only added to the confusion in this area.

Concerns have also been expressed regarding the relationship of caffeine or coffee drinking to a variety of other medical problems such as cardiac arrhythmias (Dobmeyer, Stine, Leier, Greenberg, & Schaal, 1983), cancer of the pancreas (MacMahon, Yen, Trichopoulos, Warren, & Nardi, 1981), and increased risks during pregnancy (Linn et al., 1982) as well as others. A chapter of this length cannot properly review this research. At the present time none of the proposed associations of caffeine or coffee and disease has been irrefutably demonstrated and the questions remain unanswered. However, suspicions do remain which could well provide sufficient reason for moderation in caffeine use.

CAFFEINE'S INTERACTIONS WITH STRESS

In addition to its direct effects, caffeine consumption may also affect health through its synergistic interactions with the potentially harmful effects of stress. Many of the pharmacological actions of caffeine are similar to the responses elicited by stress, and there is evidence which strongly suggests that the presence of caffeine can increase the potentially harmful effects of stress.

The strongest evidence for interactions of caffeine and stress comes from animal research. Henry and Stephens (1978) reported that the continued substitution of coffee for the drinking water provided to mice led to an intensification of the stress-related effects of living in a highly competitive social environment. The blood pressure and stress hormones such as corticosterone were elevated by caffeine above the levels produced by stress alone. Caffeine also increased the damage caused by stress on the tissues of the heart and kidney, which resulted in accelerated mortality for these mice. These effects developed over several months of chronic use, roughly equivalent to 20 years or more for humans.

Several studies with human subjects also suggest that caffeine and stress can have significant combined effects. Lane (1983) reported that 250 mg of caffeine would significantly increase the level of blood pressure elevation which occurred during the performance of a stressful, competitive laboratory task. A replication of this study (Greenberg, 1983) found the same effects for the 250 mg dose and a similar effect for a dose of only 125 mg. Further evidence suggested that subjects with a family history of hypertension were significantly more reactive to these effects of caffeine. A third study (Lane & Williams, 1985) has confirmed the interactive effects of caffeine and stress on blood pressure and also shown that the increase in muscle blood flow elicited by the stress ("fight-flight response") is magnified by caffeine.

Further evidence of the influence caffeine can have on stress is provided by Cobb (1974), who examined the effects of the real-world stress of job termination on stress hormones. These hormones were measured at the time of termination and afterward. During the stressful period of termination, the level of one important stress hormone, norepinephrine, was found to be elevated in those men who had ingested caffeine in the hours before measurement. However, in the later months when stress levels were lower, caffeine made no difference.

Although not conclusive, the studies do suggest that the effects of caffeine and stress can interact. Because stress and its consequences are thought to play an important role in the development of many diseases, the combination of stress with caffeine could increase the health risks of both. This interaction would be especially hazardous if caffeine consumption increases under conditions of greater life stress and, indeed, several studies suggest that it does. A study of the occupational stress of naval officers engaged in the training of recruits (Conway, Vickers, Ward, & Rahe, 1981) found that the officers drank significantly more coffee during weeks of high-stress work compared to more relaxed weeks. Individual coffee intake was positively correlated with reported estimates of "stress/strain" and "work load." These associations of stress and caffeine intake were very strong in some individuals and weaker in others. This suggests that not all people increase caffeine use under stress, but that some do very much.

Similar effects were found in college students (Vener & Krupka, 1982) when comparisons were made between a relatively relaxed week during the semester and finals week. The percentage of students consuming more than 500 mg daily (the level often associated with caffeinism) nearly doubled during finals week. Women were more likely to increase caffeine intake in response to stress than men, and women, but not men, reported a relationship between perceived stress and caffeine use.

These potential relationships between caffeine and stress will only be clarified by further research. However, the preliminary findings do provide a strong hint at the potential importance of this interaction for understanding the separate and combined roles of caffeine and stress in the development of disease.

SUMMARY

The information presented in this section demonstrates that caffeine abuse has significant negative consequences on health that can be expressed in several different ways. Although individuals differ in terms of the level of caffeine which can be consumed daily before these consequences develop, 500 mg appears consistently in the literature to be a dividing line between moderate use and abuse. The final section of this chapter will discuss how caffeine abuse can be treated and how the reduction of excessive caffeine use to moderate levels can be achieved.

THE TREATMENT OF CAFFEINE ABUSE

The sections above clearly demonstrate the potential harm which can result from caffeine abuse. As mentioned at the beginning of this chapter, if 500 mg of caffeine or five cups of coffee per day is taken as a rough criterion level for defining caffeine abuse, then perhaps 20% of adults in the U. S. and Canada would qualify as caffeine abusers who would benefit from a reduction in their intake of caffeine. Thus, caffeine abuse is apparently an important and widespread, although little recognized, clinical problem. The reduction of caffeine consumption in caffeine abusers should be an important public health concern.

The treatment of caffeine abuse through caffeine reduction can be managed several different ways. It is possible for many people to "go cold turkey" and totally eliminate caffeine from their diets when told to do so by their doctors. This is the method reported in many of the case studies of patients suffering caffeinism (e.g., Greden, 1974; Reimann, 1967) and it is, according to reports, successful for the treatment of caffeinism. This may not be the best approach. The abrupt cessation of caffeine intake will most likely lead to withdrawal symptoms. The unpleasantness of the withdrawal headache, irritability, and lethargy will provoke some patients to relapse and renew caffeine use since this will provide quick relief of their discomfort. This approach also has another serious limitation which reduces the likelihood of long-term success. No attempt is made to replace the consumption of caffeine with anything else that might serve the same needs for the patient, whether these needs are for increased energy and alertness or for the enjoyment of a hot beverage at mealtime. It is generally accepted that the failure to substitute new, incompatible behaviors further increases the likelihood of relapse.

BEHAVIORAL TREATMENT OF CAFFEINE ABUSE

It is apparent that more support for the person trying to reduce caffeine consumption could be provided through the use of a more complete treatment plan. To date, all of the systematic attempts to provide such a program for the reduction of caffeine consumption have been based on behavioral principles. Hyner (1979) used a relaxation training program to reduce both caffeine use and smoking in a single subject who used both caffeine (in both coffee and pill form) and nicotine to remain alert for study. During the treatment period the subject practiced the relaxation technique for 10-20 minutes in the morning and, before taking caffeine, read a card bearing a statement concerning the advantages of relaxation over caffeine. Caffeine intake dropped immediately from the equivalent of eight cups to two cups of coffee per day, and although there was a relapse during a particularly stressful exam day, caffeine intake remained well below base after treatment ended. Foxx and Rubinoff (1979) worked successfully with three coffee-drinking subjects by combining self-monitoring of caffeine intake, a behavioral contract for the step-wise reduction in daily intake level toward a final goal of moderate caffeine use, and punishment (loss of up to $20) for failing to meet the reduction criteria. Reductions from more than eight cups to less than five cups of coffee were reported for all three subjects at the end of the 4-week treatment and follow-up at 40 months suggested that the improvements were maintained. Bernard, Dennehy, and Keefauver (1981) subsequently reported success with a similar program in a subject who initially consumed over 11 cups of coffee and tea per day. The result after 1 month of treatment was a daily level of five to six cups (still perhaps excessive) and further reductions were reported during the 3-month follow-up to a final level of three to four cups per day.

Although these three studies all reported successful results for their caffeine-reduction treatments, the relative importance of the different components which were included in the treatments (instruction, relaxation, self-monitoring, gradual reduction, etc.) could not be determined by any of the authors. James, Stirling, and Hampton (1985) began such a component analysis by comparing the relative effectiveness of three treatments. The first consisted of education on the hazards of caffeine abuse and suggestions for controlling intake, the setting of a terminal goal of five cups of coffee per day, and self-monitoring of coffee and tea drinking. For another group, "caffeine fading" was added to the package and a specific weekly criterion, based on four equal reduction steps, was provided. The third group received relaxation training, consisting of a single training session with the therapist and tape-recorded instructions for home practice, in addition to the above components. All three treatments produced progressive reductions in caffeine intake during the 4-week treatment period. However, both caffeine-fading groups were more successful than the group provided only a final goal. Brief relaxation training did not significantly improve on the effect of the caffeine-fading component. These differential effects for the treatments lasted through follow-ups at 6 and 18 weeks. The clinical importance of these effects is clearly suggested by comparisons of initial and final caffeine levels. Subjects consumed an average of 18 cups of coffee or tea daily at the beginning of treatment (over 1600 mg of caffeine) but 11 of the 18 caffeine-fading subjects reached the goal of five cups per day and two more were at six cups.

Comparisons of these studies provide some initial guidelines for future treatment. Monetary rewards and

529

punishments or response-cost techniques, used by Foxx and Rubinoff (1979) and Bernard et al. (1981), are not necessary for success. Daily self-monitoring of caffeine use and the establishment of a caffeine-reduction goal can effectively produce a reduction in intake. However, the use of intermediate goals which provide for the reduction of caffeine intake in gradual steps leads to a significant improvement in treatment effectiveness. James et al. (1985) noted that the apparent benefits of a simple program which combined education on the potential consequences of chronic caffeine abuse, advice on how to control caffeine use, and the setting of a goal of moderate caffeine intake along with daily self-monitoring predicted potential success even for large-scale community interventions without individual therapist contact.

GUIDELINES FOR CAFFEINE REDUCTION

These studies clearly demonstrate the efficacy of behavioral interventions for caffeine reduction and provide the foundations for such interventions. Over all the techniques are very similar to those which have been successfully established in treatment programs for smoking and overeating.

Assessment of Baseline. The first step is the assessment of current caffeine use. Table 1 (pages 532-533) provides a list of the caffeine content in milligrams of a variety of the common sources. This information can be used to estimate the daily caffeine intake. The patient should keep daily records of every occasion of caffeine use, including both the source and amount, using a list similar to that provided in Table 1, and a description of the circumstances (time, place, situation, etc.). Because intake can fluctuate during the week, records should be kept for 2 weeks before the intervention is planned. The records will show both the actual baseline magnitude of caffeine use and the characteristic patterns of use for that person.

The assessment of caffeine use based on the daily records will have some limitations. The amount of caffeine present in a cup of coffee or tea can vary widely (Gilbert, Marshman, Schwieder, & Berg, 1976). The caffeine levels in samples of ground coffee varied from 39 to 176 mg and in sample of instant coffee from 29 to 117 mg, roughly a four-fold range. Samples of tea were even more variable, ranging from 8 to 91 mg of caffeine per cup. Part of the variation was due to differences in the size of the cup, from 140 ml to 255 (roughly 5 to 9 oz) and the rest was assumed to be due to differences in the technique of preparation, including the use of more or less coffee or tea than recommended by the manufacturer and the addition of varying amounts of milk or cream. These results suggest that use of the standard values listed in Table 1 can produce some misleading calculations of total daily caffeine. Excessive use may be especially underestimated, since many heavy coffee drinkers use larger coffee mugs that contain more than the standard 5 oz. However, a rough calculation will provide an adequate evaluation of excessive use. Furthermore, in most cases a count of cups of coffee or tea can be used for purposes of self-monitoring and goal-setting.

Goal-Setting. After a period of baseline monitoring, the therapist and patient should set a goal for caffeine reduction. This goal need not be the complete elimination of caffeine from the diet. The actual level should be determined by the elimination of symptoms of caffeinism in each patient. Although 500 mg daily may be a general guideline, Greden (1974) reported symptoms of caffeinism in some persons ingesting only 250 mg of caffeine per day. For the reduction of risk for other diseases, the value of 500 mg or less is considered acceptable. The reduction should also be planned in several gradual steps, both to minimize the possibility of withdrawal as caffeine is reduced and to maximize the likelihood that the program is adhered to. The studies cited above used four steps, each of 1-week duration. This schedule fits well into a format of weekly therapist visits. A much accelerated schedule, perhaps requiring only 1 week, should be possible but has not been studied.

Behavioral Analysis of Caffeine Consumption. Before discussing treatment interventions, it is worthwhile to consider caffeine consumption as a behavior and review the potential controlling stimuli and reinforcers. This analysis will lead directly to suggestions for interventions.

Caffeine consumption has a number of potential reinforcers. The most obvious is the drug effect, particularly the increased alertness and decreased fatigue which caffeine produces. These effects will be a positive reinforcer but will also be intermittent. The positive

531

Caffeine Abuse and Caffeine Reduction

TABLE 1: CAFFEINE LEVELS IN BEVERAGES, FOODS, AND DRUGS*

SOURCE	CAFFEINE (mg)	
	Average Level	Range
Beverages and Foods		

Coffee (5 oz) standard values

Drip	115	60-180
Percolated	80	40-170
Instant	65	30-120

Coffee (5 oz) as prepared

Drip	93	33-113
Percolated	65	29-175
Instant	49	15-84
Decaffeinated	<1	--

Tea (5 oz)

Brewed from loose or bagged	50	20-110
Instant tea	30	25-50
Iced tea (12 oz glass)	70	67-76

Cocoa and Chocolate

Cocoa (5 oz cup)	4	2-20
Chocolate milk (8 oz glass)	5	2-7
Milk chocolate (1 oz)	6	1-15
Dark chocolate (1 oz)	20	5-35
Baker's chocolate (1 oz)	26	--

Soft drinks (12 oz can)

Mountain Dew, Mello Yello	--	53-54
Cola drinks	--	36-46
7-Up, Sprite, RC-100, Fresca, Root Beer, Caffeine-free Colas	0	--

Caffeine Abuse and Caffeine Reduction

SOURCE	CAFFEINE (mg)	
	Average Level	Range
Nonprescription Drugs (per tablet or capsule)		
Stimulants		
Vivarin	200	--
NoDoz	100	--
Pain Relievers		
Excedrin	65	--
Vanquish	33	--
Goody's Headache Powders	32.5	--
Midol, Maximum Strength Midol	32.4	--
Anacin, BC Powders	32	--
Diuretics		
Aqua-Ban Plus	200	--
Aqua-Ban	100	--
Cold/Allergy Remedies		
Coryban-D, Triaminicin	30	--
Dristan-AF	16.2	--

*Note: Values are presented for estimating caffeine consumption and every effort is made to insure accuracy. However, caffeine levels in soft drinks and nonprescription drugs are subject to change by the manufacturer. Reductions are likely as public concern about caffeine use increases. Food and beverage values are from "The Latest Caffeine Scorecard" by C. Lecos, 1984, FDA Consumer, pp. 14-16 with the exception of those for "Coffee (5 oz) as prepared" which are derived from "Caffeine Content of Beverages as Consumed" by R. M. Gilbert, J. A. Marshman, M. Schwieder, and R. Berg, 1976, Canadian Medical Association Journal, 114, pp. 205-208. Nonprescription drug caffeine levels were collected from a drug-store survey of product packaging, March 1986.

effects are most apparent in the morning but as the total dose builds up during the day, the alertness will give way to the toxic symptoms. However, consumption behavior is not likely to extinguish during the day, because the positive reinforcement effects have been intermittent. The relief of withdrawal symptoms after abstinence could also provide an effective source of negative reinforcement.

It is insufficient to assume that the only reinforcers for caffeine intake are those associated with the drug effects. Coffee drinking, the most common source of caffeine in the U. S., has important reinforcing characteristics totally distinct from the drug effects. Goldstein and Kaizer (1969) found that women most frequently reported drinking coffee because they liked the taste or because they enjoyed it. Coffee drinking also has social reinforcers resulting from its use in many social situations. Going for coffee can be an avoidance or escape behavior in the presence of a difficult or monotonous task at work or home. Drinking coffee is also associated with taking a break from work. All of these could be important reinforcers for some individuals.

Caffeine consumption need not be controlled by reinforcements alone. The regular performance of a consummatory behavior often leads to the development of stimulus control which can be another cause of caffeine consumption, even in the absence of reinforcement. Coffee drinking is associated with consistent antecedent variables including the locations where it is consumed and the processes involved in preparation. These cues may elicit the behavior in the regular coffee drinker. The presence of an entire pot of fresh coffee will lead to coffee drinking. The offer of a refill of the coffee cup in a restaurant increases the likelihood that excess coffee will be taken. Stimulus control is encouraged by the socialization of caffeinated beverages and their constant presence. The automatic, almost reflexive, nature of caffeine use under such stimulus control is probably the most significant factor leading to the excessive consumption of caffeine.

Interventions. There are a variety of suggestions for reducing caffeine which can be adopted. For purposes of this discussion, the organization in terms of the antecedents of consumption, the behavior itself, and the consequences or reinforcers will be continued. These suggested strategies need not all be used at any one time. Some people will find some more helpful than others.

Changing the Antecedents. Many strategies can be used to break the association between the pre-existing cues for caffeine use and the behavior. These are similar to interventions widely used for the regulation of eating behavior.

The first strategy is to consciously limit the times and places where caffeine will be used. Evening or nighttime use of caffeine can be eliminated first, which will have the side benefit of improved sleep, and then the afternoon can be kept caffeine free. The morning coffee, most important to regular drinkers and perhaps most valuable in terms of increased alertness, can remain. This is consistent with the goal of proper caffeine use and the elimination only of excessive consumption.

The consumption of caffeine can be made more difficult. The patient should get rid of any supplies of caffeine pills. Materials and equipment for the preparation of coffee or tea should be eliminated from the office or work site. Automatic coffee makers should be put away.

The chain of cues and behaviors leading to consumption can be broken. Patients can be instructed to pause momentarily whenever coffee or tea is offered and to remind themselves of the harmful effects of caffeine abuse. The process of self-monitoring and record keeping can also provide such a pause if the notation is made before consumption.

All of these strategies and many more can help to break the link between the situational and social cues and the consumption of caffeine. This will be an important step in reducing excessive caffeine intake.

Changing the Behavior. The amount of caffeine ingested each time it is consumed can be reduced in a number of ways. Patients can substitute smaller coffee cups for the large mugs which heavy coffee drinkers tend to favor. Instant coffee, which contains 53 mg of caffeine per 5 oz, can be substituted for brewed coffee which contains 125 mg. Ground decaffeinated coffee can be blended into regular coffee in increasing proportions over time to reduce the overall caffeine level of coffee in

535

the pot. Other, uncaffeinated, beverages, such as herbal teas or some soft drinks, can be substituted for caffeinated drinks, particularly when the reasons for use are social or when the beverage is drunk for relaxation rather than for the actual drug effects of caffeine.

Changing the Consequences. Although it is not possible to alter the pharmacological effects of caffeine for purposes of reduction, a system of rewards or punishments can be instituted as part of the program. Rewards can be presented for staying below the criterion level on a daily or weekly basis. Such weekly self-rewards or response costs were part of the interventions reported by Foxx and Rubinoff (1979) and Bernard et al. (1981). Alternatively, response costs could be charged for the consumption of each cup of coffee or tea, both those which are purchased and those which are prepared. For example, the patient could set aside some small amount of money, which is later donated to a despised cause, when each cup of coffee is drunk.

The selection of interventions should, as with every behavioral intervention program, be based upon the analysis of the antecedents, behaviors, and consequences specific to the individual person. The suggestions presented here are intended only as a starting point, to stimulate the development of individualized treatment plans suited to the problem presented by each new patient. Other ideas can be borrowed from the literature of behavior therapy, especially that concerned with reduction of other consummatory behaviors such as smoking and eating.

SUMMARY

Within the constraints of this chapter it has not been possible to provide complete detail of any aspect of caffeine use or caffeine abuse. The socialization of caffeine gives this drug an importance which is shared by nothing else. It is so widely used that its drug nature is almost forgotten. However, it should be remembered that caffeinated beverages do contain a drug which has definite effects on behavior and physiology. These effects can be useful, but can also be unhealthy if caffeine is abused. The need for treatment of caffeine abuse may still be widely unrecognized, but it does exist. I hope that the suggestions provided in this chapter will provide a starting point for such treatment.

James D. Lane, PhD, is currently a Medical Research Assistant Professor in the Division of Medical Psychology of the Department of Psychiatry at the Duke University Medical Center in Durham, North Carolina. His training is in physiological psychology, psychopharmacology, and cognitive psychology. He is particularly interested in the psychophysiology of stress and the role of stress in the development of disease. Other research interests include the psychopharmacology of caffeine and nicotine and the study of Type A, coronary-prone behavior. Dr. Lane may be contacted at the Department of Psychiatry, Box 3926, Duke University Medical Center, Durham, NC 27710.

RESOURCES

American Psychiatric Association. (1980). *Diagnostic and Statistical Manual of Mental Disorders* (3rd ed.). Washington, DC: Author.

Bernard, M. E., Dennehy, S., & Keefauver, L. W. (1981). Behavioral treatment of excessive coffee and tea drinking: A case study and partial replication. *Behavior Therapy, 12,* 543-548.

Bertrand, C. A., Pomper, I., Hillman, G., Duffy, J. C., Michell, I. (1978). No relation between coffee and blood pressure. *New England Journal of Medicine, 298,* 315.

Boulenger, J-P., & Uhde, T. W. (1982). Caffeine consumption and anxiety: Preliminary results of a survey comparing patients with anxiety disorders and normal controls. *Psychopharmacology Bulletin, 18,* 53-57.

Brecher, E. M., & The Editors of Consumer Reports. (1972). *Licit & Illicit Drugs.* Boston: Little, Brown & Company.

Charney, D. S., Heninger, G. R., & Jatlow, P. I. (1985). Increased anxiogenic effects of caffeine in panic disorders. *Archives of General Psychiatry, 42,* 233-243.

Cobb, S. (1974). Physiologic changes in men whose jobs were abolished. *Journal of Psychosomatic Research, 18,* 245-258.

Cola: The real thing. (1974, January). *Psychology Today*, pp. 92-93.

Colton, T., Gosselin, R. E., & Smith, R. (1968). The tolerance of coffee drinkers to caffeine. *Clinical Pharmacology and Therapeutics, 9,* 31-39.

Conrad, K. A., Blanchard, J., & Trang, J. M. (1982). Cardiovascular effects of caffeine in elderly men. *Journal of the American Geriatrics Society, 30,* 267-272.

Conway, T. L., Vickers, R. R., Ward, H. W., & Rahe, R. H. (1981). Occupational stress and variation in cigarette, coffee, and alcohol consumption. *Journal of Health and Social Behavior, 22,* 155-165.

Dawber, T. R., Kannel, W. B., & Gordon, T. (1974). Coffee and cardiovascular disease. *New England Journal of Medicine, 291,* 871-874.

De Freitas, B., & Schwartz, G. (1979). Effects of caffeine in chronic psychiatric patients. *American Journal of Psychiatry, 136,* 1337-1338.

Dobmeyer, D. J., Stine, R. A., Leier, C. V., Greenberg, R., & Schaal, S. F. (1983). The arrhythmogenic effects of caffeine in human beings. *New England Journal of Medicine, 308,* 814-816.

Dreisbach, R. H., & Pfeiffer, C. (1943). Caffeine withdrawal headache. *Journal of Laboratory and Clinical Medicine, 28,* 1212-1219.

Foxx, R. M., & Rubinoff, A. (1979). Behavioral treatment of caffeinism: Reducing excessive coffee drinking. *Journal of Applied Behavior Analysis, 12,* 335-344.

Fredholm, B. B. (1980). Are methylxanthine effects due to antagonism of endogenous adenosine? *Trends in Pharmacological Sciences, 1,* 129-132.

Gilbert, R. M. (1976). Caffeine as a drug of abuse. In A. J. Gibbons, Y. Israel, H. Kalant, R. E. Popham, W. Schmidt, & R. G. Smart (Eds.), *Research Advances in Alcohol and Drug Problems* (Vol. 3, pp. 49-176). New York: Wiley & Sons.

Gilbert, R. M., Marshman, J. A., Schwieder, M., & Berg, R. (1976). Caffeine content of beverages as consumed. *Canadian Medical Association Journal, 114,* 205-208.

Gilliland K., & Andress, D. (1981). Ad lib caffeine consumption, symptoms of caffeinism, and academic performance. *American Journal of Psychiatry, 138,* 512-514.

Goldstein, A., & Kaizer, S. (1969). Psychotropic effects of caffeine in man. III. A questionnaire survey of coffee drinking and its effects in a group of housewives. *Clinical Pharmacology and Therapeutics, 10,* 477-488.

Goldstein, A., Kaizer, S., & Warren, R. (1965). Psychotropic effects of caffeine in man. II. Alertness, psychomotor coordination, and mood. *Journal of Pharmacology and Experimental Therapeutics, 150,* 146-151.

Goldstein, A., Kaizer, S., & Whitby, O. (1969). Psychotropic effects of caffeine in man. IV. Quantitative and qualitative differences associated with habituation to coffee. *Clinical Pharmacology and Therapeutics, 10,* 489-497.

Goldstein, A., Warren, R., & Kaizer, S. (1965). Psychotropic effects of caffeine in man. I. Individual differences in sensitivity to caffeine-induced wakefulness. *Journal of Pharmacology and Experimental Therapeutics, 149,* 156-159.

Greden, J. F. (1974). Anxiety or caffeinism: A diagnostic dilemma. *American Journal of Psychiatry, 131,* 1089-1092.

Greden, J. F., Fontaine, P., Lubetsky, M., & Chamberlin, K. (1978). Anxiety and depression associated with caffeinism among psychiatric inpatients. *American Journal of Psychiatry, 135,* 963-966.

Greden. J. F., Victor, B. S., Fontaine, P., & Lubetsky, M. (1980). Caffeine-withdrawal headache: A clinical profile. *Psychosomatics, 21,* 411-418.

Greenberg, W. P. (1983). *The Effects of Caffeine and Stress on Blood Pressure in Individuals with Parental History of Hypertension.* Unpublished doctoral dissertation, University of California, Los Angeles, CA.

Hennekens, C. H., Drolette, M. E., Jesse, M. J., Davies, J. E., & Hutchison, G. B. (1976). Coffee drinking and death due to coronary heart disease. *New England Journal of Medicine, 294,* 633-636.

Henry, J. P., & Stephens, P. M. (1980). Caffeine as an intensifier of stress-induced hormonal and pathophysiological changes in mice. *Physiology, Biochemistry, and Behavior, 13,* 719-727.

Hicks, R. A., Hicks, G. J., Reyes, R., & Cheers, Y. (1983). Daily caffeine use and the sleep of college students. *Bulletin of the Psychonomic Society, 21,* 24-25.

Hrubec, Z. (1973). Coffee-drinking and ischemic heart disease. *The Lancet, 1,* 548.

Hyner, G. C. (1979). Relaxation as a principal treatment for excessive cigarette use and caffeine ingestion by a college female. *Psychological Reports, 45,* 531-534.

James, J. E., & Stirling, K. P. (1983). Caffeine: A survey of some of the known and suspected deleterious effects of habitual use. *British Journal of Addiction, 78,* 251-258.

James, J. E., Stirling, K. P., & Hampton, B. A. M. (1985). Caffeine fading: Behavioral treatment of caffeine abuse. *Behavior Therapy, 16,* 15-27.

Jick, H., Miettenen, O. S., Neff, R. K., Shapiro, S., Heinonen, O. P., & Slone, D. (1973). Coffee and myocardial infarction. *New England Journal of Medicine, 289,* 63-67.

Klatsky, A. L., Friedman, G. D., & Siegelaub, A. B. (1973). Coffee drinking prior to acute myocardial infarction. *Journal of the American Medical Association, 226,* 540-543.

Kurppa, K., Holmberg, P. C., Kuosma, E., & Saxen, L. (1982). Coffee consumption during pregnancy. *New England Journal of Medicine, 306,* 1548.

Lane, J. D. (1983). Caffeine and cardiovascular responses to stress. *Psychosomatic Medicine, 45,* 447-451.

Lane, J. D., & Williams, R. B. (1985). Caffeine affects cardiovascular responses to stress. *Psychophysiology, 22,* 648-655.

Lecos, C. (1984, March). The latest caffeine scorecard. *FDA Consumer,* pp. 14-16.

Linn, S., Schoenbaum, S. C., Monson, R. R., Rosner, B., Stubblefield, P. G., & Ryan, K. J. (1982). No association between coffee consumption and adverse outcomes of pregnancy. *New England Journal of Medicine, 306,* 141-145.

MacCallum, W. A. G. (1979). Excess coffee and anxiety states. *International Journal of Social Psychiatry, 25,* 209-210.

MacMahon, Yen, Trichopoulos, Warren, & Nardi. (1981). Coffee and cancer of the pancreas. *New England Journal of Medicine, 304,* 630-633.

Neims, A. H., & von Borstel, R. W. (1983). Caffeine: Metabolism and biochemical mechanisms of action. In R. J. Wurtman & J. J. Wurtman (Eds.), *Nutrition and the Brain, Vol. 6* (pp. 1-30). New York: Raven Press.

Rall, T. W. (1980). Central nervous system stimulants: The xanthines. In A. G. Gilman, L. S. Goodman, & A. Gilman (Eds.), *Goodman and Gilman's The Pharmacologi-*

cal Basis of Therapeutics (6th ed., pp. 592-607). New York: MacMillan.

Reimann, H. A. (1967). Caffeinism: A cause of long-continued, low-grade fever. *Journal of the American Medical Society, 202,* 131-132.

Roberts, H. R., & Barone, J. J. (1983). Biological effects of caffeine: History and use. *Food Technology, 37,* 32-39.

Robertson, D., Frölich, J. C., Carr, R. K., Watson, J. T., Hollifield, J. W., Shand, D. G., & Oates, J. A. (1978). Effects of caffeine on plasma renin activity, catecholamines and blood pressure. *New England Journal of Medicine, 298,* 181-186.

Robertson, D., Wade, D., Workman, R., Woolsey, R. L., & Oates, J. A. (1981). Tolerance to the humoral and hemodynamic effects of caffeine in man. *Journal of Clinical Investigation, 67,* 1111-1117.

Rosenberg, L, Slone, S., Shapiro, S., Kaufman, D. W., Stolley, P. D., & Miettenen, O. (1980). Coffee drinking and myocardial infarction in young women. *American Journal of Epidemiology, 111,* 675-681.

Smits, P., Hoffman, H., Thien, T., Houben, H., & van't Laar, A. (1983). Hemodynamic and humoral effects of coffee after beta$_1$-selective and nonselective beta-blockade. *Clinical Pharmacology and Therapeutics, 34,* 153-158.

Snyder, S. H., Katims, J. J., Annau, A., Bruns, R. F., & Daly, J. W. (1981). (Untitled). *Proceedings of the National Academy of Science, USA, 78,* 3260-3264.

Sours, J. A. (1983). Case reports of anorexia nervosa and caffeinism. *American Journal of Psychiatry, 140,* 235-236.

Vener, A. M., & Krupka, L. R. (1982). Caffeine use and young adult women. *Journal of Drug Education, 12,* 273-282.

Vessey, M. P. (1972). Coffee drinking and acute myocardial infarction: Report from the Boston Collaborative Drug Surveillance Program. *The Lancet, 2,* 1278-1281.

Walker, W. J., & Gregoratos, G. (1967). Myocardial infarction in young men. *The American Journal of Cardiology, 19,* 339-343.

Weiss, B., & Laties, V. G. (1962). Enhancement of human performance by caffeine and the amphetamines. *Pharmacological Reviews, 14,* 1-36.

Whitsett, T. L., Manion, C. V., & Christensen, H. D. (1984). Cardiovascular effects of coffee and caffeine. *American Journal of Cardiology, 53,* 918-922.

Winstead, D. K. (1976). Coffee consumption among psychiatric patients. *American Journal of Psychiatry, 133,* 1447-1450.

EXERCISE AS A THERAPEUTIC MODALITY: THE EXERCISE PRESCRIPTION

Douglas D. Schocken

Physicians have long recommended physical activity as part of overall health maintenance. Physical training programs have experienced a recent great wave of enthusiasm throughout this country and elsewhere. However, exercise as a therapeutic rather than recreational or leisure activity is misunderstood by health care providers and many lay persons seeking to participate in or organize physical conditioning programs. The purpose of this chapter is to:

1. Underscore the potential health benefits of physical training.
2. Review the indications for exercise prescriptions.
3. Briefly summarize the evaluation of the patient, including exercise testing.
4. Describe the actual composition of the exercise prescription.
5. Briefly review the implementation of exercise programs as well as their potential complications.
6. Discuss the assessment and follow-up of persons enrolled in such programs.

Physical training programs produce significant alterations at many levels including changes in biochemical, anatomical, physiological, and psychological states. At the biochemical level, total cholesterol and triglyceride levels decrease, high density lipoprotein (HDL) cholesterol levels rise (hypothetically beneficial in the prevention of coronary artery disease), fibrinolysis is enhanced, glucose tolerance improves, and beta endorphin levels increase (one possible source of the runner's euphoric "high"). Anatomical effects of physical training include both a decrease in body weight and an increase in lean body mass. Physiological benefits of physical training include increased functional capacity and exercise tolerance, decreased resting heart rate, and decreased oxygen consumption at any given level of submaximal exercise (improved work efficiency) (Clausen, 1977). Psychological effects of physical training encompass the general observations of improved sense of well-being, enhanced personal confidence and self-esteem, and improved body image. Also, physical training reduces both emotional stress and anxiety and has been used successfully to decrease Type A personality measures. Regular sustained exercise may result in decreased levels of depression and provide general mood elevation, areas of study recently reviewed by Hughes (1984).

Exercise differs from other therapeutic tools. It has a broad range of indications and contraindications. As with medication, it may be titrated, and potential adverse effects may be associated with its use. Benefits in large part derive from strict compliance with the exercise prescription. However, unlike other therapeutic drugs or activities, physical exercise ought to be viewed as a life-long activity and part of a health maintenance program. Exercise prescriptions should be viewed not only as short-term but also as part of the development of lifestyle change for overall health enhancement.

INDICATIONS FOR EXERCISE PRESCRIPTION

Exercises may be broadly classified into three categories: those which increase endurance, those which improve muscle strength, and those which enhance flexibility. The first of these three modalities is primarily responsible for the significant physical and psychological changes noted above. Strength-building activities include predominantly isometric exercise and require increases in cardiac oxygen demand which are abrupt and unaccompanied by improved endurance. These abrupt changes in myocardial oxygen demand may be detrimental to those persons seeking exercise as a form of cardiac rehabilitation. Exercises to increase flexibility do not directly produce physical conditioning. This chapter will deal solely with endurance exercise.

Healthy but deconditioned persons make up the largest group of individuals seeking to participate in physical exercise programs. Guidelines for their evaluation may be found in the American Heart Association publication *Exercise Testing and Training of Apparently Healthy Individuals: A Handbook for Physicians* (1972). This group presents generally low risk for both evaluation and unsupervised exercise programs.

The second major group for whom exercise prescriptions are indicated consists of the patients either at risk for or known to have cardiac disease. Heart disease remains the leading cause of death in this country, accounting for as many as 900,000 deaths per year and utilizing 64.4 billion dollars in health care in the year 1984. Certain persons are at increased risk for the development of cardiovascular disease. Those patients with one or more of the identifiable major risk factors for cardiac disease (hypercholesterolemia, hypertension, cigarette smoking) or several minor or less well-recognized risk factors (diabetes mellitus, positive family history, obesity, Type A personality, sedentary lifestyle) ought to be regarded as at high risk for developing cardiac disease. They should be considered for primary prevention measures and physical conditioning.

A third group consists of patients with coronary heart disease (CHD) by virtue of their having sustained a myocardial infarction (MI) or having symptoms of ischemic pain (angina pectoris). Rehabilitation of this group makes up the major portion of in-hospital and medically supervised programs. Effective multidisciplinary cardiac rehabilitation beginning at the time the diagnosis of CHD or acute MI is made is essential to the process of returning the patient to as near his or her previous functional state as possible. The discussion of Step I programs (in-hospital physical activity and ambulation) is not within the scope of this chapter. Once patients have undergone initial post-MI evaluation including low-level exercise testing (if not otherwise contraindicated), they ought to be considered as candidates for implementation of a progressive out-patient exercise program (Steps II and III). Aside from the restoration of functional capacity and the benefits of improved psychological functioning following MI, physical training programs may also decrease the risk of recurrent infarction or sudden death, although the evidence for this effect is equivocal.

Other medical disorders benefit from physical conditioning. Training designed to improve functional capacity is of significant assistance to those patients with obstructive pulmonary disease, hypertension, obesity, or diabetes mellitus. Following surgery (particularly coronary artery by-pass surgery), development of a progressive physical training program may play an important part in the early restoration of functional capacity, including return to work or previous activity status. After any type of surgery, the use of a physical training program to complement physical and respiratory therapy is a valuable part of post-operative care. Exercise has received some attention in the management of psychological disorders. Specifically, depression and other mood disorders may benefit from a physical training program as part of the therapeutic plan (Greist et al., 1979).

Certain contraindications should preclude use of exercise prescriptions or enrollment in exercise programs. Table 1 lists the major contraindications for physical

---

TABLE 1:   EXAMPLES OF CONTRAINDICATIONS TO PARTICIPATION
           IN EXERCISE PROGRAMS

Acute medical illness including systemic infection
Uncontrolled chronic medical illness
      Diabetes mellitus
      Thyroid disorders: hyperthyroidism
                           hypothyroidism
      Adrenocortical insufficiency
      Anemia
      Uremic syndrome
Acute or unstable cardiac disease
      Acute myocardial infarction
      Unstable angina pectoris
      Congestive heart failure
      Severe aortic stenosis
      Atrial fibrillation with uncontrolled ventricular response
      Complex ventricular ectopy
      Sick sinus syndrome
      High degree AV block
Acute illness involving bones, joints, or ligaments
      Uncontrolled arthritis - rheumatoid, degenerative, gout
      Severe strains, sprains
      Acute fractures
Vascular disorders
      Acute stroke or transient ischemic attack
      Thrombophlebitis
      Pulmonary or systemic embolism
      Aortic aneurysms

---

exercise training. Any acute illness which would otherwise restrict one's daily activity should constitute a relative if not absolute contraindication to enrollment in such a physical training program. Cardiac problems which should similarly exclude participation include unstable angina pectoris, acute evolving myocardial infarction, active myocarditis or pericarditis, and severe aortic stenosis.

Acute or otherwise very active orthopedic or rheumatologic problems preclude participation in an active exercise program. Metabolic disorders should also be considered contraindications to program enrollment and include uncontrolled active thyroid disease, uncontrolled diabetes mellitus, and adrenocortical insufficiency. Acute and chronic disorders of the vascular system including venous and arterial insufficiency may be viewed as contraindications to exercise therapy, although physical training of patients with exercise-induced leg claudication may improve their functional capacity. Guidelines for unsupervised exercise are presented elsewhere (Williams, Miller, Koisch, Ribisl, & Graden, 1981).

EVALUATION OF THE PATIENT

Thorough evaluation of candidates for exercise prescriptions forms the foundation on which successful programs are based. Once the indication for enrollment has been identified, the patient should undergo a physician's evaluation. This evaluation will vary in its complexity depending upon the patient's health status. Of course, unfit but otherwise healthy persons do not require as detailed an evaluation as those persons recovering from acute myocardial infarction. However, the examining physician has the responsibility of making such decisions. All evaluations should include a thorough history and physical examination in order to exclude symptoms or signs of recent acute illness. In addition, the history should incorporate features of personal life habits to include daily business and leisure activities as well as an account of current and past exercise experience. Current medications constitute an important part of the medical history that may greatly modify both the interpretation of the baseline evaluation tests and the response of the patient to implementation of an exercise prescription. Routine laboratory evaluation of patients need not include great expense or detail. Asymptomatic persons under age 35 may require no specific testing. For patients over age 35, in addition to the graded exercise test recommended by the American Heart Association (1980) and the American College of Sports Medicine (1978), routine hemoglobin determination, urinalysis, and chest x-ray may be recommended, depending upon the clinical status of the individual. With increasing age, other laboratory tests including electrolytes and fasting blood glucose should be considered as part of the routine screening battery.

EXERCISE TESTING

The physiological basis of exercise conditioning rests with the exposure of the patient to large muscle dynamic exercise, thereby producing sustained increased oxygen consumption. A series of studies beginning in the 1930s have defined age- and sex-adjusted maximum values for oxygen consumption. It is widely believed that physical training effects do not occur at sustained oxygen consumption less than 60% of maximum. Within a broad range, oxygen consumption by the body as a whole and by the heart as a single muscular organ is directly proportional to heart rate (Åstrand & Rodahl, 1977). As a result of this relationship, shown in Figure 1 (page 549), the heart rate may serve as a convenient indicator of total oxygen consumption. Maximum heart rate as determined on a graded exercise test is a useful guide for writing an exercise prescription.

Exercise stress testing is a procedure undertaken by a wide variety of institutions. Health spas and community centers as well as physicians' offices and hospital cardiac diagnostic laboratories perform such testing. Each of these facilities has unique goals in mind for its subjects or patients. However, the proper conduct of exercise testing with regard to patient safety cannot be overemphasized. Guidelines for equipment and staffing of exercise laboratories are well described in the American Heart Association publication *The Exercise Standards Book* (1979).

Several principles dictate the type of exercise test chosen when developing an exercise prescription. First, the exercise should be graded, that is, featuring increasing levels of work load whether by augmenting speed or inclination of a motor-driven treadmill or by increasing

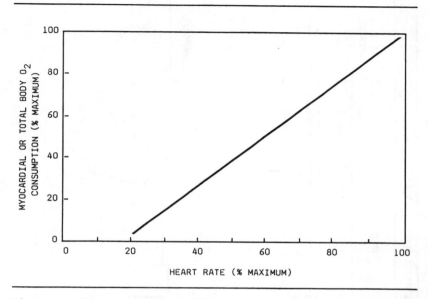

Figure 1. The relationship between total body oxygen consumption, myocardial oxygen demand, and heart rate.

tension applied to a wheel of a bicycle ergometer. Second, the type of exercise chosen for the test should closely correspond to the kind of activity that will be prescribed as the individual's exercise program. That is, bicycle ergometry is more applicable for persons choosing bicycle exercise, whereas the treadmill exercise test is more suited for those planning to walk or jog. Third, a specific testing plan or protocol should be selected and consistently followed in order to serve as a basis for comparison to other individuals as well as to the subject's own test at another occasion. Briefly, of two popular treadmill protocols, the Balke protocol (Table 2, pages 550-551) gradually increases the inclination of the moving belt used as a walking surface, maintaining a constant speed (3.4 mph). The Bruce protocol (Table 2) uses fewer fixed stages with increments of both speed and inclination between each. Examples of these and other exercise treadmill protocols are shown in Table 2.

Regardless of specific protocol, the personnel conducting the test should be well-trained in the collection of subjective and objective data from the patient. The

TABLE 2: OXYGEN REQUIREMENTS AND PROTOCOLS FOR VARIOUS EXERCISE STRESS TESTS*

FUNCTIONAL CLASS	METS	O₂ REQUIREMENTS ml O₂/kg/min	STEP TEST — NAGLE, BALKE, & NAUGHTON[1]; 2 min-stages 30 steps/min (Step height increased 4 cm q 2 min) — Height (cm)	TREADMILL TESTS — BRUCE[2] 3-min stages (mph % gr)	TREADMILL TESTS — KATTUS[3] 3-min stages (mph % gr)	TREADMILL TESTS — BALKE[4] % grade at 3.4 mph	TREADMILL TESTS — BALKE[4] % grade at 3 mph	BICYCLE ERGOMETER[4] For 70 kg body weight (kgm/min)
	16	56.0			4 22	26		
	15	52.5				24		
	14	49.0			4 18	22		
NORMAL AND I	13	45.5		4.2 16		20		1500
	12	42.0	40		4 14	18	22.5	1350
	11	38.5	36			16	20.0	1200
	10	35.0	32	3.4 14		14	17.5	1050
	9	31.5	28			12	15.0	900

Functional Class	Stage	O₂		mph	% grade	mph	% grade			kgm/min
II	8	28.0	24					10	12.5	750
	7	24.5	20	2.5	12			8	10.0	600
	6	21.0	16	1.7	10	4	10	6	7.5	450
	5	17.5	12			3	10	4	5.0	300
III	4	14.0	8			2	10	2	2.5	150
	3	10.5	4						0.0	
IV	2	7.0								
	1	3.5								

[1] Nagle, F. S., Balke, B., & Naughton, J. P. (1965). Gradational step tests for assessing work capacity. Journal of Applied Physiology, 20, 745-748.

[2] Bruce, R. A. (1979). Multi-stage treadmill test of submaximal and maximal exercise. The Exercise Standards Book. American Heart Association, Appendix B.

[3] Kattus, A. A., Jorgensen, C. R., Worden, R. E., et al. (1971). S-T segment depression with near-maximal exercise in detection of preclinical coronary heart disease. Circulation, 41, 585-595.

[4] Fox, S. M., Naughton, J. P., & Haskell, W. L. (1971). Physical activity and the prevention of coronary heart disease. Annals of Clinical Research, 3, 404.

Note. From The Exercise Standards Book (p. 11) by American Heart Association, 1979, Dallas, TX: Subcommittee on Rehabilitation Target Activity Group, M. H. Ellestad, Chairman. Copyright © 1979. Reprinted by permission.

necessity of good communication between the test subject and those conducting the test should be underscored. Exercise testing requires continuous multi-lead electrocardiographic monitoring to record heart rate, cardiac rhythm, changes in the QRS complex and ST segments. The capability to determine blood pressure quickly and accurately is also required. Some laboratories with specialized instrumentation feature gas analyzers to directly determine oxygen consumption and carbon dioxide production.

There are several methods for choosing an objective end point for an exercise stress test. The two major types of test end points are maximal and submaximal limits. The maximal end point may be based on an age-predicted maximal heart rate or on limiting symptoms, usually fatigue in otherwise healthy individuals. A submaximal end point may be based on a lower work load or lower heart rate than that generally predicted. This method has particular utility in initial low-level exercise testing after myocardial infarction and in comparing estimates of oxygen consumption at submaximal work loads on serial tests. However, in writing an exercise prescription, symptom-limited maximal exercise testing remains the most useful type of protocol. Since safety is of paramount importance in all exercise testing and programs, exercise stress tests may be concluded prematurely on the basis of numerous subjective or objective findings. An abbreviated list of reasons for discontinuing exercise testing are included in Table 3 (page 553). More inclusive lists have been developed by the American Heart Association (1975) and Ellestad (1980).

Beyond the type of illness from which the patient is suffering, other factors affect both the interpretation of the test and determination of the patient's overall exercise tolerance. Various medications (particularly digoxin, diuretics, and beta adrenegic blockers) significantly influence both exercise EKG interpretation and exercise performance. The patient's clinical status at the time of the test and the degree of personal motivation largely determine the total performance on the test. If a subject displays an inordinate degree of anxiety or poor motivation despite appropriate counseling by the testing personnel, he or she should be given the option of performing the test at another occasion rather than producing clinically suboptimal information.

TABLE 3:   SOME INDICATIONS FOR PREMATURE TERMINATION
           OF EXERCISE STRESS TESTING

Subjective
    Significant chest discomfort
    Acute dyspnea
    Claudication
    Significant musculoskeletal complaints
    Gait disturbance
    Poor communication with patient
    Patient appears inappropriately diaphoretic, pre-syncopal,
      apprehensive
Objective
    Paroxysmal supraventricular tachycardia
    Ventricular ectopic beats in groups of two or more
    Inadequate heart rate or blood pressure rise with exercise
    Significant fall in heart rate or blood pressure during exercise
    Markedly elevated blood pressure response during exercise
    Profound J-ST segment depression
Technical
    Inability to observe rhythm continuously
    Inability to determine blood pressure quickly
    Mechanical equipment malfunction

WRITING THE EXERCISE PRESCRIPTION

In order to achieve proper physical conditioning, the prescription must be individualized. The major components of this prescription include: type of activity, intensity, duration, and frequency.

The type of activity should utilize large muscle dynamic motion. Walking, or jogging, swimming, bicycling, and aerobic dancing all provide such activity. Emphasis ought to be away from static isometric exercise, which increases muscle strength but not endurance and produces rapid changes in myocardial oxygen demand that may not be well tolerated by cardiac patients. Therefore, sports such as weight lifting should be discouraged. The intensity of exercise can be measured in MET units. A MET is the oxygen uptake required for basal resting activity and approximates 3.5 milliliters O_2/kg/min. The calories expended per hour in performing a given activity can be approximated by multiplying the MET requirement by a total body mass in kg. Metabolic equivalents for various physical activities are shown in Table 4 (pages 554-555).

Aerobic exercise is that which increases peripheral muscular and myocardial oxygen transport and delivery. Activity which exceeds aerobic capacity requires

553

TABLE 4: APPROXIMATE ENERGY REQUIREMENTS OF SELECTED ACTIVITIES

Category	Self-Care or Home	Occupational	Recreational[1]	Physical Conditioning
Very light 3 mets 10 ml/kg/min 4 kcal	Washing, shaving, dressing Desk work, writing Washing dishes Driving auto	Sitting (clerical, assembling) Standing (store clerk, bartender) Driving truck[1] Crane operator[1]	Shuffleboard Horseshoes Bait casting Billiards Archery[1] Golf (cart)	Walking (level at 2 mph) Stationary bicycle (very low resistance) Very light calisthenics
Light 3-5 mets 11-18 ml/kg/min 4-6 kcal	Cleaning windows Raking leaves Weeding Power lawn mowing Waxing floors (slowly) Painting Carrying objects (15-30 lb)	Stocking shelves (light objects)[2] Light welding Light carpentry[2] Machine assembly Auto repair Paper hanging[2]	Dancing (social and square) Golf (walking) Sailing Horseback riding Volleyball (6 man) Tennis (doubles)	Walking (3-4 mph) Level bicycling (6-8 mph) Light calisthenics
Moderate 5-7 mets 18-24 ml/kg/min 6-8 kcal	Easy digging in garden Level hand lawn mowing Climbing stairs (slowly) Carrying objects (30-60 lb)[2]	Carpentry (exterior home building)[2] Shoveling dirt[2] Pneumatic tools[2]	Badminton (competitive) Tennis (singles) Snow skiing (downhill) Light backpacking Basketball Football Skating (ice and roller) Horseback riding (gallop)	Walking (4.5-5 mph) Bicycling (9-10 mph) Swimming (breast stroke)

Category	Self-Care or Home	Occupational	Recreational[1]	Physical Conditioning
Heavy 7-9 mets 25-32 ml/kg/min 8-10 kcal	Sawing wood[2] Heavy shoveling[2] Climbing stairs (moderate speed) Carrying objects (60-90 lb)[2]	Tending furnace[2] Digging ditches[2] Pick and shovel[2]	Canoeing[2] Mountain climbing[2] Fencing Paddleball Touch football	Jog (5 mph) Swim (crawl stroke) Rowing machine Heavy calisthenics Bicycling (12 mph)
Very heavy >9 mets >32 ml/kg/min >10 kcal	Carrying loads upstairs[2] Carrying objects (>90 lb)[2] Climbing stairs (quickly) Shoveling heavy snow[2] Shoveling 10/min (16 lb)	Lumber jack[2] Heavy laborer[2]	Handball Squash Ski touring over (hills)[2] Vigorous basketball	Running (≥6 mph) Bicycle (≥13 mph or up steep hill) Rope jumping

[1] May cause added psychologic stress that will increase work load on the heart.
[2] May produce disproportionate myocardial demands because of use of arms or isometric exercise.

Note. From "Design and Implementation of Cardiac Conditioning Programs" by W. L. Haskell in *Rehabilitation of the Coronary Patient* (p. 211) by N. K. Wenger and H. K. Hellerstein (Eds.), 1978, New York: John Wiley. Copyright © 1978. Reprinted by permission.

anaerobic metabolism. Physical conditioning programs to enhance endurance accomplish this goal by augmenting levels of aerobic activity. Because a threshold exists below which aerobic conditioning does not occur, intensity of the chosen activity is an important factor in exercise prescription writing. The metabolic equivalents noted in Table 4 may serve as a rough guide. However, the type of activity chosen should produce a heart rate response such that myocardial oxygen consumption will approximate 60-80% of the age-predicted maximum for that individual. Several methods may be used to calculate a target range of heart rate in which the patient should exercise to achieve aerobic affects. One convenient formula uses 70-85% of maximum heart rate achieved on the exercise stress test. Another method of determining target range is shown in Figure 2 (page 557).

The target range is also useful in teaching the patient how to monitor his or her own exercise by radial or carotid pulse palpation. In addition, an upper limitation of approximately 10-15 beats above the target range should be an absolute upper limit beyond which the patient should not exercise. Under no circumstances should a patient exercise at a heart rate greater than that observed under testing conditions.

Once the type and intensity of the exercise to be prescribed have been chosen, duration and frequency need to be determined. Thirty minutes of exercise is evidently the rough minimum necessary to produce a significant physical training effect. Thus, in addition to warm up and cool down periods, the portion of the training session devoted to aerobic exercise should consist of at least 30 minutes of vigorous exercise. Many patients with significant illness or in the early stages of their training program may not be able to sustain their exercise for 30 minutes. However, this duration ought to be one of their first goals in the training program.

Exercise sessions three to four times each week appear well-suited to produce good physical training effects. These days should preferably not be sequential. Fewer than 3 days of exercise produce significantly less physical training effect. Five or more days of exercise per week may augment training effects seen with 3 to 4 days of exercise, but frequently at the price of an increased incidence of injuries, particularly orthopedic.

As with other diagnostic or therapeutic procedures, the application of an exercise prescription in the manage-

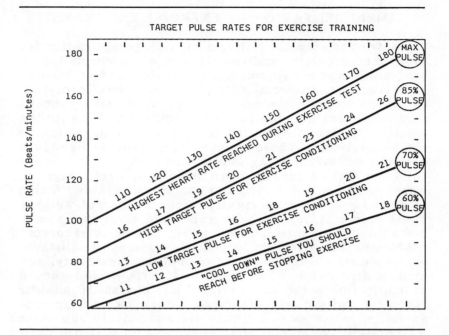

Figure 2. Target pulse rates for 10-sec counts that should be measured the first 10 sec after exercise. To convert the count to beats per minute, multiply by 6. To determine a patient's target pulse rate range, identify the highest heart rate safely achieved during the most recent exercise test on the top line (maximum pulse line); then locate the corresponding values on the 85% and 70% lines directly below. These two values represent the limits of target rate range for exercise conditioning.

Note. From "Design and Implementation of Cardiac Conditioning Programs" by W. L. Haskell in Rehabilitation of the Coronary Patient (p. 209) by N. K. Wenger and H. K. Hellerstein (Eds.), 1978, New York: John Wiley. Copyright © 1978. Reprinted by permission.

ment of medical illness requires a significant degree of understanding between the physician and patient. Informed consent should be utilized as part of all exercise prescriptions. This consent should contain information about the exercise prescription, particularly the training range and upper limits. The Appendix (page 563) of this chapter provides an example of a consent form designed by the American Heart Association (1979). The form also serves to codify a therapeutic contract between a physician and his or her patient which underscores the commitment by both parties.

IMPLEMENTATION OF EXERCISE PROGRAMS

A formal exercise program utilizes group leaders for supervised programs and specific session protocols for all programs. Whether at community service centers, schools, hospitals, or commercial enterprises, effective leadership for group sessions remains the single most readily identified factor influencing patient compliance. This leader, whether an exercise physiologist, nurse, or physician, is the single person whose motivational skills will enhance both the individual and group interactions.

Each session ideally consists of four parts: sign in, warm up, aerobic exercise, and cool down periods. A sign in period provides opportunity to check interval weights, blood pressures, resting heart rates, and gives group leaders a chance to solicit progress reports or intercurrent problems. The warm up includes low intensity calisthenics emphasizing active range of motion, flexibility, and modest stretching. The active exercise period should promptly follow the warm up and last at least 30 minutes for most individuals. In larger supervised group programs, exercise monitors may simultaneously supervise walkers and joggers as well as those who perform their exercise on stationary bicycles. At the conclusion of the exercise session, the group should participate in a cool down period consisting of calisthenics similar to those used in the warm up period. Emphasis should be placed both on the variety of the exercise and on the group supervised nature of the entire session, especially where Step II cardiac patients (post-hospital discharge after myocardial infarction) are enrolled. The greatest risk of sudden cardiac events to participants in cardiac rehabilitation programs occurs during the warm ups and cool down sessions (Haskell, 1978), and close supervision is especially necessary at those times.

There are advantages of beginning with group participation for most patients. The educational and motivational aspects of group sessions can be very beneficial. The opportunity for contact with other patients presenting similar significant functional limitation may be especially valuable. For those persons otherwise healthy but unfit, beginning in group sessions helps to assure initial appropriate compliance with warm up, exercise, and cool down techniques. All subjects should be taught how to monitor their own heart rates by counting radial or carotid pulsations for 10 seconds and multiplying by six. Group leaders and exercise monitors periodically evaluate heart rate response on all subjects to assure compliance with training range and upper limitations.

COMPLICATIONS OF EXERCISE PROGRAMS

As with other therapeutic interventions, physical training programs are not without adverse side effects. Because of the complex nature of physical conditioning and the requirements for musculoskeletal motor skills and some degree of strength, orthopedic injuries represent a major source of complications for exercise programs. Those persons at greatest risk for developing orthopedic complications include patients with past histories of joint or ligament problems. Additionally, participants in jogging or competitive sports are far more likely to incur orthopedic injuries.

The primary limitations posed by jogging include impact and stress injuries to the bones and soft tissues of the legs and feet. Strains involve pulling or tearing of musculotendonous structures (e.g., the anteromedial distal tibial strain called "shin splints"). Sprains, on the other hand, involve tearing of ligamentous structures including those of the knees and ankles. "Runner's knee" is a general term applied to a variety of pain syndromes involving the kneecap (patella) and its attachments. In younger persons, particularly females, the etiology is usually chondromalacia patellae (a degeneration of the patellar cartilage) while in older patients, excessive pronation or flexion stress commonly produces such injuries. Most strains and sprains occur as a result of overuse of poorly conditioned limbs and also from repeated impact on hard surfaces. Overzealous endurance-conditioning running programs may actually result in fractures of metatarsals, called "stress fractures."

The management of these injuries varies with their severity but begins with a foundation of rest, ice, compression, elevation, and nonsteroidal anti-inflammatory drugs. This treatment program should be supervised by a physician qualified in sports medicine and should gradually progress to reconditioning exercises. Swimming reduces impact injuries and puts aerobic stress on all extremities with the only limitations being the skill and coordination required by the activity. Bicycle riding provides excellent lower extremity training exercise and in the stationary mode eliminates the skill and reflexes otherwise demanded by this sport. Obese patients represent a special subset of persons particularly susceptible to orthopedic problems involving their weight-bearing joints.

Environmental considerations pose another source of adverse effects for patients participating in exercise programs. Emphasis should be placed on adequate hydration, evaporative heat loss, or retention of warmth, as appropriate in hot and cold climates respectively. Along with the other safety equipment available at closely monitored exercise sessions, participants should be allowed free access to water and encouraged to drink. Because of the significant additional stress which cold temperatures can impose on the cardiovascular system, exercise sessions may need to move indoors, particularly during subfreezing weather.

Cardiovascular complications present the most immediate life-threatening problems which exercise participants encounter. As noted above, the most likely time for cardiac events appears to be during the warm up or cool down portion of the exercise session. A portable defibrillator and emergency equipment recommended by the American Heart Association Advanced Cardiac Life Support guidelines should be immediately available at supervised programs. Consideration ought to be given to providing courses in Basic Cardiac Life Support for participants in both supervised and unsupervised programs. Since most persons who exercise do so in the unsupervised setting, the larger the number of persons proficient in basic cardiac life support, the greater is the likelihood of successful intervention for events which may occur in the community.

A discussion of the complications of exercise programs would not be complete without at least a brief statement about the legal considerations involved in conducting such programs. The key to avoiding legal problems resides in the usual foundations of good medical practice, proper recognition of indications of and contraindications to exercise testing and training, positive physician-patient rapport, proper use of informed consent for both exercise testing and exercise prescription writing, close attention to high risk subjects, and strict adherence to patient safety standards at all times. Liability for negligence in exercise programs may extend from the supervisors of group exercise sessions through the physicians responsible for overall supervision and emergency intervention techniques, up to the organizational level for the entire program or the corporate level for programs conducted by private enterprise. Despite the fact that national statistics suggest that a sudden cardiac event occurs only approximately once in every 40,000 participant hours for cardiac rehabilitation programs, the need for sustained vigilance and a high level of suspicion for potential high-risk patients cannot be overstated.

ASSESSMENT AND FOLLOW-UP

Because the physical training process requires both time and effort, keeping patients educated about their progress is a major source of motivation. While prescriptions might be adjusted on a weekly or bi-weekly basis, a repeat exercise tolerance test approximately 8 to 12 weeks after enrolling in the program should demonstrate significant training effects from the subject's initial test. These test results ought to be a source of encouragement and stimulation to continue the initial burst of enthusiasm which most patients bring to an exercise program. Subsequent exercise tests might be performed at more lengthy intervals such as 6 months or 1 year after enrollment. Furthermore, the topic of detraining deserves attention. The classic studies of Saltin and his colleagues (1968) clearly demonstrate the rapid loss of training effects following bed rest. This factor has particular applicability for those persons recovering from myocardial infarction, cardiac surgery, or significant systemic illness. Citation of these problems with detraining is a positive motivational tool for participants in the program as well as an educational guide for those persons long absent from the program or seeking to demonstrate their erstwhile athletic prowess. Early overuse fatigue and injuries deter many exercise trainees. For this reason, extra efforts should be focused on the concept of "start low and go slow."

When should subjects exit supervised programs? This question cannot be easily answered for all patients. Poorly motivated patients may need constant reminders and relatively continuous enrollment in supervised programs to maintain any degree of physical training. However, some subjects may require only a few instructional classes beyond which their motivation will carry them into a new lifestyle of physical training and other positive health

561

changes. Most subjects fall between these two extremes. Otherwise healthy individuals gain maximum benefit by group participation for 6 to 12 weeks. They should then be able to participate on their own schedules. Subjects recovering from myocardial infarction need a much more gradually graded program, usually requiring up to 6 months not only to return to gainful employment or previous lifestyle but also to achieve significant physical training effects.

The proper composition and implementation of the exercise prescription should serve as a cornerstone on which to build a program of overall health maintenance. For most persons enrolled in physical training programs, this prescription is one of remedial service. Nonetheless, the established framework of physical fitness programs provides a logical structure on which to base weight reduction, smoking cessation, and other behavioral modification programs. Developing a habit of life-long health maintenance should remain the primary goal of the therapeutic exercise prescription.

Exercise as a Therapeutic Modality

APPENDIX: INFORMED CONSENT FOR EXERCISE TREATMENT*

(It is recommended that this form be submitted to local counsel for review and modification to ensure that it conforms with the appropriate state and local laws governing consent.)

I desire to engage voluntarily in the _____ exercise program in order to attempt to improve my cardiovascular function. This program has been recommended to me by my physician,

Doctor _____.

Before I enter this exercise program I will have a clinical evaluation. This evaluation will include a medical history and physical examination consisting of, but not limited to, measurements of heart rate and blood pressure, EKG at rest and with effort. The purpose of this evaluation is to attempt to detect any condition which would indicate that I should not engage in this exercise program.

The program will follow an exercise prescription prepared by

Doctor _____.

I understand that activities are designed to place a gradually increasing work load on the circulation and to thereby attempt to improve its function. The reaction of the cardiovascular system to such activities cannot be predicted with complete accuracy. There is the risk of certain changes occurring during or following the exercise. These changes include abnormalities of blood pressure or heart rate, or ineffective "heart function," and possibly, in some instances, "heart attacks" or "cardiac arrest."

I realize that it is necessary for me to promptly report to the supervisor of exercises any signs or symptoms indicating any abnormality or distress. I consent to the administration of any resuscitation measures deemed advisable by the supervisor of exercise.

I have read the foregoing and I understand it. Any questions which have arisen or occurred to me have been answered to my satisfaction.

_____   _____
(Date)   (Patient Signature)

_____   _____
(Physician Signature)   (Witness)

*Note. From The Exercise Standards Book (p. 40) by American Heart Association, 1979, Dallas, TX: Subcommittee on Rehabilitation Target Activity Group, M. H. Ellestad, Chairman. Copyright © 1979. Reprinted by permission.

Douglas D. Schocken, MD, is currently Head of Clinical Cardiology at the James A. Haley Veterans' Hospital in Tampa, Florida. He is also Assistant Professor of Medicine at the University of South Florida College of Medicine. Dr. Schocken received his post-graduate training in internal medicine and cardiology at Duke University. He also served as a Clinical Associate at the National Institute on Aging. His other interests include heart disease in the elderly, cardiac rehabilitation, and receptors for adrenergic and purinergic systems. Dr. Schocken may be contacted at 13000 North 30th Street, Box 111 A, Tampa, FL 33612.

RESOURCES

American College of Sports Medicine. (1978). Position statements on the recommended quantity and quality of exercise for developing and maintaining fitness in healthy adults. *Medicine and Science in Sports, 10,* VII-X.

American Heart Association. (1972). *Exercise Testing and Training of Apparently Healthy Individuals: A Handbook for Physicians.* Dallas, TX: The Committee on Exercise, A. A. Kattus, Chairman.

American Heart Association. (1975). *Exercise Testing and Training of Individuals with Heart Disease or at High Risk for Its Development.* Dallas, TX: The Committee on Exercise, A. A. Kattus, Chairman.

American Heart Association. (1979). *The Exercise Standards Book.* Dallas, TX: Subcommittee on Rehabilitation Target Activity Group, M. H. Ellestad, Chairman.

American Heart Association. (1980). *Standards for Supervised Cardiovascular Exercise Maintenance Programs.* Dallas, TX.

Åstrand, P-O, & Rodahl, K. (1977). *Textbook of Work Physiology: Physiological Bases of Exercise* (2nd ed.). New York: McGraw-Hill.

Clausen, J. P. (1976). Circulatory adjustments to dynamic exercise and effects of physical training in normal subjects and in patients with coronary artery disease. *Progress in Cardiovascular Disease, 18,* 460-495.

Clausen, J. P. (1977). Effect of physical training on cardiovascular adjustments to exercise in man. *Physiological Review, 57,* 779-815.

Ellestad, M. H. (1980). *Stress Testing: Principles and Practice* (2nd ed.). Philadelphia, PA: F. A. Davis.

Greist, J. H., Klein, M. H., Eischens, R. R., Faris, J., Gurman, A. S., & Mortan, W. P. (1979). Running as treatment for depression. *Comprehensive Psychiatry, 20*, 41-54.

Haskell, W. L. (1978). Cardiovascular complications during exercise training of cardiac patients. *Circulation, 57*, 920-924.

Hughes, J. R. (1984). Psychological effects of habitual aerobic exercise: A critical review. *Preventive Medicine, 13*, 66-78.

Pollock, M. L., & Schmidt, D. H. (Eds.). (1979). *Heart Disease and Rehabilitation.* Boston, MA: Houghton Mifflin.

Saltin, B., Blomqvist, G., Mitchell, J. H., Johnson, R. L., Wildenthal, K., & Chapman, C. B. (1968). Response to exercise after bed rest and after training. *Circulation, 37 & 38*(Suppl. 7), 1-78.

Wenger, N. K., & Hellerstein, H. K. (Eds.). (1978). *Rehabilitation of the Coronary Patient.* New York: John Wiley.

Williams, R. S., Miller, H., Koisch, F. P., Jr., Ribisl, P., & Graden, H. (1981). Guidelines for unsupervised exercise in patients with ischemic heart disease. *Journal of Cardiac Rehabilitation, 1*, 213-217.

COMPLIANCE AND CLINICAL PRACTICE *

Rona L. Levy

Clinicians know that getting patients to follow treatment recommendations is the bottom line of clinical practice. Most procedures discussed in this book would be only useless exercises if patients did not comply with prescribed therapeutic regimens. This is true even for assessment. Patients are almost always asked to keep some records of their behavior, thoughts, or feelings. Without good compliance, assessment, like treatments, could not occur.

Despite the obvious reliance on compliance as an important part of most therapeutic regimens, considerable evidence exists that patients often do not comply. Studies which have investigated compliance rates have found rates as low as 50% or even 20% to be common (Epstein & Cluss, 1981; Haynes, Taylor, & Sackett, 1979). Problems with compliance occur across a range of medical and nonmedical regimens from appointment keeping to preventative regimens to treatment.

Let me begin by defining what I mean by "compliance." Compliance is what occurs when the patient carries out an assignment in the way it was given by the assignment giver(s). The patient adheres to the treatment assignment. Thus, adherence is another popular term for compliance. Note that I have said "in the way [an assign-

*Portions of this paper originally appeared in Behavioral Assignments and Treatment Compliance (pp. 43-76) by J. L. Shelton and R. L. Levy, 1981, Champaign, IL: Research Press. Copyright ° 1981. Permission to reproduce has been obtained from Research Press and Dr. Shelton.

ment] was given *by the assignment giver,"* not *"by the clinician."* This was deliberate because the assignment giver may be the clinician, the patient, or both in combination. As I will discuss later, it is , in fact, often advisable to have the patient involved in selecting assignments. Thus, the patient too may be an assignment giver.

This paper will begin by outlining some of the reasons for noncompliance. I will then discuss a system for structuring practice which was developed to address compliance problems. Finally, the paper will conclude with some specific recommendations for compliance-enhancement.

REASONS FOR NONCOMPLIANCE

Haynes et al. (1979) summarized patients' explanations for their noncompliance. While there is clearly a need for caution in interpreting information obtained by self-report (Barlow, Hayes, & Nelson, 1984), these findings do provide a useful starting point for looking at the causes of noncompliance. Drawing from the list provided by Haynes et al. (1979), patients' reasons for their noncompliance can be grouped into three categories.

CATEGORY 1: THE PATIENT DOES NOT HAVE THE SKILLS OR KNOWLEDGE NECESSARY TO COMPLETE AN ASSIGNMENT

Reasons patients gave for noncompliance which fall in this category include: poor instruction, incorrect or inadequate information on medications or appointments, and lost appointment slips. Simply put, patients cannot follow through on an assignment if they do not know what they are supposed to do or how or when they are supposed to do it.

Clinicians should *never* assume, without some form of check, that a patient knows how to carry out an assignment. In a later section, I will describe how and when this checking and training could occur.

CATEGORY 2: THE PATIENT'S BELIEFS ARE NOT SUPPORTIVE OF COMPLIANCE ENHANCEMENT

Reasons given by patients which fall within this category include: dissatisfaction with the clinician or treatment, believing they were getting incorrect or inappropriate medication, contradictory advice from friends, not believing the treatment was helping or believing it was making them worse (e.g., side effects), improvement and thus no further reason for treatment, dissatisfaction with clinical procedures (e.g., amount of time spent waiting), and indifference or "lack of will power."

The "will power" explanation sounds similar to the "poor motivation" explanation often given by clinicians. This author considers both of these "garbage can" explanations, where one throws a behavior when no alternate explanation can be found. I am hard on the terms "will power" and "motivation" because I believe they are useless in providing the clinician with information about future action. These terms are often used to explain a clinician's quitting in his or her efforts to obtain compliance: "What could I do? She was not motivated!" I would encourage going beyond these terms to (a) Practice in a manner that attempts to avoid noncompliance and (b) If noncompliance does occur, to evaluate why it occurs and attempt some form of remedial action. Poor knowledge, mistrust in the adequacy of the clinician, or inadequate reward for compliance are all situations which indicate a possible corrective response.

CATEGORY 3: THE PATIENT'S ENVIRONMENT IS NOT SUPPORTIVE OF, OR INTERFERES WITH, COMPLIANCE

Reasons patients gave for noncompliance which fall within this category are: financial need, sickness, child care problems, transportation difficulties, employment or housework interference, being asleep when medications should be taken, lack of family support or illness in the family, and loss of the medication.

To this list, I would add the general reason of the patient simply not receiving a sufficient reward, or even being punished for compliance. For example, a clinician may determine that a woman with a diagnosis of premenstrual tension should reduce the stressors in her life. To do this, it may be appropriate for her to discuss with her husband his participation in meal preparation and cleanup. In this case, if the behavioral homework assignment is to initiate this discussion, there is a reasonable chance that the immediate response by her husband to her compliance will be a negative one. This is one example of how many compliance behaviors have negative consequences associated with them, as the list given by patients indicates. Keeping an appointment may be extremely costly to a woman who has no child care arrangements, limited finances, no transportation, and a boss who may penalize or even fire her if she takes time off from work.

All of these reasons must be addressed if the clinician is interested in reducing potential noncompliance. In the next section, some of the ways these problems can be addressed will be discussed.

BUILDING COMPLIANCE-ENHANCEMENT INTO TREATMENT

The clinician who wants his or her patients to comply with treatment recommendations or therapeutic assignments must recognize that *compliance-enhancement activities must be built into the therapeutic contact*. This point is critical. Compliance-enhancement must not merely be adjunctive to treatment--it should be viewed as part of the treatment. Thus, when meeting with the patient, the clinician should be focused on what the patient should do outside the treatment situation. The following outline suggests how this may be accomplished.

STRUCTURING THE TREATMENT SESSION

Introduction to the Therapy. After assessment, the clinician typically informs the patient about the type of therapy he or she practices, expected timelines, and other pertinent information. It is critical that the emphasis on homework be made in this first session. Patients need to be told that the clinician does not have a magic pill or "quick fix" for the tension headache or back pain, but that the responsibility will be on them to carry out their treatment, with the assistance of the clinician or health care team. Compliance with homework assignments is at the basis of effective treatment.

Many clinicians use an initial therapeutic contract outlining both patient and therapist responsibilities (Gambrill, 1977). These contracts may include items such as "I agree to attend every session," and "I agree to complete all weekly homework assignments." Later in this chapter, I will discuss compliance-enhancement recommendations; however, the point to be made now is that this general commitment to homework completion should occur at the *beginning* of therapy.

Review of Previous Homework Assignments. Each session should begin with a review of homework which was given in the previous session. The clinician should go over any difficulties which were encountered, attempt to address these, and consistent with the recommendations listed below, praise success. This review may take considerable time but is a necessary part of the treatment process. If a patient has been asked to monitor eating behavior, for example, the clinician should take time to clarify and review information which has been recorded. Patients who have often put a good deal of time and energy into preparing such material are typically interested in discussing this information and should be positively reinforced for their efforts.

If subsequent homework seems indicated, a session will need to cover what the patient will be doing during the time between this session and the next. Within the context of the therapeutic goals, the clinician will continue to gather specific information about the patient's current situation, capabilities, and limitations which might enhance or interfere with carrying out future homework assignments. For example, the patient's work situation may make it difficult to comply with record keeping during work hours. This continuous monitoring of the patient's situation will help him or her determine additional reasons for possible noncompliance which were not discovered in the initial evaluation. Homework and compliance-enhancement recommendations are selected based on therapeutic goals and an assessment of which homework assignments are likely to be carried out or complied with. The session should conclude with a review of homework and any additional compliance-enhancement recommendations which are appropriate.

571

COMPLIANCE-ENHANCEMENT
RECOMMENDATIONS

*RECOMMENDATION 1: THE
THERAPIST SHOULD BE SURE
ASSIGNMENTS CONTAIN SPECIFIC
DETAIL ABOUT THE DESIRED BEHAVIOR*

Assignments should specify how, when, where, and for how long something is to be done. Studies in the medical literature show considerable variation in the interpretation of doctors' instructions (typically medication taking). In one study (Mazzulo, Lasagna, & Griner, 1974), it was found that patients had many different interpretations of apparently simple instructions such as "take four times a day."

When I ask patients to keep an ongoing record of some activity, I always ask where they plan to keep their monitoring sheet. This encourages them to plan the specific details of how they will keep the assignment. Many men, for example, prefer to keep a three by five card in a shirt pocket. I also encourage patients to do their recording as close as possible in time to when the event of interest occurred. Otherwise, they may forget to record or are more likely to record inaccurately.

Contracts have been very successful in obtaining compliance, as demonstrated in an antihypertensive regimen study by Steckel and Swain (1977). One way which contracts may work is that they provide a way of specifically outlining a patient's responsibilities so that the chances of misinterpretation are reduced. One caution should be noted here: Simplicity should not be sacrificed for specificity. Extreme detail and complexity may actually make a behavior too difficult (Haynes et al., 1979). For example, "At exactly 5 minutes past every hour I want you to sit in that chair in your office we were discussing and take exactly 60 seconds to relax,..." may be far too detailed to obtain compliance. If this occurred, I would most likely instruct a client that I wished her to take a relaxation period approximately 1 minute in length at the rate of once an hour, but I would usually leave the exact timing to her discretion.

RECOMMENDATION 2: THE THERAPIST SHOULD GIVE DIRECT SKILL TRAINING WHEN NECESSARY

A frequent mistake made by therapists who utilize home practice is the assumption that the patient has the skills necessary to complete the desired task. It is therefore wise to practice the behavior in the office before asking the patient to engage in the task in the natural social environment. This practice is particularly recommended in cases where the assigned behavior is so complex that verbal instructions alone are inadequate.

Direct skill training involves a chain of events that, depending on the skill level, may need repeating. In its complete form, an instructional chain consists of the following therapist behaviors:

1. The therapist assesses the level of patient skills relevant to the upcoming assignment (skill training is not always necessary).
2. If the decision is made to proceed with skill training, the therapist begins by giving the patient verbal and written instructions.
3. The therapist models the skill.
4. The patient then imitates the skill, with coaching, prompting, and reward for approximations toward the desired goal.

For example, staying with the relaxation example, a patient who is almost constantly in interaction with other people was asked to take "brief relaxes" throughout her day. She was told this could even be done when in a face to face interaction. She expressed doubt about how she could do this. Thus, it was determined that skill training was appropriate. The patient was then given verbal and written instructions (e.g., "Take a slow deep breath, exhale slowly, let your tension be released, etc."). The therapist then modeled this behavior, demonstrating that this relaxation did not need to interrupt their interaction. Finally, the patient was asked to perform the behavior, with appropriate feedback from the therapist.

RECOMMENDATION 3:
COMPLIANCE SHOULD BE REWARDED

The rate of compliance is influenced by the consequences that immediately follow compliant behavior. Missed opportunities to reward compliance may lead to a decrease in the frequency and duration of home practice activities and an overall reduction in effectiveness.

A number of reward opportunities exist for encouraging the patient to adhere to the prescribed task. The sources of reward can be the therapist, the client himself or herself, or significant others.

Therapist Reinforcement. Since the patient may not gain immediate reward from persons in his or her social environment, he or she should always be told in advance that the criterion for success is the execution of the behavior (compliance) and not the outcome of compliance. The therapist, at least initially, is frequently the most important source of reward. The therapist should keep a careful record of all prescribed assignments so that patients should never have to "fish" for reinforcement by reminding the therapist of what they were asked to do.

Initially, patients should be reinforced for *all* approximations to desirable compliance efforts. For example, if a patient were assigned to keep a daily journal of food consumed for one week but completed only one day's record he or she should be rewarded at first for this approximation to carrying out the assignment. Shaping of the patient's performance can then be carried out by rewarding gradually closer approximations to the assignment (see next recommendation).

Therapists should also make use of the telephone to deliver reward, either by calling patients or having them call in. A telephone call can provide the therapist with an opportunity to provide social reward to the client in a natural setting. Phone calls should, however, be used carefully because some patients may use homework failure as an excuse to obtain more contact with the therapist. Whenever possible, phone calls should therefore be made at a scheduled time, preferably after completion of a task rather than when there is difficulty in doing the task. Patients can be instructed to call when they finish a difficult task, not "whenever the homework doesn't go well." Thus, although problems arising from homework should be understood and empathized with, the emphasis remains on the positive aspects of performance of assigned tasks. I have found patients to be generally delighted to receive at-home calls from me. They have said that this seems to show caring when I am willing to step outside of our scheduled hour-long weekly meeting.

In addition to the therapist's praise, other avenues of therapist-initiated reward exist. A contingency statement in the homework format is one good way of assuring that the homework will be completed, and several contingencies can be designed to increase adherence. Rather than seeing the patient at a scheduled time, the therapist may not schedule the patient for the next appointment until he or she calls to say that the assignment is done. This contingency is based on the assumption, of course, that the patient finds it rewarding to talk to the therapist.

Other rewards can also be considered. For example, the therapist may give a money rebate upon completion of agreed upon homework. He or she can also make a regular appointment with the patient, but reduce the length of the session if the patient does not attempt the homework. This latter type of reinforcement is useful for agency workers who cannot manipulate the fee and also for situations in which the therapist chooses to make some contact with the patient, although for only a short time.

Reward structures should be clearly outlined. One way to do this is to use a behavioral contract. Although contracts require time and effort to construct, they can provide the additional structure and contingencies needed to foster the completion of home activities. Contracts generally emphasize the positive rewards for achieving compliance with assigned tasks. In addition, they help clarify the consequences of completing the assignment, and they provide clear-cut criteria for achievement of the stated therapeutic activities.

Contracts can be unilateral or bilateral. A unilateral contract is one in which the patient obligates himself or herself to complete the homework and is rewarded for such completion. Bilateral contracts specify the obligations and the mutual rewards for each of the parties involved.

Contracts should be very specific, determined by negotiation and fully understood and accepted by the patient. Successful contracts should have short-range goals: Two or three weeks between appointments is maximum. To be understood, contracts should be written down and both the therapist and the patient should have a copy.

Other elements of a successful contract include the following:

1. A very clear and detailed description of the homework should be stated.
2. The contract should specify the reward gained if the homework is completed.
3. Some provisions should be made for some consequence for failure to complete the assignment within a specified time limit or behavior frequency.
4. The contract should specify the means by which the contract response is to be observed, measured, and recorded.
5. An arrangement should be made so that the timing for delivery of rewards follows the response as quickly as possible.

Patient Reward. Another important source of reward is the patient himself or herself. Self-reward is vital to the success of homework and may actually be the key to maintaining therapeutic behaviors after treatment has been terminated.

Conceptually, it is helpful to look at a model first provided by Johnson (1971) in which overt behaviors and covert behaviors (thoughts) can be rewarded overtly or covertly. The reward possibilities and contingency relationships generated by this model are extensive.

1. An assertive response (overt behavior) is followed by self-praise (covert behavior) such as "I did a beautiful job on that assertive response. Dr. _____ would be proud of me."
2. A thought such as "I will be successful as long as I concentrate on the task" (covert behavior) could be rewarded by a pleasant activity, such as having something desirable to eat (overt behavior).
3. A thought such as "I am very attractive when I smile" (covert behavior) could be followed by an instance of self-praise (covert behavior) such as "Keep up the good work of thinking good thoughts."

Reward by Others. Involving others in the patient's treatment can be a very effective part of therapy. Family members or friends can help in various ways to support completion of homework assignments (Levy, 1983, 1985). Other persons' participation may even be formalized by being built into a contract.

Brownell and his colleagues (Brownell, Heckerman, Westlake, Hayes, & Monti, 1978; Brownell & Stunkard, 1981; Wilson & Brownell, 1978) have systematically involved partners of overweight spouses in weight reduction programs, with mixed results. Each week, patients are given homework assignments and partners are also given their own homework assignments, many of which include rewards to the overweight partner for compliance with assignments.

RECOMMENDATION 4: THE THERAPIST SHOULD BEGIN WITH SMALL HOMEWORK SUCCESS AND GRADUALLY INCREASE ASSIGNMENTS

This technique is sometimes referred to as the "foot in the door" technique. Patients are first asked to comply with a small request. If the request is complied with and rewarded, they are then more likely to comply with a subsequent larger task.

It is important for the reader to note that in each case the beginning assignment is simple and requires relatively little effort on the part of the patient. Each assignment is carefully planned to be within the patient's skill repertoire. For example, if a medical regimen requires a radical alteration of a patient's diet, it may be particularly useful to have a patient begin by making small dietary changes and then adding more changes on to these. Monitoring provides another example where the stepwise procedure may be useful. If my ultimate goal is to have a patient record something all day long, I may begin by selecting a 2-hour period where recording might be easy.

RECOMMENDATION 5: THE THERAPIST SHOULD USE A SYSTEM WHICH WILL REMIND PATIENTS OF THE ASSIGNMENT

The therapist should take steps to insure that the client is reminded, cued, or prompted to carry out an assignment at the appropriate time and place. One cue to assignment compliance that can be carried into the natural environment would be a copy of the written assignments. Therapists may use either a xerox copy of their own record, made in session while assignments are given, or they might utilize NCR (no carbon required) pads when writing down assignments. Thus, the therapist and the patient immediately get one copy. Patients may then be asked to post this list in a convenient place. I also have a place on my appointment cards where assignments are to be recorded. The following is printed on the cards: "Between now and _____ you have been asked to:" (if the list is long and would not fit on my card, I simply write "complete assignments on your assignment sheet").

Phone calls by the therapist, in addition to being rewards, may also be useful to remind and prompt the patient. Significant others can be helpful by providing needed reminders at appropriate times. Finally, various devices have been used as aids to compliance, including timed buzzers, calendars, and dated pill dispensers (Epstein & Cluss, 1981).

While the evidence has been mixed, several studies have found increased appointment keeping compliance when clients receive reminders in the form of postcards or phone calls (Levy & Claravall, 1977). As it likely does not decrease appointment keeping, it certainly appears worthwhile to remind patients of their appointments, if therapists have the facilities to do so.

RECOMMENDATION 6: THE THERAPIST SHOULD HAVE THE PATIENT MAKE A PUBLIC COMMITMENT TO COMPLY

Public commitments, such as verbalizations of a concrete plan, can serve two purposes. First, they can provide considerable evidence about how someone intends to behave. Such information can provide a basis for further discussion if it appears that the patient may not intend to adhere to prescribed assignments. One of the best ways to predict compliance is to simply ask the patient whether or not he or she intends to comply with the assigned outside activity. The therapist may also ask for specifics such as frequency and duration.

An overt, publicly given commitment may also serve to enhance the likelihood of compliance. In many situations such a commitment, if given verbally and written down, is sufficient to bring about completion of assignments (Levy, 1977; Levy & Clark, 1980; and Levy, Yamashita, & Pow, 1979). However, despite assurances from the patient that he or she intends to comply with the stated assignment, the therapist may doubt the accuracy of the prediction. In some cases, the patient may have repeatedly promised to complete the assignment and failed to follow through. As with reminders, the evidence is mixed on the relationship between overt commitment and improvement in compliance rates (Shelton & Levy, 1981). Yet, it "costs" so little to simply ask a patient "will you do it?" that it seems useful to use this technique in all situations along with other techniques which may be appropriate.

RECOMMENDATION 7: THE
PATIENT SHOULD BELIEVE IN THE
VALUE OF THE ASSIGNMENT FOR
TREATING HIS OR HER PROBLEM

First the patient needs to have a belief structure that supports the task. He or she must believe that the assigned task is useful, that it is acceptable to others, that it has a high probability of successful completion, and that the entire treatment program is valuable. Therapists should take considerable time to elicit the patients' beliefs, fears, and expectations regarding compliance. Questions should be encouraged and good rapport, as always, is critical. After being given the assignment, the patient should be questioned regarding his or her reaction to the assignment. This intensive discussion will also provide the opportunity to further enact other compliance-enhancement steps, such as more direct training, if needed. Well-chosen bibliotherapy regarding the benefits of treatment or the consequences of an untreated problem may alter beliefs. In addition, some people benefit from listening to audio cassettes designed especially for patients.

Any relationship-building activities in which the clinician can engage are likely to increase the chances of compliance. Kanfer and Goldstein (1975) provide a good framework for demonstrating how a patient's liking, respecting, and trusting a therapist will lead to patient change. This point seems obvious and should not be overlooked in a consideration of enhancement strategies.

A final and critical recommendation for compliance-enhancement is that patients should help select homework assignments. Rather than just hand out assignments, therapists should work with patients to develop assignments, perhaps using phrases such as "Now, what do you think would be a good way to keep track of...?" or the therapist may offer a range of assignments from which the patient can choose.

This active participation (Schulman, 1979) by the patient may have several positive consequences. First, patients should have an increased perception of control. No one is *making* them do this--they have chosen to do the assignment, and are thus more likely to follow through. Second, patients will have selected assignments that they can imagine occurring in their own world. This fact reduces the possibility that, after a reflecting on an assignment, a patient will think, "He or she doesn't really know how difficult it would be to do that," and then fail to comply.

RECOMMENDATION 8: THE
THERAPIST SHOULD USE COGNITIVE
REHEARSAL STRATEGIES

Having a patient take some time in the office to actually imagine carrying out the assignment can lead to several positive results. First, the patient may be able to raise possible difficulties which could arise and these may be "problem solved" (see Recommendation No. 9). The patient may also recognize some confusion with aspects of the assignment and may be able to ask clarifying questions. Finally, imagining a difficult activity in the relaxed atmosphere of the therapeutic office, with the support of the therapist readily available, may be an easy first step, consistent with Recommendation No. 4.

In addition to rehearsing cognitively in the office, several techniques for cognitive rehearsal outside of the therapist's office have also been recommended. With Suinn's (1972a, 1972b) approach, the client is asked to carry out a specific cognitive strategy just before engaging in a self-directed assignment. This procedure asks the client to:

RELAX

VISUALIZE (the successful completion of the assignment)

DO (the assignment)

For example, the client who is fearful of failure in some athletic event would be asked to first relax immediately before the event, then to visualize successfully completing the event, and then to do, or initiate, the athletic response.

Meichenbaum's (1977) Self-Instructional Training is considerably more complex than that just discussed, and it has shown a great deal of merit. In this approach, patients are taught to focus on the assigned task. The strategy consists of the following:

1. *Preparing for a Stressor.* In this first step the client is urged to prepare a "game plan" for anticipated anxiety and inability to focus on the assigned task (e.g., taking an exam). The client might, for example, rehearse the more frequent distractors likely to be faced when the stress mounts. The patient will then remind himself or herself what he or she plans to do when the distractors occur (e.g., "I must remember to read the directions twice and do the easiest questions first").

2. *Confronting the Stressor.* In the second phase, the patient actually activates the coping strategy rehearsed earlier. Cues such as written notes can be used as reminders of what self-control interventions to employ during the stressful time. Self-statements such as "Don't worry about the clock; just concentrate on the exam" and "Don't worry if they are already finishing; that doesn't mean they have done well" may be useful.

3. *Rewarding Self-Statements.* This third step requires the patient to reward himself or herself for the successful completion of homework.

*RECOMMENDATION 9: THE
THERAPIST SHOULD TRY TO
ANTICIPATE AND REDUCE THE
NEGATIVE EFFECTS OF COMPLIANCE*

Efforts should be made to anticipate barriers to compliance in the natural environment and facilitate the integration of the assignment into the patient's normal activities. Many potential punishment pitfalls can be avoided by following some of the strategies already discussed. For example, patients who have received thorough training in performing a task are likely to find it less difficult. Patients who have tried techniques such as Meichenbaum's (1977) or Johnson's (1971) self-reward system, discussed in Recommendations 8 and 3, respectively, are less dependent on external rewards as they generate their own reward intrinsically. Thus, a patient who complies with a very difficult task can be encouraged to say to herself something like "Good for me! That was tough, but I did it!," even if persons around her, such as a spouse, are less rewarding.

Sometimes modifications which help avoid punishment for compliance are very easy. One patient reported that it was difficult to put the yellow monitoring sheets I gave her out on her desk to monitor her task completion. She said she worked in an office where people were always writing on white sheets of paper, and if she pulled out a yellow sheet, people would know that it was something different. This was handled by simply xeroxing the form and giving her copies of the form on white sheets of paper.

RECOMMENDATION 10: COMPLIANCE SHOULD BE CLOSELY MONITORED BY AS MANY SOURCES AS POSSIBLE

Monitoring may include direct observation of the patient's compliance behavior, or some indirect method of assessing the behavior. It may be carried out by the patient (self-monitoring), by someone else in the patient's environment who has the opportunity to observe compliance (or noncompliance) behavior, or both.

Monitoring is critical because of the therapist absence feature of many behavioral medicine treatments. If the therapist cannot directly observe compliance, he or she must rely on some system of monitoring to determine that it has occurred and whether congratulations or further instructions are appropriate. Monitoring can also provide several direct benefits to the patient. He or she can engage in self-reward when monitored data are good and will also be made more aware of the importance of the task being assigned.

One example of monitoring by the patient might occur in a smoking reduction program, where the assignment might be to reduce smoking by two cigarettes per day. Compliance could be self-monitored by having the patient count the number of cigarettes smoked per day and may be co-monitored by having the client's spouse count the number of cigarettes remaining in the client's cigarette pack (assuming, of course, that the patient was not smoking any cigarettes other than his or her own).

For medication compliance, blood serum or urine assays may be directly observed. Of course, the timing on when such samples are taken will affect their accuracy as a measure of compliance (Epstein & Cluss, 1981). Tracer or marker procedures, typically used with urine-detection methods also may be employed. With this method, the clinician or others may directly observe tracers, or have patients do the monitoring of, say, urine color. Therapists could, for example, give pills to patients with tracer colors ordered in a sequence known only to the therapist. If the patient reports the correct sequence, compliance is assumed to have occurred (Epstein & Masek, 1978).

Spouses can easily monitor eating behaviors during mealtimes or other appropriate periods when the spouse is present (such as during evening TV watching or social gathering). Brownell and Stunkard's (1981) system, mentioned under Recommendation 3, relies heavily on spouse observation. If available to the therapist, trained observers may sometimes be placed in the patient's environment. Finally, other methods discussed in Gordis (1979) and Dunbar (1979), such as collecting data from permanent products (physical results from some behavior-- e.g., a candy bar wrapper may be taken as evidence that a candy bar has been consumed) or mechanical devices, may also be used to monitor compliance. Patients should be involved in the planning of any methods such as these to monitor their behavior.

When monitoring for compliance is conducted by the patient, several issues come up. One issue is that self-monitoring may be reactive--it may actually change the behaviors being observed (Barlow et al., 1984).

Another issue to consider in using self-monitoring to improve compliance is accuracy. For example, it would certainly be undesirable if the therapist were rewarding the client for desirable eating habits, as reported on the patient's self-monitoring sheet, if the patient were not eating as indicated on the assignment. In this case, the patient would be being rewarded for inaccurate recording and poor eating habits. Thus, it is important for the therapist to know how to determine and enhance the accuracy of the data received from the patient.

Monitoring by others raises many of the same issues as self-monitoring. Monitoring by others may also be reactive, and could thus be utilized by the therapist to effect compliance in a desirable direction. Observers also need to be trained in accurate recording methods. Finally, the therapist needs to be aware of many of the factors which can affect the accuracy of information.

As a final point, in working with a patient or other persons to set up many of the compliance-enhancements such as monitoring (Recommendation 10), reward (Recommendation 3), and reminders (Recommendation 5), the therapist needs to be aware of the importance of viewing these activities as assignments themselves. Thus, if the therapist wishes compliance with activities such as monitoring one's compliance, rewarding oneself after completing an assignment, or putting up reminder notes, compliance-enhancement recommendations should be utilized to enhance these activities as well.

SUMMARY AND CONCLUSION

Behavioral medicine therapists must rely on the patient's compliance with therapeutic regimens outside of the therapist's office. Therapists must begin by a careful assessment of the problems and the patient's life situation. In learning about the patient, the therapist should obtain information relevant to the possible three reasons for noncompliance:

Category 1: The patient's skills and knowledge.
Category 2: The patient's belief system.
Category 3: The patient's environmental supports.

Treatment sessions should be focused around assignments. Patients should be educated as to the importance of homework and compliance to the success of their treatment. The first part of each session should be spent reviewing homework given during the previous session. The rest of the interview should be spent on homework assignments and compliance-enhancement recommendations which are selected with sensitivity to the three problem categories discussed above. These recommendations are:

1. The therapist should be sure assignments contain specific detail about the desired behavior.
2. The therapist should give direct skill training when necessary.

3. Compliance should be rewarded.
4. The therapist should begin with small homework requests and gradually increase assignments.
5. The therapist should use a system which will remind patients of the assignment.
6. The therapist should have the patient make a public commitment to comply.
7. The patient should believe in the value of the assignment for treating his or her problem.
8. The therapist should use cognitive rehearsal strategies to improve success with assignments.
9. The therapist should try to anticipate and reduce the negative effects of compliance.
10. Compliance should be closely monitored by as many sources as possible.

Clinicians should have a checklist (and this should be written down, and then possibly memorized) of these recommendations to cue themselves to "cover" each of these points. Assuming compliance will lead to therapeutic benefit, following the recommendations in this paper will increase the likelihood that patients will receive a more positive outcome from behavioral medicine treatment.

Rona L. Levy, MSW, MPH, PhD, is currently Professor of Social Work at the University of Washington. Her training is in psychology, social work, and community mental health. She has published numerous articles and a book with Dr. John Shelton on patient compliance. Other areas of interest include women's health care, chronic pain, and the empirical evaluation of clinical practice. Dr. Levy may be contacted at the School of Social Work, JH-30, University of Washington, Seattle, WA 98195.

RESOURCES

Barlow, D. H., Hayes, S. C., & Nelson, R. O. (1984). *The Scientific Practitioner*. New York: Pergamon.
Brownell, K. D., Heckerman, C. L., Westlake, R. J., Hayes, S. C., & Monti, P. M. (1978). The effects of couples training and partner cooperativeness in the behavioral treatment of obesity. *Behavioral Research and Therapy, 16,* 323-333.

Brownell, K. D., & Stunkard, A. J. (1981). Couples training, pharmacotherapy, and behavior therapy in the treatment of obesity. *Archives of General Psychiatry, 38,* 1224-1229.

Dunbar, J. M. (1979). In S. J. Cohen (Ed.), *New Directions in Patient Compliance* (pp. 41-57). Lexington, MA: Lexington Books.

Epstein, L. H., & Cluss, P. A. (1981). A behavioral medicine perspective on adherence to long-term medical regimens. *Journal of Consulting and Clinical Psychology, 50,* 950-971.

Epstein, L. H., & Masek, B. M. (1978). Behavioral control of medicine compliance. *Journal of Applied Behavior Analysis, 11,* 1-10.

Gambrill, E. D. (1977). *Behavior Modification.* San Francisco: Jossey-Bass.

Gordis, L. (1979). Conceptual and methodologic problems in measuring patient compliance. In R. B. Haynes, D. W. Taylor, & D. L. Sackett (Eds.), *Compliance in Health Care* (pp. 23-45). Baltimore: Johns Hopkins University Press.

Haynes, R. B., Taylor, D. W., & Sackett, D. L. (1979). *Compliance in Health Care.* Baltimore: Johns Hopkins University Press.

Johnson, S. M. (1971). Self-observation as an agent of behavioral change. *Behavior Therapy, 2,* 488-497.

Kanfer, F. H., & Goldstein, A. P. (1975). *Helping People Change: Methods and Materials.* Elmsford, NY: Pergamon.

Levy, R. L. (1977). Relationship of an overt commitment to task compliance in behavior therapy. *Journal of Behavior Therapy and Experimental Psychiatry, 8,* 25-29.

Levy, R. L. (1983). Social support and compliance: A selective review and critique of treatment integrity and outcome measurement. *Social Science and Medicine, 17,* 1329-1338.

Levy, R. L. (1985). Social support and compliance: Update. *Journal of Hypertension, 3*(Suppl. 1), 45-49.

Levy, R. L., & Claravall, V. (1977). Differential affects of a phone reminder on patients with long and short between-visit intervals. *Medical Care, 15,* 435-438.

Levy, R. L., & Clark, H. (1980). The use of an overt commitment to enhance compliance: A cautionary note. *Journal of Behavior Therapy and Experimental Psychiatry, 11,* 105-107.

Levy, R. L., Yamashita, D., & Pow, G. (1979). Relationship of an overt commitment to the frequency and speed of compliance with decision making. *Medical Care, 17*, 281-284.

Mazzulo, S. M., Lasagna, L., & Griner, P. F. (1974). Variations in interpretation of prescription assignments. *Journal of the American Medical Association, 227*, 929-931.

Meichenbaum, D. H. (1977). *Cognitive-behavior Modification: An Integrative Approach.* New York: Plenum.

Schulman, B. (1979). Active patient orientation and outcomes in hypertensive treatment. *Medical Care, 17*, 267-280.

Shelton, J. L., & Levy, R. L. (1981). *Behavioral Assignments and Treatment Compliance.* Champaign, IL: Research Press.

Steckel, S. B., & Swain, M. A. (1977). Contracting with patients to improve compliance. *Hospitals, 51*, 81-84.

Suinn, R. M. (1972a). Behavior rehearsal for ski racers. *Behavior Therapy, 3*, 308-310.

Suinn, R. M. (1972b). Removing emotional obstacles to learning and performance by visuo-motor behavior rehearsal. *Behavior Therapy, 3*, 308-310.

Wilson, G. T., & Brownell, K. D. (1978). Behavior therapy for obesity including family members in the treatment process. *Behavior Therapy, 9*, 943-945.

INDEX

Index